The Subversive Science

ESSAYS TOWARD
AN ECOLOGY OF MAN

Editorial Advisor:

A. Starker Leopold

University of California,
Berkeley

69-2909

HOUGHTON MIFFLIN COMPANY
BOSTON

New York
Atlanta
Geneva, Illinois
Dallas
Palo Alto

The Subversive Science

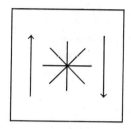

ESSAYS TOWARD
AN ECOLOGY
OF MAN

EDITED BY

Paul Shepard

Visiting Lecturer, Williams College

AND

Daniel McKinley

State University of New York
at Albany

Editor's Foreword

*My choice of title is not facetious.
I wish to explore a question of growing concern. Is ecology a phase of
science of limited interest and utility?
Or, if taken seriously as an instrument
for the long-run welfare of mankind,
would it endanger the assumptions
and practices accepted by modern
societies, whatever their doctrinal
commitments?*—PAUL B. SEARS.

It is pretty obvious that industrializa-
tion is not of itself a panacea for man's
woes, since it tends to create as many
problems as it solves. One by-product
of the industrial age has been a considerable fouling of the human environment. Another is the rapid
exploitation and expenditure of cheap
and available resources. A third is the
development of critical social problems
among the urbanized masses. The
happiness and welfare of an industrial
population is not measured by the gross
national product. There may even be
an inverse relationship. A thoughtful
evaluation of this dilemma is the purpose of the present book.

The authors have brought together
in one volume a collection of searching
and provocative essays on the ecology
of man. The central theme is that the
well-being of mankind is inescapably
associated with a healthy, productive,
and attractive environment. In addition
to material goods, people must have
pleasurable surroundings and some
measure of territorial security to be
content. The logic of this conclusion is
obvious when the human population
and its problems are subjected to the
same ecologic scrutiny as now is applied
to the study of other animal populations.
With all his technological miracles,
man is still basically an animal, with
all the natural needs, reactions, and
dependencies of an animal.

Shepard and McKinley have done a
remarkable job in selecting and integrating the essays that constitute the
body of this volume. They have put in
contemporary context the thinking of
some of the great scholars and students
of the ecology of human populations.
In this era of social unrest, chronic
poverty, resource depletion, air and
water pollution, and cluttered landscape, one may question the concept
that the growth of America's industrial

monster represents cultural progress. In many respects we seem to be trading away cultural and environmental values for the baubles and trappings of a civilization that provides poor habitat for its people.

These are some of the problems to which Shepard, McKinley, and the other authors represented in this book have addressed themselves. Educators who wish to bring to their students an environmental view of the human enterprise; laymen concerned with world survival—all will find this book not only necessary but, in some cases, frightening.

A. Starker Leopold

Berkeley, California

Like our ancestors you will certainly find that these problems can be solved only by the biologists—taking the word "biologists" in its very broadest sense, to include also the psychologists and anthropologists—and that till they have put their best efforts into the solution your theologians, philosophers, jurists, and politicians will continue to add to the existing confusion of your social organization.— WEE-WEE, 43rd NEOTENIC KING OF THE 8429th DYNASTY OF THE BELLICOSE TERMITES.

Preface

We brought this collection of papers together because we think it embodies the universality of ecology. Romanticism and primitive mythology which united men with the natural world in the past no longer teach us the unity of life. Scientific conservation, as a benign resourcism, is too narrowly and economically centered.

A truly human ecology must be consistent with the broad trans-organic scope of ecology, not merely in an analogical way but as a real extension. Much of our present intellectual and practical life isolates parts of a universal mosaic and so injures it and ourselves. No collection of essays can heal such a wound. But we may begin by acknowledging the diversity of content and implications as well as the worldwide scope of ecological processes. Perhaps some bringing together, some restoring, some juxtaposing may help to renew an ancient ecological wisdom and a vision of the world lately neglected and repudiated. We hope at least to show that the ecological concept is known or felt in different ways —ways not redundant but harmonious.

To a world which gives grudging admission of the "nature" in human nature, we say that the framework of human life is all life and that anything adding to its understanding may be ecological. It is life, not man, which is the main contour, and it is ecology in general where human ecology is to be found. Ideas themselves are inseparable from nature and the study of man in nature. Beyond the essential biological framework, the arts and social studies give human ecology its distinctive quality—its heart.

We expect the reader to find among these papers relationships not made explicit by our brief introductions. Our statements are tangential or cryptic to emphasize that ecology shapes our response to the world and we face outward from it, not inward as though it were a closed academic subject.

We hope that such a collection will stimulate the clustering of ideas which can inform philosophies of being and action, and which will generate ecological responsibility in us. Nothing less than such an ecological commitment will preserve other creatures, our earth, and ourselves.

P. S.
D. M.

*The poet, the artist, the sleuth—who-
ever sharpens our perception tends to
be antisocial; rarely "well-adjusted,"
he cannot go along with currents and
trends. A strange bond often exists
among antisocial types in their power
to see environments as they really
are.*— MARSHALL McLUHAN

Contents

v   Editor's Foreword

vii   Preface

1   Introduction: Ecology and Man—A Viewpoint / *Paul Shepard*

Part 1   Men As Populations

13   The Human Revolution / *Charles F. Hockett and Robert Ascher*

42   The Human Population / *Edward S. Deevey, Jr.*

55   Facts, Fables, and Fallacies on Feeding the World Population / *Samuel Brody*

77   The Inexorable Problem of Space / *Paul B. Sears*

93   Individual and Species: Biological Survival / *Roscoe Spencer*

99   Self-Regulating Systems in Populations of Animals / *V. C. Wynne-Edwards*

Part 2   The Environmental Encounter

115   The Seeing Eye / *Adolf Portmann*

122   The Ecology of Imagination in Childhood / *Edith Cobb*

133   Remembered Landscapes / *Grady Clay*

139   The Individual as Man/World / *Alan W. Watts*

149   God's Acre / *Erich Isaac*

158   Ghosts at the Door / *John B. Jackson*

168   The Trees and Roofs of France / *May Theilgaard Watts*

Part 3   Men and Other Organisms

179   Of Men and the Lower Animals / *Paul L. Errington*

190   On the Domestication of Cattle / *Erich Isaac*

210   Man Pressure / *Colin Bertram*

215 Fifty Years of Man in the Zoo / *G. Evelyn Hutchinson*

223 Second Thoughts on the Germ Theory / *René J. Dubos*

230 A-Bombs, Bugbombs, and Us / *G. M. Woodwell, W. M. Malcolm, and R. H. Whittaker*

Part 4   Men in Ecosystems

245 Pesticides—in Our Ecosystem / *Frank E. Egler*

268 The Impending Emergence of Ecological Thought / *LaMont C. Cole*

275 The Cybernetics of Competition: A Biologist's View of Society / *Garrett Hardin*

296 Irradiation and Human Evolution / *Earle L. Reynolds*

312 The Coming Solar Age / *Peter van Dresser*

316 The Ecological Approach to the Social Sciences / *F. Fraser Darling*

328 An Ecological Method for Landscape Architecture / *Ian L. McHarg*

333 The Preservation of Man's Environment / *F. Raymond Fosberg*

Part 5   Ethos, Ecos, and Ethics

341 The Historical Roots of Our Ecologic Crisis / *Lynn White, Jr.*

351 The New Mythology of "Man in Nature" / *Daniel McKinley*

363 The Modern Retreat from Function / *Peter van Dresser*

369 Land Use and Urban Development / *George Macinko*

384 Science and the Study of Mankind / *Laura Thompson*

395 The Steady State: Physical Law and Moral Choice / *Paul B. Sears*

402 The Land Ethic / *Aldo Leopold*

416 Fullness of Life Through Leisure / *John Collier*

437 A Woman as Great as the World / *Jacquetta Hawkes*

439 Additional Readings

Introduction: Ecology and Man—a Viewpoint

PAUL SHEPARD

ECOLOGY IS SOMETIMES characterized as the study of a natural "web of
life." It would follow that man is somewhere in the web or that he in fact
manipulates its strands, exemplifying
what Thomas Huxley called "man's
place in nature." But the image of a
web is too meager and simple for the
reality. A web is flat and finished and
has the mortal frailty of the individual
spider. Although elastic, it has insufficient depth. However solid to the
touch of the spider, for us it fails to
denote the *eikos*—the habitation—and
to suggest the enduring integration of
the primitive Greek domicile with its
sacred hearth, bonding the earth
to all aspects of society.

Ecology deals with organisms in an
environment and with the processes
that link organism and place. But
ecology as such cannot be studied,
only organisms, earth, air, and sea can
be studied. It is not a discipline: there
is no body of thought and technique
which frames an ecology of man.[1] It
must be therefore a scope or a way of
seeing. Such a *perspective* on the human situation is very old and has been
part of philosophy and art for thousands of years. It badly needs attention
and revival.

Man is in the world and his ecology
is the nature of that *inness*. He is in
the world as in a room, and in transience, as in the belly of a tiger or in
love. What does he do there in nature? What does nature do there *in
him*? What is the nature of the transaction? Biology tells us that the transaction is always circular, always a
mutual feedback. Human ecology cannot be limited strictly to biological

---

[1] There is a branch of sociology called Human
Ecology, but it is mostly about urban geography.

1

concepts, but it cannot ignore them. It cannot even transcend them. It emerges from biological reality and grows from the fact of interconnection as a general principle of life. It must take a long view of human life and nature as they form a mesh or pattern going beyond historical time and beyond the conceptual bounds of other humane studies. As a natural history of what it means to be human, ecology might proceed the same way one would define a stomach, for example, by attention to its nervous and circulatory connections as well as its entrance, exit, and muscular walls.

Many educated people today believe that only what is unique to the individual is important or creative, and turn away from talk of populations and species as they would from talk of the masses. I once knew a director of a wealthy conservation foundation who had misgivings about the approach of ecology to urgent environmental problems in America because its concepts of communities and systems seemed to discount the individual. Communities to him suggested only followers, gray masses without the tradition of the individual. He looked instead—or in reaction—to the profit motive and capitalistic formulas, in terms of efficiency, investment, and production. It seemed to me that he had missed a singular opportunity. He had shied from the very aspect of the world now beginning to interest industry, business, and technology as the biological basis of their—and our—affluence, and which his foundation could have shown to be the ultimate basis of all economics.

Individual man *has* his particular integrity, to be sure. Oak trees, even mountains, have selves or integrities too (a poor word for my meaning, but it will have to do). To our knowledge, those other forms are not troubled by

seeing themselves in more than one way, as man is. In one aspect the self is an arrangement of organs, feelings, and thoughts—a "me"—surrounded by a hard body boundary: skin, clothes, and insular habits. This idea needs no defense. It is conferred on us by the whole history of our civilization. Its virtue is verified by our affluence. The alternative is a self as a center of organization, constantly drawing on and influencing the surroundings, whose skin and behavior are soft zones contacting the world instead of excluding it. Both views are real and their reciprocity significant. We need them both to have a healthy social and human maturity.

The second view—that of relatedness of the self—has been given short shrift. Attitudes toward ourselves do not change easily. The conventional image of a man, like that of the heraldic lion, is iconographic; its outlines are stylized to fit the fixed curves of our vision. We are hidden from ourselves by habits of perception. Because we learn to talk at the same time we learn to think, our language, for example, encourages us to see ourselves—or a plant or animal—as an isolated sack, a thing, a contained self. Ecological thinking, on the other hand, requires a kind of vision across boundaries. The epidermis of the skin is ecologically like a pond surface or a forest soil, not a shell so much as a delicate interpenetration. It reveals the self enobled and extended rather than threatened as part of the landscape and the ecosystem, because the beauty and complexity of nature are continuous with ourselves.

And so ecology as applied to man faces the task of renewing a balanced view where now there is man-centeredness, even pathology of isolation and fear. It implies that we must find room in "our" world for all plants and animals, even for their otherness and their opposition. It further implies exploration and openness across an inner boundary—an ego boundary—and appreciative understanding of the animal in ourselves which our heritage of Platonism, Christian morbidity, duality, and mechanism have long held repellant and degrading. The older countercurrents—relics of pagan myth, the universal application of Christian compassion, philosophical naturalism, nature romanticism and pantheism—have been swept away, leaving only odd bits of wreckage. Now we find ourselves in a deteriorating environment which breeds aggressiveness and hostility toward ourselves and our world.

How simple our relationship to nature would be if we only had to choose between protecting our natural home and destroying it. Most of our efforts to provide for the natural in our philosophy have failed—run aground on their own determination to work out a peace at arm's length. Our harsh reaction against the peaceable kingdom of sentimental romanticism was evoked partly by the tone of its dulcet facade but also by the disillusion to which it led. Natural dependence and contingency suggest togetherness and emotional surrender to mass behavior and other lowest common denominators. The environmentalists matching culture and geography provoke outrage for their over-simple theories of cause and effect, against the sciences which sponsor them and even against a natural world in which the theories may or may not be true. Our historical disappointment in the nature of nature has created a cold climate for ecologists who assert once again that we are limited and obligated. Somehow they must manage in spite of the chill to reach

the centers of humanism and technology, to convey there a sense of our place in a universal vascular system without depriving us of our self-esteem and confidence.

Their message is not, after all, all bad news. Our natural affiliations define and illumine freedom instead of denying it. They demonstrate it better than any dialectic. Being more enduring than we individuals, ecological patterns—spatial distributions, symbioses, the streams of energy and matter and communication—create among individuals the tensions and polarities so different from dichotomy and separateness. The responses, or what theologians call "the sensibilities" of creatures (including ourselves) to such arrangements grow in part from a healthy union of the two kinds of self already mentioned, one emphasizing integrity, the other relatedness. But it goes beyond that to something better known to 12th century Europeans or Paleolithic hunters than to ourselves. If nature is not a prison and earth a shoddy way-station, we must find the faith and force to affirm its metabolism as our own—or rather, our own as part of it. To do so means nothing less than a shift in our whole frame of reference and our attitude towards life itself, a wider perception of the landscape as a creative, harmonious being where relationships of things are as real as the things. Without losing our sense of a great human destiny and without intellectual surrender, we must affirm that the world is a being, a part of our own body.[2]

Such a being may be called an ecosystem or simply a forest or landscape. Its members are engaged in a kind of

[2] See Alan Watts, "The World is Your Body," in *The Book on the Taboo Against Knowing Who You Are.* New York: Pantheon Books, 1966.

choreography of materials and energy and information, the creation of order and organization. (Analogy to corporate organization here is misleading, for the distinction between social (one species) and ecological (many species) is fundamental). The pond is an example. Its ecology includes all events: the conversion of sunlight to food and the food-chains within and around it, man drinking, bathing, fishing, plowing the slopes of the watershed, drawing a picture of it, and formulating theories about the world based on what he sees in the pond. He and all the other organisms at and in the pond act upon one another, engage the earth and atmosphere, and are linked to other ponds by a network of connections like the threads of protoplasm connecting cells in living tissues.

The elegance of such systems and delicacy of equilibrium are the outcome of a long evolution of interdependence. Even society, mind and culture are parts of that evolution. There is an essential relationship between them and the natural habitat: that is, between the emergence of higher primates and flowering plants, pollinating insects, seeds, humus, and arboreal life. It is unlikely that a man-like creature could arise by any other means than a long arboreal sojourn following and followed by a time of terrestriality. The fruit's complex construction and the mammalian brain are twin offspring of the maturing earth, impossible, even meaningless, without the deepening soil and the mutual development of savannas and their faunas in the last geological epoch. Internal complexity, as the mind of a primate, is an extension of natural complexity, measured by the variety of plants and animals and the variety of nerve cells—organic extensions of each other.

The exuberance of kinds as the setting in which a good mind could evolve (to deal with a complex world) was not only a past condition. Man did not arrive in the world as though disembarking from a train in the city. He continues to arrive, somewhat like the birth of art, a train in Roger Fry's definition, passing through many stations, none of which is wholly left behind. This idea of natural complexity as a counterpart to human intricacy is central to an ecology of man. The creation of order, of which man is an example, is realized also in the number of species and habitats, an abundance of landscapes lush and poor. Even deserts and tundras increase the planetary opulence. Curiously, only man and possibly a few birds can appreciate this opulence, being the world's travelers. Reduction of this variegation would, by extension then, be an amputation of man. To convert all "wastes" —all deserts, estuaries, tundras, icefields, marshes, steppes and moors— into cultivated fields and cities would impoverish rather than enrich life esthetically as well as ecologically. By esthetically, I do not mean that weasel term connoting the pleasure of baubles. We have diverted ourselves with litterbug campaigns and greenbelts in the name of esthetics while the fabric of our very environment is unravelling. In the name of conservation, too, such things are done, so that conservation becomes ambiguous. Nature is a fundamental "resource" to be sustained for our own well-being. But it loses in the translation into usable energy and commodities. Ecology may testify as often against our uses of the world, even against conservation techniques of control and management for sustained yield, as it does for them. Although ecology may be treated as a science, its greater and overriding wisdom is universal.

That wisdom can be approached mathematically, chemically, or it can be danced or told as a myth. It has been embodied in widely scattered economically different cultures. It is manifest, for example, among pre-Classical Greeks, in Navajo religion and social orientation, in Romantic poetry of the 18th and 19th centuries, in Chinese landscape painting of the 11th century, in current Whiteheadian philosophy, in Zen Buddhism, in the world view of the cult of the Cretan Great Mother, in the ceremonials of Bushman hunters, and in the medieval Christian metaphysics of light. What is common among all of them is a deep sense of engagement with the landscape, with profound connections to surroundings and to natural processes central to all life.

It is difficult in our language even to describe that sense. English becomes imprecise or mystical—and therefore suspicious—as it struggles with "process" thought. Its noun and verb organization shapes a divided world of static doers separate from the doing. It belongs to an idiom of social hierarchy in which all nature is made to mimic man. The living world is perceived in that idiom as an upright ladder, a "great chain of being," an image which seems at first ecological but is basically rigid, linear, condescending, lacking humility and love of otherness. We are all familiar from childhood with its classifications of everything on a scale from the lowest to the highest: inanimate matter/vegetative life/lower animals/higher animals/men/angels/gods. It ranks animals themselves in categories of increasing good: the vicious and lowly parasites, pathogens and predators/the filthy decay and scavenging organisms/indifferent wild or merely useless forms/good tame creatures/and virtuous beasts domesticated for human service. It shadows the great man-centered political scheme upon the world, derived from the ordered ascendency from parishioners to clerics to bishops to cardinals to popes, or in a secular form from criminals to proletarians to aldermen to mayors to senators to presidents.

And so is nature pigeonholed. The sardonic phrase, "the place of nature in man's world," offers, tongue-in-cheek, a clever footing for confronting a world made in man's image and conforming to words. It satirizes the prevailing philosophy of anti-nature and human omniscience. It is possible because of an attitude which—like ecology—has ancient roots, but whose modern form was shaped when Aquinas reconciled Aristotelian homocentrism with Judeo-Christian dogma. In a later setting of machine technology, puritanical capitalism, and an urban ethos it carves its own version of reality into the landscape like a schoolboy initialing a tree. For such a philosophy nothing in nature has inherent merit. As one professor recently put it, "The only reason anything is done on this earth is for people. Did the rivers, winds, animals, rocks, or dust ever consider my wishes or needs? Surely, we do all our acts in an earthly environment, but I have never had a tree, valley, mountain, or flower thank me for preserving it."[3] This view carries great force, epitomized in history by Bacon, Descartes, Hegel, Hobbes, and Marx.

Some other post-Renaissance thinkers are wrongly accused of undermining our assurance of natural order. The

[3] Clare A. Gunn in *Landscape Architecture*, July 1966, p. 260.

theories of the heliocentric solar system, of biological evolution, and of the unconscious mind are held to have deprived the universe of the beneficence and purpose to which man was a special heir and to have evoked feelings of separation, of antipathy towards a meaningless existence in a neutral cosmos. Modern despair, the arts of anxiety, the politics of pathological individualism and predatory socialism were not, however, the results of Copernicus, Darwin and Freud. If man was not the center of the universe, was not created by a single stroke of Providence, and is not ruled solely by rational intelligence, it does not follow therefore that nature is defective where we thought it perfect. The astronomer, biologist and psychiatrist each achieved for mankind corrections in sensibility. Each showed the interpenetration of human life and the universe to be richer and more mysterious than had been thought.

Darwin's theory of evolution has been crucial to ecology. Indeed, it might have helped rather than aggravated the growing sense of human alienation had its interpreters emphasized predation and competition less (and, for this reason, one is tempted to add, had Thomas Huxley, Herbert Spencer, Samuel Butler and G. B. Shaw had less to say about it). Its bases of universal kinship and common bonds of function, experience and value among organisms were obscured by pre-existing ideas of animal depravity. Evolutionary theory was exploited to justify the worst in men and was misused in defense of social and economic injustice. Nor was it better used by humanitarians. They opposed the degradation of men in the service of industrial progress, the slaughter of American Indians, and child labor, because each

treated men "like animals." That is to say, men were not animals, and the temper of social reform was to find good only in attributes separating men from animals. Kindness both towards and among animals was still a rare idea in the 19th century, so that using men as animals could mean only cruelty.

Since Thomas Huxley's day the non-animal forces have developed a more subtle dictum to the effect that, "Man may be an animal, but he is more than an animal, too!" The *more* is really what is important. This appealing aphorism is a kind of anesthetic. The truth is that we are ignorant of what it is like or what it means to be any other kind of creature than we are. If we are unable to truly define the animal's experience of life or "being an animal" how can we isolate our animal part?

The rejection of animality is a rejection of nature as a whole. As a teacher, I see students develop in their humanities studies a proper distrust of science and technology. What concerns me is that the stigma spreads to the natural world itself. C. P. Snow's "Two Cultures," setting the sciences against the humanities, can be misunderstood as placing nature against art. The idea that the current destruction of people and environment is scientific and would be corrected by more communication with the arts neglects the hatred for this world carried by our whole culture. Yet science as it is now taught does not promote a respect for nature. Western civilization breeds no more ecology in Western science than in Western philosophy. Snow's two cultures cannot explain the antithesis that splits the world, nor is the division ideological, economic or political in the strict sense. The antidote he proposes is roughly equivalent to a

liberal education, the traditional prescription for making broad and well-
rounded men. Unfortunately, there is
little even in the liberal education of
ecology-and-man. Nature is usually
synonymous with either natural resources or scenery, the great stereo-
types in the minds of middle class,
college-educated Americans.

One might suppose that the study of
biology would mitigate the humanistic
—largely literary—confusion between
materialism and a concern for nature.
But biology made the mistake at the
end of the 17th century of adopting a
modus operandi or life style from
physics, in which the question why
was not to be asked, only the question how. Biology succumbed to its
own image as an esoteric prologue to
technics and encouraged the whole
society to mistrust naturalists. When
scholars realized what the sciences
were about it is not surprising that
they threw out the babies with the
bathwater: the information content
and naturalistic lore with the rest of it.
This is the setting in which academia
and intellectual America undertook
the single-minded pursuit of human
uniqueness, and uncovered a great
mass of pseudo distinctions such as
language, tradition, culture, love, consciousness, history and awe of the
supernatural. Only men were found to
be capable of escape from predictability, determinism, environmental
control, instincts and other mechanisms which "imprison" other life.
Even biologists, such as Julian Huxley,
announced that the purpose of the
world was to produce man, whose social evolution excused him forever
from biological evolution. Such a view
incorporated three important presump-
tions: that nature is a power structure
shaped after human political hier-
archies; that man has a monopoly of

immortal souls; and omnipotence will
come through technology. It seems to
me that all of these foster a failure of
responsible behavior in what Paul
Sears calls "the living landscape" except within the limits of immediate
self-interest.

What ecology must communicate to
the humanities—indeed, as a humanity
—is that such an image of the world
and the society so conceived are incomplete. There is overwhelming evidence of likeness, from molecular to
mental, between men and animals. But
the dispersal of this information is not
necessarily a solution. The Two Culture idea that the problem is an information bottleneck is only partly true;
advances in biochemistry, genetics,
ethology, paleoanthropology, comparative physiology and psychobiology are
not self-evidently unifying. They need
a unifying principle not found in any
of them, a wisdom in the sense that
Walter B. Cannon used the word in
his book *Wisdom of the Body*,[4] about
the community of self-regulating systems within the organism. If the ecological extension of that perspective is
correct, societies and ecosystems as
well as cells have a physiology, and
insight into it is built into organisms,
including man. What was intuitively
apparent last year—whether aestheti-
cally or romantically—is a find of this
year's inductive analysis. It seems
apparent to me that there is an ecological instinct which probes deeper
and more comprehensively than science, and which anticipates every scientific confirmation of the natural
history of man.

It is not surprising, therefore, to find
substantial ecological insight in art.
Of course there is nothing wrong with
a poem or dance which is ecologically

[4] New York: W. W. Norton, 1932.

neutral; its merit may have nothing to do with the transaction of man and nature. It is my impression, however, that students of the arts no longer feel that the subject of a work of art— what it "represents"—is without importance, as was said about 40 years ago. But there are poems and dances as there are prayers and laws attending to ecology. Some are more than mere comments on it. Such creations become part of all life. Essays on nature are an element of a functional or feedback system influencing men's reactions to their environment, messages projected by men to themselves through some act of design, the manipulation of paints or written words. They are natural objects, like bird nests. The essay is as real a part of the community—in both the one-species sociological and many-species ecological senses—as are the songs of choirs or crickets. An essay is an Orphic sound, words that make knowing possible, for it was Orpheus as Adam who named and thus made intelligible all creatures.

What is the conflict of Two Cultures if it is not between science and art or between national ideologies? The distinction rather divides science and art within themselves. An example within science was the controversy over the atmospheric testing of nuclear bombs and the effect of radioactive fallout from the explosions. Opposing views were widely published and personified when Linus Pauling, a biochemist, and Edward Teller, a physicist, disagreed. Teller, one of the "fathers" of the bomb, pictured the fallout as a small factor in a world-wide struggle, the possible damage to life in tiny fractions of a percent, and even noted that evolutionary progress comes from mutations. Pauling, an expert on the hereditary material, knowing that most mutations are detrimental, argued that a large absolute number of people might be injured, as well as other life in the world's biosphere.

The humanness of ecology is that the dilemma of our emerging world ecological crises (over-population, environmental pollution, etc.) is at least in part a matter of values and ideas. It does not divide men as much by their trades as by the complex of personality and experience shaping their feelings towards other people and the world at large. I have mentioned the disillusion generated by the collapse of unsound nature philosophies. The anti-nature position today is often associated with the focusing of general fears and hostilities on the natural world. It can be seen in the behavior of control-obsessed engineers, corporation people selling consumption itself, academic superhumanists and media professionals fixated on political and economic crisis; neurotics working out psychic problems in the realm of power over men or nature, artistic symbol-manipulators disgusted by anything organic. It includes many normal, earnest people who are unconsciously defending themselves or their families against a vaguely threatening universe. The dangerous eruption of humanity in a deteriorating environment does not show itself as such in the daily experience of most people, but is felt as general tension and anxiety. We feel the pressure of events not as direct causes but more like omens. A kind of madness arises from the prevailing nature-conquering, nature-hating and self- and world-denial. Although in many ways most Americans live comfortable, satiated lives, there is a nameless frustration born of an increasing nullity. The aseptic home and society are progressively cut off from direct organic sources of health and increasingly isolated from the means of altering the course of events. Success, where its price is the misuse of landscapes, the deterioration of air and water and the loss of wild things, becomes a pointless glut, experience one-sided, time on our hands an unlocalized ache.

The unrest can be exploited to perpetuate itself. One familiar prescription for our sick society and its loss of environmental equilibrium is an increase in the intangible Good Things: more Culture, more Security and more Escape from pressures and tempo. The "search for identity" is not only a social but an ecological problem having to do with a sense of place and time in the context of all life. The pain of that search can be cleverly manipulated to keep the *status quo* by urging that what we need is only improved forms and more energetic expressions of what now occupy us: engrossment with ideological struggle and military power, with productivity and consumption as public and private goals, with commerce and urban growth, with amusements, with fixation on one's navel, with those tokens of escape or success already belabored by so many idealists and social critics so ineffectually.

To come back to those Good Things: the need for culture, security and escape are just near enough to the truth to take us in. But the real cultural deficiency is the absence of a true *cultus* with its significant ceremony, relevant mythical cosmos, and artifacts. The real failure in security is the disappearance from our personal lives of the small human group as the functional unit of society and the web of other creatures, domestic and wild, which are part of our humanity. As for escape, the idea of simple remission

and avoidance fails to provide for the value of solitude, to integrate leisure and natural encounter. Instead of these, what are foisted on the puzzled and troubled soul as Culture, Security and Escape are more art museums, more psychiatry, and more automobiles.

The ideological status of ecology is that of a resistance movement. Its Rachel Carsons and Aldo Leopolds are subversive (as Sears recently called ecology itself[5]). They challenge the public or private right to pollute the environment, to systematically destroy predatory animals, to spread chemical pesticides indiscriminately, to meddle chemically with food and water, to appropriate without hindrance space and surface for technological and military ends; they oppose the uninhibited growth of human populations, some forms of "aid" to "underdeveloped" peoples, the needless addition of radioactivity to the landscape, the extinction of species of plants and animals, the domestication of all wild places, large-scale manipulation of the atmosphere or the sea, and most other purely engineering solutions to problems of and intrusions into the organic world.

If naturalists seem always to be *against* something it is because they feel a responsibility to share their understanding, and their opposition constitutes a defense of the natural systems to which man is committed as an organic being. Sometimes naturalists propose projects too, but the project approach is itself partly the fault, the need for projects a consequence of linear, compartmental thinking, of machine-like units to be controlled and manipulated. If the ecological crisis

[5] Paul B. Sears, "Ecology—a subversive subject," *BioScience,* 14(7):11, July 1964.

were merely a matter of alternative techniques, the issue would belong among the technicians and developers (where most schools and departments of conservation have put it).

Truly ecological thinking need not be incompatible with our place and time. It does have an element of humility which is foreign to our thought, which moves us to silent wonder and glad affirmation. But it offers an essential factor, like a necessary vitamin, to all our engineering and social planning, to our poetry and our understanding. There is only one ecology, not a human ecology on one hand and another for the subhuman. No one school or theory or project or agency controls it. For us it means seeing the world mosaic from the human vantage without being man-fanatic. We must use it to confront the great philosophical problems of man—transience, meaning, and limitation—without fear. Affirmation of its own organic essence will be the ultimate test of the human mind.

Part 1 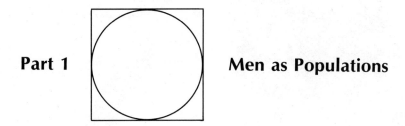 **Men as Populations**

The Human Revolution

CHARLES F. HOCKETT
ROBERT ASCHER

Men hail the freedom which raises them above animals. Our consciousness is deeper, the bondage to instinct is loosened, the limitations to place are transcended. And then there is the dream of ultimate freedom from nature itself which would be the next logical step, for the physical world seems to exert a kind of tyranny.

But this idea of tyranny misuses both ideology and nature. The uniqueness of the human species is not a great political triumph, but is itself nature. It has a biological basis and an evolutionary background. To understand human freedom is to discover its limitations. This begins with an informed, imaginative study of human evolution. Freedom grows from our animal heritage and may be traced along a series of branches from the vertebrates to the mammals to the primates and ultimately to the family of man—with freedom as we think of it intricately associated with the evolution of the nervous system, of food habits, and of habitats. "Family of man," usually narrow and homiletic, here is a profounder and more loving perspective of the zoological family Hominidae.

The "good" beginnings as well as the "bad" belong to the fundamental context of an extraordinary animal history, shaped in the ancient world of primates engaged in social carnivorousness, inseparable from the same "nature" so easily disdained.

If freedom for us be choice of action guided by knowledge, we are in a strange paradoxical situation. For our knowledge

(Left,Winnipeg Free Press, photo courtesy Food and Agricultural Organization, United Nations. Above, after Obermaier, reproduced from J. G. D. Clark, *Prehistoric Europe, The Economic Basis*, Methuen and Co., Ltd., 1952, p. 33.)

Current Anthropology, *5(3):135–168, 1964.*
Reprinted by permission.

of the intricacy of life and of our ability to destroy it links us by a thousand new ecological strands to the most minute as well as the grandest aspects of our world. In our freedom is a burden if not a bondage that no monkey was ever asked to bear.

THE EDITORS

THIS ESSAY attempts to set forth the story of the emergence of the first humans from their prehuman ancestors. A special feature is that we have tried to incorporate the various steps and stages of the evolution of language into the total picture.[1]

We dedicate this essay to the memory of Paul Fejos, whose encouragement, over a number of years, played an important part in bringing the work to fruition.

---

[1] Most paleoanthropologists have either ignored language or have tried to infer from a fossil skull or jaw that its owner could, or could not, have had "articulate speech." Childe (1936; 1951 edition: 29) fell into this error, as has Kelemen (1948); for a brief discussion, see Hockett (1956). Other examples are cited in Coon (1962:259 fn. 1, 299 fn. 5), where Coon shows his own healthy skepticism of such inferences. The basis of the trouble is that "articulate speech" does not mean anything. Bryan (1963) falls into the same trap.

Some recent discussions (e.g., Critchley 1960) try to deal with the emergence of language merely in terms of the contrast between "sign" and "symbol"; intentionally or not, these treatments give the impression that our ancestors acquired language in a single enormous leap. Anyone aware of the intricacy of design of every human language knows that such a leap was impossible; there had to be steps and stages. The contrast between "sign" and "symbol," first carefully discussed by Langer (1942), then adopted and developed by White (e.g., 1949, 1959) is too gross to serve. In White's version, the definition of the distinction is ultimately circular. A more elaborate itemization of design features found in human and animal communication will be found in Hockett (1959, 1960a, 1960b, 1963). Stuart A. Altmann, of the Department of Zoology, University of Alberta, is currently engaged in making even more subtle discriminations in this area.

The inquiry into human origins is a collective task to which hundreds of investigators have contributed. Virtually none of the proposals in the present paper are our own. Even for the ways of thinking about the evidence that seem to be fruitful, we are completely indebted to our predecessors. We do accept responsibility for the particular way in which we have chosen among alternative theories, and for the way in which we have tied them together. We believe that the time is ripe for a synthesis of this sort, if only as a clear point of departure for the further investigation of both method and detail.

The term "revolution" in our title is not intended to be flamboyant. A revolution is a relatively sudden set of changes that yield a state of affairs from which a return to the situation just before the revolution is virtually impossible. This seems to be the sense of the word intended by V. Gordon Childe (1936) when he speaks of the "Neolithic Revolution" and of the "Urban Revolution." But these two revolutions were experienced by our fully human ancestors. The second could not have occurred had it not been for the first. The first could not have taken place had it not been for an even earlier extremely drastic set of changes that turned nonhumans into humans. These drastic changes, as we shall see, may have required a good many millions of years; yet they can validly be regarded as "sudden" in view of the tens of millions of years of mammalian history that preceded them.

For the reconstruction of human evolution we have evidence of two sorts, plus certain firm and many tentative principles of interpretation.

One kind of evidence is the archeological, fossil, and geological record.

The fossil record of our own ancestry is still disappointingly sparse for the bulk of the Miocene and Pliocene. It seems unlikely that such records can ever be as complete as we might wish. But techniques of interpretation improve, and we suspect that the archeological record, in particular, holds an as yet unrealized potential.

The second kind of evidence is the directly observable physical structure and ways of life of ourselves and of our nearest nonhuman cousins, the other hominoids of today. Chimpanzees, gorillas, orangutans, gibbons, siamangs, and humans have ultimately a common ancestry not shared with any other living species. We shall refer to their most recent common ancestors as the *proto-hominoids*. Since all the hominoids of today constitute continuations of the proto-hominoids, we can attempt to reconstruct something of the physical structure and of the lifeways of the common ancestors by comparing those of the descendants. Such an effort at reconstruction must at the same time propose realistic courses of development from the ancestral group down to each of the directly observable descendant groups, and must make proper provision for those strains known only through fossils or archeological remains.

The method is very much like the comparative method in historical linguistics—and, as a matter of fact, it was first devised in the latter context, only subsequently transferred to the domain of biological evolution.[2] The term "comparative" appears also in "comparative morphology" (or "comparative anatomy"); we must therefore emphasize that the method of which we are speaking applies not only to gross anatomy but also to the fine-scale phenomena dealt with in biochemistry, and not only to structure but also to behavior.

In any domain of application, a comparative method shares with all other historical methods the fact that it can yield reliable results only insofar as one can be sure of certain key *irreversible* processes. Given information about stages A and B in the history of a single system, we can posit that stage A preceded stage B if and only if the change from A to B is the sort that happens, while a change from B to A is impossible or highly improbable. In historical linguistics, the requisite irreversibility is afforded by sound change. The philologists of the late 19th century were correct when they characterized sound change as slow, constant, inexorable, and beyond conscious control; for, as we shall see later, it is a necessary by-product of a crucial design feature of all human language, and could not be eliminated save by altering language into something unrecognizable. Whenever sound change leads to the repatterning of the phonological system of a language— and this has happened about 100 times in English between King Alfred's day and our own (Hockett 1958:457)[3]—the consequences ramify through every

[2] The first comparative grammar was published in 1799 (Bloomfield 1933: ch. 1; see also Pederson 1931). The mutual stimulation of biologists and linguists at the time of Darwin is briefly discussed by Greenberg (1959). In the literature of the last few decades we fail to find any discussion of the comparative method that properly highlights the necessary differences in its applications to language, to human lifeways other than language,

and in genetics and phylogeny. The authors are attempting to fill this hiatus in a forthcoming article; the remarks in the next few paragraphs of the present paper are only suggestive.

[3] For the nature of sound change see Hockett (1958: chs. 52–54) and Bloomfield (1933: chs. 20–21).

part of the language; soon the results are so scattered, so subtle, and from the point of view of effectiveness of communication so *trivial*, that a return to the state of affairs before the repatterning has, in effect, probability zero.

The situation in biological evolution is much more complicated, with no simple analogue for sound change. Is a particular organ in a particular species (living or fossil) vestigial or incipient? Is the swimming bladder of current teleosts a former lung, or is the lung of lungfishes a one-time swimming bladder? Evolutionists are plagued by such questions. The answers are often obtainable, but not through any simple formula. A new fossil does not automatically resolve the dispute, since one's opinions as to lines and directions of development will affect one's notions as to how the new fossil is to be fitted into the picture.

For the *mechanisms* of change we are in less trouble. We have now a good understanding of genetics, and also of the traditional transmission of lifeways. The latter was once believed to be exclusively human, but this is not so. At least for land mammals and for birds, genetics and tradition work in a constant dialectic complementation, neither being wholly responsible for anything (Hochbaum 1955; Dobzhansky 1956; 1962). We are also clearer about a point that used to be quite obscure: the domain (so to speak) within which these two mechanisms operate is not the individual but the community, which has a gene pool, a distribution of phenotypes, and a repository of lifeways, and which, as a functioning unit, faces the problems of survival (Simpson 1958).

The greatest pitfall in evolutionary thinking stems from the keenness of

hindsight.[4] For example, we know that long ago, over a long period of time, our own ancestors abandoned the trees for the ground and developed effective machinery for bipedal locomotion. This seems beyond dispute, because the prehominoid primates were arboreal and we ourselves are bipedal ground walkers. But when we ask *why* this change, we must remember that our ancestors of the time were not striving to become human. They were doing what all animals do: trying to stay alive.

Thus, in searching for causes of the change we must look to conditions pertaining at the time. There are only two possibilities. The conditions at that time may have been such that minor variations in gait and posture had no bearing on survival. We should then class the change that actually did take place as fortuitous. Or, the conditions of life at the time may have positively favored selection for bipedal locomotion and upright posture. If this is what happened, then the change was adaptive. By definition, a change that was neither adaptive nor fortuitous would lead to the extinction of

---

[4] When it comes to human evolution there is another dangerous pitfall: that of anthropomorphizing the rest of nature or (equally dangerous) of interpreting the difference between ourselves and the rest of nature in physically and biologically impossible terms. In the discussion of man's place in nature there is no place for mentalism or vitalism. The only valid assumption is that of *physicalism*: life is part of the inorganic world and subject to all the laws of physics; man is an animal and subject to all the laws of biology (Bloomfield 1936; Hockett 1948). Anthropologists still fall constantly into the error of contrasting the "cultural" and the "biological"; even Dobzhansky (1962) chooses the unfortunate terms "organic" and "superorganic" (though what he says with these terms is good). It is equally misleading to speak of "natural" versus "artificial" selection. Such pairings of terms are survivals of the mind-body dualism of an earlier day in the intellectual history of the West; they should be extirpated.

the strain that underwent it, and in the present instance we know that that did not happen.[5]

The most powerful antidote for the improper use of keen hindsight is a principle that we shall call "Romer's Rule," after the paleontologist A. S. Romer who has applied it so effectively—without giving it any name— in his own work. We phrase this rule as follows:

The initial survival value of a favorable innovation is conservative, in that it renders possible the maintenance of a traditional way of life in the face of changed circumstances.

Later on, of course, the innovation may allow the exploration of some ecological niche not available to the species before the change; but this is a consequence, not a cause.

One of Romer's examples concerns the evolution of Devonian lungfishes into the earliest amphibians (1959:93–94; 1958 *passim*). The invasion of the land was feasible only with strong fins (which in due time became legs). But strong fins were not developed "in order to" invade the land. The climate of the epoch was tempestuous; the water level of the pools in which the lungfishes lived was subject to sudden recessions. There was thus selection for those strains of lungfishes which, when stranded by such a recession, had strong enough fins to *get back to the water*. Only much later did some of their descendants come to stay ashore most of the time.

It is worthy of note that Romer's Rule is not anti-teleological. We are permitted to speak in terms of purposeful behavior whenever we are dealing with a system that incorporates negative feedback.[6] Individual organisms, and certain groupings of organisms (the kinds we call "communities"), are such systems. There is nothing wrong in asserting that a stranded Devonian lungfish tried his best to get back to the water. We are forced, however, to distinguish carefully between purposes and *consequences*, and we are not allowed to ascribe "purposefulness" to any such vague and long-continuing process as "evolution."

No principle, no matter how universal, answers all questions. Romer's Rule cuts as keenly as any razor ever devised by Occam to expose, excise, and discard unworkable pseudo explanations. Yet it is applicable, in a sense, only after the fact. For example, in this paper we follow majority opinion and trace man's ancestry back to a point of separation from the ancestors of the great apes, the gibbons, and the siamangs. Having assumed this, we elaborate one of Romer's own suggestions as to how some of the early developments may have come about. Suppose, however, that new fossil finds should convince us that man is actually more closely related to some other group of surviving primates (Coon 1962: ch. 5). We should then be confronted by a different set of

---

[5] By "extinction" we mean exclusively what Coon (1962:31) calls "utter extinction without issue"; the use of the same word for "extinction through successive evolution" is misleading, stemming from and lending support to an almost word-magical handling of the term "species."

[6] Especially since Wiener (1948), it has come to be recognized that purposeful behavior can be described as the behavior of mechanisms with certain physical properties, and that organisms are such mechanisms. On the basic assumption of physicalism (see fn. 4), we are required to speak of "purpose" only when we know, or can reasonably assume, that we are dealing with a system with the requisite physical structure. The teleological proposals in evolutionary theory, dealt with and disposed of so well by Simpson (1949: 1951 paperback edition ch. 2), do not meet these requirements.

17

putative historical facts requiring explanation; but we should evoke the same Rule as we sought that explanation. The Rule does not tell us which line of descent to postulate.

The Proto-hominoids

From the location, date, and morphology of the fossil dryopithecine *Proconsul* we infer that the proto-hominoids lived in East Africa in the Middle or Lower Miocene or, at the earliest, in the Upper Oligocene (Oakley 1962).[7] This does not mean that *Proconsul* himself—in any of the strains or species so far identified—was a proto-hominoid; indeed, he is not a good candidate as an ancestor of the gibbons and siamangs, to whom, by definition, the proto-hominoids were ancestral. But *Proconsul* was clearly an *early* hominoid, and at the moment he is the best fossil evidence available for the date and provenience we seek.

The proto-hominoids inherited certain crucial capacities from their totally tree-dwelling ancestors.[8] It is the arboreal pattern that developed the keen accommodative vision characteristic of the higher primates, de-emphasized the sense of smell, turned forelimbs into freely movable arms with manipulative hands, and built brains somewhat larger than the average for land mammals.

The balance of the characterization we are about to give—what Count (1958) would call a "biogram" of the proto-hominoids—derives mainly from the comparative method applied to

what we know of the hominoids of today (Schultz 1961 is a superb review; Sahlins 1959; Hediger 1961; Chance 1961; Spuhler 1959; Altmann 1962; Bartholomew and Birdsell 1953; Coon 1962). We shall not give all the evidence in detail. Furthermore, for the sake of vividness we shall allow some interpolations of a degree of precision that may be unwarranted. The proportion of guesswork in each statement will, we think, be fairly obvious.

Like most of their descendants, the proto-hominoids were hairy. Like all of them, they were tailless. They were smaller than we are, though not so small as present-day gibbons, whose size has decreased as an adaptation to brachiation. They had mobile facial muscles; they had neither mental eminence nor simian shelf (nor mastoid processes); they had large interlocking canines, and could chew only up and down; their tooth pattern was (2:1:2:3)/(2:1:2:3). It seems likely that there was little sexual dimorphism, although on this the comparative evidence is conflicting. The chromosome count was somewhere in the forties.

They lived in bands of from ten to thirty, consisting typically of one or a very few adult males plus females and offspring. They had a roughly defined nucleated territoriality: that is, the territory within which the members of a band moved about had only roughly demarcated boundaries, but centered on the specific arboreal sites in which they built their nests.[9] The

---

[7] *Propliopithecus*, from the Fayum Oligocene, looks like a possible ancestral gibbon rather than a pre-proto-hominoid; if so, then the proto-hominoids had to be earlier than *Proconsul* (Coon 1962:196).

[8] Apparently this suggestion was first made by Smith (1913).

[9] Students of primate behavior use the terms "band" and "troop" in technically distinct ways. Without prejudice for the subtle distinctions thus indicated, we have found it more convenient to use the term "band" throughout in a generic sense. The kind of territoriality described here is coming to be distinguished from other varieties (for instance, from the perimeter-defending territorial behavior of many birds) by the use of the term "core area." On nests: Nissen (1931); Bingham (1932); Bolwig (1959); Carpenter (1938); Hooton (1942:14–15, 155, 78–80, 124–25).

Epoch	Years*	Time Scale/Events in the History of Life†	
Recent	10,000	Urbanization Use of fossil fuels Agriculture Domestication of plants and animals New Stone Age—pottery, polished stone axes	Extinction of many birds and mammals —last of great mammoths and mastodons become extinct
Pleistocene	2 million	Planetary spread of man Modern Man (*Homo s. sapiens*) Bow and arrow Art, burials and birth of religion *Homo sapiens neanderthalensis* Wood and bone tools Clothing "Core" tools *Homo sapiens* Language "Flake" tools Jaw and skull humanized Fire as tool and cooking *Pithecanthropus*, hunting cultures (large game) Cave dwellings Perfection of human leg Advanced *Australopithecus*	Extermination of many large mammals in Europe and America Modern-sized brains ↑ Brain in transition │ │ *Zinjanthropus* ↓ *Paranthropus*
Pliocene	15 million	Early *Australopithecus* Incidental predation Pre-language Savanna dwelling Hairlessness *Kenyapithecus* and *Ramapithecus* Sexual dimorphism Ventral copulation Changes in leg, pelvis, teeth, jaw, and skull (trend toward hominid condition)	Great age of big game (Artiodactyla), large carnivores *Oreopithecus*
Miocene	25 million	*Dryopithecus* Erect posture, walking Modification of pelvis and leg Carrying *Proconsul* Bipedal, upright stance Modified foot Uric acid in blood Reduction in incisors and canines	Many kinds of elephant-like mammals Rapid evolution of modern mammals and spread of grasslands *Pliopithecus* Apes diverge from hominids
Oligocene	40 million	Proto-hominids Semi-terrestrial Forest edge habitation Generalized hand and arm	Earliest elephants

* Years given are from the beginning of the Epoch Before Present.
† Events listed are not strictly sequential but a general chronology.

(Table added by editors.)

total population was probably never very great, nor very dense, from the proto-hominoids all the way down to the first true humans.[10]

They were expert climbers and spent much of their lives in the trees of the tropical or subtropical forests which were their habitat, certainly building their nests in the trees and sleeping there. Like rodents, they climbed up a tree head first; unlike rodents, they climbed down stern first. They slept at night, from dusk to dawn, which in the tropics means nearer to one-half of each twenty-four-hour period than to the one-third characteristic of ourselves in recent times. They were active during the day. Some activities, particularly the constant search for food, led them not only among the trees—in which they may have brachiated, but with no great expertness—but also quite regularly to the ground below. On the ground, they could stand with a semi-upright posture (erect enough to raise their heads above shoulder-high grass to look about), and they could sit with arms free for manipulative motions; they could walk on all fours and could run on their feet, but bipedal walking was infrequent and awkward.

Occasionally they would pick up a stick or stone and use it as a tool. Judging from modern chimpanzees,[11] they may have reshaped such tools slightly, using nothing but their hands

and teeth to do so, and may have carried a tool for a short distance for immediate use, thereafter discarding it. They carried other things too, in mouth or hands or both, in connection with nest-building; and at least the females, perhaps on occasion the males, carried infants.

Their diet was largely vegetarian, supplemented by worms and grubs, and sometimes by small mammals or birds that were injured or sick and thus unable to escape. (We might call this "*very* slow game.") They scavenged the remains of the kills of carnivores whenever they could. Unlike all other mammals except the Dalmatian coach hound, their bodies produced no uricase; hence uric acid was not converted into allantoin before secretion in the urine, and had a chance to accumulate in the bloodstream. The structural formula of uric acid is something like that of caffein and, like the latter, it seems to be a mild brain stimulant. Since this type of purine metabolism is shared by all the hominoids, it can hardly explain our own unusual brilliance; but it may help to account for the generally high level of hominoid intelligence as compared with other primates and other mammals (Coon 1962:172 and references cited).

The males had the pendulous penis typical of the primates. Copulation was effected exclusively with the dorsal approach common to land mammals in general. Gestation required about thirty weeks. The uterus was single-chambered, and twinning was as rare as it is for us today. The placenta was of the single-disc type. The young required and received maternal care for many months. Mammary glands were pectoral; nursing females held infants to the breast in their arms,

---

[10] This is important because of the Sewall Wright effect. If the population size range is correct, random genetic drift was operative. The development of similar but independent gene pools, and the occasional gene flow across population lines, worked in favor of the selection of those mutations important for the survival of the entire population. Such circumstances favor more rapid adaptive change.

[11] Crucial recent observations by Jane Goodall were reported to us orally by L. S. B. Leakey (see fn. 16).

though doubtless the infant clung to the mother's fur also. The eruption of permanent teeth began perhaps at two and one-half or three. Menarche was at eight or nine years; general growth stopped for both sexes at nine or ten. The females showed a year-round menstrual cycle rather than a rutting season. Inbreeding within the band was the rule. The life-span was potentially about thirty years, but death was largely from accident, disease, or predation, or a combination of these, rather than old age. Corpses were abandoned, as were members of the band too sick, injured, or feeble to keep up with the rest, and were disposed of by predators or scavengers. Adult males were sexually interested in females and "paternally" interested in infants, but without any permanent family bond, and without any jealousy when they were themselves sexually satisfied.

Relations with adjacent bands were normally hostile to neutral, rarely if ever friendly; yet there was surely enough contact to provide for some exchange of genes. Social differentiation within the band turned largely on age and sex, secondarily on physical strength. In case of conflict of interest within the band, the huskiest adult males normally got their way. Collective activities required intragroup coordination, effected by various forms of communication—patterns of body motion, pushing and prodding, changes of body odor, and vocal signals. The conventions of these forms of communication were transmitted in part genetically, but in some part by tradition, acquired by the young through guided participation in the ways of the group. This implies also a certain capacity to learn from experience, and to pass on any new skills thus acquired to other members of the band by teaching and learning, rather than merely by slow genetic selection. But we may assume that usually there was very little new in any one lifetime thus to be learned or passed on.

A kind of activity called *play* is widespread among land mammals, and obviously intensified among primates; we can be sure that the proto-hominoids indulged in it, at least before maturity (Kroeber 1948:27–30; Altmann 1962 and references cited). It is very hard to characterize play precisely, beyond saying that it resembles one or another serious activity without being serious. Play at fighting, observable for example among dogs, goes through much the same gross motions as true fighting but the participants receive no injury. Sexual play has the general contours of courtship, but ends short of coitus or with mock coitus. We suspect that play is *fun*, for any species that manifests it, and that that is the immediate motive for indulging in it. But play is also genuinely pedagogical, in that the young thereby get needed practice in certain patterns of behavior that are biologically important for adult life.

The proto-hominoids did not have the power of speech. The most that we can validly ascribe to them in this respect is a call system similar to that of modern gibbons. Even this ascription may be stretching the comparative evidence somewhat. It is not hard to assume that a line of continuity from the proto-hominoids to the gibbons should have maintained such a call system essentially unchanged. It is also quite reasonable, as we shall see, to explain the evolution of a call system into language among our ancestors. The difficulty is to account for the apparently less highly developed vocal-auditory signaling of the great apes. Our hypothesis for the proto-hominoids suggests that the communicative behavior of the great apes may be somewhat more subtle and complex than has yet been realized. Be this as it may, we posit a call system for the proto-hominoids because we know no other way to proceed.[12]

The essential design features of a call system are simple. There is a repertory of a half-dozen or so distinct signals, each the appropriate vocal response—or the vocal segment of a more inclusive response—to a recurrent and biologically important type of situation. Among gibbons, one such situation is the discovery of food; another is the detection of danger; a third is friendly interest and the desire for company. A fourth gibbon call apparently does nothing but indicate the whereabouts of the gibbon that emits it: this call keeps the band from spreading out too thin as it moves through the trees. One can guess at other possible situations appropriate for a special call: sexual interest; need for maternal care; pain. Band-to-band differences in calls may help to distinguish friend from alien.

A single call may be varied in intensity, duration, or number of repetitions, to correlate with and give information about the strength of the stimulus which is eliciting it. However, the signals of a call system are *mutually exclusive* in the following sense: the animal, finding himself in a situation, can only respond by one or another of the calls or by silence. He cannot, in principle, emit a signal that has some of the features of one call and some of another. If, for example, he encounters food and danger at the same time, one of these will take precedence: he is constrained to emit either the food call or the danger call, not some mixture of the two.

The technical description of this mutual exclusiveness is to say that the system is *closed*. Language, in sharp contrast, is *open* or *productive:* we freely emit utterances that we have never said nor heard before, and are usually understood, neither speaker nor hearer being aware of the novelty.

A call system differs from language in two other ways, and perhaps in a third.[13] (1) Gibbons do not emit, say,

---

[12] Although we draw largely on Carpenter's account of gibbon calls (1940), vocal-auditory signaling of the sort that qualifies as a call system is widespread among land mammals; e.g., among prairiedogs, whose system has been partly described (King 1955). Hediger (1961) writes—using nontechnical terms that require to be properly interpreted: "Five elements of speech that by purely theoretical reasoning have been found to be the most essential are in fact contained in all animal systems of communication investigated up to date and receive added differentiation in the course of evolution, in accordance with the requirements imposed by the respective living conditions. These are the five sounds or signals: (a) warning signal (enemy), (b) mating and territorial possession, (c) mother-and-child contact, (d) social contact, (e) announcement of food." And Schultz (1961): "Without the hearing of sounds, produced by their own kind, monkeys and apes would never have become the intensely social animals that they are. Sounds of a surprising variety serve continually for the contact between the members of a group, for the orientation of mother and young, for the information of the entire group about possible danger, and, last but not least, for scaring enemies of different or the same species and even for warning rival groups away from the territories already occupied. . . . The orgies of noise, indulged in especially by howlers, guerezas, gibbons, siamangs, and chimpanzees, seemingly so repetitious and meaningless, are probably at least as informative to the respective species as most after-dinner speaking is to *Homo sapiens*."

[13] Of the thirteen design features described in Hockett (1960b), the following are shared by gibbon calls and language, hence presumably also by the call system of the proto-hominoids: vocal-auditory channel; broadcast transmission and directional reception; rapid fading (combatted by repetition in the case of gibbon calls); interchangeability; total feedback; specialization; semanticity; arbitrariness; discreteness. Hence we need not deal with any of these properties in the sequel.

the food call unless they have found food (or, perhaps, are responding to the food call from another gibbon, as they approach for their share of it). Furthermore, the gibbon that finds food does not go back to headquarters and report; he stays by the food as he emits the call. A call system does not have *displacement*. Language does: we speak freely of things that are out of sight or are in the past or future—or even nonexistent. (2) The utterances of a language consist wholly of arrangements of elementary signaling units called *phonemes* (or *phonological components*, to be exact), which in themselves have no meanings but merely serve to keep meaningful utterances apart. Thus, an utterance has both a structure in terms of these meaningless but differentiating elements, and also a structure in terms of the minimum meaningful elements. This design feature is *duality of patterning*. A call system lacks it, the differences between any two calls being global. (3) Finally, the detailed conventions of any one language are transmitted wholly by the traditional mechanism, though, of course, the capacity to learn a language, and probably the drive to do so, are genetic. On this score we are still in ignorance about the gibbons. Regional differences in gibbon calls have been noted, but various balances between tradition and genetics can yield that. We believe it safer to assume that proto-hominoid call systems were passed down from generation to generation largely through the genes, tradition playing a minor role. [14] This assumption is the conservative one—it gives us more to try to explain in later developments than would any alternative.

This completes our characterization of the proto-hominoids, which can now serve as point of departure for the story of our own evolution.

Out of the Trees

Some of the descendants of the proto-hominoids moved out of the trees and became erect bipeds. Romer's description (1959:327) of how this may have begun affords another example of the application of the Rule we ascribe to him. [15]

Geological evidence suggests that at one or more times during the East African Miocene a climatic change gradually thinned out the vegetation, converting continuous tropical forest into open savannah with scattered clumps of trees. As the trees retreated, some bands of hominoids retreated with them, never abandoning their classical arboreal existence; their descendants of today are the gibbons and siamangs. Other bands were caught in isolated groves of slowly diminishing extent. In due time, those bands whose physique made it possible for their members to traverse open country to another grove survived; those that could not do this became extinct. Thus, for those bands, the survival value of the perquisites for safe ground travel was not at all that they could therefore begin a new way of life out of the trees, but that, when necessary, they could make their way to a place where the traditional

---

[14] It is exceedingly difficult to phrase a statement of this kind in such a way as to avoid misunderstanding. We are *not* sorting out various features of structure and behavior and saying: genes are responsible for these, tradition is responsible for those. Both mechanisms of transmission contribute to everything—but with great variation in the balance and the precise nature of the interplay between the two. The best discussion we know of this is Dobzhansky (1956).

[15] We elaborate Romer's brief suggestion considerably. See also Oakley (1961).

arboreal way of life could be continued. The hominoids that were successful at this included those ancestral to the great apes and to ourselves.

Sometimes the band forced to try to emigrate from a grove would be the total population of that grove. More typically, we suspect, population pressure within a diminishing grove would force bands into competition over its resources, and the less powerful bands would be displaced. Also, when a migrating band managed to reach another grove, it would often happen that the new grove was already occupied, and once again there would be competition. Thus, in the long run, the trees would be held by the more powerful, while the less powerful would repeatedly have to get along as best they could in the fringes of the forest or in open country. Here is a double selective process. The trees went to the more powerful, provided only that they maintained a minimum ability to traverse open country when necessary: some of these successful ones were ancestral to the great apes of today. Our own ancestors were the failures. We did not abandon the trees because we wanted to, but because we were pushed out.

We are speaking here of displacements and movements of whole bands, not of individual animals. There is one thing that surely accompanied any band whenever it moved: the essential geometry of its territoriality. At any halt, no matter how temporary, whether in the trees, under the trees, or in open country, some specific site became, for the nonce, "home base"— a GHQ, a center, a focus, relative to which each member of the band oriented himself as he moved about. Headquarters was the safest place to be, if for no other reason than the safety of numbers. In a later epoch—

though doubtless earlier than will ever be directly attested by archeology— headquarters among our own ancestors came to be crudely fortified, as by a piled ring of stones;[16] it became the place where things were kept or stored; in due time it became house, village, fort, city. But earliest of all it was *home*. The tradition for this sort of territoriality is much older than the proto-hominoids, and has continued unbroken to the present day.

It is at this point in our story that we must stop referring to our ancestors as "hominoids" and start calling them "hominids." Of course, all hominids are hominoids; but we have now seen the sorting-out of the pre-apes from the pre-humans, and when we wish to speak exclusively of the latter the appropriate term is "hominid."

Carrying

It is no joke to be thrown out of one's ancestral home. If the next grove is only a few miles away, in sight, then one has something to aim for; but sooner or later movements must have taken place without any such visible target. Treeless country holds discomforts and dangers. There may not be much food, at least not of a familiar sort. There may be little available water, for the trees tend to cluster where the water is more abundant. And there are fleet four-footed predators, as well as herbivorous quadrupeds big and strong enough to be dangerous at close quarters. One cannot avoid these other animals altogether, since their presence often

[16] In a lecture at Cornell University, Wednesday, 26 March 1963, L. S. B. Leakey showed a slide of a ring of stones unearthed at a very early East African site; in conversation, he scoffed at the traditional notion that our ancestors had no homes until they moved into caves.

signals the location of water, or of food fit also for hominid consumption. The quest for food must be carried on constantly, no matter how pressing may be the drive to find a new grove of trees in which to settle. It is a wonder that any of the waifs of the Miocene savannah survived at all. Enormous numbers of them must have died out.

The trick that made survival possible for some of them was the trick of *carrying*. The proto-hominoids, as we have seen, probably carried twigs and brush to make nests, and certainly carried infants. Also, they had fine arms and hands usable for carrying as well as for climbing, grasping, and manipulating; and the comparative evidence suggests that they occasionally picked up sticks or stones to use as tools. These are the raw materials for the kind of carrying to which we now refer. But it takes something else to blend them into the new pattern. In the trees, hands are largely occupied with climbing. The infant-in-arms grabs onto the mother when the latter needs her hands for locomotion. The twig being taken to the nest is transferred to the mouth when the hand cannot at the same time hold it and grasp a tree branch. One puts down one's ad-hoc tool when one has to move.

The conditions for carrying are no better on the ground than in the trees if the hand must revert to the status of a foot. But if bipedal locomotion is at all possible, then the hand is freed for carrying; and the survival value of carrying certain things in turn serves to promote a physical structure adapted to bipedal locomotion.

Two sorts of ground carrying in the hands may have been extremely early; there seems to be no way of determining which came first. One is the carrying of crude weapons; the other is the transportation of scavenged food.[17]

The earliest ground-carrying of weapons may well have been a sort of accident. Imagine an early hominid—perhaps even a prehominid hominoid—sitting on the ground and pounding something (a nut, say) with a handy stone. A predator approaches. Our hero jumps up and runs away as best he can on two legs—there are no trees nearby to escape into—but keeps his grasp on the stone for no better reason than that he does not need his hand for anything else. Cornered, he turns, and either strikes out at the predator with the hand that holds the stone, or else throws it. The predator falls or runs off, and whatever in our hero's genes or life experience, or both, has contributed to his behavior stands a chance of being passed on to others.

The first carrying of scavenged food back to headquarters (instead of consuming it on the spot) may also have been a sort of accident. A scavenging hominoid is eating the remains of a predator's kill where he has found it, and is surprised by the predator who is coming back to make another meal from the same kill. The hominoid runs off towards headquarters, still holding a piece of meat in his hand. In due time, he or his successors develop the habit of carrying the spoils off without waiting for the predator to turn up.

As described, these two early kinds of hand-carrying involve movements of a single animal *within* the band's territory. The carrying-along of things as the whole band moves is another matter, and probably a later development. Surely the earliest carrying of this latter sort was of unshaped weapons of defense. Yet other things might have been taken along. Extra food

---

[17] On the latter, Hewes (1961) is particularly convincing.

would be a great rarity, but if some were taken along because no one happened to be hungry as a movement began, it would be important if the band reached a particularly barren region. Water-carrying would have been extremely valuable—primates in general have to drink at least once a day, in contrast to some mammalian species which can store up several days' supply. Short hauls of small quantities of water cupped in the large leaves of tropical plants may have been quite early; large-scale water transport as a whole band moves must have been a great deal later, since it requires technologically advanced containers.

The side-effects of carrying things in the hands are of incalculable importance. We have already seen that its immediate practical value helped to promote bipedal walking, which in turn selected both for carrying and for an upright posture that renders bipedal walking mechanically more efficient. A less obvious consequence is that carrying made for a kind of behavior that has all the outward earmarks of what we call "memory" and "foresight": one lugs around a heavy stick or stone despite the absence of any immediate need for it, as though one were remembering past experiences in which having it available was important and were planning for possible future encounters of the same kind. Taking scavenged meat back to headquarters without waiting for the predator to return to his kill also looks like foresight. We do not mean to deny the validity of the terms "memory" and "foresight." The point is that the outward earmarks surely came first, and only over a long period of time *produced* the psychological characteristics

to which these terms refer.[18]

A third consequence of carrying and of wandering was a change in dietary balance. The first tools to be carried were defensive weapons. Often enough, no doubt, the use of these weapons against a predator, even if successful, would only scare him off. But sometimes the predator would be killed. Why waste the meat? We can also suppose that the wandering Miocene or Pliocene hominids occasionally found themselves in open country where no suitable plant food was available. Herbivorous animals could eat the grass; quadruped predators could eat the grazers; and the hominids, if they were lucky, could eat the grazers or the predators, or else starve. Thus the hunted became the hunters, and weapons of defense became weapons of offense.[19]

The gradual increase of meat in the diet had important consequences of its own, to which we will turn after noting one further direct consequence of hand-carrying.

[18] This interpretation insists on the correctness of what has been called the "exogenic" rather than the "endogenic" theory as to the basic (though not the only) direction of causal connections in evolution (Hewes 1961:689). Our treatment is in general accord with Washburn's recent proposals (1959; 1960), which are also exogenic.

[19] It has often been proposed that the first non-scavenged meat was "slow game" (Coon 1962:80). We agree on the importance of slow game, except in one respect: the adventures that served as crucial impetus making for the carrying of weapons must have been adventures with fast and dangerous creatures, not slow and harmless ones. Once weapon-carrying was established, the weapons would obviously be used on slow game too—perhaps even predominantly so.
One other factor promoting meat in the diet should be mentioned. Oakley (1961:190) points out that a desiccating climate (of the sort that would thin out the forest) may have induced a change in intestinal flora and fauna, rendering the utilization of certain vegetable foods less efficient and thus increasing the hunger for protein.

The use of the hands for carrying implied that the mouth and teeth, classically used for this by land mammals, birds, and even reptiles, were freed for other activities. It can quite safely be asserted that if primate and hominid evolution had not transferred from mouth to hand first the grasping and manipulating function and then the carrying function, human language as we know it would never have evolved. What were the hominids to do with their mouths, rendered thus relatively idle except when they were eating? The answer is: they chattered.[20]

Remember that the proto-hominoids are assumed in this account to have had a call system, and that that system would not have been lost by the stage we have now reached. The hunting of dangerous animals is a challenge even with advanced weapons. With primitive weapons there is a great advantage if it can be done collaboratively. But this calls for coordination of the acts of the participants. Their hands hold weapons and are thus unavailable for any complicated semaphore. Their visual attention must be divided between the motions of the quarry and those of the other participants. All this favors an increase in flexibility of vocal-auditory communication.

Other factors also favor such an increase. Meat is a highly efficient and compactly packaged food, as compared with uncultivated plants. A small kill may not go very far, but with collective hunting larger quarry were caught. After such a large kill, there is often more food than can be consumed even by all the direct participants in the hunt. Sharing the food among all the members of the band comes about almost automatically, in that when the hunters themselves are sated they no longer care if the rest take the leavings. Thus the sharing of meat makes for the survival of the whole band. Collective hunting, general food-sharing, and the carrying of an increasing variety of things all press towards a more complex social organization, which is only possible with more flexible communication. These same factors also promote what we vaguely call the "socialization" of the members of the band.[21]

Another development bearing on the quality, if not the degree, of hominid socialization must have taken place during this same period. At some point during the slow morphological shift to efficient upright posture, the frontal approach for copulation must have first become anatomically possible, and it was doubtless immediately exploited. It may even be imagined that, for certain strains of the hominids at certain times, the expansion of the gluteus maximus rendered the dorsal approach so awkward that the invention of the frontal approach had the conservative value required by Romer's Rule. Humans have never shown much tendency to confine themselves to this position for intercourse, but it does seem to be universally known, and is

---

[20] Some of our guesses at the lifeways of the proto-hominoids are based on observations of modern baboons (Washburn and DeVore 1961), whose conditions of life seem to be somewhat similar. But in at least one respect there is a sharp difference: the baboons carry on their affairs in a strikingly silent way. Their vocal sounds are rare.

[21] We do not imply that there was no sharing of food or "socialization" before collective hunting. The suckling of the young is a kind of food-sharing; a food call is indicative of food-sharing; scavenged meat hauled back to headquarters, perhaps long before any use of weapons for hunting, may have been shared. The developments outlined in the text are a matter of intensification and elaboration.

almost exclusively human.[22] Just how this change may have affected hominid lifeways is not clear. Our guess is that it changed, for the adult female, the relative roles of the adult male and of the infant, since after the innovation there is a much closer similarity for her between her reception of an infant and of a lover. This may have helped to spread the "tender emotions" of mammalian mother-infant relations to other interpersonal relationships within the band, ultimately with such further consequences as the Oedipus complex.

Opening of the Call System

We have seen a changing pattern of life that would be well served by a vocal-auditory communicative system of greater complexity and subtlety. Now a call system can become more flexible, within limits, through the development of totally new calls to fit additional types of recurrent situation. But it cannot take the first step towards language as we know it unless something else happens: through a process about to be described, the closed system becomes open.

Let us illustrate the way in which this can come about by describing what may occasionally happen among the gibbons of today—although, to be sure, such an occurrence has never been observed. Suppose a gibbon finds himself in a situation characterized by both the presence of food and the imminence of danger. The factors are closely balanced. Instead of emitting either the clear food call or the unmistakable danger call, he utters a

cry that has some of the characteristics of each. Among gibbons such an event is doubtless so rare and unusual that the other members of the band have no way of interpreting it; thus, the consequences are negligible. But if we suppose that the early weapon-carrying hominids had a somewhat richer call system (though still closed), functioning in a somewhat more complex social order, then we may also assume that this type of event happened occasionally, and that sooner or later the other members of a band responded appropriately, therefore handling an unusually complex situation more efficiently than otherwise. Thus reinforced, the habit of *blending* two old calls to produce a new one would gain ground.

Indeed, we really have to believe that this is what happened, because the phenomenon of blending is the only logically possible way in which a closed system can develop towards an open one.[23] Let us represent the acoustic contours of one inherited call arbitrarily with the sequence of letters *ABCD* and those of another with *EFGH*. All we mean by either of these representations is that each call possesses two or more acoustic properties on which primate ears could focus attention; it does not matter just how many such acoustic properties are involved nor just what they are. Suppose that *ABCD* means "food here," while *EFGH* means "danger coming." Finding both food and danger, the hominid

[22] The pygmy chimpanzee, the porcupine, the hamster, and the two-toed sloth are variously known or reputed to share the human habit (Coon 1962:161). Hewes also comments on it (1961:696). The guess given here as to its consequences among the hominids is, as far as we know, our own.

[23] This is not quite true. Continuously variable features of a single call—say pitch, or volume, or duration—could become associated with continuously variable features of a type-situation, so that, in time, a specific uttering of the danger call could quite precisely specify "danger of degree seventeen, due north, three hundred yards away." The openness of a system that had developed in this way would be logically like that of bee dances (von Frisch 1950; Lindauer 1963), which is quite unlike that of human language.

comes out with *ABGH*. If this new call becomes established, then the 2 old calls and the new one are all henceforth *composite*, instead of unanalyzable unitary signals. For, in *ABCD*, the part *AB* now means "food" and the part *CD* means "no danger"; in *EFGH*, *EF* now means "no food" and *GH* means "danger"; while *ABGH* means "food and danger" because *AB* and *GH* have acquired the meanings just mentioned. One might eventually even get *EFCD*, obviously meaning "no food and no danger."

It must be asked whether this mechanism of blending can really turn a closed system into an open one. The answer is that it can start the transformation (while no other known mechanism can), but that further developments must follow. Consider the matter for a moment in a purely abstract way. Suppose the initial closed system has exactly ten calls, and that each is blended with each of the others. After the blending, there are exactly 100 calls. From one point of view, a repertory of 100 calls—or of 1,000, or of ten million—is just as closed as is a system of 10 calls. A second point of view is more important. Each of the hundred possible calls now consists of 2 parts, and each part recurs in other whole calls. One has the basis for the habit of *building* composite signals out of meaningful parts, whether or not those parts occur alone as whole signals. It is this habit that lies at the center of the openness of human languages. English allows only a finite (though quite large) number of sentences only two words long. But it allows an unlimited number of different sentences because there is no fixed limit on how long a sentence may be.

Surely the opening-up of the closed call system of our ancestors required literally thousands of years, just as all the other developments on which we have touched came about at an extremely leisurely pace. It is irrelevant that the production of a single blend, or the momentary accidental carrying of a stick or stone in the hand, is a brief episode. A potentially crucial type of event can recur numberless times with no visible effect, or with effect on a band that later becomes extinct for unrelated reasons, for every one occurrence that has minuscule but viable consequences. When the opening-up of the formerly closed call system was finally achieved, the revolutionary impact on subsequent developments was as great as that of hand-carrying.

For one thing, the detailed conventions of an open system cannot be transmitted wholly through genes. The young may emit some of the calls instinctively. But they are also exposed to various more or less complex composite calls from their elders, and are obliged to infer the meanings of the parts, and the patterns by which the parts are put together to form the whole signals, from the acoustic resemblances among the calls they hear and from the behavioral contexts in which they are uttered. (To this day, that is how human infants learn their native language.) Thus, the development of an open system puts a premium on any capacity for learning and teaching that a species may have, and selects for an increase in the genetic basis for that capacity.

If the conventions of a system have largely to be learned before the system can be efficiently used, then much of that learning will eventually be carried on away from the contexts in which the utterances being practiced would be immediately relevant. We recall the general mammalian phenomenon of play. The development of an open, largely traditionally transmitted, vocal-auditory communicative system means that *verbal play* is added to play at fighting, sexual play, and any other older categories. But this, in turn, means that situations are being talked about when they do not exist—that is, it means the addition of displacement to the design features already at hand. Speaking of things which are out of sight or in the past or future is very much like carrying a weapon when there is no immediate need for it. Each of these habits thus reinforces the other.

What was formerly a closed call system has now evolved into an open system, with details transmitted largely by tradition rather than through the genes, and with the property of displacement. Let us call such a system *pre-language*. It was still not true language, because it lacked the duality of patterning of true language. Nothing like pre-language is known for sure in the world today.[24] Any hominid strain that developed its vocal-auditory communication only to this stage has become extinct. If we could hear the pre-language of our forerunners, it would probably not sound like human speech. It would sound much more like animal calls, and only very careful analysis would reveal its language-like properties.

The development of openness, with the various consequences already mentioned, either accompanied or paved the way for some radical developments in tool habits. We imagine that tool *manufacture*—as over against the using and carrying of tools—received its single greatest impetus from this source. If carrying a weapon selects for foresight, shaping a rough weapon into a better one indicates even greater foresight. The manufacturing of a generalized tool—one designed to be carried around for a variety of possible uses—and the development of tools specialized for use in the making of other tools, certainly followed the inception of pre-language. Weapon-making and tool-shaping are further activities at which the young can play, as they learn their communicative system and other adult ways by playing with them.

We must suppose that the detailed conventions of pre-language underwent changes, and became differentiated from one band to another, much more rapidly than had the earlier call system from which it sprang (though perhaps much more slowly than languages change today). Both of these points are implied by the increased relative role of tradition as over against genetics. New blends were not uncommon. They introduced new patterns for combining elements into whole signals, and old patterns became obsolete. Any such innovation of detail spread naturally to all members of the band in which it occurred, but not readily, if at all, from one band to another. If a band fissioned into two bands—this must have happened repeatedly throughout hominoid and hominid history—the "daughter" bands started their independent existence with a single inherited pre-language, but innovations thereafter were independent, so that in course of time the two daughter bands came to have two

---

[24] But many animal communicative systems have not yet been adequately studied. There is some hint that the song systems of certain passerine birds may prove to have just the array of design features that characterized pre-language (Lanyon 1960). Of course, this would not necessarily mean that the birds in question are on their way towards the development of true language.

"mutually unintelligible" pre-lan-
guages. This is exactly—except for rate
of change—what has happened to true
human languages in recent millennia;
we must assume that the phenomena
of change and of divergence are as old
as the emergence of pre-language.

The Inception of Duality

Something else had been happening
during prehominid and hominid evolution up to this point. In apes, the glottis lies very close to the velum, and
articulatory motions anything like
those involved in human language are
structurally awkward. The development of upright posture, with the completion of the migration of the face
from the end to the ventral side of
the head, turns the axis of the oral
cavity to a position approximately at
right angles to the pharynx, and introduces a marked separation of glottis
from velum (Spuhler 1959; DuBrul
1958). Hundreds of generations of
chattering, first in a call system and
then in pre-language, increases the in-
nervation of the vocal tract and en-
riches the cortical representation of
that region. The stage is set for the
development of the kinds of articulatory motions familiar today.

Now, neither of these changes leads
directly and inevitably to duality of
patterning. Indeed, the first change is
in no sense logically required if duality is to develop; in a way, it was fortuitous, since it was a by-product of
changes taking place for a totally different set of selective reasons. In another species with a different earlier
history, duality might use some other
apparatus. If early primate history had
for some reason promoted precision of
control of the sphincter, and of the
accumulation and discharge of intestinal gas, speech sounds today might
be anal spirants. Everything else about
the logical design of human language
could be exactly as it actually is. The
failure to distinguish in this way between the logically possible and the
historically actual has led many investigators astray: they infer, for example,
that our ancestors could not have had
language until the articulatory apparatus had evolved to what it is now.
They then interpret fossil jaws in invalid ways—and offer inadequate explanations of why the speech parts
should have changed their morphology
as they actually have during the Pleistocene.[25]

However, the two changes described above did set the stage in a
certain way. The hominids were in a
state in which, if duality did develop,
the machinery used for it was in all
probability going to be the kind of
articulatory motions we still use.

We can envisage the development
of duality as follows. Pre-language
became increasingly complex and
flexible, among the successful strains
of hominids, because of its many advantages for survival. The constant
rubbing-together of whole utterances
(by the blending mechanism described
earlier) generated an increasingly large
stock of minimum meaningful signal
elements—the "pre-morphemes" of
pre-language. Lacking duality, however, these pre-morphemes had to be
holistically different from one another
in their acoustic contours. But the
available articulatory-acoustic space
became more and more densely
packed; some pre-morphemes became
so similar to others that keeping them
apart, either in production or in detection, was too great a challenge for
hominid mouths, ears, and brains.

[25] See references cited in the first paragraph of
fn. 1.

Something had to happen, or the system would collapse of its own weight. Doubtless many overloaded systems did collapse, their users thereafter becoming extinct. In at least one case, there was a brilliantly successful "mutation": pre-morphemes began to be listened to and identified not in terms of their acoustic gestalts but in terms of smaller features of sound that occurred in them in varying arrangements. In pace with this shift in the technique of detection, articulatory motions came to be directed not towards the generation of a suitable acoustic gestalt but towards the sufficiently precise production of the relevant smaller features of sound that identified one pre-morpheme as over against others.

With this change, pre-morphemes became true morphemes, the features of sound involved became phonological components, and pre-language had become true language.

Although brilliant and crucial, this innovation need not have been either as sudden or as difficult as our description may seem to imply. With openness, but as yet without duality, the hearer is already required to pay attention to acoustic detail, rather than merely to one or another convenient symptom of a whole acoustic gestalt, if he is to recognize the constituent pre-morphemes of a composite call and thus react appropriately to the whole call. In a pure call system, the beginning of a call may be distinctive enough to identify the whole call; the rest does not have to be heard. In pre-language, one cannot predict from the beginning of a call how it will continue and end. This clearly paves the way for duality. It is then, in one sense, but a small step to stop regarding acoustic details as *constituting* morphemes and start interpreting them

as *identifying* or *representing* morphemes.[26]

Here, as for all the other developments we have mentioned, we must remember Romer's Rule. The ultimate consequences of the inception of duality have been enormous. But the immediate value of the innovation was conservative. It rendered possible the continued use of a thoroughly familiar type of communicative system in a thoroughly familiar way, in the face of a gradual but potentially embarrassing increase in the complexity of the system.

The emergence of true language from a closed call system, by the steps and stages we have described, should properly be thought of not as a replacement of one sort of communicative system by another, but rather as the growth of a new system within the matrix of the old one. Certain features of the proto-hominoid call system are still found in human vocal-auditory behavior, but as accompaniments to the use of language rather than as part of language. The proto-hominoids could vary the intensity, the pitch, and the duration of a single call. We still do this as we speak sentences in a language: we speak sometimes more

[26] In recorded human history a somewhat similar transformation is observable in the evolution of Chinese characters. The earliest characters were holistically different from one another to the eye— any visual resemblances between constituent parts of different characters were unsystematic and accidental. But as the system developed, and a larger and larger number of characters had to be devised, it became impossible to keep on inventing completely different new shapes; instead, new characters came to be built by putting together pieces drawn from old ones. But this incipient "duality," as an economy measure, never developed as far as it has in languages (i.e., spoken languages). Thousands of characters in use today are built out of hundreds of recurrent parts; the tens of thousands of morphemes in any language are built out of a mere double handful of phonological components, used with amazing efficiency.

loudly, sometimes more softly, sometimes in a higher register and sometimes in a lower, and so on. Also, we use certain grunts and cries (*uh-huh, huh-uh, ow!*) that are not words or morphemes and not part of language. These various *paralinguistic* phenomena, as they are called (Trager 1958; Pittenger, Hockett, and Danehy 1960), have been reworked and modified in many ways by the conditions of life of speaking humans, but their pedigree, like that of communicative body motion, is older than that of language itself.

The phenomenon of sound change, mentioned briefly at the outset of this paper, began immediately upon the transition from pre-language to true language, continues now, and will continue in the future unless our vocal-auditory communication crosses some currently unforeseeable Rubicon. The phonological system of a language has almost as its sole function that of keeping meaningful utterances apart. But a phonological system is a delicately balanced affair, constantly being thrown into slight disbalance by careless articulation or channel noise and constantly repatterning itself in a slightly altered way. It is perfectly possible, in the course of time, for two phonemes to fall together—that is, for the articulatory-acoustic difference between them to disappear. Obviously, this changes the machinery with which morphemes and utterances are distinguished. The interest this holds for us is that it affords an example of the workings of Romer's Rule in a purely cultural context instead of a largely genetic one.

What happens seems to be about as follows. A particular phonemic difference is slowly eaten away by sound change, to the point that it is no longer reliable as a way of keeping utterances

apart.[27] This is the "changed circumstances" of Romer's Rule. The speakers of the language develop, by analogy, a way of paraphrasing any utterance that would be potentially ambiguous if uttered in the traditional way. The paraphrase is the "innovation" of the Rule. The value of the paraphrase is that the speakers can thereby continue to speak in largely the same way they learned from their predecessors. The innovation is minor and trivial, but effective in that if the phonemic contrast disappears entirely, ease of communication is in no way impaired. The inevitable and continuous process of sound change never reduces the machinery of a language to zero. A compensation of some sort is developed for every loss of contrast.

Chronology

We have now outlined a plausible evolutionary sequence leading from the proto-hominoids to our earliest truly human ancestors. For we assert that as soon as the hominids had achieved upright posture, bipedal gait, the use of hands for manipulating, for carrying, and for manufacturing generalized tools, and language, they had become men. The human revolution was over. Two important questions remain. How long did the changes take? How long ago were they completed?

It is certain that the changes we have talked about did not begin before the time of the proto-hominoids. But at present we have no way of knowing how much later than that was their

---

[27] A possible example in current American English is medial posttonic *t* versus *d*: *matter* and *madder*, or *petal* and *pedal*, or *atom* and *Adam*, are acoustically very close in the speech of many people, and absolutely identical for some. When this leads to misunderstanding, the speaker repeats with clearer articulation, or paraphrases.

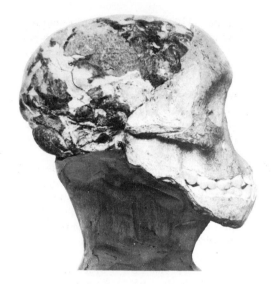

Skull of Australopithecine.
(Courtesy of the American
Museum of Natural History.
Illustration added by editors.)

inception. Conceivably the hominids of the Middle or Upper Pliocene, though already separated from the pongids, were very little more like modern man than were the proto-hominoids.

On the other hand, we are convinced that all the crucial developments of which we have spoken had been achieved by about one million years ago—that is, by the beginning of the Pleistocene.

The most important evidence for the date just presented is the *subsequent* growth of the brain, attested by the fossil record. The brain of *Australopithecus* is scarcely larger than that of a gorilla. But from about three-quarters of a million years ago to about forty thousand years ago, the brain grew steadily. Part of this increase reflects an overall increase in body size (Spuhler 1959; Washburn 1959: 27; Coon 1962: Table 37). Allowing for this, there is still something to be explained. Was the increase in relative size fortuitous or adaptive?

It is utterly out of the question that the growth was fortuitous. A large brain is biologically too expensive. It demands a high percentage of the blood supply—12% in modern man, though the brain accounts for only about 2% of the body's volume (Coon 1962: 77–78)—and all that blood, in an upright biped, must be pumped uphill. It requires an enlarged skull, which makes for difficulty during parturition, particularly since the development of upright posture resculptures the pelvis very badly for childbirth. This cost cannot be borne unless there are compensations.

We must therefore assume that if a species has actually developed a bigger and more convoluted brain, with a particularly sharp increase in the fore-brain, there was survival value in the change. For our ancestors of a million years ago the survival value of bigger brains is obvious if and only if they had *already* achieved the essence of language and culture. Continued growth would then be advantageous up to a certain maximum, but there-after unprofitable because it made for excessive difficulties in other respects but yielded no further usable gain in brainpower.

The archeological and fossil record supports our date, or even suggests that we have been too conservative. Until recently, the earliest obviously shaped tools that had been dug up were not quite so ancient, but they implied an earlier period of development that was not directly attested. Now, however, we have the direct evidence of at least crudely shaped stone tools in association with hominid fossils from Bed I at Olduvai, for which a maximum date of one and three-quarters million years ago is seriously proposed (Leakey, Curtis, and Evernden 1962). What is more, the Australopithecines show the typically human reduction in the size of the canine teeth, formerly used for cutting and tearing; and this reduction could not have been tolerated had the hominids not developed tools with which to perform such operations.

It might be suggested that, although all other crucial innovations of the human revolution were as early as we have proposed, the inception of duality may have been later. There are two reasons why we think that duality is just as old as the rest.

One side-effect of brain growth is that the top of the head is pushed forward to form a forehead. We do not see why this should in itself entail a recession of the lower part of the face, to yield the essentially flat perpendicular human physiognomy which, with minor variations, now prevails. In terms of the balancing of the head above an upright body, perhaps the recession of the snout and the decrease in its massiveness are useful. If cooking is a sufficiently old art, then perhaps this external predigestion of

food at least rendered possible the reduction in size of teeth and jaws. But it seems to us that these factors still leave room for a further influence: that of the habit of talking, in a true language that uses the kinds of articulatory motions that are now universal, requiring precise motions of lips, jaw, tongue, velum, glottis, and pulmonary musculature. If true language can be assumed for our ancestors of a million years ago, then it is old enough to have played a role in the genetically monitored evolutionary changes in what we now call the "organs of speech." And if this is correct, then "organs of speech" is no metaphor but a biologically correct description.

Our other reason for believing that duality of patterning, and the modern type of sound-producing articulatory motions, are very old, turns on time, space, and degrees of uniformity and diversity. The fossil record shows that the human diaspora from East Africa cannot be much more recent than the Middle Pleistocene. This means that several hundred thousand years have been available for a genetic adaptation to a wide variety of climates and topographies. Yet man shows an amazingly small amount of racial diversity— far less, for example, than that of dogs, which has come about in a much shorter span of time. (Of course, the difference in generation span between men and dogs must be taken into account; but when one allows liberally for this the comparison, though less striking, still seems valid.)

There is this same striking lack of diversity in certain features of language. Though we have no fossils, our observations of the languages of today, and of those few attested by written records during the past few millenia, have some relevance. Almost every type of articulation known to function in any language anywhere recurs in various other languages, with no significant pattern of geographical distribution.[28] Phonological systems— as over against individual speech sounds—show much less variety than could easily be invented by any linguist working with pencil and paper (Hockett 1963; Ferguson 1963). This uniformity precludes the independent invention of duality of patterning, and of modern articulatory motions, in two or more parts of the world. The crucial developments must have taken place once, and then spread. The innovations could have been either recent or ancient, except for an additional fact: in every language, the phonological raw materials are used with remarkable efficiency (see footnote 26). This speaks for great antiquity, since we cannot imagine that such efficiency was an instant result of the appearance of the first trace of duality.

True diversity is found in more superficial aspects of language, and in all those other phases of human life where tradition, rather than genetics, is clearly the major mechanism of change and of adaptation. We are thus led to a familiar conclusion. The human revolution, completed before the diaspora, established a state of affairs in which further change and adaptation could be effected, within broad limits, by tradition rather than genetics. That is why human racial diversity is so slight, and it is why the languages and cultures of all communities, no matter how diverse, are elaborations of a single inherited "common denominator."

[28] Coarticulated stops are commonest in west Africa, but recur in New Guinea. Clicks seem to be the least widespread: they are found only in south and east Africa, largely in languages known to be related to one another.

Additional Pleistocene Changes

The further consequences of the human revolution include, in the end, everything that we have done since. Only a few of the more striking (and earlier) of these subsequent developments need to be mentioned here.

Language and culture, as we have seen, selected for bigger brains. Bigger brains mean bigger heads. Bigger heads mean greater difficulty in parturition. Even today, the head is the chief troublemaker in childbirth. This difficulty can be combatted to some extent by expelling the fetus relatively earlier in its development. There was therefore a selection for such earlier expulsion. But this, in turn, makes for a longer period of helpless infancy— which is, at the same time, a period of maximum plasticity, during which the child can acquire the complex extragenetic heritage of its community. The helplessness of infants demands longer and more elaborate child care, and it becomes highly convenient for the adult males to help the mothers. Some of the skills that the young males must learn can only be learned from the adult males. All this makes for the domestication of fathers. This, together with the habit of paying attention to past experiences and future contingencies (which we have seen arising in the context of play, of tool-carrying, of the displacement of pre-language, and of tool-making), promotes male jealousy. The seeds of this may have been earlier, but it now becomes eminently reasonable for a male to reserve a female, even when he is not sexually hungry, that she may be available when the need arises.

In the developments just outlined we can also see contributing sources for the complex restrictions and rituals with which human sexual relations are hedged about. These include not

"Collective hunting, general food-sharing, and the carrying of an increasing variety of things all press towards a more complex social organization. . . ." Tribal aborigines in Western Australia. (Photo from BP Singer Features. Illustration added by editors.)

only all the rules of exogamy and endogamy and the varying principles controlling premarital and extramarital relations, but also the whole matter of taste—some individuals of the opposite sex are attractive, others unattractive, according to criteria learned from one's community. Any male past puberty, and any female between menarche and menopause, can, in a matter of seconds, stand a good chance of launching a new human. But child care requires time and energy thereby unavailable for other important activities. From this stem such varied modern institutions as celibate orders and beauty contests.

Among the proto-hominoids the band leaders were the strongest adult males. Language, in particular, changes this. The oldest members of the band, strong or feeble, are valued because

they have had time to learn more. They are repositories of information on which the community can call as it is needed (Sahlins 1959). This use of the elderly as encyclopedias perhaps helps to select for a greater life span, though the pedomorphism discussed earlier may also have played a part in bringing about this result. Certainly the increased social utility of the elderly promotes a protection of the old and feeble by the young and strong; it may contribute to doing something positive about the disposal of the dead.

As soon as the hominids had achieved a reasonably effective bipedal *walking* gait—not running, which is useful only for fast coverage of short distances[29]—they had the basic

[29] A point emphasized by Washburn in a talk at the Wenner-Gren Foundation for Anthropological Research, Spring 1960.

wherewithal for migrating slowly throughout all the continental territory to which they could adapt their lifeways. For the invasion of some climatic zones, protection against the cold is necessary. There are various physiological ways of doing this (Coon 1962:62–68), but the hominids developed an additional device: clothing.

The Chinese variety of *Pithecanthropus*[30] used fire for warmth. By his epoch, then, the hominid invasion of cold climates had begun. But we suspect that clothing was a much earlier invention, already available when it was first needed for warmth.

Clothing serves roughly three functions: protection, as against the cold; modesty and vanity; and *carrying*. The last of these functions was, we suggest, the one of earliest relevance. If one's way of life rests on hand-carrying, and if the number and variety of things to be carried is increasing to the point of awkwardness, then the invention of a device that helps one carry things has the conservative survival value required by Romer's Rule. The first clothing-as-harness may have been nothing more than a piece of vine pulled from the trees and draped over the shoulder or around the waist. Later, when the hominids were regularly killing small animals, the hides— useless as food—might have been put to this use. A hide cannot be eaten, but if one is hungry enough there is some nourishment to be obtained by chewing at it. Almost as early as the first use of hides as harness, it may have been discovered that a hide that has been chewed is more flexible and comfortable to wear than one that has not. This way of processing hides was still widespread only yesterday.

[30] Here and throughout we have used the taxonomic terms of Simpson (1945) and LeGros Clark (1955).

It is unlikely that any direct archeological evidence of these posited early clothing developments will ever turn up. But if clothing of sorts is actually that ancient, then it was already available, with only minor modifications, when it was first needed to help explore ecological niches characterized by cold. It may even be old enough to have played a part in permitting the development of the relative hairlessness characteristic of all strains of *Homo sapiens* today.

Abstract

Except for an introductory discussion of methodology, this paper is an effort at a narrative account of the evolution of our ancestors from proto-hominoid times to the earliest fully human stage.

[Comments on the Foregoing Article

The importance of this paper can be judged by the fact that when editors of *Current Anthropology* followed their usual practice of submitting it in manuscript to scholars, 26 responded with written comments which, together with the authors' replies, came to considerably more words than the original paper. For our purposes, in spite of the extreme interest of the comments, we feel that Hockett and Ascher generally speak best for themselves, and thus we here present only an exceedingly brief summary of criticisms and additions accepted by the authors. Readers are referred to the original article and to a full reprinting in *Culture: Man's Adaptive Dimension*, ed. M. F. Ashley Montagu (New York: Oxford University Press, 1968).

In response to comments, Hockett and Ascher admit to some hedging as to whether their proto-hominoids preceded or followed the splintering off of the line leading to the gibbons; and they defend "reconstruction via averaging" as a way of portraying proto-hominoid lifeways only because there is no better way at present to build a picture.

While some commentators suggest that the proto-hominoid forms may not have originated in East Africa, the authors reply that East Africa is the most likely area for the occurrence of the following events:

(a) A series of crucial innovations took place among our ancestors, each building on those that had preceded it. (b) Each of these innovations must have occurred in some relatively confined geographical area, among populations to which the preceding innovations had spread. (c) Each innovation would then spread to some, but not necessarily to all, allied subspecies and populations, thus coming to cover a wider or narrower geographical area. (d) Some of these innovations are of the sort that are not likely to have taken place independently in two or more places or times. (e) Many of the populations affected by some of the earlier innovations were dead ends, untouched by subsequent ones, and not ancestral to ourselves.

Citing J. Desmond Clark (1963), the authors note:

. . . we are led to East Africa as the most likely site for a number of the earliest innovations. It should be remembered that one of our chief points is the considerable antiquity of the crucial innovations that turned pre-men into men. The Human Revolution was *completed*, in our view, long before the date of the earliest hominid fossils known from anywhere in the world except Africa.

It is possible that fire-modified food was available early enough to allow evolution of tooth reduction in Peking man; but there is no archeological evidence for fire before the time of Peking man himself.

It is assumed that dialect differentiation would occur unless "curbed by *antisurvival* properties."

The authors agree with the comment that proto-hominoids probably lacked large interlocking canines. They also admit that reduction in size in the gibbon from that postulated for the proto-hominoid was not necessitated by adaptation to brachiation. They modify their statement concerning the absence of jealousy in sexually satisfied male proto-hominoids to: "if in fact the proto-hominoids were thus free of jealousy, the development of jealousy in our own ancestry is understandable in terms set forth in our paper."

Hand-carrying may possibly have preceded rather than followed the proto-hominoid level. Despite the agreement of many commentators with the authors that the frontal approach in copulation played a great role in human evolution, the authors bow to arguments put forth by Adolph Schultz and are ready to accept considerable modification of that assumption. On the other hand, they add social grooming among primates in general as a probable contributor to proto-hominoid inheritance and it becomes clear that the weakness of hominoid infants should be emphasized in considering the evolution of bipedalism.

Treeless tropical savannah was probably not necessarily short of water; it is a matter of plausibility whether one supposes the earliest tools were for defense or for food-getting and offense. A major addition to the authors' original thesis is that human hairlessness may be due to the need of a relatively large mammal, exerting himself in the chase in tropical savannahs, to lose heat rapidly at critical times.

The age at which the female can conceive is best called "nubility," not menarche; and the phrase "with a particularly sharp increase in the forebrain" ought to be deleted from "Chronology," paragraph six.

It was also pointed out that the authors should have allowed for behavioral diffusion "as well as gene flow from band to band in early hominoid and hominid times."

P. S. and D. M.]

References

Altmann, Stuart A., "Social behavior of anthropoid primates: analysis of recent concepts," in *Roots of Behavior* (pp. 277–285), ed. E. L. Bliss. New York: Harper, 1962.

Bartholomew, George A., Jr., and Joseph B. Birdsell, "Ecology and the protohominids." *American Anthropologist* 55:481–498, 1953.

Bingham, H. C., "Gorillas in a native habitat." Carnegie Institute of Washington Publ. No. 426, 1932.

Bloomfield, Leonard, *Language*. New York: Henry Holt, 1933.

———, "Language or ideas?" *Language* 12:89–95, 1936.

Bolwig, N. A., "A study of nests built by mountain gorilla and chimpanzee." *South African Journal of Science* 55:286–291, 1959.

Brace, C. Loring, "Cultural factors in the evolution of human dentition," in *Culture and the Evolution of Man* (pp. 343–354), ed. M. F. Ashley Montagu. New York: Oxford Univ. Press, 1962.

Bryan, Alan L., "The essential morphological basis for human culture." *Current Anthropology* 4:297–306, 1963.

Carpenter, C. R., Netherlands Committee for International Nature Protection, Communication No. 12:1034, 1938.

———, "A field study of the behavior and social relation of the gibbon." *Comparative Psychology Monographs* 16, No. 5, 1940.

Chance, M. R. A., "The nature and special features of the instinctive social bond of primates," in *Social Life of Early Man* (pp. 17–33), ed. S. L. Washburn. Chicago: Aldine Publishing Co., 1961.

Childe, V. Gordon, *Man Makes Himself*. London: C. A. Watts, 1936. (Reprinted 1951. New York: New American Library of World Literature.)

Clark, J. Desmond, "The evolution of culture in Africa." *The American Naturalist* 97:15–28, 1963.

Coon, Carleton S., *The Origin of Races*. New York: Alfred Knopf, 1962.

Count, Earl W., "The biological basis of human sociality." *American Anthropologist* 60:1049–1085, 1958.

Critchley, Macdonald, "The evolution of man's capacity for language," in *Evolution After Darwin*: Vol. II, *The Evolution of Man: Man, Culture, and Society* (pp. 289–308), ed. Sol Tax. Chicago: Univ. of Chicago Press, 1960.

Dobzhansky, Th., *The Biological Basis of Human Freedom*. New York: Columbia Univ. Press, 1956.

DuBrul, E. L., *Evolution of the Speech Apparatus*. Springfield: Charles C Thomas, 1958.

Ferguson, Charles A., "Assumptions about nasals: a sample study in phonological universals," in *Universals of Language* (pp. 42–47), ed. Joseph H. Greenberg. Cambridge, Mass.: MIT Press, 1963.

Greenberg, Joseph H., "Language and evolution," in *Evolution and Anthropology: A Centennial Appraisal* (pp. 61–75), ed. B. J. Meggars. Washington, D.C.: The Anthropological Society of Washington, 1959.

Hediger, Heini P., "The evolution of territorial behavior," in *Social Life of Early Man* (pp. 34–57), ed. S. L. Washburn. Chicago: Aldine Publishing Co., 1961.

Hewes, Gordon W., "Food transport and the origin of hominid bipedalism." *American Anthropologist* 63:687–710, 1961.

Hochbaum, H. Albert, *Travels and Traditions of Waterfowl*. Minneapolis: Univ. of Minnesota Press, 1955.

Hockett, Charles F., "Biophysics, linguistics, and the unity of science." *American Scientist* 36:558–572, 1948.

———, "Review." *Language*, 32:46–49, 1956.

————, *A Course in Modern Linguistics.* New York: Macmillan, 1958.

————, "Animal 'languages' and human language," in *The Evolution of Man's Capacity for Culture* (pp. 32–39), ed. J. N. Spuhler. Detroit: Wayne State Univ. Press, 1959.

————, "The origin of speech." *Scientific American* 203:88–96, Sept. 1960a.

————, "Logical considerations in the study of animal communication," in *Animal Sounds and Communication* (pp. 392–430), ed. W. E. Lanyon and W. N. Tavolga. Washington, D.C.: American Institute of Biological Sciences, Publ. No. 7, 1960b.

————, "The problem of universals in language," in *Universals of Language* (pp. 1–22), ed. Joseph H. Greenberg. Cambridge, Mass.: MIT Press, 1963.

Hooton, E., *Man's Poor Relations.* New York: Doubleday, 1942.

Kelemen, G., "The anatomical basis of phonation in the chimpanzee." *Journal of Morphology,* 82:229–246, 1948. (Reprinted in *Yearbook of Physical Anthropology,* 4:153–180, 1949.)

King, John A., "Social behavior, social organization, and population dynamics in a black-tailed prairiedog town in the Black Hills of South Dakota." University of Michigan Contributions from the Laboratory of Vertebrate Biology, No. 67, 1955.

Kroeber, A. L., *Anthropology,* New York: Harcourt, 1948.

LaBarre, Weston, *The Human Animal.* Chicago: Univ. of Chicago Press, 1954.

Langer, Susanne K., *Philosophy in a New Key.* Cambridge, Mass.: Harvard Univ. Press, 1942. (Reprinted 1948, New York: New American Library of World Literature.)

Lanyon, W. E., "The ontogeny of vocalization in birds," in *Animal Sounds and Communication* (pp. 321–347), ed. W. E. Lanyon and W. N. Tavolga. Washington, D.C.: American Institute of Biological Sciences, Publ. No. 7, 1960.

Leakey, L. S. B., "A new fossil skull from Olduvai." *Nature* 184:491–493, 1959.

————, G. H. Curtis, and J. F. Evernden, "Age of basalt underlying Bed I, Olduvai." *Nature* 194:610–612, 1962.

LeGros Clark, W. E., *The Fossil Evidence for Human Evolution.* Chicago: Univ. of Chicago Press, 1955.

Lindauer, Martin, *Communication Among Social Bees.* Cambridge, Mass.: Harvard Univ. Press, 1963.

Nissen, H. W., "A field study of the chimpanzee." *Comparative Psychology Monographs* 8, No. 1, 1931.

Oakley, Kenneth P., "On man's use of fire, with comments on toolmaking and hunting," in *Social Life of Early Man* (pp. 176–193), ed. S. L. Washburn. Chicago: Aldine Publishing Co., 1961.

————, "Dating the emergence of man." *The Advancement of Science* 18:415–426, 1962.

Pederson, Holger, *Linguistic Science in the Nineteenth Century.* Cambridge, Mass: Harvard Univ. Press, 1931.

Pittenger, R. E., C. F. Hockett, and J. Danehy, *The First Five Minutes: An Example of Microscopic Interview.* Ithaca: Paul Martineau, 1960.

Romer, A. S., "Phylogeny and behavior with special reference to vertebrate evolution," in *Behavior and Evolution* (pp. 48–75), ed. Anne Roe and G. G. Simpson. New Haven: Yale Univ. Press, 1958.

————, *The Vertebrate Story.* Chicago: Univ. of Chicago Press, 1959.

Sahlins, Marshall D., "The social life of monkeys, apes, and primitive man," in *The Evolution of Man's Capacity for Culture* (pp. 54–73), ed. J. N. Spuhler. Detroit: Wayne State Univ. Press, 1959.

Schultz, Adolph H., "Some factors influencing the social life of primates in general and early man in particular," in *Social Life of Early Man* (pp. 58–90), ed. S. L. Washburn. Chicago: Aldine Publishing Co., 1961.

Simons, Elwyn L., "Some fallacies in the study of hominid phylogeny." *Science* 141:879–889, 1963.

Simpson, George G., "The principles of classification and a classification of mammals." New York: The American Museum of Natural History, Bulletin 85, 1945.

————, *The Meaning of Evolution.* New Haven: Yale Univ. Press, 1949. (Reprinted 1951, New York: New American Library of World Literature.)

The Human Population

———, "The study of evolution: methods and present status of theory," in *Behavior and Evolution* (pp. 7–26), ed. Anne Roe and G. G. Simpson. New Haven: Yale Univ. Press, 1958.

Smith, Eliot, "The evolution of man," in *Smithsonian Report for 1912* (pp. 553–572). Washington, D.C.: The Smithsonian Institution, 1913.

Spuhler, J. N., "Somatic paths to culture," in *The Evolution of Man's Capacity for Culture* (pp. 1–13), ed. J. N. Spuhler. Detroit: Wayne State Univ. Press, 1959.

Trager, George L., "Paralanguage: a first approximation." *Studies in Linguistics* 13:1–12, 1958.

von Frisch, Karl, *Bees, Their Vision, Chemical Senses, and Language.* Ithaca: Cornell Univ. Press, 1950.

Washburn, S. L., "Speculation on the inter-relations of the history of tools and biological evolution," in *The Evolution of Man's Capacity for Culture* (pp. 21–31), ed. J. N. Spuhler. Detroit: Wayne State Univ. Press, 1959.

———, "Tools and human evolution." *Scientific American* 203:63–75, Sept. 1960.

———, and Irven DeVore, "Social behavior of baboons and early man," in *Social Life of Early Man* (pp. 91–105), ed. S. L. Washburn. Chicago: Aldine Publishing Co., 1961.

White, Leslie A., *The Science of Culture.* New York: Farrar, Straus, 1949. (Reprinted, New York: Grove Press, 1958.)

Wiener, Alexander S., and J. Moor-Jankowski, "Blood groups in anthropoid apes and baboons." *Science* 142:67–68, 1963.

Wiener, Norbert, *Cybernetics.* New York: The Technology Press and John Wiley, 1948.

EDWARD S. DEEVEY, JR.

Among headline-satiated readers, the great debate on the population explosion has lost some of its urgency. The response of the average individual was at first a test of his conviction and altruism; by now, the whole affair has become conventional, with slogans instead of facts. The "crisis" has dissipated, and we find ourselves choosing between Optimism or Pessimism, Sentimentality or Realism, Orthodoxy or Heresy.

War, crime, and the crisis of civil conflict breed interchangeable metaphors. Commentators on population overgrowth speak of the population "time bomb." But the population problem, taking the world as a whole, is quite different from anything that mankind has faced before. Militarism and its constellation of evils are old and sadly familiar in the human drama. Whether men choose to deplore or cheer the rising growth rate, human numbers in fact have already reached avalanche proportions. The "explosion" will not wait to be voted for or against; it is that roar outside: the roar that sounds like traffic.

Men and organizations of great power are competing for authority in the matter of population. Politically, the problem is too big for biologists alone, although the social use of population biology is at least as urgent and valuable as it is to medicine and agriculture.

To paraphrase Brian Hocking's stimulating book Biology or Oblivion, Lessons from the Ultimate Science,* *we*

* Cambridge, Mass.: Schenkman Publishing Co., 1965.

will have the wisdom of biology or we will have annihilation

THE EDITORS

ALMOST UNTIL the present turn in human affairs an expanding population has been equated with progress. "Increase and multiply" is the Scriptural injunction. The number of surviving offspring is the measure of fitness in natural selection. If number is the criterion, the human species is making great progress. The population, now passing 2.7 billion, is doubling itself every 50 years or so. To some horrified observers, however, the population increase has become a "population explosion." The present rate of increase, they point out, is itself increasing. At 1 per cent per year it is double that of the past few centuries. By A.D. 2000, even according to the "medium" estimate of the careful demographers of the United Nations, the rate of increase will have accelerated to 3 per cent per year, and the total population will have reached 6.267 billion. If Thomas Malthus's assumption of a uniform rate of doubling is naive, because it so quickly leads to impossible numbers, how long can an accelerating annual increase, say from 1 to 3 per cent in 40 years, be maintained? The demographers confronted with this question lower their eyes: "It would be absurd," they say, "to carry detailed calculations forward into a more remote future. It is most debatable whether the trends in mortality and fertility can continue much longer. Other factors may eventually bring population growth to a halt."

So they may, and must. It comes to this: Explosions are not made by force alone, but by force that exceeds restraint. Before accepting the implications of the population explosion, it is well to set the present in the context of the record of earlier human populations. As will be seen, the population curve has moved upward stepwise in response to the three major revolutions that have marked the evolution of culture (see graph, p. 47). The tool-using and toolmaking revolution that started the growth of the human stem from the primate line gave the food-gatherer and hunter access to the widest range of environments. Nowhere was the population large, but over the earth as a whole it reached the not insignificant total of five million, an average of .04 person per square kilometer (.1 person per square mile) of land. With the agricultural revolution the population moved up two orders of magnitude to a new plateau, multiplying 100 times in the short span of 8,000 years, to an average of one person per square kilometer. The increase over the last 300 years, a multiplication by five, plainly reflects the first repercussions of the scientific-industrial revolution. There are now 16.4 persons per square kilometer of the earth's land area. It is thus the release of restraint that the curve portrays at three epochal points in cultural history.

But the evolution of the population size also indicates the approach to equilibrium in the two interrevolutionary periods of the past. At what level will the present surge of numbers reach equilibrium? That is again a question of restraint, whether it is to be imposed by the limitations of man's new command over his environment or by his command over his own nature.

The human generative force is neither new nor metabiological, nor is it especially strong in man as compared

Years Ago	Cultural Stage	Area Populated	Assumed Density per Square Kilometer	Total Population (Millions)
1,000,000	Lower Paleolithic		.00425	.125
300,000	Middle Paleolithic		.012	1
25,000	Upper Paleolithic		.04	3.34
10,000	Mesolithic		.04	5.32
6,000	Village Farming and Early Urban		1.0 / .04	86.5
2,000	Village Farming and Urban		1.0	133
310	Farming and Industrial		3.7	545
210	Farming and Industrial		4.9	728
160	Farming and Industrial		6.2	906
60	Farming and Industrial		11.0	1,610
10	Farming and Industrial		16.4	2,400
A.D. 2000	Farming and Industrial		46.0	6,270

Population growth, from inception of the hominid line one million years ago through the different stages of cultural evolution to A.D. 2000 is shown in the chart above. In Lower Paleolithic stage, population was restricted to Africa (filled-in area on world map in third column), with a density of only .00425 person per square kilometer (fourth column) and a total population of only 125,000 (column at right). By the   Mesolithic stage, 10,000 years ago, hunting and food gathering techniques had spread the population over most of the earth and brought the total to 5,320,000. In the village farming and early urban stage, population increased to a total of 86,500,000 and a density of one person per square kilometer in the Old World and .04 per square kilometer in the New World. Today the population density exceeds 16 persons per square kilometer, and pioneering of the antarctic continent has begun. (Adapted from "The Human Population" by Edward S. Deevey, Jr. Copyright © 1960 by Scientific American, Inc. All rights reserved.)

to other animals. Under conditions of maximal increase in a suitable environment empty of competitors, with births at maximum and deaths negligible, rats can multiply their numbers 25 times in an average generation-time of 31 weeks. For the water flea *Daphnia,* beloved by ecologists for the speedy answers it gives, the figures are 221 times in a generation of 6.8 days. Mankind's best efforts seem puny by contrast: multiplication by about 1.4 times in a generation of 28 years. Yet neither in human nor in experimental populations do such rates continue unchecked. Sooner or later the births slow down and the deaths increase, until—in experiments, at any rate—the growth tapers off, and the population effectively saturates its space. Ecologists define this state (of zero rate of change) as equilibrium, without denying the possibility of oscillations that average out to zero, and without forgetting the continuous input of energy (food, for instance) that is needed to maintain the system.

Two kinds of check, then, operate to limit the size of a population, or of any living thing that grows. Obviously the environment (amount of space, food or other needed resources) sets the upper limit; sometimes this is manipulatable, even by the population itself, as when it exploits a new kind of food in the same old space, and reaches a new, higher limit. More subtly, populations can be said to limit their own rates of increase. As the numbers rise, female fruit-flies, for example, lay fewer eggs when jostled by their sisters; some microorganisms battle each other with antibiotics; flour beetles accidentally eat their own defenseless eggs and pupae; infectious diseases spread faster, or become more virulent, as their hosts become more numerous. For human populations pestilence and warfare, Malthus's "natural restraints," belong among these devices for self-limitation. So, too, does his "moral restraint," or voluntary birth control. Nowadays a good deal of attention is being given, not only to voluntary methods, but also to a fascinating new possibility: mental stress.

Population control by means of personality derangement is probably a vertebrate patent; at least it seems a luxury beyond the reach of a water flea. The general idea, as current among students of small mammals, is that of hormonal imbalance (or stress, as defined by Hans Selye of the University of Montreal); psychic tension, resulting from overcrowding, disturbs the pituitary-adrenal system and diverts or suppresses the hormones governing sexuality and parental care. Most of the evidence comes from somewhat artificial experiments with caged rodents. It is possible, though the case is far from proved, that the lemming's famous mechanism for restoring equilibrium is the product of stress; in experimental populations of rats and mice, at least, anxiety has been observed to increase the death rate through fighting or merely from shock.

From this viewpoint there emerges an interesting distinction between crowding and overcrowding among vertebrates; overcrowding is what is perceived as such by members of the population. Since the human rate of increase is holding its own and even accelerating, however, it is plain that the mass of men, although increasingly afflicted with mental discomfort, do not yet see themselves as overcrowded. What will happen in the future brings

45

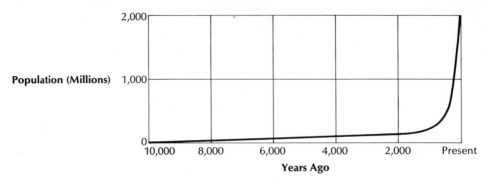

Arithmetic population curve plots the growth of human population from 10,000 years ago to the present. Such a curve suggests that the population figure remained close to the base line for an indefinite period from the remote past to about 500 years ago, and that it has surged abruptly during the last 500 years as a result of the scientific-industrial revolution. (Adapted from "The Human Population," by Edward S. Deevey, Jr. Copyright © 1960 by Scientific American, Inc. All rights reserved.)

other questions. For the present it may be noted that some kind of check has always operated, up to now, to prevent populations from exceeding the space that contains them. Of course space may be non-Euclidean, and man be exempt from this law.

The commonly accepted picture of the growth of the population out of the long past takes the form of the graph shown on this page. Two things are wrong with this picture. In the first place the basis of estimates, back of about A.D. 1650, is rarely stated. One suspects that writers have been copying each other's guesses. The second defect is that the scales of the graph have been chosen so as to make the first defect seem unimportant. The missile has left the pad and is heading out of sight—so it is said; who cares whether there were a million or a hundred million people around when Babylon was founded? The difference is nearly lost in the thickness of the draftsman's line.

I cannot think it unimportant that (as I calculate) there were 36 billion Paleolithic hunters and gatherers, including the first tool-using hominids.

One begins to see why stone tools are among the commonest Pleistocene fossils. Another 30 billion may have walked the earth before the invention of agriculture. A cumulative total of about 110 billion individuals seem to have passed their days, and left their bones, if not their marks, on this crowded planet. Neither for our understanding of culture nor in terms of man's impact upon the land is it a negligible consideration that the patch of ground allotted to every person now alive may have been the lifetime habitat of 40 predecessors.

These calculations exaggerate the truth in a different way: by condensing into single sums the enormous length of prehistoric time. To arrive at the total of 36 billion Paleolithic hunters and gatherers I have assumed mean standing populations of half a million for the Lower Paleolithic, and two million for the Middle and Upper Paleolithic to 25,000 years ago. For Paleolithic times there are no archeological records worth considering in such calculations. I have used some figures for modern hunting tribes, quoted by Robert J. Braidwood and

46

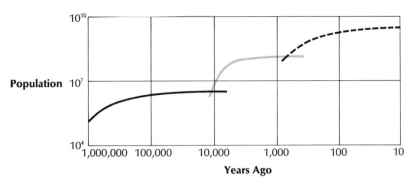

Logarithmic population curve makes it possible to plot, in a small space, the growth of population over a longer period of time and over a wider range (from 10⁴, or 10,000, to 10¹⁰, or 10 billion, persons). Curve, based on assumptions concerning relationship of technology and population as shown in chart on page 44, reveals three population surges reflecting toolmaking or cultural revolution (solid line), agricultural revolution (gray line) and scientific-industrial revolution (broken line). (Adapted from "The Human Population" by Edward S. Deevey, Jr. Copyright © 1960 by Scientific American, Inc. All rights reserved.)

Charles A. Reed, though they are not guilty of my extrapolations. The assumed densities per square kilometer range from a tenth to a third of those estimated for eastern North America before Columbus came, when an observer would hardly have described the woods as full of Indians. (Of course I have excluded any New World population from my estimates prior to the Mesolithic climax of the food-gathering and hunting phase of cultural evolution.) It is only because average generations of 25 years succeeded each other 39,000 times that the total looms so large.

For my estimates as of the opening of the agricultural revolution, I have also depended upon Braidwood and Reed. In their work in Mesopotamia they have counted the number of rooms in buried houses, allowing for the areas of town sites and of cultivated land, and have compared the populations so computed with modern counterparts. For early village-farmers, like those at Jarmo, and for the urban citizens of Sumer, about 2500 B.C., their estimates (9.7 and 15.4 persons

per square kilometer) are probably fairly close. They are intended to apply to large tracts of inhabited country, not to pavement-bound clusters of artisans and priests. Nevertheless, in extending these estimates to continent-wide areas, I have divided the lower figure by 10, making it one per square kilometer. So much of Asia is unirrigated and nonurban even today that the figure may still be too high. But the Maya, at about the same level of culture (3,000 or 4,000 years later), provide a useful standard of comparison. The present population of their classic homeland averages .6 per square kilometer, but the land can support a population about a hundred times as large, and probably did at the time of the classic climax. The rest of the New World, outside Middle America, was (and is) more thinly settled, but a world-wide average of one per square kilometer seems reasonable for agricultural pre-industrial society.

For modern populations, from A.D. 1650 on, I have taken the estimates of economic historians, given in such books as the treatise *World Population and Production,* by Wladimir S. and Emma S. Woytinsky. All these estimates are included in the bottom graph on the next page. Logarithmic scales are used in order to compress so many people and millennia onto a single page. Foreshortening time in this way is convenient, if not particularly logical, and back of 50,000 years ago the time-scale is pretty arbitrary anyway. No attempt is made to show the oscillations that probably occurred, in glacial and interglacial ages, for example.

The stepwise evolution of population size, entirely concealed in graphs with arithmetic scales, is the most noticeable feature of this diagram. For most of the million-year period the number of hominids, including man, was about what would be expected of any large Pleistocene mammal— scarcer than horses, say, but commoner than elephants. Intellectual superiority was simply a successful adaptation, like longer legs; essential to stay in the running, of course, but making man at best the first among equals. Then the food-gatherers and hunters became plowmen and herdsmen, and the population was boosted by about 16 times, between 10,000 and 6,000 years ago. The scientific-industrial revolution, beginning some 300 years ago, has spread its effects much faster, but it has not yet taken the number as far above the earlier base line.

"Intellectual superiority was simply a successful adaptation, like longer legs; essential to stay in the running, of course, but making man at best the first among equals. Then the food-gatherers and hunters became plowmen and herdsmen, and the population was boosted by about 16 times." Egyptian wall painting from Tomb of Sen-nuden, Thebes, Dynasty XIX–XX. (The Metropolitan Museum of Art.)

"Hunting Buffalo" by Alfred Jacob Miller. (Courtesy of The Walters Art Gallery.)

The long-term population equilibrium implied by such base lines suggests something else. Some kind of restraint kept the number fairly stable. "Food supply" offers a quick answer, but not, I think, the correct one. At any rate, a forest is full of game for an expert mouse-hunter, and a Paleolithic man who stuck to business should have found enough food on two square kilometers, instead of 20 or 200. Social forces were probably more powerful than mere starvation in causing men to huddle in small bands. Besides, the number was presumably adjusted to conditions in the poorest years, and not to average environments.

The main point is that there were adjustments. They can only have come about because the average female bore two children who survived to reproduce. If the average life span is 25 years, the "number of children ever born" is about four (because about 50 per cent die before breeding), whereas a population that is really trying can average close to eight. Looking back

on former times, then, from our modern point of view, we might say that about two births out of four were surplus, though they were needed to counterbalance the juvenile death toll. But what about the other four, which evidently did not occur? Unless the life expectancy was very much less than I have assumed (and will presently justify), some degree of voluntary birth control has always prevailed.

Our 40 predecessors on earth make an impressive total, but somehow it sounds different to say that nearly 3 per cent of the people who have ever lived are still around. When we realize that they are living twice as long as their parents did, we are less inclined to discount the revolution in which we are living. One of its effects has just begun to be felt: The mean age of the population is increasing all over the world. Among the more forgivable results of Western culture, when introduced into simpler societies, is a steep drop in the death rate. Public-health authorities are fond of citing Ceylon

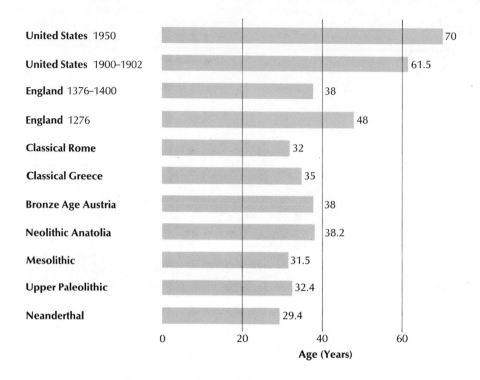

United States 1950	70
United States 1900–1902	61.5
England 1376–1400	38
England 1276	48
Classical Rome	32
Classical Greece	35
Bronze Age Austria	38
Neolithic Anatolia	38.2
Mesolithic	31.5
Upper Paleolithic	32.4
Neanderthal	29.4

0   20   40   60

Age (Years)

Longevity in ancient and modern times is charted. From time of Neanderthal man to 14th century A.D., life span appears to have hovered around 35 years. An exception is 13th-century England. Increase in longevity partly responsible for current population increase has come in modern era. In U.S. longevity increased about 10 years in last half-century. (Adapted from "The Human Population" by Edward S. Deevey, Jr. Copyright © 1960 by Scientific American, Inc. All rights reserved.)

in this connection. In a period of a year during 1946 and 1947 a campaign against malaria reduced the death rate there from 20 to 14 per 1,000. Eventually the birth rate falls too, but not so fast, nor has it yet fallen so far as a bare replacement value. The natural outcome of this imbalance is that acceleration of annual increase which so bemuses demographers. In the long run it must prove to be temporary, unless the birth rate accelerates, for the deaths that are being systematically prevented are premature ones. That is, the infants who now survive diphtheria and measles are certain to die of something else later on, and while the mean life span is approaching the maximum, for the first time in history, there is no

reason to think that the maximum itself has been stretched. Meanwhile the expectation of life at birth is rising daily in most countries, so that it has already surpassed 70 years in some, including the U. S., and probably averages between 40 and 50.

It is hard to be certain of any such world-wide figure. The countries where mortality is heaviest are those with the least accurate records. In principle, however, mean age at death is easier to find out than the number of children born, the frequency or mean age at marriage, or any other component of a birth rate. The dead bones, the court and parish records and the tombstones that archeology deals with have something to say about death, of populations as well as of people. Their testimony confirms the impression that threescore years and ten, if taken as an average and not as a maximum lifetime, is something decidedly new. Of course the possibilities of bias in such evidence are almost endless. For instance, military cemeteries tend to be full of young adult males. The hardest bias to allow for is the deficiency of infants and children; juvenile bones are less durable than those of adults, and are often treated less respectfully. Probably we shall never know the true expectation of life at birth for any ancient people. Bypassing this difficulty, we can look at the mean age at death among the fraction surviving to adolescence.

The "nasty, brutish and short" lives of Neanderthal people have been rather elaborately guessed at 29.4 years. The record, beyond them, is not one of steady improvement. For example, Neolithic farmers in Anatolia and Bronze Age Austrians averaged 38 years, and even the Mesolithic savages managed more than 30. But in the golden ages of Greece and Rome the life span was 35 years or less. During the Middle Ages the chances of long life were probably no better. The important thing about these averages is not the differences among them, but their similarity. Remembering the crudeness of the estimates, and the fact that juvenile mortality is omitted, it is fair to guess that human life-expectancy at birth has never been far from 25 years—25 plus or minus five, say —from Neanderthal times up to the present century. It follows, as I have said, that about half the children ever born have lived to become sexually mature. It is not hard to see why an average family size of four or more, or twice the minimum replacement rate, has come to seem part of a God-given scheme of things.

The 25-fold upsurge in the number of men between 10,000 and 2,000 years ago was sparked by a genuine increase in the means of subsistence. A shift from animal to plant food, even without agricultural labor and ingenuity, would practically guarantee a 10-fold increase, for a given area can usually produce about 10 times as much plant as animal substance. The scientific-industrial revolution has increased the efficiency of growing these foods, but hardly, as yet, beyond the point needed to support another 10 times as many people, fewer of whom are farmers. At the present rate of multiplication, without acceleration, another 10-fold rise is due within 230 years. Disregarding the fact that developed societies spend 30 to 60 times as much energy for other purposes as they need for food, one is made a little nervous by the thought of so many hungry mouths. Can the increase of efficiency keep pace? Can some of the apparently ample energy be converted to food as needed, perhaps at the cost of reducing the size of Sunday newspapers? Or is man now pressing so hard on his food supply that another 10-fold increase of numbers is impossible?

The answers to these questions are not easy to find, and students with different viewpoints disagree about them. Richard L. Meier of the University of Michigan estimates that a total of 50 billion people (a 20-fold increase, that is) can be supported on earth, and the geochemist Harrison Brown of the California Institute of Technology will allow (reluctantly) twice or four times as many. Some economists are even more optimistic; Arnold C. Harberger of the University of Chicago presents the interesting notion that a larger crop of people will contain more geniuses, whose intellects will find a

51

solution to the problem of feeding *still* more people. And the British economist Colin Clark points out that competition for resources will sharpen everyone's wits, as it always has, even if the level of innate intelligence is not raised.

An ecologist's answer is bound to be cast in terms of solar energy, chlorophyll and the amount of land on which the two can interact to produce organic carbon. Sources of energy other than the sun are either too expensive, or nonrenewable or both. Land areas will continue for a very long time to be the places where food is grown, for the sea is not so productive as the land, on the average. One reason, sometimes forgotten, is that the plants of the sea are microscopic algae, which, being smaller than land plants, respire away a larger fraction of the carbon they fix. The culture of the fresh-water alga *Chlorella* has undeniable promise as a source of human food. But the high efficiencies quoted for its photosynthesis, as compared with agricultural plants, are not sustained outdoors under field conditions. Even if Chlorella (or another exceptionally efficient producer, such as the water hyacinth) is the food plant of the future, flat areas exposed to sunlight will be needed. The 148.5 million square kilometers of land will have to be used with thoughtful care if the human population is to increase 20-fold. With a population of 400 per square kilometer (50 billion total) it would seem that men's bodies, if not their artifacts, will stand in the way of vital sunshine.

Plants capture the solar energy impinging on a given area with an efficiency of about .1 per cent. (Higher values often quoted are based on some fraction of the total radiation, such as visible light.) Herbivores capture about a 10th of the plants' energy, and carnivores convert about 10 per cent of the energy captured by herbivores (or other carnivores). This means, of course, that carnivores, feeding on plants at second hand, can scarcely do so with better than 1 per cent efficiency ($1/10 \times 1/10$ equals $1/100$). Eugene I. Rabinowitch of the University of Illinois has calculated that the current crop of men represents an ultimate conversion of about 1 per cent of the energy trapped by land vegetation. Recently, however, I have re-examined the base figure—the efficiency of the land-plant production—and believe it should be raised by a factor of three or four. The old value came from estimates made in 1919 and in 1937. A good deal has been learned since those days. The biggest surprise is the high productivity of forests, especially the forests of the Temperate Zone.

If my new figures are correct, the population could theoretically increase by 30 or 40 times. But man would have to displace all other herbivores and utilize all the vegetation with the 10 per cent efficiency established by the ecological rule of tithes. No land that now supports greenery could be spared for nonagricultural purposes; the populace would have to reside in the polar regions, or on artificial "green isles in the sea, love"—scummed over, of course, by 10 inches of Chlorella culture.

The picture is doubtless overdrawn. There is plenty of room for improvement in present farming practice. More land could be brought under cultivation if a better distribution of water could be arranged. More efficient basic crops can be grown and used less wastefully. Other sources of energy, notably atomic energy, can be fed back into food production to supplement the sun's rays. None of these measures

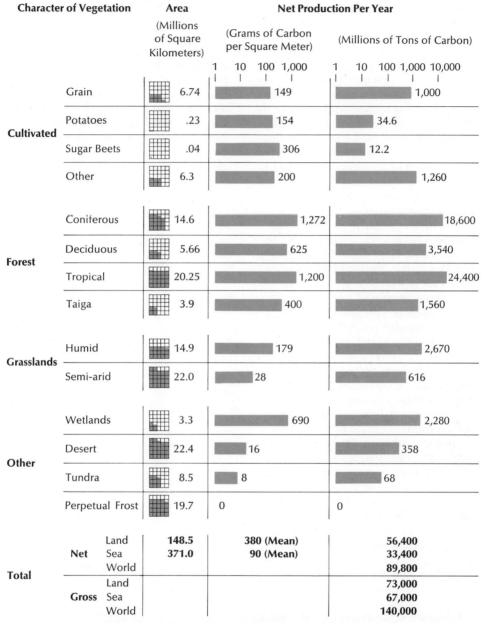

Character of Vegetation		Area (Millions of Square Kilometers)	Net Production Per Year — (Grams of Carbon per Square Meter)	Net Production Per Year — (Millions of Tons of Carbon)
Cultivated	Grain	6.74	149	1,000
	Potatoes	.23	154	34.6
	Sugar Beets	.04	306	12.2
	Other	6.3	200	1,260
Forest	Coniferous	14.6	1,272	18,600
	Deciduous	5.66	625	3,540
	Tropical	20.25	1,200	24,400
	Taiga	3.9	400	1,560
Grasslands	Humid	14.9	179	2,670
	Semi-arid	22.0	28	616
Other	Wetlands	3.3	690	2,280
	Desert	22.4	16	358
	Tundra	8.5	8	68
	Perpetual Frost	19.7	0	0

Total			Area	Net (Grams per Sq. Meter)	Net (Millions of Tons of Carbon)
	Net	Land	148.5	380 (Mean)	56,400
		Sea	371.0	90 (Mean)	33,400
		World			89,800
	Gross	Land			73,000
		Sea			67,000
		World			140,000

Production of organic matter per year by the land vegetation of the world—and thus its ultimate food-producing capacity—is charted in terms of the amount of carbon incorporated in organic compounds. Cultivated vegetation (top left) is less efficient than forest and wetlands vegetation, as indicated by the uptake of carbon per square meter (third column), and it yields a smaller over-all output than forest, humid grasslands and wetlands vegetation (fourth column). The scales at top of third and fourth columns are logarithmic. Land vegetation leads sea vegetation in efficiency and in net and gross tonnage (bottom). The difference between the net production and gross production is accounted for by the consumption of carbon in plant respiration. (Adapted from "The Human Population" by Edward S. Deevey, Jr. Copyright © 1960 by Scientific American, Inc. All rights reserved.)

is more than palliative, however; none promises so much as a 10-fold increase in efficiency; worse, none is likely to be achieved at a pace equivalent to the present rate of doubling of the world's population. A 10-fold, even a 20-fold, increase can be tolerated, perhaps, but the standard of living seems certain to be lower than today's. What happens then, when men perceive themselves to be overcrowded?

The idea of population equilibrium will take some getting used to. A population that is kept stable by emigration, like that of the Western Islands of Scotland, is widely regarded as sick— a shining example of a self-fulfilling diagnosis. Since the fall of the death rate is temporary, it is those two or more extra births per female that demand attention. The experiments with crowded rodents point to one way they might be corrected, through the effect of anxiety in suppressing ovulation and spermatogenesis and inducing fetal resorption. Some of the most dramatic results are delayed until after birth: litters are carelessly nursed, deserted or even eaten. Since fetuses, too, have endocrine glands, the specter of maternal transmission of anxiety now looms: W. R. Thompson of Wesleyan University has shown that the offspring of frustrated mother mice are more "emotional" throughout their own lives, and my student Kim Keeley has confirmed this.

Considered abstractly, these devices for self-regulation compel admiration for their elegance. But there is a neater device that men can use: rational, voluntary control over numbers. In mentioning the dire effects of psychic stress I am not implying that the population explosion will be contained by cannibalism or fetal resorption, or any power so naked. I simply suggest that

vertebrates have that power, whether they want it or not, as part of the benefit—and the price—of being vertebrates. And if the human method of adjusting numbers to resources fails to work in the next 1,000 years as it has in the last million, subhuman methods are ready to take over.

Facts, Fables, and Fallacies on Feeding the World Population

SAMUEL BRODY

I think we, in biology, must acquaint our fellow citizens with this serious world problem and aid them in working out a wise solution—ANTON J. CARLSON(1)

The burgeoning argument during the past 20 years over the capacity of agriculture to keep up with the expanding human population was surely one of the most useless discussions of the mid-twentieth century.

Much energy was dissipated that might have gone into restraining the endless flow of protoplasm from the charmed teapot of human fecundity. The brouhaha was accompanied by a phenomenal barrage of obscurantism. Special pleading, hidden motivation, and vested interest combined to demonstrate the extent to which reason could be dominated by fear and self-interest. Almost every anxiety that besets our times was hitched to the population controversy, plunging the anxious bystander into partisanship over a subject about which he was often ignorant.

And yet it was evident that some men of extraordinary patience, courage, and good will persisted in reason and clarity. They said that the human species might be better off without ten billion or more individuals, even if these masses were well fed. They observed that the fulfillment of earnest promises by agriculturists to feed everyone on earth in the year 2000 would deprive the earth of many species of larger mammals, birds, reptiles, and fish—in turn simplifying

ecosystems of which we are relatively ignorant and which may be of great practical as well as intangible value to us. They suggested that super-optimistic, though factually well informed, statements that we can feed fifty billion people are put in a new perspective in the social and political turmoil that threatens world peace and which grows to some extent from present population pressures.

THE EDITORS

Federation Proceedings, *11(3): 681–693, September 1952. Copyright 1952 by the Federation of American Societies for Experimental Biology, Bethesda, Maryland 20014. Reprinted by permission.*

THERE IS NO food shortage in the USA. Our preoccupation with the world food shortage is due to explosive political situations and menacing revolutionary fury in other parts of the world, particularly Asia, because "two-thirds of the world's people, even before the war, were undernourished all the time" (John Boyd Orr, first Secretary-General of the FAO); and "marginal millions do not get enough to eat, which means a race with death" (Norris E. Dodd, present Director-General of the FAO).

The remedy for food shortage is to increase food production. This is being done. The population in the densely populated areas is increasing, however, more rapidly than the food production, as shown by the 1951 FAO report (2):

Most of those who were hungry in the five prewar years are now hungrier. . . . Production in most of the undernourished areas is failing to keep pace with population growth. . . . This decrease means more undernourished. . . . less resistance to disease . . . more funeral processions of those who die young. . . . Hunger is steadily haunting our civilization. . . . There will inevitably be also a rising tide of unrest and revolution and war.

Furthermore, most of the world's accessible arable land is being cultivated

55

Figure 1

Population plotted on arithlog grids against calendar years, 1932–1950 (from data in *UN Demographic Year Books*). Cross-bars represent approximate positions of change in slopes of curves. Slopes of curves × 100 represent annual percentage increases in population; i.e., USA curve 1932–1950 has 3 segments of slopes, 0.008, 0.012, 0.019, representing annual percentage increases of 0.8, 1.2 and 1.9 per year. For a 1% slope population is doubled in approximately 70 years; for 2%, in 35 years; for 3%, in 23 years; for ½%, in 140 years. (Time doubling population = 0.693/*k*; thus for annual 1% increase, population is doubled in 0.693/0.01 = 70 years.) (Adapted from *Federation Proceedings*, 11(3): 681–693, September 1952. Copyright 1952 by the Federation of American Societies for Experimental Biology, Bethesda, Maryland 20014.)

Population (Millions)

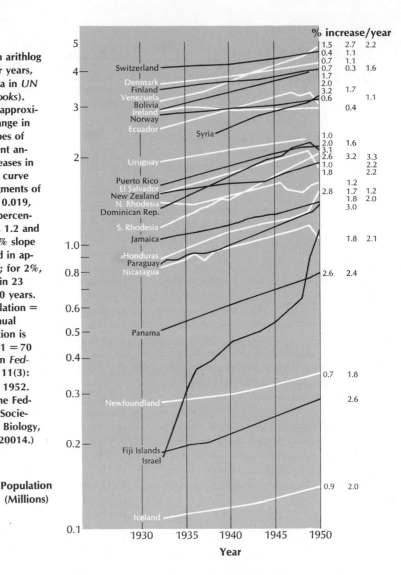

for food production and there are limitations on the ability of the earth to feed indefinitely a free-reproducing population. Therefore, an attempt should be made to reduce the pace of the population increase.

The problem of population-growth decrease is, however, unlike food production increase, bedevilled by numerous traditional and emotional taboos and confounded by many confusing fables and fallacies. Public speakers,

especially natural scientists, avoid getting involved in such complications, preferring to keep their problems simple like their laboratory researches. Unfortunately, soft-pedalling the population factor in the food/population ratio does not advance the overall solution of the problem. Hence, the following hazardous attempt to treat this situation in its broader aspects—including the population factor—even if it does involve mixing natural science with

56

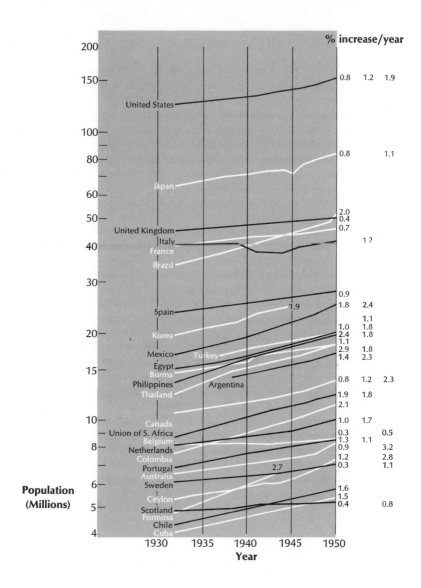

% increase/year

| | 0.8 | 1.2 | 1.9 |

United States

| | 0.8 | | 1.1 |

Japan

| | 2.0 | | |
| | 0.4 | | |
United Kingdom | | 0.7 | | |
Italy | | | 1 ? | |
France
Brazil

| | 0.9 | | |
Spain — 1.9 | | 1.8 | 2.4 |
| | | 1.1 | |
| | 1.0 | 1.8 | |
Korea | | 2.4 | 1.8 | |
| | 1.1 | | |
Mexico — Turkey | 2.9 | 1.8 | |
Egypt | 1.4 | 2.3 | |
Burma
Philippines — Argentina | 0.8 | 1.2 | 2.3 |
Thailand | 1.9 | 1.8 | |
| | 2.1 | | |

Canada | 1.0 | 1.7 | |
Union of S. Africa | 0.3 | | 0.5 |
Belgium | 1.3 | 1.1 | |
Netherlands | 0.9 | | 3.2 |
Colombia | 1.2 | | 2.8 |
Portugal — 2.7 | 0.3 | | 1.1 |
Australia
Sweden | 1.6 | | |
Ceylon | 1.5 | | |
Scotland | 0.4 | | 0.8 |
Formosa
Chile
Cuba

1930 1935 1940 1945 1950

Population (Millions)

Year

social science. The necessity for such broad treatment is due to the fact that the behavior of man is profoundly affected by ideas of his own making. His religion and his social science influence his pattern of action even as much as do purely biological factors (3).

Population Growth

It is a basic biological principle that "there is no bound to the prolific nature in plants and animals but what is made by their crowding and interfering with each other's means of subsistence" (T. R. Malthus, 1798). How does this principle apply to human populations?

1. Historical perspectives. Most Occidentals have the impression that the food shortage in Asia is due to the high percentage increase of its population. This is not true. The *percentage* growth of the population in Asia, with respect to the people there, is less than in the USA (fig. 1). The population

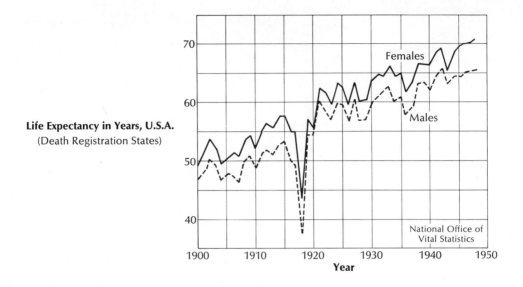

Life Expectancy in Years, U.S.A.
(Death Registration States)

Females

Males

National Office of
Vital Statistics

1900   1910   1920   1930   1940   1950

Year

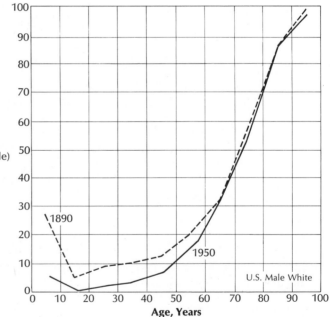

Specific Mortality
(% Living That Die During a Decade)

1890

1950

U.S. Male White

Age, Years

Figure 2

Life expectancy at birth in USA during past 50 years increased by almost 50% (about 23 years) with corresponding increase in population growth for a given birth rate. (Lower chart based on data by R. L. McNamara, University of Missouri.) (Adapted from *Federation Proceedings* 11(3): 681–693, September 1952. Copyright 1952 by the Federation of American Societies for Experimental Biology, Bethesda, Maryland 20014.)

growth in Asia, however, is extremely great *with respect to the available fertile land.*

This brings up an historical event perhaps overlooked. It is that 15th century Europe was in the same cramped condition that Asia is in now. Then something happened to relieve it: Columbus discovered America, a territory 6 times larger than Europe, with a great abundance of fertile soil and rich minerals. Australia, New Zealand, South Africa, and the many newly discovered islands belong in this category of free fertile land. These territorial discoveries rejuvenated old Europe, gave her the needed elbow room.

The new territories not only had free fertile land and other riches, but an invigorating climate—air free from kaisers, czars, kings, secret police, inquisitions, a situation unprecedent in human history. Here a novel doctrine was born[1]: "All men are endowed by their Creator with certain inalienable rights—life, liberty and the pursuit of happiness," the foundation of the "American way of life," which includes the Canadian, Australian, New Zealand, and most Western European ways of life. This way of life is now in danger because of the decline in food *per person.*

Cause and effect cannot be disentangled, but the rise in modern science and technology, beginning with the Industrial Revolution, paralleled the rise in territorial discoveries and particularly their development. A major result of the scientific progress and technology was development, first slowly then more rapidly, of public

[1] Actually this doctrine was not "born" here, but an opportunity was given for its development. It goes back to the Bible, and to John Locke (1632–1704) who spoke of "Life, liberty, and property."

health control methods with associated increases in life expectancy. These began with governmental control of communicable diseases, culminating in the modern large-scale manufacture of chemotherapeutics, antibiotics, and pesticides which virtually eliminate death from infection, and increased the average life expectancy from 30 years in the fifteenth century to over 70 years in contemporary USA. The rise in life expectancy was particularly rapid in the past 50 years (fig. 2).

This life-expectancy increase was accomplished mostly by increasing the survival rate of children who, in turn, lived to reproduce, so that the population tended to increase *autocatalytically* (exponentially, in compound-interest fashion) with time, with increasing life expectancy. In a lesser extent these developments were made available to the rest of the world. The death rate was steadily declining while the birth rate was remaining roughly constant in most of the world, with a resultant rise in the ratio of births to deaths, that is in population (table 1, fig. 1).

In brief, the increasing world food shortage *per person*, reported by the FAO, is associated with an almost pathological upsurge in world population due to declining mortality and constancy of birth rate. I say "pathological" because it is historically fantastic and, if not checked prophylactically, may affect the world population as cancer affects the individual.

To illustrate, let us assume that Adam and Eve set up housekeeping only 2100 years ago (even though it is believed that man has been on the earth at least a million years), and that the resulting population grew at the modest rate of 1 per cent per year (the present world population growth is 1.2 per

59

Table 1

Region	Estimated Population[1]				Population Increase				Percentage Distribution,[2] 1948–50		
	1936	1948	1949	1950	1949	1950	1949	1950	Popula-tion	Produc-tion	Ratio Prod. to Popul.
	millions				*millions/yr*		%	%			
Far East	1,072	1,175	1,187	1,198	12	11	1.0	1.0	54.5	32.0	0.5:1
Europe	372	390	394	397	4	3	1.0	0.8	18.0	23.5	1:1
Near East	108	124	125	127	1	2	0.8	1.6	5.5	4.4	0.8:1
Africa (ex. Near East)	127	147	150	153	3	3	2.0	2.0	7.0	4.7	0.7:1
Latin America	125	156	159	162	3	3	1.9	1.9	7.0	10.1	1:1
U. S. & Canada	140	160	163	166	3	3	1.9	1.8	7.5	22.6	3:1
Oceania	10.7	12.2	12.4	12.6	0.2	0.2	1.6	1.6	0.5	2.8	5:1
Total	1,955	2,164	2,190	2,216	26	26	1.2	1.2	100	100	

[1] Figures refer to end of each year.

[2] Percentage based on totals, excluding USSR.

cent per year as shown in table 1; see also fig. 1). The human race would then have reached in 2100 years a population, P, of 2.6 billions

$$(1a) \quad P = 2e^{0.01 \times 2100} = 2.6 \text{ billion}$$

which is greater than the present world population of 2.4 billion.

To carry this computation to an absurdity, let us assume that Adam and Eve set up housekeeping 5300 years ago, and that the population increased at 1 per cent per year. In 5300 years, the population, P, would number

$$(1b) \quad P = 2e^{0.01 \times 5300} = 1.0 \times 10^{23}$$

individuals, weighing (at 100 lbs. per person) 1.0×10^{25} lbs., equal to the weight of the entire earth. The earth's surface would then be covered miles thick with human beings. This is good arithmetical proof that the present rate of population growth is something really new under the sun; and if allowed to continue without planned controls, must be checked by the harsh natural methods that operate to maintain constant subhuman populations: starvation, disease, violence, and

premature death. Which method shall we humans choose?

Anthropologists believe that pre-literate and medieval populations were kept roughly constant by "natural causes," such as famines, epidemics, and wars. Carr-Saunders (4) reported widespread infanticide, abortion, and other crude methods for limiting offspring: "No matter in what quarter of the world we look wherever there are native races, one or more of these customs is practiced except where native customs have been destroyed by European influence." Widespread taboos against conception during lactation, which may continue for over three years, are important checks (5). The present unusually rapid population increase is due to the doubling of life expectancy during the past century.

2. Ideals and politics. In 1943, towards the end of the second World War, President Roosevelt gave the world his inspiring peace aim of world-wide "Freedom from Want," followed by the Hot Springs Conference, and the birth of the FAO of the UN.[2] These

[2] Food and Agriculture Organization of the United Nations, including representatives of about 70 nations.

activities led to widespread awareness of the seriousness of the world food problem. I recall the editorial by our own Henry A. Mattill in *Nutrition Reviews* which declared that "the world cannot long exist in peace if half its people are well fed and the rest ill fed." The symposia sponsored by the American Association for Advancement of Science on "Freedom from Want" (6), by the American Philosophical Society on the "Possibilities for Increasing the World Food Supply" (7), and this symposium on "World Food Problems" were undoubtedly partly inspired by FAO stimuli and by the world-wide freedom from want ideal. This was followed by the Point Four program in President Truman's 1949 inaugural address "for making the benefits of our scientific advances and industrial progress available for the improvement and growth of underdeveloped areas," and the 1950 British Commonwealth's Colombo Plan to help India, Pakistan, Ceylon, Malay, and Borneo (8).

The latest FAO reports (2) show that their efforts and the activities of the Point Four program made great educational and statistical contributions. The food *per person*, however, continued to decline.

An interesting feature of these aids is that the world's hungry peoples do not appreciate them. Communists characterized them as propaganda—an old imperialism in new dress. They believe, following Hobson (9), that Western powers were traditionally interested in undeveloped countries solely for their own investment opportunities.

Professor Mukerjee (10) suggested settling Indians on unused submarginal lands in other countries. Indians are used to cultivating such land and to extracting a submarginal living. In brief, one could fill up the empty spaces in America, Australasia, and Africa with hungry Indians. Had not Europeans, particularly Englishmen, filled up empty spaces displacing natives in America, Australia, and South Africa? Could not Indians do likewise? This plan refused, Mukerjee would consider the declared freedom from want aim as political hypocrisy, to counteract communistic propaganda. The Mukerjee solution, a solely verbal one, is cited only for its psychological interest, perhaps an indication of the shape of things to come, indicated by the following quotations:

"Why should we regard it of unquestionable benefit to have 400 million Indians in 1945 where there were 250 million in 1870? As they increase in numbers and as they learn to manufacture steel and the implements of war, will they not want more *Lebensraum*?" (11)."A heavily industrialized India backed up by such population pressure would be a danger to the entire world" (12).

It is not surprising for a shrewd and compassionate, as well as a publicity-conscious, world leader to suggest a reassuring world-wide freedom from want peace aim at a time when a hungry world is suffering from a murderous war. Wishful dreaming about food and peace is not unnatural for hungry people at war.

It is surprising, however, that the professional hunger fighters should believe that freedom from want can be achieved by simply "doubling the total food production." The real problem is, of course, doubling the food production *per person* in a freely-reproducing population. Judging by the FAO reports, and *equation 1* this cannot be achieved on a world-wide basis without the use of what Malthus called "powerful preventive checks" against population growth.

61

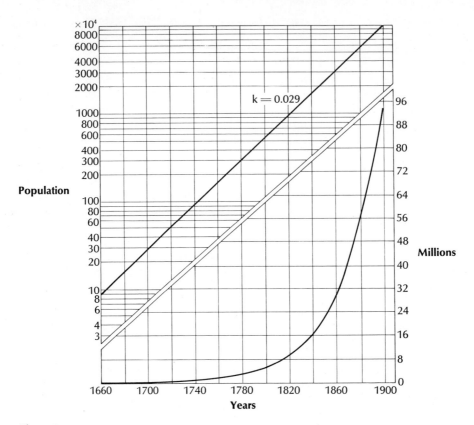

Figure 3

Time curves of growth of populations: yeast cells, fruit flies, man. Bottom two curves on p. 63 illustrate sigmoid nature of population growth. Curve on this page illustrates initial exponential phase for growth of man in USA (upper left time curve on arithlog grid and lower right on arithmetic grid). Numerical value of slope, $k = 0.029$, or 2.9% per year; it means population was doubled in about $0.693/0.029 = 24$ years. Remaining four curves on p. 63 represent growth of two human populations following bend in the curve and effect of cultural levels of the two groups on their rates of approach to maximal population density. A new discovery may raise the ceiling, or begin a new cycle from a higher base. (Adapted from *Federation Proceedings* 11(3): 681-693, September 1952. Copyright 1952 by the Federation of American Societies for Experimental biology, Bethesda, Maryland 20014.)

3. Nature of population growth. The FAO reports and *equation 1* above show that it is not possible to achieve freedom from want on a world-wide scale by increasing food production without resorting to preventive checks. The population catches up too quickly with the increased food supply. This problem was anticipated by Benjamin Franklin (13) about 1750, developed in detail by Thomas Malthus (14)

about 1800, accepted by Charles Darwin (15) about 1850, and recently confirmed (experimentally and mathematically) by the Raymond Pearl School (16).

The time curve of population growth is typically S-shaped (fig. 3). In the absence of environmental limitations the curve has a rising slope; the population tends to grow at a constant percentage rate, in proportion to the

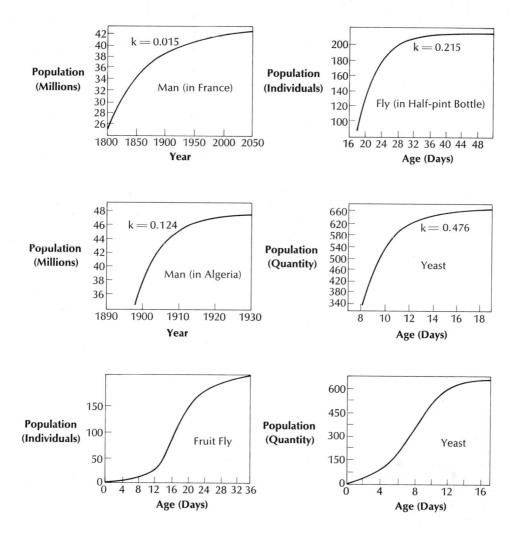

number of reproducing individuals. Reduction of space or food below a certain limit depresses the rising course of the curve to a declining one, finally bringing the population growth to a standstill, to a dynamic equilibrium with the environment (17).

The curves of *Drosophila* in a pint bottle and of man in an isolated area *tend* to have similar sigmoid shapes (fig. 3) although the immediate limiting factors may be different. The shape and upper limit of the population curve of man depend not only on available food and space but also on his cultural level, traditions, and living standard, including deliberate family planning.

4. Population data. The world population increased near 3-fold in the past 200 years, from 875 to about 2400 million. It is now increasing at the rate of 26 million or 1.2 per cent per year (table 1).

The population in India increased from 250 million in 1870 to 400 million in 1945 (11); it was increased by 83 million during the 1921–41 period (18). The population in Java was tripled between 1860 and 1930 (18). The population in Japan increased from 30 million in 1850, to 45 in 1900,

Figure 4

High infant mortality is generally associated with a high birth rate. The birth rate in Egypt and Mexico is about 2- to 3-fold that in Australia and USA, but death rates are still higher so that these population increases are no greater than in Australia or USA (cf. fig. 1). The high death rate is evidently the price for the high birth rate. (Adapted from *Federation Proceedings* 11(3): 681–693, September 1952. Copyright 1952 by the Federation of American Societies for Experimental Biology, Bethesda, Maryland 20014.)

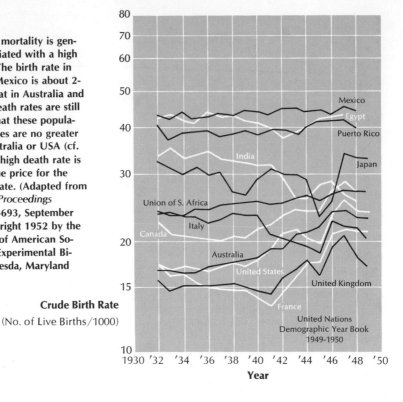

Crude Birth Rate

(No. of Live Births/1000)

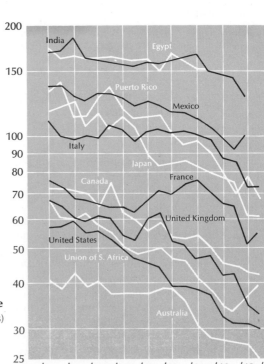

Infant Mortality Rate

(Deaths under 1 yr/1000 Live Births)

to 56 in 1920, to 73 million in 1940 (18), and 83 million in 1950 (19).

The current increase in world population, 1.2 per cent per year, is not very different in Asia than in the USA (fig. 1); prior to 1900 the increase in the USA was near 3 per cent per year (fig. 3), higher than in any Asiatic country (fig. 1).

While the current population increase is, on a percentage basis, nearly the same in the USA as in Asia, the birth and death rates are very much higher in Asia than in the USA (fig. 4). Births in Asia are not controlled, except in the highest social category. In the USA, however, especially in the middle and upper-economic classes, conception is largely controlled. Children are born for desired parental pleasures—not unlike other things they desire and acquire—if circumstances permit. Because of their realistic attitudes and freedom from traditional inhibitions, and because of relative food abundance, there is no danger of "Malthusian misery" in North America and similarly minded countries. Nor is there danger of serious population decline because most people are sufficiently fond of children to maintain the race even if they can easily avoid child bearing. The eager demand for babies by childless couples is good evidence that there is no danger of deliberate "race suicide," (cf. Kaiser and Whelpton, *Studies of Psychological Factors Affecting Fertility*).

Low birth rates are associated with low death rates (fig. 4). Low birth rates reflect the use of foresight and prudence in limiting conception rate to the parents' ability to rear their children in harmony with their child-welfare ideals, and intelligent adjustment of a birth rate pattern evolved

for preliterate, prescientific conditions when life expectancy was 14 years, to a scientific era in which the life expectancy exceeds 70 years. It appears that such ideals are lacking among the peoples half of whose children die before reaching age 13 (Ref. 18 and fig. 4) mostly as result of inadequate food supply.

Food Supply

1. Limiting factors. While awaiting the development of effective methods for retarding the rate of world-population growth, we are impelled by our ethics—and possibly by our diplomacy —to do our best towards increasing food production to feed the hungry, although this is likely to aggravate the later future by further population increase. The rate of food production can undoubtedly be increased by various technological and educational aids and developments (figs. 5 and 6). In this sense there is much good in the FAO and Point Four programs.

There are, however, definite limits to these developments. Just as limiting factors prevent conversion of 100 per cent of the coal energy into useful work of a steam engine, so limiting factors prevent cultivation of 100 per cent of the earth's surface, utilization of 100 per cent of the solar energy poured on the earth, greater exploitation of yeast and chlorella growth potentialities. Application of fertilizers increases crop yield, but their supply, especially of potassium, phosphorus, and sulphur, is limited. Certain soils are not cultivated either because they are not accessible or because of their relative sterility. The present productive ceilings can be raised, but subject to the "law of diminishing increments" (20); and while helpful locally such

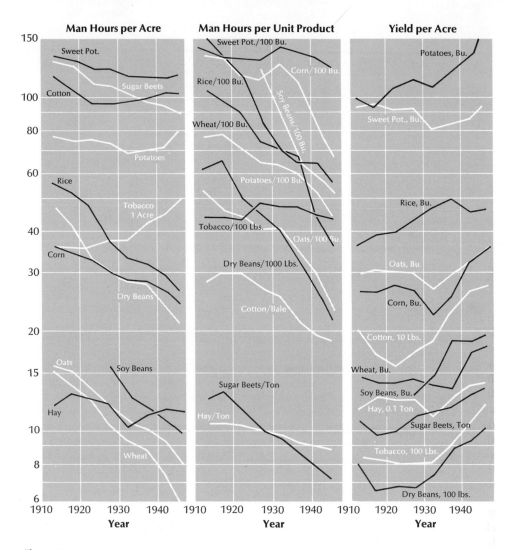

Figure 5

Impact of developing science and technology on efficiency and level of production of food of plant origin (plotted from indicated source). Most agriculturists believe accelerating crop production accelerates impoverishment of soil when food is shipped to the cities and excreta washed to the ocean or incinerated. (Adapted from *Federation Proceedings* 11(3): 681–693, September 1952. Copyright 1952 by the Federation of American Societies for Experimental Biology, Bethesda, Maryland 20014.)

elevation will be insignificant in comparison to the increasing world food needs.[3]

[3] Climatic changes may render arctic lands suitable for food production. This will be an *arithmetical* addition, quickly overtaken by *exponential* population increase.

Such "little things" as carbon dioxide concentration in the atmosphere, rainfall, temperature,[3] latitude, soil fertility, wind, topography, etc., limit greater utilization of soil and sun energy. It is theoretically possible to increase the carbon dioxide concentration in the atmosphere, to maintain

FCM Production, 1000 Lbs./Yr.

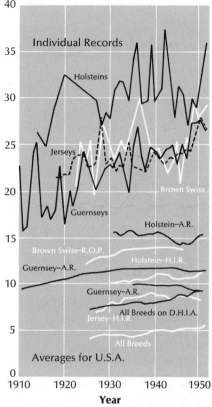

Egg Production/Hen/Year

Figure 6

Impact of developing agricultural science and technology on milk and egg production in USA (FCA = milk in terms of 4% fat). Individual records represent maximal production records. Milk production data furnished by respective cattle clubs; D.H.I.A. data of all breeds supplied by J. F. Kendrick, U.S. Department of Agriculture; average egg production, courtesy H. L. Kempster, U.S. Department of Agriculture; Missouri farm flocks, *Poultry Record Summary* 6: No. 10, University of Missouri Agricultural Extension Service; New Jersey tests, C. S. Platt, *N.J. Agric. Exper. Stn. Bull.* 720; champion data, P. H. C. du Plessis, *World's Poultry Sci. J.* 5: 150, 1949. (Adapted from *Federation Proceedings* 11(3): 681–693, September 1952. Copyright 1952 by the Federation of American Societies for Experimental Biology, Bethesda, Maryland 20014.)

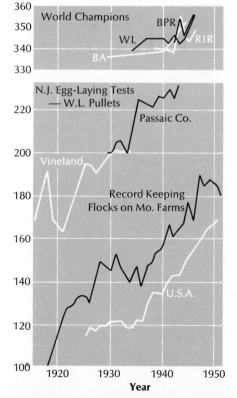

plants under optimal temperature conditions, to irrigate the deserts, to drain the swamps, to pulverize and level rocky mountains, to produce yeast and chlorella on a world-wide scale of gigantic dimensions, to increase the skill, intelligence, and ethical standards of food producers and consumers, but is it practicable?

2. *Food of plant versus animal origin and the efficiency of livestock production.* There are good reasons for livestock production, as follows:

a) Ruminants harvest the vegetation on marginal land not suitable for cultivation, and consume roughages (hay, silage, straw) and other high-cellulose feeds (bran, chaff) not suitable as food for man. Ruminants also harvest and consume cultivated grasses, which under the best conditions yield 1.5 times as much available energy per acre as potatoes and 3 times as much energy as grain. Such grasses may also yield 2 times as much protein as grain or 3 times as much as potatoes (21). Moreover, ruminants synthesize (by way of their rumen microorganisms) nutritionally essential amino acids and B vitamins. They are not only converters and refiners, but also creators of new nutrients, and so contribute mightily towards maintaining a high nutritional level.

b) Non-ruminants (pigs and chickens) which, unlike ruminants, resemble man in their dietary needs, are useful as refiners of food of plant origin, and of various wastes, such as garbage, that have nutritional value yet are not edible by man, into highly prized human foods.[4] These animals are also useful as scavengers.

c) In periods of abundance farm animals are fed surplus grain; in periods of scarcity they are liquidated, yielding their bodies and releasing the grain which they would have consumed. They thus serve as "shock absorbers" saving refined food for man against the lean years. Overpopulated regions not having such reserves are "adjusted" to the decreased food supply by the four horsemen: war, pestilence, famine, and death (22).

d) Foods of animal origin—milk, meat, egg—supply essential amino acids (particularly lysine, methionine, tryptophane) and B-vitamins (particularly B_{12}) in which foods of plant origin are deficient.

The efficiency of conversion of food of plant origin to that of animal is, however, relatively low. Many more persons can be supported from an acre of arable land when they consume the plants directly than after converting to food of animal origin. Hence, poverty is associated with a diet low in food of animal origin (fig. 7), with consequent higher child mortality.

Figure 7

(Above) Animal products in national diets. Note parallelism between "real income" and consumption of food of animal origin. (Plotted from paper of same title by M. K. Bennett, Food Research Inst., Stanford University; transmitted to author by Joseph S. Davis, Director, Stanford Research Institute) (from data published in FAO "World Food Supply, 1948," M. K. Bennett, Stanford University, 1950). (Bottom) Extension of figure to more nations, showing parallelism of nature of diet with the reciprocal of infant mortality, with "real income" and with "living standard" as indicated by use of motor vehicles (from data published by M. K. Bennett, *Am. Econ. Rev.* 41, 1951). (Adapted from *Federation Proceedings* 11(3): 681–693, September 1952. Copyright 1952 by the Federation of American Societies for Experimental Biology, Bethesda, Maryland 20014.)

---

[4] "With a garden and a cow
   Using our wastes with a sow
   Small families could get along somehow."
                              M. E. MUHRER

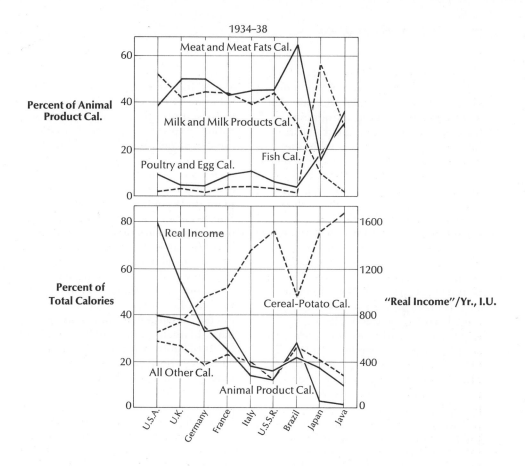

1934–38

Percent of Animal Product Cal.

Meat and Meat Fats Cal.

Milk and Milk Products Cal.

Poultry and Egg Cal.

Fish Cal.

60

40

20

0

Percent of Total Calories

Real Income

Cereal-Potato Cal.

All Other Cal.

Animal Product Cal.

80

60

40

20

0

1600

1200

800

400

0

"Real Income"/Yr., I.U.

U.S.A. U.K. Germany France Italy U.S.S.R. Brazil Japan Java

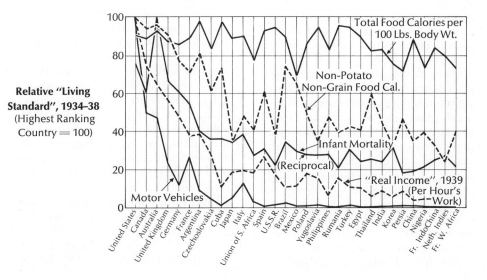

Relative "Living Standard", 1934–38
(Highest Ranking Country = 100)

Total Food Calories per 100 Lbs. Body Wt.

Non-Potato Non-Grain Food Cal.

Infant Mortality (Reciprocal)

Motor Vehicles

"Real Income", 1939 (Per Hour's Work)

100

80

60

40

20

0

United States, Canada, Australia, United Kingdom, Germany, France, Argentina, Czechoslovakia, Cuba, Japan, Italy, Union of S. Africa, Spain, U.S.S.R., Brazil, Mexico, Poland, Yugoslavia, Philippines, Rumania, Turkey, Egypt, Thailand, India, Korea, Persia, China, Nigeria, Fr. IndoChina, Neth. Indies, Fr. W. Africa

Experimental data on rats (23) and observations on man (24) indicate that mature males—or non-reproducing females—can maintain good nutrition indefinitely on an all-vegetable diet containing such foods as soybean meal. They are, however, inadequate for re-producing females and growing animals, perhaps because such foods—even soybean—lack vitamin B_{12}.

Children (Bantu in Africa) fed after weaning on a diet exclusively of plant origin (mealie-meal porridge, Kaffir corn, green vegetables) develop "malignant malnutrition" or "kwashiorkor." This is characterized by anorexia, anemia, diarrhea, enlarged fatty liver, edema, abnormally low serum protein, atrophy. Including soybean in the diet did not prevent or cure this condition. Milk is, so far, the only known prophylactic and cure for this malnutrition (25).

The soybean comes nearest to having the limiting amino acids found in food of animal origin. Its lysine and methionine-cystine levels are of the same order as in meat meal (26). Soybeans contain a trypsin inhibitor which is, however, inactivated by cooking. Although soybean diets show a high protein-efficiency ratio body weight increase/protein ingested in *short* feed experiments, there is no full agreement on the results when fed to children over *long* periods (25, 26). Fair nutrition has been achieved in China on all-plant diets using the soybean as base, perhaps because of the B_{12} in their sauces and other fermented products. Pigs, chickens, and rats have been reared on all-plant rations containing soybean fortified with vitamin B_{12} and calcium (23).

Summarizing, cereals and potatoes are the most economical dietary energy sources for man. They are, however, deficient in calcium; in vitamins B_{12} and A, in lysine, tryptophane, and methionine. Meat, eggs, and milk are rich in these nutrients; hence, optimal nutrition involves the supplementation of the cereal-potato diet with food of animal origin. Such supplementation appears to be indispensable for children and reproducing females. All-plant diets containing soybean, or Puerto Rican chick or pigeon peas (27), or tender cereal grass (28) could, perhaps, be made adequate even for children if supplemented with vitamin B_{12}. Now that the essential vitamins and amino acids that are deficient in food of plant origin are factory produced, cereal-potato diets may, perhaps, be made nutritionally complete by fortification with these nutrients. This way the great losses during conversion of plants to food of animal origin would be avoided, and the population-supporting capacity of the land would be greatly increased.

The efficiency of conversion of plants to food of animal origin varies with the animal and its product, and with the nature of the feed. With respect to the digestible feed consumed, the immediate energetic conversion efficiency for superior animals under good management on excellent feed is about 33 per cent for milk production; 17 per cent for egg production; 35 per cent for pork production (including the lard); and 5 to 33 per cent for other kinds of meat production, depending on age (29). The *protein* conversion efficiency is about 33 per cent for milk production and egg production, and about 25 per cent for pork production. The conversion efficiency is, of course, very much less, about half—3 to 17 per cent—if it is computed with respect to the *gross or total dietary energy* (including the non-digestible part). There is a large literature on the efficiency problem but it is confused by the use of different reference bases—digestible energy, gross energy, metabolizable energy, net energy—each of which gives a different efficiency value (30).

The social economy of conversion of plant feed to meat, milk, or egg, is not necessarily correlated with machine efficiency. For instance, the conversion of western range pasturage to meat is not efficient, but it is economical, because this land cannot be used for grain or potato production. Likewise, the use of swine and poultry as scavengers for producing good food from humanly useless offal may not be efficient but it is extremely economical. The production of milk on excellent grassland is highly efficient—a superior dairy cow on first grade ryegrass pasture may produce in milk energy over 50 per cent of the energy value of cereal produced on this land—but not necessarily socially economical during a period of serious food-calorie shortage, since the need for calories is primary for a starving community. This explains how consumption of food of animal origin declines rapidly with decline in fertile land per person, and with decline in real income (fig. 5). For instance, 25–35 per cent of the dietary calories is from food of animal origin in prosperous USA, Australia, and New Zealand; 15 per cent in less prosperous Europe and in most of South America; and only about 3 per cent in economically depressed Asia. The USA feeds 60 per cent of its grain to livestock; Asia feeds none of her grain to livestock (22).

Milk appears to be the most economical supplement to food of plant origin, not only because of efficiency and economy of its production, but also because it contains at a uniform level—at virtually no cost—the limiting amino acids and B vitamins, including B_{12}. It is the richest dietary

source of calcium. Its slightly soluble carbohydrate, lactose, passes into the intestine where it becomes a favorable medium for vitamin B synthesis and promotes calcium and phosphorous assimilation.

Unfortunately, milk production declines rapidly with increasing environmental temperature because cattle (unlike man) cannot increase the evaporative cooling with increasing environmental temperature above about 80°F (27°C), and so develop fever. The milk yield is, therefore, lowest where it is most needed as supplement to diets of plant origin, namely in the overcrowded tropical and semitropical regions. This problem is at present under intensive investigation (31).

Attitudes and Opposition

The attitudes of man towards the universe in general and to population growth in particular reflect his culture. Much of the history of science is history of cultural lags and struggles between old and new ways of thinking about nature and human nature (3). Our present demographic crises, with their associated social disturbances, resulted from such cultural lags, from an archaic combination of the application of modern scientific medicine for reducing child mortality with a pre-scientific rate of childbirth.

The current life expectancy at birth, at least in the USA, is about 70 years. The reproduction rate in man—its biological mechanisms and supporting traditions (including religions)—were evolved to maintain the species in an era when life expectancy was 14 years. These traditions make it praiseworthy to apply the newest methods for prolonging life but not for reducing the birth rate ("because frustration of conception is wrong" and "whoever interferes with the God-established process of perpetuating human life interferes with human life itself"). The result is an explosive human population upsurge with rise in modern medicine analogous to a rabbit population upsurge on removal of his natural enemies.

The traditionally-bound regions as regards birth rate include the Far and Near East, most of the Eastern European countries, and certain South American regions, including our own Puerto Rico, which furnishes a well documented case history (32). A Professor of Biochemistry in Puerto Rico writes (33):

The main trouble in P. R. is that while the death rate declines, birth rate remains fairly constant. Regardless of religious affiliation, the women of the upper economic classes have small, while the poor have large, families. The latter are demanding the information and facilities which the former employ in limiting the size of their families.

and a Congregational Medical Missionary in Puerto Rico writes (34):

How can we suppose that God . . . could want children to be born into homes where there is no possibility of health. It seems that God would want man to use his intellect, not his emotions and sentiments, to work out a solution of this problem. Our Christian ethic raises its head in protest against the starvation. It is unthinkable that each year an additional 30 or 40 thousand could be accommodated . . . yet this is the rate at which our population (in Puerto Rico) is increasing . . . We let children come in swarms . . . even though filth, ignorance, insecurity, will be all the days of their life . . . even though in some areas nearly half of them are doomed to die, and those who survive exist in sordidness and shame.

The above 1952 comment is similar to one by Malthus (14), an Episcopalian divine of 150 years ago:

The Creator cannot have commanded increase without relation to means of support . . . Our duty is to seek the greatest sum of human happiness . . . A common man who has read his Bible must be convinced that a command given to a rational being by a merciful God cannot be interpreted as to produce only disease and death instead of multiplication.

The following is from an Indian nutritionist (35):

The Father of our Nation, Mahatma Gandhi, was alarmed with the growth of population in India and he visualized starvation and semistarvation of the mass of people. He suggested moral restraint, but it did not work. Sex is the only recreation in their life . . . Their philosophy is that one must take the gift of God and not grumble.

The Oriental attitude is said to consider earthly life as a transient phenomenon, and there is no point in prolonging it. The present government in India, however, is encouraging procreative restriction. It has requested the UN World Health Organization for help (35) for a program of birth control. Family planning centers are being established in Delhi, Mysore, Madras, West Bengal, Poona, and elsewhere; research is being conducted on indigenous and recent contraceptive methods, and villagers seek, and are given, information. In this case leaders in India seem to be more concerned in alleviating starvation among their poor than those in Puerto Rico, who would rather see, as Dr. John Smith (34) phrased it, "half of the children doomed to die," than permit physicians to offer help for what appears as reasonable family planning that would avoid unnecessary wastage of human life.

"The human population has the capacity and 'will' for indefinite exponential growth . . . whereas the population-supporting capacity of the earth is limited." The two-year-old boy in this picture is dying from starvation caused by a drought-induced famine in the Indian state of Andhra Pradesh. (Photo by P. Pittet, courtesy of Food and Agricultural Organization, United Nations.)

Some categories of opposition towards family limitation are based on curious considerations. For instance, the latest FAO reports (2) show that it is apparently impossible to keep up the food production with population increase in free-reproducing societies in which the major human enemy, communicable disease, is controlled by governmental agencies; they indeed substantiate the operation of the old "Malthusian Principle," and refute the notion of "permanent economy of abundance."

Yet Josue de Castro, Chairman of the FAO's policy-making Executive Council, hopefully—and angrily—writes (36), as if he never heard of the FAO's reports:

The empty sleeve of the Malthusian scarecrow has flapped in the winds of prejudice for a century and a half, but science and history have finally shown that no one need take it seriously.

Starvation actually causes overpopulation . . . protein deficiency leads to cirrhosis of the liver which causes release of more estrogen . . . increases sexual appetite . . . and reproductive capacity.

Chlorella, an alga, which can be grown commercially in tanks and fed with minerals, is rich in proteins. A single installation could raise enough of it to supply the proteins needed by three million people . . . equivalent to the production of 150,000 acres of good arable land.

At the present time only about 10 per cent of the earth's arable land is being cultivated.

These statements are contrary to the facts. No one has demonstrated that the starvation or malnutrition in humans increases their sexual appetite or fertility (37), or that a nourishing diet including meat, milk, and eggs is contraceptive; no commercial installation of algae has been made; the world's accessible arable land is being cultivated as testified by John Boyd Orr, first Secretary-General of FAO, who said that "the last new land which could easily be brought under the plow was broken during World War I. . . . We have exploited the last of the world's virgin soil."

De Castro's book (38) presents a table showing that Formosa, subsisting on 4.7 gm. animal protein a day, has a high birth rate whereas Sweden, enjoying 62.6 gm. animal protein, has a low birth rate. The author concludes[5] therefrom that a poor diet causes a high birth rate and a good diet a low birth rate. This is a remarkable example of confusion between cause and effect. Is it not more logical to assume that the less tradition-bound Swedish population plans to have no more children than can be reared in harmony with their high living standard? and that this planning enables them to have 63 gm. animal protein?

General Summary

Increasing food production is meaningful only when expressed in relation to increasing population, as ratio food/

[5] This is based on the Thomas Doubleday "Law" given in his "The Law of Population" etc. (1853) in answer to Malthus: "Whenever a species or genus is indangered, a corresponding effort is invariably made by nature for its preservation and continuance, by an increase of fecundity or fertility, and that this especially takes place whenever such danger arises from a diminution of proper nourishment." (Courtesy Robert C. Cook, acting Director Population Reference Bureau, March 24, 1952.)

population. The FAO of the UN reports (2) that this ratio is steadily declining; that "production is . . . failing to keep pace with population growth . . . which means . . . more funeral processions . . . rising tide of unrest and revolution and war."

This lag in food production behind population growth, in spite of Point Four, Colombo Plan, Marshall Plan, gifts and loans, and related heroic measures, is caused by a historically unprecedented world population upsurge (39) currently at 1.2 per cent per year or 260 million per decade (table 1). A simple computation shows that such a population growth rate would soon saturate the surface of the earth.

This historically unprecedented rate of population growth is causally related to an archaic combination of modern scientific public health control (life expectancy over 70 years in the USA) with an ancient reproductive pattern evolved for a life expectancy of about 14 years. The present population upsurge associated with decline of fatal infections is analogous to an upsurge of subhuman population growth on the removal of natural enemies. Such a combination of declining death rate with constant birth rate can not long coexist. Either the birth or conception rate will be reduced prophylactically to approximate the death rate; or else the population will be scaled down to the available food supply by the ancient population-adjusting methods: hunger, disease, violence, and death. These latter patterns are now in operation in many parts of the world where half of the children die before reaching the age 13 (18)—a sacrifice to cultural lag.

The confusing details of the population-food problem result in confusing opinions about its solution. The general fact, however, is clear. The human population has the capacity and "will" for indefinite exponential growth (in compound-interest fashion) whereas the population-supporting capacity of the earth is limited. Hence, the freedom from want ideal cannot be made a world-wide reality unless the decline in birth rate is adjusted to approximate the decline in death rate. The task of adjusting the birth or conception rate to the death rate is *technically* simple as illustrated by the virtually stationary populations (fig. 1) in Ireland, France, Belgium, and can be further simplified (40). This task is, however, *culturally* formidable in most of the world because of the difficulty in enlisting the cooperation of the leaders of the traditional mass mind.

The opposition by certain religious groups to rational conception control is puzzling (3). This is particularly true since the broad, often poetic, language and spirit of the sacred writings of most of the old traditional religions encourages compassionate, humane, interpretations. For instance, we may interpret the conception-control problem with Jesus who said: "The Sabbath was made for man and not man for the Sabbath" (Mark II, 27); that man was endowed with judgment so that he may use it with compassionate discretion for solving problems developed by changing conditions. Medical knowledge and technology for family planning are already available to the literate well-to-do but not to the poor and ignorant. The latter are offered pious but unrealistic, unacceptable, advice. Such disparity in medical information is unethical, undemocratic and socially harmful, because it is promoting—indirectly but effectively—a differentially higher birth rate among the poor and ignorant.

Considerable attention was also given to the food production factor in the food/population ratio. The population-supporting capacity of the earth can be greatly increased but at progressively increasing social costs.

Grateful acknowledgments are made to my UM associates and to many correspondents, particularly J. S. Davis and H. C. Farnsworth (Food Research Institute, Stanford University) for valuable help.

References

1. Carlson, A. J., *Proc. Inst. Med. Chicago* 19: No. 1, 1952.
2. Dodd, N. E., *The Work of the FAO.* Report of Director General, Food & Agricultural Organization of U.N., Rome, 1951; also *Item III. Provisional Agenda, Conference of FAO. Nov. 19– Dec. 7, 1951.* FAO/51/10/2780.
3. Russell, B., *New Hopes for a Changing World.* New York: Simon & Shuster, 1951; also Frank, L., *Nature and Human Nature.* New Brunswick: Rutgers Univ. Press, 1951.
4. Carr-Saunders, A. M., *The Population Problem, a Study in Human Evolution; Population; World Population: Past Growth and Present Trends.* New York: Oxford Univ. Press, 1922, 1925, 1936. See also Buliard, R., *Inuk.* New York: Farrar, Straus & Young, 1951.
5. Richards, A. I., *Land, Labor and Diet in Northern Rhodesia.* New York: Oxford Univ. Press, 1939.
6. Dodd, Norris E., *Chronica Botanica* 11: 207, 1948.
7. Myrdal, A., K. Davis, J. J. Spengler, H. A. Spoehr, A. J. Stann, L. A. Walford and M. T. Jenkins, *Proc. Am. Phil. Soc.* 95: 1, 1951.
8. Fawke, V. C., *Can. J. Econ. & Pol. Sc.* 17: 501, 1951.
9. Hobson, J. A., *Imperialism: A Study.* London: Constable, 1905.
10. Mukerjee, R., *Races, Lands and Food.* New York: Dryden Press, 1948.
11. Thompson, W. S., *Ann. Am. Acad. Sci.* 249: 111, 1947.

12. Vogt, W., *The Road to Survival*. New York: Sloane, 1948.

13. Franklin, Benjamin, *Works, Vol. 2* (ed. Sparks) Boston: Hilliard, 1840.

14. Malthus, T. R., *Essay on the Principle of Population. 1st ed.* 1803; *9th ed.* 1826. London: MacMillan.

15. Darwin, Charles, *Origin of Species*. London: J. Murray, 1859.

16. Pearl, Raymond, *Biology of Population Growth*. New York: Knopf, 1925; *The Natural History of Population*. New York: Oxford Univ. Press, 1939. See also numerous other books and articles by Pearl and associates.

17. Brody, S., *Bioenergetics and Growth*. New York: Reinhold, 1945, pp. 490–92, 501, 520, 544–46.

18. Balfour, M. C., R. F. Evans, F. W. Notestein and I. B. Taeuber. *Public Health and Demography in the Far East*. New York: Rockefeller Foundation, 1950; also Davis, Kingsley. *The Population of India and Pakistan*. Princeton: Princeton Univ. Press, 1951.

19. *Demographic Yearbooks, 1949–50, 1950–51*. New York: UN Statistical Office, Depts. of Economic and Social Affairs.

20. Brody, S., *Bioenergetics and Growth*. New York: Reinhold, 1945, pp. 1 and 76.

21. Boyd, D. A., *Brit. J. Nutr.* 5: 255, 1951.

22. Pearson, F. A., and D. Paarlberg, *Starvation: Truths, Half Truths, Untruths*. Ithaca: Cornell Univ., 1946.

23. Hogan, A. G., Personal communication. See also Hogan *et al., J. Nutr.* 40: 243, 1950; *Proc. Soc. Exper. Biol. & Med.* 76: 349, 1951; *Nutr. Abstr.* 19: 781, 1950.

24. Mirone, L., *Science* 111: 673, 1950.

25. Wills, L., *Brit. J. Nutr.* 5: 265, 1951. See also Dean, R. F. A., *Id.* p. 269.

26. Carpenter, K. J., *Brit. J. Nutr.* 5: 243, 1951; also Chick, H., *Id.* p. 261.

27. Roberts, L. J., and R. L. Stefani, *Patterns of Living in Puerto Rico*. Puerto Rico: Univ. of Puerto Rico Press, 1949.

28. Brody, S., *Bioenergetics and Growth*. New York: Reinhold, 1945, pp. 749, 789.

29. Brody, S., *Bioenergetics and Growth*. New York: Reinhold, 1945, Ch. 3, also pp. 827–47, 880–89, 900–14.

30. Brody, S., *Bioenergetics and Growth*. New York: Reinhold, 1945, pp. 5–6, 24–32, 54–8. Cf. Forbes and Swift, *J. Dairy Sc.* 8: 15, 1925; Forbes and Voris, *J. Nutr.* 5: 395, 1932; Maynard, L. A., *J. Nutr.* 32: 345, 1946.

31. *Research Bulletins, Environmental Physiology Series*. Columbia: Univ. of Missouri Agricultural Experiment Station.

32. Janer, J. L., *Human Biol.* 17: 267, 1945.

33. Goettsch, Marianne, Personal communication.

34. Smith, John, Personal communication.

35. Mullick, D. N., Personal communication.

36. De Castro, J., *Nation* Feb. 16, 1952, p. 156; *Colliers*, Jan. 19, 1952.

37. Carlson, A. J., and F. Hoelzel, *J. Gerontol.* 6: 169, 1951; also *Overnutrition: Its Causes and Consequences*. Springfield: Thomas, 1950; Evans, H. M., and M. M. Nelson, *Federation Proc.* 11: 45, 1952. See also Benedict, F. G., *et al. A Study of Prolonged Fasting*. Carnegie Inst. of Washington, 1915; Keys, A., *et al. Human Starvation*. Minneapolis: Univ. of Minnesota Press, 1950.

38. De Castro, J., *The Geography of Hunger*. Boston: Little, Brown, 1952, p. 72.

39. Davis, J. S., *The Population Upsurge in the U. S.* San Francisco: Stanford Univ. Press, 1949; also *J. Farm Econ.* 31: 765, 1949.

40. Adams, R., *Science* 115: 157, 1952.

The Inexorable Problem of Space

PAUL B. SEARS

By the mid-1960's it was becoming apparent to many observers (as it had been to a very few even from the beginning) that the Great Space Race, however intrinsically challenging, lent itself to some of the most pernicious rationalizations and wretched actions of our civilization. The G.S.R. fanned the fires of competitive ideology in the form of chauvinistic industrial sufficiency and military advantage; it proved enormously costly; it extended the political manifest destiny and ethnological and ecological bigotry from an earthly to celestial scale; and it shifted intelligent attention from the deepening mess on earth to the bright new "challenge" of space.

The challenge, of course, is mastery of space techniques and subjection of the life and resources of earth's sister planets to an earthly regime. Such abuse of legitimate adventure has been chronic in the modern western world since the Portuguese and Spanish powers strove to meet the challenge of the seas, the heathens, and the unexploited lands. But our capability has greatly increased over theirs.

THE EDITORS

DISCOVERY AND COMMUNICATION are the two prime obligations of the scientist. On occasions such as this, however, the scientist has the added opportunity to examine broad issues in the light of his peculiar knowledge and experience. This I propose to do with respect to that limited segment of space in which we live, move, and have our being. For my subject was

Science, 127:9–16, 1958. Reprinted by permission.

chosen long before man's most recent and dramatic invasion of outer space.

Science and Perspective

My thesis is that, among the practical problems of humanity today, our relation to immediate space is of critical importance. In developing this idea, I shall try to show that our applications of science have been both restricted and shortsighted. In terms of moral choice, we have looked upon science as an expedient rather than as a source of enlightenment.

To be specific, our very proper concern with the applications of mathematics, physics, and chemistry may be clouding the fact that we need biology in general and ecology in particular to illuminate man's relation to his environment. At present the biological sciences are largely sustained as utilities in medicine and agriculture, the social sciences for dealing with immediate ills. But we must not forget that all science is needed to guide the process of future evolution—cultural and physical—now so largely in our own hands. The nest of anti-intellectualism is being warmed by the ignorant, but some of the eggs in it may have been placed there by those who should know better.

Science and Policy

I have no quarrel with the exploration of outer space. It is a legitimate and challenging subject for scientific inquiry and bold experiment. Our optical and mathematical studies of it have long since given us that basic confidence in order without which there could be no science. But, as we extend our astronomy by whatever celestial acrobatics we can get away with, I should like to see some consideration given to relative values. We have a vast amount of unfinished business at our feet. The golden moment for the pick-pocket comes when everyone at the county fair is craning his neck at the balloon ascension.

So far as the skies are concerned, we are feeling the natural soreness that comes from losing a sporting event we thought was in the bag. Actually, if my information is correct, the Russians had explained that they intended to launch a satellite, had indicated its probable size, and have promised to share the knowledge so gained. Since any ray of light should be welcomed in an atmosphere of gloom, it may help to recall that our Olympic ath-letes, in the face of leading questions from their interviewers, had nothing but respect to offer for the conduct of their Russian rivals.

Of course our present concern is much more than simple chagrin at los-ing a contest. What has happened in outer space raises a question about how outer space will be allocated and controlled. We fear, not unreasonably, that whoever controls the space around the earth can impose his will upon all who live on the earth's surface.

Though we grant freely the military significance of space experiments, our present hysteria seems to me to indi-cate an even deeper source of inse-curity. We are beginning to sense that the elaborate technology to which we are so thoroughly committed makes us peculiarly vulnerable. And we are not wholly confident that the ideals of our civilization—so reasonable to us—will really stand up to free competition with other systems of thought. To the extent that this is true, we suffer from an initial handicap of morale.

The pattern of conflict is much the same, regardless of scale. Whether one is watching small boys in the school yard or great powers in the world arena, the preliminaries are marked by bad manners and vituperation on both sides. Missiles are piled up and sec-onds are assembled, the advantage going to the cooler, less hysterical side. The contestant who gets rattled is asking for trouble.

I do not envy our public servants charged with the delicate business of managing international relations. But I am firmly convinced that unless one is determined on war, there is merit in self-restraint and good manners, as well as in prudent measures of self-protection. I am also convinced that the choice of policy is not limited to boasting and belligerence on the one hand or craven appeasement on the other. We have no monopoly on self-respect and other human virtues, nor is there any merit in debasing the origi-nal meaning of the word *compromise* as we have done. We should deplore every display, whether by statesman or journalist, of dunghill courage that lessens the hope of mutual under-standing, good-will, and ultimate col-laboration among human beings.

So far as purely domestic problems go, our almost hypnotic concern with outer space comes at a bad time. Outer space is one more item that diverts at-tention and energy from the prosaic business of setting our terrestrial space in order. And it has fostered an in-credible type of escapism that must be experienced to be believed. One hears too frequently for comfort the sober assertion that we need not worry about depletion of natural resources, now that interplanetary travel is just around the corner! If such a comment came from jesters or cranks, it could be dis-regarded. But we hear it uttered with the solemnity and assurance of the true believer. No doubt we shall continue to hear it, despite the chilling analysis

by Arthur Clarke, the British astronomer, in the November 1957 issue of
Harper's magazine.

Actually this obsession is not a detached phenomenon. Rather it is the
culmination of a new faith—the belief
that technology will solve any problems that may confront humanity. Curiously, it comes at a time when the
scientist is more suspect than he has
been since the days of witchcraft and
alchemy, as recent opinion studies
show. A high proportion of people consider scientists to be queer fish, if not
inhuman and immoral. For a parallel
we would have to think of a religion
which wants the favor of its gods but
does not trust them for a moment.

Opportunistic Application of Science

I do not question the tremendous accomplishments and future possibilities
of technology. I yield to no one in my
admiration for the cleverness, manual
and intellectual, of those who apply
science to meet the needs of mankind.
But faith in technology is not faith in
science or sympathy with the creative
impulse of the scientist. The direction
in which science is applied depends
upon the values of the culture applying it even while science is in turn
modifying the culture.

Our present applications of science
are selective and opportunistic, neither
wholehearted nor balanced. We are
applying it out of all proportion to the
elaboration of consumer goods, often
to such an extent that vast sums must
go into persuading people to desire
what they have not instinctively
wanted. The making of things has
become so facile that their sale creates
major problems in advertising and
credit. As Max Beerbohm once put it,
"Buy advertised goods and help pay
the cost of advertising." Some of the
keenest satire on advertising has come
from advertising men themselves.
Raymond Loewy, the famous automobile designer, has protested the
corruption in car design that has resulted from too great facility— traditionally the death of any sound art.
The current models waste space, materials, and fuel, violate good taste, and
impose needless economic burdens on
the public. And while we are applying
science in this manner, we are blandly
ignoring its highest function, which is
to give us perspective and inform us
about what we are doing to ourselves.
Even the scientist, as Kubie has so
ably shown, suffers from his lack of
self-analysis.

On the whole, a man's actions are a
response to his idea of the kind of
world he thinks he is living in and to
his concept of his own nature. That
this is true is shown very practically
in the history of human thought: No
great religion is content merely to lay
down maxims of conduct; it also develops its own cosmogony, its own
pattern of the universe, to justify those
maxims.

Our present attitude toward terrestrial space exemplifies with peculiar
clarity our selective use of science. For
living space, if we consider both its
extent and quality, subsumes all other
resources, being in that respect equivalent to the economist's technical concept of land. Yet the power of applied
science has been overwhelmingly employed to exploit space, while those
aspects of science which could illuminate its wise and lasting use are still
largely ignored.

I am assuming at the outset that the
human adventure on this planet is
worth our best efforts to keep it going
as long as possible. I am also assuming
that man is capable of responsible
judgment and conduct and that he has
at hand much of the important basic

79

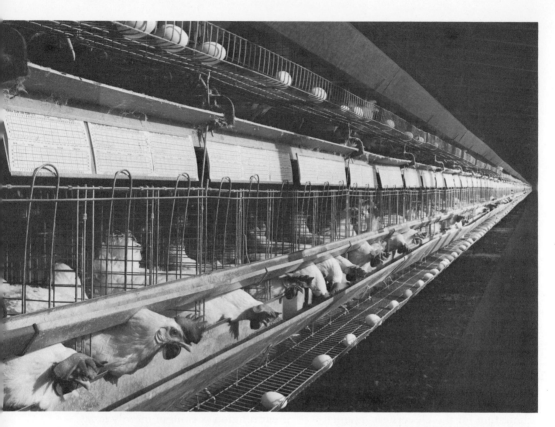

"... I am assuming that it is not enough for man to live by bread alone but that intangible, as well as tangible values are necessary to justify his persistence. If this be true, the question is, not how many people can exist on earth, but what kind of a life will be possible for those who do." (Photo by Grant Heilman.)

information he needs. Finally, I am assuming that it is not enough for man to live by bread alone but that intangible, as well as tangible values are necessary to justify his persistence. If this be true, the question is, not how many people can exist on earth, but what kind of a life will be possible for those who do.

Limiting Factors

From New Jersey to Oregon one sees great egg factories, where highly selected strains of poultry are confined at maximum density and with maximum efficiency. Every need—nutritive, environmental, and psychological—is taken care of. These gentle, stupid birds have no responsibility but to stay alive and do their stuff. Yet they are at the mercy of any break in an elaborate technological mesh that keeps them going. And should a stranger burst abruptly into their quarters, the ensuing panic would pile them up in smothering heaps in the far corners of their ultramodern apartment. The underprivileged, pre-technological hen ran many hazards, but at least she had the freedom to scratch around for food and a sporting chance to dodge under a bush to evade the swooping hawk.

People, of course, are not poultry, but they are living organisms, subject to the limitations inherent in that condition. I am unmoved by any protest against applying biological analogies to human society. Analogy is one of the most powerful tools of the scientist. From physics to physiology, and notably in the latter, analogies suggest our models which we must then test and either accept or reject as the evidence may dictate. And besides, man is a living organism, as I have said.

Fortunately, in considering man's relation to terrestrial space, our models do not all come from observing other forms of life. We have some impressive ones furnished by our own species. Let us reserve them, however, for the present, and look at the other living things. Here from students of bacteria, trees, insects, or any of the sundry groups of vertebrate animals—fish, fowl, or mammal—we get the same story. No known form of life has been observed to multiply indefinitely without bumping up against the limitations imposed by the space it occupies. These limitations involve not only quantity but quality. And quality rests upon the pattern of that complex of factors, whether known or unknown, that are necessary to sustain the species in question. So far as environment is concerned, an ancient bit of wisdom sums up the situation: "A chain is no stronger than its weakest link."

This principle was recognized by Liebig in his famous law of the minimum: the growth of a crop is determined by the essential nutrient available in least quantity. It was restated more precisely by Blackman in his law of limiting factors: physiological processes are limited by the least favorable factor in the system of essential conditions. These statements rest upon controlled experiment. They are independent of the circumstance that an English political economist and parson, Malthus by name, had suggested that human populations did

not, in fact, increase indefinitely beyond certain limitations of environment.

It should be emphasized, however, that the writings of Malthus did give the necessary clue that enabled Charles Darwin to formulate a reasonable explanation of the mechanism involved in the origin of species. Since there remain many misconceptions with regard to both Malthus and Darwin, it may be well to review the thesis of the latter. This thesis has never been successfully controverted, although there are perennial headlines "Darwin Refuted" whenever some detail of his work is brought into question. Briefly, Darwin had noted the universal tendency of organisms to vary and to transmit these variations to their offspring. Our knowledge with respect to these matters is now being applied daily by plant and animal breeders with the same effectiveness with which the phase rule is used in chemical engineering.

Darwin's second point was that organisms tend to reproduce far beyond their capacity to survive. This again in fact occurs, and is a matter of household knowledge among those who, as scientists, observe living organisms. The tagging of fish that return to the place where they began migration reveals that, despite the thousands of eggs laid by each female, not more than a few adults from each batch survive to make the return journey.

Anyone who has observed, year after year, the nesting of robins in his yard has noted the consistent toll—from cats, jays, crows, and accidents—that serves to keep numbers down. And though the clutch of eggs is fairly uniform from year to year—implying a potential doubling of the robin population—the number of nests does not increase significantly, nor do these

81

birds spread beyond a well-defined territorial range. Even though predators might fail to control their numbers, competition within the species would establish a threshold of limitation, as it did for deer when wolves were eliminated.

The final point made by Darwin was that the relatively small proportion of individuals surviving did so, not merely by random chance, but largely because they were those best fitted to cope with their environment. The less favorably endowed tended to be eliminated. Thus the better adapted lived to transmit their favorable variations. In this way he accounted for two great riddles of living nature—the immense variety of living things and the remarkable adjustments they show.

It is not my object here to justify Darwinian theory. It is enough to say that the theory coordinates more information than any alternative that has been proposed. This is all we have a right to ask in science. We need emphasize only one corollary—that the pattern of environment is built solidly into that of life. Survival rests upon this relationship. No organism known to biologists has ever, so to speak, had things completely its own way. Some, of course, are more "successful" than others, as the late L. O. Howard indicated in his famous dictum that the last survivor on earth would be a living insect on a dead weed.

Extension to Man

The rub comes when we attempt to extend these principles to our own species. As life has advanced from simple beginnings, it has played an increasing role in geological processes. Man is no exception. He is a worldwide dominant, the first such species

in earth history. And through advancing technology he is producing tremendous changes. That this should confer a sense of power is understandable. But power is not the same thing as control. Only when power is balanced by responsibility is there control, as the record of our highway accidents attests. The corrupting effect of irresponsible power is an axiom in human history.

Is there any reason to believe that man is exempt from the rules that apply to living organisms in general? Or does the difference lie in his ability to learn those rules and profit by respecting them? Can we make use of known physical and biological principles in discussing problems that involve man? Can we view psychological and sociological considerations in the light of simpler and more obvious ones, or must we rely solely upon a higher level of discourse when we speak of man? These are not idle questions. I have mentioned the indignant protests against applying "biological analogies" to sociological problems. But it is one thing to hold that man is *merely* a physicochemical system, or *merely* an animal, and quite another to insist, as I must, that he is a physical phenomenon, and a biological one too, whatever else he may be.

Man's physical body occupies space, somewhere between two and four cubic feet of it. At his present rate of increase in the United States, he is set to double the aggregate volume occupied by human bodies in about 41 years. Continuing at this rate, it would be less than 700 years—say 22 generations—until there is standing room only, with each space of 3 by 2 feet, or 6 square feet, occupied. On this basis there is room for exactly 4,646,400 people in each square mile. I have perhaps been overgenerous in estimating the per capita area, but I did wish to leave space enough to permit each individual to reach in his pocket for the rent money when it falls due. A little after this the hypothetical human population would weigh more than the planet.

In thus giving rein to imagination I have in mind sundry pronouncements regarding the potential capacity of the earth, some of them to the effect that by proper scientific management it can take care of any conceivable increase in population. The numbers I have mentioned are both conceivable and begettable. The question is, are they supportable?

Some Examples

The most densely populated continent is Europe, with 142 people per square mile, as against Asia with 78, although the most densely populated areas are yet on that continent. North America, including great areas of desert and tundra, follows with 23, while Africa and South America are nearly tied, with 17 and 19, respectively. The figure for the United States is 51, while Australia is the least densely populated of the continents, with about 3 persons per square mile. Evidently cold fact, as so often happens, has not kept pace with theory. Either people do not breed as fast as they might, or survival rates are not what they could be. Actually both of these things happen, and in curious combinations. We may, I think, allow the battered bones of the Reverend Malthus to rest in peace as we examine a few case histories quite briefly.

First, however, let us retrace our steps for a glimpse at what we pleasantly call the lower orders of life. Abstracting an item from the valuable studies of Thomas Park, we learn that when populations of flour beetles reach certain densities, their rates of increase drop sharply. Among other things, these animals begin to eat their own eggs and pupae, a very effective way of slowing down the operation of the compound interest law. Whether this practice is due to a craving for food and water or simply to the fact that hungry beetles bump into eggs oftener than before, we do not know.

The lemmings in Alaska are likewise instructive. These small rodents, living and breeding under the snow, have a kind of pulsating population record, abundance alternating with low density in fairly regular fashion. With summer melting, they are preyed upon by a variety of animals, including the Arctic fox and snowy owl. A third predator, the jaeger, a kind of sea hawk somewhat resembling a gull, has been studied by Frank Pitelka, who reported on it at the Berkeley meeting of the AAAS. When the lemming population is low or average, the jaegers space their nests and consume their prey in an orderly manner. But when the lemmings are at a peak, so that food should be no problem, the jaegers spend so much energy quarrelling over nesting space and food that relatively few of them raise normal broods. So their numbers decline, but not primarily from lack of food. They do not urbanize well—or shall we say that when they attempt to urbanize they pay the usual penalty of a greatly lowered reproductive efficiency? For it is, I believe, an open secret that few cities of major size have heretofore maintained their population by their own birth rate—a situation that is probably changing through the rapid development of suburban life. Perhaps it is time for some modern Aesop to instruct us on manners and morals, using for that purpose the verified behavior of animals instead of their imagined words. Certainly we learn that for the jaegers plenty is not an inevitable road to biological success.

Yet the idea of plenty—in food in particular, in energy and minerals to a lesser degree—dominates the discussion by scientists of man's future. Some of this material is excellent, notably that by Harrison Brown, who not only understands the physical sciences but has biological sense and a conscience to boot. Too few, however, bother to read the fine print and observe the *if*'s in such analyses as his. Those who, like Osborn, Cook, Sax, and Vogt, concern themselves with space and numbers are written off as "pessimists," as though the fixing of a label adjudicates the issue and solves the problem.

It is the merit of the men named, including Brown, that they have raised not only a material but a moral issue that is too often neglected by those who proudly label themselves "optimists." The question is not only how much but what kind of life will be possible if humanity continues to hurtle along its present course. Russell, the Huxleys, and Berrill have all warned us of the inevitable loss of freedom and personal dignity that must follow the multiplication of numbers and the depletion of resources.

Physical Limitations and Cultural Influences

The findings of archeology are in agreement with recorded observations of prefarming cultures about the space requirements of hunters, fishers, and gatherers. For such folk the space requirements are great, by modern standards, being no less than three to five square miles per person where conditions are most favorable. The best estimates for pre-Columbian United States, even with such agriculture as it possessed, do not reach three million in about the same number of square miles. Specifically, the state of Ohio, some 40,000 square miles, mostly fertile and well-watered, does not appear to have supported more than about 15,000 Indians at the time of European discovery. Even the Basin of Mexico, with a highly efficient system of horticulture and an imposing array of domesticated plants, did not have numbers exceeding a million—one-third the population of the present Mexico City, which occupies only a fraction of the modern basin.

Yet we know that this rather moderately concentrated population experienced pressures of various kinds during the centuries preceding 1519. However the situation might be rationalized, the limitations of space, with regard to both extent and quality, were stern and tangible within the Basin of Mexico. The ancient chronicles are a record of floods, drouths, volcanism, and hunger. Toward the end of the Aztec Empire, in a desperate attempt to placate the angry gods, human sacrifice was stepped up until it reached scores of thousands—suggesting the rate of emigration that today serves to stabilize the population of Ireland, whose chief export is people.

Our judgment of the whole history of agriculture has been revamped since the 1930's. Dale and Carter have done this brilliantly, showing that every great center of power and civilization has been based squarely upon fertile space, and tracing the parallel decline of culture and the nutrient capacity of the soil.

Certainly human communities have, as a matter of record, more than once run hard into the physical limitations of their environment. Often they have intensified these limitations by their own activities. That man can preserve and even enhance the potential of his environment, I do not question. But I see no warrant for asserting that he has often done it or can do so indefinitely under his present pattern of behavior.

Limiting factors are not necessarily physical in the strict sense. Cultural disruption and spiritual discouragement may likewise act as restraints. This is believed to explain the well-known decrease of the native Indian population during the century following the Spanish conquest of Mexico. With little to live for, people may simply not have families, whatever the physiological facts and urges may be. Another instance is that of the slave population in Jamaica prior to 1842. The white population, numbering less than one-tenth that of the slaves, vigorously discouraged breeding among the slaves, since it was cheaper to buy new slaves than to propagate them. Nevertheless, the apathy toward life, attested by the high suicide rate among victims of the slave trade, is believed by competent authority to have been an important factor in the low effective reproduction rate among these pathetic humans.

If we come closer home, we have the significant drop in family size during our own depression of the 1930's. In this instance, the slow-down cannot be attributed to pressure from the physical environment, for the depression preceded the great drouth. Even then there was no real scarcity of food, merely a breakdown in the mechanism for its economic distribution. Presumably the direct pressure came from cultural anxiety, or what is sometimes called "social shock." Even the "recession" of 1949–50 produced a measurable effect, total births in 1950 numbering 17,000 less than in 1949.

We have, too, the earlier decrease in the British birthrate about 1921. This was the year in which Marie Stopes, already famous as a paleobotanist, enlightened the public on responsible parenthood. It was also a time of high postwar prices, and subsequently a time of flaming individualism. But it was not, so far as I know, a period of physical pressure from environmental forces. Having myself reared a family during the 20's and 30's, I can testify that in our own country there were many cultural pressures, neither physical nor economic, that encouraged one-child or at most two-child famiIes. Not least among these pressures was increasing focus upon the personality and development of the individual child, at times to the point of morbid sentimentality.

Cultural influences can also act in the opposite direction, the classical instance being in the scriptural injunction to be fruitful and multiply and replenish the earth. Today, despite the staggering cost of education and the increasing cost of food—unchecked by our continuing agricultural surplus—the four-child family is in vogue. Incredible though it may sound, it is through the influence of fashion (call it example or prevailing custom if you prefer) that many modern families work out their response to the problem of population and space.

Certainly the record suggests that population density is influenced both by the physical and the cultural environment. However these may operate, either singly or in conjunction, they find expression in the behavior of individuals, and individuals differ greatly. Indeed, one of the most difficult of problems is to sort out the strands—cultural, physiological, intuitive, and rational—that are interwoven into the fabric of individual values and conduct. As Russell has pointed out, and as those who style themselves "human engineers" know only too well, the new psychology has little comfort to offer about the importance of reason in human conduct. This would be especially true among those least capable of using it, yet I, for one, would not give up what confidence we have in it.

Coming now more specifically to the problem of space, we find that the grim facts in certain countries which we euphemistically call "under-developed" speak for themselves, as anyone who has visited the Orient, the West Indies, or certain portions of Latin America must honestly admit. Humane and successful efforts to improve health conditions in such areas have, to date, merely intensified the problem, while equally high-minded efforts to improve food production and distribution have only deferred a solution. Ceylon, where disease control has resulted in doubling the population in less than a score of years, is a classical example. Meanwhile, food production has not kept pace, and the usable area of the island has been increased only very slightly through drainage of malarial swamps.

Technological Vulnerability

Perhaps the one bright spot in this gloomy picture is that many of the leaders in these crowded countries are now frankly recognizing the problem and trying, according to their various lights, to face it. But while I would not suggest for a moment that we allow them to stew in their own juice, I do suggest that our own problem deserves more attention than it is getting. The very fact that we have a margin of safety not enjoyed in many parts of the

world is both a challenge and an opportunity. Let me recite a few facts, even though they may be familiar.

That the productivity of our agriculture can be increased far beyond the limits of the present surplus is not questioned. But each increment in production calls for increasing capital outlays. The investment in machinery, to say nothing of that in fertilizers, feed supplements, maintenance, taxes, and insurance, frequently approaches the value of the land. The knowledge, skill, and competence of the successful farmer today rivals that tolerated in the practice of medicine fifty years ago. In that interval our farm population has diminished by more than a half, being now less than 20 percent of our total population. The pressure to keep costly machinery earning its way often results in extensive operations at the cost of personal attention to those details which prevent deterioration of the whole enterprise, and which, in the end, may make the difference between profit and loss. So meager is the margin that a significant and growing number of model farms are now owned by industrialists and other people of means to permit legitimate losses on their tax returns. So far as our ultimate food and fiber supply is concerned, we need not expect something for nothing. The late Robert Salter, surely a very conservative individual, pointed out that the high yields from hybrid corn were definitely being obtained at the expense of soil fertility. In the corn belt, yields of 100 bushels per acre are now about one-third as frequent as they once were. My guess is that farm surpluses will be only a memory within two decades.

Alternative methods of production are, of course, being proposed and investigated. Most of these involve increasing dependence upon elaborate technological devices, hence increasing energy, capital, and maintenance costs. Equally serious is the increasing vulnerability that comes from utter dependence upon elaborate technological systems. This can be illustrated by what has occurred when a brave and competent army, trained to rely solely upon mechanical transport, has faced in difficult terrain an enemy hardened to simpler and more primitive methods. It was illustrated by the comparative ease with which the Ozark hill people adjusted to a depression while their highly dependent urban neighbors were thrown completely out of gear for a long period of time.

I forbear to recite what would happen to some of our great urban centers in the event of certain entirely possible technological failures. This is information which ought to be classified if it could be. In October I observed the confusion following a two-hour power failure in the Grand Central area in New York City. Four days later an accident to a single car on the Merritt Parkway in Connecticut delayed traffic for an hour, during which time seven miles of motor cars were halted bumper to bumper. The analogy between extreme urbanites and the denizens of the egg factories mentioned earlier is too close to be comfortable. No doubt the subconscious realization of this accounts to some degree for the difference between our present mood and that of the Turks and Finns. These sturdy people proceed courageously about their simple way of life in spite of their hazardous geographical position.

We too are a brave and peace-loving people. It is entirely possible that we are not so much moved by fear of an enemy as by lack of confidence in the structure of a system in which we are so deeply committed and involved.

What I am saying is inspired by those who see in technology the complete answer to the world's problems. For I do not doubt that technology, like a human being, has the defects inherent in its own virtues. If, as I believe, it should be our servant and not our master, its advancement should be in the light of all scientific knowledge and not merely of those facets which are of immediate use. The biologist who attempted to apply his knowledge in defiance of known physical principles would be laughed out of court. Yet we seem singularly trustful of engineering projects carried out in disregard of ecological principles.

The Urban Sprawl

The most obvious and acute pressure upon space is in our great cities and surrounding metropolitan areas, whose existence and expansion depend upon technology. They and the associated industries and highways that connect them are absorbing agricultural land in the United States at the rate of some million acres a year. This means fewer orange and walnut groves in California, dairy farms in Georgia, truck and tobacco land in Connecticut, and less of the proverbially fertile valley land along the Miami in Ohio. All of these instances I have seen, as I have seen 15,000-acre tracts of the best farm land condemned for military installations when less productive sites could have been chosen.

There are some 500 major cities of over 25,000 population in the United States. Assuming that they could be evenly distributed, and neglecting smaller towns and cities, each would be in the center of a rectangle roughly 80 miles square. I have seen a fair number of them in recent years and recall very few that were not sprawling out into suburbs with little heed to

(Photo courtesy of Los Angeles Area Chamber of Commerce.)

open space, recreation, agriculture, beauty, or even the protection of future values. An exception, as a taxi driver profanely informed me, was not growing because the local university had everything sewed up!

Since this problem of urban sprawl is now receiving intelligent attention in a series of articles in *Fortune* magazine, I shall note only that it is serious, immediate, and far from simple. Municipalities generally have powers of expansion and taxation against which the rural landscape is without defense.

And between cities, across the land, highway departments are busily freezing the nation into a permanent interurban geometry. Often, in fact if not in theory, they are responsible to no one but themselves and their Euclidean rule that the shortest distance between two points is a straight line. Only through leaders who will devise and citizens who will support better use of urban and highway space can growing blight be checked. Professional planners, who, by the way, are seldom summoned until it is too late for them to be of real use, now frankly regard the entire strip from Washington to Boston as one great metropolitan area. Any lingering doubts on this score should fade at the sight of a new throughway blasting its course among rocks and homes, across land and water.

At Washington, southern end of the megalopolitan strip, fateful decisions regarding the future allocation of American space are made. One of the cabinet members who has much to do with such decisions told a recent visitor, "For one individual who, like yourself, comes here to protest the exploitation of wilderness areas, parks, and other public lands, there are a dozen who come here to press the opposing view." No matter what the sympathies of such a public official, these are elementary facts of political life with which he must reckon.

There are, moreover, numerous agencies of government, not always in close harmony, that are charged to administer space and its resources. What happens is the resultant of many forces, including the pressure put upon Congress and the advice it receives from appropriate bureaus.

The late Colonel Greeley used to relate how much of our national forest space was reserved. Congress, alarmed at the rate at which Theodore Roosevelt was setting aside forest reserves, lowered the boom on him, but the law could not become effective until he signed it. During the few weeks of grace Roosevelt, Pinchot, and Greeley spent evenings sprawled on a White House floor with maps, for all the world like kids with a comic supplement, marking out forests while the President still had power to do so.

District of Columbia

Unlike most cities, Washington was built on a definite plan and is still under close supervision. But the unremitting pressure of housing, traffic,

and waste-disposal problems is a constant threat to the space required for recreation, let alone for esthetic values, traditionally a matter of concern. Among other things, the Potomac is notoriously polluted, and the pressure for schools and other public facilities in the overflow region outside the district is a headache to all concerned. In these environs, as around growing cities all over the country, one sees a wilderness of houses built to sell. And the buyer is usually more concerned with pushbuttons and gadgets than with sound construction. It takes no prophet to visualize what the condition of these potential slums will be in less than a generation.

New York Area

Not quite midway to Boston is Jersey City and the whole complex of sleeping towns for New York. As of October 25th of this year the authorities of Jersey City were weighing the relative merits of pails versus paper milk bottles to dispense drinking water. The reserve for Jersey City and nearby places was then enough for about one month. Not even that flower of technology, the modern city, is exempt from the pressure of natural forces. Nor should this be surprising. While the per capita demand for water rises, so does the area that is waterproofed and designed to get rid of rain as fast as it falls.

Even the air is a problem. One approaches the Hudson through one of the most unsavory mixtures of gases on earth. What smells bad, with such noble exceptions as Limburger and Liederkranz, is seldom good. New York City, whose canyons full of fumes are no bed of roses, is within the same general zone of turbulence. The resulting uproar reminds one of

89

the classical dispute as to which stank worse, a goat or a tramp.

New York City illustrates what might be called a space paradox. As its population has grown, so has the per capita space, except possibly in some very congested areas. At the same time, the rural areas, whose emigration supplies the growth of nearly all major cities, have fewer people. Farms are increasing in size; fewer men are farming larger farms. Everyone is getting more space while the population rises. The answer is, of course, that the rural man who becomes urban is not getting more space than he had—simply more than he would have had had he moved into the city a generation ago.

New England

Further north, in New England, we encounter other interesting problems of space. Most of them involve conflicts of interest, often elements of minor tragedy. I have in mind the annihilation of homes for which money cannot compensate. One such, whose sturdy hand-made beauty, books, pictures, and furnishings represent the slow accretion of high cultural influence—not mere personal luxury—is now untenable because no better way has been found to dispose of the garbage of an expanding dormitory population than to burn it nearby. In southern Massachusetts I saw the occupants of a group of new homes trying to repair the damage of flood in a site which was notoriously subject to high water. The unwary newcomers who bought these houses did not know this, and no one warned them.

It was, in fact, the floods of 1955 that revealed most dramatically what can happen when important fields of science are neglected while others are being applied to the limit in technological development. Manufacturers of electronic equipment, optical instruments, and precision tools certainly keep abreast of scientific developments. Yet in locating their plants they took risks which no geologist, or competent botanist, would have sanctioned had his opinion been sought. Not only did they expand their activities upon the hazardous flood plain, but in many instances they intruded upon the channel itself, thus making bad matters worse. The old water-mill builders took no such chances. Their homes were on high land, for they knew and respected the power of water.

New England, northern end of the great metropolitan strip, offers many other examples of the pressure of humanity upon space, although it has no monopoly in this respect. The West Coast, the most rapidly growing area in the nation, may be more graphic, for it lacks any protection from past cultural inertia. But in New England one may see a losing struggle to preserve esthetic and recreational values in the face of an insistent desire to expand industry, cater to the automobile, mine for gravel and rock, convert the rivers into free sewers, and in divers other ways capture the nimble dollar.

In these respects New England is no worse—and no better—than other parts of the nation. Two-thirds of its hinterland are now covered with forests, largely of poor quality, occupying land that was once farmed and later grazed during a booming wool industry. Yet this two-thirds of the area produces not more than ten percent of the rural income. In contrast to this, I know a Danish forest of 2000 acres that furnishes year-round employment to 50 men and 20 additional during the winter months, all at a profit. True, the

New England soils are often thin and not highly fertile, but the chief trouble seems to be that we have consistently used up the finest trees, while the Danes since 1800 have been saving them for seed stock. Even though one cannot increase space, proper measures will greatly increase its yield. Inferior races of trees are just as wasteful of space as inferior breeds of livestock on pasture and farm. While New England forests even in their present poor condition add vastly to the beauty of the countryside, the time is not too far distant when their products will be needed. European experience shows that good yield is quite consistent with esthetic value.

Pressures upon Space

Across the continent, with infinite variations due to local conditions, the problem of space is growing in urgency. Ultimately we shall have to face the purely physical fact of increasing numbers on a finite area containing finite resources. Of these resources, water is now getting some of the attention it deserves. But we should keep other substances in mind, recalling that we, with less than 7 percent of the world's population, are now absorbing more than 60 percent of the world's mineral production, or ten times our quota.

Meanwhile, the general pressure is complicated by conflicts of interest. Different groups and individuals see different possibilities in the same area, and all alike wish to secure the most from it. As great cities grow they become more, rather than less, dependent upon widening circles of rural land—for water, milk and other food, transport, recreation, housing, labor, and income. It is interesting to consider the sources of support for the four world territories that have more than 10,000 people to the square mile. They are, in order, Macao, a shipping and commercial center, Monaco, a gambling resort, the District of Columbia, where taxes are collected and spent, and Gibraltar, a military post! No great concentration of people is ever self-sustaining. The Valley of the Nile, which has had perhaps 1000 people to the square mile for millenia, depends upon the vast headwater areas reaching south to Lake Victoria for its water and fertility. The same principle applies to the crowded downstream river margins of China and India.

The time must come when we shall have to deal openly, honestly, and realistically with the basic biological fact that numbers of organisms cannot multiply indefinitely within a finite area. And since our own species is under discussion, we must face the unparalleled conditions of increasing numbers and biological dominance combined with accelerating mobility, power, speed, and consumption on the part of the individual. Eventually we must come to grips with these fundamentals. Meanwhile we can, in my judgment, help matters greatly by admitting that conflicts of interest do exist, identifying them, and establishing some order of priority for conflicting claims.

I have no easy solutions to suggest. The first step in dealing with a scientific problem is to make it clear. This I have tried to do, aware of the fact that in our society solutions must be worked out by common consent—generally a painful process. There is a maxim among medical men that more mistakes come from not looking than from not knowing. So far as space is concerned, both looking and knowing are involved.

Training in Science

Much concern is now being expressed for better science training. Here at least we can make a sound, if modest, beginning. Training in the rudiments of science—asking, observing, and reasoning—should begin along with training in the mother tongue and be a part of the same process. College science, training as it does both scientist and citizen, should be taught in context with the rest of human knowledge and experience. It should certainly be a convincing and challenging aspect of education. How far it falls short of these ideals one can discover by asking those who have been exposed to it. Always excepting those who have an innate taste for science, the average college graduate, in my experience, does not retain enough for literate conversation upon the subject, let alone enough understanding to use it in civic affairs. Too often his mood is one of active distaste.

As a rule he has been required to take *a* course in *a* science weighted too often for the benefit of those who must go on in the particular field. How many times I have been told by colleagues: "We must teach it this way, or our students will not be ready for the next course." Such a philosophy misses the fact that by sacrificing insight to detail, fine intellects that might be potential candidates for further work may be lost.

Nor does the mischief stop there. No one science by itself can give that balanced view of the world of nature so essential to the citizen in our modern culture. A peep-show, no matter how good, is no substitute for a panorama. Until citizens, administrators, engineers, and businessmen become aware of the broad sweep of science, we may expect to see it applied, as it has been so largely, for immediate return rather than ultimate and lasting benefit.

Education and Self-Discipline

Let us, therefore, avoid the folly of thinking that science can be separated from the broader problem of education and self-discipline. The present hue and cry for more and better science education could easily lead us into the trap that caught the Germans in 1914. More and better science teaching we must have, not merely to produce needed scientists, but to create an atmosphere of scientific literacy among citizens at large. Only by general understanding and consent can truly creative science be sustained within our system of society and its results applied for the ultimate welfare of mankind.

Liberal education today should require not less than two years of college science, based on a skilfully planned and interwoven sequence dealing with time, space, motion, matter, and the earth and its inhabitants. Nothing less than this is adequate for a proper appraisal of the natural world and our role as a part of it. This experience should be obtained at the hands of men who believe in it, who have status with their colleagues, and who are in intellectual communication with each other. There is no place for loose ends or superficial business in such an enterprise. Nor can it be carried on without the actual contact with phenomena in laboratory and field. Science that is merely verbalized is dead stuff.

But to this end it is equally essential that the educated individual must acquire such experience in the context of history, the arts, and an understanding of his own species. As a rough objective, I would propose turning out a product aware of what is

going on around him in the world of
nature and of man, able and willing to
relate the present to the past and to
the future in both thought and action.

To do this we must recognize with
greater frankness than we have that
there are vast differences among
individuals. Let us learn to look upon
these differences with respect, as a
source of enrichment rather than discrimination, training each, honoring
each, and expecting service from each
according to his gifts. Let not the
slow impede the fast, nor the fast be-
wilder and condemn the slow.

With a population set to double in
less than half a century, with a national space which, though vast, is finite
both in area and quality, with each individual making growing demands,
moving faster and further by a factor
of at least ten, we have on our hands
a problem without precedent in
geological history. But if we sense
the problem and believe it worth
solving, we can solve it.

Our future security may depend less
upon priority in exploring outer space
than upon our wisdom in managing the
space in which we live.

Individual and Species: Biological Survival

ROSCOE SPENCER

*One of our national objectives is to banish
cancer, and then, of course, to conquer
the other great "killers." That prospect
has at times seemed to be an imminent
event, and the public is attuned with unqualified approval. What could be wrong
with perfect health, bringing in its wake
millenial contentment and equanimity?
Our economic image of this paradisiacal
goal has been an everlasting seller's market. Good business means the good life.
We want expanding markets, a bigger
Gross National Product, and more and
more and more consumers.*

*One reason it is so difficult to take
alarm at rapid population growth is that
an expanding society is euphoric. How
could anything really be wrong when
everything is going so well? Americans
particularly have difficulty comprehending
how growth can be sickness.*

*But fat-cat Americans do worry about
cancer. It is too bad that they do not
meet more microbes socially, for those
creatures, being at once single cells and
whole organisms, embody whatever close
connection there might be between cancer and population growth. In a salubrious
moment the microbe might boast that his
kind was prospering, that its gross national product was higher than ever,
that the number of consumers was rising
and bound to keep the economy lively,
and that, best of all, the Good Life was
nearly an actuality for all protozoans. But
the microbe would never ignore the possibility of tumor on the demographic body,*

The Humanist, *No. 3, pp. 155–161, 1958. Copyright 1958, by the American Humanist Association, 125 El Camino del Mar, San Francisco,
California. Reprinted by permission.*

for microbial population outbursts closely resemble cancer in multicellular organisms, and are cancer to microbes.

THE EDITORS

THE CONCEPT OF a pervasive "duality" throughout all nature is an old story in philosophy. Emerson, in his famous essay on "Compensation," declared: "An inevitable dualism bisects nature so that each thing is a half and suggests another thing to make it whole."

Thanks to modern physics we know now, beyond all doubt, that energy and matter are not absolute entities. Each is a half, a different aspect of a whole. We are also told that light consists of waves—and, in the same breath, that it consists of particles. Strange that an exact science like physics must resort to two seemingly contradictory ways of describing nature. However, the wave and the particle (matter) concepts are not mutually exclusive but mutually complementary ways of describing light. Both descriptions "fit the known facts, according to the method of observation." When the two are combined, they provide us with a truer image of our matter-energy world than either description alone.

Similarly in biology, "the philosophy of complementarity," or the merging and reconciliation of apparently irreconcilable points of view, has given us a truer image of life and living processes, because no sharp line can be drawn between living and non-living matter, between mind and body, growth and dissolution, the individual and the group. All such concepts are interdependent and interrelated; the one inevitably implies its opposite. Even in the domain of ethics and

metaphysics, science can find no clear-cut distinctions between good and evil, between the natural and the supernatural, or the sacred and the secular. The concept of an all-good God necessitated an all-bad Devil.

Good Cells and Bad Cells

In 1938, my colleagues and I became interested in the problem of cancer, and began some experimental studies which revealed interesting relationships between individual cells and the cell populations as a whole. At that time it had become clear to all investigators in this field that, first, cancer was not a contagious or communicable disease (in other words, it was not due to some parasite passing from one person to another); and second, cancer cells were invariably derived from normal cells, and all normal cells of the human body were, of course, descendants of a single fertilized ovum. It was also becoming apparent that no single chemical agent and no single internal or external environmental factor triggered the transformation of normally functioning cells of the human body into the malignant "gangster cell" stage. The inciting causes were many and varied.

However, one or two investigators have become convinced that all cancers are due to an infectious, ever-present "sleeping virus." Such a virus is thought to be activated under certain conditions favorable to its development, and it is supposed that this virus is transmitted "vertically" from generation to generation. It is well known that viruses are intracellular, self-duplicating and quite large molecular—or aggregates of molecular—nucleo-proteins. Many of them are the causes of communicable diseases such as influenza and the common cold.

If a human cancer virus is transmitted vertically, biologists and biochemists would find it extremely difficult to distinguish the behavior of such a virus from that of one or more altered or mutated genes (the organs of heredity); for genes are also self-duplicating and vertically transmitted, and are closely related chemically to viruses. Since the behavior of normally functioning cells does often become permanently altered, resulting in a non-functioning, fatal new growth, there is no theoretical reason why certain intracellular aggregates—such as the genes—might not become altered (mutated) and cause the cell, of which it had previously been a normal component, to assume the malignant form of behavior. If this turns out to be the case, we will then be forced to regard cancer as an "autosite" rather than a parasite; not as an extraneous, autonomous agent, but as an aberrant cell group obeying the universal urge of all life toward survival.

"Population Erosion" and Individual Survival

Theoretical considerations of this kind led us to study the effects of small amounts of certain well-known cancer-inducing chemicals upon populations of single-celled organisms such as paramecia and bacteria. We had a hunch that, by observing the behavior of these small, actively motile, free-living cells when they were exposed continuously, generation after generation, to these chemicals and other unfavorable environments, we might learn something about how the immobile, fixed-tissue cell-populations of man and animals respond to the same conditions. The experiments were carried out over a period of more than eight years, and the results suggested that the cancer problem might indeed be a part of the more basic biological problem of how populations of all types manage to survive under more or less harsh conditions.

Our experiments on single-celled populations revealed that a slow deterioration and final extinction of the stock could be brought about, invariably but by imperceptible degrees, under certain environmental conditions.

Populations of paramecia (motile, single-cell forms of life barely visible to the naked eye, commonly known as "lady slippers") were maintained by transferring the organisms at regular intervals in a continuous series of small glass bottles containing suitable culture media. Each population usually reached two to three thousand organisms in about ten days. A few individuals were then transferred from bottle number one to bottle number two, containing fresh culture medium; and ten days later when the population again reached several thousand, a transfer was made from bottle number two to a third bottle; and so on indefinitely.

When such a population was treated continuously with a powerful cancer-inducing chemical (methylcholanthrene) in a concentration of only one part to a million parts of the medium, a marked stimulation of cell division and a consequent rapid increase in population could be observed, whenever some of the organisms were removed from the influence of the chemical. This response was delayed, however, and did not appear until after the thirty-fifth transfer— about 350 days of continuous exposure. What seemed equally interesting was that individual organisms from the "released" cultures could be shown to be far better able to survive under starvation conditions than organisms

95

from the untreated populations or from those treated with chemicals that were not cancer-inducing. (Of course, one cannot induce cancer in a single cell or in an unorganized population of single cells. By definition, cancer is a disorganized, uncontrolled group of cells within an organized group.) Several investigators have also shown that cancer cells are more resistant than corresponding normal cells to the chemicals or the environments that induced the malignant change in the first place.

Again, when five more population series of paramecia were treated continuously with small amounts of various aniline dyes (which are not cancer-inducing), there were at first no visible effects on the organisms. All five series, however, died three and a half to five years earlier than any of the six series that were maintained as controls and not treated in any way. The populations—both treated and untreated—were kept at all times under optimum conditions and provided with an ample food supply. One would think that the control populations would have survived indefinitely. None of them did. For a period of four to six months, the control series multiplied by simple fission without showing any evidence of sexual mating. Then followed a two-and-a-half-year period of active sexual maturity during which numerous matings were observed. Then in all six of the control series there came a period of aging, during which the matings were less frequent and the rate of cell division slower. Finally the transfers failed to grow and, after surviving seven to eight years, all six populations died out, despite all efforts to keep them alive.

This result was almost identical with observations of H. S. Jennings (reported in the *Journal of Experimental Zoology* in 1945) on a closely related species of paramecia. In both experiments there is the suggestion that an environment, apparently favorable to individuals for a considerable time and extending over many cell-division cycles, may not in the long run be favorable to the survival of the stock. In other words, what may seem good for individuals may not necessarily be good for the species—that is, for the genetic material which individuals carry as temporary custodians. In more technical terms, environments apparently beneficial to *phenotypes* may be harmful to *genotypes*. The apparent "welfare" of individuals may finally be "farewell" to both species and individuals. Here we observe between phenotype and genotype an interdependence which may be thought of in terms of "the philosophy of complementarity."

Despite innumerable vicissitudes to which these small protozoa are exposed daily in nature, they stay alive indefinitely, since they may be found at any time in fresh-water ponds. One suspects that a variety of harsh experiences provides the necessary spice of life, keeping the species at all times on its toes, so to speak. In contrast, under artificial conditions in the laboratory, a perfect paradise was provided—for individuals. In time, however, the monotony of ample food secured without effort, optimum temperature, protection from all natural enemies, and ideal conditions for growth and breeding, may have been deadly—for the species. This may not be the true explanation, but there are other observations suggesting that the health and vigor of individuals (phenotypes) do not always reflect the health and vigor of the stock (genotypes). For example, whenever experimental

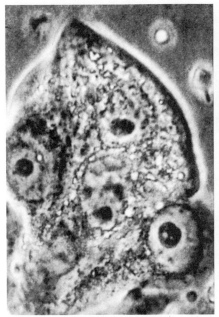
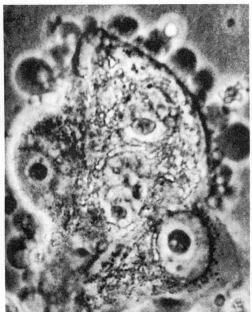

(Above) An island of living human lung cancer suddenly explodes. (Photo from American Cancer Society film "The Embattled Cell," courtesy American Cancer Society, Inc.) (Right) Paramecium dividing. (Photo courtesy Ward's Natural Science Establishment, Inc., Rochester, N.Y.)

biologists raise fruit flies in the laboratory, far more favorable conditions are provided than those experienced in nature, where selective elimination and survival take place continuously. These laboratory culture-populations of flies are filled in a short while with the weak, the halt, the lame, the partially blind, the monstrous, and the moribund. Such forms never survive in nature, but the geneticist deliberately preserves and coddles them and makes life easy for them so that he may study

the genetic mechanism of these abnormalities.

Bacteria, Rotifers, and Flatworms

"Population erosion" was more quickly demonstrated when successive populations of bacteria were used in our experiments. Under optimum conditions, most bacteria will divide every twenty minutes. Within twenty-four hours after inoculating a test tube containing beef broth with a few bacteria, one will find a population of more than five hundred million. Thereafter the population increases slowly or not at all, and soon declines. A strain of the colon bacillus (an organism commonly found in the intestines of man and animals) was used in this experiment. It had been kept in the laboratory for more than thirty years without showing any tendency to weaken or to die under usual laboratory conditions.

When successive cultures of this organism were kept constantly at 47° centigrade (ten degrees above the best temperature for growth), and transfers made every day, the organisms always grew luxuriantly in the first two test tubes of the series, but invariably failed to grow in the third. When the constant temperature was reduced to 45° centigrade, the serial-culture populations lived indefinitely, *provided the transfers were made daily.* However, when serial cultures were kept at the same 45° constant temperature but the transfers made at six-day intervals (a ripe age for test-tube populations), no series ever survived more than twenty-eight transfers or 168 days. In fact, one of the series in this experiment survived only fourteen transfers or 84 days.

These experiments, carried out in five identical series, demonstrated that a constantly high temperature was not immediately fatal to the stock, but after many generations or cell-division cycles, death was inevitable. This delayed death of the stock or species can reasonably be attributed to a gradual step-like response of the genes rather than a response of the cell material of individual organisms. Here, with bacteria as with paramecia, we see the interdependence and interrelationship (complementarity?) between individual and species. Nevertheless, the constant and normally

occurring deterioration and death of individuals seen in populations of all species may appear at times to be independent of the long-drawn-out deterioration and final extinction of the species.

This "population erosion" has been observed in widely separated species. Dr. A. I. Lansing of Washington University in St. Louis, experimenting with rotifers ("water-fleas"), showed that the offspring of the older mothers had a progressively shorter life span in each generation, and those of the "senile" (seventeen-day-old) rotifers died out entirely after the third generation. But a line of rotifers derived from young mothers (five days old) was maintained for fifty-four generations, during which the life span gradually increased to 104 days, after which the experiment ended. Speculations regarding human genetics may not be justified from these observations on lower forms of life; but Lansing cited some statistical studies, made by Louis I. Dublin for the Metropolitan Life Insurance Company, showing a tendency for the children of young mothers to live longer than those of older mothers. A Finnish investigator, E. O. Jalavisto, reached the same conclusion after an analysis of the vital statistics of her homeland.

One more experiment, reported by T. M. Sonneborn of Indiana University in 1930, suggests still another means of inducing a slow population erosion. He experimented with a flatworm (Stestoma) that multiplies by splitting into two parts, as do bacteria. The foreparts contain most of the original body, including the nervous system and most of the digestive tract; the rear section receives only a small bit of the tail. As a result, each forepart needs to grow very little,

while the tail fragment must grow almost an entire new body. Sonneborn
selected and traced successive generations of flatworms derived from
foreparts only; and another line from
tail sections only. Amazingly, the actively growing animals from the tail
fragments flourished, while those
from the front ends soon went into a
decline and died after a few splittings.

All these experiments have convincingly shown that when populations of a number of species are subjected constantly to certain artificial
conditions that appear to favor growth
and survival of individuals, the result
is not only the death of many individuals, but after a time, the extinction
of the race. Our studies of single-
celled organisms revealed a complementarity between "population erosion" and population vigor, as well as
a complementarity between the continuity of the species and the inevitable death of the individual. And,
finally, they pointed the way to a
philosophy of life—intellectually credible and emotionally satisfying—that
gives one a vision of humanity as a
passing procession having an advantage
over humanity as a permanent
assembly.

Self-Regulating Systems
in Populations of Animals

V. C. WYNNE-EDWARDS

*In the language of nature-hating, we
are informed that man is an animal because of certain black-sheep traits, like
insanity in the family closet. He shares
with the beasts: brutality, violence,
and inevitable death. Against that "biological" side of human nature, sensibility,
compassion, language, and spirituality are
claimed as peculiarly human. You do
not need to consult Plato or St. Thomas to
discover this widely-held distinction, although you could surely confirm it in their
works. That is to say, the notion belongs
to a particular history of ideas rather than
to life's immutable realities.*

*In the matter of population overgrowth
and control, "biological limitation"
means starvation and epidemic disease.
In this view, man is held to be the one
creature capable of self-limiting his numbers below the level of catastrophe. It
seems to be not so widely recognized
that restraints on birth rates (the only "humane" solution to the problem) are widespread among animals.*

*Anatomists and psychologists and more
recently endocrinologists study rats in
order to understand men. The domesticated white rat is a crude caricature of
his wild brown cousin. For behavior
characterized by subtlety, finesse and precision, one must look in the wild form
of Rattus norvegicus. Genetically, the
latter is not so badly smudged by a long
vacation from natural selection.*

*And yet the analogy between white rats
and men is probably apropos, for in
man, too, the sharpness of primeval adap-
tedness has gone out of focus—he is more*

Science, *147:1543–1548, 1965. Copyright
1965 by the American Association for the Advancement of Science. Reprinted by permission.*

*variable (or polymorphic, genetically)
than the wild ancestor of* Homo sapiens.
*Even in matters of population limitation,
men may be said to be polymorphic:
Some want to limit their numbers, others
are willing to send the surplus to the
moon or simply into space, and still others
want to see how many buyers of consumer
goods and taxpayers it takes to slow
down the earth's rotation.*

THE EDITORS

I AM GOING TO TRY to explain a hypothesis which could provide a bridge
between two biological realms (1). On
one side is that part of the "Balance of
Nature" concerned with regulating
the numbers of animals, and on the
other is the broad field of social behavior. The hypothesis may, I believe,
throw a bright and perhaps important
sidelight on human behavior and
population problems. I must emphasize, however, that it is still a hypothesis. It appears to be generally
consistent with the facts, and it provides entirely new insight into many
aspects of animal behavior that have
hitherto been unexplainable; but because it involves long-term evolutionary processes it cannot be put to
an immediate and comprehensive test
by short-term experiments.

Human populations are of course increasing at compound interest practically all over the world. At the overall
2 percent annual rate of the last decade, they can be expected to double
with each generation. In the perspective of evolutionary time such a
situation must be extremely short-
lived, and I am sure we are going to
grow more and more anxious about
the future of man until we are able to
satisfy ourselves that the human population explosion is controllable, and
can be contained.

Populations of animals, especially
when they are living under primeval
undisturbed conditions, characteristically show an altogether different
state of affairs; and this was equally
true of man in the former cultural
periods of the stone age. These natural
populations tend to preserve a continuing state of balance, usually
fluctuating to some extent but essentially stable and regulated. The nature
of the regulatory process has been the
main focus of study and speculation by
animal ecologists during the whole of
my working life, and in fact considerably longer.

Charles Darwin (2) was the first to
point out that though all animals have
the capacity to increase their numbers,
in fact they do not continuously do so.
The "checks to increase" appeared to
him to be of four kinds—namely, the
amount of food available, which must
give the extreme limit to which any
species can increase; the effects of predation by other animals; the effects of
physical factors such as climate; and
finally, the inroads of disease. "In
looking at Nature," he tells us in the
Origin of Species, "it is most necessary
. . . never to forget that every single
organic being may be said to be striving to the utmost to increase in numbers." This intuitive assumption of a
universal resurgent pressure from
within held down by hostile forces
from without has dominated the thinking of biologists on matters of population regulation, and on the nature of
the struggle for existence, right down
to the present day.

Setting all preconceptions aside,
however, and returning to a detached
assessment of the facts revealed by
modern observation and experiment, it
becomes almost immediately evident
that a very large part of the regulation
of numbers depends not on Darwin's

hostile forces but on the initiative taken by the animals themselves; that is to say, to an important extent it is an intrinsic phenomenon.

Forty years ago Jespersen (3) showed, for example, that there is a close numerical agreement between the standing crop of planktonic organisms at the surface of the North Atlantic Ocean and the distribution density of the various deep-sea birds that depend on these organisms for food. Over the whole of this vast area the oceanic birds are dispersed in almost constant proportion to the local biomass of plankton, although the biomass itself varies from region to region by a factor of about 100; the actual crude correlation coefficient is 85 percent. This pro rata dispersion of the birds must in fact depend solely on their own intrinsic efforts and behavior. Even though the dispersion directly reflects the availability of food, the movements of the birds over the ocean are essentially voluntary and not imposed against their will by hostile or other outside forces.

Turning to the results of repeatable experiments with laboratory animals, it is a generally established principle that a population started up, perhaps from one parental pair, in some confined universe such as an aquarium or a cage, can be expected to grow to a predictable size, and thereafter to maintain itself at that ceiling for months or years as long as the experimenter keeps the conditions unchanged. This can readily be demonstrated with most common laboratory animals, including the insects *Drosophila* and *Tribolium*, the water-flea *Daphnia*, the guppy *Lebistes*, and also mice and rats. The ceiling population density stays constant in these experiments in the complete absence of

predators or disease and equally without recourse to regulation by starvation, simply by the matching of recruitment and loss. For example, a set of particularly illuminating experiments by Silliman and Gutsell (4), lasting over 3 years, showed that when stable populations of guppies, kept in tanks, were cropped by removal of a proportion of the fish at regular intervals, the remainder responded by producing more young that survived, with the consequence that the losses were compensated. In the controls, on the other hand, where the stocks were left untouched, the guppies went on breeding all the time, but by cannibalism they consistently removed at birth the whole of the surplus produced. The regulating methods are different in different species; under appropriate circumstances in mice, to take another example, ovulation and reproduction can decline and even cease, as long as the ceiling density is maintained.

Here again, therefore, we are confronted by intrinsic mechanisms, in which none of Darwin's checks play any part, competent in themselves to regulate the population size within a given habitat.

The same principle shows up just as clearly in the familiar concept that a habitat has a certain carrying capacity, and that it is no good turning out more partridges or planting more trout than the available habitat can hold.

Population growth is essentially a density-dependent process; this means that it tends to proceed fastest when population densities are far below the ceiling level, to fall to zero as this level is approached, and to become negative, leading to an actual drop in numbers, if ever the ceiling is exceeded. The current hypothesis is that the adjustment of numbers in animals is a homeostatic process—that

101

there is, in fact, an automatic self-righting balance between population density and resources.

I must turn briefly aside here to remind you that there are some environments which are so unstable or transitory that there is not time enough for colonizing animals to reach a ceiling density, and invoke their regulatory machinery, before the habitat becomes untenable again or is destroyed. Populations in these conditions are always in the pioneering stage, increasing freely just as long as conditions allow. Instability of this kind tends to appear around the fringes of the geographical range of all free-living organisms, and especially in desert and polar regions. It is also very common in agricultural land, because of the incessant disturbance of ploughing, seeding, spraying, harvesting, and rotating of crops. In these conditions the ecologist will often look in vain for evidences of homeostasis, among the violently fluctuating and completely uncontrollable populations typical of the animal pests of farms and plantations. Homeostasis can hardly be expected to cope unerringly with the ecological turmoil of cultivated land.

I return later to the actual machinery of homeostasis. For the present it can be accepted that more or less effective methods of regulating their own numbers have been evolved by most types of animals. If this is so, it seems logical to ask as the next question: What is it that decides the ceiling level?

Food Supply as a Limiting Factor

Darwin was undoubtedly right in concluding that food is the factor that normally puts an extreme limit on population density, and the dispersion of oceanic birds over the North Atlantic, which so closely reflects the dispersion of their food supply, is certain to prove a typical and representative case. Just the same, the link between food productivity and population density is very far from being self-evident. The relationship between them does not typically involve any signs of undernourishment; and starvation, when we observe it, tends to be a sporadic or accidental cause of mortality rather than a regular one.

Extremely important light is shed on this relationship between population density and food by our human experience of exploiting resources of the same kind. Fish, fur-bearing animals, and game are all notoriously subject to overexploitation at the hands of man, and present-day management of these renewable natural resources is based on the knowledge that there is a limit to the intensity of cropping that each stock can withstand. If we exceed this critical level, the stock will decline and the future annual crops will diminish. Exactly parallel principles apply to the exploitation of natural prairie pastures by domestic livestock: if overgrazing is permitted, fertility and future yields just as fatally decline.

In all these situations there is a tendency to overstep the safety margin while exploitation of the resource is still economically profitable. We have seen since World War II, for example, the decimation of stocks of the blue and the humpback whale in the southern oceans, under the impetus of an intense profit motive, which persisted long after it had become apparent to everyone in the industry that the cropping rate was unsupportably high. The only way to protect these economically valuable recurrent resources from destruction is to impose, by agreement or law, a man-made code of rules, defining closed seasons, catch limits, permitted types of gear, and so on, which restrict the exploitation rate sufficiently to prevent the catch from exceeding the critical level.

In its essentials, this is the same crucial situation that faces populations of animals in exploiting their resources of food. Indeed, without going any further one could predict that if the food supplies of animals were openly exposed to an unruly scramble, there could be no safeguard against their overexploitation either.

Conventional Behavior in Relation to Food

When I first saw the force of this deduction 10 years ago, I felt that the scales had fallen from my eyes. At once the vast edifice of conventional behavior among animals in relation to food began to take on a new meaning. A whole series of unconnected natural phenomena seemed to click smoothly into place.

First among these are the territorial systems of various birds (paralleled in many other organisms), where the claim to an individual piece of ground can evoke competition of an intensity unequaled on any other occasion in the life of the species concerned. It results, in the simplest cases, in a parceling out of the habitat into a mosaic of breeding and feeding lots. A territory has to be of a certain size, and individuals that are unsuccessful in obtaining one are often excluded completely from the habitat, and always prevented from breeding in it. Here is a system that might have been evolved for the exact purpose of imposing a ceiling density on the habitat, and for efficiently disposing of any surplus individuals that fail to establish themselves. Provided the territory size is adequate, it is obvious that the

rate of exploitation of the food resources the habitat contains will automatically be prevented from exceeding the critical threshold.

There are other behavioral devices that appear, in the light of the food-resource hypothesis we are examining, equally purposive in leading to the same result—namely, that of limiting the permitted quota of participants in an artificial kind of way, and of off-loading all that are for the time being surplus to the carrying capacity of the ground. Many birds nest in colonies—especially, for example, the oceanic and aerial birds which cannot, in the nature of things, divide up the element in which they feed into static individual territories. In the colony the pairs compete just as long and keenly for one of the acceptable nest sites, which are in some instances closely packed together. By powerful tradition some of these species return year after year to old-established resorts, where the perimeter of the colony is closely drawn like an imaginary fence around the occupied sites. Once again there is not always room to accommodate all the contestants, and unsuccessful ones have to be relegated to a nonbreeding surplus or reserve, inhibited from sexual maturation because they have failed to obtain a site within the traditional zone and all other sites are taboo.

A third situation, exemplifying another, parallel device, is the pecking order or social hierarchy so typical of the higher animals that live in companies in which the individual members become mutually known. Animal behaviorists have studied the hierarchy in its various manifestations for more than 40 years, most commonly in relation to food. In general, the individuals of higher rank have a prior

Gannets on Bonaventure Island, Gaspé. (Photo by Robert C. Hermes from National Audubon Society.)

right to help themselves, and, in situations where there is not enough to go round, the ones at the bottom of the scale must stand aside and do without. In times of food shortage—for example, with big game animals—the result is that the dominant individuals come through in good shape while the subordinates actually die of starvation.

The hierarchy therefore produces the same kind of result as a territorial system in that it admits a limited quota of individuals to share the food resources and excludes the extras. Like the other devices I have described, it can operate in exactly the same way with respect to reproduction. In fact, not only can the hierarchical system exclude individuals from breeding, it can equally inhibit their sexual development.

It must be quite clear already that the kind of competition we are considering, involving as it does the right to take food and the right to breed, is a matter of the highest importance to the individuals that engage in it. At its keenest level it becomes a matter of life and death. Yet, as is well known, the actual contest between individuals for real property or personal status is almost always strictly conventionalized. Fighting and bloodshed are superseded by mere threats of violence, and threats in their turn are sublimated into displays of magnificence and virtuosity. This is the world of bluff and status symbols. What takes place, in other words, is a contest for conventional prizes conducted under conventional rules. But the contest itself is no fantasy, for the losers can forfeit the chance of posterity and the right to survive.

Conventionalized Rivalry and Society

It is at this point that the hypothesis provides its most unexpected and striking insight, by showing that the conventionalization of rivalry and the foundation of society are one and the same thing. Hitherto it has never been possible to give a scientific definition of the terms *social* and *society*, still less a functional explanation. The emphasis has always been on the rather vague element of companionship and brotherhood. Animals have in the main been regarded as social whenever they were gregarious. Now we can view the social phenomenon in a new light. According to the hypothesis the society is no more and no less than the organization necessary for the staging of conventional competition. At once it assumes a crisp definition: a society is an organization of individuals that is capable of providing conventional competition among its members.

Such a novel interpretation of something that involves us all so intimately is almost certain to be viewed at first sight a bit skeptically; but in fact one needs no prompting in our competitive world to see that human society is impregnated with rivalry. The sentiments of brotherhood are warm and reassuring, and in identifying society primarily with these we appear to have been unconsciously shutting our eyes to the inseparable rough-and-tumble of status seeking and social discrimination that are never very far to seek below the surface, bringing enviable rewards to the successful and pitiful distress to those who lose. If this interpretation is right, conventional competition is an inseparable part of the substance of human society, at the parochial, national, and international level. To direct it into sophisticated and acceptable channels is no doubt one of the great motives of civilized behavior; but it would be idle to imagine that we could eliminate it.

A corollary of the hypothesis that deserves mention is the extension of sociality that it implies, to animals of almost every kind whether they associate in flocks or seek instead a more solitary way of life. There is no particular difficulty of course in seeing, for example, cats and dogs as social mammals individually recognizing the local and personal rights of acquaintances and strangers and inspired by obviously conventional codes of rivalry when they meet. In a different setting, the territory-holding birds that join in the chorus of the spring dawn are acting together in social concert, expressing their mutual rivalry by a conventional display of exalted sophistication and beauty. Even at the other extreme, when animals flock into compact and obviously social herds and schools, each individual can sometimes be seen to maintain a strict individual distance from its companions.

Social Organization and Feedback

We can conveniently return now to the subject of homeostasis, in order to see how it works in population control. Homeostatic systems come within the general purview of cybernetics: in fact, they have long been recognized in the physiology of living organisms. A simple model can be found in any thermostatic system, in which there must of course be units capable of supplying or withdrawing heat whenever the system departs from its standard temperature and readjustment is necessary. But one also needs an indicator device to detect how far the system has deviated and in which direction. It is the feedback of this information that activates the heating or cooling units.

Feedback is an indispensable element of homeostatic systems. There seems no reason to doubt that, in the control of population density, it can be effectively provided simply by the intensity of conventional competition. Social rivalry is inherently density-dependent: the more competitors there are seeking a limited number of rewards, the keener will be the contest. The impact of stress on the individuals concerned, arising from conventional competition and acting through the pituitary-adrenal system, is already fully established, and it can profoundly influence their responses, both physiological and behavioral.

One could predict on theoretical grounds that feedback would be specially important whenever a major change in population density has

to take place, upsetting the existing balance between demand and resources. This must occur particularly in the breeding season and at times of seasonal migrations. Keeping this in mind, we can obtain what we need in the way of background information by examining the relatively long-lived vertebrates, including most kinds of birds and mammals, whose individual members live long enough to constitute a standing population all the year round. The hypothesis of course implies that reproduction, as one of the principal parameters of population, will be subject to control—adjusted in magnitude, in fact, to meet whatever addition is currently required to build up the population and make good the losses of the preceding year. *Recruitment* is a term best used only to mean intake of new breeding adults into the population, and in that sense, of course, the raw birth rate may not be the sole and immediate factor that determines it. The newborn young have got to survive adolescence before they can become recruits to the breeding stock; and even after they attain puberty, social pressures may exclude them from reproducing until they attain a sufficiently high rank in the hierarchy. Indeed, there is evidence in a few species that, under sufficient stress, adults which have bred in previous years can be forced to stand aside.

There are, in fact, two largely distinct methods of regulating reproductive output, both of which have been widely adopted in the animal kingdom. One is to limit the number of adults that are permitted to breed, and this is of course a conspicuous result of adopting a territorial system, or any other system in which the number of permissible breeding sites is restricted. The other is to influence

Sharptail Grouse mating dance. (Photo by Ed Park from National Audubon Society.)

the number of young that each breeding pair is conditioned to produce. The two methods can easily be combined.

What we are dealing with here is a part of the machinery for adjusting population density. What we are trying to get at, however, is the social feedback mechanism behind it, by which the appropriate responses are elicited from potential breeders.

Birds generally provide us with the best examples, because their size, abundance, and diurnal habits render them the most observable and familiar of the higher animals. It is particularly easy to see in birds that social competition is keenest just before and during the breeding season, regardless of the type of breeding dispersion any given species happens to adopt. Individuals may compete for and defend territories or nest sites, or in rarer cases they may engage in tournaments in an arena or on a strutting ground; and they may join in a vocal chorus especially concentrated about the conventional hours of dawn and dusk, make mass visits to colony sites, join in massed flights, and share in

other forms of communal displays. Some of these activities are more obviously competitive than others, but all appear to be alike in their capacity to reveal to each individual the concentration or density level of the population within its own immediate area.

Communal Male Displays

Some of these activities, like territorial defense, singing, and the arena displays, tend to be the exclusive concern of the males. It has never been possible hitherto to give a satisfactory functional explanation of the kind of communal male displays typified by the arena dances of some of the South American hummingbirds and manakins, and by the dawn strutting of prairie chickens and sharp-tailed grouse. The sites they use are generally traditional, each serving as a communal center and drawing the competitors from a more or less wide surrounding terrain. On many days during the long season of activity the same assembly of males may engage in vigorous interplay and mutual hostility, holding tense dramatic postures

107

for an hour or more at a stretch without a moment's relaxation, although there is no female anywhere in sight at the time. The local females do of course come at least once to be fertilized; but the performance makes such demands on the time and energy of the males that it seems perfectly reasonable to assume that this is the reason why they play no part in nesting and raising a family. The duty they perform is presumably important, but it is simply not credible to attribute it primarily to courting the females. To anyone looking for a population feedback device, on the other hand, interpretation would present no difficulty: he would presume that the males are being conditioned or stressed by their ritual exertions. In some of the arena species some of the males are known to be totally excluded from sexual intercourse; but it would seem that the feedback mechanism could produce its full effect only if it succeeded in limiting the number of females fertilized to an appropriate quota, after which the males refused service to any still remaining unfertilized. I hope research may at a not-too-distant date show us whether or not such refusal really takes place.

The conclusion that much of the social display associated with the breeding season consists of males competing with males makes necessary a reappraisal of Darwinian sexual selection. Whether the special organs developed for display are confined to the males, as in the examples we have just considered, or are found in both sexes, as for instance in most of the colony-nesting birds, there is a strong indication that they are first and foremost status symbols, used in conventional competition, and that the selective process by which they have been evolved is social rather than

sexual. This would account for the hitherto puzzling fact that, although in the mature bullfrog and cicada the loud sound is produced by the males, in both cases it is the males that are provided with extra-large eardrums. There does not seem much room for doubt about who is displaying to whom.

Communal displays are familiar also in the context of bird migration, especially in the massing and maneuvering of flocks before the exodus begins. A comparable buildup of social excitement precedes the migratory flight of locusts. Indeed, what I have elsewhere defined as *epideictic* phenomena—displays, or special occasions, which allow all the individuals taking part to sense or become conditioned by population pressure—appear to be very common and widespread in the animal kingdom. They occur especially at the times predicted, when feedback is required in anticipation of a change in population density. The singing of birds, the trilling of katydids, crickets, and frogs, the underwater sounds of fish, and the flashing of fireflies all appear to perform this epideictic function. In cases where, as we have just seen, epideictic behavior is confined in the breeding season to the male sex, the presumption is that the whole process of controlling the breeding density and the reproductive quota is relegated to the males. Outside the breeding season, when the individuals are no longer united in pairs and are all effectively neuter in sex, all participate alike in epideictic displays— in flighting at sundown, like ducks; in demonstrating at huge communal roosts at dusk, like starlings, grackles, and crows; or in forming premigratory swarms, like swallows. The assumption which the hypothesis suggests, that the largest sector of all social behavior must have this fundamentally epideic-tic or feedback function, gives a key to understanding a vast agglomeration of observed animal behavior that has hitherto been dubiously interpreted or has seemed altogether meaningless.

Maintaining Population Balance

Having outlined the way in which social organization appears to serve in supplying feedback, I propose to look again at the machinery for making adjustments to the population balance. In territorial birds, variations in the average size of territories from place to place and year to year can be shown to alter the breeding density and probably also the proportion of adults actually participating in reproduction. In various mammals the proportion of the females made pregnant, the number and size of litters, the survival of the young and the age at which they mature may all be influenced by social stress. Wherever parental care of the young has been evolved in the animal kingdom, the possibility exists that maternal behavior and solicitude can be affected in the same way; and the commonly observed variations in survival rates of the newborn could, in that case, have a substantial functional component and play a significant part in regulating the reproductive output. This would, among other things, explain away the enigma of cannibalism of the young, which we noticed earlier in the guppies and which occurs sporadically all through the higher animals. Infanticide played a conspicuous part in reducing the effective birth rate of many of the primitive human peoples that survived into modern times. Not infrequently it took the form of abandoning the child for what appeared to be commendable reasons, without involving an act of violence.

Reproduction is of course only one of the parameters involved in keeping the balance between income and loss in populations. The homeostatic machinery can go to work on the other side of the balance also, by influencing survival. Already, in considering the recruitment of adults, we have taken note of the way this can be affected by juvenile mortality, some of which is intrinsic in origin and capable of being promoted by social pressures. Conventional competition often leads to the exclusion of surplus individuals from any further right to share the resources of the habitat, and this in turn compels them to emigrate. Research conducted at Aberdeen in the last 8 years has shown how important a factor forced expulsion is in regulating the numbers of the Scottish red grouse. Every breeding season so far has produced a population surplus, and it is the aggressive behavior of the dominant males which succeeds in driving the supernumeraries away. In this case the outcasts do not go far; they get picked up by predators or they mope and die because they are cut off from their proper food. Deaths from predation and disease can in fact be substantially "assisted" under social stress.

On the income side, therefore, both reproductive input and the acquisition of recruits by immigration appear to be subject to social regulation; and on the loss side, emigration and what can be described as socially induced mortality can be similarly affected. Once more it appears that it is only the inroads of Darwin's "checks to increase," the agents once held to be totally responsible for population regulation, which are in fact uncontrollable and have to be balanced out by manipulation of the other four components.

109

Attention must be drawn to the intimate way in which physiology and behavior are entwined in providing the regulatory machinery. It seems certain that the feedback of social stimulation acts on the individual through his endocrine system, and in the case of the vertebrates, as I have said, this particularly involves the pituitary and adrenal cortex or its equivalent. Sometimes the individual's response is primarily a physiological one—for example, the inhibition of spermatogenesis or the acceleration of growth; sometimes it is purely behavioral, as in the urge to return to the breeding site, the development of aggressiveness, or the demand for territory of a given size. But often there is a combination of the two—that is to say, a psychosomatic response, as when, for instance, the assumption of breeding colors is coupled with the urge to display.

Sources of Controversy

There is no need for me to emphasize that the hypothesis is controversial. But almost all of it is based on well-established fact, so that the controversy can relate solely to matters of interpretation. Examples have been given here which show the ability of the hypothesis to offer new and satisfying interpretations of matters of fact where none could be suggested before. Some of these matters are of wide importance, like the basic function of social behavior; some are matters of everyday experience, like why birds sing at dawn. Very seldom indeed does the hypothesis contradict well-founded accepted principles. What, then, are the sources of controversy?

These are really three in number, all of them important. The first is that the concept is very wide-ranging and comprehensive; this means that it cannot be simply proved or disproved by performing a decisive experiment. There are of course dubious points where critical tests can be made, and research is proceeding, at Aberdeen among many other places, toward this end. Relevant results are constantly emerging, and at many points the hypothesis has been solidified and strengthened since it was first formulated. On the other hand, there has been no cause yet to retract anything.

The second source of controversy is that the hypothesis invokes a type of natural selection which is unfamiliar to zoologists generally. Social grouping is essentially a localizing phenomenon, and an animal species is normally made up of countless local populations all perpetuating themselves on their native soil, exactly as happens in underdeveloped and primitive communities of man. Social customs and adaptations vary from one local group to another, and the hypothesis requires that natural selection should take place between these groups, promoting those with more effective social organizations while the less effective ones go under. It is necessary, in other words, to postulate that social organizations are capable of progressive evolution and perfection as entities in their own right. The detailed arguments (5) are too complex to be presented here, but I can point out that intergroup selection is far from being a new concept: It has been widely accepted for more than 20 years by geneticists. It is almost impossible to demonstrate it experimentally because we have to deal with something closely corresponding to the rise and fall of nations in history, rather than with success or failure of single genes over a few generations;

it is therefore the time scale that prevents direct experiment. Even the comparatively rapid process of natural selection acting among individuals has been notoriously difficult to demonstrate in nature.

The third objection is, I think, by far the most interesting. It is simply that the hypothesis does not apply to ourselves. No built-in mechanisms appear to curb our own population growth, or adjust our numbers to our resources. If they did so, everything I have said would be evident to every educated child, and I should not be surveying it here. How is this paradox to be explained?

The answer, it seems clear, is that these mechanisms did exist in primitive man and have been lost, almost within historic times. Man in the paleolithic stage, living as a hunter and gatherer, remained in balance with his natural resources just as other animals do under natural conditions. Generation after generation, his numbers underwent little or no change. Population increase was prevented not by physiological control mechanisms of the kind found in many other mammals but only by behavioral ones, taking the form of traditional customs and taboos. All the stone age tribes that survived into modern times diminished their effective birth rate by at least one of three ritual practices—infanticide, abortion, and abstention from intercourse. In a few cases, fertility was apparently impaired by surgery during the initiation ceremonies. In many cases, marriage was long deferred. Mortality of those of more advanced age was often raised through cannibalism, tribal fighting, and human sacrifice.

Gradually, with the spread of the agricultural revolution, which tended to concentrate the population at high densities on fertile soils and led by degrees to the rise of the town, the craftsman, and the merchant, the old customs and taboos must have been forsaken. The means of population control would have been inherited originally from man's subhuman ancestors, and among stone age peoples their real function was probably not even dimly discerned except perhaps by a few individuals of exceptional brilliance and insight. The continually expanding horizons and skills of modern man rendered intrinsic limitation of numbers unnecessary, and for 5,000 or 10,000 years the advanced peoples of the Western world and Asia have increased without appearing to harm the world about them or endanger its productivity. But the underlying principles are the same as they have always been. It becomes obvious at last that we are getting very near the global carrying capacity of our habitat, and that we ought swiftly to impose some new, effective, homeostatic regime before we overwhelm it, and the ax of group selection falls.

References

1. Wynne-Edwards, V. C., *Animal Dispersion in Relation to Social Behaviour.* New York: Hafner, 1962.
2. Darwin, C., *The Origin of Species.* London: Murray, 1859. (Quoted from 6th edition, 1872.)
3. Jespersen, P., "The frequency of birds over the high Atlantic Ocean." *Nature* 114: 281, 1924.
4. Silliman, R. P., and J. S. Gutsell, "Experimental exploitation of fish populations." *U.S. Fish Wildlife Serv. Fishery Bull.* 58: 214, 1958.
5. Wynne-Edwards, V. C., "Intergroup selection in the evolution of social systems." *Nature* 200: 623, 1963.

Part 2 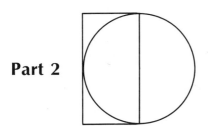 **The Environmental Encounter**

The Seeing Eye

ADOLF PORTMANN

How does one define human ecology? Does it refer to general ecology as shared by humans, or to a specific aspect of general ecology? Whichever we choose, there are two distinguishing characteristics of human, as opposed to plant or animal, ecology. One deals with the nature of the environmental encounter—the complexity of the sentient response—as it seems or feels or appears. The other is the element of choice or decision as it affects this encounter.

The encounter or confrontation almost by definition involves perception, a perception that is essentially visual. Having as primates subordinated our other sensory modes, we must now admit that we move in a visual world and that our relationship to it—our ecology—is in part shaped by the nature and limitations of vision. Sight is of course only the beginning of the encounter, for it is linked to memory and to history and to other characteristics of our sensibility. We are confronted by a world which for us was made to be seen, and for our minds was made to be understood.

THE EDITORS

WHEN WE SAY that our experience of the world comes to us chiefly through the eye we do not mean to belittle the power of music or poetry; we mean simply that the eye is the organ which transmits to us our basic perceptions of the world outside. No matter how much is contributed by speech and hearing, whatever is uttered or heard is constantly supplemented by what is observed. We are surrounded by innumerable forms in

(Photo by Elizabeth B. Hecker.)

Landscape, *9(1):14–21, Autumn 1959. Reprinted by permission.*

nature, by an immense treasury of works of art, and all these speak to our eyes.

It is as a biologist that I would like to survey the world of the optic senses —the world of colors and forms. We know that in our environment there are electro-magnetic waves of different lengths, some of which we are able to see as colors. On either side of the colors of the rainbow there are further wave lengths which we identify as infrared and ultraviolet. We also know through experiment that many creatures—numerous insects, for instance—see ultraviolet rays as colors. Those which our human senses register are therefore only a fragment of the total spectrum. Nevertheless we live according to the concept of a complete range of colors which, moreover, our optic sense orders in complementary, interacting pairs.

Colors and Forms

The manner in which we pair off colors is a physiological problem; a problem of a different sort is how we integrate this inherited characteristic into our sensory image of the world. The intellect teaches us which wave lengths correspond, for example, to red or blue, but the fact that yellow and red affect us as warm, stimulating colors, whereas their complementary colors, blue and green, have a cooling and subduing effect, is something we do not have to learn—it is knowledge we already possess with a kind of inherited certainty. It is therefore not surprising that our various psychic reactions to color provide the bases for more than one psychological test, or that they have determined the use of color in advertising and packaging. These are merely practical applications of what we already know about one unconscious inherited characteristic.

How early in life the perception of color matures has been shown in the way new born babies respond. It was long held that a child developed a color sense only after six months; some even believed after two or three years; but a Swiss pediatrician a few years ago measured the length of time a newborn child would gaze at a pure color painted on a card. The time for red was 11.5 seconds; for yellow, 4.5; for green, 13.4; and for blue, 16 seconds. The "cool" colors were preferred. The children also responded quickly to forms; when a black or white figure—a line or circle—was superimposed on the colored card, the length of time a child gazed at red was increased from 9.5 seconds to 31. Pure yellow held its attention for 3.8 seconds, but when a black circle was added, this time increased to 46 seconds, or about twelve times as long! In some cases the child's reaction was marked by movements of the eyes and head.

Sensitivity to color is thus active from the moment of birth, and it can only have developed in a pre-natal stage. No less innate is the perception of forms and shapes. Whatever may be said of some aspects of Gestalt psychology, no one will deny that laws are at work organizing our field of vision. The capacity which has been ours since the earliest times to compose groups of stars into constellations is still functioning, even when the intellect seeks to discredit it. Likewise the capacity to order our image of the environment in relation to the vertical and horizontal seems inborn. Our sense of gravity helps in the process, but the eye responds in its own particular way to the two chief directions in space. Combined with primary colors, these two elements have been composed by Piet Mondrian into pictures of a joyous simplicity and directness.

Experiments with animals show that heredity often prepares an advance awareness of many objects later encountered in the visible world. Some animal mothers have an instinctive knowledge of some important characteristic of their young, even without preliminary experience; and the young themselves are informed in advance, as it were, of the distinguishing marks of their parents. The image of the future mate, of other members of the species, of edible plants, of suitable quarry, and of hereditary enemies are very often inborn and await only the discovery of the living prototype.

Any naturalist aware of these hereditary relationships with the environment will reject the notion that man's innate relationships with *his* environment are any less rich than those of animals. I emphasize this point because some theorists have been inclined to believe that our own inborn structures are insignificant—as if the traits so obvious in an animal had somehow been lost or destroyed in us. The truth is much more complex: in the case of human beings, as with animals, many visual concepts are certainly prepared in advance, but it is also clear from observing the behavior of the more highly developed animals that this advance preparation is not rigid; it always allows for possibilities of learning, and of true experience.

The idea that our sensory perception of the world is in a large measure determined by an inherited structure coincides with certain aspects of Jung's notion of the Collective Unconscious. It was in fact to describe this assumed structure that he created the word "archetype." It is not my task here to discuss the archetype problem, but we must face a fundamental fact: there exist within each of us many inherited structures for the apprehension of outer reality. I am thinking, for instance, of that capacity of ours to anthropomorphize our entire environment, to discover a human figment even in the stars, and to endow many things in our surroundings with gender. It is obvious that tradition plays an important part in this process, as it has in the varied ways man has anthropomorphized the heavenly bodies. Among one group of people the sun is feminine and the moon masculine; among the neighboring group it will be the other way around. In such notions tradition is clearly at work. Yet beyond tradition and prior to it, the urge of the anthropomorphic imagination can be discerned.

When we contemplate the inherited structures designed to adjust us to the world we become aware of the miracle of organic life. It is then that the eye ceases to be a neutral sort of organ for receiving and registering electromagnetic stimuli, like a photographic plate; and it is then that we begin to know that it is not the eye alone which sees; it is Man, the whole living organism.

Things Designed to Be Seen

Up to now we have been discussing the inherited relationships which exist within ourselves, and which enable us to establish contact with the environment and with other human beings. But this is only one aspect of the optic function. Among all the creatures in the world there are many which almost seem to demand that they be looked at; many forms of life are fashioned as if the gaze of others were essential to their being. They possess "organs to be seen."

These have been much studied of

late under the term of "visual structures." Contemporary biology, in fact, concerns itself just as much with the organs made to be seen as with the organs of sight, and among the former there are a number familiar to us all: flowers whose form and color are meant to attract insects and birds, animal patterns and coloring meant to serve as a signal for those of the same species; other patterns meant to enable the animal to hide, to melt into the background—meant for an eye, but for an enemy eye, and meant to deceive it.

These visual traits have been studied because there is a widely held belief in some biological circles that certain colors and patterns among animals have been chosen and perfected by the process of selection; that they have, in a sense, been screened by millions of years of watchful eyes. What interests us here is the fact that some optical traits must have existed prior to this screening process, and how are we to explain *them*? In brief, we are chiefly interested in the laws of form which originally determined those visual traits, those so-called optical organs.

The connections in nature between the sense of sight and the object seen are beyond counting; yet these are merely a part of the whole visible world. The production of forms intended especially to be seen is not confined to animals having some vital relationship to the watching eye. For those who think only in terms of function and utility—concepts which in a too exclusive interpretation have had so unwholesome an influence on our relation with nature—it will come as a surprise that this ability to produce visual features is native to organisms whose exterior has no connection with any eye at all. The great number of unperceived and all-but-invisible

forms in nature (which come to our notice only in the course of research) teaches us one important principle. It is this: the appearance of every living organism serves a fundamental purpose: self-expression, or *self-projection* of that organism in form and color. This, together with a particular, individual perception of the world, is the mark of the highest group of living creatures.

I find myself comparing the colors and brilliant designs of some of the remoter forms with the work of artists of the so-called non-objective school of art, in particular Hans Arp and Paul Klee. These two, and many others, each in a different way, have turned for inspiration to instinctive sources of form that could well stimulate in all of

". . . We must observe and learn to know the varied ways plants and animals proclaim their identity, by projecting themselves before the optic sense of higher forms of life." (Photo of nighthawk by Hal H. Harrison.)

us a basic capacity for fresh visual experience, for it is the function of the artist to reactivate the powers which once compelled us to experience the starry sky of night as an ordered group of constellations, and to expand our vision.

If we wish to comprehend the world of sight in all its uniqueness we must formulate an overall image of the living being in which the miracle of vision has its rightful place. We must observe not only those aspects of nature which particularly appeal to our technological way of thinking—the streamlined form, the camouflage, the flight structure, the photographic apparatus of the eye—we must observe and learn to know the varied ways plants and animals proclaim their identity, by projecting themselves before the optic sense of higher forms of life.

The Uneducated Eye

Why am I so concerned with this matter of self-projection? Because it involves the training of our capacity to see; it involves the realization that the living world is designed to be seen, and our awareness of what an astounding natural phenomenon confronts us in this coordination between the eye and the objects it sees. One of the greatest tasks ahead of us is to develop our psychic relationship to these forms and to increase our participation in the optic abundance at our disposal. What we are actually seeking is a heightened experience of the world of the senses, a fuller life in the world of nature and art.

The first years of our contact with the environment witness the formation of our own individual private world, which to a great extent is determined by the inherited structure of images—Jung's Collective Unconscious. The general diffusion of this heritage is a powerful guarantee of social cohesion, since it provides a common basis of experience. It is during this period that a primary world comes into being for each of us, a world in which all things are living, and in which our imagination works by means of pictures or images or analogies. It is the world of immediate experience where the sun always "rises" in the East, and where the sky is always a dome, and the stars always move. This is the concept which, since primitive times, has determined the images common to a group, and out of which the first scientific theories arose.

But it is a concept which the astronomical teachings of Copernicus shattered for the Occident in the 16th century. We may therefore define it in terms of pre-Copernican concepts: as the world of Ptolemy. We are all Ptolemaic when we are born, and for years thereafter our powers of reasoning are attuned to that ancient and primary way of thinking. The decisive early period in our contact with nature is strongly influenced by the Ptolemaic point of view, in which our inherited traits and responses find a congenial outlet.

We should, moreover, never forget that throughout a great portion of our lives we remain essentially Ptolemaic. No matter how skillfully our intellect may be at understanding the series of electro-magnetic variations from 10^{-8} to 10^{-14} meters, to our sensory perceptions the color range still extends from red to blue through purple and no farther. Nor is the Ptolemaic world merely a phase to be outgrown, a kind of animal experience; it is an integral part of our total human quality, and the fullness of any human existence depends on how fruitful has been its influence on our imagination. The hardest task for any of us is to integrate this

original phase of our existence into another entirely different phase which unfolds in later life. A few decades ago we would have called the second phase the "Copernican World"; now we must speak of the "Einsteinian World," and in the future it will doubtless have still other names. The difficulty is not so much how to preserve the Ptolemaic concepts intact as it is how to harmonize their lasting values with those of the equally necessary second phase—and thereby insure a well-balanced life. How to combine the primary experience of form and color with the subsequent intellectual process of knowing and analyzing?

The undertaking is all the harder today because our visual sense is being allowed to revert to a sort of wilderness state. The language of form and color is being abused to the point where a new kind of illiteracy is emerging, and this is true not only of childhood and adolescence; the new illiteracy is invading the adult sphere as well. The present flood of illustrated publications threatens to increase to an enormous extent the number of the visually ignorant and the visually apathetic.

It may sound strange to emphasize this danger at a time when an unparalleled flood of nature documentation is overwhelming us—books, magazines, films, television—photographs everywhere, everywhere possibilities of seeing as never before. Can this actually be a menace? Yes, precisely because this deluge of pictures rarely encourages a genuine relationship with nature, and because any true education of the spirit lies in a totally different direction. The most important developments in biology now have to follow the lead of physics and chemistry; they have to take us to the invisible aspects of nature, to the structures lying beyond the microscope, and every day we are led farther from the familiar forms surrounding us. This is the road of the Einsteinian world, passing far beyond all frontiers of everyday sensory observation. Progress of this sort is our destiny, but it is also our destiny that we are all born and live as human beings in the world of the senses, and that only by conforming to an inherited way of life can we achieve a satisfying existence. This calls for an intensive contact with all living things, a contact which cannot be based exclusively on knowledge of the invisible.

The inevitable immersion of research in the zone of the sub-microscopic brings us close, however, to the dangers of a false perspective. If, as doctors or research scientists, we are involved in the processes of life we must of course know and master the submicroscopic universe and its laws, but the experience should ultimately help us to recognize the living forms around and within us.

If in these times of increasing techniques any scale of values is to be preserved, if the living being as manifested in form and color, odor and sound, is to retain its full worth, this can only come about through a strong determination on our part to experience those forms as intensively, as freshly, as possible. This in turn demands new thinking on the whole subject of schooling, and especially of the schooling of vision. In such an undertaking the teacher of biology meets with the teacher of art on a common ground; both are concerned with demonstrating form as a manifestation of light, and the eye as an essential part of the process. It is finally a matter of emerging from the realm of the invisible into our own world once more, where there is the leaf, the flower, the fruit, the diversity of colors and forms among living creatures. We must bring into being a kind of nature study which belongs in the world of our senses—in the world where our Ptolemaic aspect must also stay, no matter what new views of the cosmos may evolve. Natural forms are a constant source of stimulation for the imagination, a constant incentive to lead a life of sensory joy in a sensory world. In the light of this understanding these forms are themselves transformed into something new: expressions of the mysterious realities around and within us.

The Ecology of Imagination in Childhood

EDITH COBB

The relationship of mind to nature is the crucial question for man's ecology. If we deny that mind requires anything in its environment save other minds, we imply that the quality of natural surroundings is not very important and that, indeed, place is expendable. If the uniqueness of place were only a phenomenon, like a passing play of colors, then we could explain esthetic experience as a matter of attitudes and opinions. If beauty is relative and only skin deep and the beauty of nature actually a kind of recent human invention—a matter of taste—our inherent sense of relationship to it gets lost in a flux of artiness, mode, and fashion.

How nearly true this is may be appreciated if you consider the "little old ladies" fighting against billboards. Human sanity requires some less-than-obvious connections to nature as well as the necessities of food, water, energy, and air. We have hardly begun to discover what those connections may be, but the ladies are braver than hypocritical politicians, kept lampooners, and cynical scholars when it comes to putting what they feel into the limited forms of available action.

THE EDITORS

THE PRESENT ESSAY is an abridgment of a longer work in process, which attempts the difficult task first of defining what we mean by the genius of childhood as a common human possession; and second of showing that a major

Daedalus, *88(3):537–548, Summer 1959. Reprinted by permission from DAEDALUS, Journal of the American Academy of Arts and Sciences, Boston, Mass.*

clue to mental health lies in the spontaneously creative imagination of childhood both as a form of learning and as a function of the organizing powers of the nervous system. Of necessity, the exploration includes tracing the relationship of this early psychophysical force in human development to those uncommon forms of genius which constitute the high point of achievement in human growth potential, with roots, as I believe, in the child's perceptual relations with the natural world.

I propose to argue in this paper that children are born animals and mature biologically, but evolve culturally into human individuality, reaching widely different levels and norms. This use of the term "evolution" must be taken literally—that is, as a "true metaphor" (1), a description of an experiential continuation of nature's own strivings toward a transcendence of biological levels through culturally elaborated relations with environment. The difference between animal and human nature would then be seen to consist of the uniqueness of every human individual as a species in himself, while nature's drive toward speciation and variation in forms could be interpreted as continuing in individual form into human life, first in the child's speculative play with nature's plasticity, and ultimately in man's individual striving to create forms *not* found in nature, in the arts, sciences, technology, and thought.

Historically speaking, individual genius has played the principal role in the achievement of a general cultural transcendence of previous levels, both psychological and cultural, by introducing higher forms of ability, purpose, and aim into the cultural continuum. The genius of childhood, in the sense of extreme personal originality and the creation of private worlds, is discontinuous and persists into adult life only as a specialized, highly cultivated condition. But the gift of our prolonged human childhood to the family of man is plasticity of response to environment. This plasticity of response and the child's primary aesthetic adaptation to environment may be extended through memory into a lifelong renewal of the early power to learn and to evolve.

If we examine the statements made by adult geniuses about their own childhood and compare them with references to the child in myth and religion (in particular in the Christian religion), it seems clear that there is and always has been a widespread intuitive understanding that certain aspects of childhood experience remain in memory as a psychophysical force, an élan, which produces the pressure to perceive creatively and inventively. For from this position, creative and constructive mental processes do not result from an accumulation of information, but from the maintaining of a continued plasticity of response of the whole organism to new information and in general to the outer world. Perhaps we have arrived at a new age in which this condition of mind and purpose can no longer be optional or left to the gifted few, but must be recognized as a common human need in adapting to life and society.

My position is based upon the fact that the study of the child in nature, culture, and society (the evolution of social attitudes toward childhood into present realization of its importance in everyone's life history) reveals that there is a special period, the little-understood, prepubertal, halcyon, middle age of childhood, approximately from five or six to eleven or twelve—

"... there is a special period ... —between the strivings of animal infancy and the storms of adolescence—when the natural world is experienced in some highly evocative way ..." (Photo by
Elizabeth B. Hecker.)

between the strivings of animal infancy and the storms of adolescence—
when the natural world is experienced
in some highly evocative way, producing in the child a sense of some profound continuity with natural processes
and presenting overt evidence of a
biological basis of intuition (2).

These concepts have evolved from
four principal sources: first, biographi-
cal and autobiographical memories of
gifted people; second, the Freudian
concept of childhood as the core of human development, particularly as this
is treated in social casework (3), which

furthers adaptation of the unique individual to his total environment; third, a
study of the plastic, dynamic nature of
imagery in contrast to the more static
condensed simultaneity of the symbol;
last, and as a tool for the implementation of these sources, an investigation
of studies of the changing imagery in
the language of natural description,
which disclosed this special trend in
perception, a trend in the cultural evolution of attitudes toward nature which
has produced the concept of ecology,
the study of mutual relations, the give-
and-take between organisms and their

complete and total environment. The science of ecology provides us with a plastic image of behaving organisms in a behaving world, and a tool for synthesis as well as analysis of the system of meaning and verbal imagery which we use to describe nature.

In my collection (4) of some three hundred volumes of autobiographical recollections of their own childhood by creative thinkers from many cultures and eras, ranging from a fragment from the sixteenth century to the present, it is principally to this middle-age range in their early life that these writers say they return in memory in order to renew the power and impulse to create at its very source, a source which they describe as the experience of emerging not only into the light of consciousness but into a living sense of a dynamic relationship with the outer world. In these memories the child appears to experience both a sense of discontinuity, an awareness of his own unique separateness and identity, and also a continuity, a renewal of relationship with nature as process. This apprehension is certainly not intellectual; I believe it is rational at least in a limited sense, a preverbal experience of an "aesthetic logic" both in nature's formative processes and in the gestalt-making powers of the child's own developing nervous system, aesthetic powers that overlap meaningfully in these moments of form-creating expansion and self-consciousness.

"Form is the magic of the world," as Dalcq has expressed it, whether in nature, play, art, or thought. But it is the activity of creating form which has fascinated the mind of man, most particularly as the power to animate the inanimate, the ability to make things move in the shape of working models and refined machines, the power to produce animation even in the "still"

image of the plastic arts. This shaping force, this desire to master and to create motion, not only is at the basis of all human technical invention but also is the prime characteristic of effective metaphor: "Those words set a thing before the eyes that show it in an active state," said Aristotle.

It is especially interesting to note, therefore, that in dictionary terms the word "animate" derives from a Latin word signifying "soul" or "breath" (a metabolic action pattern), and that among its meanings are "to give spirit to" or "to put in motion or operation" or, synonymously, "to energize" (Webster). The term "genius" plays with all these threads of meaning, including mental power or energy, but in its earlier usage it referred most frequently to the spirit of place, the *genius loci*, which we can now interpret to refer to a living ecological relationship between an observer and an environment, a person and a place.

Instead of working backward from the adult's position to the child's, I found it necessary in my exploration of the genius of the living child to set up methods of investigating creative purpose in the child's play and art. The value of forms produced was secondary to the importance of the response to "aesthetic logic" in the child's gestalt-forming action patterns with the instrument of the self. Using various forms of so-called projective methods and play techniques (in particular, modified versions of the Lowenfeld World-Play Technique and the Thematic Apperception Test, accompanied by a continual reference to the Rorschach categories of Form, Color, Motion, Time and Space, Animal and Human Response), I became acutely aware that what a child wanted to do most of all was to make a world in which to find a place to discover a self. This ordering reverses the general position that self-exploration produces a knowledge of the world. Furthermore, while observing the passionate world-making behavior of the child when he is given plastic materials and working dimensions which are manageable and in proportion to his need, accompanied by a population of toys, fauna and flora, and artifacts that do duty as "figures of speech" in the rhetoric of play, I have been made keenly aware of those processes which the genius in particular in later life seeks to recall.

The tendency to play may be said to be characteristic of animals reared in a nidicolous (i.e., a specifically nestlike) domestic ecology. The important point about the child's play is that it includes the spontaneous effort to be something other than what he actually is, to "act out"[1] and to dramatize speculation, which is in effect to take play out into the four-dimensional continuum by adding motion and sequence, and therefore time, to its procedures.

As lay people, we probably think with greater ease about biological evolution in terms of continuity; and, as Julian Huxley reports, "Life is and must be a continuum because of its basic process of self-reproduction: in the perspective of time all living matter is continuous because every fresh portion of it has been produced from pre-existing living matter" (5). However, he adds, "Discontinuities of various sorts have been introduced into the continuity," the study of which should be of great value, for they are of first-rate importance to a long-term view of evolution. "The chief of these discontinuities," Huxley continues, "are those of the cell, the multicellular individual, the species, and the ecological community"—that is, the "ecological niche," the preferred perceptual world in which the organism functions. Each one of these discontinuities is of major significance to the psychobiological nature of man's individual organism and to his psychosomatic personality. In nature, continuity of species is maintained by interbreeding; the discontinuities with previously related forms are maintained by absence of interbreeding brought about by isolating mechanisms, which in animal life also include psychological barriers to mating. Man must create his own psychological identity in order to survive, and he represents a climax in the historically related achievements in discontinuity. His psychosocial history shares in this process; one need only remember the discontinuous nature of such social mechanisms as monogamy, celibacy as a social ideal, or the role of the incest motif, found in one form or another throughout civilization.

When Freud defined childhood's middle age as the latency period, he referred only to latent sexual drives, which, according to psychoanalytic interpretation, become less purposive when the child's mastery of body and speech directs his energies toward other types of cognitive satisfaction. Energy remains libidinal, and creativity a substitute for sex. I suggest that this period is also a time of far more general latent awareness or "half-knowledge" (6), a period of plasticity of perceptual response and "biological memory" which when employed in original gestalt-building processes must be described as intuition (in contrast to other instinctual biological drives).[2] In infancy the impulse to love is aroused

---

[1] An important term, which now is unfortunately also the metaphor for delinquency and neurotic behavior.

[2] Intuition is not necessarily benign. It is relational and structural; its value depends upon the purposes to which it is addressed.

to the level of passion and yet must remain unfulfilled and unformulated in any direct sense. The passion of infancy is therefore addressed to goals and purposes unknown but not entirely "unperceived," for in ordinary experience in early childhood, the parents (more specifically the nurturing figure of the mother) are the targets of love, a fact that evokes some latent foreknowledge of sexual form and function. The "distance" between the self and the objects of desire, and the natural pressure for fulfillment, are equally real, although "out of sight." The child fills in the distance between the self and the goals of desire with imagined forms. The basic evolutionary characteristics of perceptual processes, also latent in the human nervous system, become dominant as the child emerges more consciously into a perceptual participation in external nature. The reproductive urge is undoubtedly also represented in the desire "to body forth the forms of things unknown," but the biological urge toward growth becomes the psychophysical urge toward transcendence, the urge to create higher and ever more complex gestalten in perception and cultural meaning.

Freud has made plain to us that the problem of maintaining our individual transcendence of levels above our biological heritage of animal instinct and impulse is a matter of life-long effort. It begins with the cultural demand for the discontinuity of instinct, which he has described as the Oedipal situation, a climax in nature's use of isolating mechanisms in culturally elaborated form. While the child's expression of reproductive mechanisms is biologically delayed and culturally restricted, the psychological growth mechanisms have been culturally elaborated,

speeded up, and highly differentiated. The child's will and need is to use energy for purposes of growth, thus following nature's own biological pattern of alternating the use of energy between self-reproduction and self-increase. Energy in itself cannot be described as "libidinal," although the body's purpose in the use of energy may be addressed to libidinal ends. It is the process we know as metabolism, which furnishes "the energy system which is the body" (to use Sir Charles Sherrington's phrase) with what D'Arcy Thompson has called "the power to do work."

In his study of prenatal and neonatal infancy (7), Gesell finds that the development of genius is a true growth phenomenon, a continuation of the earliest prenatal morphological strivings. The embryology of mind, according to him, is to be sought in the embryology of behavior, even in the earliest postural mechanisms and the first prenatal adjustment to the ceaseless pull of gravity. Genius, he finds, is an achieved "personal possession," an extension of the body's own growing corpus of behavior into nature's continuum. We would say here that genius is a personal achievement rather than a possession, a personal "reading" of nature extended into the semantic unknown. But, as Gesell states, the action patterns of growth are continuous and analogous; the unfolding experience becomes a part of all metaphor. We would extend this idea to stress the individual uniqueness of human psychological and cognitive growth, in spite of the fact that the recognition of growth or learning ultimately depends upon culturally standardized methods. The child's early perceptual continuity with nature, the innate gestalt-making powers of the nervous system, then remain the biological basis of intuition.

127

The cognitive process which differentiates man from all other animals is the source of his predictive, prefigurative imagination, enabling him to learn and evolve culturally. As Norbert Wiener, whose genius has been directed to the understanding and "modeling" of the mind as mechanism, has remarked, "It remains a miracle that children do learn," that they do match perception and language so successfully. For every child this relational behavior is an act of genesis, the genesis of his real world as a personal yet culturally conditioned image.

Thorpe's recent summary of works on animal learning and perception (8) provides a significant re-enforcement of the present concept of a perceptual basis of human intuition and learning. Perception, he finds, must now be considered to be a primary drive in evolution, and the exploration of environment to be an innate appetite deriving from a principle of expectancy within the animal's neural tissue. However, the exploratory tendency in the animal, which Thorpe identifies as "latent learning," is not addressed to primary survival needs. For the animal as for man, the ultimate satisfaction of perceptual expectancy and perceptual exploration is the organization of the perceptual world into the "good gestalt," into environmental shapes that "hold," that are populated with forms and are rich in perceptual meaning. In bird, fish, beast, or man, the need to make a world is intricately related to the sense of identity. Perception even on lower levels of animal life is not a response to simple sense data, "but an active organizing process, itself possibly including an element of purpose, tending all the time to build up primary perceptions into more and more complete and unitary systems." Thorpe states that "purpose" here has the usual meaning, "a striving after a future goal retained as *some kind of image* or idea" [italics mine]. Plasticity of response is again the important feature in perception, for "in as far as the original faculty of perception retains or increases plasticity during evolutionary development, it becomes the various learning processes that we know."

But most significant to our argument here is the idea that perception is a comparative activity which contains a neural experience of duration, and that "perception of a time dimension including an element of expectancy is as fundamental to organisms as is perception of space." Perception is a kind of temporal scanning, a translation of spatial into temporal patterns after the manner of scanning as performed by a television apparatus. Time and space dominate all perceptual activities. In this activity "perception of relations is primary while sensation is the result of secondary analysis." In human life the primary perceptual activity is not the photochemical synthesis of a prefabricated gestalt, but a creative imagination of form.

The child, like the poet, is his own instrument. His whole body, erotized and highly sensitized by the necessities of nurture and touch, is the tool of his mind, and serves with a passionate enjoyment in a creative engagement with the forces of nature. Examination of the psychobiography of genius suggests that the perception of wholeness has been a characteristic of all individuals who have thought more closely with the instrument of the body. Perceptual unity with nature is, of course, not a new concept.[3] As Conrad Aiken

[3] The false metaphors of "contest" and "conquest" of nature continue to interrupt our perceptions of nature's aesthetics.

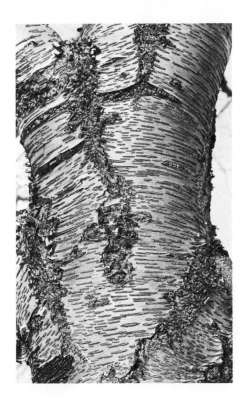

"... adult memories of childhood ... refer to a deep desire to renew the ability to perceive as a child and to participate with the whole bodily self in the ... sights and sounds of the external world of nature and artifact." (Photos by Arthur Ambler from National Audubon Society.)

has expressed it, drawing upon the philosophy of ancient China:

The landscape and the language are the same
For we ourselves are landscape and are
    land. (9)

Taken together, the child's intuitive sense of a perceptual continuity with nature and the often expressed hope that the poetic and the scientific aspects of our culture may be evolving toward a new synthesis with nature suggest that the "unmediated vision" of childhood is the primary evidence, perhaps the source, of the predictive, prefigurative imagination of man, and that the exercise of this imagination is dependent upon autobiographical recall in some form. Geoffrey H. Hartman, pursuing this thought in his analysis of

the work of four poets (10), points out that Wordsworth was not only the first English poet to treat autobiography poetically, but also the first to separate personal experience from the impersonal element within autobiographical recollection in order to obtain a vision of the basic creative process, "the motion that impels and rolls through all things" in the order of nature, using himself as a recording instrument. Perhaps it is significant that this was the point in recent social history at which the social reality of the concept of individual uniqueness was beginning to assert itself, coinciding with the emergence of the autobiographical impulse (until then something of a rarity in printed discussion) as a form of the "education of the poetic spirit"

129

(Hourd's phrase [11]), with roots in the perceptions of childhood.

In an important study, John Oman (12) comments that in every genius whose special gift is perception, either time or space seems to be a dominant intuition in childhood. We would say here that genius consists in the continuing ability to recall and to utilize the child's primary perceptual intuition of time and space. Oman recalls that his own exodus, his first sense of discontinuity and aloneness with respect to other individuals but equally one of continuity with nature, occurred when as a child of six he stood at the edge of the sea on a Sunday morning in summer. His own awakening to a sense of nature as infinity and yet as a part of himself seems to have occurred quite directly in relation to the earlier experience of a Sunday morning in church. This was not a specifically religious experience, but simply a response to an open-system attitude, a state of temporal and spatial inquiry— Where am I? Who am I?—an attitude toward nature which is frequently evoked within or as a result of religiously conditioned circumstances described in childhood recollection.

In a charming autobiographical account of the birth of his own genius (13), Giordano Bruno recounts his "acting out" of this particular version of childhood experience, the intuition that drove him to continue to relate "depth of potentiality to the sublimity of action" and held him in a state of enchantment even to his death at the stake. In Bruno's allegory the sense of a deceptiveness of appearances across time and space is described as a colloquy between two mountains, his "parents" in nature—Mount Cicada on whose slopes he lived, and Mount Vesuvius

opposite. To satisfy himself he journeyed on foot across the distance between Cicada and Vesuvius, to find each of them barren at a distance, but rich in texture close by. "Thus did his parents [the two mountains] first teach the lad to doubt, and revealed to him how distance changes the face of things." In later life, Bruno averred, "No matter in what region of the globe I may be, I shall realize that both time and space are distant from me."

It is significant that adult memories of childhood, even when nostalgic and romantic, seldom suggest the need to be a child but refer to a deep desire to renew the ability to perceive as a child and to participate with the whole bodily self in the forms, colors, and motions, the sights and sounds of the external world of nature and artifact. The nonanthropomorphic position, the ability to see and think in terms of process as well as in terms of myth and allegory or personal drama, is the basis for separating process in nature from psychological motivation. This, the gift of the ancient Greeks to the world, is assumed to be open only to intellectual understanding. While the Greek discovery represents a great step forward in intellectual and cultural evolution, the basic neural potential for performing this distinction and differentiation is, I suggest, a functional part of childhood everywhere. The experiences remain largely nonverbal— although not entirely so, if we take into consideration some of the astonishing and beautiful cosmic questions of the child. But such experience is subject to recall in remarkably similar terms by gifted or creative people from the most widely differing eras and backgrounds—social, cultural, and geographical.

In his autobiography (14), Bernard Berenson gives an exceptionally full and rich description of his discovery in early childhood of the sense of "Itness" as an integration with the on-going process in nature. The position achieved by the child in this experience of "psychological equipoise" became a stabilizing influence, a life-long goal, and also the basis of a highly skillful method of observing and learning. His experiences continued through childhood and boyhood. In particular, one balmy summer morning he "climbed up a tree stump and felt suddenly immersed in Itness.[4] I did not call it by that name, I had no need for words. It and I were one." Of these moments of exodus into the temporal and spatial continuum, Berenson says that "in consciousness this was due not to me, but to the not-me, of which I was scarcely more than the subject in the grammatical sense." As an adult he sees himself "as an energy of a given force in radiation and of a certain power of resistance," but adds that "he seems to be the same in these respects as I remember being at the end of my sixth year," when he became latently aware that the form-creating harmony of his perceiving body and the form-creating harmony of nature were one and the same process, the process which eventually enabled him to perceive and to estimate value in art as the appearance of living motion in his perceptual "readings," even of a stone fresco. The experience at the dawn of conscious life remained the "guardian angel," returning in memory to remind him that "It was my goal, It was my real happiness," the happiness of perceptual creation upon which all other creativity depends.

Further examples are to be encoun-tered in autobiographical recollections from Africa, Asia, Europe (North and South), and the Americas. These descriptions—some fleeting, some lengthy—of the inception of a relationship with nature express not only a deep need to make a world the way the world was made, but also the need to make a piece of the real world in which one lives with others. This is, I suggest, the only truly effective counter-agent to the forces of internal conflict which until recently were considered the major subjects of study, the main background to purpose in life. Once the theme of world-making is seen as a basic human goal, the emphasis upon discontinuity and the pressure toward self-knowledge represented by the Socratic axiom "Know thyself," so essential to the differentiation of the idea of man into the image of the unique self, seems to diminish in value, or to have reached a saturation point as a useful psychosocial concept. This is not to say that the concept of the individual or of individuality is outmoded or even fully realized in social aims, but that, as a tool for the shaping of thought about human behavior, self-exploration as an aim in itself is not merely less and less effective but is unconsciously supporting a dangerous trend toward neurotic self-interest on a world-wide scale.

This point of view calls for a re-definition of human individuality, not only in terms of human relations, but also in terms of man's total relations with "outerness," with nature itself. Such a redefinition seems feasible in terms of the developing intellectual climate. The pattern of cultural evo-lution that has been long in the making is one in which the concept of ecology, the study of the relations between or-ganisms and their total environment, will play a major part.

---

[4] It may be remembered that Rilke as an adult at Duino underwent a similar experience in a tree cleft.

References

1. "What is true metaphor?" Owen Barfield inquires (*Poetic Diction: A Study in Meaning* [London: Faber and Faber, 1952], p. 86); and in replying to his own question, he refers to Bacon's statement in *The Advancement of Learning:* "Neither are these only similitudes, as men of narrow observation may conceive them to be, but the same footsteps of nature treading or printing upon several subjects or matters." Barfield's conclusions are quoted here as typical of a kind of thinking that is central to my thesis, for this treatment of perception and the making of meaning leads to the observation that it is these very footsteps of nature "whose noise we hear alike in primitive language and in the finest metaphors of poets."

2. I am here following especially the leads of Albert M. Dalcq, "Form and Modern Embryology," and Konrad Z. Lorenz, "The Role of Gestalt Perception in Animal and Human Behaviour," in L. L. Whyte, ed., *Aspects of Form* (London: Percy Lund Humphries & Co. Ltd., 1951); also of L. L. Whyte on formative processes in his many publications, particularly *The Unitary Principle in Physics and Biology* (London: Cresset Press, 1949).

3. Practice of social work in the fullest sense is in fact the only field of applied human ecology that I know of. In direct relation to the ideas presented here, I find that in 1940 Dr. Eduard C. Lindeman, Professor of Social Philosophy at the New York School of Social Work, saw "Ecology" as "an instrument for the integration of science and philosophy" in a paper of that title ("Ecology: An Instrument for the Integration of Science and Philosophy," *Ecological Monographs, 10* [July 1940] pp. 367–372), although he did not apply this directly to social work.

4. The Edith Cobb Collection, now in the possession of the New York School of Social Work, Columbia University.

5. Julian Huxley, *Evolution: The Modern Synthesis*. New York: Harper & Brothers, 1943.

6. Keats' term for intuition. His *Letters* embody a highly developed theory of cognition, resembling also Wordsworth's and Traherne's.

7. Arnold Gesell, *Embryology of Behavior*. New York: Harper & Brothers, 1945.

8. W. H. Thorpe, *Learning and Instinct in Animals*. Cambridge: Harvard University Press, 1956.

9. Conrad Aiken, *A Letter from Li Po and Other Poems*. New York: Oxford University Press, 1955.

10. Geoffrey H. Hartman, *The Unmediated Vision*. New Haven: Yale University Press, 1954.

11. Marjorie L. Hourd, *The Education of the Poetic Spirit*. London: William Heinemann, Ltd., 1949.

12. John Oman, *The Natural and the Supernatural*. New York: The Macmillan Company; and Cambridge: Cambridge University Press, 1931.

13. Dorothy Waley Singer, *Giordano Bruno, His Life and Thought*. New York, Abelard-Schuman, Limited, 1950.

14. Bernard Berenson, *Sketch for a Self-Portrait*. New York: Pantheon Books, Inc., 1940.

Remembered Landscapes

GRADY CLAY

Edith Cobb has said that the "embryology of mind" requires landscapes. What can be said then of the mind's later growth, when landscapes become remembered landscapes?

The image of youth as a lost paradise is ancient and widespread. Resplendent with recollection of golden moments of leisure, the images are inextricably connected with places that gave them significance.

Since about 1870 the dream of youthful paradise has been more and more frequently judged puerile, sentimental, maudlin, and even neurotic. A conflict has arisen between the necessity of recollection and the ban on sweetness, but it has not stopped the memories. From Marcel Proust to the endless autobiographical flow of cool introspection and self-analysis in the modern novel and the New Yorker, the result has been more "objective" recollection.

Whether told in the warm colors of now outmoded passion or anesthetized and dissected, the important things remain: something of continuing significance in the texture of remembered landscapes will always be deliberated and conjured up for ourselves and others.

THE EDITORS

ALL ACROSS A CONTINENT the bulldozers wait for spring. In the drafting rooms, the landscape architects trace out the contour lines of vast new neighborhoods; the surveyors stomp indoors with muddy boots and notebooks full of figures to be translated into a new suburban landscape.

Wherever frost, mud and ice prevail, an entire industry marks time until it

Landscape, *7(2):7–10, Winter 1957–58. Reprinted by permission.*

can open up another building season and carve its desires upon the landscape. In the south, the earth-movers never stop for weather; but further north, men must wait, repair their scoops and scrapers, their dozers and diggers, and stay indoors until the season opens.

And finally, by the season's end, another million or so acres will have been subjected to the currently most-popular treatment: "urbanization." Another million acres, more or less, will have been converted from open farmland, field, swamp, and wooded hillside into a newly urbanized landscape. The contours will have disappeared; man will have cut down the intervening hills, dug into the resisting slopes, filled up the marshes and swamplands, smoothed out the rough spots, and installed in their place a new angularity, a new geometry.

This will be a rawer, yellower, dustier landscape by midsummer; a landscape of houses and sidewalks, for-sale signs, airport runways and hardstands, express highways cutting precisely across a random wilderness, slicing exactly through cluttered cities; a landscape of asphalt, concrete, angularity, predictability.

Already the promises are being made, and options taken by the advance men who draw pretty pictures of "planned industrial districts," or "Your Home in The Country" as they act out the ancient pageantry of the salesman-developer of land. "Without the jobs we bring, you won't be able to afford all this," they argue, waving their hands over a suburban map, while a reluctant planning commission listens wearily. "Let us in, and your land will be worth double," they confide to possible objectors in the neighborhood.

In the face of all this—the bulldozer, the advance man, the job promise—the landscape crumbles, the trees and grass disappear, the random quality of the countryside becomes more predictable. We know that around the next corner will be, neither cornfield nor open plain, but more developments, more structures.

And yet, deep within many of us is the knowledge (carefully and deliberately pushed underground as we grow older) that the miracles of lush grass, tangled undergrowth, a running brook, a tree to climb, a view to enjoy—these should somehow be protected and preserved for yet another generation, as our world moves ponderously toward a totally-urbanized landscape.

This feeling, this knowledge, is an esthetic one, and has been discounted by land-developers until lately. Now, in this "tight-money" era, they are discovering a wide resistance among millions of families shopping for new homes, new neighborhoods. "We want more trees," clamour the housewives attending a "Women's Congress on Housing" in Washington. Even the highway-builders, notorious for, and proud of, their disregard for trees and running brooks, are now being admonished by the Federal Highway Administrator Bertram D. Tallamy to improve the looks of their roads because it is "just as cheap or cheaper to use the advantages nature has given."

The Scenery of Childhood

Man's need for a bit of wilderness among the concrete, for a respite from angularity and aridity, is a deep need, long recognized by poet and artist, and noted by sensitive men for ages. But now a research project at Massachusetts Institute of Technology has produced some findings which may even impress developers themselves—men who never believe a fact unless it is statistical.

In the summer of 1955, a class of architects and planners at M.I.T. wrote short papers on their memories of their childhood environments. These papers tempted two men, Alvin K. Lukashok and Kevin Lynch, to undertake a series of detailed interviews with 40 persons, none of them professionally involved in urbanism or design. These ranged from 18 to 32 years in age, had come mostly from the Boston area, but included a few persons from New York, and as far distant as Vienna. The Lukashok-Lynch study grew out of one assumption: *"that present adult memories reflect actual childhood preoccupations."* Or —that memories of childhood are important emotional underpinnings of modern man's life, and are to be laughed away or disregarded at our peril and great loss.

What they discovered would gladden the hearts of all concerned with creating a decent, pleasant environment out of America's crowded and ugly cities, and of insuring such surroundings in the new Outer and Inner Suburbias.

For these people remember most vividly those elements of their childhood which involved landscape—lawns and pavement surfaces, foliage, woods and green hills, and water in the landscape. Among these childhood memories, lawns were associated with spaciousness, a sense of freedom. "I was very happy," recalls one of those interviewed. "I remember the first day we got there I was running over the lawns, up the slopes because it was so much of a change."

"Of the various types of (landscape) floor coverings mentioned, grass is the best liked, then dirt that can be dug or molded, and after that, any smooth surface that allows roller-skating or bicycling." (From the report.) . . . "The floor surfaces a child seems to dislike

(Photo by Elizabeth B. Hecker.)

are asphalt on open spaces that otherwise would remain grassy, and brick, gravel and cobblestones placed where he can suffer a fall. Of the few people who mention brick-paved surfaces, none talk about the visual quality of such surfaces, all dislike the uneven texture it provides. . . . This surface, rarely the conscious concern of the designer, so often left to the surveyor contractor, or to sheer custom, thus turns out to be the most important sensuous element of all."

Trees, trees and more trees reappear in these childhood memories, and are mentioned with great warmth. For children, trees offer ideal places for play, shade, climbing, carving, hiding, and for creating wonderful childhood fantasies. Hardly a single interview failed to reveal this affinity for trees.

"We had a big oak tree in front of our house which was sort of a favorite. Then they were planting these small ones which were supposed to grow into these big ones someday but never got a chance because we would hang on them or try to climb them and break them off. During the latter part of the spring, when they used to get real bushy, they almost covered the street in a sort of tunnel. It gave a nice feeling of security. You could walk on the outside of the trees and be blocked off from the road. Yet it wasn't the same thing as barriers you encountered in Brookline, it was sort of a friendly thing. We carved our initials in them. You could do a lot of things with them, climb them, hit them, hide behind them . . . you could see out between the trees, but none could see in, and we used to hide in there and watch people. . . . I always liked to watch people."

"I can remember in summertime it was beautiful along Saratoga and Bennington Streets because it was shaded. We used to play on the front stoop of somebody's house, and it was so nice to get under the trees for shade. . . ."

Or: "There were maple trees along our street. It's about the only tree I've ever been conscious of; it's the first tree I remember the name of, I've thought of it all my life. White birch trees, too, have a special meaning. But when I think of Scarsdale, I think of maple trees."

This may cause shudders among professional recreationalists, for these interviews showed clearly that "children seem to prefer to play anywhere but the playground." Some comments: "We would rather play in the foliage. . . . Our idea when I was 9 or 10 years old was not to play on the playground, but to find some place where

there were rocks and broken bottles . . . a lot of trees and holes to fall into. . . . Out in back was a big field where the grass was over your head. They have cut that down now, and made a playground out of it so it isn't as romantic."

And: "I remember Riverside Park before it turned into developed areas. . . . I remember there being a lot more space to play in. The big change, the big spurt of playground building had gone up. I was sort of pleased with having all these nice places to play in, the nice things that moved and worked, etc., but there simply wasn't enough space just to go and play in and do idiotic things in. You couldn't dig, for example; I like to dig. There weren't many places to dig because of the hard asphalt on the playground."

"So many people remember with pleasure, the overgrown lot, thick brush and woods," say the authors. "It is sufficient to give us pause in our treatment of 'waste' or 'untidy' areas or in the design of play spaces."

"On the whole, people remember keenly and with pleasure the hills that were in the vicinity. . . . Because so often a hill is not the best site for a building, it is the last part of an area developed, allowing it to remain wild and therefore attractive to children."

What Do These Findings Mean?
Oddly enough, none of the persons interviewed complained about too much space. Most professional designers nowadays seem to be avoiding excessively big, open spaces, in replanning cities ("prairie planning" has become a dirty word among many American planners, especially those influenced by the C.I.A.M. city-square tradition). But few children remembered too much space—perhaps because there are so few urban spaces with "too much" open space. In fact,

(Photo by Lorraine Burgess.)

the authors conclude that "There is so little open space left in our cities that, in their hunger for it, most people cannot afford to be concerned with the quality of the space, they are grateful that it is there." And, as one of those interviewed put it:

"Boston Common is one of the best parks in New England. They'll never get that."

Finally, "The feelings and key elements that run through all the interviews on childhood memories have strong similarities. The remembered children were sharply aware of lawns and floor surfaces; they delighted in foliage, woods and green. There is a strong and pleasant memory for hills and for water in the landscape. A somewhat ambiguous fascination with the big transportation vehicles is equally clear. There was conscious alertness to spatial qualities, a definite preference for openness and spaciousness, and distaste for crowdedness. Even in childhood, perception is strongly colored by associations of social status: by 'niceness,' by cleanliness, by upkeep and by money."

To my mind, the most disturbing thing coming out of this study was the authors' conclusion that most of the people interviewed "rarely conceive of the city as something that might

"... something of continuing significance in the texture of remembered landscapes will always be deliberated and conjured up for ourselves and others." (Photo by Joyce R. Wilson from National Audubon Society.)

give pleasure in itself. They hardly expect to have an enjoyable city environment, as if a mild civic nausea were a normal burden of man's existence."

If this conclusion may be justified in America, what must one expect from the great booming cities of the world—Johannesburg, Singapore, Agadir in Morocco, São Paulo, Hong Kong—where a flood of villagers and farmers is inundating whole square miles of cities, wiping out the green corners,

the open lots, with overcrowding of appalling intensity?

One is forced to conclude from the M.I.T. studies, if not from a knowledge of the world as it exists without benefit of such research, that somehow the delights of waste spaces, of odd lots, of tangled woodlands left in the midst of housing developments—somehow these must be protected and preserved. For the city—not merely the Exurbs, the Suburbs, the Rolling

Knolls and other high-income area neighborhoods—must keep these delights if it is to keep the affections of its people.

Under the impact of housing shortages, of get-rich-quick pressures on city officials, the urban green spaces are disappearing at an appalling rate. And with the disappearance of these "wastes" we lose trees, hills, water, fields of tall grass, the hidden and hiding places of the world, and in the end, an important part of life itself.

The Individual As Man/World

ALAN W. WATTS

There is a poignancy in remembering scenes of childhood that only adults can experience. Maturity is necessary for cherishing far-off places and times. The spilling over of self into the world during childhood prevents that kind of consciousness.

In animals, too, it seems that juveniles take place for granted. They become territorial—aware of spatial bounds and the adult dimensions of occupancy—and are fully cast in their life roles only at sexual maturity. Without a territory they do not so mature and gain self and identity.

The crisis of anonymity that preoccupies so much of contemporary drama and literature is, then, an art that can issue only from "adult" minds that lack some essential element, minds anguished by dreadful isolation, unable to form a new continuity with the universe and unwilling to escape the problem by seeking to become a child again. There is little enough in Jean-Paul Sartre's memories of his early years, for instance, to elicit anything but a kind of faint mal-de-mer. *Childhood is no longer something to feel poignant about; it is absurd, nauseating.*

But fortunately pessimistic existentialism is not the only attitude open to an adult mind. Indeed, alienation and absurdity may be inevitable only in a certain form of egomania which increasingly focuses the individual's attention upon himself. A fanatic preoccupation with self leads not to discovery but to an abysmal lack of identity. It would appear that the self is discoverable only in its own loss and that it is not identifiable without an intense sense of environment.

THE EDITORS

The Psychedelic Review, *1(1):55–65, June 1963. Reprinted by permission.*

(*Prefatory Note*: The following was originally delivered as an impromptu lecture for the Social Relations Colloquium at Harvard University on April 12th, 1963. Although the subject was not discussed in the lecture itself, its theme is closely related to the expansion of consciousness achieved through psychedelic substances. With proper "set and setting," the psychedelics are very frequently successful in giving the individual a vivid sensation of the mutual interdependence of his own behavior and the behavior of his environment, so that the two seem to become one—the behavior of a unified field. Those who uphold the impoverished sense of reality sanctioned by official psychiatry describe this type of awareness as "depersonalization," "loss of ego-boundary," or "regression to the oceanic feeling," all of which, in their usual contexts, are derogatory terms suggesting that the state is hallucinatory. Yet it accords astonishingly well with the description of the individual which is given in the behavioral sciences, in biology and in ecology.

(Theoretically, many scientists know that the individual is not a skin encapsulated ego but an organism-environment field. The organism itself is a point at which the field is "focused," so that each individual is a unique expression of the behavior of the whole field, which is ultimately the universe itself. But to know this theoretically is not to *feel* it to be so. It was possible to calculate that the world was round before making the voyage that proved it to be so. The psychedelics are, perhaps, the ship, the experimental instrument by which the theory can be verified in common experience.)

THERE IS A colossal disparity between the way in which most individuals experience their own existence, and the way in which the individual is described in such sciences as biology, ecology, and physiology. The nub of the difference is this: the way the individual is described in these sciences is not as a freely moving entity within an environment, but as a process of behavior which *is* the environment also. If you will accurately describe what any individual organism is doing, you will take but a few steps before you are also describing what the environment is doing. To put it more simply, we can do without such expressions as "what the individual is doing" or "what the environment is doing," as if the individual was one thing and the doing another, the environment one thing and its doing another. If we reduce the whole business simply to the process of doing, then the doing, which was called the behavior of the individual, is found to be *at the same time* the doing which is called the behavior of the environment. In other words, it is quite impossible to describe the movement of my arm except in relation to the rest of my body and to the background against which you perceive it. The relations in which you perceive this movement are the absolutely necessary condition for your perceiving at all. More and more, a "field theory" of man's behavior becomes necessary for the sciences.

Yet this is at complete variance with the way in which we are trained *by our culture* to experience our own existence. We do not, generally speaking, experience ourselves as the behavior of the field, but rather as a center of energy and consciousness which sometimes manages to control its environment, but at other times feels com-

"... a conception of the individual ... as a reciprocal interaction between everything inside the skin and everything outside it, neither one being prior to the other, but equals, like the front and back of a coin." (Photo courtesy Head Ski Co., Inc.)

pletely dominated by the environment. Thus there is a somewhat hostile relationship between the human organism and its social and natural environment, which is expressed in such phrases as "man's conquest of nature," or "man's conquest of space," and other such antagonistic figures of speech.

It would obviously be to the advantage of mankind if the way in which we feel our existence could correspond to the way in which existence is scientifically described. For what we feel has far more influence upon our actions than what we think. Scientists of all kinds are warning us most urgently that we are using our technology disastrously, eating up all the natural resources of the earth, creating incredibly beautiful but wholly non-nutritious vegetables by altering the biochemical balances of the soil, spawning unbelievable amounts of detergent froth which will eventually engulf cities, overpopulating ourselves because of the success of medicine, and thus winning our war against nature in such a way as to defeat ourselves completely. All this advice falls on deaf ears, because it falls on the ears of organisms convinced that war against nature is their proper way of life. They have to be unconvinced, and can be, to some extent, by intellectual propaganda, scientific description, and clear thought. But this moves relatively few people to action. Most are moved only if their feelings are profoundly affected. We need to *feel* this view of our individual identity as including its environment, and this must obviously concern scientists who are trying to find ways of controlling human feelings.

This problem has an important historical background. It is curious how the ancient philosophical debates of the Western world keep coming up again and again in new forms. Any question of the definition of the individual always becomes involved with the old argument between nominalism and realism. I do not wish to insult the intelligence of this learned audience, but, just to refresh your memories, the realistic philosophy of the Middle Ages and of the Greeks was not what today we call realism. It was the belief that behind all specific manifestations of life such as men, trees, dogs, there lies an archetypal, or ideal, form

of Man, of Tree, of Dog, so that every particular man is an instance of that archetypal form, and that behind all men is something which can be called Man with a capital M, or the "substance" of man, of "human nature."

The nominalists argued that this was a mere abstraction, and that to regard Man (capital M) as possessing any effective existence was to be deluded by concepts. There are only specific, individual men. This idea is carried on in one of the most remarkable forms of modern nominalism, General Semantics, which argues that such abstractions as "The United States," "Britain," or "Russia," are so much journalistic gobbledygook.

Most people working in the sciences tend to be nominalists. But if you carry nominalism to its logical conclusion, you are involved in awkward problems. Not only would there be no such thing as Man, Mankind, or Human Nature, but it would also follow that there are no individual men, because the individual man is an abstraction, and what really exists is only an enormous amalgamation of particular molecules. If you pursue this further and inquire about the individual entities composing the molecules, there is an interminable array of nuclear and sub-nuclear realities, and if *these* in turn are to be regarded as the only realities, then the reality which we call a man is simply the association of discontinuous particles. This is the *reductio ad absurdum* of nominalism carried too far. The nominalist and realist viewpoints are actually *limits*—to borrow a term from mathematics. I have often thought that all philosophical debates are ultimately between the partisans of structure and the partisans of "goo." The academic world puts a heavy emphasis on structure: "Let's be definite, let's have rigor and precision, even though we are studying poetry." But the poets will reply: "We are for goo, and you people are all dry bones, rattling in the wind. What you need is essential juices, and therefore more goo is necessary to liven you up." But when we want to know what goo is, and examine it carefully, we eventually turn up with a structure, the molecular or atomic composition of goo! On the other hand, when we try to examine the structure itself to study the substance of its bones, we inevitably come up with something gooey. When the microscope focus is clear, you have structure. But when you reach beyond the focus and what confronts you is vague and amorphous, you have goo because you cannot attain clarity. Structure and goo are essential limits of human thought; similarly, the nominalist-structural and the realist-gooey will always be essential limits in our thinking. We must be aware that today, the particular academic and scientific fashion leans heavily in the direction of structure and nominalism.

To take a specific example, we all know that in modern medicine nominalism and structuralism hold the field. When you go to a hospital, you are liable to go through a process of examination by specialists working upon you from different points of view. They will treat you as a non-person, from the very moment you enter. You are immediately put in a wheelchair—a symbol of the fact that you are now an object. You will be looked at piecemeal, X-rays will be taken of various organs, and special tests will be made of their functioning. If anything is wrong, you will be taken to a medical mechanic, i.e., a surgeon, who will use his equivalents of wrenches, screwdrivers and blowtorches to make certain mechanical alterations in your organism, and it is hoped you will get along fairly well with these repairs!

But the opposite, minority school of medicine will say: "This is all very well, and the services of the surgeon are sometimes greatly welcomed, but man must be considered as a whole. He has complicated metabolic and endocrine balances, and if you interfere with him seriously at one point, you will affect him unpredictably at many others, for man is an organic whole." Such are accused of being woolly-minded, old-fashioned doctors, mostly from Europe, with a kind of nature-cure background, who will use diet, complicated fasts, and massage. The poor layman doesn't know whether to deliver himself over to these old-fashioned naturalistic doctors or to Mr. Sawbones with his very up-to-date qualifications.

Fortunately, precise science is coming to the rescue of our man-as-a-whole. More recent studies are showing just how diseases formerly regarded as specific entities, or afflictions of a particular organ or area, are actually brought about by responses of the central nervous system, acting as an integrated whole. We are beginning to see how man, as a complex of organs, is not an *addition* of parts, like an automobile. His various organs are not to be treated as if they were assembled together, but by seeing the physical body as a unified or integrated pattern of behavior—which is just what we mean when we talk about an entity or thing. What happens when we have the feeling that we understand something, when we say, "Oh, I see"? If a child asks, "Why are the leaves green?" and you answer, "Because of the chlorophyll," and the child says, "Oh!," that is *pseudo*-understanding. But when the child has a jigsaw puzzle and sees how it all fits together, then the "Oh!" has a different meaning from the "Oh!" following the chlorophyll explanation. To understand anything is to be able to fit various parts into a system which is an integrated whole, so that they "make sense."

As organic diseases are fitted into a whole, and problems of crime or psychosis in individual behavior are fitted in with a pattern of social behavior that makes sense, that is consistent with those kinds of behaviors, we say "Aha! —now I see!"

Fascinating work is being done in studying the ways in which the individual as a system of behavior is related to his biological and social environments, showing how his behavior may be explained in terms of those environments. One of the people who has done very important work in this sphere is our distinguished colleague, B. F. Skinner. I cite his work because it brings out these ideas in a marvellously clear, crucial, and provocative way, and because it is evidence for conclusions which he himself does not seem to have realized. One of his most important statements is in his book, *Science and Human Behavior:*[1]

The hypothesis that man is not free is essential to the application of scientific method to the study of human behavior. The free inner man who is held responsible for the behavior of the external biological organism is only a prescientific substitute for the kinds of causes which are discovered in the course of a scientific analysis.

He is talking, of course, about the chauffeur inside the body, or what Wittgenstein called the little man inside the head: this is for him a prescientific substitute for the kinds of causes for behavior which are discovered in the course of scientific analysis. He continues:

All these alternative causes lie *outside* the individual. The biological substratum itself is determined by prior events in a genetic process. Other important events are found in the nonsocial environment and in the culture of the individual in the broadest possible sense. These are the things which *make°* the individual behave as he does. For them he is not responsible and for them it is useless to praise or blame him. It does not matter that the individual may take it upon himself to control the variables of which his own behavior is a function or, in a broader sense, to engage in the design of his own culture. He does this only because he is the product of a culture which *generates°* self-control or cultural design as a mode of behavior. The environment determines the individual even when he alters the environment.[1] [° Emphasis mine —A.W.W.]

I am not going to quarrel with this finding. I am not a clinical or experimental psychologist and am therefore unqualified to criticize Skinner's evidence. Let's take it for Gospel, simply for the sake of argument.

But there is a rather heavy emphasis upon the individual being the puppet. "All these alternative causes," i.e., the kinds of causes discovered in the course of scientific behavior, "lie outside the individual," i.e., outside this wall of flesh and bag of skin. The individual is therefore passive. This is psychology in terms of Newtonian physics. The individual is a billiard ball upon which other balls impinge, and his seemingly active behavior is only a passive response. Skinner admits the individual does and can alter the environment, but when he does so, he is *being made* to do so. This is put forth in such a way as to make the individual appear passive and the things *really* controlling his behavior outside him.

[1] New York: Macmillan, 1953, pp. 447–448.

But the reciprocal relationship between the knower and the known, common to all the sciences, is set aside here although he mentions it elsewhere.

A laboratory for the study of behavior contains many devices for controlling the environment and for recording and analyzing the behavior of organisms. With the help of these devices and their associated techniques, we change the behavior of an organism in various ways, with considerable precision. But note that the organism changes our behavior in quite as precise a fashion. Our apparatus was designed by the organism we study, for it was the organism which led us to choose a particular manipulandum, particular categories of stimulation, particular modes of reinforcement, and so on, and to record particular aspects of its behavior. Measures which were successful were for that reason reinforcing and have been retained, while others have been, as we say, extinguished. The verbal behavior with which we analyze our data has been shaped in a similar way: order and consistency emerged to reinforce certain practices which were adopted, while other practices suffered extinction and were abandoned. (All scientific techniques, as well as scientific knowledge itself, are generated in this way. A cyclotron is "designed" by the particles it is to control, and a theory is written by the particles it is to explain, as the behavior of these particles shapes the nonverbal and verbal behavior of the scientist.)[2]

In one of his essays, he has a cartoon of one mouse saying to another, "Boy, have I got that guy up there fixed! Every time I press this bar, he gives me some food!"

Although Skinner seems in general to be stressing heavily the point of view that the individual is the puppet in the field in which he is involved, he is nevertheless stating here the opposite point, that the individual organism, mouse, or guinea pig, in the experiment is nevertheless determining the environment even when, as in a laboratory, the environment is designed to control the specific organism. The environment of a rat running in a barn is not designed to control the rat, but the more it is so designed, the more the rat is involved in and shaping its environment. He writes elsewhere that what he has been saying

does not mean that anyone in possession of the methods and results of science can step outside the stream of history and take the evolution of government into his own hands. Science is not free, either. It cannot interfere with the course of events; it is simply part of that course. It would be quite inconsistent if we were to exempt the scientist from the account which science gives of human behavior in general.[3]

Now we might well object: "Look, Professor Skinner, you say we are completely conditioned behavior-systems. We cannot change anything. At the same time, you are calling upon us to embark upon the most radical program of controlling human behavior. How can you write *Walden II*, a utopia? Are you not a monstrosity of inconsistency by calling for responsible human action and at the same time saying that we have no freedom?" But is this actually a contradiction? He is saying two things, both of which can be valid, but he does not provide a framework in which the opposed points of view can make sense. Similarly, the physicist says light can be considered as a wave or as a particle system. These sound mutually exclusive to the nonphysicist. In the same way, the advocacy of a planned development of

---

[2] "The Design of Cultures," *Daedalus*, Summer 1961, p. 543.

[3] *Science and Human Behavior*, p. 446.

human resources and potentials, coupled with the idea that the individual is not a self-controlling, skin-encapsulated ego, needs some further concept to help it along. The following passage clinches the problem.

Just as biographers and critics look for external influences to account for the traits and achievements of the men they study, so science ultimately explains behavior in terms of "causes" or conditions which lie beyond the individual himself. As more and more causal relations are demonstrated, a practical corollary becomes difficult to resist: it should be possible to *produce* behavior according to plan simply by arranging the proper conditions.[4]

There is the contradiction which necessarily arises in a psychology with a language system which incorporates into present scientific knowledge an outmoded conception of the individual —the individual as something bounded by skin, and which is pushed around by an environment which is not the individual. Skinner is naturally aware that his emphasis on our passive relationship to conditioning causes is rather unpalatable.

The conception of the individual which emerges from a scientific analysis is distasteful to most of those who have been strongly affected by democratic philosophies . . . it has always been the unfortunate task of science to dispossess cherished beliefs regarding the place of man in the universe. It is easy to understand why men so frequently flatter themselves—why they characterize the world in ways which reinforce them by providing escape from the consequences of criticism or other forms of punishment. But although flattery temporarily strengthens behavior, it is questionable whether it has any ultimate survival value. If science does not confirm the assumptions of freedom, initiative, and responsibility in the behavior of the individual, these assumptions will not ultimately be effective either as motivating devices or as goals in the design of culture. We may not give them up easily, and we may, in fact, find it difficult to control ourselves or others until alternative principles have been developed.[5]

There the book ends, and there is no suggestion as to what those principles might be, even though they are implied in his conclusions.

When an individual conspicuously manipulates the variables of which the behavior of *another*° individual is a function, we say that the first individual controls the second, but we do not ask who or what controls the first. When a government conspicuously controls its citizens, we consider this fact without identifying the events which control the government. When the individual is strengthened as a measure of counter-control, we may, as in democratic philosophies, think of him as a starting point. [°My emphasis—A.W.W.]

Isn't this political nominalism?

Actually, however, we are not justified in assigning *to anyone or anything* the role of prime mover. Although it is necessary that science confine itself to selected segments in a continuous series of events, it is *to the whole series* that any interpretation must eventually apply.[6] [My emphases—A.W.W.]

We are now listening to a man who represents himself as a behavioristically oriented, non-mystical, on-the-whole materialistic, hard-headed scientist. Yet this passage is the purest mysticism, which might have come straight from Mahayana Buddhism: "We are not justified in assigning to anyone or anything the role of prime

[4] "Freedom and the Control of Men," *The American Scholar*, Vol. 25, No. 1, Winter, 1955–56, p. 47.

[5] *Science and Human Behavior*, p. 449.

[6] *Ibid.*, pp. 448–449.

mover." No segment, no particular pattern of integrated behavior within whatever universe we are discussing can be called the prime mover. Now this is the *Dharmadhatu* doctrine of Mahayana Buddhism, that the universe is a harmonious system which has no governor, that it is an integrated organism but nobody is in charge of it. Its corollary is that everyone and everything is the prime mover.

In Skinner's language, the popular conception of the inner self, the little man inside the head who is controlling everything, must be replaced by the whole system of *external* causes operating upon the individual, the whole network of causal relationships. But this language obscures a very simple thing: when there is a certain cause in the external environment whose effect is always a particular individual behavior, you are using very cumbersome language for something you can describe more simply. For when you find these two things going together, you are actually talking about one thing. To say that Event A causes Event B is a laborious way of saying that it is one Event C. If I lift up this book by a corner, all the corners are lifted up at the same time. If I lift up an accordion, there is an interval between cause and effect. Similarly when we study the individual's behavior, we are studying a system of relationships, but we are looking at it too close up. All we see is the atomic events, and we don't see the integrated system which would make them make sense if we could see it. Our scientific methods of description suffer from a defective conception of the individual. The individual is not by any means what is contained inside a given envelope of skin. The individual organism is the particular and unique focal point of a network of relations which is ultimately a "whole series"—I suppose that means the whole cosmos. And the whole cosmos so focused is one's actual self. This is, whether you like it or not, pure mysticism. Skinner is saying that although science is a method of observation which, by reason of the blinkers of the head, is limited to our one-thing-at-a-time method of thought, science can only look at the world area by area. But science also becomes the method of understanding its own limitations. When you conduct any experiment, you must be careful to exclude variables you cannot measure. When you want to keep something at a constant temperature, you must put it into some kind of heat-and-cold-proof or shock-proof, or cosmic-ray-proof system. So by excluding variables and by having to do it rigorously, you begin to understand how really impossible it is to do except in very special cases. In this way, the scientist, by attempting to isolate events and by looking as rigorously as he can at one segment of the world at a time, becomes aware of the fact that this looking at things simply in segments, although it is a form of very bright, clear, conscious knowledge, is also a form of ignorance. For it is a form of "ignore-ance," ignoring everything that is not in that segment. Therefore he becomes aware of the fact that just this is *ultimately* what you can't do. You *can* do it only to discover you *cannot* do it.

I commend these observations to you simply to show how a scientific thinker whose whole stance is in the direction of mechanism, of regarding the human being as a kind of biological puppet, must be forced by the logic of his own thinking to conclusions of a rather different kind. He states these questions in veiled language, so that neither he nor his colleagues will see their disastrously unrespectable implications!

Suppose, then, it becomes possible for us to have a new sense of the individual, that we all become conscious of ourselves as organism-environment fields, vividly aware of the fact that when we move, it is not simply my self moving inside my skin, exercising energy upon my limbs, but also that in some marvelous way the physical continuum in which I move is also moving me. The very fact that I am here in this room at all is because you are here. It was a common concurrence, a whole concatenation of circumstances which go together, each reciprocally related to all. Would such an awareness be significant? Would it add to our knowledge? Would it change anything, make any difference? Seriously, I think it would; because it makes an enormous difference whenever what had seemed to be partial and disintegrated fits into a larger integrated pattern. It will of course be impossible finally to answer the question, "Why does that satisfy us?," because to answer this question exhaustively I would have to be able to chew my own teeth to pieces. In the pursuit of scientific knowledge, always watch out for that snag. You will never get to the irreducible explanation of anything because you will never be able to explain why you want to explain, and so on. The system will gobble itself up. The Gödel theory has roughly to do with the idea that you cannot have any system which will define its own axioms. An axiom in one system of logic must be defined in terms of another system, etc., etc. You never get to something which is completely self-explanatory. That of course is the limit of control, and the reason why all systems of control have ultimately to be based on an act of faith.

The problem confronting all sciences of human behavior is that we have the evidence (we are *staring* at it) to give us an entirely different conception of the individual than that which we ordinarily feel and which influences our common sense: a conception of the individual not, on the one hand, as an ego locked in the skin, nor, on the other, as a mere passive part of the machine, but as a reciprocal interaction between everything inside the skin and everything outside it, neither one being prior to the other, but equals, like the front and back of a coin.

God's Acre

ERICH ISAAC

What appears repeatedly to have saved Christianity from itself is the fecklessness of Christians and the vitality of heathen ideas available to them. Christianity has unblushingly incorporated wisdom from all manner of pagan lumber yards and competing theologies.

The sanctity of place is probably as old as totemism and the caves of Altamira. Both pre-Classical Greece and the Hebrew ethos have important elements of that kind of reverence and wonder. Post-Roman Christianity evolved the blithe notion that places on earth are all more or less alike. To prove the point, it set about destroying unique myths associated with Roman shrines and utilizing the shrines themselves as Christian temples for the contemplation of distant matters and nearby souls.

But Christianity never triumphed entirely over the essentially religious experience of nature which links men to their immediate, particular environments. Nor has it been able to outgrow its own primitive traditions of pilgrimage and its imagery of a Holy Land. It is only when such steersmen as the spirits of Platonic mysticism and industrial technology have brought them to the verge of truly homogenizing their environment that Christians show their refractory streak and think of preserving nature.

THE EDITORS

TO BROACH THE theme of holiness or the sanctity of place in geography always verges on the trite or the impertinent. Geographers are, of course, well aware that there are holy places and that landscapes have been modi-

Landscape, *14(2):28–32, Winter 1964–65.*
Reprinted by permission.

fied under the pressure of religious beliefs or dogmas. To elaborate on the theme of holiness is to intrude on a domain preempted by theology, and few ventures are as dangerous as the transgression of that sacred boundary. One's armor consists in the time-honored incontrovertible assertion that holy places are *places* and therefore properly within the geographic sphere. As for triteness, consolation lies in a celebrated slogan of linguistic philosophy that "philosophy begins and *ends* in platitude"—its conclusions are only the repetition of what we normally say. The platitude with which I am going to begin and end is that holy places belong to God.

Many current views hold that religious knowledge is not what it purports to be but is a disguised way of stating something else, or is a device, often described as rather underhanded, for effecting certain changes in society or in individuals. The root of these views is in the conviction that religion corresponds to no objective reality but is a psychological aberration, a disease of mind or language, or a means of political control, economic exploitation, etc. In general, such views are expressive of a pervasive popular positivism known as "commonsense," but also are a reflection of the analytical difficulties of dealing with the "holy."

The studies of R. R. Marett, R. Otto, L. O. J. Söderblom, G. van der Leeuw, S. Mowinckel and others have established that the experience of the "holy" is absolutely empirical and that such difficulties as exist in its definition are mainly analytical. As far as we know, everywhere that he exists man reports experiences of reality which impress themselves upon him as highly exceptional—what is felt is an extremely impressive "Other." The state produced by such experience is described in various ways—a sense of absolute dependence, amazement and in extreme cases fear and terror.

The attempt to explain the religious experience as a facet of normal or abnormal psychology, popular though it has been, does not really come to grips with the phenomenon. It has been asserted, for example, that the fear described in association with the experience of the holy is really the fear associated with some danger such as a threatening natural calamity. However, the "Otherness" which provokes the fear has no single mode of appearance and can come as in the Second Book of Samuel "The Lord thundered from heaven" or in absolute silence—the still small voice in the First Book of Kings.

One knows of states of fear for which there is no apparent cause, such as claustrophobia, but in such instances it is often possible to trace the disorder and even cure it. Psychology has no cure for religious fear. Of course, by transgressing the boundaries of its positive findings, psychology in effect creates its own metaphysics and describes religious experience in terms of its own metaphysical categories, reducing the likelihood of religious fear being recognized as such even by the experiencing subject. Freud's attempt to explain away religious fear by saying "the whole thing is patently infantile" fails to take into account the possibility that religious fear is not a projection of childhood fear of one's father—even if one feared one's father —but can have its origin in a "holy encounter." Freud himself makes a metaphysical judgment regarding religious experience as a projection of an "ideal authority derived from our childhood guardians." The absence of clear and present dangers alone does not justify this conclusion.

But if the fear of the holy is not the ordinary fear experienced in the presence of a clear threat nor a pathological state nor yet a projection of childhood experience of authority, what is this fear? In the plethora of studies on the essence and nature of religion and religions, the component of "power," "might" and "overwhelmingness" are stressed. The experience of the holy produces, according to Rudolph Otto (*The Idea of the Holy,* Galaxy Book, 1958), a peculiar quality of the "uncanny" and "aweful," this "even on the highest level of all, where the worship of God is at its purest." Otto tries to suggest the quality of the emotion by comparing it to the element of horror and shudder in ghost stories experienced even among the more sophisticated. The feeling of numinous terror toward the holy brings out a characteristic of the holy important in the Bible—the Wrath of God, a concept clearly analogous to the *ira deorum* of many religions. "It is . . . 'like a hidden force of nature,' like stored up electricity, discharging itself upon anyone who comes too near . . ." Wrath is not anger in the sense of moral retribution upon wrongdoers, but is experienced as part of the nature of the deity. One accustomed to think of the deity's power in terms of popular contemporary religiosity, that is to say, in moral categories as power applied righteously in retribution and as punishment for moral transgression "must see in this 'wrath' mere caprice and wilful passion." (*Idea of the Holy.*)

Religious language itself uses the analogy of force and power, e.g., Mark and Matthew use the term *a dunamis* while similar use is found frequently in the Hebrew Bible in the word *koach.*

It is evident that the Biblical language refers to Power in a highly exceptional sense. In discussing this Power, as well as parallel concepts of primitives, one cannot use our concept of supernatural, for the verification of the power is entirely empirical. Indeed, S. Mowinckel (*Religion und Kultus*, Göttingen 1953) regards the notion of Power or powers as the basic experience of the magic world view. The importance of this notion in primitive thought and the phenomenology of religion was first stressed by the missionary R. H. Codrington in 1878 in a letter in which he discusses the Melanesian *mana*. In all cases, in the event of anything unusual, whether bad or good, the natives speak of *mana*. "Magic is certainly manifested by Power; to employ power, however, is not in itself to act magically." *Mana's* power is not of the ordinary kind, nor does it enjoy any moral value, for it resides alike in European medicine and in the poisoned arrow. Similarly the *orenda* of the Iroquois is used to bless and curse alike—it is simply a matter of power, for good or ill. The same is true of other concepts found among the American Indians: the *wakanda* of the Sioux and the Algonquin *manitu* are examples. The ancient German *hamingja* corresponds to these as well.

The reaction to the experience of the holy is an ambivalent one. Possibly Bertholet (*Theologische Zeitschrift*, 1958) is right in seizing on the ambivalence of love as at least the psychic equivalent from which the experience of the holy may be understood. The fear is inextricably bound to the attraction, the one feeding the other. One fears to be consumed in the overwhelming character of the experience. The ambivalent attitude toward "Power" is seen in Hebrew usage. The word "on" means power, strength, wealth (Isaiah, Hosea). But "aven" derived from the same root, means mischief, calamity and evil. It is likely that a distinction between the good and bad aspect of Power has led to a differentiation of a formerly "neutral" word. Mowinckel and van der Leeuw both have remarked on the ambivalent character of the experience of the holy, G. van der Leeuw finding the best analogy in love and hate. (*Religion in Essence and Manifestation*, Harper Torchbooks, 1963.) In India the god Shiva is both destroyer and procreator, his spouse Durga is both destroyer and eternal mother. On the highest levels of contemporary religion the relation with the supernatural is interpreted in the same ambivalent terms in which we experience people, and that relation is held to be explicable only in terms of confrontation with God as a Person.

Places are frequently thought to possess, or be possessed by, the power of the holy. On almost all levels of culture there are segregated, dedicated, fenced, hallowed spaces. The holy, or hallowed, means separated and dedicated: *sanctus* means exceptional or that which has to be placed within boundaries. The peculiar repulsion and attraction which are experienced in the face of the power of the holy are reflected in the attitude towards the holy place which combines an element of absolute unapproachability and an element of fascination and attraction. Innumerable examples could be cited of this ambivalence in ritual directives for the approach or shunning of sacred places, many of which must be both approached and shunned according to prescribed patterns and according to selected characteristics

151

of the believer. Geographically this has been of the greatest importance, not only because of the effect upon the particular place designated as holy but in all the incidental effects on other places which participate in the ceremonial safeguards or participate in other ways in the economic or political aspects of the ritual system.

Yet ritual prohibitions of access or the demand for cultic purity in the approach to a holy place should not obscure the fact that the holy is neither primarily clean or unclean, pure or impure, but a dynamic potency. It is as if "its powerfulness creates for it a place of its own." (van der Leeuw) The sacred is neither completely moral nor without further qualification pure or desirable. Uzzah was struck down not because of a divine arbitrariness and still less because of divine justice. In a manner of speaking, he was struck down by the morally neutral potency of the Lord "Af 'Hashem'." Holiness may indeed defile. G. van der Leeuw points out that the Roman *tribunis plebis* was so sacred that merely to meet him in the street made an individual impure. In the Biblical view the prescribed participation in sacrificial rites is sometimes actually defiling (Numbers 19). The contrast pure-impure is not the equivalent of sacred versus profane. In no religious system is purity and impurity a simple dyad but rather elements in a threefold distinction between that which is pure, that which is impure and that which is neither. Moreover, the pure is by no means always holy. Common bread is pure, but only showbread is holy (Numbers 4:7). Pure and impure are both aspects of the holy, so that to derive the concept of holiness from a contrast of pure and impure is certainly mistaken. It is similarly wrong to regard the contrast between sacred

and profane as arising out of the distinction between what is dangerous and what is not. "Power has its own specific quality which forcibly impresses men as dangerous. Yet the perilous is not sacred, but rather the sacred dangerous."

Perhaps nowhere is the holy more bound up in spatial categories than in early Greek thought. The overwhelming impression derived from both early Greek religion and "science" is that the sanctity of the spatial order is fundamental. The very concept of *Nomos*, or law, is probably based upon the division of land. A sacred enclosed tract in ancient Greece was called *nemos* and its sanctity was derived from the powerful and threatening forces invested in it. One ancient name for this force is *Nemesis* and in the archaic period when nemos was the typical holy place, *Nemesis*, as F. M. Cornford has plausibly suggested (*From Religion to Philosophy*, London, 1912) was probably the automatic avenger of trespass. In the religion of Homer and Hesiod, gods as well as men are confined by the bounds set by destiny or *moira*, which itself means "allotted portion." Each god has a province within which his supremacy cannot be challenged. "The original conception of moira thus turns out to be spatial rather than temporal. We are to think of a system of provinces, coexisting side by side, with clearly marked boundaries." (Cornford)

The extent to which the spatial conception of the divine order had become rooted in the Greek mind is reflected in the writings of Anaximander who believed that all life constituted a transgression—which must eventually be paid for—of the spatially allotted domains of the elements. The creation

"On almost all levels of culture there are segregated, dedicated, fenced, hallowed spaces." The Tholos at Delphi. (Photo courtesy Greek National Tourist Office.)

or birth of any of the things of the world according to Anaximander is only brought about by the malappropriation of the elements of earth, air, fire and water from their proper domain. Thus, to take an animal body, its proper substance is earth, while water is appropriated for blood, air for breath and fire for warmth. The dissolution of death constitutes proper repayment, for each stolen portion returns to its original place. What is an "element" in Anaximander is a god in Homer and Hesiod, and in both Anaximander's "science" and in Homeric and earlier religions the elements or gods are themselves only transient phenomena destined to make reparation and return into that from which they came. What Anaximander calls the "limitless thing," the ultimate stage of existence, which alone is incorruptible and un-

dying is in Homeric religion *moira*. Anaximander uses a deceptively moral language in speaking of the elements making "reparation" and paying "the penalty of their injustice." But there is no personal moral responsibility involved any more than there is in Greek myth and drama, for all is ordained and the very fact of existence means that the sanctified structure of things is disturbed and it will and must be restored.

The spatial aspect of the holy was apparently a minor theme in late Greek philosophy and in the best known discussion, Sextus Empiricus dismisses even relatively sophisticated discussions of the relation of God and space:

And so far as regards these statements of the Peripatetics, it seems likely that the First God is the place of all things. For

153

according to Aristotle the First God is the limit of Heaven. Either, then, God is something other than the Heaven's limit, or God is just that limit. And if He is other than the Heaven's limit, something else will exist outside Heaven, and its limit will be the place of Heaven, and thus the Aristotelians will be granting that Heaven is contained in place; but this they will not tolerate, as they are opposed to both these notions—both that anything exists outside of Heaven and that Heaven is contained in place. And if God is identical with Heaven's limit, since Heaven's limit is the place of all things within Heaven, God—according to Aristotle—will be the place of all things; and this, too, is itself a thing contrary to sense.

It seems remarkable that in Jewish theology with its heavy stress on the universal and absolutely transcendental nature of God, one finds an extremely common substitution of "place"—*makom*, for the name of God, a usage which continues in contemporary orthodox Judaism. This usage probably derives from "holy place," *makom kadosh*, and presumably reflects earlier spatial associations for the sacred. It is striking how the discussion of Sextus Empiricus seems to echo a discussion found in the Midrash Rabbah. R. Huma said in R. Ammi's name: Why is it that we give a changed name to the Holy One, blessed be He, and that we call him "the place"? Because He is the place of the world. R. Jose b. Halafta said: We do not know whether God is the place of His world or whether His world is His place, but from the verse "Behold, there is a place with me" (Exodus) it follows that the Lord is the place of His world, but His world is not His place. R. Isaac said: It is written "The eternal God is a dwelling-place" (Deuteronomy); now we do not know whether the Holy One, blessed be He, is the dwelling place of His world or whether His world is

His dwelling place. But from the text, "Lord, Thou hast been our dwelling place" (Ninetieth Psalm) it follows that the Lord is the dwelling place of His world but His world is not His dwelling place. (Midrash Rabbah, and Genesis II.)

Max Jammer in his *Concepts of Space* pointed out that this metonymy is not simple metaphorical usage, but the result of a theological process which widened the boundaries of the holy to encompass the world. The early rabbis gave Moses the credit for widening the sphere of the holy: "Say the Rabbis, 'Moses made Him fill all the space of the Universe, as it is said, The Lord He is God in the heaven above, and upon the earth beneath; there is none else.'" (Deuteronomy.)

It seems evident that since the concept of holiness is so inextricably bound up with a spatial order the notion of property and boundary may well be grounded in a religious attitude. In Indonesia and Polynesia, for example, taboo quite commonly is a means for establishing possession in land. In Amboina, it is reported, trespassers are supposed to be struck by leprosy. The seemingly sophisticated notion that taboos are inventions of a "power élite" to protect their property, or that they arose solely, or even primarily, for utilitarian reasons is not in accord with the facts. This attitude is expressive of modern myths based on our economic life in which acquisition is more important than possession, and in which "property" can always be translated into "commodity." Indeed, the economistic myth is an inadequate explanation even in the context of "western" economies. It is certainly wrong for societies where property "is a 'mystical' relation between owner and owned" and where "the possessor is not the *beatus possidens*, but the depository of a power that is superior to himself." (van der Leeuw) The psyche of contemporary man too reveals emotions and feelings in regard to property which may be independent of its market value. There is a plus of value attached to gifts received; there are sentimental attitudes to objects which do not permit the owner to consider the idea of parting with them under any circumstances or which lead him to place a value on things astronomically above any conceivable market value. In a negative sense, the property of a despised person can arouse strong reactions—thus the fine gesture of the Dutch admiral Tromp who used to remark, "I spit into the ocean to spite the British." There are analogous attitudes towards the body, which while not identical with a person—the "I" of the person is really not identical with its anatomy—is yet in law and custom held to be, if not identical with the person, his very own. Assault on the body or maltreatment of one of its parts is considered assault on the person. Beyond the body we regard the belongings of a person, or at least certain objects he has used or made as bound up with his personality.

What is a psychic datum in modern man has been shown by J. Pederson (*Israel, Its Life and Culture*, 1926) as characteristic of the old Hebrew attitude to property in general. All of a man's possessions, including his tools, his house, his animals, are permeated by his soul; and, as O. R. Jones has noted, his entire household is regarded as a whole—the extended personality of the man who is its head. (*The Concept of Holiness*, London, 1961.) It is interesting to note in this connection that the association of holy place with the personality of the god has been felt by some writers so strongly that they have believed the holy place was selected because it suited characteristics the god supposedly had, or the reverse, that the physical characteristics of the holy place actually determined certain attributes bestowed upon the god. Paula Philippson in her discussion of Greek gods and landscapes tends to the former view; and W. Robertson Smith in his studies on the religion of old Arabia to the other.

The stress thus far has been on classical, Biblical and later materials, as well as on general psychological considerations about the relationship between personality and property. Ethnological materials reveal similar attitudes on a wide scale. Indeed we find among very primitive gathering and hunting cultures a strong sense of personality which manifests itself in extreme form in attitudes toward personal possessions. That, in spite of a maximum of cooperation and mutual sharing, there is a strong sense of individuality and property is not at all in accord with the romantic picture of the primitive. But, although ethnopsychology and studies on the foundations of property among primitive peoples are still in their infancy, such a generalization seems to be warranted on the basis of studies of particular cultures, and on the basis of systematic inquiries into the problem of property.

In primitive hunting and gathering groups, in spite of the fact that utensils and implements are not products of specialized craftsmanship and each makes the tools he uses, these are clearly recognized as his sole property. Ownership is often signified with special marks; thus Semang women in Malaya notch their combs and similar ownership marks are known among

155

Bushmen. Women have personal property and men are neither free to use nor dispose of it without their consent. Personal property rights can also be established by the finding of a fruit tree, a bee hive, termites, etc. Ownership by an individual can be extended to such intangibles as songs and dances. On the Andaman Islands only the owner can recite and sing his songs and his proprietary right is not extinguished by death. Similarly among the Bushmen, Nippold points out that rock paintings of an individual cannot be tampered with even after his death. (*Die Anfange des Eigentums bei den Naturvölkern*, etc., The Hague, 1954.)

W. Robertson Smith, in his classic *Lectures on the Religion of the Semites,* sought to examine the idea of holiness as the connection thought to exist between particular deities and holy places. Noting that gods were generally conceived as being in possession of a land and holy places, he stressed that certain aspects of this possession could be equated with our legal concepts of property. He felt that ethnological evidence pointed to the probability that ownership in crops preceded ownership in land and that particular places whose "crops" were tended by the gods came to be the property of the gods. In Jewish and much later in Islamic agricultural law, a grainfield was described as Baal's field, or "house of Baal" or "field in the house of Baal," the pagan terminology surviving (indeed into modern Hebrew) long after its pagan associations were forgotten. In other words, land where crops grow, metaphorically speaking, through the efforts of the god rather than through extensive application of human labor, became eventually the property of the deity. Robertson Smith pursued this as a suggestive analogy, but felt that holy places belonged to

the world of taboo, a realm of ideas quite separate from and antecedent to legal concepts of individual property. But in view of our discussion, it seems that W. Robertson Smith's analogy of personal property with the god's relation to a sacred place had more validity than he was willing to allow. Certainly in the Biblical view the holy is that which *belongs* to God. The frequent Biblical combination of the possessive pronoun with "holy" actually indicates property ownership and is not merely a matter of usage. Boundaries were set so that people should not approach Sinai, the holy mountain, "or touch the border of it." (Exodus) These boundaries were property lines, for whenever reference is made to a holy mountain in the Bible it is spoken of as the property of God. (Isaiah, Exodus, Daniel, Joel.)

The notion of divine property in a place is of course different from common concepts of property. Sacred places are not identified by deeds nor are they transferable. Perhaps the only earmark of private property in land as commonly understood is the boundary. But trespassing is invited under certain circumstances, for some holy places in the Bible and elsewhere bestow sanctuary, e.g. Heracleum on the Canobic Nile, Phoenician, Greek and Roman centers of refuge for lawbreakers, etc. In this respect, public rather than private property constitutes the more appropriate analogy to divine property.

Suggestive though the hypothesis is, the question must remain open whether the concept of distinct property boundaries in land has religious roots. Certainly, as far as we know, "personal" property boundaries in land were conceptually associated at an early stage with divine property. Open tracts of sacred land, on which it was forbidden to cut fodder, fell trees or limit game were, and still are for that matter in popular superstition, exceedingly common in the Arabian peninsula and elsewhere in the Arab world. These pre-Islamic usages regarding sacred tracts were in some instances confirmed by Muhammed, e.g., for the Haram of Mecca and the Hima of Wajj at Taif. These data are suggestive for they deal with lands distinctly experienced as belonging to "somebody" and imbued with his "personality" as distinct from the lands which are held to be the property of the tribe as a whole. Among hunting and gathering peoples territorial boundaries, not of the tribe (which is but a linguistic and culture-historical unit) but of the separate bands, are well established. Land is indeed the only property which can be called communal and such communal property ends at the borders of the band's territory, this being the property for which the people will fight as a group. This does not mean that there is no "personal" property within the group's territory. The band's communal ownership of its territory does not mean that there is an organized communal exploitation of its resources. Such exploitation is entirely an individual matter. Individual claims to trees and other resources are established and recognized, and they are sometimes honored for years, even if the individual does not exploit them. Indeed there are distinct religious sanctions against infringement of private property. Theft on the Andaman Islands is avenged by Puluga, whose punishment extends not only to the thief but to the whole community. The Semang of Malaya and the Bushmen apparently also consider theft as a serious transgression and among Pygmies awesome divine retribution is expected

to be the result. The sacred place or site is known in these cultures too, and demarcation objects are recognized as boundary markers just as we have posted warnings against trespass.

No matter how much data are accumulated from contemporary primitive or ancient societies, it is not possible to decide whether the notion of personal property is rooted in the experience of a divine personality. In the first place contemporary primitives are not primordial and have had as long an "historical life" as contemporary civilized man. More important, however, is the inescapable methodological impasse involved in any attempt to say whether personal private property in land came before or after the bestowal of "property rights" in land upon a deity. To me it seems most probable that the limits of the holy place were the first property lines honored by man, but whether this is true or not, what is certain is that the notion of property sacred to the god is extremely early and nearly universal. The concept has psychological roots in the experience of the deity as a personality. In the spatial structuring of man's world, the god's personality finds an extension in a portion of the landscape deemed appropriate in some fashion to the nature of the god. The impact of the experience of the "holy place" was important not in early Greek and Jewish thought alone, for this thought gave rise to Judæo-Christian ideas about space which in turn played a part in the development of the concept of absolute space.

I have stressed the "experience of the holy" as the source of sanctity imputed to a place. Always and everywhere the claim to religious knowledge rests upon the belief that an

Ghosts at the Door

actual encounter occurred at a certain place and to certain people. Individual experience, of course, may not lead to permanent sanctification and segregation of holy places. Within the data that can be studied by comparative religion, however, the earliest sanctification of a place arises from the religious experience of charismatic patriarchs. The "founded" religious places are sanctified by a religious leadership, hereditary or not, which bases its authority upon the founder. It should be evident that custom often replaces the original sense of awe; pure formalism is much more widespread than any experience of the holy, and such formalism may serve nonreligious practical and social ends without arousing any fervor. As Claude Levi-Strauss put it: "Emotion is indeed aroused, but only when the custom, in itself indifferent, is violated." Yet observance and indifferent custom too can be the source of religious experience though not the historically primary one as some students of comparative religion used to claim. Observance *per se* may indeed benumb awe, but observance may also fan it again. For customs given by society as external norms may, and often do, give rise to sentiment.

JOHN B. JACKSON

Some things are more fashionable than others. Not, that is, more in vogue at a particular time, but more vulnerable to changing judgments. The landscape arts (and therefore the landscape itself) may be looked upon as though styles were drawn and withdrawn by an arbitrary hand—the capricious dictates of a master arbiter or the whims of a clique such as that which designs women's clothes.

The study of the history of landscape architecture (that is, of gardens) may be approached in that way, as though it were a sequence of earth costumes. Although each style can be seen to have been appropriate to its day, it is also considered as somehow determined by "taste" and the independent creativity of contemporary artists.

Since about 1910 a predominant temper in art has held the "world of art" answerable only to itself. Art was analyzed in abstract concepts so completely removed from life that a kind of inner esoteric reality found in mathematical games was created. Said Henri Focillon, there is a "life of forms in art" which has its own independent dynamics. One may wonder, as a consequence, how many students in college art courses and innocent participants on guided tours in museums have been misled into thinking that, if they knew about symmetry and mass and form and line, or about Rococo or Romanesque or Expressionist, they would know what it was all about.

Such is the history of criticism. The artists themselves are something else. Landscape architects are not intimidated by the smell of the earth or seduced by anti-organic intellectuality. They know

Landscape, *1(1):3–9, Autumn 1951. Reprinted by permission.*

*that a certain combination of lawn and
tree may be labeled "The Pastoral," but
also that it was something more than a
term for a Renaissance literary posture,
and that it was and is too deeply connected with the nonfashionable to be
explained as mere style. The Pastoral is
one of the environmental configurations
to which we respond out of profound
biological and cultural depths.*

THE EDITORS

THE HOUSE STANDS by itself, lost
somewhere in the enormous plain.
Next to it is a windmill, to the rear a
scattering of barns and shelters and
sheds. In every direction range and
empty field reach to a horizon unbroken by a hill or the roof of another
dwelling or even a tree. The wind
blows incessantly; it raises a spiral of
dust in the corral. The sun beats down
on the house day after day. Straight as
a die the road stretches out of sight
between a perspective of fence and
light poles. The only sound is the
clangor of the windmill, the only movement the wind brushing over the grass
and wheat, and the afternoon thunder-
heads boiling up in the western sky.

But in front of the house on the side
facing the road there is a small patch
of ground surrounded by a fence and
a hedge. Here grow a dozen or more
small trees—Chinese elms, much
whipped and tattered by the prevailing gale. Under them is a short ex-
panse of bright green lawn.

Trees, lawn, hedge and flowers—
these things, together with much care
and great expenditure of precious
water, all go to make up what we call
the front yard. Not only here on the
Western farmstead, but on every one
of a million farms from California to
Maine. All front yards in America are
much the same, as if they had been
copied from one another, or from a
remote prototype.

They are so much part of what is
called the American Scene that you are
not likely to wonder why they exist.
Particularly when you see them in the
East and Midwest; there they merge
into the woodland landscape and into
the tidy main street of a village as if
they all belonged together. But when
you travel west you begin to mark the
contrast between the yard and its surroundings. It occurs to you that the
yard is sometimes a very artificial
thing, the product of much work and
thought and care. Whoever tends them
so well out here on the lonely flats
(you say to yourself) must think them
very important.

And so they are. Front yards are a
national institution—essential to every
home, like a Bible somewhere in the
house. It is not their size which makes
them so. They are usually so small that
from a vertical or horizontal distance
of more than a mile they can hardly be
seen. Nor are they always remarkable
for what they contain. No; but they are
pleasant oases of freshness and moving shade in the heat of the monoto-
nous plain. They are cool in the summer and in the winter their hedges and
trees do much to break the violence of
the weather. The way they moderate
the climate justifies their existence.

They serve a social purpose, too.
By common consent the appearance
of a front yard, its neatness and luxuri-
ance, is an index of the taste and enterprise of the family who owns it. Weeds
and dead limbs are a disgrace, and the
man who rakes and waters and clips
after work is usually held to be a
good citizen.

So this infinitesimal patch of land,
only a few hundred square feet, meets
two very useful ends: it provides a
place for outdoor enjoyment, and it

159

indicates social standing. But in reality does it always do those things?

Many front yards, and by no means the least attractive, flourish on the Western ranches and homesteads many miles from neighbors. They waste their sweetness on the desert air. As for any front yard being used for recreation, this seems to be a sort of national myth. Perhaps on Sunday afternoons when friends come out from town to pay a visit chairs are tentatively placed on the fresh cut grass. For the rest of the week the yard is out of bounds, just as the now obsolete front parlor always used to be. The family is content to sit on the porch when it wants fresh air. It admires the smooth lawn from a distance.

The true reason why every American house has to have a front yard is probably very simple: it exists to satisfy a love of beauty. Not every beauty, but beauty of a special, familiar kind; one that every American can recognize and enjoy, and even after a fashion recreate for himself.

The front yard, then, is an attempt to reproduce next to the house a certain familiar or traditional setting. In essence the front yard is a landscape in miniature. It is not a garden; its value is by no means purely esthetic. It is an enclosed space which contains a garden among other things. The patch of grass and Chinese elms and privet stands for something far larger and richer and more beautiful. It is a much reduced version, as if seen through the wrong end of a pair of field glasses, of a spacious countryside of woods and hedgerows and meadow.

Such was the countryside of our remoter forebears; such was the original, the proto-landscape which we continue to remember and cherish, even though for each generation the image becomes fainter and harder to recall.

Loyalty to a traditional idea of how the world should look is something which we not always take into account when analyzing ourselves or others. Yet it is no more improbable than loyalty to traditional social or economic ideas or to traditional ideas in art. The very fact that we are almost completely unaware of our loyalty to a proto-landscape allows us to express that loyalty with freedom. We have not yet been made ashamed of being old-fashioned. But what precisely is that landscape which our memory keeps alive and which an atavistic instinct tries to recreate?

It is not exclusively American. It is not New England or Colonial Virginia or Ohio, it is nothing based on pictures and vacation trips to the East. It is northwestern Europe. Whatever the ethnic origin of the individual American, however long his family may have lived in this country, we are all descendants, spiritually speaking, of the peoples of Great Britain and Ireland, of the Low Countries, and to a lesser extent of northern France and western Germany. It was from those countries that the colonists transferred the pattern of living which is still the accepted pattern of living in North America. It may not remain so much longer, but that is something else again. We are all of us exiles from a landscape of streams and hills and forests. We come from a climate of cold dark winters, a few weeks of exuberant spring, and abundant snow and rain. Our inherited literary and popular culture both reflect that far-off environment, and until recently our economy and society reflected it too.

For almost a thousand years after the collapse of the Roman Empire the history of Europe was the history of a slow and persistent de-forestation.

When the Classic civilization began to die, Europe ceased to be one unit and became two. The region around the Mediterranean preserved a good deal of the Roman heritage; for the most part its population did not greatly change; and the land remained under cultivation. But for several reasons the entire northwestern portion of the Empire—Great Britain, the Lowlands, northern France and western Germany began to revert to wilderness. Roads, towns, cities and farms were gradually abandoned, fell into ruin, and in time were hidden by brush and forest. The peoples whom we call the Barbarians and who later moved in from the East had thus to reclaim the land all over again. They were obliged to take back from the forest by main force whatever land they needed for farms and pastures and villages. They were pioneers no less tough than those who settled our own West. Their numbers were so few and their means so primitive that every lengthy war and every epidemic saw much newly cleared land revert to undergrowth once more. It was not until a century ago that the last wastelands on the continent were put under cultivation. The whole undertaking was an extraordinary phase of European history, one which we know very little about. How well it succeeded is shown by the fact that Holland, now a land of gardens, originally meant "Land of Forests."

Could this incessant warfare with the forest fail to have an effect on the men who engaged in it? Does it not help to explain an attitude toward nature quite unlike that of the peoples farther south? The constant struggle against cold and solitude and darkness, the omnipresent threat of the wilderness and the animals that lived in it in time produced a conviction that there was no existing on equal terms with nature. Nature had to be subdued, and in order to subdue her men had to study her and know her strength. We have inherited this philosophy, it sometimes seems, in its entirety: this determination to know every one of nature's secrets and to establish complete mastery over her; to love in order to possess and eventually destroy. It is not a point of view which has worked very well here in the West. If we had thought more in terms of cooperation with a reluctant and sensitive environment, as the Mediterranean people still do, and less in terms of "harnessing" and "taming," we would have not made such a shambles of the Southwestern landscape.

That aggressive attitude is however only part of what the earliest farmers in northern Europe bequeathed us. Since they created the human landscape themselves and under great difficulties, they had a deep affection for it. They looked upon the combination of farmland and meadow and forest as the direct expression of their way of life. It was a harsh and primitive landscape, just as by all accounts it was a harsh and primitive way of life, but it was not lacking in a sentiment for the surrounding world, nor an element of poetry. The perpetual challenge of the forest stirred the imagination as did no other feature in the environment. It was the forest where the outlaw went to hide, it was there that adventurous men went to make a new farm and a new and freer life. It teemed with wolves, boars, bears and wild oxen. It contained in its depths the abandoned clearings and crumbling ruins of an earlier civilization. It was a place of terror to the farmer and at the same time a place of refuge. He was obliged to enter it for wood and game and in search of pasture. For hundreds of years the forest

161

determined the spread of population
and represented the largest source of
raw materials; it was an outlet for
every energy. Its dangers as well as its
wealth became part of the daily existence of every man and woman.

When at last it was removed from
the landscape our whole culture began
to change and even to disintegrate. A
Frenchman has recently written a book
to prove that the decline in popular
beliefs and traditions (and in popular
attitudes toward art and work and
society) in his country was the direct
outcome of the destruction a century
ago of the last areas of untouched
woodland. If he is correct, how many
of those traditions can be left among us
who have denuded half a continent in
less than six generations? The urge to
cut down trees is stronger than ever.
The slightest excuse is enough for us
to strip an entire countryside. And yet
—there is the front yard with its tenderly cared-for Chinese elms, the
picnic ground in the shadow of the
pines, and a mass of poems and pictures and songs about trees. A Mediterranean would find this sentimentality
hard to understand.

The old ambivalence persists. But
the reverence for the forest is no longer
universal. Our household economy is
largely free from dependence on the
resources of the nearby forest, and any
feeling for the forest itself is a survival
from childhood associations. Until the
last generation it might have been said
that much of every American (and
northern European) childhood was
passed in the landscape of traditional
forest legends. Time had transformed
the reality of the wilderness into myth.
The forest outlaw became Robin Hood,
the vine-grown ruins became the castle
of Sleeping Beauty. The frightened
farmer, armed with an ax for cutting
firewood, was the hero of Little Red

Riding Hood and the father of Hänsl
and Gretl. In a sense, our youngest
years were a re-enactment of the formative period of our culture, and the
magic of the forest was never entirely
forgotten in adult life. Magic, of course,
is part of every childhood; yet if a
generation grew up on the magic of
Superman and Mickey Mouse and
Space Cadet instead, if it lived in the
empty and inanimate landscape which
provides a background for those figures,
how long would it continue to feel the
charms of the forest? How long would
the Chinese elms be watered and
cared for?

After the forest came the pasture,
and the pasture in time became the
lawn. When a Canadian today cuts
down trees in order to start a farm he
says he is "making land." He might
with equal accuracy say that he is
"making lawn," for the two words have
the same origin and once had the same
meaning. Our lawns are merely the
civilized descendants of the Medieval
pastures cleared among the trees. In
the New Forest in England a "lawn"
is still an open space in the woods
where cattle are fed.

So the lawn has a very prosaic background, and if lawns seem to be typically northern European—the English
secretly believe that there are no true
lawns outside of Great Britain—that is
simply because the farmers in northern
Europe raised more cattle than did the
farmers near the Mediterranean, and
had to provide more feed.

As cattle and sheep-raising increased
in importance, the new land wrested
from the forest became more and more
essential to the farmer; he set the highest value on it. But to recognize the
economic worth of a piece of land is
one thing: to find beauty in it is quite
another. Wheat fields and turnip

162

(Photo courtesy Vermont Development Department.)

patches were vital to the European
peasant, yet he never, as it were, domesticated them. The lawn was different. It was not only part and parcel of
a pastoral economy, it was also part of
the farmer's leisure. It was the place
for sociability and play; and that is
why it was and still is looked upon
with affection.

The common grazing land of every
village is actually what we mean when
we speak of the village common, and it
was on the common that most of our
favorite group pastimes came into being. Maypole and Morris dances never
got a foothold in northern America,

and for that we can thank the Puritans.
But baseball, like cricket in England,
originated on the green. Before cricket
the national sport was archery, likewise a product of the common. Rugby,
and its American variation football, are
both products of the same pastoral
landscape, and golf is the product of
the very special pastoral landscape of
lowland Scotland. Would it not be possible to establish a bond between national sports and the type of terrain
where they developed? Bowling is
favored in Holland and near the Mediterranean—both regions of gardens and
garden paths. A continental hunt is

163

still a forest hunt; the English or Irish hunt needs a landscape of open fields and hedgerows. Among the many ways in which men exploit the environment and establish an emotional bond with it we should not forget sports and games. And the absence among certain peoples of games inspired by the environment is probably no less significant.

In the course of time the private dwelling took over the lawn. With the exclusion of the general public a new set of pastimes was devised: croquet, lawn tennis, badminton, and the lawn party. But all of these games and gatherings, whether taking place on the common or on someone's enclosed lawn, were by way of being schools where certain standards of conduct, and even certain standards of dress were formed. And in an indefinable way the lawn is still the background for conventionally correct behavior. The poor sport walks off the field; the poor citizen neglects his lawn.

Just as the early forest determined our poetry and legend, that original pasture land, redeemed from the forest for the delectation of cows and sheep, has indirectly determined many of our social attitudes. Both are essential elements of the proto-landscape. But in America the lawn is more than essential; it is the very heart and soul of the entire front yard. We may say what we like about the futility of these areas of bright green grass; we may lament the waste of labor and water they represent here in the semi-arid West. Yet to condemn them or justify them on utilitarian or esthetic grounds is to miss the point entirely. The lawn with its vague but nonetheless real social connotations is precisely that landscape element which every American values most. Unconsciously he identifies it with every group event in his life: childhood games, commencement and graduation with white flannels or cap and gown, wedding receptions, "having company," the high school drill field and the Big Game of the season. Even the cemetery is now landscaped as a lawn to provide an appropriate background for the ultimate social event: How can a citizen be loyal to that tradition without creating and taking care of a lawn of his own? Whoever supposes that Americans are not willing to sacrifice time and money in order to keep a heritage alive regardless of its practical value had better count the number of sweating and panting men and women and children, pushing lawn-mowers on a summer's day. It is quite possible that the lawn will go out of fashion. But if it does it will not be because the toiling masses behind the lawn-mower have rebelled. It will be because a younger generation has fewer convivial associations with it; has found other places for group functions and other places to play: the gymnasium, the school grounds, the swimming pool or the ski run. It will be because the feeling of being hedged in by conventional standards of behavior has become objectionable.

To hedge in, to fence in; the language seems to shift in meaning and emphasis almost while we use it. Until not long ago neither of those words meant to keep in. They meant to keep out. A fence was a de-fense against trespassers and wild animals. The hedge was a coveted symbol of independence and privacy. Coveted, because it was not every farmer who could have one around his land.

Like the lawn and the tree, the hedge is something inherited from an ancient agricultural system and an ancient way of life. The farming of the Middle Ages is usually called the open-field system.

Briefly, it was based on community ownership (or community control) of all the land—ownership by a noble amounted to the same thing—with fields apportioned to the individual under certain strict conditions. Among them were rules as to when the land was to lie fallow, what day it was to be plowed, and when the village cattle were to be allowed to graze on it. Much modified by social and economical revolutions, the open-field system still prevails over much of northern Europe. Fences and hedges, as indications of property lines, naturally had no place in such a scheme.

In the course of generations a more individualistic order came into being, and when for several good reasons it was no longer desirable to have the cattle roaming at will over the country-side the first thing to appear, the first change in the landscape, was the hedge. With that hedge to protect his land against intruders of every kind the individual peasant or farmer began for the first time to come into his own, and to feel identified with a particular piece of land. He did not necessarily own it; more often than not he was a tenant. But at least he could operate it as he saw fit, and he could keep out strangers.

Each field and each farm was defined by this impenetrable barrier. It served to provide firewood, now that the forests were gone, shelter for the livestock, and a nesting place for small game. Most important of all the hedge or fence served as a visible sign that the land was owned by one particular man and not by a group or community. In America we are so accustomed to the fence that we cannot realize how eloquent a symbol it is in other parts of the world. The Communist governments of Europe do realize it, and when they collectivize the farms they first of all destroy the hedgerows—even when the fields are not to be altered in size.

The free men who first colonized North America were careful to bring the hedge and fence with them, not only to exclude the animals of the forest, but as indications of the farmers' independent status. Hedges and fences used to be much more common in the United States than they are now. One traveller in Revolutionary New England enumerated five different kinds—ranging from stone walls to rows of up-ended tree stumps. In Pennsylvania at the same period fields were often bordered with privet. As new farms were settled in the Midwest every field as a matter of course had its stone wall or hedge of privet or hawthorn, or permanent wooden fence. And along these walls and fences a small wilderness of brush and vine and trees soon grew, so that every field had its border of shade and movement, and its own wild life refuge. The practice, however inspired, did much to make the older parts of the nation varied and beautiful, and we have come to identify fences and hedges with the American rural landscape at its most charming.

As a matter of fact the hedge and wooden fence started to go out of style a good hundred years ago. Mechanized farming, which started then, found the old fields much too small. A threshing machine pulled by several teams of horses had trouble negotiating a ten acre field, and much good land was wasted in the corners. So the solution was to throw two or more fields together. Then agricultural experts warned the farmers that the hedge and fence rows, in addition to occupying too much land, harbored noxious animals and birds and insects. When a farm was being frequently reorganized,

"And along these walls and fences a small wilderness of brush and vine and trees soon grew, so that every field had its border of shade and movement . . ." (Photo by J. C. Allen and Son.)

first for one commercial crop then another, depending on the market, permanent fences were a nuisance. Finally Mr. Glidden invented barbed wire, and at that the last hedgerows began to fall in earnest.

There were thus good practical reasons for ridding the farm of the fences. But there was another reason too: a change in taste. The more sophisticated landscape architects in the mid-century strongly advised homeowners to do away with every fence if possible. A book on suburban gardening, published in 1870, flatly stated; "that kind of fence is best which is

least seen, and best seen through." Hedges were viewed with no greater favor. "The practice of hedging one's ground so that the passer-by cannot enjoy its beauty, is one of the barbarisms of old gardening, as absurd and unchristian in our day as the walled courts and barred windows of a Spanish cloister."

Pronouncements of this sort had their effect. Describing the early resistance to the anti-fence crusade during the last century a writer on agricultural matters explained it thus: "Persons had come to feel that a fence is as much a part of any place as a walk or a wall is.

It had come to be associated with the idea of home. The removal of stock was not sufficient reason for the removal of the fence. At best such a reason was only negative. The positive reason came in the development of what is really the art-idea in the outward character of the home . . . with the feeling that the breadth of setting for the house can be increased by extending the lawn to the actual highway."

Utilitarian considerations led the farmer to suppress the fences between his fields; esthetic considerations led the town and city dwellers to increase the size of their lawns. Neither consideration had any influence on those who had homesteaded the land, lived on it and who therefore clung to the traditional concept of the privacy and individualism of the home. The front yard, however, had already become old-fashioned and countrified fifty years ago; the hedge and picket fence, now thought of as merely quaint, were judged to be in the worst taste. Today, in spite of their antiquarian appeal, they are held in such disrepute that the modern architect and the modern landscapist have no use for either of them; and they are not allowed in any housing development financed by FHA.

Why? Because they disturb the uniformity of a street vista; because they introduce a dangerous note of individualistic non-conformity. Because in brief they still have something of their old meaning as symbols of self-sufficiency and independence. No qualities in Twentieth Century America are more suspect than these.

It is not social pressure which has made the enclosed front yard obsolescent, or even the ukase of some housing authority, egged on by bright young city planners. We ourselves have passed the verdict. The desire to identify ourselves with the place where we live is no longer strong.

It grows weaker every year. One out of a hundred Americans lives in a trailer; one out of every three American farmers lives in a rented house. Too many changes have occurred for the old relationship between man and the human landscape to persist with any vigor. A few decades ago the farmer's greatest pride was his woodlot, his own private forest and the forest of his children. Electricity and piped-in or bottled gas have eliminated the need for a supply of fuel, and the groves of trees, often fragments of the virgin forest, are now being cut down and the stumps bulldozed away. The small fields have disappeared, the medium sized fields have disappeared; new procedures in feeding and fattening have caused meadows to be planted to corn, range to be planted to wheat; tractors make huge designs where cattle once grazed. A strand of charged wire, a few inches off the ground, takes the place of the fence, and can be moved to another location by one man in one day. The owner of a modern mechanized farm and even of a scientific ranch need no longer be on hand at all hours of the day and night. He can and often does commute to work from a nearby town. His children go to school and spend their leisure there, and the remote and inconvenient house on the farm is allowed to die.

All this means simply one thing: a new human landscape is beginning to emerge in America. It is even now being created by the same combination of forces that created the old one: economic necessity, technological evolution, change in social outlook and in our outlook on nature. Like the landscape of the present, this new one will in time produce its own symbols and its own beauty. The six lane highway, the aerial perspective, the clean and spacious countryside of great distances and no detail will in a matter of centuries be invested with magic and myth.

That landscape, however, is not yet here. In the early dawn where we are we can perhaps discern its rough outlines, but we cannot have any real feeling for it. We cannot possibly love the new, and we have ceased to love the old. The only fraction of the earth for which an American can still feel the traditional kinship is that patch of trees and grass and hedge he calls his yard. Each one is a peak of a sinking world, and all of them grow smaller and fewer as the sea rises around them.

But even the poorest of them, even those which are meager and lonely and without grace, have the power to remind us of a rich common heritage. Each is a part of us, evidence of a vision of the world we have all shared.

Reading the Roof-Lines of Europe

MAY THEILGAARD WATTS

Ever since Jacquetta Hawkes wrote her beautiful book, A Land, *the question of the relationship of culture to environment has emerged from its disreputable phase, where it was considered a problem of free will against determinism. Miss Hawkes showed that where we had been right in seeking a relationship we had been wrong in trying to make universal generalizations about the role of climate, geology, soil, and geography on the character of the human society and its products. Thus, she said, we must keep the effects of environment and the creativity of response both in perspective. Rebecca West did just that when she wrote:*

"As I passed one of the points towards the end of the walk where the bridge is in full view I felt great pleasure because of the attitude of a girl of sixteen who was playing with a child of about five. She had picked the child up in her arms, and it was trying to force her to put it down on the grass again, by putting its hands on her head and throwing its whole weight on them, and bouncing its laughing body up and down. The girl of sixteen, though strongly built, was short; and to withstand these assaults she had planted her feet wide apart and stiffened her neck. It happened to strike my eye that while she stood thus the line of her leg, and the line of her neck from the ear to the collarbone, was very like the line of the cantilevers which supported the Forth Bridge which was a tremendous black diagram across the western sky behind her. That matter in such different forms as this soft, rosy girl, and the vast and harsh assemblage of metals were adopting the same method of

Landscape, *10(3):9–14, Spring 1961. Expanded by the author. Reprinted by permission.*

resisting strain caused me pleasure; and I have noticed since that most people feel some such pleasure when they see in one and the same composition (whether an artistic composition or merely a section of the real world which the senses can take in comfortably at one time) two or more objects using the same method to overcome some difficulty offered by the nature of the universe." (The Strange Necessity, p. 122.)

Now let us look at the roofs of France through the eyes of another gifted woman.

THE EDITORS

IGLOOS, TEPEES, prairie sod-huts, hogans, pueblos—have ecology in their roof-lines.

These shelters for families, like such individual protectors as sunbonnets, sombreros, serapis, are oriented to a landscape, to weather, and to local materials.

No such orientation marks American roof-lines. They offer no comment on wind, or rain, or local quarries, or forests. They speak only of style and solvency. A roof has become only another piece of merchandise, as unrelated to environment as its owner's creased trousers, his wife's spike heels, or their son's space-suit.

That is why the American traveler can find unexpected pleasure in reading the roof-lines of Europe. Their structure, pitch, overhang, chimneys, substance, and mosses, describe their environment so adequately that one may look at them, and then be ready to predict the feel of local leaf between the fingers—any leaf of the dominant native vegetation, but especially the feel of the local oak leaf—leathery, harsh, prickly, silky, thin, or thick. Perhaps, if one should need to gauge a landscape by one bit of evidence, the feel of the native oak leaf would be as revealing as any single facet.

But there are other aspects of a landscape, besides the harshness or silkiness of its leaves, to be deduced from the roof-lines. There are human aspects, such as the preference for certain colors; or the prevalence of fire over water in religious ritual, for example.

A desirable sequence for reading the roof-lines of Europe, starts with northern France, in Normandy, and reads southward to the Mediterranean, and then northward into Norway, and Scotland.

In Normandy, the roofs of moderate pitch, moderate overhang, raising chimneys of only moderate importance, indicate a like moderation in rainfall, temperature, wind, and humidity. Such a moderation favors forests of beech trees. A traveler from western or midwestern America, where beech trees are denied us by our dry west wind, can seldom resist stroking the smooth gray surface of a beech bole, while inspecting the inevitable hearts and initials that it wears. (Some day, some psychologist may find that some quality of American midwestern characters, some strength, some inhibition, or inferiority, stems back to our environment's lack of any tree with a smooth bark receptive to the declaration of our names and our loves. The corky ridges of a midwestern bur oak, and the rough surfaces of the oaks of our western mesas and desert rims, are frustrating to any outlet for self-expression.)

The leaves of the beech and of the hornbeam (the chief understory tree) and of the two oaks that inhabit the less-favorable slopes of Normandy, all feel thin and silky. On the forest floor is the patterned ground-cover of pink oxalis that clothes the spreading roots of beeches in both hemispheres. Ivy,

169

The roof-lines and leaves of Northern France. Left to right: hornbeam; beech; English oak; Durmast oak. Below hornbeam: oxalis. (Illustration by the author.)

on the forest floor, gives evidence of winters that are mild enough to permit the survival of this hardy broad-leaved evergreen.

But there is plenty of evidence that the weather is neither blandly mild nor enervatingly constant. It provides those changes that are so necessary in developing a vigorous, active people. The orange tiles of the roofs are tightly-fitted. The windows are shuttered against the night air. Every fallen twig has been collected in the forest, and every willow has been pollarded, for firewood. The invigoration of the climate keeps long lines of bent backs working low across the fields, and keeps the gardener's pruning shears compulsively active, and seems to prevent inhibitions from thawing so that no one sings aloud, outdoors, in the daylight, and no Norman child will return the wave of a stranger.

But the wheat waves, with its company of red poppies and cornflowers. Where apple orchards are setting their fruit, and cows are starting the production of Camembert cheese, the traveler can be served lunch outdoors in a regimented garden, with geometric trees, surrounded by moderate roof-lines. The lunch will include such products of the landscape as crusty bread, Camembert cheese, apple cider, and strawberries.

As the road widens and straightens for Paris, roofs, like men, cease commenting on local weather. The roofs of Paris are as divorced from environment as is city life itself. The mansard roof does not deign to comment on rainfall or quarries or wind or forests. This mansard-roof realm has achieved a unity that is restful, though dictated— a unity that democracy and advertising do not seem able to achieve.

The plant associates of the mansard roof are the typical eclectic assemblage of a city: horse chestnuts from the Balkans; black locusts and blue spruces from America; geraniums from Africa; the Oriental plane tree, because it endures city life so well; and the native linden, because it endures shaping— almost as well as a French poodle does.

Here one eats trout from the north, with almonds from the south, and beef from the Argentine, and oranges from Africa.

Southward from Paris the roof-lines change—they flatten and broaden, with wide eaves that shade the windows. Those windows are smaller, with shutters firmly closed against the heat of the day. The rust-coloured curved half-tiles do not form an airtight covering, and are too hot to offer a foothold to mosses, such as soften the contours of the roofs of Normandy; but these roofs suit the small yellow stone-crop, with its succulent leaves plump with stored water.

The leaves of the countryside have become smaller—or thicker, or narrower, or prickly, and are of a paler green. And instead of extending horizontally, they dangle.

Among flowers there is an abundance of yellow, especially on such legumes as the laburnums along the road, and on the masses of broom. The Lombardy poplars grow more abundantly— the same Lombardy poplars that winter-kill so easily in the American midwest. The pines are diffuse and sparse-looking, and there are junipers in chalky places.

The local oak leaf feels thick and leathery between the fingers, and somewhat resembles a holly leaf. Another oak, no more than a shrub, bears holly-like leaves less than an inch long. True holly, too, is present in fence-rows. A similar occurrence of holly-form leaves is apparent as one travels in our American Southwest, finding its culmination in the silvery leaves of the desert holly of alkaline flats.

Bent backs are no longer a part of the scenery (unless the back is bent to conform to the curves of a chaise longue). And pruning shears no longer subdue the vegetation. It is possible to hear a Frenchman singing outdoors after sundown; and to have a French child return a friendly wave.

For paint color, blue is favored (the same blue that is noticeable in the American Southwest, especially in Old Mexico).

A nightingale's song is certain to remind the American traveler of the

The roof-lines and leaves of Provence. Left to right: chestnut; Italian cypress; olive; rosemary; holm oak; cork oak; umbrella pine. (Illustration by the author.)

171

Traveling south in Europe		Traveling south in America
	flatter roofs	
	smaller windows	
	more shutters	
	more red flowers	
	flat-topped trees	
	thicker leaves	
	smaller leaves	
	grayer leaves	
	holly-form leaves	
example: Kermes oak, holm oak		**example:** Emory oak, desert holly
	more aromatic leaves	
examples: rosemary, lavender, thyme		**examples:** sagebrush, desert lavender
	more legumes (especially the yellow-flowered ones)	
	more improbable-looking birds	
examples: hoopoe, bee-eater		**examples:** road-runner, humming birds
	louder music	
	wider balconies	
	bigger guitars	
	more reclining seats	
example: chaise longue		**example:** rocking chair
	more tanned skins without a hat-line or a sleeve-line (people who work in the sun wear hats and sleeves)	
	more water in religious rituals (as compared with more hell-fire in religion as one travels north)	
example: for sprinkling Catholics		**example:** for dipping Baptists
	more dogs asleep on their sides	

mockingbird. If he hears the song from his bed in a small rural inn, where his windows are swung open under wide eaves beside a dark fragrant garden, he is likely to ruminate on the many similarities in the changes in the landscape, as one travels south in Europe, or southwest in America. He might make up a list [such as that shown on p. 172].

In Provence, as he continues south, the traveler will observe a change that has no parallel in our Southwest. Something has happened to roofs. They have pulled in their eaves. And windows, even small ones, are absent from the north walls of houses. Some roofs have rocks on them.

This is the area of the mistral, that bitter wind that comes from the northwest in the winter and spring, blowing cold and strong for days off the Alps, scourging Provence and the Rhone Valley.

Against the mistral every small field is barricaded, with a closely-woven fence of tall reeds. Van Gogh is said to have ventured out into the mistral, even though it kept most people indoors. He painted the woven-reed barricades into his pictures. Perhaps it was the mistral which caused him to see the cypresses of San Remy whirling with Fourth-of-July pinwheels.

The flat tops of the umbrella pines present a thin edge to the wind. Many plants present small, thick, gray foliage to the sun. While vacationers are wearing dark glasses and rubbing their skins with oil, the trees are wearing thick corky bark and are full of oil. They stand widely-spaced, as in our mesa country, and it is hardly possible to walk among them without pressing out a richness of rosemary, and thyme, and lavender, with a tinge of garlic.

There are goats feeding on this gray-greenness, and there are many artists painting in the sun, for this country has long belonged to them—Cézanne, Matisse, Picasso, Toulouse-Lautrec, Van Gogh.

In Italy's watery Po Valley, roofs take on added responsibilities. The tiled roofs of the two-story farm-houses stretch out into an "L" shape. One wing of the house accommodates cattle downstairs and the family upstairs, and is provided with an outside stairway. The other wing is open, except for its roof and one side, which is built up with open-work brick lattice. The open wings are empty in June, but are stuffed to capacity with baled hay in late summer, before the rainy season.

The productive croplands spreading flat under the sun, with their rows of poplar trees, fail to hold any traveler long (as croplands everywhere tend to fail). The Italian hill towns beckon, from above the long slopes of olive trees and grape vines.

As in most cities, the roof-lines in Italian cities offer little comment on weather or crops. As the mansard roofs of Paris recorded style, so the roof-lines of Italian cities record conflict, pride, hope, and territorial imperative. Castle battlements present rows of teeth for the Guelph party; or rows of fish-tails for the Ghibelline party. Spires, domes, and intricate façades raise crosses, or angels, or saints against the sky. Square towers raise bells, or a hopeful bid for eminence. Columns raise soldiers and statesmen, wolves and horses, gods and goddesses against the sky's dependable blueness. Dove-cotes, and decorative chimney-pots, and lines of laundry, all help to complicate the sky-line.

The roof-lines and leaves of Switzerland. Left to right: Norway spruce; mountain ash; alpenrose; larch; sycamore; maple. (Illustration by author.)

To see a contrast to these roof-lines one should turn northward and westward and skyward, into the Alps. Here the spreading roofs hold thick chunks of slate used for shingles, and boulders used to anchor the slates against the wind; and thick feather-beds of snow for additional warmth. The eaves are wide. They spread like the wings of a brooding hen. Travelers are glad to find refuge from rain under their spread; and to eat lunch under their shelter; and later to fall asleep listening to their slow drip in the foggy night.

It is easy to understand why these roofs have been built wider and why balconies have been tucked under the eaves for shelter. There is plenty of lumber for balconies from the forests which thrive in this rainfall; and there is time for wood-carving in the isolation of long winter nights on the mountains. These balconies are bedecked with red paint and red geraniums. In this cold, where Nature achieves the bluest flowers on earth and the bluest crevasses, men favor red flowers and red paint.

As the traveler descends from the Alps and enters the Black Forest of Germany, the roofs are conspicuous for their long steep slopes. These roofs accompany dripping forests of Norway spruce, of beech carpeted richly in mosses and ferns, with an atmosphere like a conservatory. In the towns the roofs are often so steeply-pitched that several stories of dormer windows interrupt them. But on the heights overlooking the Rhine the castle roofs record protection from men rather than from weather, with their notches for weapons and slots for pouring hot oil or molten lead on invaders.

In Denmark, and in England, many cottages wear their roofs like stocking-caps, pulled low around their ears. The use of thatching indicates an abundance of moisture, which reduces the danger of fire in those roofs which would otherwise be so vulnerable. These roofs accompany beech forests, and velvet lawns and tall spikes of delphinium that last for days and days in that cool humidity.

In Norway one can look down the mountainside to the roof of a small farmhouse on a minuscule farm and observe that roof materials have changed; tiles have given way to wood shingles.

Top: the roof-lines and leaves of England. Left to right: English oak; beech; cowslip; hawthorn; ash. Bottom: the roof-lines and leaves of Norway. Left to right: Scots pine; Norway spruce; birch; Norway maple; oak. (Illustration by author.)

One can look up the mountainside to where a log cabin perches beside a mountain meadow. Pine and spruce furnish the building materials in this deeply-forested land. Usually the pitch of the roof is steep enough to let the snow and rain slide off; but sometimes a farmer builds a roof with little pitch, so that he can cover it with sod. The sod roofs are green and often flowery, and sometimes a goat grazes there. But the old stave churches offer the rain and snow a series of descending slopes. And, whatever the slope of the roof, it is rewarding to come close to inspect the carving of frames and lintels and beams, and even shingles.

Evidently long nights, cold winters, and mountains have induced their inevitable handiwork; and have evoked the inevitable hell-fire in the religion of those unheated churches. (If those sea-faring Lutherans of both Denmark and Norway tend to take their religion with a grain of salt, might that not be just another effect of the Gulf Stream?)

In Scotland, chimneys become more and more dominant, with more and more smoke pouring into the fog out of clustered chimney-pots. Then coats become thicker and shaggier on sheep and Highland cattle and Britons. Then hell-fire is warming on the bleak Sabbath; and a strong and steaming cup of tea becomes important; and there are bag-pipes, and gorse, and thistles and (therefore?)—Scotch.

The traveler turns from such reading of roof-lines and comes home to the incongruity of ranch-house roofs on mountain dwellings and highway taverns; to the confusion of nursery-grown Norway spruce planted between muscular native giant of a bur oak, selected by dry prairie winds, and an elm with the long whip-like twigs that belong to the easy life of a river bottom. Technology has given us media that are facile, and transportation that is efficient.

Such progress will not be denied to Europe. It will reach quickly from Normandy to Provence and the Black Forest and Denmark; and then climb more slowly to the hill towns, and to the Alps, and Norway; and then creep across the moors of Scotland.

Part 3   Men and Other Organisms

Of Man and the Lower Animals

PAUL L. ERRINGTON

In his capacity for over-population, even when manifest as a scourge of the biosphere, man must suffer comparison to lower creatures. Among many of them eruptions of numbers occur commonly, individuals exhibit syndromes of stress and physiological breakdown (nervousness, high blood pressure, poor digestion, neuroses, ulcers, and infertility), social systems deteriorate (resulting in poor mothering and fights with neighbors), and the organisms pollute and exhaust their own environments. But, unlike men, they do not observe or anticipate the catastrophic death that inevitably follows population explosions.

The humble muskrat, among some other species of mammals, is occasionally beset by population overgrowth and the tragedies that end it. Given our advantage in perspective, can we ameliorate the grief such a doom holds for us? That is, is the muskrat, besides being interesting in itself, part of a society whose destiny is truly homologous to ours? From the time of Aesop to that of Pogo, animals have been identified with particular human virtues and vices; their purpose on earth has commonly been presumed to exhort human behavior or illustrate human foible.

It is highly improbable that the special destiny of muskrats is to serve as a model for man. Yet, as a mammal with both his savage and his sweeter sides and with needs and capabilities contingent upon a neutral universe, the muskrat may have something to say to the judicious, loving observer who would learn by insight and observation the mutual aspects of life between muskrats and men.

THE EDITORS

The Prince of Wales visiting the Monkey Temple, Benares. (From Radio Times Hulton Picture Library.)

The Yale Review, *51(3):370–383, March 1962. Copyright Yale University Press.*

MAN IS A most special animal. However much disagreement may exist as to his origin or purpose (if any), we can agree that he has both simplified and complicated his way of living and has made a great impact on his surroundings. The phenomenon of man, whether we think of it with exultation or despair or with some emotion in between, remains strong stuff and has prospects of getting stronger. Man may fancy himself exempt from natural laws or well on the way toward becoming so; his technological advances seem to promote delusions as to what he is and can do.

Man can, on at least some logical grounds, rate himself as a higher animal. He has already named himself the wise, *Homo sapiens,* and he can at times show capabilities for wisdom. He is special, but he should not assume that he is higher, wiser, or more special than he is. An unrealistic attitude of man toward himself as an animal can be, I think, most dangerous. If twentieth-century society really values the things that it proclaims essential to a civilized culture—peace, human dignity, intellectual activity, a reasonable degree of freedom and security, and a reasonable standard of living—it cannot afford to ignore the natural laws by which life continues to be bound.

It is particularly when thinking about the increase of human beings over the habitable areas of the earth that I am afraid not only for man's physical future but also for the values that go furthest toward making human life worth living.

I confess to further disquieting thoughts as to how much moral right man actually has to regard the earth as his exclusive possession, to despoil or befoul as he will. Man has or should have some minimal responsibility toward the earth he claims and toward the other forms of life that have been on earth as long as or longer than he has.

Public attitudes toward the recent, current, and future increase of the earth's human populations may hardly be summarized briefly or neatly. People may joke that the so-called population explosion will not matter to any of us a hundred years hence. Or Providence or scientific gadgetry will save us, if we are to be saved. Or the attitude may be that the earth could support many times its present human population and that the era of human colonization of other worlds in space awaits us; and that continued population growth is necessary to assure us of anything rightly identifiable with progress. But whether the public view is that of fatalists caught in an irresistible current or of boosters convinced that not even the sky need be the limit, seldom is any evidence to be detected that the public knows much about populations, about its own or any other populations. Seemingly, it should be appropriate for the public, as participating in this great increase, to concern itself more with what it is doing, afraid of, or aiming for.

This essay proposes no panaceas. It is mainly to develop the by-no-means-novel thesis that man could learn from consideration of the basic biology and sociology of animal populations.

The population dynamics of man and what man calls lower animals may not show detailed parallels throughout. The life equation of modern man can be subject to an all but unending array of qualifying conditions. Within the framework of the laws of life, he can be a breaker as well as a maker of rules. He is a product of diverse cultures and blends of cultures and offshoots of cultures. He may be as intolerant of crowding as an American frontiersman who wanted no neighbors in sight or as tolerant as a metropolitan to whom crowds represent a normal environment. He may demand and be sensitively adjusted to a high standard of living. He may be materialistic when having much or philosophical when in want. Man is venturesome and conservative, patient and volatile, reasoning and unreasoning.

If man is to learn anything about populations of lower animals so that he may better understand his own populations, it may just about have to be at the more elementary levels. This might not impress some who feel that we need more than an elementary understanding. We do need understanding on the highest plane that we can reach, but I feel that we can ill afford to be scornful about what we can learn that is elementary as long as we as a public continue to demonstrate so little understanding of that. If man knew more about population fundamentals, I doubt if he would so blindly make certain of the mistakes that he does make.

A tremendous amount of work has been done in following the population fortunes of wild mammals and birds living their own lives under more or less natural conditions. The work has been chiefly on gamebirds, songbirds, fur bearers, and rodent pests; and their habits and vital statistics have been recorded for the same tracts of land year after year and discussed in the biological literature for a quarter-century or longer.

My research specialities among these species have included two native North Americans: the bobwhite quail and the muskrat. They both illustrate population resiliences and rigidities concerning which misconceptions may persist.

Some of the most misleading of misconceptions relate to food as a limiting factor of populations. Granted that some species of animals do increase up to the limits of their food supply, that animals must eat, and that, if they do not get enough to eat, they may starve, or that populations may otherwise decline because of food deficiencies, it may still be an unsafe assumption that the upper limits of a population must necessarily be determined by lack of food, or, for that matter, by lack of other palpable environmental constituents that we customarily think of as limiting factors.

Not so very many years ago, the wintering fortunes of bobwhite populations in the north-central and northeastern United States were considered almost exclusively in terms of weather, natural enemies, food, and cover.

It is true that severe weather emergencies may now and then practically eliminate the bobwhite as a species over wide areas of its geographic range. Two feet of heavy snow or an inch-thick seal of ice over everything for a couple of weeks or longer may pose their understandable threats to susceptible wildlife. So may twenty to forty below zero temperatures accompanied by blizzard winds and eight-foot snowdrifts. Yet a given area—a whole region—may not have any weather emergencies of lethal intensity for bobwhites for years, and, even so, the bobwhite populations tend to increase up to a certain level and no higher.

The thesis that bobwhites are limited in numbers and distribution by the depredations of flesh-eating enemies has long been a public favorite. Predatory flesheaters do kill and eat bobwhites about as often as they have opportunities, and they may have many or conspicuous opportunities to do so. Nevertheless, this predation, when closely studied, has proved to be more a symptom of insecurity in a wintering bobwhite population than a primary limiting factor.

The food and cover—those essential constituents of wintering environment for the bobwhites—must be present when, where, and in the quantity and quality and combinations needed, or the birds cannot long live anywhere. But excess food or cover is unlikely to be accompanied by any corresponding increase in numbers of the bobwhites that are able to winter. The chief limiting factor becomes the psychology of the bobwhites themselves.

Such a population picture does not have its fully traceable counterparts throughout the animal kingdom. Psychological intolerances do not always prevent increases up to levels where food does become the limiting factor—as in those insects the abundance of which is governed by food supply and in those human populations to whom subsistence-living and starvation are commonplace. It does apply, however, to that wide variety of mammals and birds that we think of as being territorial, those we classify as the property owners, those making claims that they are willing to defend. This territoriality is manifested by the fights and displays of songbirds settling their rights of possession on a city lawn and by some remarkably human-like behavior. An animal's own psychological intolerance toward its own kind can be a mighty factor in determining what lives where, when, how, and at what densities.

Another distinction emphasized by the bobwhite data: although there can be fighting (including fighting between social groups that may not be dissimilar to human warfare), the limiting factor of social intolerance need not always take the form of overt antagonism or fighting. Some of the most significant intolerance can have such benign bird-between-bird manifestations as frictionless avoidance or withdrawals on the part of individuals or groups that recognize their own superfluity in places where they do not belong.

Even so, manifestations of social overpopulation can include plenty of trouble. Bobwhite equivalents of displaced persons wander in strange places or try to live in uninhabitable areas. In their wanderings, they tend to be harassed by and vulnerable to predatory attacks. Not only may they be vulnerable to such formidable predators as great horned owls and dashing blue-darter hawks and agile and clever foxes but also to rather weak and clumsy predators having no special aptitudes for preying upon grown bobwhites unless something goes wrong. To a considerable extent, it may not seem to make much difference what kills the birds that are trying to live under highly adverse, if not hopeless, conditions. They are the have-nots and they do not need to have human intelligence to know it. They may lack food or cover; they may lack both; but, possibly as contributory as anything to their serious troubles, they lack what might be called the sense of rightness that enables them to do the best they can with what they have.

Not only are wanderers affected but also those among an area's wintering bobwhites that are relatively sedentary but trying to live at too-high densities for peace and security, even as bobwhites know peace and security. This may be true in places having far more than sufficient food and cover for all the bobwhites that conceivably would ever live or visit there. One can see it

Quail roost in a tight circle facing outward. (Photo by Charles W. Schwartz.)

about an Iowa cornfield having tons of the best all-around food for wintering bobwhites and lying conveniently adjacent to a woodlot full of the best of refuge cover for the birds—a place having food enough to feed thousands and cover enough to afford mechanical protection to hundreds, but having only perhaps thirty to forty birds that act as if they know when they are enough.

Long-term data on bobwhite populations of Iowa and Wisconsin have tendencies to line up with remarkable fidelity to numerical patterns, often for many consecutive years. For a period of years, not more than a fairly definite number of bobwhites would be able to winter on a given tract of land under the best weather conditions, and the numbers trying to live there in excess of that figure would soon be whittled down by predation or be forced to leave

or would withdraw of their own volition. After elimination of the vulnerable surplus, the remaining bobwhites would stand a good chance of wintering securely, despite the presence and activities of native enemies that would be entirely willing to feed upon them if they could do so. In the event that the bobwhite population entered the winter and stayed at a level well below the threshold of security, those particular birds might not suffer any wintering loss or only the trifling losses that might occur through age or accident.

An actual case history for a tract of about a thousand acres demonstrated a threshold of security at about fifty bobwhites for the six winters that I made detailed observations. During one winter of heavy snowfall, this tract had the best food supply in its whole neighborhood and it was repeatedly visited by hungry quail coveys from outside its boundaries. Each such visit resulted in the local population exceeding the threshold of security for the thousand-acre tract and, unless extremely temporary, was followed by a reduction down to the threshold level, until the birds losing their lives there outnumbered the even fifty that did survive.

Differences in the wintering fortunes of secure and insecure populations may show up in still greater contrast. Another six-year case history relates to a covey range that was rich in food though lethally poor in protective cover and a site of chronic unrest for the quail whenever any lived there. For the five winters of the six that it attracted quail, it wintered two birds out of a total of eighty-four. About a third of the decline was due to birds abandoning the tract while alive and able to do so. The rest of the decline occurred through predation. For the season that the two birds wintered, virtually the whole loss of twenty-one was traced to a pair of great horned owls. Yet, in the center of the nesting territory of the owls, thirty-two of thirty-two bobwhites wintered. Another neighboring but strong and well-balanced covey range wintered thirty-three birds without a single loss. Elsewhere in the same neighborhood during the same winter, the two other covey ranges nearest the scene of the practically annihilative predation lost six birds out of thirty-nine, which represented just about the elimination of a vulnerable surplus on the range of these birds.

In detailed analysis, the story of what happens at times of a bobwhite population crisis can become too involved to discuss in a short article, but I want to emphasize the social intolerance underlying so much of the trouble associated with overpopulation. There

need not be any overt friction manifested even when the appearance of newcomers puts a population dangerously over the threshold of security that applies to a given tract of wintering range. Newcomers may even join with resident "homesteaders," roosting tail to tail in a common circle. But uneasiness and the preoccupation of birds with each other may divert atten- from the proper business of living, whether in getting along well or in staying alive at all.

The apparent role of food as a limiting factor in muskrat populations may differ with the area and with the subspecies of muskrat. In the coastal marshes of Maryland and Louisiana (which comprise two population centers for Southern forms of muskrats), the animals may eat themselves out of their habitats in the accepted Malthusian sense. Conversely, the population increases of the muskrats studied in Iowa were almost invariably damped before the onset of frankly Malthusian stages.

Nor does the mechanism basically limiting the population growth of the Iowa muskrats especially conform to the Darwinian version of the balance of nature. It has nothing that I can see of predation any more than it has of Malthusian-type food limitation working as a master factor to remove enough of the annual production of muskrats to keep populations within bounds—despite the fact that predation upon vulnerable parts of populations may be heavy. On areas where predatory enemies were virtually absent (or did little or no preying upon the muskrats), the muskrats did not show an unrestrained increase.

The reproductive changes shown by the Iowa muskrats have been particularly informative. Average numbers of young conceived by or born to adult females of given populations during a given year varied from about a dozen young up to about three times that many. Generally, the average litter size may reflect more the health and nourishment of the females, whereas the average number of litters born per adult female during a breeding season may more reflect the collective dispositions or states of mind or social tensions of the population or maybe something else not so satisfactorily labeled.

A changing birth rate in a muskrat population does not have to signify any genetic change, nor any irreversible trend either up or down. Change may be expected whenever biological conditions induce change. Broadly, when social tensions increase, the birth rate falls; when tensions are relieved, the birth rate rises.

The adult females in overcrowded muskrat populations typically stop breeding after giving birth to averages of about two litters. This would be about the first of June in Iowa, in the middle of the breeding season shown by the calendar. The mere presence of many young underfoot or sneaking around or getting into trouble or being a distracting influence in the sociology of the population seems to inhibit further breeding.

The weaned young of uncrowded populations have better opportunities for dispersing away from the properties of their elders and not only spare themselves trouble but also reduce their own chances of causing trouble. Populations that do not have their breeding production inhibited by the presence of excessive numbers of young might give birth to averages approaching four litters per adult female for the season, or about twice the average for the crowded populations.

Or, crowded populations suffering heavy losses of their early-born young (as through late-spring and early-summer floods drowning most of the young born before midsummer) might give birth to additional, late litters in compensation for the loss of the earlier ones. Death may thus serve the biological function of a moderate degree of underpopulation insofar as it similarly results in lowered social tensions, at least to the extent of there being fewer young to be getting in the way of their elders and thus inhibiting reproduction.

The commonly-held supposition that fecund animals need their fecundity to outbreed their heavy loss rates, to keep ahead of their enemies, or to compete with their fellows should not be accepted without question.

Case histories of muskrat populations do show how animals producing the larger numbers of young stand better chances of filling up underpopulated habitats with their own progeny. Following droughts, for example, the return of surface water may put the lakes and marshes of a whole region in superior condition for muskrats at a time when only a few muskrats may be present to live in them. Muskrats thus living in places characterized by splendid resources and minimal social tensions may rear nearly all of the young born to them; and, in the accelerating stages of a population rise, a breeding season's production of young may show such impressive results as averages exceeding twenty young successfully reared per adult female. That would occur when the animals would be sufficiently abundant to have full opportunities for mating yet still be below the levels of crowding at which the psychological brakes start tightening.

Muskrat as shown in natural habitat. (Photo by V. B. Scheffer, courtesy U.S. Department of Interior, Fish and Wildlife Service, Bureau of Sport Fisheries and Wildlife.)

Once the muskrats fill up their habitat, they do not need a high reproductive rate to keep their population at a capacity level. Even the lower birth rates shown by the Iowa muskrats—such as an average of a dozen young born per adult female—ordinarily are sufficient to replenish a population; and the survival rate of these young need not be especially high.

For a crowded population beset by much social tension, averages as low as four young successfully reared per female may be all that can be expected, even when nothing goes seriously wrong with the habitat. Such a reproductive rate would be attained through rearing an average of half the young born in a single litter per adult female.

The relatively slow breeders can still have all the fecundity that they need to hold a population at a saturated level, especially in view of the fact that an adult female almost always takes better care of a few young than she does of many young.

Some of the postulated biological advantages of high fecundity therefore cancel out as social tensions build up. For a population that cannot withstand crowding and has no more livable frontiers to spread into, greater fecundity can mean greater wastage.

The natural shaking-down of the muskrat population to fit its habitat and its social mold may be bloodily messy, even when the only deadly muskrat enemies are other muskrats.

Compared with the troubles of many other species, muskrat troubles may have more savage violence in them if only because the muskrats possess murderous teeth and dispositions commensurate with the teeth whenever social conditions become intolerable. When matters really go wrong for the muskrats, all their nightmares come true.

Excess or misfit or strange adults may circulate about a marsh, finding trouble and making trouble. They may have gashes around their rumps or tails bitten through. They may have bites into kidneys, bites into livers, intestines, or into any body parts that teeth can reach and penetrate. They may try to walk on elbows after having had forelegs hamstrung. They may have face wounds, feet swollen out of shape from wounds, and wounds that fill with maggots or provide sites of bulging abscesses. They hobble around and sit in improvised nests on shore or ice; they bleed where they go and where they rest; and now and then one dies.

Strife victims may include huge animals of either sex at the height of physical prowess but not able or disposed to live in peace. They may include sick or injured or simply those too immature to take good care of themselves, the animals that could not keep away from other animals that did not want them around. Some victims may be among the aggressively troublesome; some may be only those offering inviting targets for the abuse of their fellows—the timid, the hesitant, the blundering.

A weaned young enters its home lodge and eats the hindquarters off a member of a new-born litter that it finds unprotected. A mother kills a couple of her own weaned young in driving them away before the birth of another litter. A mother may see a young muskrat swimming on the far side of the cleared space surrounding her lodge, swim out to it, and bite it to death with the utmost viciousness. Or a mother on a crowded marsh may enter a lodge containing another mother's young, kill them in the nest, and take over the lodge for the housing of her own young.

Life can be very cheap among the muskrats of an overpopulated area. In addition to the young victims that are murdered outright, many young die as a result of parental carelessness when the parents have no reason to be careful. Members of a single helpless litter have been found left lying around in as many as four different lodges. It not infrequently happens that a litter may be divided and the parts kept in nest chambers of two different lodges fifty yards or farther apart; and, when this happens, the mother sometimes neglects the occupants of one of the nests, and they do not grow any more.

With increased distractions, mothers become increasingly forgetful of the numbers and whereabouts of their helpless young. When litters are being moved under pressure, a mother may carry two or three to a safe place. She may casually retrieve another young or two, if she swims past them and they are complaining. Ultimately, she may gather together half her litter, and, if so, that may be enough to satisfy her. She still has young muskrats to look after, and her type of mass production does not call for exacting standards of motherhood.

The mistake should not be made of taking for granted that such troubled lives are merely the ordained lot of muskrat flesh, or that the troubles of muskrats increase in direct proportion to the numbers of the muskrats. The troubles increase out of all proportion

to the numbers of muskrats as populations become top-heavy in terms of
what muskrats recognize as crowding.
In the other direction, lowering of
populations down to levels that the
muskrats find socially more tolerable
means proportionally much less
trouble.

This is not to say that muskrat (or
bobwhite or any other) populations that
contain naturally irascible individuals
ever live in idyllic peace, at any population levels. There are always the
aged, the ailing, the unlucky, the misfit, and their dispositions need not be
of mellow contentment. Nevertheless,
it is generally basic behavior for a
mammal or bird population to live more
peaceably when it feels that things are
right than when subject to endless
stress.

What, specifically, could civilized
man learn from population phenomena
of the so-called lower animals that
might help him understand population
phenomena of his own kind? What,
specifically, might help him in his
seeking for "the better life"?

In their essential features, the lessons from the lower animals look rather
simple. I shall not try to say how many
of them reflect anything really new
philosophically. Many of them look
like homely truths, and, whether or
not they are of sorts that thinking
people have always thought about, I
know that they are not original with
me.

A frequently quoted passage from
Isaiah reads: "Woe unto them that join
house to house, that lay field to field,
till there be no place, that they may
be placed alone in the midst of the
earth!" The ancients had some experience with frustrations, too, and not
all of the problems in their lives were
manifested by shortages of food.

The modern concepts of "pathological togetherness" as a population
phenomenon seem to have developed
chiefly in connection with recent work
on physiological and psychological
stress.

The lessons of the lower animals
could help us get rid of naivetés concerning fundamentals. We could recognize that there may be more to meeting a population problem than increasing the production or improving the
distribution of food or other material
goods. There are the estimates as to
how many times the present world
population could be fed if we could
make more efficient use of the resources of the sea, if algae could be
adapted for human diet, if we could
accomplish technological miracles in
mass-producing foods without soil, and
so on and so on. To me, this reasoning
neglects some of the most serious
problems of overpopulations, the social
evils.

We could do well in getting away
from misconceptions as to the biological significance of changes in birth
rates. A declining birth rate should not
be regarded as a calamity to be avoided
by all possible means. It may be a
symptom of something being wrong
without being menacing in itself—indeed, it may be, of itself, exactly what
is needed to better a situation.

For all of the boom-talk about space
travel and the unlimited horizons
awaiting mankind's expansion, it might,
for the present, befit human intelligence to think more about the world
we still happen to be living in and filling up so rapidly with people and their
by-products. What ultimate billions
do we expect our populations to reach,
according to a booster philosophy of
always bigger and bigger? What, with
such a philosophy, are we committing
ourselves to?

I think that it would be more befitting human intelligence for man to take for granted that his population growth curve will level off some time, however much he may postpone it by his technological ingenuity. Moreover, if a top-heavy human population collapses through a cataclysm instead of merely leveling off, what are the limits to which mass desperation may not go, on a scale such as our earth could never experience before it had the billions of people to become involved?

Apart from any threat—distant or not, as the case may be—of actual collapse in our population structure, the present pyramiding stage produces enough trouble and prospects of more trouble at best. Puerto Rico, the South Pacific, Africa, the metropolitan congestions that we already have in North America —we do not have to look to the congestions of Old World cultures for dismaying examples of evils associated with mankind's overpopulations. I confidently expect the troublous aspects of our population situation to be compounded the higher our numbers go, until the laws of life absolutely put a stop to further increase.

This much is from the lower animals: the upper asymptote of a population growth curve almost always represents forced retrenchment, and the forcing represents suffering for the living forms possessed of enough nervous system to suffer. The upper asymptotes for the animals that I have studied operated through no mysteriously benign process of falling birth rates; they reflected a tightening up of many things, including, especially, psychological tensions. There is no reason I can see that man, with his capacities for irascibility and suffering, could have an upper asymptote forced on to his population curve without expecting intensification of the

tensions that add nothing to any legacy of human happiness.

Man, as well as the lower animals, has plenty in his collective and individual destinies that he cannot expect ever to control, but it seems ironical that he cannot do better than the lower animals in at least seeing the menace in irresponsible increase.

There may well be questions as to exactly where dangers lie, as to what man can hope to do about his population problems, as to what practical measures he could take or be ethically justified in taking. At any rate, he could break away from the fallacy that his enormous population increase must necessarily be identified with progress.

If the lower animals have any one, simple, major lesson for us, it would seem to be that moderation is, or is the nearest approach to, a biological basis for any kind of "good life." The idea that adaptable mankind may be able to adapt to a new, crowded, tightly integrated, superlatively artificialized way of living still does not answer questions as to why this way of living should be a goal so desired, so worthy of attainment. Surely, we have what it takes to fill the earth with people to its habitable limits, but why must we, if we can possibly avoid it?

For what goals should we be willing to allow our numbers to increase up to the point where we have less and less worth living for? More dangers of appalling political and economic dislocations? Speeded-up complexities and frantic entertainment, even the search for peace of mind at a breathless tempo, instead of more wholesome ways of living? Countrysides that are no longer in the country, opportunities to enjoy solitudes existing only farther and farther away from home, if there?

With the intelligence that man has in him, why must he in the face of danger

189

signals give obeisance to the shaky
doctrine that his population growth
must never cease? Why not some
goals that leave for man some of the
things worth living for, not just imposing statistics or material necessities or universal gadgetry? Why, before it becomes too late, can we not
at least try to do what is within our
capabilities to hold our populations
within some reasonable limits?

Ultimately live on algae? I suppose
so, if that is what we must do, but
why must we as rational beings get
ourselves into the position of having
to do it? Dream dreams about conquering space? I suppose that it would
be considered reactionary to discourage
that, but first we might concern ourselves with not making a complete
mess of our heritage on earth. A philosophy of conscientious husbandry
should be consistent with a civilized
and progressive attitude.

On the Domestication of Cattle

ERICH ISAAC

*It is not easy for a modern scientist to put
himself in the frame of mind of his counterpart of, say, the last 40 years of the
17th century. If there were no records of
the motives of John Ray or Isaac Newton
we might assume that their attitude was
the same dispassionate, skeptical, self-
contained, inductive, highly technical inquiry that now characterizes research.
Most present-day scientists would feel that
the peculiar mixture of religious and intellectual and emotional animation of an
earlier day was not only embarrassing but
an impediment to clear thinking. The
suffusing sense of wonder as worship and
of discovery as movement toward God
has been lost or discarded. More than
the material circumstances, it is the motives of scientific endeavor that have
changed.*

*From more distant times, before there
was writing, there are no corrective documents to prevent us from supposing that
men's motives were the same as Newton's
or ours. The biases we project upon
those lost generations—painters in caves,
hunters, domesticators of animals—are not
likely even to be recognized as biases. To
say that things were done in the name of
God is our corrupt way of imagining the
interplay of thought and thing that may
have composed the mood of the Paleolithic hunter, Assyrian farmer, Crusader,
or even Pilgrim Father. It permitted incredible cruelty and simultaneously endowed life with a unity and purpose
scarcely imaginable today. To know this
is not to yearn to go backward—as so
many critics of such "romanticism" claim*

Science, *137:195–204, 1962. Copyright 1962
by the American Association for the Advancement of Science.*

—but to retain the perspective that makes advance possible.

Our children are led to believe that ancient hunters and farmers would be us if they could, and that everyone the world over is striving not only for our kind of prosperity but also for the ideology that is presumed to create prosperity. Eccentric individuals who object to such ideas are not only "romantic" but "unpatriotic," "unprogressive," "egghead," or worse. However, those eccentrics are mutants in the cultural foliage, oddities today, but our only source of viable ideas when the climate changes.

THE EDITORS

THE PROBLEM OF animal domestication has proved a challenging one to the disciplines concerned with the history of man's economic and social development, for animal domestication has had a revolutionary impact on man's ecumene. Culture historians, geographers, and ethnologists, in particular, have been intrigued by the host of psychological and technological questions inherent in the problem of animal domestication. Necessarily, however, in view of the darkness which shrouds the original achievement, their analysis has depended upon the construction of hypotheses. To the extent that they support one another, these offer a coherent picture (1).

The problem of animal domestication has also been of increasing concern to geneticists and zootechnologists. For not only does domestication show the enormous potential variability in a given animal, hardly to be demonstrated in the wild state, but it also poses a whole set of questions, the answers to which could provide fundamental insights into basic problems of general zoology, taxonomy, and other disciplines. Thus, for example,

why are there no barriers to crossing in widely differing domestic species of animals and plants which intercross to yield fertile hybrids, whereas natural species often distinguished by only minute differences are intersterile (2)? The province of zoology up to the present, in a field beset by problems of verification, has been to define and explain the changes domestication has produced in animals by comparing present-day domestic animals or wild animals raised in captivity with their wild relatives, by studying the fossil record, and more recently by studying modes of inheritance.

Of all the problems of animal domestication, none has been so extensively discussed by culture historians and cultural geographers as that of the domestication of cattle. Moreover, despite great advances in the study of heredity and domestication, the major cultural theory of the domestication of cattle has not required any important revision as the result of zoological study. Zoology, indeed, has little to say about the social conditions of domestication, and for clarification of this problem we must rely on the hypotheses of the culture historians. In the absence of conclusive evidence, they have constructed their theory of the origin and process of domestication of cattle largely on the basis of deductive reasoning (3–5; 6, p. 35).

The cultural thesis which has been most widely accepted is that which asserts that cattle, probably the first of the great herd animals to be domesticated, were originally domesticated in western Asia. The thesis further argues that the domesticators of cattle were sedentary farmers rather than nomadic hunters, that domestication was deliberately undertaken and not haphazard, and that the motive was religious (7).

191

Fig. 1. Milking scene, from al-'Ubaid, Iraq, about 2600 B.C., part of a frieze of limestone on bi-
tumen with copper borders, representing the cattle farm of the goddess Ninkhursag. The milker
is seated behind the cow. Height of frieze, about 8⅝ inches; length of entire mosaic, 3 feet 9¼
inches. (The University Museum, University of Pennsylvania.) (From "On the Domestication of
Cattle," Erich Isaac, *Science*, Vol. 137, pp. 195–204, 20 July 1962. Copyright 1962 by the Amer-
can Association for the Advancement of Science.)

Arguments for Agricultural Origin

There are a variety of suggestive facts
which, taken together, support an agricultural origin for domestication.

(1) Harnessing methods used by a
nomadic society are clearly modifications of harnessing methods of nearby
farmers, devised for handling herd
animals in the field (8, p. 441).

(2) All wild bovines that have been
domesticated lived in the realm of the
ancient peasantry of western Asia,
whereas no wild bovines whose range
was primarily in the realm of nomadic
hunters have been domesticated, despite the fact that these animals (for
example, the bison) are easily domesticated (6, p. 35).

(3) Neither the European elk nor the
African eland, both demonstrably easy
to domesticate, has been domesticated
by nomadic hunters. No deer or antelope species, with the exception of the
reindeer, has been domesticated (9),

and even reindeer do not belong to the
oldest group of domestic animals (10,
11).

(4) Milking practices which have
been considered peculiar to pastoral
nomads, such as presenting the cow
with a straw-stuffed calfskin to stimulate milk flow, blowing into the anal
passage, and milking from behind (Fig.
1), are now known to have been common in the realm of West Asian peasants
and are presumably derived from that
realm (12).

(5) The problem of feeding captured
animals could have been solved only
by an agricultural society producing a
food surplus that might be used to
supplement pasture.

(6) The pastoral nomad's complete
absorption in his herd animals, which
has been cited by those who argue that
domestication originated from nomadic
hunting, has been shown to be irrelevant. American Indian hunters became

horse-riding nomads shortly after the Spaniards introduced the horse into North America (13).

Arguments for Asian Location

The archeological evidence supports the view that cattle were first domesticated in western Asia (8, 14, 15). Unfortunately, osteological study often leaves it unclear whether remains are those of domestic or those of wild animals. For this reason, an increasingly refined statistical approach has been used since the turn of the century. As Dyson observes (14, 16), the significance of this approach is that "an analysis of the fauna of a site over a period of time may indicate at some point a shift from reliance on small or 'wild' game to reliance on 'prodomestic' game, by which is meant potentially domesticable . . . i.e., those animals known as domestic in later periods. Subsequently a second shift, this time in the age at which prodomestic animals are killed, may be indicated. When accompanied by a constant increase of the percentage of the prodomestic group in the total these two shifts would seem to be reasonably good evidence for inferring cultural control over the animals in question."

Students using this method have found that a shift from a reliance on wild animals to a reliance on domestic animals had taken place in the Near East by the beginning of the 5th millennium B.C. (17, 18). In Europe, similar shifts in faunal deposits occur at least one millennium later, while in central, eastern, and southwestern Asia the shift occurs closer to two millennia after that in the Near East.

Support for the conclusions of the statistical approach lies in the discovery of evidence that it was in West Asia that cattle were first used as a source of animal power. It is here that sledge, wagon, yoke, and plow are first found (8, pp. 441, 449, 478; 19, 20). Wagons and representations of wagons are found at Tell Halaf, the ancient Gossan, in the extreme north of Mesopotamia and at Ur in the southeast (21, 22). In Mesopotamian sites the burial of wheeled vehicles is firmly associated with royal funerals by 3000 B.C. (23). At Susa, in Elam, a wagon was unearthed and dated to 2500 B.C. (21). By the beginning of the 2nd millennium cattle and wagons are always associated on representations of the Indus culture. The sledge was apparently the earliest vehicle to be developed, and records of sledges are found in Mesopotamia in pre-Warka IV layers. By the Warka IV period (3000 to 2800 B.C.), an ideograph for "wagon" was in use; thus, the wagon must have been in use by the end of the 4th millennium. Indeed, that cattle were used in Mesopotamia for traction, at least from the late 5th millennium onward, is indicated by the symbolism of the zodiac, which can be traced that far back. The constellation Taurus was then already interpreted as a bovine harnessed to a sledge or wagon. The earliest representations of plows show a similar regional distribution. They are found in Warka IV and in Egypt from about 2700 B.C. on. Plow figurines dated 2300 to 1900 B.C. have been recovered from Vounous Bellapais on Cyprus. Sumerian seals of uncertain date also depict plows. Representations of plows are more recent than those of wagons or sledges, but to which of these vehicles animal traction was first applied is not certain (8, pp. 412, 436).

The oldest type of harness strongly suggests that cattle were the first animals to be used for traction. This is the double neck yoke, with which it is

Fig. 2. Urus skull from Bur-well Fen near Cambridge, England. Length of horns along horn contour and across forehead, 5 feet 9 inches. (Courtesy American Museum of Natural History.) (From "On the Domestication of Cattle," Erich Isaac, *Science*, Vol. 137, pp. 195–204, 20 July 1962. Copyright 1962 by the American Association for the Advancement of Science.)

possible to control and utilize the great muscular power concentrated in the cervicothoracic region in cattle. This yoke has been found in Mesopotamia, associated first with wagons and later also with plows. The earliest representations of plowing, also from Mesopotamia, show that cattle were attached either by ropes tied directly to the horns or by ropes attached to a beam lashed to the horns (8, pp. 412, 436). The neck yoke was not known in Egypt until about 1600 B.C., and only the more rudimentary methods of harnessing (methods also used in Mesopotamia) were employed up to that time. When, subsequently, the onager was used for traction, the cattle harness, although inappropriate, was used (8, p. 431; 19).

Only One Ancestral Strain

Zoological study of remains has cast little light on the question of when or where cattle were first domesticated. Zoology asserts that present-day types of domestic cattle are all derived from one ancestral strain, *Bos primigenius* Bojanus, or the wild urus, an animal which survived in Europe until the late Middle Ages (the last known remaining specimen died in 1627). *Bos namadicus* Falconer et Cautley, whose relics are found in Asia, and *Bos opis-thonomous* Pomel, found in North Africa, are assumed today to be the same animal. The urus formerly ranged from the Pacific through Asia and Europe and from the Eurasian tundra to the Indian Ocean and into North Africa. The vast range occupied by the urus from the Pleistocene to the 17th century A.D. could well account for minor differences in the animal, and hence the names denote little more than its geographic range (24).

Early cattle remains reveal considerable differences in size. Fossil remains indicate that the wild urus, whose presence in Europe is first proven in the Riss glacial, was a large, long-horned and powerful animal (Fig. 2) (25). Remains of individual urus have been found, for the whole period of early domestication, which indicate that the animal stood over 2 meters high at the withers. But alongside remains of these enormous animals, fossil remains of considerably smaller cattle have been found (26). Similarly varied finds have been made throughout North Africa and western Asia. The diversity in size has been interpreted in more than one way. It has been asserted that the smaller animals represent a dwarf urus, that they represent a separate ancestral strain of contemporary longifrons or brachyceros types, or that the size difference is due to the great sex dimorphism of the urus, the small animals being females, as in the case of the Tibetan yak. Certainly, dwarf varieties of other wild animals are known, especially in isolated locales—for example, dwarf elephant, crocodile, hippopotamus (*Hippopotamus liberiensis*), buffalo (*Syncerus caffer nanus*), and antelope (*Neotragus pygmaeus*). In all cases, however, the animals are found in relatively restricted habitats (27) and do not have the wide range that the small bovine evidently had. The view that the smaller animal is indicative of a non-urus bovine has found least favor among zoologists. It seems fairly clear that animals domesticated between, roughly, 2000 B.C. and the present, including animals domesticated in this century, are of monophyletic origin (for example, the cat, rabbit, silver fox, and

nutria), and the argument goes that it is unlikely that cattle and other old domestic animals should be of polyphyletic origin (28). Although this argument constitutes no proof, recent studies have confirmed the view that the small animal was probably the female of the urus, the size difference largely disappearing in domestication (29).

As to the social or economic conditions under which domestication of cattle arose, zoology has not made any serious attempts to critically analyze the postulates of culture history. Some —Herre, for example—accept the conclusion of culture history (11), while others, such as Zeuner, content themselves with a general statement concerning the inevitability of symbiotic relationships developing between animal and man, who is assumed to be "an integral part of his physico-biological environment" (30).

In the last 50 years great strides have been made in the comparative study of domestic and wild individuals of a species, and many changes which are the result of domestication, including changes in the soft parts of the body reflected in skeletal remains, have been clearly established, so that theoretically it should be possible to distinguish between wild and domestic animals in early finds and representations (31). But the usefulness of the criteria which have been established in the examination of skeletal remains from the dawn of domestication is severely limited in that cultural domestication must have antedated any impact upon the osteological components of the animal. The difficulty is aggravated by the fact that osteological elements to which such diagnostic criteria might be applied are unfortunately missing in most of the earliest archeological finds, and one cannot exclude the possibility that the changes occurred in wild mutants, for in fact almost all the changes that occur in domestication are known to occur (though rarely, to be sure) in wild individuals (32). Thus, for all the progress that has been made in determining characteristics which develop in domestication, these criteria are insufficient for determining whether domestication had in fact occurred in the earliest sites in which prodomestic animals are found. Indeed, as Epstein, a leading student of African domestic animals, has pointed out, the study of anatomic characteristics has been inadequate even for determining the racial history of long-horn cattle (33).

Arguments for Religious Motivation

The geographer Eduard Hahn, in a series of writings at the turn of the century, posed the basic questions involved in study of the domestication of cattle (4). These are the questions still raised today, and they are still answered by culture historians substantially in the way he answered them. Hahn pointed to the exceptional position of cattle among animals that have been domesticated. In the case of some animals, domestication may have come about spontaneously. For example, the ancestor of the dog as well as that of the domestic pig probably, as scavengers, sought out man, and gradually man assumed the leadership in the relationship. One may indeed ask, "Who then initially domesticated whom?" (34). Domestication, again, may have been furthered by instincts which make us cherish our own infants and which are aroused by young mammals of somewhat similar bodily proportions. Piglets and dog pups are nursed by women in some primitive societies. But the domestication of wild cattle cannot be explained

as an inadvertent process. Wild cattle presumably did not seek human company, and the initiative must have come from man (6, p. 33). Furthermore, man must have had a strong motivation, since the wild urus was a powerful, intractable animal of whom it is said in Job (35): "Will the urus be willing to serve thee, or abide by thy crib? Canst thou span him into a plowing harness or will he harrow the valleys after thee?"

Eduard Hahn has postulated that the motive for capturing and maintaining the urus in the captive state was to have available a supply, for sacrificial purposes, of the animal sacred to the lunar mother goddess worshipped over an immense area of the ancient world. The economic uses of the animal would then have been a by-product of a domestication religious in origin. Why the urus was selected as the animal sacred to the deity is uncertain, but this was probably because its gigantic curved horns resembled the lunar crescent (Fig.3). Studies in prehistoric and early historic religion have shown that the bovine was early regarded as an epiphany of the goddess or her consort and was slain in the ritual reenactment of the myth of her death. This myth involves the notion of the death and resurrection in new life of the deity. Of course, if cattle were domesticated because the horns of the urus resembled the moon's crescent, it is possible that other horned animals, such as sheep and goats, were also domesticated for their horns. Again, it is possible that an unsuccessful attempt to domesticate crescent-horned gazelles (17, 18) was made for the same reason. On the other hand, the bison, domesticable but lacking crescent-shaped horns, was never domesticated (36). The old 19th-century theory that animals were domesticated through

196

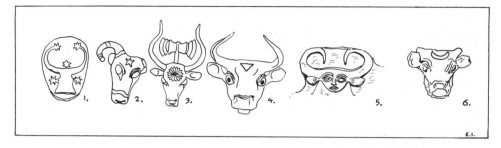

Fig. 3. A group of heads indicating the ritual significance of cattle. 1. Gerzean slate palette with the head of Hathor as the heavenly cow, about 3300 B.C. 2, Clay bull's head with astral symbol, Old Kingdom period, Egypt. 3, Bull's head with rosette, Mycenaean period, Greece. 4, Bull's head from Tell Khafaje, Iraq, with pearl triangle, about 2800 B.C. 5, Head of Hathor with cow's ears and horns on a votive plate of King Narmer, Hierakonpolis (Kom el Ahmar), about 3200 B.C. 6, Bull's head with lunar crescent, al-'Ubaid, about 3100 B.C. (Art courtesy Erich Isaac. From "On the Domestication of Cattle," Erich Isaac, *Science*, Vol. 137, pp. 195–204, 20 July 1962. Copyright 1962 by the American Association for the Advancement of Science.)

being corralled for food was dismissed by Hahn as raising more problems than it answered (37). It failed to explain the choice of certain animals and the rejection of others equally abundant, more easily captured, and more easily raised in captivity (38). Hahn's theory, moreover, has the merit of fitting current attitudes toward cattle of many African and Asian peoples.

Conjectures on Domestication

Hahn's followers have conjectured that the process by which the urus was transformed into a domestic animal was as follows. The captured animals were kept in corrals, for sacrificial use. Types different from the original strains of captured urus developed, since the sacrificial stock, protected from predators and free to multiply, would have been either more inbred or more outbred than under natural conditions. As every zoo keeper knows, this factor alone would produce deviations from the wild parent stock (39). Obviously, animals with more infantile characteristics, such as foreshortened heads, long legs, and relatively straight backs, as against the high withers and massive build of the wild cattle, could

grow to maturity under the protective conditions of the sacred corral. Indeed, the selection of mature long-horned animals as epiphanies of the deity and thus the best animals for sacrificial purposes perhaps initially encouraged the survival of such individuals. Moreover, pied coats, which occur among many species as the result of domestication, developed in cattle as a result of breeding in confinement. Thus, the argument runs, *Bos taurus longifrons*, the first cattle to be economically exploited, emerged. On the other hand, the desirability for sacrifical purposes of the massive long-horned animal led to the perpetuation of a urus-like animal in the well-known sacred primigenius herds of the ancient Near East.

The development of infantile-appearing strains of sacred cattle more tractable than the parent stock widened the range of ritual uses to which the animal could be put. Representations indicate that the first known harnessing of cattle was to sleighs or wagons in religious processions. Mesopotamian frescoes show priests plowing and performing other tasks of husbandry. Priests are also shown performing rites involving cattle, either in the sacrifice

197

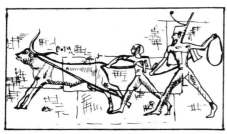

Figs. 4–6. Fig. 4 (top). Bull hunt on painted sunk relief carved on the mortuary temple of Rameses III at Medinet Habu, western Thebes. The king dispatches wounded (probably wild) bulls in papyrus thickets on a stream bank, about 1150 B.C. (× 1/60) (Oriental Institute, University of Chicago). Fig. 5 (center). Urus and gazelles hunted by charioteer. The figures are embossed in prominent relief on a gold bowl from Ugarit, 14th century B.C. (Schaeffer, Collège de France). Fig. 6 (bottom). Rameses II and a prince lasso a bull (probably semi-domestic), temple of Sethos I at Abydos (Farshut), about 1300 B.C. (E. Isaac). (From "On the Domestication of Cattle," Erich Isaac, *Science,* Vol. 137, pp. 195–204, 20 July 1962. Copyright 1962 by the American Association for the Advancement of Science.)

of an animal or in processions in the temple precincts. The notion of using cattle for secular labor seems to have been derived from the use of cattle to pull sacred vehicles. Castration of the bull, which led to one of the most significant of agricultural developments, the ox, also had a religious origin. Neither the taming effect of castration nor its effect in improving the texture of meat could have been foreseen (6, p. 37). Human ritual castration, a reenactment of the fate of the deity in certain cults of Near Eastern ritual mythology (Tammuz, Attis, and so on) probably served as the model for the castration of bulls.

The earliest indication, apart from the osteological record, of the development of a domestic type distinct from the wild urus lies in representational art. From representations we find that the earliest strains of domestic cattle strongly resembled the urus. In many cases, of course, it is difficult to determine whether the animal portrayed was wild or domestic. On the famous standard of Ur, a bull is shown, and that it was probably domestic may be inferred from the ring through its nose. Certainly, some reliefs leave no doubt that the animal was domestic, as, for example, the copper relief of the temple of Mesannipadda (6, p. 43), founder of the first dynasty of Ur (about 3100 B.C.), which shows priests milking. Other representations, such as the well-known victory tablet of King Narmer of Hierakonpolis (Kom el Ahmar, Egypt), undoubtedly depict wild bulls. However, much of the representational evidence, especially that which shows hunting scenes, is ambiguous (Figs. 4–6). We may infer that the scenes depicting the hunt of cattle by Ashurnasirpal (884–860 B.C.) show the hunting of wild cattle, from the existing lists of the game killed and captured.

On a single hunt this king killed 50 urus bulls and captured eight live ones. From other Assyrian texts we learn that young cattle captured in the hunt were bred in captivity. In the existing lists, different symbols are used for wild and for domestic animals; the representations alone would not tell us conclusively that the animals were wild and not semidomestic cattle kept on the open range. Even when a hunt is shown, or where the scene is that of an animal trapped in nets or trapped through the use of decoy cows, the capture that is shown may well be of animals from a semidomestic herd on the range. Boettger stresses that the capture of bulls depicted on two gold cups found in a tomb of Vaphio near Sparta and dating back to about 1500 to 1250 B.C. is very probably a capture not of wild bulls, as was previously supposed, but of bulls kept in a state of semidomestication. Again, the long-horned massive cattle depicted in the bull-game scenes of Cretan frescoes probably are semi-domestic animals, for they are pied. Indeed, on a picture of late Minoan times a cow of the same massive configuration is shown being milked in the old (and dangerous) Mesopotamian fashion—through her hind legs. This method is employed even today in Africa (6, pp. 35, 47, 49).

There is still another reason why one cannot rely completely on representational art as a source of information: styles in art may have persisted when they ceased to convey an accurate picture of the cattle of the period. The maintenance of conventions characterizes religious art in particular. In Austrian churches, until recent times, peasants offered little statuettes of long-horned cattle, although such cattle had been unknown in Austria for many centuries (40). Herre's comparative

study of skeletal remains, and of pictures of domestic animals contemporary with the remains, from medieval Hamburg revealed that very different conclusions would be drawn from the study of either alone (41). That Egyptian representational art was characterized by the same maintenance of artistic conventions has been pointed out by Boessneck (42).

Although there are thus difficulties in judging from early representational art what kind of cattle were in fact used, it is possible to distinguish domestic cattle in later representations, when the specifically domestic characteristics are stressed—in representations of cattle with pied coats or extremely large udders, or of short-horned or polled cattle (*Bos taurus akeratos*) such as we find represented on the mural relief of King Ti and Queen Neferhotpes at Saqqara (25th century B.C.).

Primigenius and Longifrons Emerge

From the wild urus two races of domestic cattle emerged early. The heavy horns of the urus caused the development of wide and flat parietal bones, so that the top of the skull, when the animal is seen head on, appears almost horizontal. Domestic cattle which retained a urus conformation of skull and body are called "primigenius" cattle, descendants of *Bos taurus primigenius*, the earliest domestic cattle. When shorter-horned domestic cattle developed, the frontal and parietal bones, released from the excessive weight of horns, became domed; this is, of course, most evident in polled animals. This type of animal, because of its characteristic long and narrow face and upward convex parietals, is called *Bos taurus longifrons* (Figs. 6–9) (43).

Longifrons cattle, differing markedly from primigenius cattle, like the latter

199

Fig. 7. Urus from a seal impression from the Indus Valley, about 2500 B.C. (Art courtesy Erich Isaac. From "On the Domestication of Cattle," Erich Isaac, *Science,* Vol. 137, pp. 195–204, 20 July 1962. Copyright 1962 by the American Association for the Advancement of Science.)

first appear in Mesopotamia. While it is difficult, in the early Mesopotamian representations, to distinguish between urus and primigenius cattle, in the case of longifrons it is clear that a domestic type is represented. Generally, moreover, longifrons cattle are depicted in association with agricultural performances or symbols. Probably the first representation of longifrons is on a bowl of the Jemdet Nasr period, and subsequently longifrons cattle are depicted more and more often, although never so frequently as primigenius types. Boettger has proposed that the distinction between longifrons and primigenius was one between an economically exploited breed and a strain maintained primarily for ritual purposes. The distribution of longifrons cattle outside the Near East is taken by Boettger to indicate that longifrons was spread intentionally and did not originate independently in a number of places. In spite of the fact that longifrons cattle appear much later than primigenius in Mesopotamia, their docility, their manageability, and their overall usefulness account, according to Boettger, for their having reached both the Atlantic and the Pacific peripheries of the Old World continents before primigenius cattle did (6, p. 52).

With the spread of longifrons into the European periphery, a number of dwarf varieties appeared, constituting, in the view of the culture historian, a deterioration of the introduced strain. This deterioration may have been initially the result of inexperience in handling, and of inadequate feeding before a proper balance of feed crops was grown or before pasture systems were developed. Dwarf longifrons cattle, formerly called *Bos taurus brachyceros*, occur in the Swiss Neolithic, and in the Balkans and Caucasus in the 2nd millennium B.C. (44). Certain present-day cattle (still kept under relatively poor conditions of husbandry) are counted among the modern representatives of this type—for example, the Polish Maydan and Hutsul cattle, Polesian and Polish Red, Spanish Mountain, Italian Piedmont, Brown Mountain (Austria), and Bulgarian Rhodope cattle. Eventually, animals larger than longifrons or its dwarf varieties developed. Crosses with wild cattle undoubtedly occurred, and the products of such crosses resembled in conformation the primigenius types of West Asia. These were favored in some areas and through selective breeding gave rise to *Bos taurus frontosus*, a broad-faced type which is represented today by some economically very important European breeds such as the Dutch Friesian and the Meuse-Rhine-Yssel, the Swiss Fribourg and Simmentaler, the German Yellow Hill, and the Austrian Pinzgau. Elsewhere, cattle with a dwarfed primigenius conformation but a short skull developed —*Bos taurus brachycephalus* Wilkens, whose modern representatives include the French Tarentaise, the Swiss Hérèns, and the Austrian Tux-Zillertal (45).

Thesis Consistent with Zoology

There is no fundamental disagreement between zoology and culture history on the question of how domestic breeds of cattle developed, even though the notion of a religious motive is not germane to zoological analysis. Of course, to find out if there was even a possibility that the urus voluntarily joined human society, zoologists would have to recreate the animal by back-crossing. Apparently successful attempts to recreate the urus have been made. Both H. Heck, at the Hella-brunn Zoo of Munich, and his brother L. Heck, at the Berlin Zoo, were able from different breeding stock to create bovines which bore a remarkable resemblance to medieval representations of the urus. Unfortunately, however, we have no precise knowledge of the physiology and psychology of the urus, so that even if one produced an animal that looked exactly like the urus (and medieval representations are generally stylized), it would not be possible to know whether the animal behaved like the urus (46).

The zoologist, like the culture historian, asserts that new strains would almost necessarily appear as a result of the accidental capture of foundation stock from different breeding groups and the establishment of larger breeding units. Even under wild conditions, where there are animals heterozygous for numerous genes, segregation of deviating individuals occurs constantly. But although as a rule deviant individuals are eliminated by natural selection, the protection against predators afforded by the simplest enclosure would suffice to allow deviating animals to develop and reproduce. Polled cattle, whose senses are poorly developed in comparison to those of wild individuals and who lack a primary defense, would survive. Even in the case of nonsocial animals, such as cats, living in a human settlement, the increase in population density has the effect of increasing variability (11).

The history of the domestic rabbit is known with some completeness and shows the same pattern of changes taking place under conditions of enclosure. In fact, the rabbit is taken by students of domestication to illustrate the process of change in a wild animal under the influence of domestication (47). The domestic rabbit is derived

Fig. 8. Sumerian marble bowl with primigenius bulls carved in relief, about 2700 B.C. (The Metropolitan Museum of Art, Fletcher Fund, 1939.) (From "On the Domestication of Cattle," Erich Isaac, Science, Vol. 137, pp. 195–204, 20 July 1962. Copyright 1962 by the American Association for the Advancement of Science.)

Fig. 9. Relief of longifrons cattle from the tomb of Ra-em-kai, Saqqara, Egypt, Vth Dynasty. (The Metropolitan Museum of Art, Rogers Fund, 1908.) (From "On the Domestication of Cattle," Erich Isaac, Science, Vol. 137, pp. 195–204, 20 July 1962. Copyright 1962 by the American Association for the Advancement of Science.)

Fig. 10. Woodcut of a urus, highly stylized, in Johan Prüss' *Hortus sanitatis,* published in 1495 by Jacob Meydenbach in Mainz. The text reads: "Isidor says of the urus: urus are wild cattle so strong that they can lift trees as well as armed knights with their horns. They are called urus from the Greek word oros meaning mountain . . . Helynandus says . . . In the Hercynian Forest of Germany the urus is found. These animals are nearly as large as elephants: in appearance, color and conformation they are like cattle. The force of their horns is great and their speed is great. They spare neither man nor animal. One catches them in pits and kills them." (From "On the Domestication of Cattle," Erich Isaac, *Science,* Vol. 137, pp. 195–204, 20 July 1962. Copyright 1962 by the American Association for the Advancement of Science.)

Ro. Jſidorᵒ. Uri ſunt boucs agreſtes adeo fortes vt arbores z armatos milites i cornib cleuét. Jdé vri Dictiſut apoton orion.i.a montib. Sūt boues aūt agreſtes i germania bītes cornu in rantum prenſa:vr regīs mēſis inſigni capa citate ex eis gerule fiant. ¶Delynandus libro viceſimoſexto. Jn hyrcinia ſilua germanie ſunt vri. Di ſunt magnitudine paulo clephantos:ſpecie z colore z figura tauri. Magna vis corū eſt z magna velocitas necꝫ bomini necꝫ fere quā aſpexerint parcunt. Dos ſtudioſe foueis captos interficiunt.

from wild rabbits, imported from Spain during the period of the Roman Empire, which were enclosed in leporaries where they lived as in the wild but were accessible to hunting parties. From old engravings it is apparent that hunting rabbits in leporaries was held to be a suitable and safe pastime for ladies. Not until the 17th century had the rabbit changed by mutation from wildness to tameness and assumed the characteristics of the present-day rabbit. That the urus differentiated under conditions of domestication into primigenius and longifrons is thus not unlikely, even if the degree of control and selection was less than the thesis of religious motivation assumes.

What Was Transmitted— Animal or Idea?

Although the culture historian assumes that the small cattle which are the first to appear in Old World strata outside West Asia were longifrons which West Asian migrants brought with them, all that zoology can state with certainty is that a pronounced diminution in size differentiates this animal from the urus; such diminution could, of course, come through local domestication. In fact, in Europe a steady diminution in size continued until the Middle Ages. While the urus had stood at more than 2 meters at the withers, the average height at the withers in the Iron Age is given by Herre as 1.10 meters, and the average in the Middle Ages, as 1 meter or less. Herre asserts that domestication must have been local, since the earliest domestic cattle in Europe, occurring long after domestic characteristics were well developed in Near Eastern cattle, were transitional forms with respect to the local representatives of the urus (48). Herre does not deny that domestication first occurred in the Near East but asserts that the technique and idea of domestication were transmitted rather than actual

Fig. 11. Drawing of urus copied from a 16th century oil painting found in 1827 by the English zoologist Hamilton Smith in an Augsburg antiquities shop. The painting was subsequently lost, but this drawing was widely reproduced. (Courtesy of the American Museum of Natural History.) (From "On the Domestication of Cattle," Erich Isaac, *Science,* Vol. 137, pp. 195–204, 20 July 1962. Copyright 1962 by the American Association for the Advancement of Science.)

domestic animals. He supports his view with reference to "substitute" domestications ("*Ersatzhaustieren*")—animals domesticated outside the range of the wild form of an already domesticated animal, such as the ass (*Asinus africanus* Fitzinger 1857) in place of the horse (*Equus cab. przewalski* Poliakov 1881), the yak (*Bos* [*Poëphagus*] *grunniens* Przewalski 1883) in place of the urus, and so on (11).

There are additional weighty arguments put forth in support of the thesis of local domestication of the urus in disparate areas. The general average decline in size of the early European cattle was accompanied, as the osteological record shows, by a great overall variability in size and conformation. Such remarkable multiplication in conformational types and increase in the growth range of adult animals follows, even today, upon the domestication of wild animals, as practical work with domestic fur-producing animals has shown. Thus, the silver and blue fox, themselves mutants of the red fox, have in a short time given rise to a series of other types: platinum, white-faced, golden platinum, pearl, perlatina, glacier blue, Washington platina, radium, and pastel fox (47). Similar results have been achieved with mink and nutria. The great variability observed in early European domestic cattle remains a strong argument against the thesis of

the introduction of a developed domestic strain.

Should, then, the thesis of the introduction of longifrons into Europe be thrown out? Were it not for the appearance simultaneously with domestic cattle of tools, pottery, and art stylistically related to and often demonstrably imported from the prehistoric and early historic Near East, the thesis of actual introduction of the earliest domestic cattle would undoubtedly receive even less attention than it does in current treatment of the racial history of European cattle. And, of course, even where contact, trade, and migrations have occurred, actual movement of cattle cannot be proven. Nonetheless, there remains much to support the introduction thesis. Ersatz domestication, while it has occurred in many instances, has taken place in areas where the domestic animal cannot be introduced because of conditions of excessive physiological strain and stress, local bacterial faunas, dangers of worm infestation, and so on. Such conditions make it economically unfeasible to introduce many of the classical domestic animals into tropical or high-altitude areas even today, but there was never any bar to the introduction of cattle into Europe. Moreover, although local wild strains (Figs. 10 and 11) undoubtedly contributed to the formation of the earliest European domestic cattle, accounting for the "dwarf urus" which appears rather abruptly in stratigraphic layers (49), unless domestic cattle were brought into Europe and crossed with the local urus, the difficulty of domestication would have been scarcely less in Europe than it had been millennia previously in West Asia. It is conceivable, in fact, that the European wild urus played a smaller part in the formation of frontosus and primigenius types than was formerly assumed. Certainly in historic times efforts have always been made to prevent cross breeding between the urus and domestic cattle so as not to increase the wildness of the domestic races (6, p. 48). Perhaps the locally occurring European primigenius and frontosus races are, after all, products of selection from the early introduced longifrons, and from the subsequently introduced West Asian or Mediterranean primigenius cattle.

Of interest in this connection is the fact, pointed out by Nobis, that in regions dominated by the Roman camps of the European *limes*, primigenius or "pseudoprimigenius" cattle are found (50). These may be introductions from the Mediterranean world, or products of the application to local stock of the more expert Roman husbandry, or the result of both. There was no lasting improvement in the near-dwarfed local cattle of the surrounding areas, and after Roman times pseudoprimigenius all but vanishes from the osteological record of these areas. It is tempting to draw an analogy with the more recent history of cattle in southern and central Africa. After the disastrous rinderpest epidemic of 1896, there were massive introductions of European stock (51), but in spite of large-scale cross-breeding, the contribution of the European stock to the conformational characteristics and productive capacity of native cattle was all but negligible. Under the

rigorous conditions of the African veld, natural selection operated in favor of animals of overall ruggedness rather than of animals of indifferent stamina though of higher potential as a source of meat and milk (52).

Explanation of Variability
Great variability in size and even in conformation of a herd may be taken to imply a low level of animal-husbandry skill and does not necessarily mean that domestication has been recent. African domestic cattle today are almost entirely derived from repeated introduction of West Asian domestic races (51, 53). Yet among Sanga cattle, the most important breed type in central and southern Africa and represented as far west as Nigeria and as far north as the Sudan, the variation in conformation, in animal size, and in horn size is enormous. Often gigantic-horned, long-horned, short-horned, and polled animals occur in a single herd (54). Some Sanga, such as the Shona or Karanga cattle of Southern Rhodesia, have truly dwarfed and short-horned representatives (55), whereas another Sanga, Bechuana cattle, includes gigantic specimens (56) whose enormous horns approach and even exceed in length those of Indian Pliocene ancestors of the urus (57). The fact is that where, for whatever reason, the herder selected for small size, a small Sanga appeared. Similarly, megaloceratic horns in African Sanga herds persist only because of continued careful selection for gigantic horns. Where there is no selection for special points, the Sanga herds are made up of generally small, although widely divergent, individuals. This state of affairs obviously does not prove that the Sanga was locally domesticated. Thus, perhaps the dwarfing and variability of European

neolithic cattle indicates that an introduced race—longifrons—deteriorated under conditions where a desire for a large number of animals outweighed considerations of carrying capacity and productive potential of the individual animal—as it so often does in African husbandry.

It is noteworthy that recent and more sophisticated methods of investigation have tended to support the thesis that cattle were introduced into Europe from western Asia. Electrophoretic studies of the distribution and mode of inheritance of different types of hemoglobin in cattle (58) support the thesis that Jersey (59) (a brachycephalus type) as well as Guernsey and South Devon cattle (the former brachyceros, the latter brachycephalus) had an African, and ultimately a Mesopotamian, origin. The superior performance of Devon and Jersey cattle at high temperatures, demonstrated in studies at agricultural research centers in Africa, as well as the exceptionally high butter-fat content of milk from these breeds, characteristic also of milk from cattle native to tropical regions, tends to reinforce the argument that these types had a western Asian origin.

Conclusion

The thesis of Eduard Hahn and of those who have followed his lead has stood up well in the light of progress made in zootechnology, animal psychology, the comparative anatomy of domestic and wild species, and the study of non-European native cattle. On the other hand, Hahn's hypothesis can in no way be said to have stimulated work in the zoology of domestic species, although such work has gone far to confirm its plausibility. But if Hahn's thesis has had no particular bearing on the zoological study of domestication, in what can its value be

said to lie? Like all cultural theses, it provides an insight into historical processes. Specifically, Hahn's thesis also constituted a protest against the materialistic assumptions underlying 19th-century German social and economic theories. Hahn affirmed the importance of irrational forces in major technological advances of mankind. His thesis, moreover, has stood up better than most of the broad and more spectacular cultural theses of our day, where close examination by experts in any specific and relevant area has led to steady erosion of the overarching argument. In the study of domestication the scientist and the cultural historian join forces, each playing a role which the other discipline, by its very nature, cannot fill.

References

1. This article grew out of research in the larger problem of the origin and distribution of the breed groups of domestic cattle. I am indebted to the Ford Foundation, which supported a year's study in Africa devoted in part to the study of African animal husbandry and breeds.

2. A. Müntzing, *Proc. Am. Phil. Soc* **103**, 190 (1959).

3. The classical statement of the theory is that of E. Hahn (4).

4. E. Hahn, *Die Haustiere and ihre Beziehungen zur Wirtschaft des Menschen* (Leipzig: Duncker and Humblot, 1896); *Die Entstehung der Pflugkultur* (Heidelberg: Winter, 1909).

5. The most recent statement is that of C. R. Boettger (6).

6. C. R. Boettger, *Die Haustiere Afrikas* (Jena: Fischer, 1958).

7. The old ethnological view, dating back to the Greek geographer Dicaearchus (about 310 B.C.), that cattle were domesticated by nomadic hunters has been shown to be untenable, notably by Georg Cancrin (1774–1845), Alexander von Humboldt (1769–1859), and Eduard Hahn (1856–1928). None of the steppes of the New World gave rise to herding complexes, although they were

occupied by hunters and wild herd animals for an extensive period of historical
time. The nomadic complexes of the
Old World steppes were always con-
tiguous to land areas of sedentary farmers who had the same domestic animals as the nomads. Conversely, in no
steppes not adjacent to areas occupied
by animal-using peasantry has pastoral
nomadism developed from hunting nomadism (the steppes of Australia are an
example). The South African Hottentots
are only an apparent exception; they
originated in the East African steppes
occupied by other herding peoples.
Moreover, present-day nomadic hunters
do not domesticate animals; the use of
animals in hunting (such as the cormo-
rant, the hawk, the cheetah, and the
mongoose) is an invention of peasant
cultures, whether the animals are used
as decoys, as trackers, or as agents of
the kill. Primitive hunters do not even
use dogs in the hunt. On the subject of
the land areas occupied by peasants and
nomads, see K. J. Narr, in *Historia
Mundi*, ed. F. Valjavec (Bern: Francke,
1953), vol. 2, pp. 60–100. On Hottentot
origins, see T. F. Dreyer and H. J. D.
Meiring, *Soologiese Navorsing van die
Nasionale Museum Bloemfontein* (1937),
vol. 1, p. 81, and *Navorsing van die
Nasionale Museum Bloemfontein* (1952),
vol. 1, p. 19; P. V. Tobias, *African
Studies* **14**, 1 (1955); J. C. Trevor, *J.
Roy. Anthropol. Inst.* **77**, pt. 1, 61 (1947).

8. F. Hancar, *Das Pferd in Prähistorischer
und Früher Historischer Zeit* (Vienna:
Herold, 1956).

9. Eland has recently been successfully
domesticated in Southern Rhodesia by
J. Posselt, near Gwanda and in the
Union of South Africa. I owe my intro-
duction to domesticated eland to Paul
Donnelly, provincial agriculturist,
Bulawayo, Southern Rhodesia. See
Onslow, *Man* **55**, 24 (1945).

10. W. Herre, *Das Ren als Haustier* (Leipzig: Geest and Portig, 1955), pp. 15–33.

11. _____, *Naturw. Rundschau* **12**, 88
(1959).

12. On African milking methods, see S.
Lagercrantz, *Studia Ethnographica
Upsal.* (Stockholm 1950), vol. 1; T. M.
Bettini, *Beitr. Kulturgesch. Linguist.* **6**,
126 (1944); G. W. B. Huntingford, *The*

Southern Nilo-Hamites (London: International African Institute, 1953), pt. 8,
pp. 21, 29. On ancient sources, see H.
Plischke, *Ethnol.* **79**, 1 (1954); J. L.
Benson, in *The Aegean and the Near
East*, ed. S. S. Weinberg (Locust Valley, N.Y.: Augustin, 1956), p. 65, note
27.

13. Homer Aschman has recently described
the nearly complete absorption in pastoral husbandry of a society which was
formerly a sedentary society of cultivation, in *Ann. Assoc. Am. Geographers*
50, 408 (1960). See also K. J. Narr in
Historia Mundi, ed. F. Valjavec (Bern:
Francke, 1953), vol. 2, pp. 77–78; J.
Weisner, *Gnomon* **31**, 289 (1959).

14. R. H. Dyson, Jr., *Am. Anthropol.* **55**,
662 (1953).

15. C. A. Reed, *Science* **130**, 1629 (1959).
Proponents of the nomadic-hunter domestication theory have argued that the
archeological record constitutes no
proof, since the transient sites of early
nomads are not likely to be identified.
Certainly the archeological record is
haphazard for vast areas, but as Narr
pointed out, such evidence as there is
does point to the agricultural origin of
herd animal domestication.

16. A statistical approach to determination
of the presence of domestic animals
has been used at least since the 1890's.
See H. Krämer, *Rev. Suisse zool.* **7**
(1899); J. U. Duerst, *Arch. Anthropol.*
2 (1905); A. Pira, *Zool. Jahrb. Abt.
Allgem. Zool. Physiol. Tiere* **28**, suppl.
10 (1909).

17. Material currently being studied by
Charles A. Reed at the Peabody Museum, Yale University, indicates that
a shift from wild to domestic sheep occurred in northern Iraq as early as the
9th millennium B.C. Reed questioned
recently [*Science* **130**, 1635 (1959)] the
universal applicability of the statistical
approach, for we find similar concentrations of submature individuals in instances where the animals never became
domestic. Such finds, on the other hand,
may mean that an attempt at domestication was made which was ultimately
found to be impractical (see 18).

18. F. S. Bodenheimer, *Hachai bearzot
Hamikra* (Jerusalem: Bialik Foundation,
1949), vol. 1, pp. 56–57.

19. C. W. Bishop, *Smithsonian Inst. Publs. Rept. No. 3477*, pp. 531–547.

20. V. G. Childe, *Ethnographisch-Archäologische Forsch.* **2**, 14 (1954); A. G. Haudricort, *Rev. geog. humaine et d'ethnol.* **1** (1948); P. Leser, *Enstehung und Verbreitung des Pfluges* (Münster: Anthropos, 1931).

21. V. G. Childe, *Proc. Prehistory Soc. for 1951* (1951).

22. L. C. Watelin and S. Langdon, *Excavations at Kish* (Paris: Geuthner, 1934), vol. 4, pp. 30–34; C. L. Wooley, *Ur Excavations* (London: Oxford Univ. Press, 1934), vol. 2, p. 64.

23. S. Foltiny, *Am. J. Archaeol.* **63**, 55 (1959).

24. H. Epstein, in *The Indigenous Cattle of the British Dependent Territories in Africa*, ed. D. E. Faulkner (London: Her Majesty's Stationery Office, 1957), p. 40; W. Herre, *Verhandl. Deut. Zool. Ges.* (1949); *Handbuch Tierzüchtung* (Berlin; Parey, 1958), vol. 1.

25. V. Lehman, *Neues Jahrb. Mineral. Geol. Palaeontol.* B, 90 (1949).

26. W. Herre, *Zuechtungskunde* **28**, 223 (1956).

27. M. D. W. Jeffreys, *S. African J. Sci.* **47**, 227 (1951).

28. A. Müntzing, *Proc. Am. Phil. Soc.* **103**, 208 (1959).

29. W. La Baume, *Eclogae Geol. Helv.* **40**, 308 (1947); *Forsch. Fortschr.* **26**, 43 (1950); O. von Leithner, *Ber. Intern. Ges. Erhalt. Wisent.* **2**, 1 (1927).

30. F. Zeuner, in *A History of Technology*, ed. C. Singer *et al.* (London: Oxford Univ. Press, 1954), vol. 1, p. 327.

31. In cattle a foreshortened and widened skull, decrease in the dimension of eye and ear openings, shortness of backbone, decrease in size—in short, overall infantilism—distinguishes domestic from wild varieties. It is remarkable that many changes are common to animals of different species that have been domesticated: curly hair instead of straight; retention of baby hair; pied coats instead of monocolored; reduction in differences between male and female; variability in size between different breed groups, leading to a pronounced contrast between giants and dwarfs; extremely one-sided development of certain characteristics, such as milk production, and sometimes pathological alterations, such as the short-leggedness of Dexter cattle, in which the responsible gene is lethal when homozygous. Some changes in the soft parts are reflected in skeletal remains. Muscular development or atrophy and changes in brain volume due to environmental modifications, such as differences in food supplied by man, or due to the specialized physiological performance required of domestic animals, mark the skeleton and lead to the development of characteristic processes, crests, or ridges. The changes are comprehensively summarized by H. Nachtsheim, *Vom Wildtier zum Haustier* (Berlin: Parey, 1949) and treated in M. Hilzheimer, *Natuerliche Rassengeschichte der Haussäugetiere* (Berlin: de Gruyter, 1926); C. Darwin, *The Variation of Animals and Plants under Domestication* (London, 1868); B. Klatt, *Entstehung der Haustier* (Berlin: Borntraeger, 1927); *Haustier und Mensch* (Hamburg: Hermes, 1948), pp. 54–59; A. Müntzing, *Proc. Am. Phil. Soc.* **103**, 207 (1959).

32. H. Bohlken, *Zool. Jahrb. Abt. Allgem. Zool. Physiol. Tiere* (1958); M. Röhrs, *Verhandl. Deut. Zool. Ges. Graz. Zool. Anz.* **21** (1957); H. Kelm, *Z. Anat. Entwicklungsgeschichte* **108** (1938).

33. H. Epstein, *Z. Tierzücht. Züchtungsbiol.* **71**, 59 (1958).

34. B. Klatt, *Haustier und Mensch* (Hamburg: Hermes, 1948), p. 32.

35. Job 39: 13–14.

36. It is interesting to note that B. Klatt suggests (in *Haustier und Mensch*, p. 34) that the arni buffalo (*Bubalus bubalis*) was the first bovine to be domesticated in Mesopotamia, and that the reason for this was the near-perfect crescent shape of its horns, which made it a suitable epiphany of the lunar deity. The urus, according to Klatt, was probably domesticated as a substitute for the arni, which disappeared from Mesopotamia in early historic times. One might suggest that capture and subsequent sacrifice contributed to the disappearance of the arni, while the urus survived ritual domestication. It was J. U. Duerst, in *Die Rinder von Babylonien, Assyrien*

*und Agypten und Ihr Zusammenhang
mit den Rindern der Alten Welt* (Berlin:
Reimer, 1899) who first pointed out that
there was a relative abundance of representations of arni buffalo and a scarcity
of representations of urus in early Mesopotamian art, and that subsequently
representations of urus increased,
whereas the arni vanished as a subject.
The topic is also treated by M. Hilzheimer, *Die Wildrinder im alten Meso-
potamien* (Leipzig: Pfeiffer, 1926).

37. J. F. Downs, in "Domestication: An
Examination of the Changing Social
Relationships between Man and Animal," *Kroeber Anthropol. Soc. Publ.
No. 22* (1960), pp. 18–67, restated the
enclosure-for-food concept. Hahn and
subsequent authors were dubious about
this view, at least in so far as it concerns cattle, partly because of the rejection of meat and animal products by
many of the great cattle-keeping cultures on religious grounds.

38. The mummified cat interments of Egypt
(at Bubastis near Zagazig and at the
Alexandrinian Serapeum) are probably
the best example of domestication for
religious reasons. A complete record of
mummified cats (the cat was the epiphany of the goddess Bast) exists, showing
a sequence of development from the
ancestral Libyan wild cat (*Felis catus
libyca*) to the domestic cat. Domestic
forms appear first in the course of the
XIIth and XIIIth dynasties. Nowhere
outside of Egypt were wild cats domesticated. It has been argued that the
Libyan wild cat entered into some kind
of symbiotic relationship with ancient
grain-storing Egyptians [see K. Z. Lorenz, *Man Meets Dog* (London: Pan,
1959), pp. 22–24]. The argument is not
convincing, since even today there is a
symbiotic relationship between the wild
cat and man in southern Nubia, but despite the long history of this relationship no development toward domesticity
has taken place. The rodent killer of
ancient Egypt, as of the Mediterranean
basin and most of Europe, was the
housesnake, and the cat did not succeed
in displacing it in many areas until the
post-Christian era. The cat does not
seem to appear in the Bible, but I think
it is significant that the post-Biblical
Hebrew term for cat is "the swaddled,"
undoubtedly referring to the tradition

of mummification. Moreover, it is likely
that our word *cat* ultimately derives
from the old Semitic word for cotton,
the material in which the mummy was
swaddled. (On the cat in Egypt, see 18,
p. 1962.) On the spread of the cat, see
E. Werth, *Grabstock, Hacke, Pflug*
(Ludwigsburg: Ulmer, 1954), p. 324.
The cat is found in the Germanic culture area as sacred to Freya and has survived in folklore as the familiar of the
witch.

39. H. Spurway, *New Biol.* **13,** 11 (1952).

40. O. Antonius, *Grundzüge einer Stam-
mesgeschichte der Haustiere* (Jena:
Fischer, 1922), p. 184.

41. W. Herre, *Hammaburg* **4,** 7 (1950); *Zool.
Garten* **17,** 103 (1950).

42. J. Boessneck, *Veröffentl. zool. Staats-
sammlg. München* **3** (1953).

43. Fundamental studies on horn and skull
conformation were made by J. U.
Duerst, *Das Horn der Cavicornia* (Zü-
rich: Fretz, 1926). Duerst's later views,
especially those on the parietal angle,
are quoted by H. Epstein in *Z. Tierzücht. Züchtungsbiol.* **71,** 61 (1958).

44. On the stunted growth of cattle on
mountain pastures, see V. Vezzani and
E. Carbone, *Report of the 4th International Grassland Congress,* ed. R. O.
Whyte (Aberystwyth, Wales, 1937).

45. A. Schmid, *Rassenkunde des Rindes*
(Bern: Benteli, 1942), vol. 1. Names of
breeds and breed groups are given according to I. L. Mason, "A World Dictionary of Breed Types and Varieties of
Livestock," *Commonwealth Bur. Animal Breeding Genet. (Gt. Brit.) Tech.
Commun. No. 7* (1951).

46. H. Heck, *Oryx* (1951); Heck's popular
claims have been severely criticized by
O. Koehler [*Z. Tierpsychol.* **9** (1952)]
and by W. Herre.

47. A. Müntzing, *Proc. Am. Phil. Soc.* **103,**
205 (1959).

48. W. Herre, *Züchtungskunde* **28,** 223
(1956).

49. *Verhandel. Deut. Zool. Kiel* **1948,** 312
(1949).

50. G. Nobis, *Petermanns Geogr. Mitt.* **99,**
2 (1955).

51. E. A. Nobbs, *S. African J. Sci.* **24,** 331
(1927).

52. I am greatly indebted to D. A. Robinson, director of the Department of Native Agriculture, Southern Rhodesia, and to the scientific personnel of that department's animal husbandry research centers. I also wish to express my gratitude to the many individuals who were associated with Institut National pour l'Etude Agronomique du Congo Belge (INEAC) and Institut pour la Recherche Scientifique en Afrique Centrale (IRSAC) centers at Luiro, Bukavu, and Nioka in the Belgian Congo, and with breeding centers at Entebbe in Uganda; at Sangalo, Maseno, Kibigori, Kisii, and Kabinga in Kenya; and at West Kilimanjaro and Arusha in Tanganyika. I wish to express my special thanks to the department of agriculture, University College of Rhodesia and Nyasaland, for its hospitality, especially to its chairman, Prof. C. Davis, and to Dr. John Oliver, senior lecturer in animal husbandry.

53. H. Curson and R. W. Thornton, *Onderstepoort J. Vet. Sci.* **1936**, 618 (1936); J. H. R. Bisschop, *S. African J. Sci.* **33**, 852 (1937); H. H. Curson and H. Epstein, *Onderstepoort J. Vet. Sci.* **1934**, 3 (1934); H. Epstein, *J. Heredity* **24**, 449 (1933); ———, *J. S. African Vet. Med. Assoc.* **5**, 1 (1934); ———, *E. African Agr. J.* **21**, 83 (1955); D. E. Faulkner and H. Epstein, *The Indigenous Cattle of the British Dependent Territories in Africa* (London: H. M. Stationery Office, 1957).

54. H. Epstein, *E. African Agr. J.* **22**, 149 (1957); *Z. Tierzücht. Züchtungsbiol.* **71**, 65 (1958).

55. Dwarfed Sanga, *Tumombe mapako*, are by now probably extinct in Southern Rhodesia. In 1946 E. A. B. McLeod, a Rhodesian rancher, tried to obtain government assistance in collecting a remnant of the dwarfed animals, but failed.

56. Bechuana cattle from the Lake Ngami area stood nearly 6 feet high at the withers. The Africana Museum, Johannesburg, possesses a skull whose horns measure 8 feet 8 inches from tip to tip. The total length along the contour of the horns and across the forehead is 13 feet 7 inches.

57. These ancestors were *Bos planifrons* Rütim. and *B. acutifrons* Lydekker.

Descriptions of them appear in L. Rütimeyer, *Abhandl. schweiz. Palaeontol. Ges.* **4**, 4 (1877).

58. A. D. Bangham, *Nature* **179**, 467 (1957).

59. E. J. Boston, in *Jersey Cattle*, ed. E. J. Boston (London: Faber, 1954), pp. 19–42.

Man Pressure

COLIN BERTRAM

The claim by economists, agriculturists, and others that the world can support several times its present human population at a level above minimal food requirements is probably true. Such a proposition also has the curious distinction of becoming irrelevant only if it is ever realized. So long as people do starve in crowded lands, it is at least an appropriate comment of concern. But when the prophets of plenty are at last proved right, the naiveté of their position will be apparent. That is to say, "Can we feed them?" may not be the most important question to ask about human population.

The question of the quality of life draws attention to a possible optimum rather than maximum number. To the rejoinder that it would be presumptuous to decide where the optimum lay, the only relevant response is to open the question of responsibility in its broadest context, to the whole of life. The indignant righteousness of laissez faire *lacks precisely that view. To those who have not looked carefully at anything but human faces and printed words, the world's magnitude, diversity, and richness are difficult to communicate. At least the idea of responsibility toward life or for life is as old as Noah and a part of, if not central to, Western thought. It is difficult to prove in advance that this altruism—the concern that we do not devastate the green earth and its inhabitants—is in the long view essential to our own survival.*

THE EDITORS

Oryx, *7(2–3):97–101, August 1963. Reprinted by permission.*

THOSE WITH the enthusiasm and zeal for fauna preservation and conservation even yet, I believe, remain inadequately aware of the enormity of the human tide which sets against them. This essay is intended to help towards a fuller perspective, biologically frightening though it is.

Whereas it is true that the minute calcareous-shelled marine planktonic organisms have had the greatest topographic influence on the earth's surface in the formation of chalk, mankind's overwhelming influence on his environment has so far been in the alteration of the world's vegetational cover, and in the decimation and extinction of other species, chiefly the larger vertebrates. What may come from his radioactive wastes, or purposes, is not for discussion here.

Why is it that *Homo sapiens* is so unprecedently destructive of other species? The answer is that quite apart from man's powers and potentialities, he is by far the most numerous of the larger animals. To name another species of vertebrate of comparable total numbers—at present 3,000 million—is not easy and is probably impossible except among the smaller marine fishes. No other species of world-wide terrestial vertebrate has ever existed and been co-existent in comparable numbers—and, in addition, been large and therefore excessively demanding.

Is there any species of vertebrate of which if may truly be said that a significant proportion of all the individuals there have ever been are alive simultaneously? The answer is indubitably negative, with the sole exception of our own species. So great has been, and is, the recent multiplication of human kind that it is calculated that of all the individuals of the species that there have ever been since *H. sapiens* emerged, between 3 and 4 per cent are alive at this moment.[1]

Human multiplication, the population surge, is in process of explosion. The present 3,000 million are conservatively expected to reach 6,000 million within the present century. The average world-wide figure for increase is about 2 per cent per annum, a figure which itself increases annually, and which already in particular regions exceeds 3 per cent per annum—a doubling of local population in under twenty years.

The reasons for this human surge are not for discussion here.[2] A population crash for *H. sapiens*—perhaps through some virus mutation rather than hunger alone—will most certainly come unless the rate of increase can be checked. Having very substantially, by beneficent effort, greatly reduced mortality, the crash is inevitable at some stage *unless* we are equally successful in limiting human fertility.

Nuclear warfare may "solve" the species' excessive reproduction, but we all must strive to avoid it. Lesser warfare will not "solve" this problem. Two world wars killed between them perhaps 50 million people: that is now the world's net increase of a mere 400 days. Crash and chaos can only be avoided, by means acceptable to people of goodwill, by the deliberate control of fertility. At what point—or at what human population level—this will be achieved remains to be seen. However, so far as we are concerned with the conservation of our heritage of fellow species, we must expect that some decades at the very least will elapse before there is even a significant deceleration of the human surge. In passing, it may be remarked, with sadness and surprise, that, in this great population surge, there are no discernible positive advantages[3] to anyone, while the disadvantages are so numerous yet so little realized in the present ocean of ignorance. Our population increase was never planned: it is a mere by-product of technology and beneficence. Fundamental antagonisms exist between quantity of human lives and the quality of life for the individual. They concern the whole range from the importance and dignity of the individual, through matters of freedom and human relationship, to crowd psychology and personal stress.

H. sapiens, in addition to being now world-wide[4] in distribution, is omnivorous with a strong predilection for animal flesh and products. When man succeeds in this it is called affluence, a state which is highly prized and much sought. The immediate result of course, of this deliberate seeking to change in any degree from a mainly vegetarian to a more largely animal diet, is that the individual "occupies" or requires more space. The use of livestock, as intermediaries between vegetation and the human stomach, adds a new link to the food chain with all the inherent

---

[1] Of human scientists, those creatures of knowledge, power and potentiality for good or ill, 90 per cent of all those who have ever existed are calculated to be alive to-day.

[2] A convenient general summary is provided in *World Population and Resources*. Political and Economic Planning, London, 1955. This work satisfactorily covers not only food and other biological resources but mineral and energy resources in addition.

[3] These matters are conveniently set out by the present author in a chapter "What are People For?" in the symposium volume *The Humanist Frame*, ed. Sir Julian Huxley, 1961.

[4] Antarctica, the last continent to be colonized, now regularly has a few overwintering males, and male summer migrants are numerous. Female visitors are still very scarce. Conception is known to have occurred, but as yet no birth has been recorded in Antarctica.

losses. Thus, not only does humankind press progressively more heavily on the biological environment by reason of the enormous increase in the numbers of our species, but additionally because every effort is made to bring about dietary changes which inevitably result in the individual effectively occupying more space.

Further, since a large proportion[5] of mankind is at present underfed or undernourished, kind hearts and international zeal are at present seeking to improve the nutritional status of individuals world-wide. The Food and Agricultural Organization of the United Nations asserts, for example, that with population doubled by the end of the century, a fourfold increase in food production in Asia will be necessary. Further, the recommendation is and the effort will be made, enormously to increase the cattle population of the world in the hope of achieving for the many something of the nutritional affluence already accepted as normal by the Western world. Yet remember, that the end of the century is less than forty years ahead; and A.D. 2000 is a point of mere verbal significance within a continuous process.

Not only does mankind thus progressively take more space on account of surging numbers and seeking nutritional affluence, but additionally requires ever-increasing areas of agricultural land to produce crops yielding textiles and tobacco, rubber, fibres and so on. Further, there are timber requirements which ravage the forests of the world, the hardwoods from the tropics and the softwoods from the temperate zones. The coniferous softwoods serve to produce those fantastic quantities of newsprint whose excessive use in affluent lands is far from admirable.

Good agricultural practice, with increasing yields from the same area of land through growing technical enterprise—manuring, weed and pest control,[6] genetic advance, etc.—is at least rational from the point of view of food production. But much environmental damage is not even that. Agricultural and pastoral practices which lead to gross soil erosion, the over-cutting of forests and the over-fishing of aquatic stocks, are all world-wide examples of irrational action. Over the years less is gained than would be available with lesser exploitation on a basis of sustained yield.

That is the picture and the prospect for our own species, so numerous and so destructive. Turn then to other species which share with us the earth. As a first example it is asserted that in Africa 90 per cent of all the large mammals, that incomparable fauna, have already gone within the present century. Yet Africa is still "backward" in its rate of human population increase compared with many parts of the world.

The world prospect for faunal conservation is dismal indeed on a numerical basis. There is nothing to cheer except the recent rise of minority understanding, effort and spirited endeavour through IUCN, the World Wildlife Fund and associated activities. Whether the rate of increase of benevolent and conservationist influence can remotely match the fast growing man-made danger and destruction is not here for prophecy. Optimism has no basis in fact: pessimism is useless: it is for us to strive now with all the zeal we can muster: our sons will see

---

[5] The exact proportion (whether one-third, one-half or two-thirds) is debatable and lacking in definition, and is irrelevant to the present discussion.

[6] The faunistic dangers of chemical control are at last becoming more widely recognized.

"The world prospect for faunal conservation is dismal indeed on a numerical basis." Whooping Crane in pursuit of another that has invaded his territory. (Photo by Luther C. Goldman, courtesy U.S. Department of Interior, Fish and Wildlife Service, Bureau of Sport Fisheries and Wildlife.)

the result. Examples fill the pages of this journal of species already extinct in recent times as a result of human predation and competition and of the many species now in jeopardy.

All in all, the prospects for other large vertebrates, and for small ones, too —to say nothing at all of other animals and plant communities—could scarcely be worse than they are to-day in the face of overwhelming competition from human kind. The force of competition increases geometrically— each year the rate of increase itself increases—because that is what man's numbers do.

Now as to ameliorative action by that minority which appreciates the loss in the quality of life for the individual man and woman when other species are extinguished. This minority realizes that increase in human numbers is the greatest hazard even to the maintenance of the present quality of life of all people, let alone its improvement which is the natural, if subconscious, goal of all men. Quite certainly, in wisdom, there must be no reliance whatever on one method of preservation or conservation of other species, and plant and animal communities too. To assume that, in a complex situation, the favourable adjustment of a single factor will solve a problem is nearly always an erroneous judgment. Many methods must be tried even if each one of us has his own predilection as to which should have priority.

213

"... species already extinct in recent times as a result of human predation and competition and ... species now in jeopardy." California Condor. (Photo by Carl Koford from National Audubon Society.)

Preservation of a community of species by the formation of national parks and nature reserves, in Africa and elsewhere, may do much. But, to be realistic, the "erosion" of those special areas is all too easy and probable. The London green belt is diminished little by little by developers, with the sanction of the relevant Ministry; and the reserve in Africa suffers likewise by the pasturage of cattle. Where people grow rapidly in numbers, where food supplies need increase, where governments are "emergent," tribalism strong, and law enforcement feeble, there may reserves not long remain intact. Game reserves and forest reserves will go together. The realist will see not only Africa full of instances. Education in the value of the cropping of wild herbivores, and the glitter of the tourist trade, must both be pressed but may not be enough.

Conservation through rational exploitation may in some instances be the strongest form of protection. The Fur Seals of the Pribilof Islands and the Saiga antelopes of Siberia are fine examples within the sovereignty of single nations. Even the Fur Seals, however, because of their migrations, depend upon the backing of an international treaty, which might not, in all circumstances, be enforceable. Likewise, international treaties at present allow the rational exploitation of the Mackenzie river salmon and the halibut of the American Pacific coast. On the other hand, international treaties and commissions and an abundance of knowledge and scientific co-operation have failed alike to prevent irrational over-exploitation of the whales of the world's oceans and the fishes of the North Sea.

Preservation by domestication in an alien environment is far better than extinction in the natural habitat. Pere David's deer is a leading example. Okapi and Giraffe are free breeders in captivity and could thereby be preserved with effort in distant lands. The aviculturists in these matters are perhaps more advanced than those with their main interest in the mammals which so commonly require more space and money. All should be encouraged, just as the last individuals of the Arabian Oryx are now transported to Arizona in a desperate attempt to build a breeding herd in safety. Special limited enthusiasms likewise should be fostered and lead to efforts such as those of our Wildfowl and Pheasant Trusts.

Even the minority, the preservationists and conservationists, in my opinion, have as yet failed to see in full the awful vividness of the red light before them. Education is indeed essential everywhere, in fauna preservation,[7] but it can rarely be relied upon to be enough alone. Man pressure, with all its deleterious influence on the fauna and flora which grace our earthly home, will continue to increase geometrically until man's actual fertility is controlled to the extent that his mortality already is. The huge present surge of population of our own species is a mere by-product of our own beneficent effort. We must and shall strive to avoid a "natural" population crash. If we succeed, for a few decades more without sufficient fertility control,[8] we lose inevitably and for ever most of the remaining larger mammals of the world, very many of the birds, the larger reptiles and so many more both great and small. The more the delay in fertility control for our own species the worse our prospects in every way, in the quality of life for the individual just as in the hopes for survival of other species. The good of man and beast in the end are one.

[7] Crowding may now be such that even the enthusiasm of the cognoscenti must be checked: the Royal Society for the Protection of Birds has had some recent distressing examples.

[8] The International Planned Parenthood Federation is the co-ordinating central pressure group. As yet Japan is the only country in which the change from high fertility to low (from thirty-four to seventeen per thousand of population per year) has been brought about in a short time by deliberate intention. India is one of the countries now in which really strenuous efforts are being made, under governmental leadership, to bring population growth under rational control. Some others strive but success is slow to come. Indubitably a sensible momentum is developing in these matters in many parts of the world, but fundamentally what matters is that the rate of change of attitude and practice shall match the ever-increasing need.

Fifty Years of Man in the Zoo

G. EVELYN HUTCHINSON

THIRTY-SIX YEARS AGO the writer was invited to dine with Professor Punnett. The guest of honor was Thomas Hunt Morgan, the most celebrated biologist that America had produced. Punnett had just confirmed, characteristically working with sweet peas, the main results of the chromosomal theory of inheritance, elaborated over the two previous decades by Morgan, Bridges, and Sturtevant from the results of their studies of the genetics of the pomace-fly *Drosophila*. Equally characteristically Punnett had a superb cellar. At the last moment a Russian expert on artificial insemination, then applied mainly to horses, was included in the party. When asked by this Russian guest if there would be opportunities for practicing his art in the New World, Morgan, evidently misunderstanding the true meaning of Punnett's claret, unwisely replied, "Only if you can apply it to Ford cars." The machine age had come upon us. Perhaps *Drosophila* could teach us everything we needed to know about life, and it lived conveniently in rows of cream bottles in a thermostat. Today the same attitude is exhibited by those who look to bacteria and viruses to provide the universal intellectual stimulus of the living world.

It is the purpose of the present article to show, without too much nostalgic wearing of the Old Lascaux tie, that this attitude, which grew up during the past half-century, has also proved itself, during that time, to be wrong.

The Yale Review, *51(1): 56–65, Autumn 1961. Copyright Yale University Press.*

By considering man as an animal, we may see how essential is the animal kingdom, in its incredible diversity, to a proper understanding of man.

Man possesses bones, and we may conveniently begin by putting him in perspective as a fossilizable animal.

The last million or more years of the earth's history were characterized by the development of great ice sheets over parts of the temperate regions. These ice sheets waxed and waned four to six times and at least some of the mild interglacial periods were a little warmer than the present. The evolution of our own species *Homo sapiens* from its immediate precursors evidently took place during this dramatic time which is geologically termed the Pleistocene.

In 1911 a number of fossil skeletons of more or less modern types of man were available; these included remains of the famous Cromagnon people, who have achieved a reputation, perhaps a little undeserved, for physical perfection and brain size. There were also known some good skeletons of the related beetle-browed *Homo neanderthalensis*, the true cave man of cartoons and comic strips. A huge jaw from Mauer near Heidelberg had been described as a third species of *Homo, H. heidelbergensis*. Outside Europe, Dubois, following an extraordinary intuition, had discovered at Trinil in Java the skull cap and associated femur on which he based the famous *Pithecanthropus erectus*, the first real ape-man, but he became so worried by his discovery that in 1911 it was still not properly described. There were also known by 1913 Mr. Dawson's skilful artifacts from Piltdown, which later did so much to impede a clear understanding of human evolution. None of these finds could be dated absolutely in years, and in many cases there was great doubt as to the relative antiquity of the different specimens.

The modern period of palaeoanthropology really began in the 1920's when the great series of bones of the Peking apeman, now known as *Pithecanthropus erectus pekinensis*, began to appear from the cave at Chou-kou-tien and when Young discovered and Dart described as *Australopithecus africanus*, an infant skull from Taung in South Africa. Since then a seemingly endless series of fossils has been found in Asia and Africa. As a result of Leakey's brilliant investigation of Olduvai Gorge in Tanganyika, new material is turning up so fast that anything written at the moment is likely to be out of date by the time that it is printed. We also have available, from the method of radiocarbon dating, a reliable chronology for the last 50,000 years of our history, and the promise of other radiochemical methods applicable to the entire Pleistocene and beyond.

What we know is very briefly as follows. At the beginning of the Pleistocene there lived in Africa a series of what have been called, rather misleadingly, man-apes, scientifically termed the *Australopithecinae*, who walked erect, and some of whom made simple chopper-like stone tools. The tools found in the lowest bed at Olduvai are believed to be the oldest human artifacts known from anywhere in the world today, and the fossil australopithecines (*Zinjanthropus* and the more recently discovered slightly older unnamed fossils) may therefore be regarded as fairly close to the extremely low-browed ancestors of the reader and writer. Several species of australopithecines lingered on somewhat later in South Africa; all were small-brained, comparable to modern anthropoid apes in cranial capacity, and there has been much controversy as to their toolmaking capacities.

A little later at Olduvai typical early stone age hand axes appear and these are associated with what Leakey regards as the first true fossil man of the genus *Homo*. Whether he arose from *Zinjanthropus* on the ground is as yet uncertain.

In Asia there now appear the ape-men related to Dubois' *Pithecanthropus*. As well as the Peking form, today considered as only a sub-species of *P. erectus*, there is also a number of new Javanese fossils. *Pithecanthropus* was bigger-brained than the australopithecines but in certain minor anatomical details seems to be off the main line of human descent and probably represents a side branch that came to nothing. The great mandible from near Heidelberg and certain North African fossils have been supposed to be related Western forms.

We then find in the middle Pleistocene in Europe, from Steinheim in Germany, Fontéchevade in France, and Swanscombe in England, a group of imperfect skulls, to which Leakey has compared his Olduvai *Homo*, that are quite modern in character, though with thicker, heavier bone than we ourselves possess. From some such stock two lines seem to have developed: one became the beetle-browed caveman *H. neanderthalensis*, the other gave rise to the modern types. Both species or sub-species clearly had developed an elaborate culture with religious beliefs early in their history, for both practiced burial. When portraiture first appears, the first portrait sculpture, from an open last-glacial site in Czechoslovakia, seems to depict an intellectual young woman, who today might be doing brilliantly in graduate school. She is clearly European in facial characters. The various subspecies of *Homo*

sapiens, whose existence gives rise to so many practical problems today, seem therefore to have arisen before the last retreat of the ice, probably in response to the very varied climates that man was beginning to experience at this time.

A few rather curious hints about evolution in the Pleistocene can be gathered from certain physiological and anatomical facts. Darwin knew that man is the only animal that blushes. Goodhart has pointed out recently that blushing is a fairly complex physiological process known in all living men, though useless as a signal if the skin is black or if it were covered with hair. It is therefore probable that all existing human populations had a relatively light-skinned and fairly hairless common ancestor. The detailed distribution of such hair as is retained on the human body does not correspond to the pattern of well-developed hair tufts in any other anthropoid. It is not unreasonable to suppose that the deeply pigmented skins of some African and other peoples are secondary adaptations. Leakey has made the astonishing discovery, in the lowest Olduvai bed, of what seems to be a tool for scraping skins. Modern great apes spontaneously use large leaves as hats, and young chimpanzees in captivity take great delight in wearing human clothing. These facts taken in conjunction with Goodhart's ideas suggest, at least as an interesting speculation, that clothing, with all its immense psychological significance, may have first been made, though not with a needle, before man's brain had reached its full size.

When we try to go further back in time the record is extremely disappointing for some ten million years. During the geological period known as the Miocene, ten to twenty million years ago, there lived in Africa an assemblage of primitive apes or monkeys, placed in the genus *Proconsul,* which seem fairly well qualified as human ancestors. They were clearly animals of the open country, though no doubt on occasion they climbed trees. Their gait was certainly quadrupedal; the hand had not yet been fully freed by its possessor getting up on the hind feet. Among their numerous primate contemporaries they would not have appeared as particularly remarkable. They had generalized simian teeth with moderate canines, the molars arranged in two parallel rows, and not in the neat parabolic line that the australopithecines share with ourselves. They lacked the simian shelf, a ridge of bone that strengthens the mandibles of the modern great apes and which makes stripping bark with their great canines a less jawbreaking occupation. In the fine technical details of the tooth cusps *Proconsul* suggests a human ancestor, and most investigators think it must have been close to the human line. Leakey has discovered two jaws of apes with simian shelves in a deposit which was evidently laid down in water bordered by forests, rather than open country. These strongly suggest that at the time of *Proconsul* the line leading to the modern great apes was already distinct; these two fossils in fact are all that we have to elucidate the descent of the chimpanzee, a much more obscure matter than the descent of man.

In time and in structure there is unhappily very little yet to show how a form like *Proconsul* developed into the *Australopithecinae.* It is in this region that at the moment most links are missing. We do have in *Oreopithecus,* from the intervening period in Italy, an arboreal animal with an astonishing human jaw and pelvis; we also have two fragments from India which also suggest the australopithecine jaw. *Oreopithecus* has a habit of getting into American magazines and newspapers, but it is almost certainly in its hominid characters a strange parallel development. The Indian form *Ramapithecus* looks promising; there is not enough of it to provide any serious difficulties, save that it did not live in Africa.

Before *Proconsul* the problem consists of elucidating the whole history of the early Primates. There are dozens of fragmentary fossils representing what must have been charming animals in life. In a general way they show us, as their survivors among the lower primates also do, the gradual process of the eyes turning forward, that permitted binocular vision, the focusing of attention on a single object, a necessary prerequisite for the development of the hand and the mind.

Dry bones can clearly be made to live, if one has an enormous amount of material, great knowledge, enough love for the subject, and a lively but controlled imagination. The process is however difficult and the results still rather meager. To get further we must turn to studies of behavior. At least four major approaches to behavior have been developed in the past fifty years, though all have their roots in the late nineteenth century. These are the study of brain physiology, of academic experimental psychology, of psychiatry, and of the kind of scientific natural history that is nowadays called ethology. Unfortunately until recently many of the proponents of the various schools of psychological study devoted too much energy to attacking each other rather than getting on with the problems to be solved. Curiously enough perhaps the greatest unifying force in recent years has come from an initially entirely different field of study. The use of self-regulatory machines had begun early in the nineteenth century but reached an extraordinary development during the Second World War. In this development new and complicated kinds of applied mathematics had to be invented. Since a missile guided by photocells to seek a target is behaving very much like a man guided by his eyes, walking across a room and putting his hand on a door knob, it is not surprising to find that some of the theory developed in one case applies to the other. In particular it is known deductively that if too great demand is put on any self-regulatory system, it is apt to go into oscillation, and that the best way to avoid this is to have a hierarchy of regulatory devices. This arrangement is exactly what the brain physiologists and neurological surgeons have been exploring, while the psychiatrists have had to deal with all sorts of cycloid conditions looking like cases of too great demand being placed on self-regulatory systems. The academic psychologist in his attempt to establish quantitative laws of the way behavior is learnt, has come to realize that the simplicity of his systems is only apparent. A higher organism, even a laboratory white rat, giving simple responses to simple stimuli, does so largely because at every stage from perception to motor response an intricate system of controls is operating to keep the system stable and therefore dependable in everyday situations. This point of view is a healthy reminder that we must never say glibly that something is nothing but something else that is supposed to be simpler.

It is very difficult to summarize the work on behavior relative to our theme; there is so much of it but it is still far too compartmentalized. What is clear is that in so far as immediate emotions can be recognized in objectively recordable behavior, man differs very little from most of his primate relations. Some are more social than he is, some less, some exhibit aggression more, some less easily than man does, but as far as one can tell there is not a great deal of difference. Everyone who has worked at all extensively with chimpanzees feels that in all non-intellectual ways they are beings like ourselves, and the same is true with increasing limitations as we go from the higher to the lower primates. Recent events have tended to make people skeptical of *Homo sapiens* as the rational animal that the schoolmen and the *philosophes* believed him to be, but it is quite certain that he is much more intellectual than any other animal and that in no other important way is he unique. The evolution of the hand and of speech certainly are physical prerequisites of intellectual ability, but without the latter they would merely be curious adaptations comparable to hundreds of other elaborate specializations found up and down the animal kingdom.

It is becoming clear that all large mammals capable of learning are potentially able to develop dispositions and capacities quite different from what they ordinarily develop in nature. Elsa, in Mrs. Adamson's wonderful book, became a civilized lioness; she had clear limitations and remained a lioness, but was unlike any lioness that had ever lived before. A single unfavorable review of *Born Free* dismissed the book as dealing with the least pressing problem of the twentieth century. It is possible that it dealt with one case, and a very illuminating case, of a class of problems which includes all the really pressing issues of our time.

What good is a rhinoceros? Who *needs* a rhinoceros! But, who needs a panda? "Or a trumpeter swan? Or an Ainu? Or a Pigmy? Or a Bushman? Or a Laplander? Or an Eskimo? Or —?" (Paul Brandwein in *Future Environments of North America*, ed. F. Fraser Darling and John P. Milton.) (Photo on left by W. Brindle, courtesy Australian News and Information Bureau. Photo on p. 221 by A. W. Ambler from National Audubon Society.)

In considering both man's evolution and his behavior we inevitably face another related field where zoological analogies have proved fruitful in illuminating a region of the utmost practical importance. Man is an animal that exhibits a quite extraordinary tendency to what zoologists call subspeciation, the tendency to produce locally distinct populations. These are usually referred to as races, but that word is so charged with emotions that the more neutral term subspecies is preferable in the present context. The phenomenon occurs in most widely distributed animals; an ornithologist can easily tell a robin that has bred in Newfoundland from those of Connecticut, Virginia, or California. It is, however, probably more strongly developed in man than in any other species, doubtless on account of his great geographical range. Originally in man, as in other organisms, the subspecific characters were probably partly adaptations to climate; stocky individuals with short extremities in cold regions conserved heat, while in hot countries long spindly legs help to dissipate heat. All the circumstances that promoted these adaptations can now be taken care of by artifacts more effectively. The morphological adaptations have largely lost their meaning, and probably started to do so more than 10,000 years ago. There has been much movement of populations since then, so that it is now hard to trace the original meaning of the variations. A black skin may once have been an advantage in hunting by night. Now it is a disadvantage on an ill-lit road traveled by automobiles. Unhappily this is not the only disadvantage of being heavily pigmented in North America. Since for about four-fifths (say 40,000 out of 50,000 years) of their duration as subspecific entities, all men were living by their wits in the stone age, the amount of wits needed was probably everywhere much the same. We find, therefore, if we look without prejudice, no evidence of differences in *average* innate intellectual ability among the principal human subspecies. What we find, and nothing would lead us to suspect this a priori, is that within populations there is an enormous individual amount of variation. Man is highly polymorphic, to use the technical term, in intellectual ability. Until recently this fact, though obviously of great sociological importance, has never been

taken very seriously. In order to learn more about it, other cases of polymorphism must be studied. The classical cases are in the color patterns of butterflies and moths, and it is these which provided the initial suggestions in studying human polymorphism. With this acknowledgment to the Lepidoptera, we can consider first some human cases. The best known ones concern blood groups, because survival after transfusion appeals to people more than intellectual distinction, and appals them less than congenital feeble-mindedness. The most interesting cases involved, however, are the peculiar conditions of the red blood corpuscles known as sickling and thalassaemia. These conditions occur mainly where certain forms of malaria are or have been prevalent. They are inherited in such a way that if an individual receives a sickling gene from each parent he dies early of a serious

form of anaemia, if from one parent he has functionally normal blood but with red corpuscles that, when collapsed in certain solutions, have a characteristic sickle or half-moon shape. An individual receiving the sickling gene from neither parent is of course in almost every case normal with respect to the condition. The evolutionary question that arises is why if the individuals receiving the sickling gene from both parents always die young, the condition does not disappear from the population, as Darwin would lead us to think. The answer appears to be that the blood corpuscles of the hybrids with one sickling gene, though functional, are just abnormal enough chemically to provide bad homes for certain stages of the malaria parasites, to which therefore the hybrid individuals are immune. Normal individuals therefore get malaria, hybrids do not, people with two sickling genes get anaemia;

the hybrids are therefore the fittest that survive. When they mate, according to Mendel's law, they produce on an average one normal prone to malaria, two hybrids, and one anaemic. The polymorphism therefore persists. There is more than a suggestion that most of the multifarious inherited blood types behave in a comparable though much less extreme way.

The question now arises as to whether psychological diversity can be due to the same sort of mechanism. Though the expression of intelligence is certainly enormously influenced by upbringing, morons and intellectuals appear in the most unexpected places. The woefully inadequate work on the characteristics of identical twins reared apart moreover shows clearly that there is an inherited influence in determining at least the scores in intelligence tests. Penrose has found that among the Scots, a group traditionally committed to encouraging intellectual capacities, the population of any generation tends to be recruited from the people of middle ability in the previous generation. The moron and the genius contributed less than the *homme moyen sensuel*. Here then we seem to have a polymorphic situation of the greatest social significance, comparable to the sickling gene case, but doubtless dependent on many pairs of genes, which goes far to explain the distribution actually observed in all large human populations. If we introduced social mechanisms to encourage the production of more intellectuals, possibly society might perish from a dearth of stupidity.

There is one final zoological case which shows how possibly temperamental and emotional differences might be in part of genetic origin but in a very unobvious way. King and Shea, in a recent but already classical study,

have examined the basis for an inherited difference in capacity to climb in two subspecies of a single species of deermouse. The open country subspecies opens its eyes a little earlier in its career than does the woodland form. If the two kinds of mice are reared in the laboratory with no opportunity for vertical movement till they are relatively mature, both forms climb. If however the opportunity to climb is present from the beginning, the open country form tries to climb as soon as it can see, but is inadequate to the task, falls down and learns that climbing is a bad thing to do. The woodland form, developing vision and muscular coördination more slowly and harmoniously, climbs well from the beginning and goes on doing so. If we were deermice and the tendency to climb had great social significance, while ethical considerations prevented direct experimentation, we should have two rival schools, environmentalists who claimed that the difference was due to upbringing, which it is, and geneticists who claimed that it was due to heredity, as indeed it is. There would be much emotion involved; the situation would be typically human. It is more than a guess that this sort of thing does indeed occur in man.

As yet it is not possible to summarize all the diverse themes of this essay in a concise and formal set of statements. Yet there is one conclusion, as to method if not results, that is of great importance. The themes that have been developed have been illuminated by studies on butterflies, deermice, robins, a lioness, and by implication all the primates living as well as fossil. It would have been quite possible to develop other themes involving snails, waterbugs, birds of paradise, dolphins, giraffes, and rhinoceroses. We are only at the beginning of this kind of study. A world containing none of these animals would be intellectually impoverished to a degree that we are only just beginning to realize. We are, however, rapidly approaching such a world. Most Western countries, the USSR, and Japan are becoming alive to the danger. Unfortunately a great many of the new countries, where a vast number of the most interesting animals live, regard them as a nuisance to be rid of, and interest in them as a symbol of colonialism.

In view of the desire of the United States, both altruistic and practical, to help these countries, it is of great importance that those concerned in such aid should understand their responsibility in helping to maintain an adequate diversity of living beings on our planet, for without this diversity it will be immeasurably more difficult to understand ourselves.

Second Thoughts on the Germ Theory

RENÉ J. DUBOS

The modern mind seems to have a very limited awareness of other, non-human life: its abundance, complexity, and interpenetration with humanity. The soil, the landscape, the atmosphere are parts of an organic continuum. Even the human brain is profoundly connected to non-human life; it was derived from a brain peculiar to the three-dimensional sea of jungle life; it was founded in a million years of hunting and gathering; its idiom speaks of an intricate dependence on domesticated plants and animals over seven thousand years of rural life; it is perennially excited by monsters and demons.

Since demons are usually defined as ugly but unseen spirits, demonology is hardly a branch of biology. Our imaginations, however, are incapable of attributing animation to such spirits except in familiar form. Chemist and science-fiction writer Isaac Asimov once pointed out how uninspired are our pictures of life on other planets and in general how limited our fictional ideas of monsters.

Perhaps the only important change in demonology since the 15th century has been the discovery of the similarity of demons to germs. Indeed, those invisible creatures have been given most of the idiosyncracies, especially the vices, of the old demons. The wizard's robes now hang in the clinic. Much of modern medicine involves incomprehensible machinery, ritualized behavior, prescriptions in hieroglyphics, treatment with invisible

Scientific American, *192(5):31–35, May 1955.*
Reprinted with permission. Copyright © 1955 by Scientific American, Inc. All rights reserved.

rays and injections, mysterious concoctions to swallow, all cloaked in the professional secrecy and superciliousness of the shaman. This is from the viewpoint of the patient, of course, cowering in the waiting room and cringing in the clinic, his million-year-old psyche in as much need of shamans as it is of demons.

THE EDITORS

THE GERM THEORY of disease has a quality of obviousness and lucidity which makes it equally satisfying to a schoolboy and to a trained physician. A virulent microbe reaches a susceptible host, multiplies in its tissues and thereby causes symptoms, lesions and at times death. What concept could be more reasonable and easier to grasp? In reality, however, this view of the relation between patient and microbe is so oversimplified that it rarely fits the facts of disease. Indeed, it corresponds almost to a cult—generated by a few miracles, undisturbed by inconsistencies and not too exacting about evidence.

Historians usually give a biased account of the heated controversy that preceded the triumph of the germ theory of disease in the 1870s. They barely mention the arguments of those physicians and hygienists who held that clinical observations could not be completely explained by equating microbe with causation of disease. The critics of Louis Pasteur and Robert Koch pointed out that healthy men or animals were often found to be harboring virulent bacteria, and that the persons who fell victim to microbial disease were most commonly those debilitated by physiological disturbances. Was it not possible, they argued, that the bacteria were only the secondary cause of disease—opportunistic invaders of tissues already weakened by crumbling defenses?

It is entertaining to note that this doctrine was recently revived in an English court of justice. According to an account published in *The Lancet* of November 6, 1954, a lacquer sprayer, aged 36, sued his employers on the ground that he had contracted pneumonia and pleurisy because the spraying room in which he had worked was cold and drafty. His lordship the judge found that the plaintiff's work place was indeed cold, drafty and damp in the early morning. He accordingly awarded damages totaling 401 pounds, feeling satisfied that the plaintiff's illness was caused by the absence of heating. There is little doubt that the pneumonia and pleurisy of which the workman complained were manifestations of the activities of some microbial agent—virus or bacterium or probably both. Furthermore, it is probable that the workman had not contracted infection in the shop but had been harboring the guilty microbes in his organs for weeks, months or perhaps even years. The ruling that the deficient heating had *caused* the pneumonia brings to mind the view expressed by George Bernard Shaw in the preface to *The Doctor's Dilemma:* "The characteristic microbe of a disease might be a symptom instead of a cause."

Fortunately for the prestige of the germ theory, another case involving a microbial disease was being tried at the same time before a French court. Readers of SCIENTIFIC AMERICAN will recall that the myxomatosis virus, which has killed off immense numbers of rabbits in Australia, was recently introduced in France by a doctor who wished to get rid of the rabbits on his estate, and that the disease soon spread over most of Western Europe [see "The Rabbit Plague," by Frank

Fenner; February, 1954]. The too-enterprising French doctor was sued for huge sums of money by enraged hunters, fur dealers, rabbit breeders and others whose interests had been affected. The trial brought out many fine points of legal responsibility, but there was no doubt in anyone's mind that the myxomatosis virus—not some climatic or physiological factor—was the cause of the destruction of rabbits. The germ theory had been vindicated.

History offers many examples which, like myxomatosis, illustrate the operation of the germ theory of disease in its simplest and most direct form. The epidemic that ravaged Athens during the Peloponnesian War has not been convincingly identified, but Thucydides' vivid description makes clear its immensely destructive power. According to Edward Gibbon, the Justinian plague killed most of the European population during the 6th century, and plague reappeared with the same virulence in Western Europe under the name of "The Black Death" in the 14th century. Other illustrations could be selected from more recent historical events: the immense mortality caused by smallpox among the American Indians when they came into contact with the disease, introduced first accidentally, then willfully, by the European invaders; the decimating effect of measles in the Sandwich (Hawaiian) Islands in 1775, in the Fiji Islands a century later and among the Columbia River Indians in 1830; the death from tuberculosis of some 90 per cent of the Indians of the Qu'Appelle Valley in Western Canada within a decade. These instances, selected at random, provide tragic evidence that a microbial agent may strike down the weak and the healthy alike when newly introduced in a susceptible population.

Yet what shall we say of the case of pneumonia that came before the English court? There are many situations in which the microbe is a constant and ubiquitous component of the environment but causes disease only when some weakening of the patient by another factor allows infection to proceed unrestrained, at least for a while. Theories of disease must account for the surprising fact that, in any community, a large percentage of healthy and normal individuals continually harbor potentially pathogenic microbes without suffering any symptoms or lesions. This type of dormant infection seems to occur widely, not only among men and animals, but also probably among plants and even microscopic cells. Only a few examples need be quoted to illustrate the theoretical interest and practical importance of the phenomenon.

All the healthy-looking mice raised for medical research under highly standardized and hygienic conditions carry a multiplicity of viruses capable of causing in them severe and often fatal pulmonary disease. Under normal circumstances the viruses remain dormant in the form of so-called "latent infections." But they can be "evoked," as the expression goes, by the simple artifice of dropping certain sterile fluids into the nasal cavity of the mouse. There is another disease, called pseudo-tuberculosis, which can be evoked in normal mice by subjecting the animals to radiation, to certain nutritional deficiencies or to a number of other stresses. Pseudotuberculosis results from the unrestrained multiplication of a diphtheria-type bacillus, which exists in a latent form in normal mouse tissues.

Like the mouse, normal man carries throughout life a host of microbes which now and then start proliferating and cause disease—under the influence of factors rarely if ever well understood. For example, a large percentage of the readers of this article harbor virulent tubercle bacilli and staphylococci, but very few will ever become aware of the microbes' presence. Most likely the infections will remain dormant unless brought into activity by some other intervening factor causing a "loss of general resistance"—an expression useful by virtue of its vagueness. Uncontrolled diabetes, life in a concentration camp, overwork, overindulgence, even an unhappy love affair, may precipitate an attack of disease, much as exposure to drafts and to damp air was judged by the English court to be the cause of pneumonia. An example familiar to most of us is provided by the benign but recurrent lesions known as fever blisters or cold sores, caused by the herpes virus. Many people contract the herpes infection early in life, and the virus persists somewhere in the tissues from then on. It lingers idly until some provoking stimulus causes it to manifest its presence in the form of blisters. The stimulus may be a fever of unrelated origin, excessive irradiation, certain types of surgery, menstruation or improper food. Thus the herpes virus is merely the agent of *infection:* the instigator of the *disease* is an unrelated disturbance of the host.

It has been easy to demonstrate experimentally that the tubercle bacillus, the staphylococcus and the herpes virus are capable of causing progressive disease and even death in animals without the apparent participation of other contributory factors. For this reason these microbes are said to be virulent. But there are many other types of microbes not regarded as virulent which also can play an important part in the causation of disease under special circumstances. C. P. Miller of the University of Chicago School of Medicine has shown, for example, that some of the manifestations of radiation sickness are due to invasion of the blood and certain organs by bacteria normally present in the intestinal tract; indeed, he succeeded in protecting experimental animals from radiation death by controlling this infection of intestinal origin with antimicrobial drugs. In contrast, it has been repeatedly observed that vigorous treatment with drugs of almost any type of virulent infection in a human being may have the paradoxical effect of bringing about another type of infection, caused by the proliferation of otherwise innocuous fungi and bacteria. We are beginning, in fact, to witness the appearance of man-made diseases, caused by the rapid changes in human ecology brought about by the new therapeutic procedures.

The classical doctrines of immunity throw no light on precisely what mechanisms determine whether dormant microbes will remain inactive or begin to act up. What is needed to analyze this problem is some understanding of the agencies responsible for natural resistance to infection, and of the factors that interfere with the operation of these agencies. Fortunately interest in this area of research is increasing rapidly. Several independent trends of thought appear clearly in current programs of investigation.

One approach is a search of normal animal tissues for substances possessing antimicrobial activity. There are many such substances. One of the best known is lysozyme, discovered some 30 years ago by the late Alexander Fleming of penicillin fame. But the difficulty is not to discover antimicrobial substances; it is rather to gain information as to what role, if any, they play in the body's resistance to infection. The most interesting information on this point has come from studies at Western Reserve University Medical School by a group of immunologists under the leadership of Louis Pillemer. They have separated from human and animal sera a peculiar protein, "properdin," which can destroy or inactivate a few types of bacteria and viruses under certain conditions in the test tube. They have established, furthermore, that the concentration of properdin in serum is not constant. Particularly exciting is the finding that when animals are exposed to weakening radiation, properdin disappears almost completely within four to six days, precisely at the time when the animals become highly susceptible to the bacteria normally present in their intestinal tract.

Another determinant of susceptibility and resistance is the individual's nutritional state. History shows that famine and pestilence commonly ride together, but the links that bind them are neither obvious nor simple. This has been well demonstrated by a thoughtful analysis carried out by Howard Schneider at the Rockefeller Institute for Medical Research. I should like to cite the effect of diabetes, a metabolic disorder. It has long been known that patients with uncontrolled diabetes are extremely susceptible to certain bacteria, notably staphylococci and tubercle bacilli, whereas diabetics receiving proper insulin treatment are just as resistant to these bacteria as are normal individuals. In other words, susceptibility to infection in these cases appears to be linked in a reversible manner to the metabolic state. It is tempting to postulate that the biochemical abnormalities brought about by uncontrolled diabetes create an environment favorable for the activities of the bacteria. In fact, experiments carried out at Bryn Mawr College and at the U.S. Air Force School of Aviation Medicine by J. Berry and R. B. Mitchell, and in our own laboratory at the Rockefeller Institute, have shown that one can increase the susceptibility of mice to microbial disease by metabolic manipulations as simple as temporary deprivation of food, or feeding an unbalanced diet rich in citrate. Furthermore, resistance can be brought back to normal within two to three days by correcting the nutritional disorder.

It is clear, therefore, that susceptibility to infection is not necessarily inherent in the tissues, or dependent on the presence of antibodies, but is often the temporary expression of some physiological disturbance.

All in all, a new look at the biological formulation of the germ theory seems warranted. We need to account for the peculiar fact that pathogenic agents sometimes can persist in the tissues without causing disease and at other times can cause disease even in the presence of specific antibodies. We need also to explain why microbes supposed to be nonpathogenic often start proliferating in an unrestrained manner if the body's normal physiology is upset.

To guide one's thinking on these problems it is well to keep in mind a fact so simple that it is never talked about—namely, that the tissues of man and animals contain everything required for the life of most microbes. This is well shown by the ability of tissue cells to support the growth of bacteria and viruses in the test tube. It is therefore surprising that microbial disease is the exception rather than the rule, for we continually come into contact with all kinds of microbes. The problem, in other words, is not merely, "How do some microbes cause disease?" but rather, "Why are not all microbes capable of causing disease?"

We have already cited evidence of the tendency for a new kind of microbe to run riot in a population exposed to it for the first time. Even more striking in this regard are the observations made by James Reyniers and his colleagues at the University of Notre Dame. They found that animals born and raised in a sterile environment died when they were exposed to common bacteria such as are always present in a normal environment. For example, some of the banal microorganisms present in ordinary food products were virulent for them.

Thus the simple fact that a population survives and flourishes in a given environment implies that its members are endowed with a high degree of natural resistance to the microbes normally present in that environment. This natural resistance stems in part from evolutionary selection of the strains best endowed with mechanisms for withstanding the infections, and probably in part from the development of adaptive reactions in response to early exposure to the microbes. We cannot discuss here the workings— still very obscure—of these various protective mechanisms. Suffice it to say that their over-all effect is the establishment of a state of biological equilibrium between man or animals on the one hand, and the microbes endemic in the community on the other.

Whatever their nature, the mechanisms responsible for natural resistance are in general most effective under the narrow range of conditions constituting the "normal" environment in which the population has evolved. Any shift

from the normal is likely to render the equilibrium unstable. I have already mentioned examples of disturbances that may upset the equilibrium—irradiation, metabolic abnormalities, treatment with antimicrobial drugs and so on. Psychosocial factors could have illustrated the point just as well. Although the precise mode of these factors is still unknown, there is no reason to doubt that they act by changing the environment, especially the *milieu intérieur,* in which higher organisms and microbes have evolved to a state of biological equilibrium.

During the first phase of the germ theory the property of virulence was regarded as lying solely within the microbes themselves. Now virulence is coming to be thought of as ecological. Whether man lives in equilibrium with microbes or becomes their victim depends upon the circumstances under which he encounters them. This ecological concept is not merely an intellectual game; it is essential to a proper formulation of the problem of microbial diseases and even to their control.

To be sure, there are situations where a microbe itself is a sufficient cause of disease irrespective of the physiological state of the exposed individual. Infancy exemplifies one such situation. The child, arriving so to speak as an immigrant in the human herd, comes into contact with certain microbes which are not yet fully integrated in human life by evolutionary forces and with which he as an individual has not had any experience. We have noted another type of situation where people may be defenseless against the disease agent: namely, the introduction of a new microbe in a previously unexposed population. This type of relationship is certainly in the mind of all scientists concerned with bacteriological warfare. Untold harm might follow the introduction of types of infectious agents to which we have never been exposed as a group in the past. Our farm animals or our crops would prove equally susceptible to plagues and pests so far kept at bay by unending vigilance.

However, dramatic as these special cases of complete lack of resistance may be, they do not constitute the main problem of microbial disease in ordinary life. As we have seen, practically all the common microbes already present, though ordinarily harmless, are capable of producing disease when physiological circumstances are sufficiently disturbed. These ubiquitous microbes rarely cause death, but they are certainly responsible for many ill-defined ailments—minor or severe—which constitute a large part of the miseries and "dis-ease" of everyday life. They establish a bridge between communicable and noncommunicable disease—a zone where presence of the microbe is the prerequisite but not the determinant of disease, a situation in which the fact of infection is less decisive in shaping the course of events than the physiological climate of the invaded body. For reasons that cannot be discussed here, it is unlikely that antimicrobial drugs can control this aspect of the relationship between man and microbe. What is most needed at the present time is some knowledge of the physiological and biochemical determinants of microbial diseases. For we cannot possibly hope to eliminate all the microbes that are potentially capable of causing harm to us. Most of them are an inescapable part of our environment.

The views of those who still deny the microbial causation of disease altogether are epitomized in a saying they are fond of repeating: "If the germ theory of disease were correct, there would be none on earth to believe it." I have attempted to show that this statement implies a narrow and incomplete understanding of the germ theory. Much more perceptive—indeed prophetic—was the conclusion reached by John Caius in his essay on the English "sweating sickness" in 1552: "Our bodies cannot . . . be hurt by corrupt and infective causes, except ther be in them a certein mater apt . . . to receive it, els if one were sick, al shuld be sick."

A-Bombs, Bugbombs, and Us

G. M. WOODWELL
W. M. MALCOLM
R. H. WHITTAKER

The transmission of violence in nature, such as the flow of poisons to plants and animals and men for whom they were not intended, follows pathways called eco-systems. The term denotes a highly ordered functional pattern of flow in nature. The structures of these ecosystems are neither incidental nor merely compensatory in the coming and going of life, but are essential to the survival of the organisms taking part. They are fundamental charac-teristics of the community structure of life, and their complexities demand careful attention and study.

Controversy over pesticides has brought ecological interdependence to the atten-tion of perhaps more people than had heard of it during the preceding century. The ground over which we had earlier advanced was not entirely barren, how-ever. A familiar image, the "balance of nature," is a legacy of nature study and the great naturalists. Although it has long since proved too static a concept to suit most biologists it had at least stimulated some awareness of what we now call eco-systems. The "balance" turned out to be a variable but self-adjusting flow of energy and materials along organized lines.

In spite of that background, the storm over Rachel Carson's Silent Spring *marked a historical moment in our society's rela-tionship to its natural environment. It was tragically appropriate that a dying woman should have given four years to the crea-tion of a classic document in defense of an endangered environment. Without her the issue would have drawn to a culmina-tion anyway, but she formulated the dan-ger so skilfully as to become one of those uncommon people who embody a move-ment or an idea.*

Rachel Carson's candor and innocence brought on her the fury reserved for those who neither connive nor conciliate. Her brother biologists, almost to a man, did excellent imitations of people frightened by big money and authority and deserted her before the Establishment which con-trols the funds that keep scientists fat. It remained for the amateurs, the natural-ists, and the rare scientist of independent temperament to support the contentions of her brilliant book and the cause of ecological reason which it represented.

THE EDITORS

Brookhaven National Laboratory, *Publication No. 9842, 1966. Work carried out at Brook-haven National Laboratory under the auspices of the U.S. Atomic Energy Commission.*

THE WORLD IS SMALL. This is the les-son of the Bomb and the rockets, of hunger and of exploding populations. And it is the lesson that the problems of POLLUTION also teach. We once thought that dilution of man's wastes into the earth's vast currents of air and water was the simple answer to all problems of waste disposal. We know now that these currents are not vast enough to handle safely all the wastes and poisons man is releasing into them.

Two aspects of environmental pol-lution—radioactivity and pesticides—illustrate the problem most effectively.

The lessons from these call for re-straint and a gradual revolution in the use of environment and in pest control. It is these twinned problems that are our subject.

Two ecological ideas are at the heart of these pollution problems: First

What happens to fallout and pesticides in our environment? Some of it decays—the rest accumulates. (All art in this article by W. M. Malcolm, courtesy the artist. From the original publication.)

is the principle that substances released into environment move in pathways loosely described as "cycles" and often return, concentrated, to threaten man himself. Second, the poisons used to control pests have effects on many populations, not merely the pest; effects of these poisons include: (a) killing of some wild animal populations, especially those of predatory animals which regulate populations of other animals; (b) causing population eruptions of other species, which may become new pests, while (c) the old pests remain and evolve new ability to survive the poisons.

Much of what we know about biological, geological and chemical cycles of the earth has come from studies of radioactive tracers, and especially fallout from bombs. What these studies have taught us is closely related to what we have been learning more recently about movement of pesticides.

For this reason a brief review of the lessons of radioactivity is appropriate.

Biologists have long known that substances are carried from place to place in environment by currents of moving water, air and by moving organisms, and that substances also are transferred from one kind of organism to others. It took an unfortunate series of mishaps in the Pacific in the mid-1950's to demonstrate the meaning of such cycling for man. These events brought rapid quickening of interest in environment and even forced governments to examine these questions.

The bomb test at Bikini in 1954, known as BRAVO, due to unexpected winds at upper levels dropped radioactive fallout on Rongelap Atoll and exposed the inhabitants including several U.S. servicemen to significant radiation (8, 10). A Japanese fishing vessel was also in the fallout field and its crew was exposed as well. At the

It gets into plants, then plant-eaters, then meat-eaters.

time that these events were being reported in the world press, fish in Japanese markets were discovered to contain fallout radioactivity in easily measurable, if not genuinely hazardous, amounts. Public reaction was rapid and intense, especially in Japan. A Japanese oceanographic vessel and later an American one, were sent on large sweeps through the Pacific and found that the contamination was considerable and was widespread (10). Wind and water had spread the radioactive material from this and earlier tests across wide areas of the Pacific. In each area that radioactive dust fell into the ocean, the material was taken up by small plants, the plants were eaten by small animals, the animals were eaten by other animals, and these in turn were eaten by such large animals as tuna fish, which accumulated the radioactive material passed up to them along the food chain. Migrating tuna fish could carry their radioactivity considerable distances, even to the last link in the chain, man.

Although the real hazard to human health was small, the Japanese, who depend heavily on food from the sea, were understandably alarmed. Most people had been acutely aware for years of the problem of direct radioactive fallout. The hazard to man from cycling in currents of wind and water and in organisms was a less obvious, disturbing discovery. The incident gave dramatic proof that there are limits to the capacity of wind and water to dilute pollutants potentially harmful to man.

Since then there have been many efforts to clarify the biogeochemical cycles of the earth using isotopes from fallout (2, 6, 12, 14). Most of the knowledge of these cycles, fragmentary though it is, has been gleaned from researches started since 1954 by a very large program of environmental research within the AEC costing many millions of dollars.

There is no simplified general rule describing the movement of radioactive materials in the environment. Each chemical element and each substance travels its own peculiar path, largely independent of pathways of other elements. Time and place of release, size of particles, chemical composition, environmental conditions, and kinds of organisms present are all important in determining patterns of movement.

While the substances released tend first to be diluted in the water, air, or soil, they are frequently concentrated again later by organisms, often in unexpected places. It is often the case that a substance which is very dilute in the water is picked up by algae and transferred along food chains at concentrations many thousands of times as high as those in the water (3, 5, 13, 18). The tendency to move (even substances normally considered "insoluble" move) and to be concentrated presents the dual hazard of wide dispersal and potentially hazardous local concentrations of pollutants. This means that there is continuing and expanding need for rigorous checking of environmental concentrations, and especially of man's own food chains for a wide variety of pollutants. From

All along this food chain it's concentrated because animals eat many times their own weight in food.

the studies of radioactivity we know that the "cycles" of the biosphere in which pollutants travel are too complex for easy or safe prediction, and that we cannot simply trust dilution to protect man against the persistent poisons he releases into environment.

With radioactivity, pesticides, and other poisons, the principal direct hazard to man arises from contamination of food chains that man taps. A few of these have been studied in detail. Radioactive iodine (iodine[131]) for instance is a particularly serious hazard because it emits gamma rays and is strongly concentrated in the thyroid gland of man and other mammals. Iodine[131] has an 8-day half-life and is a hazard only during the first weeks following its release, but in those weeks it may reach high levels in man even though the contamination in environment was low. It enters several of man's food chains but the most important route is through cow's milk. The food chain in this instance is short and simple—involving only grass, cattle, milk and man—but it is difficult to predict the extent of iodine[131] concentration into man's thyroid gland. The rate of movement to man is affected by (a) the density of the grass the cow eats (if the forage grows densely and the cow covers little ground, she picks up less iodine), (b) rain, which may wash some of the radioactive particles off the forage into the soil, (c) the diet of the cow (she may be eating heavy supplements of grain or stored hay), (d) the efficiency with which iodine is secreted in the milk, and (e) the amount of milk consumed by individuals who may differ greatly in their consumption, and other factors. It is not easy, first, to predict the concentration into man or, second, to predict the possible long-range meaning to the human body of a given concentration.

There is another lesson from these studies—they are full of surprises, sometimes tragic ones. One such surprise of recent years was discovery of tumors of the thyroid gland in children caused by radiation exposures at levels that had been assumed to be safe. The effect was discovered in studies of children whose thyroids were irradiated when they were treated with radiation years ago for enlarged thymus glands. Recognition that the thyroid may be damaged after relatively low exposure to radiation (either by x rays or from the emissions of iodine[131]) led to issuance of the Radiation Protection

So the last guy in the chain gets quite a load. WE'RE LAST GUYS.

234

Poisons kill other last guys, too, making nature simpler and less stable.

Guide by the Federal Radiation Council in 1961, setting limits at less than 1/10 previously acceptable levels (7). The wisdom of this step was demonstrated when studies of the children exposed at Rongelap Atoll in 1954 showed occurrence in them of thyroid tumors—tumors that did not appear until about 10 years after irradiation . . .

These experiences involved an isotope whose environmental pathway to man is relatively simple and whose clinical effects seem comparatively clear cut. Yet even here, where biologists had reasonable assurance that they knew the mechanisms, we have been surprised. (It may well be that only *because* we know the mechanisms well were we able to recognize the problem.) The lesson is an important one: apparently even when we think we know the pathways and the concentrations that are safe, there is reason

for conservatism in estimating hazards to man. When hazards are less clearly known, as is the case with pesticides, there is greater cause for caution. It is unusual to be able to link a pollution cause to a health effect ten years later. Such effects could be established for radioactive materials only because of a very large body of background data on radiation effects and because of an unusual and unequivocal, if unfortunate, series of radiation exposures. It may be many years before equivalent knowledge of pesticides in relation to environment and man's health is available. Pesticides are intensely poisonous, and must be poisonous to control pests effectively. There is little evidence now that they produce cancer or are (except for special cases of extreme exposure) damaging to health. But it is certainly not true that hazard to man is unlikely. It is more accurate

**Imagine a simple food chain:
posies→sheep→people.**

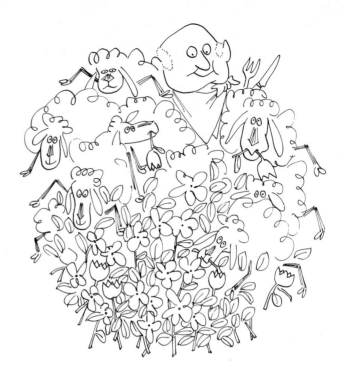

to say, first, that we do not know now the long-range hazard of pesticides to man and, second, that analogies with radioisotopes and cancer-producing substances in cigarette smoke and atmospheric pollution suggest we are likely to encounter unpleasant surprises.

There is one more important point about food chains as they affect both radioactive materials and pesticides. This is the fact that there is often a step-by-step increase in concentration along a food chain. In the step from pasture to milk in our example of I^{131}, the cow gathers fallout from many square yards of grass and deposits it in 10–20 quarts of milk daily. In the next step iodine from a quart of milk daily is concentrated in the small volume of a child's thyroid gland. With other isotopes and in other food chains parallel patterns of increasing concentration are common. Greatest concentrations often occur in the last links of the chain, which may be man

and the animals he eats. Generalizations, however, are difficult because the behavior of each element must be considered individually before its hazard to man can be appraised. The best survey of this work with radionuclides is the 1962 UNSCEAR Report and its 1964 supplement (15, 16).

No such authoritative document outlining hazards to man is available for pesticides, although the problem is an even more difficult one. Pesticides, which emit no easily measured signal similar to a radioactivity, are very difficult to detect. Further, the significance of pesticides as contaminants of the biosphere has been recognized only recently, and broad-scale research on the cycling of pesticides has really only barely started. Indeed, the greatest steps have been made in this work since 1960 when a very sensitive analysis technique for pesticides (gas chromatography) first became widely available for this application. And even now our knowledge is largely restricted

236

to the persistent chlorinated hydro-carbons, especially DDT.

There are a few instances where studies of food chains have given indications of step-by-step increase in pesticide concentrations along food chains. For instance, in the food web in which the herring gull is a scavenger in Lake Michigan, DDT (DDE and DDD) concentrations in the bottom muds at 33–96 feet averaged 0.014 parts per million. In a shrimp (*Pontoporeia affinis*) they were 0.44 ppm, more than ten times higher. Levels increased in fish to the range of a few ppm (3.3 ale-wife; 4.5 chub; 5.6 whitefish) another tenfold increase, and jumped in the scavenging, omnivorous herring gull to 98.8 ppm, twenty times higher still, and 7000 times as high as in the mud (9). There are numerous less complete examples of this type of concentration of pesticides, especially the chlorinated hydrocarbons in birds (17, 20, 21).

This food chain effect is especially serious among birds, and predatory birds (hawks, owls, ospreys, and the eagle, our national emblem) are in real danger of extinction in the United States. Accumulation of pesticides can kill adult birds directly, as has repeatedly been observed in robins and other species in areas sprayed with DDT. The more serious effect, however, is a less obvious one—lower levels of pesticide accumulation appear to cause the birds to fail to reproduce successfully. The peregrine falcon, for instance, no longer breeds in the Northeastern United States, although there were numerous breeding sites there a decade ago (17). The Northeastern strains appear to have been wiped out, probably an example of

Take away one————? In na-ture: Simplicity = Instability

pesticide extinction of a wild species over a wide area. Populations of ospreys or fish hawks and eagles appear also to be declining seriously.

It is a widely-accepted ecological principle that the stability of populations is related in complex ways to the number of different kinds of organisms present. The greater the number of kinds of organisms (diversity), the greater the stability. In somewhat oversimplified terms diversity is thought to introduce stability by including predators and competitors of each species, thereby guaranteeing natural controls of population size. Reducing the number of species may remove predators or competitors, and allow spectacular increases in the populations that survive. The most abrupt changes occur in species that have short life cycles. Insects are among the most conspicuous of these rapidly reproducing populations. Populations of mites often erupt in farm fields after spraying with DDT, and there are numerous other examples (4). The principal point about pesticides is that control of pests with broad-spectrum poisons not only reduces the pest population but also reduces its competitors and predators. This decreases the stability of the populations, increasing the probability that populations of other resistant species may themselves reach "pest" proportions. Furthermore, this removal of predators and competitors implies that the species against which the pesticide was used is even more likely to erupt out of control after the spraying stops, than it was before. Pesticide spraying thus tends to intensify the pest problems the spraying was intended to control. Once pesticide use has begun, continued or increased use of pesticides is likely to be needed to control population instability which was in part produced by the pesticides.

But short life cycles mean something else—capacity for rapid evolutionary change. When fields are sprayed with pesticides, the individuals of the pest species that are most resistant are the ones that survive. They are also the ones that reproduce, and the population of the pest in that field the next year consists of their descendents which are, on the average, more resistant to the pesticide. Year by year the pest population becomes more resistant to the pesticide. There is consequently need either for heavier use of the pesticide, or for different kinds of pesticides to control its population. Meanwhile, new pest species may be appearing. Use of pesticides is thus a double-edged sword. On one side it has great short-range advantage for simple, effective control of farm pests. On the other, long-range side, it is a kind of treadmill, or a constantly escalating chemical warfare. Because it creates new pest problems and pest resistance, there is need for constantly increasing amounts and variety of pesticides to control pests.

If it were not for the cycling effects, this warfare might be accepted without concern. The observations on birds suggest, however, that steadily increasing use of pesticides will cause extinction of increasing numbers of more vulnerable wild species. Furthermore, the cycling effects imply increasing consumption of pesticides in food by man.

Two ominous facts should be placed side by side. First, is the rapid increase in pesticide use. Money spent for pesticides in the U.S. increased between 1962 and 1964 from about $734 million to $944 million (it is encouraging that DDT use in this period declined; most of the increase was in organic phosphate insecticides) (19). Second is the fact that certain pesticides such as DDT

What's more, pests get immune to poisons, and we must forever beef up the poisons or find new ones.

can now be found in tissues of animals from the sea. The problem works this way:

1) DDT and some other pesticides are stable chemicals. They do not simply break down into harmless forms in the soil or water, but tend to accumulate there in increasing amounts.

2) Rapidly increasing pesticide use implies increasing amounts of pesticides accumulated in such reservoirs.

3) From farm soils they may be carried as dust (1) and by moving water into streams, where they kill some fresh water life. (Devastating kills of millions of fish in the Mississippi, appear to have resulted from careless contamination of that river by endrin, one of the pesticides. The deleterious effects of DDT spraying for the spruce budworm on salmon runs in the Miramichee River in New Brunswick,

Canada, have been very carefully documented) (11).

4) Rivers and winds carry the pesticides into the ocean. There is a steady movement of pesticides from farm fields through streams into the ocean, and consequent increasing accumulation of pesticides there.

5) In the ocean pesticides are concentrated by food chains into animals. Man eats some of the animals which are last links of food chains.

6) Gradually increasing accumulation of pesticides from food into human tissue is implied. Man is also receiving some pesticides in food he eats that was grown on land.

7) So far as the ocean is concerned, some nations are now dependent on it for an important part of their food; and

as man's population grows, this dependence will increase.

Even the oceans are not so large that man can assume he will not, because of dilution effects, be affected by pesticide cycling. As we have indicated, the long-range meaning to the human body of a variety of different pesticides accumulated in its tissues is not known. Use of pesticides has great and compelling short-range, practical advantage. It is unfortunately also true that pesticide use has marked long-range disadvantage in its effects on natural populations and pest evolution and (probably, with due allowance for what we cannot now know) on human health.

Steadily increasing contamination of environment with radioactive materials from bomb fallout would be, in long-range terms, foolish and reckless. This is one reason for the treaty banning tests of atomic bombs in the atmosphere. Uncontrolled, constantly increasing contamination of environment by persistent pesticides would be, in long-range terms, equally foolish. Yet use of some pesticides is almost essential as a part of the means of controlling pests. What can we do? These steps seem necessary:

1) Restriction of the persistent, broad-spectrum poisons such as the chlorinated hydrocarbon insecticides to uses that cannot contaminate the biological, geological and chemical cycles of the earth.

2) Replacement of these pesticides by others that are not persistent (and whose breakdown products are not toxic) and are specific (kill only the pest they are aimed at). There is need for extensive research in developing such pesticides.

3) Above all, learn to use pesticides with restraint as only one tool in a wide range of possible control techniques that include use of a diversity of resistant crop strains, use of natural enemies to control pests, and use of a greater diversity of crops in any area. Maintenance of the full range of species in the natural communities of an area is probably one important step toward this shift in pest control practices. Research on the implications of biological diversity (number of species per unit area) for controlling pests is being pressed at present and will doubtless contribute new techniques enabling the transition.

More broadly, we must restrain the use of pesticides for the sake of our own future. The world is now too small for rapidly increasing human populations to release rapidly increasing amounts of persistent poisons into environment. Man needs to begin a quiet revolution in his thinking, which recognizes the crowding of our world and seeks to govern man's own effects on environment with foresight, long-range wisdom, and restraint. In an age when we can reach for the moon, such a revolution seems possible. There is no doubt that it is necessary.

References

1. Antommaria, P., Corn, M. and DeMaio, L., "Airborne particulates in Pittsburgh: association with p,p –DDT." *Science* **150**, 1476–7, 1965.

2. Caldecott, R. S. and Snyder, L., *Radioisotopes in the Biosphere*. Minneapolis: University of Minnesota, 1960.

3. Corcoran, E. F., and Kimball, J. F., Jr., 1960. "The uptake, accumulation and exchange of strontium-90 by open sea phytoplankton," *Radioecology* (pp. 187–191), V. Schultz and A. Clement. New York: Reinhold; and Washington: American Institute of Biological Sciences, 1963.

4. DeBach, P., *Biological Control of Insect Pests and Weeds*. New York: Reinhold, 1964.

5. Donaldson, L., Seymour, A. H., Held, E. E., Hines, N. O., Lowman, F. G., and

Wilander, A. D., "Survey of radioactivity in the sea near Bikini and Eniwetok atolls, June 11–24, 1956." University of Washington, Seattle. US AEC Report UWFL-46, 1956.

6. Eisenbud, M., *Environmental Radioactivity.* New York: McGraw-Hill, 1963.

7. Federal Radiation Council, "Background material for the development of radiation protection standards." Report No. 2, 1961.

8. Glasstone, S., *The Effects of Nuclear Weapons.* Washington, D C.: USAEC, 1962.

9. Hickey, J. J., and Keith, J. A., "Pesticides in the Lake Michigan ecosystem," in *The Effects of Pesticides on Fish and Wildlife* (p. 11). U.S. Fish and Wildlife Service, Washington. G.P.O. No. 896–932, 1964.

10. Hines, N. O., *Proving Ground: An Account of Radiological Studies in the Pacific, 1946–1961.* Seattle: University of Washington Press, 1962.

11. Kerswill, C. J., Elson, P. F., Keenleyside, M. H. A., and Sprague, J. B., *Effects on Young Salmon of Forest Spraying with DDT.* USPHS Technical Report W 60.3, 1960.

12. Kulp, J. L., and Schulert, A. R., *Strontium-90 in Man and His Environment.* Volume 1: Summary. Lamont Geological Observatory, Columbia University, Palisades, New York, 1962.

13. Lackey, J. B., *The suspended microbiota of the Clinch River and adjacent waters in relation to radioactivity in the summer of 1956.* Oak Ridge National Laboratory, Oak Ridge, Tenn. ORNL-2410, 1957.

14. Schultz, V., and Klement, A. W., Jr., *Radioecology.* New York: Reinhold; and Washington: American Institute of Biological Sciences, 1963.

15. UNSCEAR, Report of the United Nations Scientific Committee on the Effects of Atomic Radiation. General Assembly. Official Records: 17th Session, Suppl. No. 16, 1962.

16. UNSCEAR, Report of the United Nations Scientific Committee on the Effects of Atomic Radiation. General Assembly. Official Records: 19th Session, Suppl. No. 14, 1964.

17. U.S. Fish and Wildlife Service, *The Effects of Pesticides on Fish and Wildlife.* U.S. Fish and Wildlife Service, Washington, D.C. GPO No. 896-932, 1964.

18. Whittaker, R. H., "Experiments with radiophosphorus tracer in aquarium microcosms." *Ecol. Monographs* 31, 157–188, 1961.

19. Wills, H., Data compiled for Pesticides Control Board Meeting, December 15, 1965, from Census of Manufacturers, U.S. Department of Commerce, and U.S. Department of Agriculture, 1965.

20. Wurster, C. F., Wurster, D. H., and Strickland, W. H., "Bird mortality after spraying for Dutch elm disease with DDT." *Science* 148, 90–1, 1965.

21. Wurster, D. H., Wurster, C. F., and Strickland, W. H., "Bird mortality following DDT spray for Dutch elm disease." *Ecology* 46, 488–99, 1965.

General Bibliography

For detailed and authoritative discussions of the "Pesticides Problem" see:

Carson, R., *Silent Spring.* Boston: Houghton Mifflin, 1962.

Carson, R., Statement before the Subcommittee on Reorganization and International Organizations of the Committee on Government Operations, U.S. Senate, Washington, D.C. June 4, 1963. Part I, pp. 207–12, 1963.

DeBach, P., *Biological Control of Insect Pests and Weeds.* New York: Reinhold, 1964.

Rudd, R. L., *Pesticides and the Living Landscape.* Madison: University of Wisconsin Press, 1964.

Part 4   **Men in Ecosystems**

Pesticides—in Our Ecosystem

FRANK E. EGLER

(Left, photo courtesy U.S. Forest Service, U.S. Department of Agriculture. Above, after Obermaier, reproduced from J. G. D. Clark, *Prehistoric Europe, The Economic Basis,* Methuen and Co., Ltd., 1952, p. 34.)

THE PROBLEM OF pesticides in the human environment is 95 per cent a problem—not in the scientific knowledge of pesticides, not in the scientific knowledge of the environment—but in the scientific knowledge of human behavior. The problem has come into existence because of a revolt of an intelligent minority against the growing pseudo-scientific technology of our age, a revolt in which the knowledgeable scientists are peculiarly silent. In recognition of such problems as this, Professor Loren Eiseley, historian and philosopher, writes of the need for "an enlightened campaign not only against apathy but—what is worse—an apparently organized stupidity in areas where that attitude is most unbecoming."

This paper will be primarily an inquiry into pertinent aspects of that 95 per cent portion, the sociological. Concerning the remaining 5 per cent, the scientific knowledge of pesticides and of the environment, and of the interrelationships of the two, is rapidly advancing and readily available in the literature (Anon., 1960; Anon., 1963; Burke, 1963; Carson, 1962; Carson, 1963; Consumer Reports, 1963; Cottam, 1959; Cutler, 1963; Dale, *et al.,* 1963; Dale, *et al.,* 1963; George, 1963; Johnson, *et al.,* 1963; Residue Reviews, 1963; Wiesner, 1963). When a persistent biocide is set loose to ramify through the ecosystem, we are confronted by a danger of such obvious

American Scientist, *52(1):110–136, March 1964. Reprinted by permission. Footnotes indicating omissions are those of the* American Scientist *editor, not of the editors of this anthology.*

proportions that governments should take immediate action.

In interpreting and accepting that literature, the source of publication should be borne in mind. The two last-published references (Dale, *et al.*, November 1963, and Dale, *et al.*, December 1963) form an interesting pair. In the first, two additional chlorinated hydrocarbons are found in the body fat of a random sample of people. In the second, poisoning and death in rats is correlated with concentrations of such hydrocarbons in the brain rather than in the body fat, which body fat is reduced by starvation, while the hydrocarbons apparently move into the nervous system.

The problem will be discussed in five parts. The first two will be in the nature of a definition of terms; I on the ecosystem, II on pesticides. The interaction of these two is discussed in III "Revolution in the Environment." In section IV we enumerate various "Social Units" that play important roles in this human ecosystem web. Section V portrays the "communication" between and among these social units and thus opens the door to lights which can add meaningfulness to the present pesticide controversy. There are scientists, too many of them, who believe that once they have published their research in a professional journal, all the world will know of it. The science of communications studies the movement of that knowledge into and among the facets of society. Unfortunately, "communication specialists" have too often limited themselves to theoretical and actual studies of communication media, of retrieval systems for libraries and published material, of radio, television, and the press (Menzel, 1960; Wiesner, 1963).

I. The Ecosystem

The *idea* of the ecosystem, like so many ideas in human society, could undoubtedly be traced back to the origins of society itself. In its simplest form, it means nothing more than that a whole is greater than the sum of its parts, that a molecule of water is "more than" the simple addition of hydrogen and oxygen, that a human being is "more than" the simple addition of its chemical components, its tissues and its organs. These higher integrated wholes have been variously called organizations, organisms (not necessarily biologic), systems, and now ecosystems.

In philosophy and thought, the idea received two considerable stimulants in the 1920's. Morgan (1922) elaborated the idea as "emergent evolution" in the sense that new properties and characteristics emerged in the process of evolving integration of those larger more complex units. J. C. Smuts (1926) expanded his own approach under the designation of "holism," which emphasized the properties of wholes, rather than of component parts. Such ideas were applied, perhaps too literally, by certain plant ecologists of the succeeding decade, who confused analogies with identities, and who looked for and found in the plant-community all the characteristics of the individual biologic organism.

On the other hand, within the natural sciences we find a small but significant trickle of critical papers that are attaining increasing recognition. Forbes (1887) wrote on "The Lake as a Microcosm." William Morton Wheeler (1911) discussed "The Ant-Colony as an Organism," and later (1927) extended the discussion to "Emergent Evolution of the Social." Egler (1942) applied the idea in "Vegetation as an Object of Study." Nevertheless, the concept never became really popular. It was either misunderstood, or considered impractical for scientific research.

The term *ecosystem* was coined by the British plant ecologist, Tansley, in 1935, as a holistic unit comprised not only of the vegetation, but also of the environment of that vegetation including climate, soils, and animals. The word is not etymologically unreasonable, if we consider the eco- not as meaning environment of, or something around something else, but as the totality of a site or habitat and everything in it. Tansley did little more than give birth to the word, but, since then, it is appearing with increasing frequency in the scientific literature. The 1953 textbook of Odum (*Fundamentals of Ecology,* 2 ed., 1959) is molded firmly on the concept. I note two relatively distinct trends in contemporary scientific publication. The one emphasizes productivity and energy relationships in the ecosystem; the second is grappling with the methodologically challenging problems of describing the ecosystem in its entirety. In this second field, we hear more and more of the "human ecosystem," with psychology and sociology playing prominent roles.

The first trend, that of productivity and energy relationships, is receiving understandable popularity. Its research can be designed and planned. Its methods are related to those of the chemist and the physicist. Its data can be treated quantitatively, and tested statistically. Its problems are meaningful: the intake of energy into the system, the energy flow as it passes through the food chain, the total biomass of that system, and the eventual consumption and loss of energy to the exterior. These studies are unquestionably one of the most fertile fields of contemporary research, because, for the first time, our focus on these matters is

upon the entire ecosystem, and not upon some one plant or animal species which, in a sense, does not exist as a totally independent entity in nature. It should not be necessary to add that the emphasis on the whole should not blind us to the fact that recognition of the components is also essential. More than once I have been concerned, feeling that the approach can be likened to understanding a cow by running the entire live animal through an enormous meat grinder, and scientifically analyzing the resultant hamburger. A monkey might slip in, and never be noticed. The resultant science might express a perfect bovine placidity, but it would take a sharp mental eye to be aware of the monkey business.

The second trend, that of recognizing and describing ecosystems, in all their manifestations, is also gaining recognition, but with different concepts, different methods, different researchers. Evans (1956) surveyed the matter in his "Ecosystem as the Basic Unit in Ecology." I believe many others would like to sink their teeth into these problems, but they are discouraged if not foiled, by a wealth of near-insurmountable obstacles. The very subject matter is not organizable, analyzable, researchable by the orderly, precise, quantitative methods which are so very much the substance of scientific life today, from the proposal for a research grant, to the published paper that improves the scientist's stature and security among his peers.

Furthermore, the very modes of thinking run counter to much that is ingrained in the training and practice of the scientist of today. He is taught to take apart, and study the parts. He is taught to factor, to analyze. He has methods to study the relationship of two factors (cause and effect); and there are mathematical methods for studying

247

the effects of several interacting factors. Quite simply, however, the study of ecosystems is the study of wholes first, and parts later. The study of those wholes cannot start, cannot proceed, by methods traditionally acceptable to chemists, physicists, and mathematicians, who, in turn, are likely to belittle concepts and methods which in their own fields might be "inexact," "subjective" and not amenable to statistical treatment. Even worse, these wholes are intrinsically changed by factorial analysis. They are no longer wholes when so studied. Would you, for example, break down water into hydrogen and oxygen, and study those parts in order to comprehend the nature of water? Would you study the parts of an automobile in order to comprehend the functioning of the complete car on the highway and in traffic?

That scientists in the natural sciences have not solved this problem, and are still thinking, teaching, and researching at the factorial level is interestingly evident from the organization of many textbooks. I have in mind such books as start out with a preface indicating a high integrative approach. Then, chapter after chapter deals with the various factors of the environment or of the ecosystem. Finally, in the very last chapter, the ecosystem or its analogue is paraded out, in a not very convincing fashion. This conclusion, to me, is where the book should begin, not end.

That international science is progressing in the field of ecosystematics, however, is clearly evident. What in my opinion was a milestone was attained last year in F. R. Fosberg's (1963) symposium on "Man's Place in the Island Ecosystem." Dr. Fosberg has long been operating on the international scene, strongly linked with UNESCO symposia in human ecology,

and quietly but certainly developing a solid basis for the ecosystem, and for "Ecosystem Management" in our human society. His brief but effective plea for "The Community Ecologist" (1957), for example, is widely known. The idea of the Community Ecologist was carried on by Roland Clement (1963). Considering the complexity of the ecosystem in continental areas, it is no accident that island phenomena have lent themselves to productive studies. And of all islands, coral atolls are some of the most discrete and integrated land ecosystems, little piles of sand tossed upon a submerged coral life, bearing their plants, animals and man, in an environment of sea and air. Here, also, the name of Fosberg comes to the fore, for he has been Editor, since its inception, of the *Atoll Research Bulletin,* issued by the Pacific Science Board of the U.S. National Academy of Sciences, with No. 100 appearing on November 15, 1963. His introductory 6-page article in the Honolulu symposium (1963) on "The Ecosystem Concept" and on "The Island Ecosystem" may well become a classic both for the brevity and quality of its statements.

It is essential to diverge at this time, and consider the relation of the ecosystem to "ecology." The problem of "ecology" among scientists and in human society is first a problem of semantics. "Ecology" to a European student of plant-communities is that subdivision of his science dealing only with the relations of his communities to the external environment. To an American botanist, it is the entire science of plant-communities. To a bio-ecologist, (usually a zoologist), it is the study of plant-and-animal communities, but sometimes it is only the study of animal or plant populations, or even of separate plant or animal species. To another type of ecologist, whom I would prefer to call an ecosystematist, it is the study of entire ecosystems, even if these are relatively poorly integrated in nature. Many add man to this ecosystem, and talk about the "human ecosystem," and the significance of fire, agriculture, forestry, fisheries, wildlife management, and urban developments.

We will progress one step farther in this analysis. Our interest in the human ecosystem will be not only in the movement of pesticides through that ecosystem. We will seek the causes of that movement through the varying operations of different human social units, such as industry, government, academia, citizen groups, and eventually the individual citizen.

One step farther. We will seek the *causes* of those variations among the different social units in terms of their own local environments. Specifically this is a problem in the *flow of knowledge* to such social units. *This paper is, therefore, a contribution to an empirical and descriptive science of communications, in which the flow of different but related bodies of knowledge is traced through and among the human social units of the human ecosystem.*

We must again return for some general comments concerning "ecology." I do not believe I am incorrect in saying that "ecology" has not been the most respected of the biologic disciplines. It has smacked of being glorified, old-time natural history. It dotes on the "natural," on virgin conditions untouched by the hand of man. It has reveled in comfortable and comforting armchair theories. It has not always attracted the cream of the intellectual student crop. At one of the times that I was completely disgusted with the field, I wrote (1951) what was intended

to be my swan-song. The reaction, to my complete astonishment, was favorable enough to keep me in the field. Nevertheless, even now, over a decade later, I cannot say that the situation has changed significantly. Even in 1963, there has been a recrudescence of the extremely simple plant-succession-to-climax theories that leaves me quite baffled. Clearly we have here a psychologic problem, one involving "wishful wisdom," the urge to believe in which transcends even what is perfectly obvious to untrained laymen.

The problems of the human ecosystem are making the most urgent demands upon the science of "ecology." It is my sincere opinion that these demands are surprising "ecology." Ecology has not yet risen, not to its own needs, but to the needs of human society. I can end this section on a fruitful note, however. Peter Farb's book *Ecology*, has recently appeared (1963) in Life Nature Library. The academicians may protest that it is a picture book, rather scatteringly unorganized. It does, however, draw well upon a wealth of knowledge on the part of its author. It will probably do more than the entire body of ecologic literature in bringing both the word "ecology," and ecosystemic thinking, to the general public. In turn, I am hoping that, from this general public, a new type of scientific individual will rise to the occasion, and help to form the ecosystem ecology of the future. In the words of Marston Bates (in *The Nation*, October 6, 1962) "Ecology may well be the most important of the sciences from the viewpoint of long-term human survival, but it is among those least understood by the general public, and least supported by research."

II. Pesticides

Pesticides have probably existed ever since the first cave dweller by the side of the sea noticed that salt water, flung far in a storm, killed plants; and then used that knowledge to effect the intentional killing of plants. Other pest killers were found, and exploited.

The tempo, the variety, and the effectiveness of pesticides, could they be graphed, would appear like our own human population curve, the rate of increase itself increasing. DDT was first synthesized in 1874; its insecticidal properties were not discovered until 1939. During World War II, research in chemical warfare was enormously stepped up. The chemists searched for chemicals by which man could kill man, his crops, his livestock.

From these indubitably sinister origins developed the post-World War II pesticide industry. It was found that what poisoned man also poisoned insects. It was found that some substances could kill insects, without killing man, at least immediately. It was found that, with pests so controlled, crop production burgeoned and yields per acre shot up. The race was on. Farmers produced more. Farm prices were supported, while excesses were stored, given away, or destroyed. And with it, the pesticide industry mushroomed. Synthetic pesticide production in the United States was 124,259,000 lb. in 1947. It soared to 637,666,000 lb. in 1960. It is still soaring, as chemicals ever more effective are synthesized to combat the forms of life that have developed immunities to the present chemicals. The wholesale value of these products is now stated as being close to 400 million dollars. The big chemical concerns have much at stake. Monsanto Chemical's business in agricultural chemicals (which includes chemical fertilizers) reportedly

has had an average growth rate of about 20 per cent annually over the last decade. Dow Chemical's business in this field showed a moderate but still healthy growth at 12 per cent a year. Stauffer Chemical's volume in agricultural chemicals, comprising 18 per cent of its total sales, approximated 40 million dollars in 1962, more than double the 1961 figure. Hercules Powder's farm chemicals volume has tripled in the last decade. And American Cyanamid derives 17 per cent of its over all sales from agricultural chemicals. Sales of pesticides in 1962 revealed a slow down in growth rate, but still an increase over 1961. To the hopes and plans of the industry, this is but a small beginning, as they eye the underdeveloped countries, with their unfertilized and pest-ridden crop-lands, their proliferating human populations, and the toll of human disease. It is understandable, if not forgivable, that those whose ecological nonsophistication is restricted to a simple equation involving "more food—for more people —with less disease—today" should look upon themselves as the saviors of mankind, and should look upon the profits of the pesticide industry as a moral and righteous source of private profit.

If this degree of ecological nonsophistication shall prove to have been insufficient for the good of mankind, then the fault lies not only with industry, but with the science which has failed to produce and to communicate the proper knowledge, and with the society that has failed to educate its citizenry and that tolerates the offending industries.

In the years before 1962, many scientists were expressing great concern as to the side-effects, the indirect effects, and the long-term effects of these pesticides, not only on the target organisms themselves, but on other organisms, as the pesticides moved through the environment, interacting among themselves, following food chains as predator ate predator, and acting upon man himself, as in cancer-producing substances, in ways most difficult to document in a factual manner.

The struggling scientists, however, were ridiculed or ignored or silenced in a variety of ways, even by their own colleagues, and especially by the chemical industry and by its chief disciples in the U.S. Department of Agriculture and the Food and Drug Administration. In any event their work was not entirely lost to society. There came a change.

The years 1962 and 1963 are so completely dominated by one person and one book that historians of the future may well refer to this period as the Carsonian Era of "Silent Spring" (1962). With initial appearance of excerpts of the book in the June *New Yorker* magazine, the world has been treated to the most absorbing and instructive body of scientific and pseudo-scientific literature it has ever known. There has been defense and counter-defense, a focusing upon minutiae, distortion, innuendo, bias, claims of emotionalism themselves written with extreme and apparent emotion. The book rose to the Best Seller lists, and stayed there for months. With it all, I seriously wonder how many of the most vocal have really read the book! I have made it a point to ask everyone who expresses a strong opinion about it to me, whether he has really read the book. The replies unfortunately were never taped by modern recorders. In all truthfulness, I here report that I have yet to find the pro-pesticide man who admits to reading the book. (Maybe

this statement will elicit affirmative replies—but, after all, a year and a half has passed.) The case is typified by the Director of Research of a large chemical manufacturer who, when asked about the book, stammered apologetically that he really had not read it; he tried; several times; but he just could not bring himself to read it. It is abundantly clear from some of the anti-reviews, that the reviewers themselves really had not read it through. They read into it what they feared to find, what the anti-chemical alarmists said they had found. In short, they criticized it for what they *thought* was in it. One of the most interesting reviews that has come to my attention is that of Dill, *et al.* (1963), in which quotations from anti-Silent Spring reviews are paired with and refuted by quotations from the book itself.

Another milestone was reached on May 15, 1963, with the Report of the President's Science Advisory Committee, published by the White House. This Report did not alter the pesticide picture as Rachel Carson had portrayed it. It vindicated that picture, and lent a stature to it that one person alone, even Dr. Carson, could not have given.

The story of pesticides in 1962–1963 is that of the angry, emotional, and sales-conscious reaction of the industry and of its disciples in government agriculture, abetted albeit innocently by the obsessively scientific, not that of the cool and calm progress of scientific knowledge through a democratic society.

We have at this point discussed (I) the idea of the ecosystem, a relatively new concept in the natural sciences; and (II) pesticides, and their burgeoning use in the human ecosystem within the past 15 years. It is now time to combine these two ideas, to stand off as it were, and to view this whole in the light not of one minute, one year, or a decade, but in the light of the human race, its past, present, and future.

III. Revolution in the Environment

An organism without an environment is inconceivable.

A successful organism without a suitable environment is an irrational thought.

An organism unable to adjust to a *changing* environment becomes an extinct organism. So it was with dinosaurs, lords of creation in their time, when their swamps dried up. So it was not with cockroaches, which have successfully adjusted to changing environments, as geologic era succeeded geologic era. We have much to learn from the cockroach.

As the history of the human race unfolds, the rate-of-change in all its activities appears to be increasing. There is a constant acceleration. The phenomenon is most obvious in human population itself. We have removed the natural checks and balances due to war and disease. Disease no longer wipes out children; war no longer kills off the warriors and the civilian populations (though the greatest threats of war continue to exist); disease no longer keeps the old from getting much older. Population levels are getting out of control, even while traditional forces, particularly in religion, are trying to keep "natural" what is otherwise most unnatural, thus preventing any logical solution to the problem.

Any slow change is called "evolution"; any rapid change, "revolution." We have a right to refer not only to a revolution in human populations, but also to a Revolution in the Environment, in the human environment. I refer at this time to those changes produced by man himself. Our earth-

moving machinery is becoming increasingly powerful, with shovels now commanding 18,000 horsepower. These goliaths are taller than a 20-story building, longer than a city block, and wider than an eight-lane highway, with a dipper that can dig 200,000 tons of earth a day. We are draining our swamps at an alarming pace. Our river systems are becoming a set of step-like rises of dams alternating with lakes, with new dams now planned to rise even in the middle of existing reservoirs, and with national legislation needed to preserve a stretch of wild river as a rare "museum piece." Water tables are being lowered, to create critical water shortages particularly in regions already arid. Cropland soils are being altered by nutrient changes, by destroying the original microbiota, and by loading them with such long-lasting biocides that only the crop plant itself can survive, sometimes not without changes in its nutrient value to man, even while (as with arsenic in some tobacco), the biocide reappears in the crop plant itself. The wastes and effluvia of our homes and industry are polluting the streams and the underground water supplies, to reappear, often with chemically significant changes, in our wells and our reservoirs. Our cities are taking over more and more of the landscape, and in doing so are radically altering every aspect of that landscape. The testing of atomic bombs has made us conscious of unusual radioactive materials in the environment, even while industrial uses of nuclear energy increase, and with that increase the problem of removing nuclear wastes from our immediate environment. Along with all these problems is that of pesticides, of lethal biocides affecting all forms of life, which are remarkably persistent in the environment, which kill or harm much more than the target organism, and which have the unpleasant habit of distributing themselves far from their point of application, into the polar regions and out to sea.

The revolution in the environment is not to be questioned. It is here, with us, to be accepted. Up to this time, it has occurred with the inexorable inevitability of natural forces. True, it is being occasioned by an organism, whereas other revolutions in the history of the earth appear to have been occasioned by volcanic and mountain building forces, by changes in the distribution of land and sea, by climatic changes of aridity and glaciation. But, being occasioned by an organism does not automatically make it well-planned, rational, or necessarily sound for the organism involved, even for the organism self-named *Homo sapiens*.

In general, we have acted with remarkable arrogance to the whole-nature of which we are a part. Any part which we do not want, we seek to destroy, completely and utterly, be it the bison, the snake, the mosquito or a human enemy. The human enemy may be individual, city-state, tribe, nation, or race. With the destruction of each such "pest," by the use of the handiest, cheapest, most quickly acting "pesticide," goes the destruction of anything else about which we do not care at the moment, or the eventual destruction of other things about which we may care, but by such remote side-effects that the actual connection can be disputed. The result of all this destruction, of what is not immediately and obviously of use to us is what can be called a "simplification of the habitat." One of the cardinal axioms of the natural sciences is that a simplified habitat is extremely unstable. Like a child's house of blocks, one block pulled, and the whole topples.

Accepting the revolution to a simplified and possibly poisoned environment as—not necessarily an actuality today, but at least a possibility with a high probability—then mankind is faced with (1) the most challenging problem yet to confront his self-acclaimed intelligence, and (2) the most interesting train of events yet to be described and recorded by objective scientists.

To dispense with the second point first, since it is beyond the scope of this present inquiry:—Whether future generations of mankind will be able to survive and thrive in the changed environment which his so-called ingenuity is producing is—to put it honestly—an open question. Man-plus-that-environment forms a new "whole" never before in existence. To observers outside this planet (imagining that such exist) the experiment would be highly interesting, if not exciting.

The first point is the challenge to our supposed intelligence so to direct and control this Revolution in the Environment that we here and after thrive and survive in it. The problem is not one of growing and selling at a suitable profit this year's surplus crop of wheat. The problem is not in destroying the rats in your cellar, the cockroaches in your kitchen, the mosquitoes on your lawn, or even the bats in your belfry. The problem is not in growing timber on a 70-year rotation. The problem is not in saving your child from a lethal disease, or the unreasonable perpetuation of your own life. The problem is not in the continuing growth of our national economy. The problem is not in the balance of payments for a nation, or whether that nation and all nations are to survive under communism or under capitalism. The problem is whether the entire earth, man and the environment he is modifying can persist successfully and happily, generation after generation, meaningfully, without man either destroying himself, or losing himself in a whirling dervish of economic prosperity, linked with individual nonentity made tolerable only by perpetual tranquilization. This latter is the world prophesied by Aldous Huxley, which even he admitted, before his recent death, seemed to be coming into existence far more rapidly than he had ever anticipated.

Insofar as this is a problem—to be described only, or to be directed—it is a problem of the ecosystem, for the ecosystematist. Ecology as a science is only barely ready to assume this tremendous role. Ecology, however, is noted by its absence from the council tables of those who are deciding the fate of mankind.

We cannot understand this interplay of forces and phenomena within the web of the pesticide-modified human ecosystem unless we identify some of the strands of that web. Such identification by no means implies the "independence" of such strands. To the contrary, it only reveals their dependence on the whole. It also reveals the limitations and bias inherent in any attempt to interpret the entire ecosystem in terms of one or a few strands.

IV. Some Strands of the Human Ecosystem Web

The web of the human ecosystem—the web in which persistent pesticides have been introduced at certain points by man and have ramified throughout the web so extensively as to be causing a "revolution" in all those strands that are collectively to be called the "environment" of man—this web is a highly complex phenomenon. It is not only more complex than we think. It

is more complex than we *can* think. Nevertheless, there are certain strands, and certain combinations of strands, which are sufficiently integrated into themselves to have attained a certain distinctness in our scientific thinking and action. *That they are thought to be completely independent of the rest of the ecosystem is precisely at the root of the entire pesticide-ecosystem problem.* I refer specifically to those fields of science and technology (often involving more of the latter than the former) known as agriculture, forestry, horticulture, and certain aspects of medicine. Through these four fields runs a common strand, that of entomology. It is entomology which has spawned the field of "Pest Control." There is no phrase in this entire paper which is more loaded with emotionalism than this. It sets up a great evil; then destroys it. It creates both the dragon, *and* St. George. (The fire ant was not a pest until the commercial sprayers told the believing Department of Agriculture that it was.) It is the web-strand-crossings of entomology-agriculture, entomology-forestry, entomology-horticulture, and entomology-medicine (where insects have been the vectors of disease) that have served as *the four major focal points for the entry of pesticides into the human ecosystem, and the spread therefrom.* They are worth further consideration.

Agriculture is the basis of our food supply. It is the hope of our burgeoning populations, even though we now grow too much, store too much, give away too much, destroy too much. Any threat to agriculture is couched in alarmist terms, and immediately arouses alarmist reactions in the general public. There is no question that our agriculture is dependent upon the use of chemical pesticides, even as there is no question that what the ecologist is asking for is a gradual reduction in the use of broad-spectrum persistent chemicals, and a gradual increase in various biological means of control that affect the target organism alone. On the other hand, agriculture is one of the most non-ecological of these fields, and agriculturists are some of the most non-ecological of these technicians. We must realize that agronomists are a one-species-oriented people. Their efforts are to plough, plant, and harvest the greatest crops at the least cost, within one year or even several months. In their training and in their thinking, they are strangers in time and space to the complex ecosystem. They want a simplified, if highly unstable environment.

Agriculture is extremely effective in communicating to the general public through its "extension services." The relationship between them and ecosystem ecology does not always express compatibility. Ian McMillan (in *The Condor,* 1960) says that "... Extension Services, more than any other forces, are responsible for this (unwise) land-use picture. What they have done, however innocently, is to encourage and advise toward maximum, immediate, economic exploitation of the land, without regard for end results. They have demonstrated and advocated only that which is most profitable economically. I have never noted any real concern for conservation of the future. Through their influence and tutelage we have, on the local level, a leadership of prosperous ignoramuses." A specific instance of problems of this kind is indicated in a release by the Connecticut Area Citizens for Biological Control (1963).

Forestry has certain things in common with agriculture, even though the time-scale for growing timber crops is far greater. Insect damage takes enormous toll of our forest resources. Insecticides "control" (but rarely eradicate) those insects. The costs of that damage in terms of the costs of insecticide control present irrefutable, sound, and logical arguments for the widespread use of pesticides—as long as only two strands of the web are considered. On the other hand, foresters can be remarkably ignorant of other strands, of the ramifying effects of wildlife changes within the forest, of long-term reactions from the loss of nitrogen-fixing "pest plants" such as alder. Silvics, as an ecological science and as the foundation of silviculture, is as undeveloped as classical "ecology." So-called control of the gypsy moth is one of the most informative case histories in this forestry-entomology ganglion. This restricted picture is presented admirably by Worrell (1960) in a tightly documented essay that links this forest economist with an Ivy League university and a respected conservation organization. We all recognize the gypsy moth as an unmitigated nuisance which should certainly be controlled without affecting the rest of the ecosystem. But, even in this rigid cost-benefit study, there is no figure for the timber losses involved, for areas where the timber value is often the least important of all ecosystem values, and where other effects in the ecosystem are simply not considered. It is an illuminating study.

Horticulture and bug control are congenial bed-fellows. He who has picked Japanese beetles endlessly off his roses, and who needs only go to the nearest supermarket to pick up a can of "harmless" (to himself) spray that will "kill everything" (he does not want), is easily convinced. I am not saying that these pesticides should never be used by the homeowner. I am only saying that they should be used wisely, that the too-fine print should be read, that alternate means should be used whenever and as soon as available. It is wisest not to drive 80 miles an hour on glare ice, even for an emergency, if alternate means are available. And it is even wiser to avoid, or not to create, such emergencies. Horticulturists and horticultural societies have been easily wooed to marriage with pesticides. They themselves are generally laymen with no professional training in any of the sciences. Too often they are gullible to the blandishments of the quick-kill-salesmen of pesticide hucksters. Frankly, I believe industry has a point when it says that the collective effect of all the homeowners putting pesticides in the ecosystem is infinitely worse than of the agriculturists. Agriculture, watching its profits, cannot afford a 5 per cent increase in pesticide use unless absolutely necessary for its immediate crop. But the home owner, finding that one spritz "works," will give 900 per cent more for good measure, often with arms and legs bare, and mouth wide open. I know the reactions of these new ex-city suburbanites, especially in town meetings when voting on gypsy moth control and when whipped into fear by the vested interests of the local agricultural experiment station. It is here, more than anywhere else, where one sees a corrosive contradiction between science and a democracy, a democracy of human beings who are apathetic, or credulous, or both. One mosquito bite where they cannot scratch in public, one fuzzy-wuzzy caterpillar on a darling baby threatening his health, and they soon turn into lawn lizards or barbecue pit vipers, which in all scientific seriousness I consider two of the most dangerous races of wildlife

which can vote to affect vast areas of forest land far beyond their own quarter-acre lots.

Professional horticulturists often abet this situation. It is my sober opinion that the peak of ecological ignorance is attained in those too-numerous instances where it is recommended that one part of a garden not be sprayed, so as to protect the beneficial insects. It is, of course, reassuring to realize that these people are aware that beneficial insects exist. It is, however, very difficult to accept their implication that nature was so created for man that bad insects will go where they can get killed, and good insects where they will thrive, not to mention the intelligence of the chemicals themselves to stay where they are put, and not move past the garden wall in ground water, surficial runoff, and in the bodies of other animals in the food chain, and not react with other chemicals to form more critical compounds.

Medicine comes into our discussion from three vantages: insect-borne diseases, the field of nutrition, and pollen-caused allergies. All three may be heavily dominated, directly and indirectly, by industry.

Insect-borne diseases strike terror in the heart of man. Pesticides strike the insect-borne diseases. Ergo, pesticides are marvelous. There is no question that lives saved from malaria by DDT spraying are to be reckoned in the millions. For example, the population of Madagascar, which had been stationary for many years, doubled in a dozen years following the initiation of an antimalaria campaign. I suppose this is "good." In terms of a two-strand science, pesticides and human disease form a most successful combination. An excellent recent expression of this non-ecologic view was contributed a few months ago by Thomas Jukes

(1963), formerly nutritionist and bio-chemist of American Cyanamid.

Nutrition itself has been the battle ground between the powerful food in-dustry, and those who are concerned about pesticide residues in their diet. The food industry in turn has heavily invaded some of our campuses. Fur-thermore, the trade organizations of this industry have been extremely ef-fective in distributing literature in saturation campaigns. Of "the genius of the American food industry," we are endlessly reminded. I have had such literature forwarded to me from strange places, small town libraries, local na-ture centers, school teachers. With it all, as is true in this entire field, the companies themselves keep as pure as possible. It is difficult to pinpoint the corporate source of trouble.

Allergy, as a medical field, is closely related for our purposes to the control of ragweed with herbicides. Ecosyste-matically speaking, ragweed control is an absurdly simple procedure. The plant is a pioneer, growing only on bare soil, not growing where it is crowded out by other plants. In crop-lands, it is controlled by known farm-ing procedures. On roadsides, it is only increased by such spraying, as spraying kills its competitors as well as it, while it disappears when the rubble strip at the side of the road is itself re-moved by better road design. Never-theless, this two-strand part of our ecosystem has developed to prepos-terous dimensions, to be mentioned again in Part V of this paper. Much of the "action" arises in the industry-sustained weed control conferences. My acquaintance with the public health sections of these conferences leads me to say that two groups of people attend them, M.D.'s who are concerned about the pollen counts in the atmosphere but who have absolutely no knowledge about ragweed as a component of plant-communities, and commercial sprayers. The latter teach the former, and woe betide any mere botanist who dares to rear his head on the simple botanical facts of ragweed life.

In addition to forestry, agriculture, horticulture, and medicine, three other pesticide-land parts of the ecosystem are deserving of mention: wildlife, ranges and pastures, and right-of-ways and roadsides. All three of these are suffering from a lack of ecosystematic sophistication, often within their own ranks, most certainly on the part of public and other scientific groups who should be supporting them.

In behalf of wildlife, it is under-standable that wildlife agencies should be the leaders in opposing unnecessary introduction of persistent broad-spec-trum pesticides into the ecosystem. Wildlife is one of the first to suffer, often conspicuously and continuously so. The original fears of these agencies have been amply documented by a continuing barrage of scientific studies confirming not only actual kills, but pesticide movements through the food chains to affect every stage in the re-production cycles of animals far re-moved from those initially affected. In this role, the U.S. Fish and Wildlife Service has taken a lead, and should be commended. On the subject of kills, I continue to be disgusted at the out-raged replies of the non-ecologic oppo-sition. They often represent the "Big Stiff" school of thought. Unless they have a cold corpse before them, they belittle the effect. And even if they do, they call it an "accident." It seems impossible to convince these people that nature disposes of dead bodies far quicker than they can find them. Simple reflection should indicate their errors. Assume, for example, a bird that raises six nestlings, such as the

257

common chickadee. At the end of the season, that bird population will be 400 per cent greater. Yet by the next nesting season, the population will be the same; 75 per cent will have died. Who has seen a dead chickadee, or one in the process of feeding a predator? Now take a pesticide which destroys 90 per cent of that remaining population, and you have a population imbalance which can be extremely critical. Even worse, an empty habitat will drain into it birds from surrounding areas, very possibly to be killed by the persistent pesticides. The crime is compounded. On the matter of bird populations, there is still another highly unscientific and illogical approach by those to whom . . . well, I am not sure what has gone wrong, except that I am highly interested in this aberrational thinking and cannot explain it away to the credit of the parties involved. I refer to the misuse being made of the figures from the National Audubon Society Christmas Bird Counts (Nat. Aud. Soc., 1963). These Bird Counts are taken each winter at the Christmas season (when most birds have gone south). They are essentially number-counting outings by amateur bird watchers. Through the years, better places have been found by more birders. (Hence, higher counts.) It is quite true that some of these increased counts may be of significance to population scientists. For example, more herring gulls (more garbage in our harbors); more blackbirds (more grain crops); higher counts (more human counters). All these factors would have to be weighed carefully. What disturbs me (or amuses me—I am not sure which is the greater reaction) is the way non-ecologists are using these counts as scientific "data," to be treated statistically, in support of their pesticides-don't-harm arguments. I recall

being in the audience during one public pesticide debate, when these counts were brought up by an able industry representative, and ably refuted by the opposition. On the platform after the debate, the industry representative seemed conspicuously alone, so I went up to him and, according to my usual policy, told him I was extremely interested in everything he had to say. He took the comment as a compliment, did not recognize my face (I try to keep it unknown), never asked for my name, never asked for my opinion, and discussed at some length his own views. I still feel confused, but I suspect that he believed "numbers" do not lie. They are "data." They can be treated statistically, to give infallible conclusions. I could only feel—as I do with so much of the mathematical turbulence in my own field of plant ecology—that the concepts and the methods are indeed flawless; and that all may depend on arbitrary subjective and personal elements in the very first steps of the methodology, often hidden from the observer himself, if not manipulated by a subconscious "wishful wisdom." The mind of man is still the determining factor, and not the electronic computer which only feeds on what is given it. It cannot answer questions that it is not asked.

On the range lands of this country, the cattle and sheep industry play dominant roles. Zoicides have played dominant roles in predator control, often leading to unanticipated disruptions of the ecosystem. These extremely virulent poisons are not only carried through the food chain to still other animals. Man is learning the hard way what a good ecologist could have told him in the first place, that irruptions of rodents and rabbits are part of this ecosystemic upset. One of the clearest recent studies on this subject is that of Niering, Whittaker, and Lowe (1963) in the cactus country near Tucson. In this case, it took two outside ecologists to see at once what local specialist-researchers had long been missing—that persistent cattle grazing had totally upset the original ecosystem, resulting in a new, and to a great extent irreversible, ecosystem without cactus reproduction and with more rodents. Since the land in question is a national heritage, for cactus, not cows, it remains to be seen whether this ecologic knowledge is applied without delay by those who guard our national heritages. The case has some points in common with my study of the role of fire, kinds of fires in producing, maintaining, and destroying the Everglades of Florida.

Another facet of range land management is associated with invading brush and with brush control. The role of pre-whiteman fires in conditioning the original grasslands is gradually being accepted (Humphrey, 1962) over the edapho-climatic climax jargon of an American ecology fast becoming obsolete (or so I hope). "Brush control" was heavily dominated by the aerial herbicide sprayers, and nonecologic scientists were quite vocal in their researches on "kill" of woody plants. We hear less about that these days. Strangely, I hear more of bulldozing, and mechanical means of ripping out the unwanted plants, in recent years. Without hesitation, I say that such techniques of brush control indicate a woeful lack of ecological knowledge of the nature of plant-communities and of vegetation management. I do not say that alternative and successful methods could be applied at once; I do say that they need research by ecologists, and not by agronomists, physiologists, sprayers, or engineers.

With right-of-ways and roadsides—occupying more of our country than all six New England states put together—I have been peculiarly involved in this field of Right-of-way Vegetation Management as long as anyone in the nation. It is 95 per cent a human social problem, and 5 per cent a botanical problem, as I have amply demonstrated in various publications. The botanical solution rests on vegetation situations which are all too obvious to intelligent observers of the outdoors, and yet are contrary to certain tidy textbook and armchair theories on "plant succession" that old-time American-ecologists just hate to discard. Complications on the human social scene are formidable. Herbicide manufacturers and spray contractors are extremely effective. Highway and utility engineers know but two kinds of plants: "grass" which does not grow up; and "brush" which does. (I remember the time that I failed to convince an otherwise intelligent engineer that a shrub would not grow up into a tree.) The world's most colossal corporation, American Telephone and Telegraph, which spent 3.5 million dollars in eight years unwisely spraying 200,000 acres in one subsidiary alone, runs the largest industrial research laboratory in the world, Bell Telephone Laboratories. Yet, to my most recent knowledge, they have not one investigator evaluating the ecological results of this spraying on the vegetation! Their philosophy, as that of many other companies with which I have dealt in many capacities is that "they have the weeds," "herbicides are good for weeds," so "we use herbicides—as the salesman tells us, because he should know." A new chapter appears to open in 1962 with the formation of Rightofway Resources

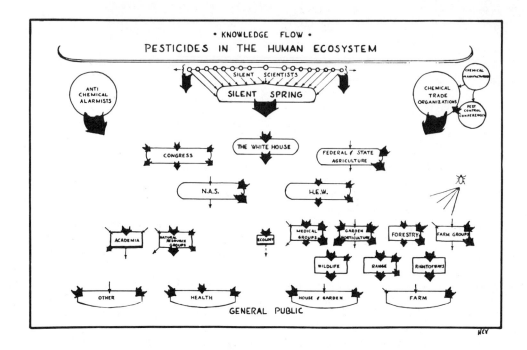

KNOWLEDGE FLOW
PESTICIDES IN THE HUMAN ECOSYSTEM

of America. The founder of the organization aimed to bring together the leading scientists in the field, as a research and advisory committee. The organization has served very efficiently in communicating scientific knowledge to various citizen groups. On the other hand, it has shown certain weaknesses —typical of such scientific groups— which are anything but complimentary to the scientific fraternity. It remains to be seen whether scientists, even though the "best" in their field, have the knowledge, the courage, and the freedom, to present a united front to the public—even though industry, with a minute fraction of that knowledge, has presented an overwhelming front to the public for years.

There are two other strands in the human social ecosystem that play, or could play, significant roles. I refer first to the citizen groups dealing with the conservation of natural resources, and second our universities collectively referred to as "academia."

Conservation organizations are maturing rapidly in recent years. It is

perfectly true that many of them can trace their historical origins to specialist interests, sometimes encumbered and overcast with a sickly sentimentality. On the other hand, these citizen organizations are rapidly enlarging their interests to include all strands of the ecosystemic web. The more critical ones have already attained to a degree of ecologic sophistication, in acceptance of factual knowledge, in keeping abreast of legislation activities, in communicating to the general public, far superior to that of their confreres in academia. Although the record is still spotty, and surprising blunders still occur, I feel that the greatest hopes lie in this direction. It may be unwise to single any one out for mention. If I were to judge by the number of references in my files, and by the absence of instances that I consider ecologically and sociologically unsound, I believe I would give top honors to the National Audubon Society. The academic world unfortunately too often knows this group only from its bird-feeding bird-counting members. That

Fig. 1. Flow of Knowledge Concerning Pesticides in the Human Ecosystem.

Chart based on a survey made in 1962–1963 of all available literature from the social units involved, including articles and notices in newspapers, magazines, television, and radio. The social units were of the following major categories: the "silent scientists" supplying much of the basic ecologic knowledge; the "Silent Spring" by Rachel Carson; a group referred to as "anti-chemical alarmists" including the extremists of the left; the pro-pesticide industry of the right (including chemical manufacturers, pest control conferences, and chemical trade organizations); government (in which the principal actors were the White House, Congress, federal and state agriculture, the National Academy of Sciences, and the Dept. of Health, Education and Welfare (including the Public Health Service, and the Food and Drug Administration). Then there was a large group of social units forming three separate clusters: (1) our colleges and campuses (excluding agriculture); (2) a group that might be called ecology, ecologists, and the Ecological Society of America; and (3) a complex of seven, involving medical groups, gardens and horticulture, forestry, farm groups (these four are tied to each other, and heavily influenced by entomology), wildlife, range, and rightofways. Lastly are the general public and the individual consumer, among whom we must segregate those of the farm, of house and garden, the ones concerned with health, and a catch-all for the remainder. Three types of knowledge must be recognized: (1) that of ecosystem ecology and general ecology, represented by *vertical* arrows; (2) that of the anti-chemical extremists, represented by *diagonal* arrows of the *left;* and (3) that of the pro-pesticide elements, represented by *diagonal* arrows of the *right.* The role of each social unit in the flow of pesticide knowledge is indicated by the size and kind of arrows entering and leaving that social unit, as estimated by the author as a result of his studies. (Actual connecting lines between units are not shown, because of their great numbers.) The chart is extremely revealing of the roles in our society of the three types of knowledge. The overwhelming abundance of heavy arrows of the "right" is everywhere evident, not only in government, but also in the general public. The extremists and alarmists of the "left" have made little impression on government, little impression on other social groups except for gardening and horticulture, but considerable impression on the general public. The role of "vertical" ecosystem ecology is the most instructive aspect of this chart, for it is in this direction that the fundamental scientific knowledge is moving. At the top of the chart we find the "silent scientists," who supplied their information for "Silent Spring." "Silent Spring" in turn is represented as the largest unit of the chart, in my opinion the most important single study in ecosystematics that has been written. For other social units, the role of ecology gives many surprises. It is the dominant factor in the White House, but only the thinnest of lines in federal and state agriculture, and even in the pest-control-philosophy-dominated National Academy of Sciences. Natural resource and conservation groups have shown unusual success in receiving, and giving out, sound ecological information. Our campuses make a poor showing beside them, for although much ecologic knowledge goes in to academia, but little goes out (to wit, the "silent scientists"). The role of "ecology" as a social unit in America is unquestionably the most illuminating feature of the entire chart. Whereas this science should be playing a leading role on the social scene, it is represented as the smallest of social bodies which, altho sound knowledge goes in, so little comes out to influence the public that that little is indicated only by a dotted line. (Figures 1, 2 and 3 were prepared by Harry E. Van Deusen, Research Associate, Aton Forest. From the original article.)

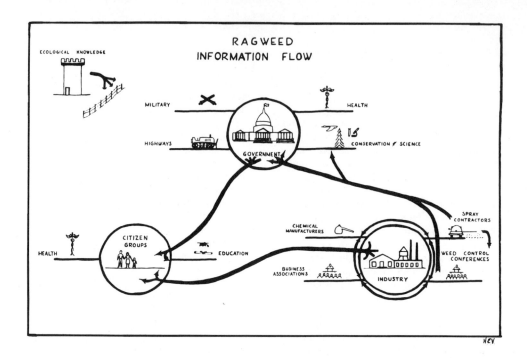

RAGWEED
INFORMATION FLOW

Fig. 2. Flow of Roadside Ragweed Control
Knowledge.

Chart based on a questionnaire survey made in
1958–1959, to over 200 social units involving
two federal governments, seven states and
provinces, five counties, 2 major cities, and
miscellaneous individuals and organizations.
Each social unit was asked from whom they
did get or would get information, what literature they had published or released, and to
whom it was distributed. The social units
recognized were of three major categories:
government (including military, highways,
health, and conservation & science); citizen
groups (including health and education); and
industry (including chemical manufacturers,
business associations, spray contractors, and
weed control conferences). Two kinds of
knowledge were segregated. The first was
ecological (blue-line)* knowledge, which recognizes the ragweed (Ambrosia artemisiifolia)
is a pioneer plant of sterile sites, the "symptom" of a "site disease." It will disappear if
the site itself is altered; but will become more
abundant if its competitors are destroyed by
spraying. This knowledge is not communicated
to government, industry, or citizen groups. The
second type of knowledge is that associated

with commercial herbicide blanket-spraying
(red-line)* which does kill ragweed but also
kills its competitors, so opening the site to
more ragweed and to grassy weeds. Separate
work sheets were prepared for the flow of
information in each of the states, provinces,
and federal governments. The present chart is
a generalized diagram abstracted from these
worksheets, and includes only the more important flow lines. It will be noticed that the
basic ecologic knowledge (upper left of chart)
is restricted to its source, and is not communicating itself to the rest of society. Commercial
blanket-spray knowledge (rest of chart) appears to arise in industry, though even there
the knowledge goes round and round and
round and there is no definitive source. There
is a heavy flow-line out of the spray contractors and the weed control conferences (and
from the contractors *to* the weed control conferences) to government, especially to conservation and science. This same information
in turn is communicated to the citizen groups,
reinforced by heavy communication directly
from industry.

° Blue-line indicated by white lines; red-line by
black lines (See Fig. 3).

262

field known as the "conservation of natural resources" is coming closer and closer to an "applied ecosystem ecology." Two recent and excellent summaries of this subject occur in Dasmann's *The Last Horizon* (1963) and Secretary Udall's *The Quiet Crisis* (1963).

To discuss *academia* in the pages of AMERICAN SCIENTIST, on the subject of pesticides in the ecosystem, is a task from which I would prefer to withdraw in a sort of courteous but dishonest silence. I feel this is "my" world; I would like it to be my world; yet it is my candid opinion that on this subject it is failing *the* world.[1]

The last social unit in this section I term "ecology." In a sense it is embodied in all the social units already discussed. However, it seems reasonable to question and consider whether "ecology" exists as an effective social strand in this ecosystem. The answer quite simply is "no," for more reasons than the immaturity of the science already discussed in section I of this paper. This time I would say it is the social immaturity of the ecologists.[2]

Four strand-complexes in the human ecosystem also merit discussion. They are: the alarmist groups; government; industry; and *Silent Spring* itself.[2]

V. Communication

The "social units" enumerated in part IV are of significance to the problem of pesticides in the human ecosystem, only if *communication* of knowledge from one social unit to another is itself

[1] In the original manuscript Dr. Egler documented this opinion in a five-page discussion. The Editor has assumed the responsibility of eliminating it.

[2] Discussion of these topics and the *Conclusion* have been abbreviated—Ed.

studied objectively and descriptively. This aspect of scientific investigation, involving questionnaire surveys and personal interviews, with analyses for the units as to opinions held, from where information is sought or from where it comes, and to whom it goes, has been the subject of three studies by the author, as yet largely unpublished. One concerns ragweed control knowledge in northeastern North America, a second involves gypsy moth control knowledge in a New England state, and the third embraces the wealth of pesticide literature triggered by the publication of *Silent Spring*. Summarizing charts are here presented. For all three charts, it must be remembered that the recognition of Social Units is necessarily "arbitrary" (as with any plant-and-animal-communities) and depends on their apparent distinctness in nature. The nature and size of the flow lines are not necessarily arithmetically or statistically determined (though charts based on questionnaire returns have been prepared), but are here generalized on the basis of the judgment of the author. (See Figs. 1, 2 and 3.)

Conclusion

The scientific awareness of the problem of pesticides in the human environment is not new. For example, Lyle Thorpe, Director of the Connecticut State Board of Fisheries & Game, has told me of his concern, during the World War II spraying of Pacific islands, when he found large dead lizards soon after such spraying. Nevertheless, coordinated scientific and social concern within the sphere of general ecology is very largely a post-Silent Spring phenomenon since mid-1962.

As a scientific subject, the phenomenon lies in the field of general ecology,

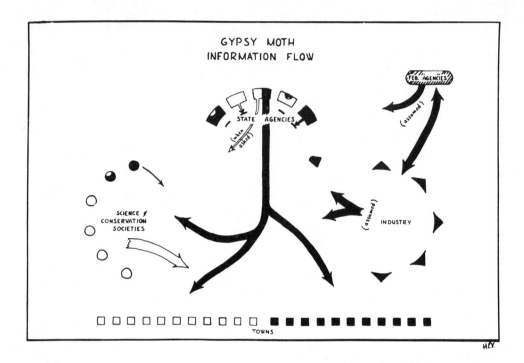

GYPSY MOTH
INFORMATION FLOW

FED. AGENCIES

STATE AGENCIES

(when asked)

(assumed)

SCIENCE &
CONSERVATION
SOCIETIES

(assumed)

INDUSTRY

TOWNS

HEY

here often called ecosystematics to distinguish it from minor and obsolescent fields that may also carry the name "ecology."

What has developed, especially in the last two years and is revealed in the three communication charts, is not only the feebleness of an existing science of ecology, but also the rather disturbing inability for needed ecologic research to be carried out by both government and universities. Furthermore, there is the very disturbing inability of this ecologic knowledge to communicate itself to other parts of the human ecosystem once it does exist. And finally, there is the even more disturbing flood of literature supported by specialist-"experts" who speak from their one-strand vantages on the ecosystem web. What shows up especially and incontrovertibly is the non-existence of suitable teaching and research in our universities.

In the light of this undesirable situation, I trust that somewhere, somehow, an Institute for the Study of

Ecosystem Ecology will arise, with sufficient intelligence, money and energy to carry on research and to communicate that research throughout our society. It might be affiliated with a university. It might be affiliated with a government agency, although both our state (with few exceptions) and our federal governments are themselves split into specialist groups, and lack the coordinating power of a Department of Natural Resources, or of Ecosystem Ecology. To date, only a lone woman, and a special White House panel, have shown the necessary scientific sophistication.

In our human ecosystem, the dislocation of one strand of this web, though possibly for the short-term good of that strand and of its short-sighted and narrow-minded custodians, can result in adverse readjustments through the whole web. The entire integrated ecosystem of life on earth is being weighed in the balance.

Fig. 3. Flow of Gypsy Moth Control Knowledge.

Chart based on a questionnaire survey made in 1962, of approximately 100 social units in a single New England state. Each social unit was queried as to its publications if any, as to whether they recommended or wanted broadcast aerial spraying with DDT of large acreages, or wished alternative chemical or biological controls in local spots of high infestation or research directed to such alternatives. Other values of the human ecosystem were considered, involving timber, wildlife, water supplies, and human health. Each social unit was also queried as to from where, and to whom its information was communicated. The social units recognized were of five major categories: state government agencies, federal government agencies (when mentioned by others), science and conservation citizen societies, industry (when mentioned by others), and the various Towns themselves (which voted on aerial spraying). Two kinds of knowledge were segregated: ecological (blue-line) knowledge represented on the chart by white lines, opposed to indiscriminate broadcast aerial spraying with DDT; and red-line knowledge represented on the chart by black lines, favoring indiscriminate broadcast aerial spraying with DDT. The present chart is a generalized diagram abstracted from the questionnaire returns and interviews, and includes only the more important flow lines. All except two of the reporting science and conservation units (symbolically represented by six units on the chart) were blue-line in their knowledge, and the two red-line exceptions clearly showed the influence of one state agency on people simply unable to judge the ecological nature of the problem. The Towns are shown equally divided between blue- and red-orientation. (The exact number of each is not given, so as to preserve the anonymity of the state involved.) Only one Town made an intelligent effort to obtain expert advice from national authorities; it voted against aerial spraying. Voting in other Towns was rarely significant, since the die was often cast by a handful of uninformed emotional or selfish citizens, influenced only by a pro-spraying representative. "Industry" and "Federal Agencies" are included in the diagram. Although they were not directly queried, they were frequently referred to by others. Furthermore, since there was no actual scientific source of information in the state, it must be assumed that pro-spraying "knowledge" arose either in industry, or federal agencies, or both. The situation with the State Agencies was clearly the most revealing and significant part of this sociological study! The agencies queried were those involved with agricultural research teaching and extension, with fisheries, game, forests, parks, and health. The "official line" from each agency, without exception, was that they make no recommendations whatever concerning aerial spraying. This was empirically true of four of the agencies. These four, despite the soundness of their ecologic knowledge, or the enthusiasm of their unecologic knowledge, did what they wanted; and kept mum. It was the fifth state agency however which eventually supplied the secret to the entire problem in the state. This tax-supported agency, and essentially only one department in it, and essentially only the head of that department, appeared to be the one and only source of such pro-aerial-spraying information as led others to report that "the state" recommended such spraying. On the other hand, when in the presence of or queried by a blue-line citizen, this agency gave the winning impression of being 100% blue-line itself. Although such an agency must be referred to as being two-phased, its effect on the social scene was however 100% red-line.

Publications by the Author Concerning the Communication of Scientific Knowledge

"Science, industry and the abuse of rights of way." *Science 127:* 573–580, 1958.

"Roadside ragweed control knowledge, and its 'communication' between science, industry and society" (Abstract). IX Intern. Botanical Congress Proc. IIA: 11–12, 1959.

"Human ecology, and Connecticut's two roadside bulletins." *Ecol. 41:* 820–822, 1960.

"Roadside ragweed control knowledge, and its 'communication' between science, industry and society." Pp. 1430–1435 in *Recent Advances in Botany*, Univ. Toronto Press, 1961.

"Pesticides and the National Academy of Sciences" (A review of pesticide bulletins I and II). *Atlantic Naturalist 17:* 267–271, 1962.

"On American problems in the communication of biologic knowledge to society." 30th Biologisch Jaarboek Dodonaea (Belgian Royal Natural History Society), 263–304, 1962. (Reprints at cost, 50¢ from Litchfield Hills Audubon Society.)

"What is the 'suburban forest'?—A national problem." (Review of the Lockwood Conference on the Suburban Forest and Ecology.) *Ecol. 44:* 625–627, 1963.

"Pesticides and the National Academy of Sciences. A Sequel" (A review of pesticide bulletin III). *Atlantic Naturalist 18:* 229–231, 1963.

"Conversations on Ecology. Vegetation Management VI." (Communication.) *Garden Journal* (N.Y. Bot. Garden) *13:* 219–220, 224, 1963.

The Free and the Led. Book manuscript, in preparation.
(Reprints available at cost, 3¢ per page, from Aton Forest, Inc., Norfolk, Connecticut.)

References

Anon., "Pesticides and public safety." Natl. Agric. Chemicals Assoc., 1960.

Anon., "Agricultural chemicals: what they are, how they are used." Manufacturing Chemists Assoc., 1963.

Atoll Research Bulletin, National Academy of Sciences, Pacific Science Board.

Bates, Marston, "Man and other pests." *The Nation 195:* 202–203, 6 October 1962.

Burke, Albert E., "The pests" (text of television program). Burke Enterprises Inc., 1963.

Carson, Rachel, *Silent Spring.* Boston: Houghton Mifflin, 1962.

———, "Environmental hazards. Control of pesticides and other chemical poisons." (Statement before the Senate Subcommittee on Reorganization and International Organizations.) Repr. by Garden Club of Pennsylvania, 1963.

Clement, Roland C., "Man, his environment, and wildlife." Mass. Audubon, 1963.

———, Papers in a symposium on use and effects of pesticides. Albany, New York, September 23, 1963. Mimeogr. National Audubon Society, October 1963.

Conn. Area Citizens for Biological Control, Letter to visitors on Field Day of Agric. Exper. Sta. Mimeogr. Area Cit. for Biol. Control (Box 283, Trumbull, Conn.), 1963.

Cottam, Clarence, "Chemical pesticides—a national problem." Natl. Wildlife Fed., 1959.

———, "*Silent Spring*: an appraisal." *Natl. Parks Magazine* 36 (182): 16–17, 21, 1962.

———, "A noisy reaction to *Silent Spring*." *Sierra Club Bull.* 48, January 1963.

Cutler, M. Rupert, "Some progress seen on the pesticides front." *Conservation News* (Natl. Wildlife Fed.) 28 (22): 609, 1963.

Dale, Wm. E., and Griffith E. Quinby, "Chlorinated insecticides in the body fat of people in the United States." *Science* 142: 593–595, 1963.

———, Thomas B. Gaines, Wayland J. Hayes, and Geo. W. Pearce, "Poisoning by DDT: relation between clinical signs and concentration in rat brain." *Science* 142: 1474–1476, 1963.

Dasmann, Raymond, *The Last Horizon.* New York: Macmillan, 1963.

Dill, Norman H., et al., "The spray around us." *Bull. Torrey Bot. Club* 90: 149–152. (See also: same title, Rutgers Botany Dept. Seminar Report, in which quotations for anti-S.S. reviews are paired with and refuted by quotations from the book itself, in parallel columns.)

Egler, Frank E., "Vegetation as an object of study." *Philosophy of Science* 9, 245–260, 1942.

———, "A commentary on American plant ecology, based on the textbooks of 1947–1949." *Ecol.* 32: 673–694, 1951.

Eiseley, Loren, letter to author, 1963.

Evans, F. C., "Ecosystem as the basic unit in ecology." *Science* 123: 1127–1128, 1956.

Farb, Peter, *Ecology.* Life Nature Library. New York: Time, Inc., 1963.

Forbes, S. A., "The lake as a microcosm." *Peoria Sci. Assoc. Bull.*, 1887. (Repr. *Illinois Nat. Hist. Surv. Bull.* 15: 537–550, 1925.)

Fosberg, F. R., "The community ecologist." *Amer. Inst. Biol. Sci. Bull.*, pp. 24–25, April 1957.

———, ed., *Man's Place in the Island Ecosystem: A Symposium.* Honolulu: Bishop Museum Press, 1963.

George, J. L., ed., "Pesticide-Wildlife studies. A review of Fish and Wildlife Service investigations during 1961 and 1962." *U.S.D.I., F. & W.S.* Circ. 167, 1963.

Humphrey, Robt. R., *Range Ecology.* New York: Ronald, 1962.

Johnson, Oscar, Norman Krog, and J. Lloyd Poland, "Pesticides," Part I: Insecticides, miticides, nematocides, rodenticides; Part II: Fungicides and herbicides. *Chemical Week*, pp. 117–148; 55–90, 1963.

Jukes, Thomas H., "People and pesticides." *Am. Sci.* 51: 355–362, 1963.

Menzel, Herbert, "Review of studies in the flow of information among scientists." Prepared for Natl. Sci. Found., Columbia Univ. Bur. of Applied Social Research. Two vols., mimeogr., 1960.

Morgan, C. Lloyd, *Emergent Evolution.* New York: Holt, 1931 (not 1922).

Natl. Acad. of Sciences, "Pest control and wildlife relationships," Parts I, II, and III. N.A.S. Publ. 920 A.B.C., 1962–1963.

Natl. Audubon Soc., "Memo on N.A.S. Christmas Bird Counts." N.A.S., 1963.

———, "Memo on 'Abraham Ribicoff's statement on persistence of residual action of pesticides." N.A.S.—the statement in full, with comment by staff biologist Roland C. Clement, 1963.

Niering, W. A., R. H. Whittaker, and C. H. Lowe, "The saguaro: a population in relation to environment." *Science* 142: 15–23, 1963.

Odum, Eugene P., *Fundamentals of Ecology*, 2nd. ed. Philadelphia: Saunders, 1959.

Residue Reviews, Vol. 2, 1963. New York: Academic Press; Berlin: Springer-Verlag.

Ribicoff, Abraham, "Statement on pesticide control bill S. 1605." Congressional Record—Senate: 19080–19083, October 22, 1963.

Smuts, J. C., *Holism and Evolution.* New York: Macmillan, 1926.

Tansley, A. G., "The use and abuse of certain vegetational concepts and terms." *Ecol.* 16: 284–307, 1935.

Udall, Stewart L., *The Quiet Crisis.* New York: Holt, 1963.

Wheeler, Wm. Morton, "The ant-colony as an organism." *Journ. Morph* 22: 307–325, 1911.

———, "Emergent evolution of the social." *Proc. Sixth Intern. Congr. Philosophy*, 1927.

Wiesner, Jerome B., Chairman, President's Science Advisory Comm. "Science, government, and information: the responsibilities of the technical community and the government in the transfer of information." The White House, January 10, 1963.

———, "Use of pesticides." The White House, 1963.

Worrell, Albert C., "Pests, pesticides, and people." *Amer. Forests*, 1960. A study sponsored by the Conservation Foundation, publ. by American Forestry Assoc.

The Impending Emergence of Ecological Thought

LaMONT C. COLE

To any biologist who occasionally hob-nobs with other scholars, it soon becomes clear that his friends are not frightened or offended so much by science as by certain philosophical hobgoblins which wear a mask of scientific authority. One such goblin is Reductionism, the attempt to explain something by one or more of its components; for example, human personality on the basis of diet. Fear of reductionism might be called the Nothing-But phobia, for it is commonly triggered by some such statement as "Men are nothing but collections of molecules."

There are other reductionisms that are not so obvious, as when scientific description seems to undermine humanism or theology. To say, for instance, "Man is a member of natural food chains which link him to other forms of life, just as all other creatures are members of food chains," implies to some people that man is an undignified captive in a mechanistic system not of his or of God's devising.

A still more intricate type of Reductionism is simply the discussion of biological processes in a human context. To say to a group of historians, for example, that animals communicate or have traditions usually ends a conversation. Few men can face daring speculation in every aspect of their lives and seem to need the solid ground of dogma in those areas which they themselves are not exploring. There are some, even so, who will surely wel-

come information from any source that will illuminate the human situation. The marvelousness of man may be a visible part of the mystery and beauty of animal life rather than an exception to it. Indeed, what was thought to be reduction may be elevation; the grace of life in which men share may compensate for the vileness much of contemporary literature finds in man.

THE EDITORS

BioScience, *14(7):30–32, July 1964.*
Prepared under an assignment from the Ecology Study Committee, Ecological Society of America. Grateful acknowledgment is made for the support of the committee from the National Science Foundation under grant G-6073.

Prologue

ECOLOGY AS AN autonomous science has existed about as long as genetics, but ecologists have been exceedingly timid about becoming involved in public affairs. Individually, they have lent support to conservation groups in protesting the destruction of natural areas and some of the more flagrant cases of environmental pollution. But only rarely have they shown signs of genuine outrage as many did over some of the programs of predator control in the West.

For the most part, we have gone on learning more and more in the field and laboratory and ivory tower while adopting a somewhat detached and sometimes bemused attitude toward the activities of an ill-informed public. It is not a matter of any great import if people want to believe that the songbirds are protecting us from insect pests, and we do not begrudge a livelihood to those "exterminators" who make their living by harvesting rats. There is even something amusing about "sportsmen's" groups doing their civic duty by shooting crows or planting fishes, as though the female bass' 10,000 eggs per spawning or the pike's 100,000 is somehow inadequate—it conjures up a picture of someone importing acorns to scatter among the oaks.

"The human population of the world has entered a potentially disastrous cycle of growth; we are polluting the environment at an unprecedented rate . . ." (Photo by Grant Heilman.)

But, in recent years, things have been happening that make the widespread ignorance of ecology seem more alarming than amusing. The human population of the world has entered a potentially disastrous cycle of growth; we are polluting the environment at an unprecedented rate, and with biologically active materials such as pesticides and radioisotopes to which the earth's biota has never before had to adapt; and, in one way or another—through erosion or paving or poisoning, we are removing vast areas from the cycle of photosynthetic productivity. Worst of all, our policy makers are seeking and obtaining advice on these problems from groups of scientists who do not even recognize the existence of ecology. Those of us who have spent our professional lives trying to understand the intricate mechanisms that regulate

population size and the composition of biotic communities are not amused when chemists can obtain space in reputable scientific journals to assert that their employer's product is what regulates population size and community composition.

It will take volumes to bring even the scientific public up to date with what ecologists have learned that should be considered in seeking solutions to the crises facing mankind. But permit me to use the minuscule space allotted to me here to indulge in ecological meditation about one little problem—our current fascination with residual pesticides.

A Parable
In a small town where as a boy I spent several summers, there lived an old gentleman who professed the belief

269

that a high concentration of ethyl alcohol in the blood would protect him from infectious diseases. The old man was ahead of his time; he was the first person of my acquaintance to advocate what we now call systemic pesticides.

A few years later, "wonder drugs," in the shape of the sulfas, appeared and showed much greater antibacterial activity than alcohol; then a great many physicians and veterinarians endorsed the old man's hypothesis that an animal body loaded with such chemicals would be protected from an assortment of important diseases. The chemicals became ingredients of such diverse products as foot powders and animal foods. Soon it was learned that sulfas might have side-effects even more undesirable than those of alcohol, but this was not too discouraging because, by this time, penicillin had appeared and seemed to be about as toxic as physiological saline to vertebrates. But there is no need here to review the history of chemoprophylaxis.

The old man's hypothesis is with us now in a slightly different form, represented by the intensive search for systemic insecticides. The rationale, of course, is to grow plants that will kill insects that touch them or bite them, and, for example, cattle that will cause bot flies to drop dead before they can damage the cowhide. It is argued that, even if people do not want to eat protected organisms, the approach can still be valuable for protecting ornamental plants, species producing fiber and lumber, and dogs, cats, and horses. A poisonous soil or atmosphere can be regarded as sort of a systemic pesticide for the biotic community or superorganism so, in effect, our present practices are simply the analog of a clinical technique that has been tried and quite generally abandoned.

If the chemical defenses had lived up to expectations, a number of the most important infectious diseases would already have moved from the textbooks to the history books, but I am not aware that even one disease has done so as a result of all these efforts. What went wrong? Even in those pioneer days when penicillin was a novelty almost unavailable to civilians, a few geneticists were predicting (though not very loudly) that the bacteria would evolve resistant strains. But, to the best of my knowledge, ecologists were completely reticent about saying that these prophylactic measures were not very sensible ways of attacking such problems in the first place.

Some ecologists must have had doubts about these practices from analogy with the many broad-spectrum chemical defenses in nature that fail to defend. Toads will gorge on such poisonous insects as blister beetles, while snakes and crows eat the toads (poisonous skin glands and all) and so do skunks, which also eat the snakes, and which, in turn, are eaten by owls. And someone surely must have paused to wonder why, to obtain nicotine as an insecticide, it was necessary to treat the tobacco plants with lead arsenate to protect them from insects.

This is simply a manifestation of one of the most familiar of ecological generalizations. All ecological niches, or roles in the economy of nature, tend to be filled, and, if there is a way for another species to make a living in a community, we expect some species to evolve the mechanisms for doing so even if it requires drastic morphological and physiological modifications. Thus, all ecologists are aware of marsupials and placentals occupying comparable niches, even specialized ones such as the mole and anteater niches, in different regions. We teach about the finch that has learned to exploit the woodpecker niche, of lizards that substitute for grazing mammals, and of euphorbias that look like and live like cacti.

The general principle should be deducible *a priori* from the observation that, once a certain threshold is reached, organic matter is used up as rapidly as it is produced. It is true that organic matter accumulates continuously in peat bogs and that special conditions permit coal and petroleum to form, but these cases are clearly exceptional. The caloric value of the soil in a tropical rain forest or temperate deciduous forest or of arctic tundra is remarkably stable from year to year, and the same is probably true of most marine sediments. How very different things would be if even a few species had evolved chemical defenses that prevented digestion by any other species!

When once we accept the proposition that natural selection will operate in the direction of filling vacant ecological niches, we must logically begin to wonder whether total eradication of destructive forms is desirable. I have been fascinated to note that some leaders in medical research have recently arrived independently at the sound ecological conclusion that it might be more desirable to replace harmful viruses and bacteria with innocuous types than to leave niches open by trying to keep our bodies free of these forms.

". . . we must logically begin to wonder whether total eradication of destructive forms is desirable." (Photo by Leonard Lee Rue from National Audobon Society.)

By the same principle, the broad-spectrum antibiotic or pesticide is likely to empty not just one niche but several. Ever since antibiotics came into use, physicians have been plagued by secondary infections resulting from the destruction of an innocuous intestinal flora thus leaving ecological niches available for drug-resistant and pathogenic staphylococci. The same applies to biotic communities, and we have a wealth of examples of such secondary infections in which, for example, orchard mites replace the codling moth as the pest of apples and spider mites replace the spruce budworm as the defoliator of fir trees following the application of insecticides.

Another generalization of ecology, which has actually been noted for centuries by amateur naturalists, is that an environment with an ample food supply but special characteristics that make most organisms unable to adapt to it typically harbors enormous populations of a few species. Witness what Mark Twain said of a California lake containing "venomous water that would eat a man's eyes out like fire":

There are no fish in Mono Lake—no frogs, no snakes, no polliwogs—nothing, in fact, that goes to make life desirable . . . no living thing exists *under* the surface, except a white feathery sort of worm, one-half an inch long, which looks like a bit of thread frayed out at the sides. If you dip up a gallon of water, you will get about fifteen thousand of these. They give to the water a sort of grayish-white appearance. Then there is a fly . . . these settle on the beach to eat the worms that wash ashore—and any time, you can see there a belt of flies an inch deep and six feet wide, and this belt extends clear around the lake—a belt of flies one hundred miles long . . .

The principle illustrated is of wide generality. Arctic waters contain fewer species than tropical waters, but far more individuals of each. The same applies to the tundra as contrasted with the tropical rain forest. This trend can be traced from cold springs to thermal springs and from low-altitude to high-altitude situations. And genuinely difficult environments, not only saline lakes but also sewage beds, sulfur waters, and the like, produce almost incredible concentrations of one or very few species. This would have to be so in view of our conclusion that organic matter tends to be used up. In an easy environment, many species participate in the task but, as the environment becomes more rigorous, fewer species occur and each is able to build up larger populations.

Now, as a general rule, about the last thing an agriculturist wants on his land is a tremendous concentration of individuals of one species of animal. Yet this is what he is asking for, under the laws of nature, when he makes the plants or the environment toxic and difficult to adapt to. Only a few kinds of animals can inhabit saline lakes, or eat blister beetles or hairy caterpillars, or attack skunks with impunity, but the specialists that can do these things find little competition and can build up populations commensurate with the food supply. So the animals that succeed in adapting to DDT or other toxins reach population levels far beyond what they could achieve without the toxin. I suspect that this would have become obvious and this general approach to pest control abandoned if it were not for the time factor. So many commercial crops are annuals, subject to damage only over a brief growing season, that the farmer who succeeds in avoiding pest damage for this critical period fails to recognize that his protective measures may be producing the counterpart of a saline lake. The problems are more difficult and

"And genuinely difficult environments, not only saline lakes but also sewage beds, sulfur waters, and the like, produce almost incredible concentrations of one or very few species." (Photo courtesy Florida Game & Fresh Water Fish Commission.)

the difficulties more apparent for perennial crops. Objective entomologists are aware (1) that chemical treatment has greatly reduced the number of pest species in orchards without necessarily reducing the amount of pest damage to the crop and (2) that the problems of dealing with, for example, the pests of apples are continuously increasing in complexity as chemical treatment increases. Most of my apple-growing neighbors now spray their orchards twelve times per year with mixtures of some five chemicals, and they worry incessantly about outbreaks of pests. They must worry because they are producing environments comparable in inhospitality to the tundra, where populations of voles and lemmings and foxes erupt and migrate and crash to an extent that has inspired legends.

Population eruptions do not occur in the tropical rain forest where there are a great many ecological niches, and all of these are filled. Every species there is beset by an assortment of predators and parasites which can turn on any adjacent species that begins to increase in numbers. Without alternative foods to maintain their numbers, predators are likely to be ineffectual in holding down prey populations. Consequently, as we move from the rain forest to simpler biotic communities with fewer alternative foods, we note instability of the predator-prey systems growing and reaching an extreme in the arctic.

All this suggests to an ecologist that clean cultivation, routine pesticide application, and other agricultural practices that reduce the diversity of species in the community may be working in exactly the wrong direction. A healthy,

273

diverse biotic community is not easily invaded by exotic forms and has considerable ability to adjust to invaders. Thus we have seen the Japanese beetle invade new areas, become a major pest, and then decline to a minor status without human intervention. Similarly, our pondweed *Elodea* invaded England and choked major rivers, then declined and ceased to be a pest. Nonselective toxins must inevitably reduce the possibility of such mutual adjustment.

Turning again to the clinical analogy, we find that physicians have now largely discarded the old man's hypothesis of chemical defense except as a temporary emergency measure, as in cases of exposure to plague. They now treat the patient only when needed and, by preference, will use the most highly specific drug available for the particular infectious organism. This is ecologically sound and is the very way nature has designed our own bodies to function. Our bodies do subsidize predators, maintaining large populations of phagocytes which are quite non-selective of the invaders they attack. But when the body brings out its chemical pesticides, in the form of antibodies, these are exceedingly specific, as they should be. Too broad a spectrum of chemical defense results in allergic reactions in the human body and, I suggest, in the biotic community also.

Epilogue

For two years, the Ecological Society of America has had a Committee on Public Affairs, so now there is a place that our administrators and the public can turn to for competent advice on ecological problems. Another committee of the Society has in the planning stage an Information Center on Environmental Pollution. These, and other signs, indicate that ecologists are

at last going to lend their specialized fund of knowledge to the attack on important public problems. My little discourse here has been intended to suggest that some of these problems will change in appearance when seen from the viewpoint of an ecologist. It is safe to predict that such viewpoints are about to emerge in increasing numbers from their sheltered retreats.

The Cybernetics of Competition: a Biologist's View of Society

GARRETT HARDIN[1]

SCIENCE FICTION depends heavily on the postulation of Martians, who are invariably assumed to be more advanced intellectually than we. The psychological reason for this assumption seems clear: the whole apocalyptic myth of the men from Mars fulfils needs that were earlier satisfied by the idea of an imminent Kingdom of Heaven. To the objective eye of an anthropologist, our fictional Martians are manifestly gods, and science fiction is a kind of theology.

The odd thing is that before another human lifetime has passed, we may have a chance to see what Martians are really like (if they exist). And if we do, will it be gods that we are finding, or something less than human? I predict the latter, on the grounds that we have not yet heard from them, as we should have if their technology were really more advanced than ours. If they exist and if they trail us in knowledge, we will then be faced with an interesting complex of problems. Should we educate them? Can we educate them? How?

[1] Professor of Biology, University of California, Santa Barbara. Based on a paper presented to the Symposium on Central Planning and National Goals, directed by James W. Wiggins and Helmut Schoeck at Sea Island, Georgia, in September, 1962. An earlier version of this article is part of a volume in the William Volker Fund series in the Humane Studies published by D. Van Nostrand Company in 1964. The present draft has benefited by the criticisms of Mortimer Andron, William Kennedy, and Carl Stover, in addition to the symposiasts in Georgia.

Perspectives in Biology and Medicine, *7(1): 58–84, Autumn 1963. Reprinted by permission of the University of Chicago Press. Copyright 1963 The University of Chicago.*

In the past, in dealing with the backward peoples of the earth (a similar problem), we have taken the easy path and have given them the answers ready-made. But suppose for once we decide to give our backward brethren, not the answers, but the *questions*—and let them work out their own answers? Suppose we expose the men from Mars to all the complexities of our technological situation and let them figure out the explanations? Watching them, we should learn a great deal about epistemology!

This *Gedankenexperiment* is introduced for nontrivial reasons. The point I wish to make is this: Martians faced with the riddle of our technology would have a far harder time than we did in creating the underpinning of physical theory, even if they are as intelligent as we. Faced with airplanes, how could they arrive at a theory of gravitation? Listening to the radio, would it occur to them that the intensity of electromagnetic radiation obeyed an inverse-square law? In the presence of an atomic explosion, how could they conceive of a conservation law? They might, of course. After all, we found the laws of nature. But in our search we were fortunate in this respect: most of the time invention was only a very little bit ahead of theory; often it was even behind. We were able to discover theory because the world was simple. A theory-poor Martian confronted with our invention-rich world would have a much harder time discovering theory than we did. He might fail utterly.

Picture if you will a convention of Martians, reading scientific papers to each other, papers concerned with the theory of the Earth. One of them proposes a universal law of gravitation. Pandemonium breaks loose. In the absence of all knowledge about combustion, Newton's three laws of motion, electricity, magnetism, superconductivity, radioactivity, and all the rest, it would be all too easy for the Martian auditors to cite evidence upon evidence to refute the idea of universal gravitation. Only a total complex of theory ("model") can be tested against a factual complex. If the elements of a theoretical construct are tested one by one against the complex world, they will, one by one, be "disproved." Probably our visitors from Mars could arrive at a workable theory only if we earthlings agreed to play "Twenty Questions" with them—to give them a nod of approval whenever they stumbled across a fruitful element of theory. (They would, of course, have to have faith in us; for how could they know that we were not merely playing tricks on them?)

The relation of our hypothetical Martians vis-à-vis the physical world is, I submit, our relation to the social world we have created. Over a period of thousands of years, out of necessity and our unconscious, we have elaborated fantastically complex mechanisms of social interaction, inventions so subtle and pervasive that much of the time we cannot even *see* them, much less explain them. In trying to discover or invent social theory we are in the position of the Martians of our thought-experiment. We have too many facts and not enough theory. Data-rich and theory-poor—that is the social world. And there is no one to play "Twenty Questions" with us.

I. The Nature of Theory

Popular writing commonly pictures the great scientist as an extremely critical person. There is much truth in this, but the contrary is also partly, and significantly, true. I know a chemist who frequently says to his graduate students, "Don't let a fact stand in the way of a good hypothesis." This is certainly dangerous advice, but inasmuch as the speaker has won a Nobel Prize for his revolutionary chemical theories, we must assume that he knows something of the requirements for creativity. A good scientist should be a good critic part of the time; but he cannot be a good critic all of the time, not if he hopes to discover new and surprising truths. Different occupations require different temperaments. In mentally reviewing a large roster of successful scientists, I am struck with the fact that it includes no men who were ever lawyers. I can recall scientists who in their early years were artists, musicians, actors, machinists, carpenters, businessmen, and even wearers of the cloth—but no lawyers. From the past, Advocate Fermat is the nearest to an exception I can think of —but he became a mathematician, not a scientist.

A good critic must be tough-minded, to use William James's term. Good lawyers are like other good critics. The successful developer of scientific theory, on the other hand, must be *tough-motivated.* A scientific theory, in its early stages at least, is incapable of explaining all the data it is confronted with. This fact may be illustrated by a joke that was standard in engineering circles for several generations: "The bumble bee doesn't have large enough wings to fly, but fortunately the bee doesn't know this, and so he flies anyway." This was a way of acknowledging that the theory of aerodynamics was inadequate to explain the facts. But engineers did not abandon their theory. Instead they retained it (because of its many successes) in the hope—indeed, in the *faith*—that it

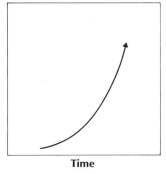

**Amount of
Money or
Numbers of
Organisms**

Time

Fig. 1. The result of positive feedback. (From *Central Planning and Neomercantilism* by Schoeck and Wiggins, D. Van Nostrand Co., Inc., 1964. Courtesy D. Van Nostrand Co., Inc.)

would one day be enlarged in such a way as to make possible an explanation of the flight of the bumble bee. How scientists decide which theories to have faith in, and which not, is a problem of great subtlety, which has been courageously attacked by Polanyi (1).

In the development of social theory we must follow the path that has proven successful in the natural sciences: we must be critical but not too critical. We must be willing to *entertain* partial theories while we see whether they are capable of fruitful enlargement. In the early stages we must expect to be confronted with markedly different theoretical models. What is offered here is one biologist's conception of the foundations of social and economic theory. "What presumption!" social scientists may say. Admitted; but biology, as Warren Weaver has put it, is "the science of organized complexity" —and what is the social scene if not one of organized complexity? Some of the principles worked out in one field should be at least part of the theoretical structure of the other. Particularly relevant are the principles of *cybernetics*, the science of communication and control within organized systems. Let us see what some of these are, as they have been developed in the natural sciences, and how they may apply to the social sciences.

II. Postive Feedback

Money put out at compound interest and the unimpeded reproduction of any species of living organism are both examples of systems with positive feedback. Mathematically they are most conveniently represented by equations of the form

$$(1) \qquad y = C\,e^{bt}$$

where C represents the initial amount (of money or organisms), y is the number or amount after time t, e is the base of natural logarithms (2.71828 . . .), and b is a measure of the rate of increase—the greater the rate, the greater is b. (For example, if there is no increase at all, $b = 0$; when the rate of increase is 10 per cent, $b = .0953$.)

The exponential function just given may be graphed as shown in Figure 1. Notice that the curve rises ever more steeply with the passage of time. Money which is initially interest becomes principal-money, earning more interest-money. Children become parents and produce more children. Hence the use of the term "feedback." The output (part of it, at least) feeds back as input. When the exponent b is positive, we speak of positive feedback. To persist indefinitely, a species must be capable of positive feedback reproduction. To attract investment, a borrower must offer the same possibility for the sums invested.

The exponential equation can be represented by a family of curves, one curve for each value of b. But we can generalize the graph shown and say that if we imagine a flexible abscissa—the time axis—one curve stands for all positive exponential functions. With elephants, the scale would read in decades; with bacteria, in minutes. Similarly, with money at compound interest, we have only to stretch or contract the scale on the abscissa to make one curve fit all rates of interest.

In all cases, we should note this: the curve of unimpeded positive feedback "approaches infinity" with the passage of time. This is true no matter how slow the rate of reproduction, no matter how low the rate of interest. *But ours is a finite world.* Therefore it is clear that positive feedback is not tolerable as a permanent state of affairs. It can be tolerated only for short periods of time. In biology no species can indefinitely increase in keeping with its potential, or soon all the world would be nothing but salmon, elephants, men, or whatever. In economics no sum of interest can be allowed to earn compound interest except for very short periods of time. Suppose, for example, that the thirty pieces of silver which Judas earned by betraying Jesus had been put out at 3 per cent interest. If we assume these pieces of silver were silver dollars, the savings account would today amount to a bit more than 9×10^{14} dollars, or more than $300,000 for every man, woman, and child on the face of the earth. Since the real economic wealth of the world is certainly much less than that amount, it would be quite impossible for Judas' heirs (all of us, I presume) to close out the account. The balance in the bankbook would be largely fictional.

A modern William Paley (2) contemplating bank failures, embezzlements, business collapses, runaway inflation, and revolutions might well argue that these catastrophes are examples of "Design in Nature," for by their presence the impossible consequences of perpetual positive feedback are avoided. A professional economist would be more likely to suggest that we could achieve the same end by falling interest rates, which could fall to zero if need be. Historically, however, this more pleasant possibility has seldom, if ever, developed. Failures, inflation, and revolution have been the historically important counteractants to positive feedback.

In contemplating the implications of the exponential growth function, we see also a fundamental criticism of all forms of "Growthmanship" (to use William H. Peterson's term). Plainly the idea of continuous national growth is a dangerous myth. Recent public debate as to whether our economy should grow at a rate of one or two or three per cent annually deals with a question which is, in the time scale of human history, of only evanescent interest. Continuous economic growth of the order of magnitude hoped for is possible only for a short period of time—a few centuries at most. If a political and economic unit can achieve enduring stability—and we don't know that it can—it could only be with *zero* per cent growth. Not a bit more. Not if growth is measured in material terms, with statistics that are corrected for the effects of inflation. (If growth is in nonmaterial terms, that is another, and a far more interesting, question, which will be neglected here.)

III. Negative Feedback

If a system that includes positive feedback is to possess stability, it must also include "negative feedback." The meaning of this term can be made clear by an example from engineering.

The temperature of a room is kept constant by the combined operation of a furnace and a thermostat. The result is a cybernetic system which can be represented by a type of diagram previously introduced (3). As indicated in

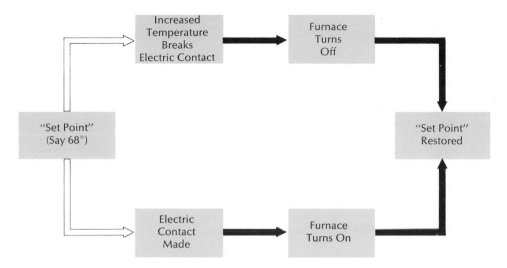

Fig. 2. Cybernetic equilibrium maintained by negative feedback. (From *Central Planning and Neomercantilism* by Schoeck and Wiggins, D. Van Nostrand Co., Inc., 1964. Courtesy D. Van Nostrand Co., Inc.)

Figure 2, when the temperature rises, a bimetallic strip in the thermostat is distorted, thus breaking an electric contact, thus turning off the furnace, and so lowering the temperature. On the other hand, a lowering of the temperature leads to a re-establishment of the electric contact, thus starting the furnace, thus raising the temperature. The temperature of the room will thus fluctuate about the "set point" of the thermostat—and this is what we mean when we say "the temperature is held constant." The variations do not exceed certain limits.

Now for an example from biology. In any natural setting, the population size of a given species·is relatively constant for long periods of time— usually thousands, or even millions, of years. How this constancy is maintained is shown in Figure 3. If the population should increase above the "natural" population size—which we may call the "set point" of the population—various kinds of negative feedback will be brought into play. Shortage of food may lead to starvation. Fighting may lead to deaths or to

interference with breeding. And so on. The result of all this will be more deaths, and perhaps fewer births, and the population will fall. The consequence of a decrease in population can be read from the diagram. Again we have a cybernetic scheme that produces fluctuations about a "set point." What determines the "set point" is not so easy to tell. That is, our knowledge of the interactions of the natural controls of population size is usually insufficient to enable us to *predict* what the "carrying capacity" of the land will be. We have to go into the field and measure it; we determine it *ex post facto*. Nevertheless, we retain this model and interpret our inability to make an a priori determination of the set point as indicating a deficiency in our knowledge rather than a defect in the model.

The cybernetic model can be carried over into economics, as shown in Figure 4, which depicts the control of price in the Ricardian economic scheme. The well-known course of events can be read from the figure. Again we see that negative feedback

279

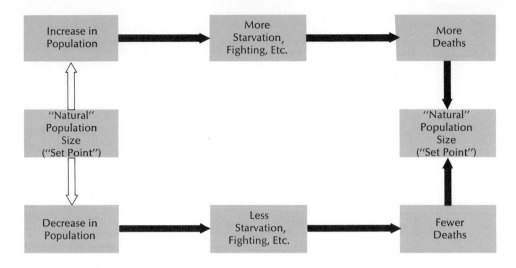

Fig. 3. Cybernetic maintenance of population equilibrium. (From *Central Planning and Neo-mercantilism* by Schoeck and Wiggins, D. Van Nostrand Co., Inc., 1964. Courtesy D. Van Nostrand Co., Inc.)

produces stability about a "set point," which Ricardo called the "natural price." The model would be more realistic if it were constructed in terms of *profit* rather than price, but for historical continuity we retain the classic Ricardian element *price*. As with the biological example previously used, the meaning of "natural" can, in general, only be determined *ex post facto*. The word "natural" is here (as elsewhere) a verbal cloak for ignorance. Nevertheless, it or an equivalent word is needed to remind us of the state of affairs. There is mystery here. It was this mystery together with the un-premeditated consequences of the economic cybernetic system that led Adam Smith to speak of an "Invisible Hand."

An effective cybernetic system produces stability, i.e., fluctuations within limits, and this we esteem. A system that produces a stable temperature, or a stable population, or a stable price, seems to us somehow *right*. When we examine any cybernetic system we discover that it is more or less wasteful.

The thermostated room wastes heat; the natural population wastes lives; the economic system produces price wars and business bankruptcies. We may refine the controls and minimize the losses (of heat, or of money, for example), but a close examination of the system convinces us that there must always be some losses, waste in some sense. This is so because the controls that serve to produce equilibria are themselves so many modes of loss. Accounting procedures, insurance programs, police forces, sweat glands, electric fans, predation, crowd diseases, delicate thermostats—all these are forms of waste. We do not regret them, for the negative feedback produced by each of these elements acts as a check to some kind of uncontrolled and ruinous positive feedback. But each negative feedback device has its price, and we cannot get rid of one form of loss without incurring another. In a deep sense we see that some waste is inevitable and natural, and we recognize as immature the man who compulsively tries to do away with all waste.

We recognize as pathological the goal of a waste-free world. This recognition is an important element in that complex of temperament that we label "conservative." Insofar as we think deeply, we all, of necessity, partake of this temperament to some extent.

But because the mature person acknowledges the inevitability of some waste, it does not follow that he must be reconciled to any amount and kind of waste. In the first excitement of discovering the beauties of economic cybernetics, David Ricardo quite naturally made such an error. In speaking of the cybernetic system that stabilizes the population of laborers, Ricardo (4) wrote: "When the market price of labour is below its natural price, the condition of the labourers is most wretched: then poverty deprives them them of those comforts which custom renders absolute necessaries. It is only

after their privations have reduced their number, or the demand for labour has increased, that the market price of labour will rise to its natural price. . . ."

Attention should be called to the use of the word "natural" in this question. It would be antihistorical to expect Ricardo to speak of the "set point of labor" inasmuch as the term "set point" was not used for another century; but that is not the only criticism that can be made of the word "natural." Looking at the problem through the eyes of Stephen Potter (5), what do we see? Plainly, that an advocate is likely to use the word "natural" in order to insinuate approval of the "natural" thing into the mind of his auditor. By so doing, the advocate frees himself of the necessity of developing a defensible argument for the "natural" thing—for who can disprove that which is "natural"?

Fig. 4. Cybernetic regulation of price, in the Ricardian model. (From *Central Planning and Neo-mercantilism* by Schoeck and Wiggins, D. Van Nostrand Co., Inc., 1964. Courtesy D. Van Nostrand Co., Inc.)

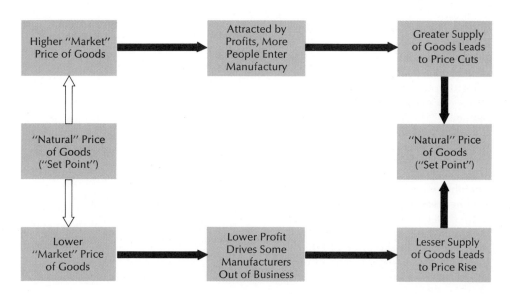

This attack on the use of the word "natural" is more than a mere Potterian counterploy, as is clearly shown by the following defense given by Ricardo (6).

Labour, like all other things which are purchased and sold, and which may be increased or diminished in quantity, has its natural and its market price. The natural price of labour is that price which is necessary to enable the labourers, one with another, to subsist and perpetuate their race, without either increase or diminution.

These then are the laws by which wages are regulated, and by which the happiness of far the greatest part of every community is governed. Like all other contracts, wages should be left to the fair and free competition of the market, and should never be controlled by the interference of the legislature.

This passage leaves no question in our mind that Ricardo identified the momentary state of things in his own time as "natural" and that all attempts to modify it further by new legislation were "unnatural" and hence improper in some deep sense. With rare exceptions, most of us post-Ricardians have been unwilling to accept this view. We will accept the starvation of field mice; but not that of human workers: Ricardo, at least on paper, accepted both. But— perhaps because of a delicate consideration of the feelings of others?— he used a most elegant euphemism for the facts. "It is only after their privations have reduced their number," he wrote; and insisted that "wages should be left to the fair and free competition of the market." The market must be free, that we may enjoy the blessings of cybernetic stability. Most of us now think that Ricardo's price is too high. We are willing to make use of "unnatural" controls of the price of labor even if it means losing some of our

freedom. The history of the labor movement since Ricardo's time may be regarded as one long struggle to substitute other forms of waste for the "natural" form which Ricardo, who was not a laborer, was willing to accept.

IV. The Competitive Exclusion Principle

Perhaps more important than the humane argument just given against the Ricardian model is a theoretical argument which indicates that the cybernetic system he described is fundamentally unstable. Before we can discuss this matter we need to introduce a biological principle known by various names but recently (3) called the "competitive exclusion principle." The historical origin (7) of this principle is complex; no one man can be given credit for it. In the last decade it has become increasingly clear that it is a basic axiom of biological theory; and it will be my argument here that it is basic also to sociological and economic theory. But first, let us develop the principle in an exclusively biological context.

Consider a situation in which two mobile species, X and Z, live in the same habitat and also live in the same "ecological niche," i.e., live exactly the same type of life. Species X multiplies according to this equation:

$$(2) \qquad x = Ke^{ft},$$

where x is the number of individuals of species X at time t; e is the base of natural logarithms; K is a constant standing for the number of x at $t = 0$; and f is a constant determined by the "reproductive potential" of the species.

Species Z multiplies according to this equation:

$$(3) \qquad z = Le^{gt},$$

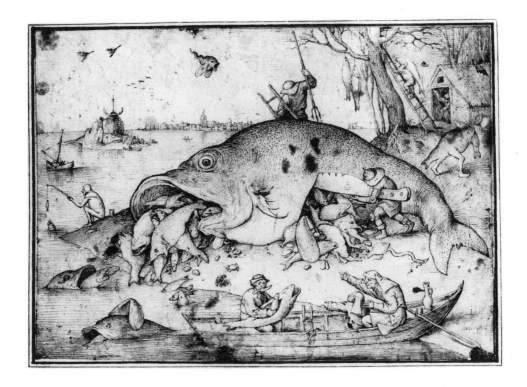

"Suppose . . . two species are placed in the same universe to compete with each other. What will happen?" ("Big Fish Eat Little Fish" by Pieter Brueghel d. Ä., 1556, pen in gray ink; H 216 mm, W 302 mm. Courtesy Graphische Sammlung Albertina, Vienna, Austria.)

in which the constants have the same meaning as before (though, in the general case, with different values).

Suppose these two species are placed in the same universe to compete with each other. What will happen? Let us represent the ratio of the numbers of the two species, x/z, by a new variable, y. Then:

$$(4) \qquad y = \frac{Ke^{ft}}{Le^{gt}}.$$

Since K and L are both constants, they can be replaced by another constant, say C; and making use of a well-known law of exponents, we can write:

$$(5) \qquad y = Ce^{ft-gt} = Ce^{(f-g)t}.$$

But f and g are also constants, and can be replaced by another constant, say b, which gives us:

$$(6) \qquad y = Ce^{bt},$$

which is, of course, our old friend equation 1 again, the equation of exponential growth. The constant b will be positive if species X is competitively superior, negative if it is species Z that multiplies faster.

What does this mean in words? This: in a finite universe—and the organisms of our world know no other—where the total number of organisms of both kinds cannot exceed a certain number, a universe in which a fraction of one living organism is not possible, one species will necessarily replace the other species completely if the two species are "complete competitors," i.e., live the same kind of life.

Only if $b = 0$, i.e., if the multiplication rates of the two species are *precisely* equal, will the two species be able to coexist. Precise, mathematical equality is clearly so unlikely that we can ignore this possibility completely. Instead we assert that the *coexistence of species cannot find its explanation in their competitive equality.* This truth has profound practical implications.

V. Have We Proved Too Much?

It is characteristic of incomplete theory that it "proves too much," i.e., it leads to predictions which are contrary to fact. This is what we find on our first assessment of the competitive exclusion principle. If we begin with the assumption that every species competes with all other species, we are forced to the conclusion that one species—the best of them all—should extinguish all other species. But there are at least a million species in existence today. The variety seems to be fairly stable. How come?

There are many answers to this question. I will discuss here only some of the answers, choosing those that will prove suggestive when we later take up problems of the application of the exclusion principle to human affairs. The following factors may, in one situation or another, account for the coexistence of species.

Geographic isolation. Before man came along and mixed things up, the herbivores of Australia (e.g., kangaroos) did not compete with European herbivores (rabbits). Now Australians, desirous of retaining some of the aboriginal fauna, are trying desperately to prevent the working out of the exclusion principle.

Ecological isolation. English sparrows introduced into New England excluded the native bluebirds from the cities. But in very rural environments bluebirds have, apparently, some competitive advantage over the sparrows, and there they survive today.

Ecological succession. It is not only true that environments select organisms; in addition, organisms make new selective environments. The conditions produced by a winning species may put an end to its own success. Grape juice favors yeast cells more than all others; but as the cells grow they produce alcohol which limits their growth and ultimately results in new predominant species, the vinegar bacteria. In the growth of forests, pine trees are often only an intermediate stage, a "subclimax," being succeeded by the climax plants, the hardwood trees, which out-compete the pines in growing up from seeds in the shade of the pine tree.

Lack of mobility. The universal application of the exclusion principle to plants is still a controversial issue, which cannot be resolved here. It may be that the lack of mobility, combined with certain advantages to being first on the spot, modify the outcome significantly. Although this explanation is questionable, it is a fact of observation that a pure stand of one kind of plant hardly ever occurs.

Interbreeding. If two competing populations are closely enough related genetically that they can interbreed, one group does not replace the other, they simply merge. This does not end competition; it merely changes its locus. The different genes of the formerly distinct groups now compete with each other, under the same rule of competitive exclusion.

Mutation. Continuing with the example just given, one gene never quite eliminates another because the process of mutation is constantly producing new genes. The gene for hemophilia, for example, is a very disadvantageous gene; but even if hemophiliacs never had children (which is almost true), there would always be some hemophiliacs in the population because about three eggs in every 100,000 produced by completely normal women will be mutants that develop into hemophilic sons.

VI. The Cybernetics of Monopoly

We are now ready to take a second look at the Ricardian thesis. The model implicit in his writings may not unfairly be stated as follows. We conceive of a single product manufactured by a number of entrepreneurs, each of whom must, for simplicity in theory construction, be imagined to be engaged in the manufacture of this product only. Under these conditions the Ricardian cybernetic scheme diagrammed in Figure 4 will prevail—but only for awhile. History indicates that the number of entrepreneurs is subject to a long-term secular trend toward reduction. In the early days there were many scores of manufacturers of automobiles in the U.S.; today there are less than a dozen. Ball-point pens, transistors— every new product—have followed the same evolution. The history of the oil industry (to name only one) indicates that under conditions of perfect laissez faire, competition has a natural tendency to steadily decrease the number of competitors until only one is left. In industries with heavy overhead this tendency is a consequence of the economy of size. But even without this size effect, a simple extension of the competitive exclusion principle into economics shows that a reduction in the number of competitors will take

place as the more efficient entrepreneurs squeeze out the less efficient, until ultimately only one is left. If this were not so, we would have to conclude that the free enterprise system has no tendency to produce the lowest possible price; or, to put it differently, that it has no tendency to produce the maximum efficiency. Either conclusion would deny the claims to virtue put forward by the defenders of the free enterprise system.

If a monopoly is produced, what then? Here is a question which Ricardo did not face. At first glance one might say that the monopoly price should be stable, because if it were to rise, new entrepreneurs would be attracted to the field and would lower the price. But this is a naïve view. We know that it is more difficult to start a business than to continue one, and consequently a monopolist can maintain a price considerably above the "natural price." Furthermore, a realistic model must include much more than we have indicated so far. We must consider the whole complex of phenomena that we include under the word "power." *Social power is a process with positive feedback.* By innumerable stratagems a monopolist will try to manipulate the machinery of society in such a way as to ward off all threats to re-establish negative feedback and a "natural" cybernetic equilibrium. And, as history shows, the monopolist in one field will seek to extend his power into others, without limit.

What has just been said about business monopolies applies equally to labor monopolies, *mutatis mutandis.* Insofar as they meet with no opposition, there is little doubt that labor monopolies seek to produce an ever higher price for labor. At the same time, they protest the appearance of business monopolies. Contrariwise,

285

unopposed businessmen seek to promote a free market in labor while restricting it in their own field (by "Fair Trade" laws, for instance). It is not cynicism but simple honesty that forces us to acknowledge that Louis Veuillot (1813–1883) was right when he said: "When I am the weaker, I ask you for liberty because that is your principle; but when I am the stronger I take liberty away from you because that is my principle." In other words, such verbal devices as "principles," "liberty," and "fairness" can be used as competitive weapons. Each purely competitive agent, were he completely honest and frank, would say, "I demand a free market—but only for others." It is, in fact, a natural part of *my* competitive spirit to seek to remove from *my* field the natural competition on which the validity of the Ricardian scheme rests.

Such an analysis, which is based on the observed behavior of competing groups, may seem depressing. Rather than dwell on the possible emotional consequences of the facts, let us see what we can do about arranging the world to our satisfaction. Let us try to enlarge the model of our theory. To do this we acknowledge that we are *not only* unconscious "purely competitive agents," but that we are also capable of being conscious. We can predict the results of our own actions, as well as the results of the actions of those opposed to us. We acknowledge that *words are actions*, actions designed to influence others. Because we can see that others resort to high-flown rhetoric when they want to influence us, we become suspicious of our own arguments. We operate under the basic and parsimonious rule of the Theory of Games (8), which says that we must impute to others intelligence equal to our own. Under these conditions we seek the *boundary conditions* within

which the rule of laissez faire can produce stability.

VII. The Limits of Laissez Faire

Laissez faire has a strong emotional appeal; it seems somehow right. Yet we have seen that, in the limit, the rule fails because of the positive feedback of power. Can we *rationalize* the rule of laissez faire by harmonizing it with boundary conditions?

I suggest that there is, in biology, a useful model already at hand (9). Consider the cybernetic system that controls the temperature of the human body, a system that is enough like that shown in Figure 2 so that it need not be diagrammed here. This system works admirably. So well does it work that, for the most part, we can safely adopt a laissez faire attitude toward our body temperature.

The system works without conscious control or planning. But only within limits. If the environmental stress is too great, temperature control fails. At the upper limit, too great a heat input raises the body temperature to the point where the physiological thermostat no longer functions. Then higher temperature produces greater metabolism, which produces more heat, which produces higher temperature, which— and there it is, positive feedback, leading to death, to destruction of the whole system. Similarly with abnormally low temperatures. The working of the system is shown in Figure 5. There is a middle region in which a laissez faire attitude toward control of the environment works perfectly; we call this middle region the *homeostatic plateau*. (The word "homeostatic" was coined by W. B. Cannon to indicate constancy-maintained-by-negative-feedback.) Beyond the homeostatic plateau, at either

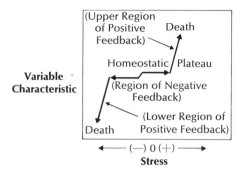

Variable
Characteristic

(Upper Region
of Positive   Death
Feedback)

Homeostatic / Plateau

(Region of Negative
Feedback)

(Lower Region of
Death   Positive Feedback)

◄─── (—) 0 (+) ───►
Stress

Fig. 5. The cybernetics involved in the survival of a system. (From *Central Planning and Neomercantilism* by Schoeck and Wiggins, D. Van Nostrand Co., Inc., 1964. Courtesy D. Van Nostrand Co., Inc.)

extreme, lies positive feedback and destruction. Plainly, our object in life must be to keep ourselves on the homeostatic plateau. And insofar as it is within our power to affect the design of a system, we would wish to extend the plateau as far as possible.

Is this not the model for all cybernetic systems, sociological and economic as well as biological, the model on which ethics must be based? The desire to maintain *absolute* constancy in any system must be recognized as deeply pathological. Engineering theory indicates that excessive restraints can produce instability. In psychiatry also, the desire for complete certainty is recognized as a most destructive compulsion. And in the history of nations, attempts to control rigidly all economic variables have uniformly led to chaos. The psychologically healthy human recognizes that fluctuations are unavoidable, that waste is normal, and that one should institute only such explicit controls as are required to keep each system on its homeostatic plateau. We must devise and use such controls as are needed to keep the social system on the homeostatic plateau. On this plateau—but not beyond it—freedom produces stability.

We can do this only if we explicitly give up certain superficially plausible objectives which are incompatible with stability. In the realm of economics, the most dangerous will-o'-the-wisp is the word "efficiency." Consider

the classical Ricardian economic system. If we decide that all waste is bad and that we must maximize efficiency, then we will stand admiringly by and watch the competitive exclusion principle work its way to its conclusion, leaving only one surviving entrepreneur, the most efficient. And then? Then we find that we have a tiger by the tail, that we have allowed the positive feedback of power to go so far that we may be unable to regain anything that deserves the name of freedom. It is suicidal to seek complete efficiency. The Greek Solon said, "Nothing in excess," to which we must add, *not even efficiency*. Whatever it is that we want to maximize, it cannot be efficiency. We can remain free only if we accept some waste.

How are we to keep a social system on its homeostatic plateau? By laws? Not in any simple way, for the effect of an action depends on the state of the system at the time it is applied—a fact which is, I believe, not systematically recognized in the theory of law. An act which is harmless when the system is well within its homeostatic boundaries may be quite destructive when the system is already stressed near one of its limits. *To promote the goal of stability, a law must take cognizance not only of the act but also of the state of the system at the time the act is performed.* In his effort to obtain the maximum individual freedom, it is to be expected, of course, that "economic man" will try to defend his actions in terms of some tradition-hallowed "absolute" principles that take no cognizance of the state of the system. Absolutists of all sorts may, in fact, be defined as men who reject *systematic* thinking.

287

Consider this question: Should a man be allowed to make money, and keep it? In the history of Western capitalism our first approximation to an answer was an unqualified *Yes*. But as we became aware that money is one means of achieving the positive feedback of power, we looked around for curbs. One of these is the graduated income tax, which most men would now defend as a reasonable brake to the positive feedback of economic power. Yet it can easily be attacked as being "unfair," and in fact has been so attacked many times. As late as 1954 (according to a press report) the industrialist Fred Maytag II, speaking to a meeting of the National Association of Manufacturers on the subject of discriminatory taxes, issued this clarion call for action: "The hour is late, but not too late. There is no excuse for our hesitating any longer. With all the strength of equity and logic on our side, and with the urgent need for taking the tax shackles off economic progress, initiative is ours if we have the courage to take it."

One cannot but have a certain sympathy for the speaker. He is right when he says that the existing tax structure is contrary to "equity." But if discussion is to be carried on in terms of such abstractions, Mr. Maytag would find his opponents introducing the word "justice" and saying that this is more precious than equity. Rather than use such verbal bludgeons, we should think operationally in terms of the homeostatic plateau. We should think in terms of systems rather than individual acts. That this sort of thinking presents difficulties for the law is admitted; but it is clear also that we have made some progress in the solution of these difficulties, e.g., in the graduated income tax. It is clear also that our systematic

thinking has not produced perfect solutions to our problems (e.g., it is still possible to become a millionaire via the capital gains route).

Indeed, the recognition of the relevance of the whole system in judging the desirability of an individual act can be traced back to antiquity. One of the greatest of the technical social inventions of ancient Athens was that of *ostracism*, which was invented by Cleisthenes. We are told (10):

Once a year the popular Assembly deliberated on whether any citizen should be required to go into exile for ten years on the grounds that his presence in Athens was a threat to the constitution. If the Assembly voted to hold an ostracism, a second vote was taken. Then, if six thousand citizens wrote the same name on an *ostrakon*, or potsherd, the man named must leave Athens for ten years. But he did not lose his citizenship, his goods were not confiscated, he did not even suffer disgrace. In fact, it was only the man of great ability who was likely to be ostracized, yet the possibility of ostracism was a constant deterrent to overweening political ambition.

In other words, ostracism was a device aimed at stopping the positive feedback of power, a tool designed to maintain the political system on a homeostatic plateau. Recognition of the dangers of this positive feedback must surely be almost universal among practical men and produces the most diverse strategems, many of which would seem quite paradoxical to one who was ignorant of the positive feedback of power (as adolescents in our society often are). For instance, we are told (11) that "in the early history of the Church, bishops had to take two solemn oaths at the time of their ordination. The first oath was that they would discharge the duties of that office faithfully in the sight of God and man. The second oath was called the oath of

'Nolo episcopari'—'I don't want to be a bishop.' . . ." Those who frequent the university campuses of our own time will surely have noted that one of the best ways to achieve a deanship is to insist that one doesn't want to be dean (but not too loudly!). Competition and the desire to limit power produce strange strategies.

VIII. The Persistence of Variety

An important part of the unfinished work of theoretical biology revolves around the question of variety: how are we to account for the variety of the living world? The competitive exclusion principle points always toward simplification; yet the world remains amazingly, delightfully complex.

The same problem exists in economics. Why do there continue to be so many competing units? The economist's problem is, I suspect, even further from solution than the biologist's, but we can briefly list some of the social factors, which resemble those mentioned earlier in the biological discussion.

Geographic isolation. A less efficient company may be able to coexist with a more efficient one if it is at a considerable distance and if transportation charges are heavy, as they are, for instance, in the coal and steel industry. (It is interesting to note that major steelmakers of the United States two generations ago tried to negate this factor by enforcing the "Pittsburgh-plus" system of pricing.)

Product differentiation. In biology, ecological differentiation is the necessary condition for coexistence; in economics, product differentation (12) plays the same role. Patents, copyrights, and mere advertising gimmicks enable entrepreneurs partially to escape pure competition.

Mergers prevent extinction in economics in the same sense that interbreeding prevents extinction in biology.

In the social realm we have in addition various peculiarly human characteristics that contribute to the persistence of variety. Curiosity, envy, dislike of boredom, yearning for destruction are a few of the factors which work against the efficiency of the market and hence tend to perpetuate variety. We are a long way from understanding the economic system. It is, however, transparently clear that any satisfactory over-all theory of economics must include a large measure of psychology in it. The *Homo economicus* of classical theory has been useful as a first approximation only.

IX. The Idea of a System

One of the most important ideas in modern science is the idea of a *system;* and it is almost impossible to define. There are a number of good essays available on this subject (13). Here we will try to define by example.

Our first example is a caricature from the nineteenth century—the idea of a system that connects the welfare of England with the existence of old maids. The argument is simple: old maids keep cats, cats eat rats, rats destroy bumblebee nests, bumblebees fertilize red clover, and red clover is needed for horses, which are the backbone of English character training. Ergo the strength of England depends on a bountiful supply of old maids. Now that is a caricature, but it gets across the idea that the many cybernetic systems of nature are connected in complex ways. So complex are they that we can seldom predict exactly what will happen when we introduce a new element into a system. By way of illustration, consider the following examples from three different fields of biology.

Ecology. Charles Elton (14) tells the following history.

Some keen gardener, intent upon making Hawaii even more beautiful than before, introduced a plant called *Lantana camara*, which in its native home of Mexico causes no trouble to anybody. Meanwhile, someone else had also improved the amenities of the place by introducing turtle-doves from China, which, unlike any of the native birds, fed eagerly upon the berries of *Lantana*. The combined effects of the vegetative powers of the plant and the spreading of seeds by the turtle-doves were to make the *Lantana* multiply exceedingly and become a serious pest on the grazing country. Indian mynah birds were also introduced, and they too fed upon *Lantana* berries. After a few years the birds of both species had increased enormously in numbers. But there is another side to the story. Formerly the grasslands and young sugar-cane plantations had been ravaged yearly by vast numbers of army-worm caterpillars, but the mynahs also fed upon these caterpillars and succeeded to a large extent in keeping them in check, so that the outbreaks became less severe. About this time certain insects were introduced in order to try and check the spread of *Lantana* and several of them (in particular a species of Agromyzid fly) did actually destroy so much seed that the *Lantana* began to decrease. As a result of this, the mynahs also began to decrease in numbers to such an extent that there began to occur again severe outbreaks of army-worm caterpillars. It was then found that when the *Lantana* had been removed in many places, other introduced shrubs came in, some of which are even more difficult to eradicate than the original *Lantana*.

From this example (and scores of comparable ones are known) it is easy to see why it is so difficult to secure the permission of the U.S. Department of Agriculture to import any species of plant or animal. However, though we are very conservative about the introduction of biotic elements into our ecological systems, we show the most juvenile irresponsibility in our attitude toward new chemicals. To get rid of insects, we spray promiscuously with such potent poisons as Malathion. As a result, we kill not only millions of insects, but also thousands of birds. Because birds are a great natural negative feedback for insect populations, using insecticides often causes a secondary *increase* in the numbers of insects later. We may refer to this as a "flareback"—thus verbally acknowledging our failure to think in terms of systems. We are only now beginning to see the magnitude of the problems we have created for ourselves by *unsystematic* thinking, for which belated insight we are significantly indebted to Rachel Carson's book *Silent Spring* (15).

Embryology. Beginning about 1960 a drug known as "thalidomide" became an increasingly popular sedative in Europe. It seemed superior to all others in effectiveness and harmlessness. But by the end of 1961 a most painful disillusionment had set in. When taken during the early weeks of pregnancy, it frequently interfered with the development of the limb buds of the child, resulting in the birth of a child suffering *phocomelia*—seal-limbs, little flipper-like hands, without long arm bones. In addition, there were other variable defects of the ears, digestive tract, heart, and large blood vessels; strawberry marks were common (16). Only a minority of the children whose mothers took thalidomide during the first trimester developed phocomelia, but so widespread was the use of the drug that the number of cases produced in West Germany alone in two years' time probably exceeded 6,000. This experience contributed to a reevaluation of the whole idea of therapy, particu-

"This is the dog that bit the cat that killed the rat that ate the malt that came from the grain that Jack sprayed." (Reproduced by permission of *Punch*.)

larly of newly pregnant women. The developing embryo is a set of cybernetic systems of the greatest complexity. Coupled with the high rate of change during the early weeks is a high sensitivity to foreign chemicals inserted into the system. To a growing extent, physicians are loath to permit a newly pregnant woman to take any drug if it can possibly be avoided.

When we think in terms of systems, we see that a fundamental misconception is embedded in the popular term "side-effects" (as has been pointed out to me by James W. Wiggins). This phrase means roughly "effects which I hadn't foreseen, or don't want to think about." As concerns the basic mechanism, side-effects no more deserve the adjective "side" than does the "principal" effect. It is hard to think in terms of systems, and we eagerly warp our language to protect ourselves from the necessity of doing so.

Genetics. When a new gene is discovered, it must be named; this is accomplished by naming it for some conspicuous effect it has on the organism. But when a very careful study is made, it is found that a mutant gene has not one effect but many. For example, close analysis of one mutant gene in the laboratory rat has shown (17) no less than twenty-two well-defined effects, including effects on ribs, larynx, trachea, vertebrae, lungs, red blood cells, heart, teeth, and capillaries. Yet all these effects spring from a single chemical change in the genetic material of the fertilized egg. In the early days, geneticists often used the word "pleiotropy" to refer to the multiple effects of genes. Now it seems scarcely worthwhile to use this word because we are pretty sure that all genes are pleiotropic. The word "pleiotropy" is a fossil remnant of the days when geneticists failed to have sufficient appreciation of the developing organism as a system.

Pleiotropy presents animal and plant breeders with one of their most basic and persistent problems. The breeding performance of the St. Bernard dog will serve to illustrate the problem. Crosses between St. Bernard and other breeds of dogs produce a large proportion of stillborn or lethally malformed puppies. The trouble apparently lies in the pituitary gland, which is overactive. When we look closely at the adult St. Bernard, we see that its abnormally large head and paws correspond to "acromegaly" in humans, a condition also caused by an overactive pituitary. The St. Bernard breed is, in fact, standardized around this abnormality. Why are not the causative genes more deleterious to the breed? Undoubtedly because there are other, "modifier," genes which alter the whole genetic system so that it can tolerate the effects of the "principal" genes. The production of a new breed built around some distinctive gene often takes a long time because the breeder must find, and breed for, a multitude of modifier genes which create a genetic system favorable to the principal gene. This work is almost entirely trial and error; along the way the breeder must put up with large losses in the way of unsuccessful systems of genes.

X. The Feasibility of Human Wishes

The dream of the philosopher's stone is old and well known and has its counterpart in the ideas of skeleton keys and panaceas. Each of these images is of a single thing which solves all problems within a certain class. The dream of such cure-alls is largely a thing of the past. We now look askance at anyone who sets out to find the philosopher's stone.

The mythology of our time is built more around the reciprocal dream—the dream of a highly specific agent *which will do only one thing.* It was this myth which guided Paul Ehrlich in his search for disease-specific therapeutic agents. "Antitoxins and antibacterial substances are, so to speak, charmed bullets which strike only those objects for whose destruction they have been produced," said Ehrlich in voicing this myth. Belief in the myth has inspired much fruitful research; but it *is* a myth, as the phenomena of allergies, anaphylaxis, autoimmunization, and other "side-effects" show us. It is *our* myth, and so it is hard to see.

One of the inspired touches in Rachel Carson's *Silent Spring* is her use of "The Monkey's Paw," a story which W. W. Jacobs built around our modern myth. In this story a man is allowed three wishes. He wishes first for money. He gets it. It is brought to his door as compensation for his son's death in the mill. Horrified, the father wishes his son alive again. He gets that wish too—his son comes to the door looking as he would after such an accident. In desperation, the father wishes everything back as it was before he was given the three wishes.

The moral of the myth can be put in various ways. One: wishing won't make it so. Two: every change has its price. Three (and this one I like the best): *we can never do merely one thing.* Wishing to kill insects, we may put an end to the singing of birds. Wishing to "get there" faster, we insult our lungs with smog. Wishing to know what is happening everywhere in the world at once, we create an information overload against which the mind rebels, responding by a new and dangerous apathy.

292

Systems analysis points out in the clearest way the virtual irrelevance of good intentions in determining the consequences of altering a system. For a particularly clear-cut example, consider the Pasteurian revolution—the application of bacteriology and sanitation to the control of disease. We embarked on this revolution because we wished to diminish loss of life by disease. We got our wish, but it looks now as though the price will be an ultimate increase in the amount of starvation in the world. We could have predicted this, had we taken thought, for Malthus came before Pasteur, and Malthus clearly described the cybernetic system that controls populations. The negative feedbacks Malthus saw were misery and vice—by which he meant disease, starvation, war, and (apparently) contraception. Whatever diminution in effect one of these feedbacks undergoes must be made up for by an increase in the others. War, it happens, is almost always a feeble demographic control; and contraception is not yet as powerful as we would like it to be; so, unless we exert ourselves extraordinarily in the next decade, starvation will have to take over. Like the father in "The Monkey's Paw," we wanted only one thing—freedom from disease. But, in the system of the world, we can never change merely one thing.

Suppose that at the time Pasteur offered us his gift of bacteriology—and I use the name "Pasteur" in a symbolic way to stand for a multitude of workers —suppose at that time that some astute systems analyst had drawn a Malthusian cybernetic diagram on the blackboard and had pointed out to us the consequences of accepting this gift. Would we have refused it? I cannot believe we would. If we were typically human, we would probably have simply called forth our considerable talent for denial and gone ahead, hoping for the best (which perhaps is what we actually did).

But suppose we had been what we like to dream we are—completely rational and honest, and not given to denial? Would we then have rejected the gift of disease control? Possibly; but I think not. Is it not more likely that we would, instead, have looked around for another gift to combine with this one to produce a new, stable system? That other gift is well known, of course: it is the one Margaret Sanger gave us, to speak symbolically again. It is a gift we are now in the process of accepting.

In terms of systems, we can give this analysis:

System	Stability
Malthusian	Yes
Pasteurian	No
Sangerian	Possibly
Pasteurian-Sangerian	Yes

A systems analyst need not, when confronted with a new invention, reject it out of hand simply because "we can never do merely one thing." Rather, if he has the least spark of creativity in him, he says, "We can never do merely one thing, *therefore we must do several* in order that we may bring into being a new stable system." Obviously, in planning a new system he would have to examine many candidate-ideas and re-examine our value system to determine what it is we really want to maximize. Not easy work, to say the least.

XI. Is Planning Possible?

Some of the most excruciating questions of our time hinge on feasibility of planning. Is good planning possible? Is it possible to devise a planned system that is at least as good as a free system? Can the free market be dispensed with without losing its desirable virtues?

There is no dearth of literature supporting and condemning planning. Rather than add to this double battery of polemic literature, I would like to take a different approach. I would prefer to adopt an agnostic attitude toward the principal question and ask a second question: *If* successful planning is possible, what are its preconditions? If we can see these clearly, we should be in a better position to answer the principal question. The major points at issue seem to me to be the following.

1) Can it be shown, before instituting a plan, that all significant factors have been taken account of? It is not easy to see what the nature of the proof would be; and in any case, the consequences of past planning attempts do not make us optimistic.

2) Are we sure that we can predict all possible interactions of factors, even when we have complete knowledge of them? This is not as disturbing a question now as it was in the past. Any system of equations that can be solved "in principle" can be turned over to computing machines, which are immensely faster, more patient, and more reliable than human beings; and all computing machines operate under the Magna Charta given them by A. M. Turing (18).

3) Granted that we can predict a new and better stable system, can we also devise an acceptable transition? The many social systems known to historians and anthropologists represent so many points in space and time. The transitions from one to another are usually obscure; or, when recorded, are known to involve great human suffering and immense wastage of human resources. In general, transitions seem more feasible for small populations than large—but will small populations ever again exist?

4) Can we take adequate account of the reflexive effect of knowledge and planning on the actions of the planned and the planners? I have argued elsewhere (19) that a satisfactory theory of the social sciences must be based on recognition of three classes of truth. No one, to my knowledge, has tackled this fundamental problem.

5) Can it be shown that programming, in the light of the reflexive effect of knowledge, does not lead to some sort of infinitive regress? Only so can solutions be achieved.

6) Can the calculations be carried out fast enough? Modern calculating machines, with their basic operations measured in microseconds, are marvelously speedy. But the number of operations required may be astronomical, and the 3.1557×10^7 seconds available in each year may not be enough.

7) Can we persuade men to accept change? A casual survey of important reforms effected in the recent past (20) shows that each of them took about seventy-five to one hundred years for completion. It is a general impression (and a correct one, I think) that the speed at which social problems *appear* is now accelerating. But is there any indication that the rate of solution is also accelerating? We seem to need some basic reform in people's reaction to proposed changes. Would this demand a new sort of faith? And in what? Science? Truth? Humanism?

8) Will any plan we adopt have adequate self-correcting mechanisms built into it? It is one of the virtues of a market economy that any error in judgment as to what people want is soon corrected for. Price fluctuations *communicate* needs to the managers.

But in a planned economy, it has been often noted, planners who make errors are likely deliberately to interfere with the free flow of information in order to save their skins. Can a planned system include uncloggable channels of information?

Such seem to me to be the principal difficulties in the way of planning. Whether they will ultimately prove insuperable, who can say? But for the foreseeable future, I suggest there is much to be said for this analysis (21) by Kenneth Boulding:

> . . . I believe the market, when it works well, is a true instrument of redemption, though a humble one, not only for individuals but for society. It gives the individual a sense of being wanted and gives him an opportunity of serving without servility. It gives society the opportunity of coordinating immensely diverse activities without coercion. The "hidden hand" of Adam Smith is not a fiction.
>
> There are forces operating in society, as there are within the human organism, which make for health. The doctor is merely the cooperator with these great forces in the body. The doctor of society—who is equally necessary—must also be a humble cooperator with the great forces of ecological interaction, which often restore a society to health in spite of his medications. It is precisely this "anarchy" which Professor Niebuhr deplores which saves us, in both the human and the social organism. If we really established conscious control over the heartbeat and the white blood cells, how long would we last? Health is achieved by the cooperation of consciousness with a largely unconscious physiological process. Selfconsciousness is not always an aid to health, either in the individual or in society.

The problem of planning will not soon be disposed of, nor soon solved, but perhaps some false issues can be avoided if we make a distinction between "planning" and "designing." By *planning* I mean here what I think most people have in mind, the making of rather detailed, rather rigid plans. The word *designing* I would like to reserve for the much looser, less detailed, specification of a cybernetic system which includes negative feedbacks, self-correcting controls. The classical market economy is such a design. Kenneth Boulding when he speaks of "the market, *when it works well*" is, I believe implicitly referring to the biologist's model of homeostasis shown in Figure 4. The classical market should not be called *natural*, for it is truly human invention, however unconsciously made. It is not universal. It has been modified continually as men have groped toward better solutions. I would submit that the proper role for conscious action is the ethical evaluation of many possible homeostatic systems, the selection of the best *possible* one, and the refinement of its design so as to make the homeostatic plateau as broad as it can be, thus maximizing both social stability and human freedom.

References

1. Polanyi, M., *Personal Knowledge*. London: Routledge & Kegan Paul, 1958.

2. Paley, W., *Natural Theology: or Evidences of the Existence and Attributes of the Deity Collected from the Appearances of Nature*. London: R. Faulder, 1802.

3. Hardin, G., *Nature and Man's Fate*. New York: Rinehart, 1959.

4. Ricardo, D., *The Principles of Political Economy and Taxation* (1817), p. 53. London: J. M. Dent (Everyman's Library), 1911.

5. Potter, S., *Lifemanship*. New York: Holt, 1950.

6. Sraffa, P., ed., *The Works and Correspondence of David Ricardo*, I, 93. Cambridge: Cambridge University Press, 1951.

7. Hardin, G., *Science* 131: 1292, 1960.

8. von Neumann, J., and O. Morgenstern, *Theory of Games and Economic Behavior*. Princeton: Princeton University Press, 1944.

9. Hardin, G., *Biology: its Principles and Implications*, p. 489. San Francisco: W. H. Freeman, 1961.

10. Barr, S., *The Will of Zeus*, p. 78. Philadelphia: Lippincott, 1961.

11. Gregg, A., *J. Nerv. Mental Dis.* 126: 3, 1958.

12. Chamberlin, E. H., *The Theory of Monopolistic Competition*, 6th ed. Cambridge, Mass.: Harvard University Press, 1948.

13. von Bertalanffy, L., and A. Rapoport, eds., Yearbook of the Society for the Advancement of General Systems Theory, Volume I. Ann Arbor, Mich.: Mental Health Research Institute, 1956.

14. Elton, C., *Animal Ecology*, pp. 54–55. New York: Macmillan, 1927.

15. Carson, R., *Silent Spring*. Boston: Houghton Mifflin, 1962.

16. Taussig, H. B., *Sci. Amer.* 207: 29, August 1962.

17. Grüneberg, H., *Animal Genetics and Medicine*. New York: Paul B. Hoeber, 1947.

18. Turing, A. M., *Proc. London Math. Soc.* 42: 230, 1937.

19. Hardin, G., *ETC.* 18: 5, 1961.

20. Turner, E. S., *Roads to Ruin: The Shocking History of Social Reform*. London: Michael Joseph, 1950.

21. Boulding, K. E., *The Organizational Revolution*. New York: Harper, 1953.

Irradiation and Human Evolution

EARLE L. REYNOLDS

Ionizing radiation was a normal element of man's ecology long before there were atomic bombs or x-ray machines. But with the invention and explosion of nuclear devices, a new problem in worldwide pollution of air, soil, plants, and animals emerged. Each time a bomb went off (especially in the air), the amount of radioactivity circulating at the earth's surface was increased.

Debate centered on how to weigh the military desirability of those explosions against potential human detriment. The possibility of damage to other life—particularly to the soil life and other organisms which build up concentrations of radioactive substances—was scarcely mentioned in the controversy. Years passed before research put even the human danger into biological perspective.

Perhaps the willingness of many people and our government to be satisfied with the advice of physicists on probable biological effects was the second demonstration within a century of misplaced confidence in physics, the first having been the creation of a general image of science derived from physics as a model. Historically it was physicists who convinced other scientists and educated men everywhere that science ought not to ask the teleological questions "What for?", "Why?", and "How come?", but only the question "How?" The adherence of science to this doctrine, and contemporary popular trust in that doctrine, came close to delaying the modern development of the life sciences, particularly environmental studies, until it was too late

Human Biology, *32(1): 89–108, February 1960. Reprinted by permission of the Wayne State University Press. Copyright 1960 by Wayne State University.*

*to give sound counsel on the matter of
radiation effects.*

*The issue quieted down during the mid-
1960's, because of the Russian-American
moratorium on bomb testing, then revived a little with the explosion of French
and Chinese bombs. The capacity of nuclear fissions to poison the lives of generations to come has begun a new era in
pollution that may last as long as mankind.*

THE EDITORS

Introduction

AS IS OFTEN THE CASE when attempts
are made to bridge two diverse aspects
of knowledge, the chairman of a symposium such as this is faced with a
problem: shall he obtain a specialist in
formal evolutionary theory, who may
perhaps fail to devote a proper share
of his attention to ionizing radiation,
or shall he invite, say, a radiation
physicist, who dimly recalls having

heard something about evolution when
he was in high school? Or should he
ask a geneticist, who might just possibly equate a minute increase in
radiation with the extinction of humanity? Or a radiologist, who will sternly
remind us that radiation is an indispensable boon to mankind? Or perhaps a gentleman from the government, who will cheerfully advise us to
"keep smiling"?

Your chairman has solved his problem by bravely inviting a speaker who
cannot qualify as an expert in any of
these areas. Whether this is an elegant
solution remains to be seen.

There is a large literature related to
ionizing radiation,[1] some of it in official
reports.[2] Much of this material is rather
technical and somewhat removed from
the normal reading matter of the
anthropologist. Nevertheless, we must
bring the relevant aspects of the subject into our area, since data meaningful to evolutionary theory are rapidly
accumulating.

[1] The word "radiation," as used in the present
report, does not refer to the process of the same
name which has a secure place in the literature of
evolution. As here used, it refers throughout to
ionizing radiation or to irradiation.

The purpose of the present report is to give a
brief general survey of the subject, and to offer
certain opinions on the problems involved. It is
hoped that the distinction between the two objectives has been clearly made.

Problems of human evolution, as they relate to
ionizing radiation, are reached only by passing
through a number of disciplines, with a constantly
accumulating and overlapping literature. The
selected list of references, through June 30, 1957,
worked up by Little (1957: 1996-2053), is very
useful, as are the references listed in the recent
United Nations report on the effects of atomic
radiation (1958). A number of surveys (Dean,
1954; Lapp, 1956; Titterton, 1956; Alexander,
1957; Schubert and Lapp, 1957; Wallace and
Dobzhansky, 1959), more or less pertinent to our
interests, have been written. Pauling (1958a) and
Teller and Latter (1958) may be considered as
representing opposing points of view.

Several periodicals, such as Bulletin of the
Atomic Scientists (Selove and Elkind, eds., 1958)
and Scientific American, Sept. 1959, have given

entire issues to the subject of radiation and man.
In the latter journal, articles by Beadle (1959),
Crow (1959), Hollaender and Stapleton (1959)
and Platzman (1959) are particularly relevant.

[2] Principal governmental and official publications, in addition to special and semi-annual
reports by the U.S. Atomic Energy Commission,
include Volume 11 of the United Nations (1956)
report on peaceful uses of atomic energy; the report by the British Medical Research Council
(1956) on the hazards to man of nuclear radiations;
publications by the National Academy of Sciences
on pathologic (1956b) and biologic (1956a) effects
of atomic radiation; and the report by the World
Health Organization (1957) on the effect of radiation on human heredity. See also reviews by
Glass (1956, 1958).

Particularly important is the voluminous "Hearings on the Nature of Radioactive Fallout," held
before the Joint Committee on Atomic Radiation
(1957). The definitive report of the United Nations
Scientific Committee on the Effects of Atomic
Radiation (1958) was summarized in Science
(1958). Most recent is the report made to the
A. E. C. by the General Advisory Committee
(1959), reviewed in Science (1959b).

However, as an act of charity, some of the references and mathematics have been banished to the footnotes.

First, a preliminary paragraph may be useful. Ionizing radiation consists of either particles or electromagnetic waves which have enough energy to remove electrons from atoms or molecules, the ejected products being known as ions. This action can be destructive to biologic organization, by injuring or killing the living cell in any of a number of ways.[3] The biologic effects may be somatic or genetic—and the latter area is our particular concern. Ionizing radiation, operating on the genetic mechanism, inducing possible mutations, opens the door to a consideration of evolutionary consequences.

It is generally accepted that there is a lineal relation between gonadal radiation and mutation, that even the smallest dose may have genetic effects, that the consequences are cumulative, and that there is no recovery. Mutations are considered to be usually deleterious. It has been suggested that "man may prove to be unusually vulnerable to ionizing radiations, including continuous exposure at low levels, on account of his known sensitivity to radiation, his long life, and the long interval between conception and the end of the reproductive period" (United Nations, 1958: 39).

Having said this, we must make the startling confession that there is, in man, "no completely convincing evidence that mutations are induced by radiation" (Wallace and Dobzhansky, 1959: 85). However, while we await the evidence, it would be wise to proceed in our thinking and acting as if the proof had in fact been obtained. Failure to do so might give us the dubious honor of locking the biggest barn on earth after the theft of the world's largest horse.

Meanwhile, as Neel (1958) reminds us, this area is one of the most actively discussed topics in human biology; furthermore, the biological effects of radiation appear to be one of those unhappy subjects, wherein the more we learn the less we like it. It is not reassuring to read that DNA (the desoxyribonuclear acids), genetically the most important part of the chromosome, normally contains phosphorus, and that if a radioactive isotope of phosphorus gets into the chromosomal DNA, "the affected molecule is doomed" (Wallace and Dobzhansky, 1959: 66). It is small comfort to know that in a few days the isotope of phosphorus changes into sulphur, which we are told has no place in DNA.

It is a bit of a shock, having been assured that strontium-90, for all its dangers, is not a genetic threat, to read in the A. E. C.'s 23rd semi-annual report (1958, p. 413), that there may be some "minor" effect from its incorporation into the chromosomes themselves. "Until more is known about such possibilities, calculations about genetic damage must continue to be based on the increase of background radiation due to long-lived gamma-ray emitting isotopes in the fallout." We will save a place in our calculations for

[3] The roentgen is the unit of exposure dose of X- or gamma radiation. The rad is the unit of absorbed dose. The rem (roentgen-equivalent for man) is the measurement of biological effectiveness. The table below (Gladstone, 1958: 595) gives relationships:

RELATIONSHIP AMONG RADIATION UNITS

TYPE OF RADIATION	R	RADS	REMS
X-rays and Gamma rays	1	1	1
Beta particles	—	1	1
Fast neutrons	—	1	10
Thermal neutrons	—	1	4-5
Alpha particles	—	1	10-20

General studies of the actions of radiation on cells are given in Hollaender (1954), volume 1 (2 parts) and Lea (1955). The United Nations report (1958) reviews information in this area.

the genetic damage caused by the replacement of calcium trace elements by strontium-90.

We have no time to pursue these intriguing topics, and must turn to our subject, evolutionary theory, which, as we all know, is highly objective, completely impersonal, and deals with things and people far away and long ago, or yet unborn.

Particularly, we might be interested in these questions: Has ionizing radiation played any role in past evolution, particularly in the formation of human races? What changes have taken place in man's environment since 1900, due to man-made ionizing radiation? What are the possible evolutionary consequences of such changed environment, under differing future circumstances?

Before proceeding, however, we must face the fact that not only is knowledge as yet fragmentary and unorganized, but the nature of radiation is such that factors of politics and ethics intrude.[4] The motivation for certain statements on the amount and effect of radiation on man must be questioned. Reports have been made which contain value judgments under the guise of scientific dicta. Bias, both conscious and unconscious, can be seen, and the speaker naturally is not immune, being just as prejudiced as most scientists. In these days, even ivory towers have separate entrances, and if I must enter either by a door marked Pauling or a door

marked Teller, I will choose the former.

There is reason to hope, however, that the peak of difficulties may have passed and that, barring a tragic reversal of recent trends, there will be a slow return to attitudes, motives, methods of research and publication of findings, which we may once again call scientific.

Past Evolution: Race Differences

So far as we know, life on earth has always been exposed to small amounts of ionizing radiation, and considerable information exists as to types, amounts, distribution and possible effects of radiation from natural sources.[5]

The United Nations Report (1958: 9) lists the average annual gonad dose to man from natural radiation as about 100 mrem, as follows: rocks and soil, 47; cosmic rays, 28; atmosphere, 2; internal sources, 23. This would total 3 rem for a 30-year span.[6]

It is not surprising that, stimulated by Muller's (1927) discovery that mutations can be induced by x-radiation, the possible significance of natural radiation to evolution should have been explored.[7] Crow (1959: 160), however, appears to represent the

[4] As examples of specific incidents, see Haldane's (1955) comments on Cockcroft, Sturtevant's (1954) criticism of Strauss' statement of March 31, 1954, Lapp's (1957) analysis of the Lucky Dragon case, the analysis by Rienow and Rienow (1959) of the A. E. C. program, and Mumford's (1959) criticisms. For an account of the "snafu"—as Strauss called it—in which Strauss admitted responsibility for refusing to permit Muller to participate in the 1955 International Geneva Conference, see Muller (1955a). For a report defending the A. E. C., see Hughes (1957).

[5] See bibliography by Lowder and Solon (1956), and reports by Libby (1955), Spiers (1956), Stehney and Lucas (1956) and Schaefer (1956). The Joint Committee Hearings (1957), Appendix J (1647–1654) give the British report on radiation doses from natural sources.

[6] The chief sources of background radiation are the radioactive elements radium, thorium (and their decay products) and potassium-39, found in the crust of the earth. Extra-terrestrial radiation comes from cosmic rays and their secondary radiations. Internally, radioactive elements such as potassium-40 and carbon-14 are contained in the body, and radon and thoron are taken in from the atmosphere.

[7] See, for instance, Calvin (1956), Beadle (1957) and Sagan (1957) for recent speculation and conclusions.

299

consensus (Newell, 1956; Miller and Urey, 1959) when he concludes that "ionizing radiation is probably not an important factor in animal and plant evolution. If it is important anywhere it is probably in those species, such as man, that have a long life span and at least for man it is a harmful rather than a potentially beneficial factor."[8]

Turning to the part ionizing radiation may have had in human race formation, we note first the wide variability shown by various types of background radiation. For instance, cosmic rays increase in intensity with altitude and with geomagnetic latitude. Even greater variability is shown in the radioactivity in rocks and soils. Thus, the mean dose-rate for thorium in igneous rocks is 37 mrad per year, nine times that in limestones.

In some regions, where thorium-containing sands are found, high levels may exist, as in Kerala, where the average was determined to be 1270 mrad per year (United Nations, 1958: 55), with an upper limit of 84 mrad over a 30-year period.

Other studies still in progress may give us clues. Gentry (1959), for instance, in a study of $1\frac{1}{4}$ million babies born in New York State, is reported to have found an association between a higher incidence of malformed infants at birth and a higher radioactive content in rock and soil. If a causal relationship is confirmed, the implications are important. We know too that other variables—on which research has

scarcely begun in man—may add to the intensity of radiation effect. Thus, starvation may increase radiosensitivity, and temperature may be related to genetic effects (United Nations, 1958: 20, 21).

Obviously much more work is needed. It would be most valuable to have careful studies of high background radiation areas, such as in Kerala and Brazil. Such studies have not been made in detail, and thus recent reports (General Advisory Committee, 1959) stating "human beings have lived for generations" in such regions, are very misleading.[9]

The problems of research in these fields, requiring the search for small differences in large groups over long periods of time, are evident. Thus, the fact that Neel and Schull (1956) did not turn up a battalion of two-headed babies in their F_1 Hiroshima population should not be taken as evidence that the population was unaffected genetically—although I am sorry to say that this position has been taken, and by men who should know better.

In any event, it is not too far-fetched, I think, to imagine an early human group, in an area of relatively high natural radiation, geographically isolated from other human groups, racially differentiating through normal evolutionary processes, but with an assist from increased mutations due to higher levels of background radiation. Of course, these levels are quite small, in terms of their presumed mutagenic capabilities, but it is suggested only that radiation, rather than being an offstage voice, may have played at least a minor supporting role in the formation of human races.

[8] These views are derived in part from research on Drosophila and on mice, in which it has been determined that the rate of spontaneous mutations from natural radiation is extremely low. Crow (1959: 140) estimates that in man less than 10% of mutations are due to natural radiation, but cautions that because of the uncertain state of our present knowledge "it cannot be ruled out that even a majority of human mutations owe their origin to radiation."

[9] Lapp's (1959b) critique of the Advisory Committee report to A. E. C. concludes ". . . it would appear that the statement on radiation hazards by the General Advisory Committee to the Atomic Energy Commission is misleading." (p. 320)

Man-Made Radiation: A New Environment

It is a most disturbing mathematical exercise to add an insignificant amount of radiation from Source A, a reassuringly low level of radiation from Source B, a permissible exposure from Source C, and a safe percentage from Source D, to arrive at a total which in the United States averages about three times the mean natural rate (Wallace and Dobzhansky, 1959: 76). Eventually we are going to have to face the fact that two new radioactive contaminants, each amounting to only 5% of the natural background, do not cancel each other out, as we are sometimes seemingly led to believe, but add up to 10%, and that the total now becomes 110%.[10]

Working one's way through myriad attempts to evaluate differential radiation exposure in man, trying to equate a brick house with a wooden one, brown rice with white, radiography of the pelvis with that of the lumbar spine, tropospheric with stratospheric fallout, one is tempted to agree with the little old lady, who surely by now must have said, "If the Good Lord had intended us to be irradiated, we'd have been born with built-in radiation counters."

At present, the main source of man-made radiation is from medical uses, principally diagnostic x-rays.[11] In x-ray using countries, the mean annual genetically significant dose is about 100 mrem, thus doubling the background rate. In the United States, the figure is about half again as much. The use of x-rays will spread, and at present we can only hope that self-policing medical policies will keep exposure down.

Radioactive wastes from atomic energy plants loom as the greatest peacetime radiation threat. At the moment, there is "no general population hazard" (United Nations, 1958: 15), but present disposal through smoke, burial and dumping at sea may only postpone a crisis. Regulation depends on agreements at the national and international level. Judging from the past, when economic exploitation clashed with forces of conservation, the prognosis is not good.[12]

---

[10] Beyond this, we may have to change our concept of background radiation itself, in which man has evolved, from that of a benign and inert standard, to an active and possibly damaging source of radiation to man (United Nations, 1958: 36). See also Crow's testimony at Joint Committee Hearings (1957: 1013), and Lewis (1957) on relation of leukemia to natural background. Natural background is a base against which additional radiation contamination can be measured, but not necessarily a "safe" level of radiation.

[11] Varieties of radiation hazard to man in the United States are listed by the U. S. Public Health Service in the Joint Committee Hearings (1957: 477–479), together with a bibliography. Exposure from occupational hazard, not mentioned in the text, is at present low, on a population basis, although individual exposures may be high, as in airplane pilots or uranium miners (Alexander, 1957), and individuals who work with radiation-emitting machines, who may receive as much as 1 r per hour (Braestrup and Mooney, 1959: 1074). Occupational hazards will rise as the use of ionizing radiation in industry, medical work and research expands. For an idea of what this expansion involves (with a complete omission of any mention of radiation hazards) see Hafstad (1957).

As examples of the wide range of individual problems, taken from a large collection, see Haybittle (1958) on problems of luminous watches; Fritsch, et al. (1958) on radiation in French spas; Weiss and Shipman (1957) on concentration of cobalt-60 in killer clams, due to contamination of sea water. For a discussion of the concentration of low-level contamination in plankton see Rienow and Rienow (1959: 44).

[12] Glass (1957: 245) says: "It is stated on good authority (Anderson, et al., 1957) that a 100 megawatt heat reactor will produce annually the same quantity of long-lived fission products as the detonation of a 1-megaton fission bomb." See also DuShane, in an editorial (1957) in Science. The New York Times (1959a) cites the serious nature of high-level radioactive waste disposal problems, pointing out that with an underground tank capacity of 110 million gallons, 65 million gallons have already been used.

Thermonuclear detonation during the Pacific Tests in 1958, Hardtack Series I. (Photo by Los Alamos Scientific Laboratory, courtesy U.S. Atomic Energy Commission.)

Millions of words have been written on the problem of fallout, and I will add only a hundred or so more. Relatively, the amount of radiation released by fallout from nuclear weapons tests is small, but, like natural radiation, it is world-wide. Its principal threat lies in the continuation of testing programs, and the entry of new nations into the nuclear club. Above all, the chief threat to mankind stems from the purpose of testing, which is to perfect nuclear weapons for the mass killing of man.

A vast amount of research has been done on the effects of these "nuclear events," as they are somewhat delicately called.[13] Reports, however, are scattered, uncoordinated and difficult to interpret. Some information has not

[13] The tabulation of "nuclear events" is given as 173,760,000 tons of TNT equivalent, about one-half being fission (New York Times, 1959b).

For a general survey of effects of fallout, see Pirie (1957), the lengthy testimony in the Joint Committee Hearings (1957) and Lapp (1957). Japanese research has been reported in a detailed fashion in the publications of the Japan Society for the Promotion of Science (1956). See also the recent report on fallout (United States, 1959), and Lapp's (1959a) résumé of this report. Snyder has given a reasoned position on testing programs (1957). For a recent report contending that fallout problems have been too strongly emphasized, see Morgan (1959).

been available to independent scientists. Since 1946, the A. E. C. has spent 125 million dollars on biomedical investigations on radiation, including fallout. According to Science (1959a: 1210), "no comprehensive up-to-date account of all the A. E. C. radiation control work is available."

The reports which are available are not reassuring. For instance, carbon-14 (Totter, Zelle and Hollister, 1958), with its half-life of about 5600 years, to which Pauling (1958b) has called particular attention, should interest any student of evolution. Carbon-14 may be a greater genetic hazard than any other isotope, even the better publicized caesium-137. And again, at the risk of being repetitive, it must be said that the two contaminants—and others not mentioned—are additive in their effects; they do not cancel each other out.

The testing of nuclear weapons involves ethical, legal and political questions which transcend national policies. For the moment testing has ceased, pending negotiations. The sentiment of the world is, I believe, in favor of a continuation of this cessation.[14]

As we wander through the wilderness of radioactive contamination we become lost in a forest of luminous watch dials, shoe-fitting gadgets, television sets, electron microscopes, radioactive killer clams, high voltage rectifiers, hot plankton, atomic submarines and prison "Inspectoscopes." I wonder if the public is really aware of the amount of radioactivity man lives with.

This we do know: At the moment our wallets are bulging with atomic credit cards. But, if we are to believe the geneticists, in due time the bill will be presented, and not one radiation-induced mutation will be omitted. For the debt, whatever it may be, must be paid; on this point there appears to be little argument.[15] Even the proponents of continued nuclear testing have shifted their position from an earlier claim that there was no danger, to the grounds that the end justifies the means.

Diligent and conscientious efforts have been made to quantify this debt.[16] The results, hypothetical though they are, and admittedly based on sketchy evidence, nevertheless provide us with a framework for our thinking. For instance, it is useful to know that a permanent doubling of man's mutation

[14] Recent evidence of public opinion may be seen in the Gallup (1959) poll reports, in which 77% favored a continuation of the present ban on H-bomb tests. The recent actions of the United Nations, the unanimous Senate Resolution, and the many recent statements by the State Department and the President, are evidence of a marked change in public opinion since the summer of 1958. This change came about through the release to the public of official information on the dangers of radiation, through such publications as the United Nations report (1958).

[15] For general surveys, see Dobzhansky (1955) and Auerbach (1956). Carter (1956) and Muller (1956) both report on the genetic problem in man in the United Nations (1956) report on peaceful uses of atomic energy. See also Bulletin of the Atomic Scientists, editorial, (1955), and Glass (1957) and Dunn (1957). Muller, since 1927, has repeatedly warned of genetic dangers to man from excessive radiation (1950, 1955b, 1957).

Surveys of human populations are tabulated in the United Nations report (1957: 195). Problems of human evolution and genetics have been discussed by Strandskov (1950), Kraus and White (1956), Dobzhansky and Allan (1956), Oliver and Howells (1957), Garn (1957) and Hunt (1959).

[16] Recent examples of attempts at quantification are Inglis (1958) on radiation dosage from future weapons tests under three differing circumstances; Buck (1959) on the population size required for investigation of threshold in radiation-induced leukemia; and Muller and Meyer (1959) on incidence of "invisible" detrimental mutations. The United Nations report brings together significant research in this area (p. 32). In the Joint Committee Report (1957), the National Academy of Sciences presents a discussion of radiation hazards and estimates (1831–1847), including the famous dictum: *"keep the dose as low as you can"* (1845).

303

rate might increase the 4% of children born with important detectable genetic defects to between 5 and 8% (United Nations, 1958: 32). It is more than a clever exercise in mathematics to estimate, after trying to reconcile the imponderables, that each rad of additional exposure per generation could cause as many as 10 million affected persons, at equilibrium (p. 33).

Many of the estimates attempt to grapple with possible future conditions.[17] A permanent world-wide exposure of 10 rad appears to be the most popular estimate, assuming there is no nuclear war. Beadle (1959: 232) is more optimistic, feeling an average of less than 1 r above natural background could be achieved. At the opposite pole, Braunbek (1959) postulates a steadily increasing contamination, century after century, ending in the gradual extinction of mankind.

On the whole, I think the Saturday Review (1959a: 73) offers mankind a better deal: a choice of extinction, survival in small numbers, or being changed "beyond our recognition." There are many who feel the last possibility would be a definite improvement.

But all predictions falter before the prospect of nuclear war.[18] The recent Joint Committee meetings (1959) concluded that "a nuclear war might result in a doubling of the deleterious genes the human race already possesses" (Lapp, 1959c: 341). Neel (1959), assuming a constant post-attack population of 40 million in the United States, estimated defective births over the next 1000 years between 17 million and 1.2 billion. But each estimate literally depends, as General Gavin bluntly said, "on which way the wind blows" at the time of the attack.

We may be stimulated to consider a few of the factors involved. There would of course be the direct and traumatic genetic effect, and its evolutionary consequences, whatever they may be. Part of the process, its importance impossible to assay, would be the pressure of conscious selection, operating on two levels: first, as we now see it in Hiroshima, where identification as a survivor of the bomb appears to be a factor in the marriage market; and second, at the international level, since it is certain that prompt action would be taken by the unbombed portions of the world—if such remained—to set up barriers against the mass entry of genetically damaged victims. The protection of mankind might necessitate either physical segregation or rigid prohibition against procreation. Mankind can absorb, perhaps, Hiroshima and Nagasaki; the involvement of the

---

[17] Wallace and Dobzhansky (1959) have recently calculated mutation rates in man at various levels of radiation under differing circumstances, for varying numbers of generations. For comments on A. E. C. estimates, see Rienow and Rienow (1959: 158).

[18] The most recent estimate is in Joint Committee Report (1959), on effects of nuclear war, issued August 31, 1959, reported in Science (1959c: 696). See also Saturday Review (1959b), based on this report, and Lapp's (1959c) article. An earlier government report (United States, 1950) is based on the Hiroshima and Nagasaki bombs. Kissinger

(1957) discusses the possibility of "limited" nuclear war. The enormous literature on nuclear war, much of it having relevance in any consideration of man's future, ranges from Cousins' early (1945) and eloquent declaration that "modern man is obsolete" to such recent analyses as Mills' (1958) on possible causes of World War III. See also Schweitzer (1957, 1958) and Russell (1959).

General Gavin's remarks on the direction of the wind are found in Hearings before Senate Committee on Armed Services in 1956. See also Bulletin of Atomic Scientists, Sept. 1956, p. 270. Neel's estimates were reported in Newsweek for July 6, 1959, p. 17.

"... aeons from now ... will our successors bless us or curse us for defending with H-bombs what we now so positively claim to be their interests?" (Photo of Nagasaki courtesy U.S. Atomic Energy Commission.)

survivors from the northern hemisphere would be a vastly different problem.

We now live in an age where man has the power to alter instantly the evolutionary prospects of his species. Moreover, the capable and incapable, the adaptable and the unadaptable, the potential evolutionary success and the potential evolutionary failure, can all become extinct together in an instant. It might be difficult for man to eliminate man entirely, but being the patriotic and determined animal he is, he would give it a good try.[19]

Possible Futures for Man

Speaking strictly in terms of direct relation of radiation to evolution, one might think as follows: Over a very

[19] If war, as has been claimed, has been an important factor in human evolution, the addition of the new element—radiation effects—will cause a drastic revision of theory.

long time, man has evolved through evolutionary processes now fairly well understood, which include certain relations between mutation and selection. These mutations were derived at least partly from background radiation. Presumably we receive a sufficiently steady supply of mutations from our background, to take care of future evolution, without calling in additional mutagenic processes, not just from man-made radiation, which is only a part of the picture, but from such other sources as smog, food preservatives, drugs and cranberry insecticides.

To me, therefore, anything beyond the background radiation seems super-fluous, from an evolutionary viewpoint. Excess mutations are functionally unnecessary, probably harmful, and possibly acutely dangerous. Using as standards the characteristics suggested by the United Nations report (1958) as

likely consequences of man-made radiation—excess defects at birth, smaller
birth weight and stature, reduced intelligence, shortened lifespan, reduction
in ability to survive or reproduce—I
would cast my vote with those who
have said, "Keep the dose as low as
possible" (National Academy, 1956a).

I can imagine man as adapting to all
these factors which we usually consider as defects; I can imagine circumstances under which these things
might be considered as advantages,
and an entity known as man continue
to exist. I can imagine it, but I would
rather not.

I think that man, as a species, could
absorb quite a bit of radiation punishment, from a constant level of 10 rad to
the holocaust of nuclear war. I can
imagine man adapting himself, not to a
4% incidence of birth defects, but to a
load of 40%. It would not be the kind
of world we know, and I wouldn't
want to live in it, but I can imagine it.

I can imagine humanoid creatures,
banded in small groups, chewing the
bark off trees—the inner, less radioactive bark. I can imagine an anthropologist, in that distant time, diligently
scratching in the dirt, trying to work
out the precise level of radiation at
which man may be said to have ceased
to be human.

I can imagine extreme adaptation to
an atomically vicious environment,
with man, anthropologically recogniz-
able, still existing. To me, this isn't
quite the point. To me the question is,
not whether man *can* adapt, but must
he? Does he want to? Are his present
goals so important, his contemporary
prizes so valuable, that he will mort-
gage his evolutionary future to obtain
them?

Again, I can understand man dying
for an ideal—or killing for it. This is a

distinguishing human trait. My problem is this: aeons from now, when
present nationalistic and ideological
differences are but footnotes in world
history, will our successors bless us or
curse us for defending with H-bombs
what we now so positively claim to be
their interests?

I do not think these are frivolous
questions. We should look for answers,
before we have so committed ourselves, by action or inaction, that our
range of adaptation is severely limited.
Since man can direct his own destiny
—or likes to think he can—it is important that he learn as far as possible the
alternatives.[20]

Of course, it may be that even now
it is too late; that the forces leading
inevitably to man's extinction have already been set in motion. It may be
that this caterwauling creature, man,
has at last goaded the cosmos into
stepping on him. But even if this were
so, we would still ask our questions,
striving to derive what satisfactions we
could from understanding the processes
by which man fell even though we
could not prevent the fall.

Conclusions

I prefer to believe that it is not too
late, and that man can do something. I
suggest three areas—within the framework of our topic, ionizing radiation—
wherein we can better prepare ourselves to answer problems of man's
evolution.

[20] Recently a scientist high in government circles
(Warren, 1959) announced that radiation will increase and man must learn to live with it (see also
Warren 1957). He held out the hope that medical
science will curb the bad effects, and that man
himself might ultimately build defenses against
radiation. This point of view hardly seems to
come to grips with the problem. It is less a question of learning to live with it, than of living to
learn about it.

1. We must educate ourselves on the facts of radiation. This means education unhampered, uncensored and unexpurgated. Man now knows about this invisible and sensorially undetectable force. He fears it, but he has been given no chance to learn about it. Now, after a political detour, he can begin to learn.[21]

The pressure of honest education will inevitably force a saner use of radiation for man's benefit. Non-radioactive techniques to achieve the same results in medicine will be devised. For example, from yesterday's newspaper: the use of soundwaves, rather than x-rays, to detect tissue changes in cancer diagnosis, is being perfected. We are told by the press that the photographs "look like a series of jumbled white blips on a black surface"—which certainly sounds scientific enough.

2. We must accept the responsibilities of a nuclear age. At a national level, this may be difficult, because as Beadle (1959: 231) cogently remarks: "A nation accused of such contamination is naturally reluctant to face the issue squarely. The temptation is rather to avoid the issue by alleging that the harm does not exist or that it is insignificantly small. Once significant harm is admitted, the issue can no longer be evaded, for morality is qualitative, not quantitative."

Accepting our responsibility, we must try to make amends to humanity. Recently a commissioner of an agency described how methods are being developed to lessen damage to the human system from strontium-90. At a news conference he jauntily predicted how this treatment would be given to us—the "us" referring to U. S. citizens. I can imagine nothing worse than the usurping of such a discovery for the exclusive use—or even the first use— of a nuclear nation. The first recipients of such a boon should be the innocent bystanders in non-nuclear nations. This would not be a favor granted, but the payment of an installment on a debt incurred against humanity.

A portion of man's responsibilities include cooperation on a world-wide scale, through such negotiations as are now going on in Geneva, through the wider use of international agencies, and through conferences such as those on the peaceful uses of atomic energy —with the elimination, of course, of political maneuvering.

It is no treason, I hope, to suggest that just as every individual is a part of a community, and must sacrifice some individual liberty for the benefits of that association, so too each nation is a part of a world community, and must likewise give up certain pre-atomic privileges.[22] Which brings us to the third point.

3. We must remove temptation from ourselves. Man must do away with his nuclear weapons, or face the eternal prospect of a nuclear war. If the first

[21] This learning has now begun to reach the grass-roots level, as witness the recent articles on fallout in the Saturday Evening Post (August 29, September 5, 1959) and Redbook (November, 1959). Some magazines have, of course, followed policy rather than unbiased news reporting throughout the period of debate on problems of radiation. See, for instance, the U. S. News (1955: 46–48) report on Hiroshima, claiming no A-bomb effects.

At the national level, it is encouraging to learn that a national tabulation of malformations at birth will be started in 1960 by the office of Vital Statistics. This program, it is announced, resulted mainly from the wide interest which has been shown in the hereditary effects of radioactivity.

[22] One of the most important privileges the United States may have to give up is that of continuing to defend the thesis that the bombing of Hiroshima was "necessary." For debate on this most touchy of subjects see the contrasting views of Blackett (1949) and Compton (1956). Jungk (1958), Amrine (1959) and Laurence (1959) have written recent accounts of the building and use of the first A-bombs, which bear on this problem.

idea is impossible, and the second unthinkable, then mankind has no recourse but the escape of the pathologically thwarted rat—insanity. I would assume that man, a creature whose neural evolution has developed to an exquisitely delicate degree, would be highly vulnerable, in an evolutionary sense, to the long-continued effects of a world-wide fear neurosis. The wider context of being scared to death is being frightened into extinction.

These are my three suggestions. They are not particularly inspired, but neither, I believe, are they unimportant. There is one more point.

Tatum (1959: 1714), when receiving the Nobel award, said: "Selection, survival and evolution take place in response to environmental pressure of all kinds, including social and intellectual. In the larger view, the dangerous and often poorly understood and poorly controlled forces of modern civilization, including atomic energy and its attendant hazards, are but more complex and more sophisticated environmental challenges of life. If man cannot meet these challenges, in a biological sense he is not fit to survive."

These words are clear enough, but I would go a bit further. Survival in a biological sense alone is not enough for man. Survival as a "victor" in a nuclear war is not enough. Survival as a genetically crippled monument to an ancestral history of stupidity and greed is not enough.

Survival in a world in which the best a man can leave his son is an atomic power plant, a higher probability of producing a deformed baby, and a nuclear pistol for atomizing fellow humans who happen to disagree with him, is, to my mind, not enough.

In our evolution, we have acquired a few things we do not share with our fellow creatures. For instance, man appears to have a vague but universal desire to leave the world what he would call a "better place" in which his children can live—or to die believing he has done so. Today I think a generation exists which dimly suspects that, in spite of all our gadgets, radioactive and otherwise, we are not leaving to our children a better world. More than that, our children, in spite of slick, high-pressure atomic salesmanship, also suspect it.

It is time, I suggest, for us as anthropologists to take a sober look at what man is letting himself in for, thanks to an ionized atom.

References

Alexander, Peter, *Atomic Radiation and Life*. London: Penguin, 1957.

Amrine, Michael, *The Great Decision*. New York: G. P. Putnam's, 1950.

Anderson, E. C., *et al.*, "Radioactivity and people." *Science* 125: 1273–1278, 1957.

Auerbach, Charlotte, *Genetics in the Atomic Age*. New York: Essential Books, 1956.

Beadle, G. W., "Uniqueness of man." *Eugenics Quart.* 4: 24–29, 1957.

———, "Ionizing radiation and the citizen." *Scientific Am.* 201: 219–232, Sept., 1959.

Blackett, P. M. S., *Fear, War and the Bomb*. New York: Whittlesey House, 1949.

Braestrup, Carl B., and Richard T. Mooney, "X-ray emission from television sets." *Science* 130: 1071–1074, 1959.

Braunbek, Werner, *The Pursuit of the Atom*. New York: Emerson Books, 1959.

Buck, Carol, "Population size required for investigating threshold dose in radiation-induced leukemia." *Science* 130: 1357–1358, 1959.

Bulletin of the Atomic Scientists, Editorials and various articles: "Genetics and the atom." 11: 314–343, 1955.

Calvin, Melvin, "Chemical evolution and the origin of life." *Am. Scientist* 44: 248–263, 1956.

Carter, T. C., "The genetic problem of irradiated human populations." United Nations Reports 11: 382–386, 1956.

Compton, A. H., *Atomic Quest.* New York: Oxford Univ. Press, 1956.

Cousins, Norman, *Modern Man Is Obsolete.* New York: Viking, 1945.

Crow, James F., "Ionizing radiation and evolution." *Scientific Am.* 201: 138–163, Sept., 1959.

Dean, Gordon, *Report on the Atom.* New York: Alfred Knopf, 1954.

Dobzhansky, Th., *Evolution, Genetics and Man.* New York: John Wiley, 1955.

Dobzhansky, Th., and Gordon Allan, "Does natural selection continue to operate in modern mankind?" *Am. Anthrop.* 58: 591–604, 1956.

Dunn, L. C., "Radiation and genetics." *Sci. Monthly* 84: 6–10, 1957.

DuShane, Graham, "Loaded dice." *Science* 125: 963, 1957.

Fritsch, A., J. Pinset-Harstrom, and J. Coursaget, "The concentration of radioactivity in water and air from hot springs at Bourboule, Mont-Doré and Royat." *J. Radiol. and Electrol.* 39: 148–151, 1958.

Gallup, George, "Public opinion poll on continuation of H-Bomb tests." *Star-Bulletin* (Honolulu), December 10, 1959.

Garn, Stanley, "Race and evolution." *Am. Anthrop.* 59: 218–224, 1957.

General Advisory Committee, Report to the Joint Committee on Atomic Energy, made public May 7, 1959. Washington.

Gentry, John, Reported in the New York *Times*, April 18, 1959, p. 24c.

Gladstone, Samuel, *Source Book on Atomic Energy.* New York: D. Van Nostrand, 1958.

Glass, Bentley, "The hazards of atomic radiations to man." *J. Hered.* 47: 260–268, 1956.

———, "The genetic hazards of nuclear radiation." *Science* 126: 241–246, 1957.

———, "Effect of radiation on human heredity." *Science* 128: 999, 1958.

Hafstad, L. R., "Uses of atomic radiation and energy." *Sci. Monthly* 84: 11–17, 1957.

Haldane, J. B. S., "Genetical effects of radiation from products of nuclear explosions." *Nature* 176: 115, 1955.

Haybittle, J. L., "Radiation hazards from luminous watches." *Nature* 181: 1422, 1958.

Hollaender, Alexander, *Radiation Biology.* New York: McGraw-Hill, 1954.

Hollaender, Alexander, and G. E. Stapleton, "Radiation and the cell." *Scientific Am.* 201: 95–100, Sept., 1959.

Hughes, D. J., *On Nuclear Energy: Its Potential for Peacetime Use.* Cambridge, Mass.: Harvard Univ. Press, 1957.

Hunt, E. J., "Anthropometry, genetics and racial history." *Am. Anthrop.* 61: 64–87, 1959.

Inglis, D. R., "Future radiation dosage from weapon tests." *Science* 127: 1222-1227, 1958.

Japan Society for the Promotion of Science, *Research in the Effects and Influences of the Nuclear Bomb Test Explosions.* Tokyo: Committee for Compilation of Report on Research in the Effects of Radioactivity, 1956.

Joint Committee on Atomic Energy, *Hearings on the Nature of Radioactive Fallout and its Effect on Man.* Washington: Special Subcommittee on Radiation, 1957.

———, *Report on Effects of Nuclear War.* Washington, August 31, 1959.

Jungk, Robert, *Brighter Than a Thousand Suns.* New York: Harcourt, 1958.

Kissinger, H. A., *Nuclear Weapons and Foreign Policy.* New York: Harper, 1957.

Kraus, B. S., and C. S. White, "Micro-evolution in a human population." *Am. Anthrop.* 58: 1017–1043, 1956.

Lapp, Ralph, *Atoms and People.* New York: Harper, 1956.

———, *The Voyage of the Lucky Dragon.* New York: Harper, 1957.

———, "Fallout hearings: second round." *Bull. Atom. Scientists* 15: 302–307, 1959a.

———, "A criticism of the G. A. C. report." *Bull. Atom. Scientists* 15: 311–312, 1959b.

———, "What is the price of a nuclear war?" *Bull. Atom. Scientists* 15: 340–343, 1959c.

Laurence, William L., *Men and Atoms.* New York: Simon and Schuster, 1959.

Lea, Douglas E., *Actions of Radiations on Living Cells.* Cambridge (Eng.): University Press, 1955.

Lewis, E. B., "Leukemia and ionizing radiation." *Science* 125: 965–972, 1957.

Libby, W. F., "Dosage from natural radioactivity and cosmic rays." *Science* 122: 57–58, 1955.

Little, Ruth A., Selected list of references. In Hearings, Joint Committee 1957: 1996–1998, 1999–2053, 1957.

Lowder, Wayne M., and L. R. Solon, "Background radiation: a literature search." New York, U.S.A.E.C. (NYO 4712), 1956.

Medical Research Council. *The Hazards to man of Nuclear and Allied Radiations.* Special Report. London: H. M. Stationery Office, 1956.

Miller, Stanley L., and H. C. Urey, "Organic compound synthesis on the primitive earth." *Science* 130: 245–251, 1959.

Mills, C. Wright, *The Causes of World War Three.* New York: Simon and Schuster, 1958.

Morgan, Karl Z., "Human exposure to radiation." *Bull. Atom. Scientists* 15: 384–389, 1959.

Muller, H. J., "Artificial transmutation of the gene." *Science* 66: 84–87, 1927.

———, "Our load of mutations." *Am. J. Human Genet.* 2: 111–176, 1950.

———, "Comments on the genetic effects of radiation on human populations." *J. Hered.* 46: 199–200, 1955a.

———, "Genetic damage produced by radiation." *Science* 121: 837–840, 1955b.

———, "How radiation changes the genetic constitution." *United Nations Reports* 11: 387–399, 1956.

———, "Man's place in living nature." *Sci. Monthly* 84: 245–254, 1957.

Muller, H. J., and Helen U. Meyer, "Further evidence of the relatively high rate of origination of 'invisible' detrimental mutations." *Science* 130: 1422, 1959.

Mumford, Lewis, "The morals of extermination." *Atlantic Monthly* 204: 38–44, 1959.

National Academy of Sciences, *The Biological Effects of Atomic Radiation.* Washington, 1956a.

———, *Pathologic Effects of Atomic Radiation.* Washington, Publication No. 452, 1956b.

Neel, James V., "The study of natural selection in primitive and civilized human populations." *Human Biol.* 30: 43–72, 1958.

———, Report in *Newsweek*, July 6, 1959, p. 17.

Neel, James V., and W. J. Schull, *The Effect of Exposure to the Atomic Bombs on Pregnancy Termination in Hiroshima and Nagasaki.* Washington: National Academy of Sciences, 1956.

Newell, Norman D., "Catastrophism and the fossil record." *Evolution* 10: 97–100, 1956.

New York Times, "Radioactive waste." September 3, p. 19: 7, 1959a.

———, "Nuclear events." August 24, p. 14, 1959b.

Oliver, Douglas, and W. W. Howells, "Micro-evolution: cultural elements in physical variation." *Am. Anthrop.* 59: 965–978, 1957.

Pauling, Linus, *No More War!* New York: Dodd Mead and Co., 1958a.

———, "Genetic and somatic effects of carbon-14." *Science* 128: 1183–1186, 1958b.

Pirie, A., *Fallout.* New York: Greenberg, 1957.

Platzman, R. L., "What is ionizing radiation?" *Scientific Am.* 201: 74–83, Sept., 1959.

Rienow, Robert, and Leona T. Rienow, *Our New Life with the Atom.* New York: Thomas Y. Crowell Co., 1959.

Russell, Bertrand, *Common Sense and Nuclear Warfare.* New York: Simon and Schuster, 1959.

Sagan, Carl, "Radiation and the origin of the gene." *Evolution* 11: 40–55, 1957.

Saturday Review, "The Research Frontier," Nov. 14, pp. 72–73, 1959a.

———, "The bombing of St. Louis," Nov. 28, pp. 15–18, 1959b.

Schaefer, Hermann J., "Biological significance of the natural background of ionizing radiation." *J. Aviation Med.* 26: 453–462, 1956.

Schubert, Jack, and R. E. Lapp, *Radiation.* New York: Viking, 1957.

Schweitzer, Albert, "A declaration of conscience." *Sat. Rev.* May 18, 1957, 17–20.

———, *Peace or Atomic War?* New York: Henry Holt, 1958.

Science, "News of science." 128: 402–406, 1958.

———, "Report on A.E.C." 129: 1210–1212, 1959a.

———, "Reports disagree on radiation hazards." In: News of Science, 129: 1473–1474, 1959b.

———, Report on Joint Committee Report. 130: 696, 1959c.

Selove, Walter, and M. Elkind, eds., "Radiation and man." *Bull. Atom. Scientists* 14: No. 1. Entire issue, 1958.

Snyder, Laurence H., "What we most need to know." *Sci. Monthly* 84: 17–23, 1957.

Spiers, F. W., "Radioactivity in man and his environment." *Brit. J. Radiol.* 29: 409–417, 1956.

Stehney, A. F., and H. F. Lucas, Jr., "Studies on the radium content of humans arising from the natural radium of their environment." United Nations Reports, 11: 49–54, 1956.

Strandskov, H. H., "The genetics of human populations." Cold Spring Harbor Symposia on Quantitative Biology, 15: 1–12, 1950.

Sturtevant, A. H., "Social implications of the genetics of man." *Science* 120: 405–407, 1954.

Tatum, E. L., "A case history in biological research." *Science* 129: 1711–1715, 1959.

Teller, Edward, and A. L. Latter, *Our Nuclear Future.* New York: Criterion Books, 1958.

Titterton, E. W., *Facing the Atomic Future.* London: Macmillan & Co., Ltd., 1956.

Totter, John R., M. R. Zelle, and H. Hollister, "Hazard to man of carbon-14," *Science* 128: 1490–1495, 1958.

United Nations, *Peaceful Uses of Atomic Energy.* Proceedings of the International Conference in Geneva, August, 1955. New York: United Nations, 1956.

———, *Report on the Effects of Atomic Radiation.* The United Nations Scientific Committee on the Effects of Atomic Radiation, New York, 1958.

United States, *The Effects of Atomic Weapons.* Washington: Superintendent of Documents, U. S. Govt. Ptg. Office, 1950.

———, *Fallout from Nuclear Weapons Tests.* Washington: U. S. Govt. Ptg. Office, 44272, 1959.

United States Atomic Energy Commission, Semi-annual report, 1958.

U. S. News and World Report, "Report on Hiroshima: Thousand of babies, no A-bomb effects." (Apr. 8) 38: 46–48, 1955.

Wallace, Bruce, and Th. Dobzhansky, *Radiation, Genes and Man.* New York: Henry Holt, 1959.

Warren, Shields, "Radiation and the human body." *Sci. Monthly* 84: 3–6, 1957.

———, Report in New York *Times,* Sept. 30, p. 22: 5, 1959.

Weiss, H. V., and W. H. Shipman, "Biological concentration by killer clams of cobalt-60 from radioactive fallout." *Science* 125: 695, 1957.

World Health Organization, *The Effect of Radiation on Human Heredity.* New York: Columbia University Press, 1957.

The Coming Solar Age

PETER van DRESSER

The phrase "conquest of nature" may represent a normal misunderstanding of the meaning of technology instead of nature. Neither nature nor gravity is conquered, for example, when we use a lever to lift a stone. All technological achievement derives from leaning with nature. Technological disaster, the other end of the continuum, comes when energy so gained is used to disrupt other systems and other patterns, to hurt the environmental bystanders.

The idea of mastery implicit in the Western world-view and the implication of dominance and control through power and knowledge give technology as we know it a malignant life of its own. The persistant spirit of aggression and hostility with which we confront the natural world is appropriate to a state of war. It reflects a "hard" view of life, a belief in historical progress from a primitive state upward by means of an indomitable, autonomous drive spurring man against a resisting universe. A misreading of the Darwinian theory of evolution envisions all creatures as rapacious, supports a tooth-and-claw philosophy of life.

In the West at least, technology itself has joined doctrine to split man from nature. We may never know if practice preceded philosophy, but belief in an essentially adverse world is probably as ubiquitous as machines and as old as cities. Whether the "hard" view is an inevitable concomitant of machines and cities is not clear. Are industrial civilizations that are not violent and destructive possible?

THE EDITORS

Landscape, 5(3): 30–32, Spring 1956. Reprinted by permission.

NUCLEAR TECHNOLOGY, now so indisputably in the limelight of world attention, may be thought of as the ultimate development of that drive toward the conquest of nature and the mastery of demiurgic forces, which began in the time of Roger Bacon and led through the steam and iron age to the emerging era of electronics and automation. The kind of civilization which we can foresee as fission-produced power comes more into play is an intensification of that which is already at work about us: one in which precision and intensity of rational control are the factors of achievement and survival; one in which the machine of necessity is the pattern of life, and centralization and co-ordination the watchwords. For how long this drive, which Spengler aptly called Faustian, will continue, we cannot, of course, tell, but it is interesting to be made aware of the birth-stirrings of a new orientation which in time may lead us along a route quite different from that which seems so inevitable at the moment.

Solar energy, in the last analysis, has always been the basis not only of civilization, but of life; from the primeval sun-basking plankton to modern man harvesting his fields and burning coal and oil beneath his boilers, solar energy has provided the ultimate moving force. But its direct utilization at a higher level of technology is a new phenomenon, and rich with new potentialities at this stage of human affairs. Should it become feasible and usual within the next generation or two for man to heat a large proportion of his structures in the colder climates, and cool those in the hotter ones, by solar absorption and storage techniques; should he find it possible to energize industrial and metallurgical processes through an intensification of these techniques; should the generation of electrical or mechanical power from the same source become practicable—then sweeping changes in the economic and social future would be inevitable, changes as powerful in their effect on the landscape as were those which accompanied the industrial revolution.

Most obviously, the pattern of distribution of utilizable solar radiation is very different from that of deposits of coal, oil and, latterly, uranium ores. Zones of clear atmosphere and steady insolation would be the favored ones in a solar-oriented economy; the vast arid and semiarid belts and uplands, the hitherto energy-poor tropical lands, would come into their own. And over these great regions, the distribution of this new wealth of energy would be uniform and utterly impartial. No strategic locations of site or geologic accident would occur; the entire pattern of urban industrial concentration at coal-rich centers, around which our present national economies crystallized, would be nullified, and a new pattern of dispersion and decentralization would emerge in its place.

The second significant characteristic of solar radiant energy at the earth's surface is its relatively low intensity. Here again is implicit a fresh techno-logical *esprit*. Controlled violence is the essence of contemporary mechanism; the violence of fire under forced draft, of exploding gases, of super-heated steam, of high-voltage electricity, and bombarded atomic nuclei. This is the technology of Vulcan closely allied to, and often arising directly out of, the demands of war.

A future solar technology would appear to be largely free of this core of violence. Utilizing fluxes of low-gradient energy controlled by diurnal and seasonal cycles, its processes would of necessity be akin to the processes of plant growth. A society built around them would tend to reflect, on a higher level of science and organization, the esthetic values and the virtues traditionally associated with sylvan and agrarian cultures. A greater intimacy with, and respect for, the subtle phenomena of the natural world would be enforced by the geographic dispersal of the homes and work places utilizing solar energy, and their necessary affinity to climatic and celestial rhythms. A logical and close relationship to the husbandry of field and forest would develop, as biologic raw materials displace mineral raw materials with the further evolution of the plastic and kindred industrial techniques. The intensive organic cultivation and on-the-spot consumption or preservation of diversified food crops would integrate naturally into the living pattern of this earth-and-sunlight-oriented society. A diminution of the role of massive transportation, which dominates our present economy, would tend to result, and this in turn would serve to further demechanize the landscape.

Whether or not such a vision will displace—or at least modify—the faintly nightmarish atomic age that now looms before us, it does seem a fact that at long last a good deal of scientific and engineering attention is being focused on the problem of effective solar-energy utilization—a proposition which has engaged the attention of occasional visionary individuals for centuries. Last fall's World Symposium on Applied Solar Energy, held in Tucson and Phoenix, Arizona, seems to have brought together an array of talent, and to have concentrated a degree of public attention that is quite unprecedented in connection with this subject.

Sponsored by the Stanford Research

At the National Physical Laboratory in New Delhi experiments have been made with this commercial type of solar cooker. (Photo courtesy Food and Agricultural Organization, United Nations.)

Institute and the newly organized Association for Applied Solar Energy, this international symposium occupied in November 1955 an intensive week of lectures, papers, and panel discussions presented by researchers and engineers mainly from government services of a chain of low-latitude countries that virtually encircle the globe. The material ranged from highly mathematical discussion of optical absorption and emissivity phenomena to the techniques of boiling rice in solar cook-stoves and the harvesting of mass-cultured algae for fuel and food. The physics and economics of distillation of sea water, of space heating and refrigeration, of mechanical and electrical power generation, of irrigation water pumping, of photosynthesis, of high-temperature metallurgy—all by solar

activation—were treated at considerable length. An accompanying exposition of working solar machines and devices at the Phoenix Civic Center, probably the first of its kind in the world, served as an interesting peephole into a possibly realizable future.

One general reflection engendered by the wealth of material so presented was on the tremendous structural change necessary in our living and social-organizational techniques to make effective use of the principal discussed. Our economy is, above all, a mass-transportation complex, evolved to transmute concentrated sources of mineral energy into an ever-increasing industrial dynamism. Our rail, highway, and air networks, our pipelines and transmission grids, interconnecting and energizing vast urban, manufacturing, and mineral-processing centers, are the very essence of our civilization. Our economists, businessmen, and engineers are conditioned to think of such complexes as synonymous with civilization. Our financial institutions are developed almost entirely around the function of channeling investment into their operation, while the citizen invests in them emotionally through ownership of his automobile and daily participation in the psychodrama of fast highway traffic.

By contrast, the utilization of solar energy usually requires extensive static installations, handling energy-fluxes of low intensity, and yielding useful work or products primarily for localized consumption. Although the ultimate in efficient and nondestructive utilization of natural resources, such installations are inefficient from the point of view of capital investment, since their relative throughput is small and they are incapable of the high returns which intensive operations can yield. They are in fact the antithesis of the "capital-saving" technique, which contemporary economists see as characteristic of a progressive industrialism.

It is perhaps for such reasons that the most marked interest in solar technology seems to be associated with the underdeveloped areas of the world, where at present largely agrarian peasant or shepherd populations prevail. In such regions, the extensive but relatively simple structures needful for many sun-powered operations may be built by local labor, with the minimum importation of high-cost machinery. Once constructed, the yield of such installations would be free of fuel costs and the attendant complexity of fuel or power transmission, and would contribute to the local economy without burdening it with credit and import costs. Thus one finds engineers and

administrators from India, North Africa, Israel, and kindred lands much more aware of the potentialities of solar energy than their counterparts in the highly industrialized countries, although owing to the technical inferiority of their economies they have been unable so far to carry out extensive pilot installations.

It is also interesting to note that leadership in solar metallurgy and power generation has appeared in France, a nation of high culture and prestige, which seems nevertheless in process of withdrawing from the ambitions of a "major power" and perhaps for this very reason is turning toward the development of nonexploitive resources. The Laboratoire de L'Energie Solaire in Montlouis in the French Pyrenees, with that of Algiers in North Africa, comprises by far the most complete installation for high-temperature solar metallurgy in the world. Similarly, the Claude-system power plant

"... direct utilization [of solar energy] at a higher level of technology is a new phenomenon, and rich with new potentialities at this stage of human affairs." (Photo by Jerry Rose Studio of Albuquerque, New Mexico, courtesy Bridgers and Paxton, Consulting Engineers, Inc.)

now under construction near Dakar, and designed to serve as a municipal plant operating from the energy of sun-heated water, is unique.

One also notes in Israel, a tiny newly-formed country intent on developing an advanced economy in a resources-poor land, a striking concentration on the potentialities of solar energy. At the Physics Laboratory in Jerusalem, some of the most interesting work described at the Arizona symposium has been carried on in the field of solar-energy absorption, to the end of developing more efficient surfaces for the construction of power-collectors.

It seems still too early to guess intelligently whether the economic revolution implicit in these slight beginnings will maintain itself. Certainly in terms of total energy available, the promise of solar technology far exceeds that of nuclear technology; in terms of total benefits to mankind, it ranks at least equal. But whether we can accomplish the profound changes in our technical, economic, and psychological structure orientation to realize these potentials it is at present impossible to know.

The Ecological Approach to the Social Sciences

F. FRASER DARLING

Many historians and geographers have been environmentally-minded for many years, but one of the curious things about that awareness is its one-sidedness. It seems that the environmental factor in history has been studied largely from the point of view of geographic effects on a society—on the way it developed or failed to develop. The emphasis, in short, is on a stable relationship with some critical element, whether it be mountain passes, seacoasts, coal deposits, alluvial soils, or reindeer herds. Such analyses have never been as much in fashion in America as in Europe and, except in the hands of talented students, seem somewhat too simple. But their banality is a standing reproach to the social sciences for failing to go beyond the obvious, and is a constant challenge to their fear of determinism in appraising the relationship between the "physical" world and man.

Rarely are the consequences of the relationship considered in the opposite direction, in terms of the intricate effects of humanity on the natural community. At one level, for example, we know that some creatures—and not others—become extinct under the impact of pioneering; this in turn affects the quality of human life. Following this line of reasoning we might ask: What is the effect of replacing oxen with horses and horses with tractors on soil fertility or on the fish life in streams? What is the relationship of property tax laws to the health of the forest, of clothing fashions to animal populations, of the character of a board of directors to the purity of air and water?

American Scientist, *39(2):244–256, April 1951. Reprinted by permission.*

A multitude of such questions, many of them fundamental, remain to be asked. They cannot be scorned as of interest only to dicky-birders, although, indeed, the dicky-birders are likely to be among the first to recognize the importance of such connections between the populations of wild plants and animals and the habitability of a place by man.

By posing the questions in this reverse order—the effects of a human society on nature—foundations are laid for seeking the consequences of human activity. The patterns of new activity are shaped by reactions to what has been done, and that is perceived and felt in many ways—some conspicuous, such as floods, and others subtle and pervasive, such as modification of the composition of the atmosphere. This kind of thinking will result in a vision of nature and man bound in an organic set of interpenetrating resonances.

THE EDITORS

SOME YEARS AGO there was a great advance in Britain in the methods of growing grass, the basic food of livestock. We learned how to grow more grass, how to lay down new pastures, to select leafy strains, and to compound seed mixtures which would give early and late grazing. Indeed, such was the thrill of power, some agricultural scientists became grass fanciers and forgot the livestock in what should have been a cow's millenium.

Nobody asked the cow.

Nevertheless, the grass fanciers were sure they were in the position to supply the best of all possible cows' worlds and could point to results in increased stocking capacity, more beef, more milk. The problem of cows' lives was solved.

But was it? The cows had a habit of searching diligently in the hedge bottoms and some were so perverse as to break out of heaven and graze the roadside roughage. And lately, investigators have come upon a number of digestive disturbances and conditions which can really only be called poisoning, occurring on these improved, artificial pastures.

Within the last five years, students of animal behaviour have begun to study cows and record their observations. You can present the cow with a questionnaire, but she is inarticulate, like most human beings. Yet she has quite decided opinions and all sorts of little preferences, dislikes, and fussinesses which are important to the good life— of cows. We are learning more of how to keep cows in mental and physical health by watching them. When do they feed, when do they rest, what is it they seek in the hedge bottoms; and if they find it, how much of it do they want; what is the physical and chemical quality of the plant sought? Do cows like trees, and if so, what for—cover, browse, back-scratchers, or what? What is the structure and nature of their community life? A cow's world, you will see, is becoming a complex one, and it is quite difficult to assess scientifically the various environmental factors which influence her well-being. Her life cannot be planned from the material end with such omniscience that she can be popped down in the environment which we are assured provides the greatest good for the greatest number—of cows. She has shown us that the environment should be planned around her as a sentient organism and a personality in a social group. She had forest-roaming ancestors.

So had we.

The much greater complexity of human communities and the more baffling mental and physical sicknesses we suffer as a result of having tried to create for ourselves a grass fancier's world, are the reasons for my choosing this title for my paper. You cannot turn a highly bred dairy cow back into the forest again, and it is quite certain that *we* are not going "back to nature." Yet we must go on learning something of the natural history of man.

I am merely a biologist whose main interest is ecology and animal behaviour in relation to conservation, but during the last seventeen years I have been applying the methods of ecology to studying the life of the West Highland people among whom I have lived; the study was desultory for ten years or more, but has been intensive since then. The underlying principle in conservation today is to study the complexity of the habitat, the wholeness of the environment, and the relations and behaviour of the animals within it in time as well as in space; and if you can keep the habitat going, in sufficient quantity that it is not dying on the fringes, there is no difficulty in conserving any particular animal within it. The social life of the animal is now recognized as being an important part of its environment. Conservation in this sense is closely associated with the pressures between human communities and their environment and between themselves. The study of these is human ecology.

At the end of these six years the conviction has grown that the ecological approach to a study of human communities can be an illuminating one, but I would not be so bold as to say that I could now set down a sound statement of what human ecology is. Rather I have learned what a great deal we do not know, and the good idea of human ecology will need much hard thinking and careful discipline before it is good science. That is what many

of us are seeking in our different ways: to make the social investigation of man into good science. Human ecology deals with the structure of animal communities which man dominates and their development through the ecological principle of succession. As Paul Sears says, "The social function of ecology is to provide a scientific basis whereby man may shape the environment and his relations to it as he expresses himself in and through his culture patterns." Perhaps in these early days of human ecology it would be better not to set it up as a science, but rather to say that human problems may be nearer solution if we tackle them ecologically.

I believe that human ecology and social science can be good science, but we should not confuse it with social service. If I may say so, the natural history of man and the emergent social sciences are not missionary endeavour. If, as scientists, we come upon an outbreak of wife-beating, the men's immortal souls and the women's suffering backs are not our primary concern, as investigators. We would seek causes for the phenomenon, and possibly find it in a hectoring foreman and the operation of peck-orders. Doormats among animals and men have a habit of being hard on their females and children.

There are different levels in what might be called the social management of man. These are exploration and fact-finding, research and the development of ideas, application, and maintenance. We should not confuse the first two of these strata with the second two.

I was once asked by a social anthropologist what human ecology was that social anthropology was not. This was a very right and proper question to which the reply should be that there is no difference. But I ventured to say that human ecology deals essentially with *process*. The value of the ecologist in society will be in his power and accuracy in elucidating causes and forecasting consequences.

The West Highland Problem

The relatively small West Highland and Hebridean populations live close to their physical elemental environment, and to the natural resources on which they have largely depended for their existence. It seemed to me, when I began the West Highland Survey seven years ago, that the problem of the Highlands should be investigated from the biological point of view, looking on the people—without the least disrespect—as members of the indigenous fauna and social animals, and inquiring what were the factors of change in the environment, or in them, which were rendering man a slowly failing species in that environment. This was an essay in human ecology, the approach of a naturalist in conservation as contrasted with the economic attitude of mind which tends to be that of the grass fancier towards the cow. The West Highland problem cannot be described here in detail, but will serve for illustration of what I consider to be the ecological approach to the study of social behaviour.

Broadly, the Highland problem is that of *a very old and in many ways primitive human culture existing in an administratively awkward and physically refractory terrain set on the fringe of a highly industrialized urban civilization,* which itself is situated in one of the greenest, kindest lands on earth. Highlanders have been part and parcel of our national structure for only two hundred years, having until then lived a very different kind of life, in standards, laws, language, and techniques,

than had the rest of Britain. Yet Highlanders are not New Hebrideans or Eskimos over whom, try as we may to the contrary, we feel some kind of mental superiority. Here is a race of people of probably greater average intelligence and intellect than the dominant group, indistinguishable from it in physical appearance. And as members of this race moved so smoothly and successfully in the dominant civilization, it was overlooked how different were the inner rhythm of life and the style of thought and tradition. The new centralized British government of that day merely extended its administrative, economic, and social regime to include the Highlands, and with some ameliorations and some encrustations this applies today.

In human ecology we can never neglect history, for we are studying process; I would say, therefore, that a cross-sectional social survey is not ecological unless it studies origins and successions, in other words, process. We must always remember the significance of political action as an environmental factor. For example, the manipulation of the Salt Tax in the last part of the eighteenth and early nineteenth centuries had profound results on the lives of Highlanders, and the transposition of the English system of poor relief had some fantastic consequences. Again, imagine the island of Islay being immune from Spirit Duty, as it was in the late eighteenth century: distillers flocked in, the bread corn of the people was deflected to whisky, the distillers were soon making money advances (at their own rates) on the barley crops of small tenants; drunkenness was rife and the people were reduced to an appalling social state. The detailed research into population movement conducted by the West Highland Survey shows that this favoured island

319

A flock of Blackface sheep on the move near Douglas, Lanarkshire. (Photo by John Topham Ltd., Kent, England.)

has suffered more than any other part of the Highlands from excessive emigration.

Another historical factor at the root of the Highland problem of today, is the exploitation which the natural resources suffered in the past. The Tudor monarchs in England were already conscious that the supply of oak was dwindling, and there were prohibitions on the felling of English oak. This sent the shipbuilders northwards to the Scottish forests; and a hundred years later, when the iron districts of Surrey and Sussex had lost their trees, there was a determined attack on Highland forests to provide fuel and charcoal. The iron ore was shipped up there.

The ultimate disappearance of the forests followed the introduction of sheep-farming on the extensive, extractive system in the second half of the eighteenth century.

The countryside was one of steep hills, initially poor rocks, and of high rainfall. The climax vegetation which conserved fertility was broken, and there was rapid deterioration of the habitat. That is the core of the problem today: the people are living in a devastated habitat. And now we come to another important ecological factor, the age of the culture. The Gael is living where he has lived for several thousand years and is tenacious of place and culture. How different from

North Wisconsin, where settlers went in to still virgin forests in the 1920's, devastated their environment in a very short time, and left! "Ghost towns" remain. The administration which furthered the movement had forgotten the podsol conditions of the soil in relation to climate. A heterogeneous aggregation of people would not continue to inhabit a devastated terrain in the way an old culture hangs on to its place, even in decay.

Before leaving the historical aspect, we might consider briefly the effect of a change of food habits. Dr. Salaman of Cambridge has recently published his great book, *The History and Social Influence of the Potato;* it is a mine of wealth for the human ecologist. The acceptance of the potato as the staff of life allowed an immense increase in the number of mouths so long as a low standard of existence was accepted. The history of the west of Ireland and the West Highlands and islands of Scotland—both places where wheat was not grown and where the bread corn was relatively difficult to harvest —shows that the potato, coinciding with the practice of vaccination, did bring about a swarming of the population and a very marked depression in the standard of living. Potatoes and maize meal were staples of diet at the most chaotic period. Arthur Young tried to make the potato the food of the rural working class in England; Cobbett fought the potato school tooth and nail, and the English labourer stood firm by his wheaten loaf.

We may take it for granted that when a countryside begins to feed on much the same diet as its pigs, social problems are piling up ahead. And that is the right order; the change in diet precedes the social trouble. The human ecologist will never neglect the belly of the people. Professor Paul

Sears has noted an interesting situation that occurred in Mexico. The government had prohibited the fermentation of a beer, pulque, from a plant called maguéy that is grown as a stiff hedge of spiky leaves. The result of the prohibition was a high incidence of diseases associated with deficiency of vitamin B, and only when the plant was ceasing to be grown was it discovered that it was one of the most efficient anti-erosion plants on the plateau.

To return to the Highlands: the destruction of the forests has meant the removal of cover, and this environmental factor is of great importance in human lives. Humanity needs cover for all sorts of things—shelter for crops and stock; cover to enable a man to do a little experimentation which he dare not try if the eyes of every household in the township are upon him; and cover for courting and love-making. It is obvious what a social problem lack of cover imposes in certain types of urban communities. In the Highlands it has imposed a set of conventions almost the exact opposite of our own. Darkness is the only cover, but this is supplemented by a build-up of psychological cover. The Tiree crofter visits the Duke of Argyll's factor on the nights of no moon, though he could just as well go in the day. A fellow and a girl in the Hebrides will ignore each other in daytime should they meet on the road, but he will be calling at her home just about the time of night when in our culture we should have taken our leave. Good manners require that he be gone before it is light.

I have mentioned the value of cover in experimentation. We tend to forget how important it is in primitive communities that people should not be different, and the initial attempts to be different are the most dangerous ones.

Think how in our own lives we like to experiment in private and avoid being different in the beginning. The Anglo-Saxon races have a firm belief in the power of demonstration in changing methods of doing things. This is a fallacy. The Gael or the Mexican is wiser. It does not matter that a changed practice will reap him a bigger material reward. That is not recompense for having to that extent placed himself outside his group. If the material reward is real, he will be envied by his fellows, and that is not a good state to be in. If the reward is illusory, he will be ridiculed, and that is not good either in a society where there is no privacy.

I have seen the sudden loss of cover depress a small community psychologically, because of the sudden cessation of the opportunity to grow flowers and fruit. Nor should we neglect an animate factor such as the rabbit as a creator of deserts, and as an animal weed of poor land. I have seen a community give up all effort at gardening because of rabbits, and looking forth on a deteriorating habitat fostered psychological ills of frustration and ultimate indifference. Village halls do not correct this kind of situation. The first requirement is a coordinated scheme of habitat rehabilitation. It is in this way that the Tennessee Valley Authority has been such a splendid ecological project.

Deterioration of the Habitat

The science of ecology deals with causes of observed biological phenomena, and it should be expected to lay bare multiple-factor causation, which is a very difficult field. But it is also concerned with consequences and ramifications. The practical value of ecology, as I have said, is the ability to forecast consequences of certain courses of

action and of observable trends. The politician has to be very careful here, and I would suggest that the ecologist is as necessary a servant to the statesman as the economist. Let me take examples from the Highland problem. I have said that the destruction of the region's greatest natural wealth, its forests, was followed by the establishment of large-scale sheepfarming on the ranching, extractive system. The immediate social consequences of this were unfortunate, in that the people were pushed to the coast and suffered a forcible social break. This kind of sheepfarming meant a very heavy preponderance of sheep over cattle, and I have managed to discover in detail how this style of grazing destroys the habitat over a period of a century or so.

The soil is in general sour and peaty, and the roots of trees reaching down to the rock and possible glacial drift were an essential means of bringing mineral matter of a basic nature to the surface. First it went to the leaves, and as a proportion of the calcium-rich young leaves were eaten by caterpillars, there was a rain of their faeces onto the surface of the ground, where they were consumed by earthworms, which are so necessary in the British terrain to the production of a porous, well-mixed soil. Removal of the trees has broken the circulatory system of basic salts and destroyed the continuum. Earthworms disappear if the calcium level of their medium is not maintained; the soil becomes a tough, peaty skin and loses its absorptive as well as its nutritive qualities. Sheep graze much more selectively than cattle and tend to remove the more palatable components of the herbage, especially the ameliorative legumes. Sheep also neglect tall and toughened herbage, so that burning of the terrain is necessary when the sheep-cattle ratio is wide. This practice in itself impoverishes the variety of the herbage, helps the spread of the bracken fern, and tends to produce a biotic climax of a few dominants of poor nutritive quality. Burning on peat slopes also tends to produce an impervious surface which accelerates lateral runoff. This runoff water, being heavily charged with carbonic acid as it runs over the acid peat, itself helps in souring the land in the glens. This is a story of impoverishment of habitat by imposing a foreign land use.

Where the sheep-cattle ratio is grossly disturbed, conditions for a peasantry become desperate. I have now reached the stage in the Highlands when I can say: "Tell me the cattle-sheep ratio in an area, and I shall know the social health of the people." If the ratio is wide, 30–50 or more sheep to one cattle-beast, there is serious trouble; if it is under 10, things are not so bad. One can also correlate the cattle-sheep ratio with the age-structure of the population. Another thing that becomes evident is that it is the children who keep milk cows on the land; when the age-structure gets top-heavy like that of Assynt in 1931 (Fig. 1), down goes the number of milk cows.

The descending spiral of fertility of the general habitat, as outlined above, is continued on the inbye land of the croft: when a man replaces his cattle with sheep, he finds he has no manure for his arable plot, and the yields go down so far that his capacity for winter cattle is decreased. He also finds that he must bring his ewes onto the inbye land to lamb, and there they stay, nibbling the heart out of the grass until the end of May. Such meadow land cannot be expected to yield a good crop of hay, and being relieved of grazing so late means that the hay crop is not ready to cut until a time when heavy rain is general. This means the hay will not be gotten well and its nutritive value will be poor, so that once more the ability to maintain a cattle stock and the fertility of the arable land is being assailed. It is quite definitely an ecological story, and to attempt to study social and economic problems apart from the biological background would be to blindfold oneself.

Now, where do the politician and economist conflict with the ecologist in the example just given? You may have heard that ten years ago hill sheepfarming was not paying, yet a supply of hill sheep was necessary for the stratification of crosses leading to the low-ground farms, which were paying. The economist finds many good reasons for the discrepancy, though deterioration of the habitat by the hill sheep is not one of them. He says: "We must take some of the high profit from the fat-lamb end of the chain and put it back at the fountainhead." And this has been done by giving a substantial subsidy to hill ewes. The idea may have worked well in the Southern Uplands of Scotland, but in the poor terrain of the Highlands the ewe subsidy might have been specially designed for further deterioration of the habitat and for fostering social unhealth. The politician says we cannot start differentiating between one countryside and another in a measure of this kind. All he could do was to slap a still bigger subsidy on hill cattle and another new one on calves. The economists here will admit that this is a dangerous path to follow, and I as an ecologist will say, from close observation of this particular measure, that the ultimate good it can do is negligible unless it is linked with vigorous rehabilitation of habitat, which is the basis of social health.

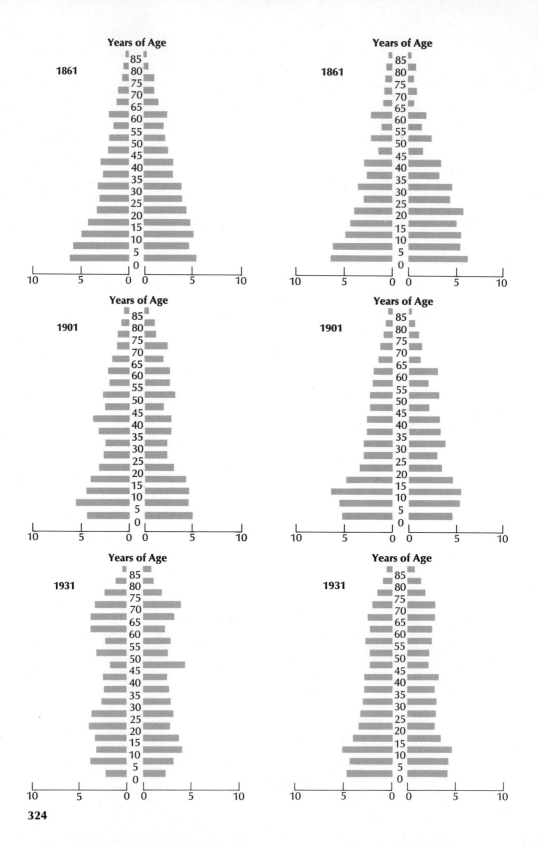

Other Sources of Social Problems

Depopulation and distortion of the age-structure go together and bring a new set of social problems. People in and out of the Highlands have said often enough that industries should be established there, industries of the kind where wheels go round in an important way. But what do we find? Where such industry has been established, there has been even greater depopulation in the adjacent rural areas, yet the big problem is how to maintain dispersion. Fort William and Kinlochleven may have provided Britain with aluminum, but they have created new social problems and solved none.

The remoter areas of the Highlands need roads and better transport, and scarcely anyone can be found to question the benefit that might accrue. But again, this obvious measure of amelioration must be considered ecologically. For example, I happen to know well the townships on either side of a long sea loch, one side of which has a road and the other has not. The living conditions of the people either side are different. Those on the road buy Glasgow bread (untouched by hand) and packeted goods of all sorts, and I have seen tinned porridge sold from the vans. The communities are absolutely dependent on the vans, and their standard of husbandry is low. On the other side of the loch, more cows are kept; cheese and butter are made; homemade oatcakes and porridge are the cereal staple rather than bought

bread; the men fish more, and the standard of husbandry is higher. So what has the road done? It has given those people the benefit of our well-known brands of this and that and a daily paper. But it has not so reorganized the habitat that the so-called higher standard of living can be paid for out of the greater amount of produce exported. Indeed, quite apart from the loss of social health and skills, these people are in a worse economic plight. On the roadless side there is still self-sufficiency, competence, and a realization that the croft must be well farmed. A road can be a benefit only if the environmental factors are closely studied and integrated. Here is seen clearly the effect on this small, old, subsistence culture, of being on the fringe of the most highly developed urban culture of its day. Had most of Britain been like the Highlands, the impact might have been less severe.

The ecologist asks that unquestioned beliefs should be questioned. Good communications is one of these; education is another. Consider, for example, the problem of educating the Reindeer Lapps in Scandinavia. How do you do it? The convenient way is to put the children in schools in the winter season when the Lapps are at the southernmost end of their pastoral migration. But if this is done the families and their reindeer are unduly immobilized, and the secret of pastoralism in poor terrain is to keep on the move. The winter range of the Reindeer Lapps is

Fig. 1. Population pyramids for two localities in the West Highlands. Age classes have been reduced to percentage of total population, with males represented at the left and females at the right of each pyramid. Series at left is for Assynt, a village on the mainland, showing top-heavy age structure in a deteriorated habitat. Series at right is for the island of South Uist, Outer Hebrides, a somewhat healthier social environment. (From *American Scientist* 39(2): April 1951, reprinted by permission.)

thus being overbrowsed, and as it is the amount of winter range which determines numbers of livestock, the damage to the birch and willow forests means that the high summer potential of the tundra is being less used. We can still believe in education, of course, but at least let us ponder methods of applying it, in terms of consequences on the habitat.

I have mentioned depopulation and the distortion of the age-group pyramids. The problems of human ecology arising from the phenomenon in small communities are manifold. In the first place, the old remain in power and so prevail that they can initiate an era of reaction in the life of a community, so that in a region of hard-shell Presbyterianism all gaiety for the young is frowned upon. And nowhere do the young show greater consideration for the old than in the Highlands. I know of townships where there are but few married couples now. Brothers and sisters have cared for their old folk, and now that they are gone they continue living in their parents' houses and cannot bring themselves to the considerable upset of getting married. The social urge and necessary gaiety are not there. This depression of the vivid social life of man is likely to lead to such undesirable consequences as burning of the hills in an excitement bordering on hysteria. The crass burnings of the heather are made ostensibly to further the growth of young grass; in actual fact they further the devastation of the habitat. The fires occur at Beltane, which was once the breeding season. Where the social life is in better order, burning is under control. That great American ecologist, Charles Adams, who has now turned his attention to mankind, told me recently of an almost identical phenomenon in one of the southern states, and of how the

problem had solved itself with improvement in social conditions.

It is difficult to avoid the impression that religion is a considerable ecological factor, but it must always be related with other environmental characteristics. The areas of most pronounced depopulation in the Highlands have the harshest sects of Presbyterianism; but I do not want to overdo this idea or give a wrong impression, because the area of greatest congestion, Lewis, follows the same faith. What I would say is this: that in the Highlands a small, remote community with poor services would have more chance of survival if it were Catholic than if it were Free Presbyterian. This is because there is more sense of community to be found in the districts of the old, liberal—almost Columban—style of Catholicism. The culture is stronger altogether; music and folk tales have not been dimmed, and the status of women is higher. Birth rates are exactly the same. It is in these small, isolated communities, where the social pattern of humankind can scarcely be completed, that a factor which is associated with the old culture can be critical.

The human ecologist must always be on the lookout for these marginal factors, the comprehension of which may illuminate a much wider field where complexity defeats scientific investigation.

There is one more illustration that I want to give from the Island of Lewis, which, as I have said, is a congested island. The terrain is poor, but the people have been there for 4000 years or so, with various immigrant waves which have accepted the old culture and have not imposed their own. The old Celtic custom of subdivision of land, and the intense conviction that the land is theirs, have resulted in the island's being entirely held by crofters, all doing much the same things. It is a one-class society worthy of very close study. Weaving has given prosperity, and though the land is tending to be neglected because it is more profitable to weave, the people cannot effect the social revolution of relinquishing at least lip service to subsistence husbandry, and thereby achieving division of labour and social stratification. There is an intense social life from house to house among the young in Lewis, who are numerous enough to maintain a fine gaiety in the face of religious proscription, but there is little knowledge of the constructive or artistic use of leisure. Nearly everybody is a peasant except for a handful of professional people in Stornoway. Prosperity has come as money—pound notes—but in rural Lewis there is nothing much to spend money on.[1] Social evolution would seem to have stuck, and needs a catalyst. Lewis will not allow itself to evolve, and the observer cannot help comparing the tremendous social vitality maintained by the good proportion of young folk, with the stricken life of the dying communities on the mainland shore. The right hand of Lewis reaches out for all that the world can offer, but her left hand holds fast to the croft in the unenclosed township, and she is anchored in time. The fact that the crofting townships are unenclosed, precludes differentiation of husbandry and agricultural improvement.

I want to close these remarks on the natural history of society by pointing the obvious: that tradition and accumulated experience are part of man's environment, and for all the

importance of the physical and biological factors I have mentioned, the ethos is still the biggest ecological factor of all on the life of the individual. Here I would digress for a moment on methods of approach in gathering data. The ecologist must distrust the questionnaire so beloved of the sociologists, because it fails to take sufficient notice of the ethos of a people. The questionnaire will not necessarily give you scientific data. In the course of the West Highland Survey we compiled a punch-card Domesday of factual data about crofting townships and it is immensely valuable, but we never asked questions on personal household matters or questions of opinion. Had we done so we should either have come up against a brick wall or, with such a sensitive and penetrating people, we should have got the answers they thought we should like. Much the best way is observation and soaking in the culture. Ability to observe closely and interpret accurately, by way of a large grasp of the organism of a society in its habitat, is the essence of human ecology. It is an integrative science as much as an analytical one, with observation as its basis.

If the psychologists could devise courses in development of the power of observation as part of the training for a research career, we should at least be able to pick out at an early stage those graduates who are fitted to study man as a social animal. After that must come the faculty to use several disciplines. Teamwork in human ecology will be essential, but still each specialist will have to have the quality of delighting in another man's work and linking his own to it; and he cannot be the traditionally remote academic type, but must be inquisitive about what humankind is doing to itself.

[1] At the moment of going to press, the export market for Harris tweed has suffered a relapse; there is depression in the weaving districts of Lewis.

An Ecological Method for Landscape Architecture

IAN L. McHARG

IN MANY CASES a qualified statement is, if not the most propitious, at least the most prudent. In this case it would only be gratuitous. I believe that ecology provides the single indispensable basis for landscape architecture and regional planning. I would state in addition that it has now, and will increasingly have, a profound relevance for both city planning and architecture.

Where the landscape architect commands ecology he is the only bridge between the natural sciences and the planning and design professions, the proprietor of the most perceptive view of the natural world which science or art has provided. This can be at once his unique attribute, his passport to relevance and productive social utility. With the acquisition of this competence the sad image of ornamental horticulture, hand-maiden to architecture after the fact, the caprice and arbitrariness of "clever" designs can be dismissed forever. In short, ecology offers emancipation to landscape architecture.

This is not the place for a scholarly article on ecology. We are interested in it selfishly, as those who can and must apply it. Our concern is for a method which has the power to reveal nature as process, containing intrinsic form.

Ecology is generally described as the study of the interactions of organisms and environment which includes other organisms. The particular interests of landscape architecture are focussed only upon a part of this great, synoptic concern. This might better be defined as the study of physical and biological processes, as dynamic and interacting, responsive to laws, having limiting factors and exhibiting certain opportunities and constraints, employed in planning and design for human use. At this juncture two possibilities present themselves. The first is to attempt to present a general theory of ecology and the planning processes. This is a venture which I long to undertake, but this is not the time nor place to attempt it. The other alternative is to present a method which has been tested empirically at many scales from a continent, a major region, a river basin, physiographic regions, subregional areas, and a metropolitan region town to a single city. In every case, I submit, it has been triumphantly revelatory.[1]

First, it is necessary to submit a proposition to this effect: that the place, the plants, animals and men upon it are only comprehensible in terms of physical and biological evolution. Written on the place and upon its inhabitants lies mute all physical, biological and cultural history awaiting to be understood by those who can read it. It is thus necessary to begin at the beginning if we are to understand the place, the man, or his co-tenants of this phenomenal universe. This is the prerequisite for intelligent intervention and adaptation. So let us begin at the beginning. We start with historical geology. The place, any place, can only be understood through its physical evolution. What history of mountain building and ancient seas, uplifting, folding, sinking, erosion and glaciation have

[1] Australia; Rhodesia; the United Kingdom; the Gangetic Plain; the Potomac River Basin; Allegheny Plateau; Ridge and Valley Province; Great Valley Province; Piedmont; Coastal Plain; the Green Spring and Worthington Valleys, Philadephia Standard Metropolitan Statistical Area; and the City of Washington.

Landscape Architecture, *pp. 105–107, January 1967 Reprinted by permission.*

passed here and left their marks? These explain its present form. Yet the effects of climate and later of plants and animals have interacted upon geological processes and these too lie mute in the record of the rocks. Both climate and geology can be invoked to interpret physiography, the current configuration of the place. Arctic differs from tropics, desert from delta, the Himalayas from the Gangetic Plain. The Appalachian Plateau differs from the Ridge and Valley Province and all of these from the Piedmont and the Coastal Plain. If one now knows historical geology, climate and physiography then the water regimen becomes comprehensible—the pattern of rivers and aquifers, their physical properties and relative abundance, oscillation between flood and drought. Rivers are young or old, they vary by orders; their pattern and distribution, as for aquifers, is directly consequential upon geology, climate and physiography.

Knowing the foregoing and the prior history of plant evolution, we can now comprehend the nature and pattern of soils. As plants are highly selective to environmental factors, by identifying physiographic, climatic zones and soils we can perceive order and predictability in the distribution of constituent plant communities. Indeed, the plant communities are more perceptive to environmental variables than we can be with available data, and we can thus infer environmental factors from the presence of plants. Animals are fundamentally plant-related so that given the preceding information, with the addition of the stage of succession of the plant communities and their age, it is possible both to understand and to predict the species, abundance or scarcity of wild animal populations. If there are no acorns there will be no squirrels; an old forest will have few

deer; an early succession can support many. Resources also exist where they do for good and sufficient reasons—coal, iron, limestone, productive soils, water in relative abundance, transportation routes, fall lines and the termini of water transport. And so the land use map becomes comprehensible when viewed through this perspective.

The information so acquired is a gross ecological inventory and contains the data bank for all further investigations. The next task is the interpretation of these data to analyze existing and propose future human land use and management. The first objective is the inventory of unique or scarce phenomena, the technique for which Philip Lewis[2] is renowned. In this all sites of unique scenic, geological, ecological, or historical importance are located. Enlarging this category we can interpret the geological data to locate economic minerals. Geology, climate and physiography will locate dependable water resources. Physiography will reveal slope and exposure which, with soil and water, can be used to locate areas suitable for agriculture by types; the foregoing, with the addition of plant communities will reveal intrinsic suitabilities for both forestry and recreation. The entire body of data can be examined to reveal sites for urbanization, industry, transportation routes, indeed any human land-using activity. This interpretive sequence would produce a body of analytical material but the end product for a region would include a map of unique sites, the location of economic minerals, the location of water resources, a slope and exposure map, a map of agricultural suitabilities by types, a similar map for

---

[2] See "Quality Corridors for Wisconsin," by Philip H. Lewis Jr., LANDSCAPE ARCHITECTURE, January, 1964.

forestry, one each for recreation and urbanization.

These maps of intrinsic suitability would indicate highest and best uses for the entire study area. But this is not enough. These are single uses ascribed to discrete areas. In the forest there are likely to be dominant or co-dominant trees and other subordinate species. We must seek to prescribe all co-existent, compatible uses which may occupy each area. To this end it is necessary to develop a matrix in which all possible land uses are shown on each coordinate. Each is then examined against all others to determine the degree of compatibility or incompatibility. As an example, a single area of forest may be managed for forestry, either hardwood or pulp; it may be utilized for water management objectives; it may fulfill an erosion control function; it can be managed for wildlife and hunting, recreation, and for villages and hamlets. Here we have not land use in the normal sense but *communities* of land uses. The end product would be a map of present and prospective land uses, in communities of compatibilities, with dominants, co-dominants and subordinates derived from an understanding of nature as process responsive to laws, having limiting factors, constituting a value system and exhibiting opportunities and constraints to human use.

Now this is not a plan. It does not contain any information of demand. This last is the province of the regional scientist, the econometrician, the economic planner. The work is thus divided between the natural scientist, regional planner-landscape architect who interprets the land and its resources, and the economics-based planner who determines demand, locational preferences, investment and fiscal policies. If demand information

is available, then the formulation of a plan is possible, and the demand components can be allocated for urban growth, for the nature and form of the metropolis, for the pattern of regional growth.

So what has our method revealed? First, it allows us to understand nature as process insofar as the natural sciences permit. Second, it reveals causality. The place is because. Next it permits us to interpret natural processes as resources, to prescribe and even to predict for prospective land uses, not singly but in compatible communities. Finally, given information on demand and investment, we are enabled to produce a plan for a continent or a few hundred acres based upon natural process. That is not a small accomplishment.

You might well agree that this is a valuable and perhaps even indispensible method for regional planning but is it as valuable for landscape architecture? I say that any project, save a small garden or the raddled heart of a city where nature has long gone, which is undertaken without a full comprehension and employment of natural process as form-giver is suspect at best and capriciously irrelevant at worst. I submit that the ecological method is the sine qua non for all landscape architecture.

Yet, I hear you say, those who doubt, that the method may be extremely valuable for regional rural problems, but can it enter the city and reveal a comparable utility? Yes, indeed it can but in crossing this threshold the method changes. When used to examine metropolitan growth the data remain the same but the interpretation is focussed upon the overwhelming demand for urban land uses and it is oriented to the prohibitions and permissiveness exhibited by natural process to urbanization on the one hand and the presence of locational and resource factors which one would select for satisfactory urban environments on the other. But the litany remains the same: historical geology, climate, physiography, the water regimen, soils, plants, animals and land use. This is the source from which the interpretation is made although the grain becomes finer.

Yet you say, the method has not entered the city proper; you feel that it is still a device for protecting natural process against the blind despoliation of ignorance and Philistinism. But the method can enter the city and we can proceed with our now familiar body of information to examine the city in an ecological way. We have explained that the place was "because" and to explain "because," all of physical and biological evolution was invoked. So too with the city. But to explain "because" we invoke not only natural evolution but cultural evolution as well. To do this we make a distinction between the "given" and the "made" forms. The former is the natural landscape identity, the latter is the accumulation of the adaptations to the given form which constitute the present city. Rio is different from New Orleans, Kansas City from Lima, Amsterdam from San Francisco, because. By employing the ecological method we can discern the reason for the location of the city, comprehend its natural form, discern those elements of identity which are critical and expressive, both those of physiography and vegetation, and develop a program for the preservation and enhancement of that identity. The method is equally applicable when one confronts the made form. The successive stages of urbanization are examined as adaptations to the environment, some of which are successful, some not. Some enter the inventory of resources and

contribute to the *genius loci*. As for the given form, this method allows us to perceive the elements of identity in a scale of values. One can then prepare a comprehensive landscape plan for a city and feed the elements of identity, natural process, and the palette for formal expression into the comprehensive planning process.

You still demur. The method has not yet entered into the putrid parts of the city. It needs rivers and palisades, hill and valleys, woodlands and parkland. When will it confront slums and overcrowding, congestion and pollution, anarchy and ugliness? Indeed the method can enter into the very heart of the city and by so doing may save us from the melancholy criteria of economic determinism which have proven so disappointing to the orthodoxy of city planning or the alterative of unbridled "design" which haunts architecture. But here again we must be selective as we return to the source in ecology. We will find little that is applicable in energy system ecology, analysis of food pyramids, relations defined in terms of predatorprey, competition, or those other analytical devices so efficacious for plant and animal ecology. But we can well turn to an ecological model which contains multi-faceted criteria for measuring ecosystems and we can select health as an encompassing criterion. The model is my own and as such it is suspect for I am not an ecologist, but each of the parts is the product of a distinguished ecologist.[3] Let us hope

[3] "Simplicity, complexity; uniformity, diversity; independence, interdependence; instability, stability," thesis by Dr. Robert MacArthur.
"Stability, instability," thesis by Dr. Luna Leopold.
"Low and high number of species," thesis by Dr. Ruth Patrick.
"Low and high entropy," thesis by Dr. Harold F. Blum.
"Ill-health, health," thesis by Dr. Ruth Patrick.

that the assembly of the constituents does not diminish their veracity, for they have compelling value.

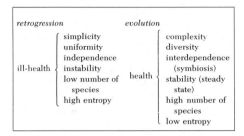

retrogression		evolution	
ill-health {	simplicity uniformity independence instability low number of species high entropy	health {	complexity diversity interdependence (symbiosis) stability (steady state) high number of species low entropy

The most obvious example is life and death. Life is the evolution of a single egg into the complexity of the organism. Death is the retrogression of a complex organism into a few simple elements. If this model is true, it allows us to examine a city, neighborhood, community institution, family, city plan, architectural or landscape design in these terms. This model suggests that any system moving towards simplicity, uniformity, instability with a low number of species and high entropy is retrogressing; any system moving in that direction is moving towards ill health.

Conversely, complexity, diversity, stability (steady state), with a high number of species and low entropy are indicators of health and systems moving in this direction are evolving. As a simple application let us map, in tones on transparencies, statistics of all physical disease, all mental disease and all social disease. If we also map income, age of population, density, ethnicity and quality of the physical environment we have on the one hand discerned the environment of health, the environment of pathology and we have accumulated the data which allow interpretation of the social and physical environmental components of health and pathology. Moreover, we

have the other criteria of the model which permit examination from different directions. If this model is true and the method good, it may be the greatest contribution of the ecological method to diagnosis and prescription for the city.

But, you say, all this may be very fine but landscape architects are finally designers—when will you speak to ecology and design? I will. Lou Kahn, the most perceptive of men, foresaw the ecological method even through these intractible, inert materials which he infuses with life when he spoke of "existence will," the will to be. The place is because. It is and is in the process of becoming. This we must be able to read, and ecology provides the language. By being, the place or the creature has form. Form and process are indivisible aspects of a single phenomenon. The ecological method allows one to understand form as an explicit point in evolutionary process. Again, Lou Kahn has made clear to us the distinction between form and design. Cup is form and begins from the cupped hand. Design is the creation of the cup, transmuted by the artist, but never denying its formal origins. As a profession, landscape architecture has exploited a pliant earth, tractable and docile plants to make much that is arbitrary, capricious, and inconsequential. We could not see the cupped hand as giving form to the cup, the earth and its processes as giving form to our works. The ecological method is then also the perception of form, an insight to the given form, implication for the made form which is to say design, and this, for landscape architects, may be its greatest gift.

The Preservation of Man's Environment

F. R. FOSBERG

*Antoine de Saint-Exupéry has written, in
A Sense of Life, that spiritual life "begins
when a human being is conceived as an
entity over and above his component parts.
The love of home, for example—a love
that is unknowable in the United States—
belongs to the spiritual life." Paradoxically
this defect seems to foster within us a
sense of superiority and a patronizing attitude toward the natives of other lands.
Then again, it engenders an alienation
which has little to do with society directly, and a form of materialism symp-
tomized by an inability to appreciate and
enjoy the material uniqueness of things
and places.*

*But America learned from Europe. All
westerners away from home impose an
uprooted, destructive familiarity on
foreign landscapes which disregards the
indigenous unity of those regions. Such a
unity is internally oriented and buttressed,
but it is vulnerable to penetration by professional specialists in subversion, be
they missionaries, medicine men, mer-
chants, or technologists. The more exotic
(i.e., unlike our own) the culture and
landscape, the more calamitous is the
result. Activities normal to the economy
of one society may become poisonous
when transplanted as part of a program
into the new environment and society.
Just as the Great Space Race is a misuse
of adventure, and jingoism an abuse of
feelings for homeland, so are the legitimate
virtues of the handyman debauched by the
flagrant expedient of dredge and bulldozer.*

*The error of the pioneer is self-propa-
gating. Complex cultural attitudes or non-
verbalized restraints (which may be
translated as love) cannot be transmitted
as techniques. They are, in their homeland,
the necessary background for survival,
but there are often no words for them.
Since people of other environments do
not need precisely the same restraints, they
would not recognize or value words for
them anyway. The result is that pioneering
can sell its techniques to "undeveloped"
nations for exploitation; but we find it
hard to make machines or to limit
their use so as to show the conservative
side of our culture.*

THE EDITORS

ONE OF THE BASIC preoccupations of
human ecology in the humid tropics,
as elsewhere, is the effect man has on
his environment. Contemplation of this
relationship leads, inevitably, to the
question: how long can man continue
to exert such an effect and still have
this environment capable of supplying
his needs? When we ask this question,
we enter the area of applied human
ecology commonly known as *conservation.* This is a subject with immense
practical interest, and in which emotion plays an essential part. It can be,
and should be, treated in a scientific
manner by the ecologist. He should,
however, keep in mind that emotion is
a vital and universal characteristic of
the human part of the system with
which he is dealing. Emotional considerations must, therefore, be ac-
corded their place in any attempt to
consider man's relations with his environment and its resources.

Conservation is usually approached
by serious students from the standpoint of economics, or at best, from
that of philosophy or aesthetics. These
are both necessary and laudable approaches, as they stem from and appeal

Proceedings, 9th Pacific Science Congress, 20:
159–160, 1958. Reprinted by permission.

"... how long can man continue to exert such an effect [on his environment] and still have this environment capable of supplying his needs?" (Photo courtesy Federal Water Pollution Control Administration, U.S. Department of the Interior.)

to two of the great sources of motivation in human society. The derivation of wealth from the resources of our environment and the appreciation of the beauty of this environment are two of our most obvious and easily grasped areas of contact with what we conceive as reality. Both are of fundamental concern to the human ecologist. The approach to conservation by human ecology, however, must be both broader and more penetrating than this to achieve the fullest understanding of the relation between man and his environment.

Perhaps the essential problem is that of man's ecological behavior. Most organisms occupy a very definite, usually rather restricted, position on a scale that ranges from the pioneer types who inhabit raw newly available habitats to the so-called "climax" organisms of mature stable communities. An important distinction separating these types is the duration of their occupancy of a habitat. The pioneer exerts a strong effect on its environment and tends to change it relatively rapidly, soon rendering it unsuitable for its own further occupancy. The climax organism, on the contrary, does not bring about or further such change, but lives in such adjustment with its environment that it is able to occupy it relatively permanently without serious modification. Indeed, such organisms may even tend to stabilize their environments and maintain equilibrium with them indefinitely.

The physiology of most organisms determines their patterns of ecological behavior and only changes in the organisms' genetic makeup can alter these patterns. Perhaps a possible exception to this is *Homo sapiens*. In man the emergence of the faculty of intelligence makes possible self-determination or choice of type of ecological behavior, probably for the first time in the course of organic evolution. Man, as a species, has it within his power to fulfill the role of a pioneer, but in all probability a temporary, member of the world biotic community, on the one hand, or the role of a permanent climax species, preserving or even renewing his habitat and living in equilibrium with it, on the other.

Modern man seems clearly to be following the role of a pioneer species.

His numbers are increasing geometrically. His ability to modify his environment is likewise growing geometrically and is being used without restraint. His rate of consumption of the resources of his environment naturally follows the curve of the product of the two factors just mentioned.

Two points in this picture are of especial concern here. First, most of the resources essential to man's life or well-being are definitely limited in amount, and some are already in short supply. Second, man was physically and emotionally evolved to fit a particular range of habitats. By means of his technology he has managed to increase vastly this range. Physically little changed, he has spread into most of the natural environments on the earth's land surfaces and into a great diversity of those of his own making. Technologically it is probably feasible to modify almost any environment to accommodate human physical occupation. This will be true, as long as resources hold out, of all except, perhaps, habitats highly contaminated with radioactive materials. Man's physiology is reasonably well understood and his physical requirements are the preoccupation of most of the constructive effort of applied science. The limiting factor here is likely to be increasing scarcity or exhaustion of essential resources.

The adjustment between man's emotional and nervous makeup and these profound changes in his environment is a more immediately serious matter. The enormous rise in incidence of insanity and less acute nervous, mental, and emotional disorders in the most technologically advanced countries is an indication that all is not well. Neither the physiology of the nervous system nor the functioning of the human mind and emotions are understood

335

"How to achieve a stable biotic community with man as a member is certainly the most important single question ever to face any branch of applied science." (Photo of Indian birth control clinic by P. Pittet, courtesy Food and Agricultural Organization, United Nations.)

nearly as well as are the physical requirements of man. His nervous system, and its product, the mind, have shown themselves to be very resilient and have adapted to an amazing amount of change from the situations they were evolved to meet. But the percentage of failure grows higher with the degree of change of the environment from what the human organism was evolved to fit.

It is entirely possible, even probable, that this is the modern form assumed by natural selection in the continued evolution of man. If so, this means that the surviving portion of the human race will be different from man as we know him now. What he will become as a result of this process is not easy to predict. Certain it is that to meet the strain of the new environ-

ment and the disappearance of the quiet and beauty of the old, man's nature will be changed. He will be harder, and the gentler traits that we now admire, as well as the appreciation of and need for the beauty of nature, will be bred out of him.

It is entirely possible that man will not survive the changed environment that he is creating, either because of failure of resources, war over their dwindling supply, or failure of his nervous system to evolve as rapidly as the change in environment will require. Or he may only survive in small numbers, suffering the drastic reduction that is periodically the lot of pioneer species, or he may change beyond our recognition. All these alternatives have plenty of precedent among pioneer plant and animal species in nature.

If these fates are not palatable to man, the possibility of assuming another role than that of the pioneer may still be open to him. If this is true, it will be the part of the sciences of geography and ecology, especially the latter, to show him the way. These, as well as the other sciences now give him the power to change his habitat. These two, alone, have as a principal function the building up of knowledge and understanding of the environment as such. Ecology studies the nature of and differences between pioneer and climax species. The changes in man's treatment of his environment necessary to establish a permanent equilibrium with it can only be formulated through a broad ecological approach. The understanding of biotic communities is the ecologist's major potential contribution. How to achieve a stable biotic community with man as a member is certainly the most important single question ever to face any branch of applied science.

How this question may be answered will not be discussed at length, as no answer is yet available. It must certainly involve some means of stabilizing or even reducing the human population of the world. It will involve the elimination or control of greed and the rational, balanced use of natural resources. Management and utilization of the environment on a true sustained yield basis must be achieved. And all this must be accomplished without altering the environment beyond the capacity of the human organism as we know it to live in it.

This will require, on a scale not imagined heretofore, the functioning of ecology in its traditional role of utilizing and integrating the data provided by other sciences. To accomplish the task here outlined will require use of information from the usual physical and biological sciences, as well as the data and principles of ecology itself. Perhaps even more important eventually may be the findings of the social sciences. As the task progresses and basic understanding develops, the human factor will loom larger and larger. As the physical and biological framework is outlined, the task of fitting man into it and establishing his role in the new system will become paramount. Even more critical will be the educational task of influencing man to assume this role.

The undertaking, admittedly, appears impossible. It does seem to be the only road toward preservation of an environment satisfactory for the continued existence of the sort of man that we know. Whether as a scientific community we are sufficiently interested, farsighted, or courageous to attack such a problem may well determine the future of man on the earth.

Part 5 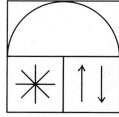 **Ethos, Ecos, and Ethics**

"The Emperor Kuang Wu
Fording a River" by Ch'iu
Ying (active first half 16th
century; Chinese—Ming Dy-
nasty), 67¼" × 25¾". From the
National Gallery of Canada,
Ottawa.

The Historical Roots
of Our Ecologic Crisis

LYNN WHITE, JR.

For a long time ecology dealt only with communities of plants and animals. With the ecosystem concept its view broadened and its focus shifted. Cycles of elements and the flow of energy were seen as the main structures of nature. Only lately has ecology recognized that information also flows in such systems. Just as a gene may convey information to a cell and light reflected from a pond surface may inform a kingfisher, a concept may (or may not) inform people about their environment.

An ecosystem is a concept. So far, it is substantiated by studies of the patterns of natural relationships. The ideas that natural forms are emblems placed on earth for man's moral edification, that crops will grow only after a ritual sacrifice or marriage, that sentient spirits reside in all things, that man's destiny is to control all life in the biosphere—these ideas too have influenced men's behavior. That is to say, they have been and are parts of the ecosystems to which we belong. They have even contributed to the kinds of landscapes we have made, and have thus influenced, however indirectly, natural selection in human populations. Historians and others with a special knowledge of the history of ideas are in a unique position to tell us about this aspect of ecology.

THE EDITORS

A CONVERSATION WITH Aldous Huxley not infrequently put one at the receiving end of an unforgettable monologue. About a year before his lamented death

---

Science, *155:1203–1207, 1967. Copyright 1967 by the American Association for the Advancement of Science. Reprinted by permission.*

he was discoursing on a favorite topic: Man's unnatural treatment of nature and its sad results. To illustrate his point he told how, during the previous summer, he had returned to a little valley in England where he had spent many happy months as a child. Once it had been composed of delightful grassy glades; now it was becoming overgrown with unsightly brush because the rabbits that formerly kept such growth under control had largely succumbed to a disease, myxomatosis, that was deliberately introduced by the local farmers to reduce the rabbits' destruction of crops. Being something of a Philistine, I could be silent no longer, even in the interests of great rhetoric. I interrupted to point out that the rabbit itself had been brought as a domestic animal to England in 1176, presumably to improve the protein diet of the peasantry.

All forms of life modify their contexts. The most spectacular and benign instance is doubtless the coral polyp. By serving its own ends, it has created a vast undersea world favorable to thousands of other kinds of animals and plants. Ever since man became a numerous species he has affected his environment notably. The hypothesis that his fire-drive method of hunting created the world's great grasslands and helped to exterminate the monster mammals of the Pleistocene from much of the globe is plausible, if not proved. For 6 millennia at least, the banks of the lower Nile have been a human artifact rather than the swampy African jungle which nature, apart from man, would have made it. The Aswan Dam, flooding 5000 square miles, is only the latest stage in a long process. In many regions terracing or irrigation, overgrazing, the cutting of forests by Romans to build ships to fight Carthaginians or by

Crusaders to solve the logistics problems of their expeditions, have profoundly changed some ecologies. Observation that the French landscape falls into two basic types, the open fields of the north and the *bocage* of the south and west, inspired Marc Bloch to undertake his classic study of medieval agricultural methods. Quite unintentionally, changes in human ways often affect nonhuman nature. It has been noted, for example, that the advent of the automobile eliminated huge flocks of sparrows that once fed on the horse manure littering every street.

The history of ecologic change is still so rudimentary that we know little about what really happened, or what the results were. The extinction of the European aurochs as late as 1627 would seem to have been a simple case of overenthusiastic hunting. On more intricate matters it often is impossible to find solid information. For a thousand years or more the Frisians and Hollanders have been pushing back the North Sea, and the process is culminating in our own time in the reclamation of the Zuider Zee. What, if any, species of animals, birds, fish, shore life, or plants have died out in the process? In their epic combat with Neptune have the Netherlanders overlooked ecological values in such a way that the quality of human life in the Netherlands has suffered? I cannot discover that the questions have ever been asked, much less answered.

People, then, have often been a dynamic element in their own environment, but in the present state of historical scholarship we usually do not know exactly when, where, or with what effects man-induced changes came. As we enter the last third of the 20th century, however, concern for the problem of ecologic backlash is mounting feverishly. Natural science, conceived as the effort to understand the nature of things, had flourished in several eras and among several peoples. Similarly there had been an age-old accumulation of technological skills, sometimes growing rapidly, sometimes slowly. But it was not until about four generations ago that Western Europe and North America arranged a marriage between science and technology, a union of the theoretical and the empirical approaches to our natural environment. The emergence in widespread practice of the Baconian creed that scientific knowledge means technological power over nature can scarcely be dated before about 1850, save in the chemical industries, where it is anticipated in the 18th century. Its acceptance as a normal pattern of action may mark the greatest event in human history since the invention of agriculture, and perhaps in nonhuman terrestrial history as well.

Almost at once the new situation forced the crystallization of the novel concept of ecology; indeed, the word *ecology* first appeared in the English language in 1873. Today, less than a century later, the impact of our race upon the environment has so increased in force that it has changed in essence. When the first cannons were fired, in the early 14th century, they affected ecology by sending workers scrambling to the forests and mountains for more potash, sulfur, iron ore, and charcoal, with some resulting erosion and deforestation. Hydrogen bombs are of a different order: a war fought with them might alter the genetics of all life on this planet. By 1285 London had a smog problem arising from the burning of soft coal, but our present combustion of fossil fuels threatens to change the chemistry of the globe's atmosphere as a whole, with consequences which

we are only beginning to guess. With the population explosion, the carcinoma of planless urbanism, the new geological deposits of sewage and garbage, surely no creature other than man has ever managed to foul its nest in such short order.

There are many calls to action, but specific proposals, however worthy as individual items, seem too partial, palliative, negative: ban the bomb, tear down the billboards, give the Hindus contraceptives and tell them to eat their sacred cows. The simplest solution to any suspect change is, of course, to stop it, or, better yet, to revert to a romanticized past: make those ugly gasoline stations look like Anne Hathaway's cottage or (in the Far West) like ghost-town saloons. The "wilderness area" mentality invariably advocates deep-freezing an ecology, whether San Gimignano or the High Sierra, as it was before the first Kleenex was dropped. But neither atavism nor prettification will cope with the ecologic crisis of our time.

What shall we do? No one yet knows. Unless we think about fundamentals, our specific measures may produce new backlashes more serious than those they are designed to remedy.

As a beginning we should try to clarify our thinking by looking, in some historical depth, at the presuppositions that underlie modern technology and science. Science was traditionally aristocratic, speculative, intellectual in intent; technology was lower-class, empirical, action-oriented. The quite sudden fusion of these two, towards the middle of the 19th century, is surely related to the slightly prior and contemporary democratic revolutions which, by reducing social barriers, tended to assert a functional unity of brain and hand. Our ecologic crisis is the product of an emerging, entirely

343

novel, democratic culture. The issue is whether a democratized world can survive its own implications. Presumably we cannot unless we rethink our axioms.

The Western Traditions of Technology and Science

One thing is so certain that it seems stupid to verbalize it: both modern technology and modern science are distinctively *Occidental*. Our technology has absorbed elements from all over the world, notably from China; yet everywhere today, whether in Japan or in Nigeria, successful technology is Western. Our science is the heir to all the sciences of the past, especially perhaps to the work of the great Islamic scientists of the Middle Ages, who so often outdid the ancient Greeks in skill and perspicacity: al-Rāzī in medicine, for example; or ibn-al-Haytham in optics; or Omar Khāyyám in mathematics. Indeed, not a few works of such geniuses seem to have vanished in the original Arabic and to survive only in medieval Latin translations that helped to lay the foundations for later Western developments. Today, around the globe, all significant science is Western in style and method, whatever the pigmentation or language of the scientists.

A second pair of facts is less well recognized because they result from quite recent historical scholarship. The leadership of the West, both in technology and in science, is far older than the so-called Scientific Revolution of the 17th century or the so-called Industrial Revolution of the 18th century. These terms are in fact outmoded and obscure the true nature of what they try to describe—significant stages in two long and separate developments.

By A.D. 1000 at the latest—and perhaps, feebly, as much as 200 years earlier—the West began to apply water power to industrial processes other than milling grain. This was followed in the late 12th century by the harnessing of wind power. From simple beginnings, but with remarkable consistency of style, the West rapidly expanded its skills in the development of power machinery, labor-saving devices, and automation. Those who doubt should contemplate that most monumental achievement in the history of automation: the weight-driven mechanical clock, which appeared in two forms in the early 14th century. Not in craftsmanship but in basic technological capacity, the Latin West of the later Middle Ages far outstripped its elaborate, sophisticated, and esthetically magnificent sister cultures, Byzantium and Islam. In 1444 a great Greek ecclesiastic, Bessarion, who had gone to Italy, wrote a letter to a prince in Greece. He is amazed by the superiority of Western ships, arms, textiles, glass. But above all he is astonished by the spectacle of water-wheels sawing timbers and pumping the bellows of blast furnaces. Clearly, he had seen nothing of the sort in the Near East.

By the end of the 15th century the technological superiority of Europe was such that its small, mutually hostile nations could spill out over all the rest of the world, conquering, looting, and colonizing. The symbol of this technological superiority is the fact that Portugal, one of the weakest states of the Occident, was able to become, and to remain for a century, mistress of the East Indies. And we must remember that the technology of Vasco da Gama and Albuquerque was built by pure empiricism, drawing remarkably little support or inspiration from science.

"Man Plowing." From north French manuscript, after 1291. (Illustration from Bibliothéque Royale de Belgique, BBR 1175, f. 156V).

Il a dem boniv de tere en campaigne . tenant a letere lair Ghillam
tenant a le boie de papenghien averbauf

In the present-day vernacular understanding, modern science is supposed to have begun in 1543, when both Copernicus and Vesalius published their great works. It is no derogation of their accomplishments, however, to point out that such structures as the *Fabrica* and the *De revolutionibus* do not appear overnight. The distinctive Western tradition of science, in fact, began in the late 11th century with a massive movement of translation of Arabic and Greek scientific works into Latin. A few notable books—Theophrastus, for example—escaped the West's avid new appetite for science, but within less than 200 years effectively the entire corpus of Greek and Muslim science was available in Latin, and was being eagerly read and criticized in the new European universities. Out of criticism arose new observation, speculation, and increasing distrust of ancient authorities. By the late 13th century Europe had seized global scientific leadership from the faltering hands of Islam. It would be as absurd to deny the profound originality of Newton, Galileo, or Copernicus as to deny that of the 14th century scholastic scientists like Buridan or Oresme on whose work they built. Before the 11th century, science scarcely existed in the Latin West, even in Roman times. From the 11th century onward, the scientific sector of Occidental culture has increased in a steady crescendo.

Since both our technological and our scientific movements got their start, acquired their character, and achieved world dominance in the Middle Ages, it would seem that we cannot understand their nature or their present impact upon ecology without examining fundamental medieval assumptions and developments.

Medieval View of Man and Nature

Until recently, agriculture has been the chief occupation even in "advanced" societies; hence, any change in methods of tillage has much importance. Early plows, drawn by two oxen, did not normally turn the sod but merely scratched it. Thus, cross-plowing was needed and fields tended to be squarish. In the fairly light soils and semiarid climates of the Near East and Mediterranean, this worked well. But such a plow was inappropriate to the wet climate and often sticky soils of northern Europe. By the latter part of the 7th century after Christ, however, following obscure beginnings, certain northern peasants were using an entirely new kind of plow, equipped with a vertical knife to cut the line of the furrow, a horizontal share to slice under the sod, and a moldboard to turn it over. The friction of this plow with the soil was so great that it normally required not two but eight oxen. It attacked the land with such violence that cross-plowing was not needed, and fields tended to be shaped in long strips.

In the days of the scratch-plow, fields were distributed generally in units capable of supporting a single family. Subsistence farming was the presupposition. But no peasant owned eight oxen: to use the new and more efficient plow, peasants pooled their oxen to form large plow-teams, originally receiving (it would appear) plowed strips in proportion to their contribution. Thus, distribution of land was based no longer on the needs of a family but, rather, on the capacity of a power machine to till the earth. Man's relation to the soil was profoundly changed. Formerly man had been part of nature; now he was the exploiter of nature. Nowhere else in the world did farmers develop any analogous agricultural implement. Is it coincidence that modern technology, with its ruthlessness toward nature, has so largely been produced by descendants of these peasants of northern Europe?

This same exploitive attitude appears slightly before A.D. 830 in Western illustrated calendars. In older calendars the months were shown as passive personifications. The new Frankish calendars, which set the style for the Middle Ages, are very different: they show men coercing the world around them—plowing, harvesting, chopping trees, butchering pigs. Man and nature are two things, and man is master.

These novelties seem to be in harmony with larger intellectual patterns. What people do about their ecology depends on what they think about themselves in relation to things around them. Human ecology is deeply conditioned by beliefs about our nature and destiny—that is, by religion. To Western eyes this is very evident in, say, India or Ceylon. It is equally true of ourselves and of our medieval ancestors.

The victory of Christianity over paganism was the greatest psychic revolution in the history of our culture. It has become fashionable today to say that, for better or worse, we live in "the post-Christian age." Certainly the forms of our thinking and language have largely ceased to be Christian, but to my eye the substance often remains amazingly akin to that of the past. Our daily habits of action, for example, are dominated by an implicit faith in perpetual progress which was unknown either to Greco-Roman antiquity or to the Orient. It is rooted in, and is indefensible apart from, Judeo-Christian teleology. The fact that Communists share it merely helps to show what can be demonstrated on many other grounds: that Marxism, like Islam, is a Judeo-Christian heresy. We continue today to live, as we have lived for about 1700 years, very largely in a context of Christian axioms.

What did Christianity tell people about their relations with the environment?

While many of the world's mythologies provide stories of creation, Greco-Roman mythology was singularly incoherent in this respect. Like Aristotle, the intellectuals of the ancient West denied that the visible world had had a beginning. Indeed, the idea of a beginning was impossible in the framework of their cyclical notion of time. In sharp contrast, Christianity inherited from Judaism not only a concept of time as nonrepetitive and linear but also a striking story of creation. By gradual stages a loving and all-powerful God had created light and darkness, the heavenly bodies, the earth and all its plants, animals, birds, and fishes. Finally, God had created Adam and, as an afterthought, Eve to keep man from being lonely. Man named all the animals, thus establishing his dominance over them. God planned all of this explicitly for man's benefit and rule: no item in the physical creation had any purpose save to serve man's purposes. And, although man's body is made of clay, he is not simply part of nature: he is made in God's image.

Especially in its Western form, Christianity is the most anthropocentric religion the world has seen. As early as the 2nd century both Tertullian and Saint Irenaeus of Lyons were insisting that when God shaped Adam he was foreshadowing the image of the Incarnate Christ, the Second Adam. Man shares, in great measure,

God's transcendence of nature. Christianity, in absolute contrast to ancient paganism and Asia's religions (except, perhaps, Zoroastrianism), not only established a dualism of man and nature but also insisted that it is God's will that man exploit nature for his proper ends.

At the level of the common people this worked out in an interesting way. In Antiquity every tree, every spring, every stream, every hill had its own *genius loci*, its guardian spirit. These spirits were accessible to men, but were very unlike men; centaurs, fauns, and mermaids show their ambivalence. Before one cut a tree, mined a mountain, or dammed a brook, it was

Illustration of windmill from the margin of a 14th century manuscript now in the Bodleian Library, Oxford. (Ms. Bodley 264, folio 81 recto.)

important to placate the spirit in charge of that particular situation, and to keep it placated. By destroying pagan animism, Christianity made it possible to exploit nature in a mood of indifference to the feelings of natural objects.

It is often said that for animism the Church substituted the cult of saints. True; but the cult of saints is functionally quite different from animism. The saint is not *in* natural objects; he may have special shrines, but his citizenship is in heaven. Moreover, a saint is entirely a man; he can be approached in human terms. In addition to saints, Christianity of course also had angels and demons inherited from Judaism and perhaps, at one remove, from Zoroastrianism. But these were all as mobile as the saints themselves. The spirits *in* natural objects, which formerly had protected nature from man, evaporated. Man's effective monopoly on spirit in this world was confirmed, and the old inhibitions to the exploitation of nature crumbled.

When one speaks in such sweeping terms, a note of caution is in order. Christianity is a complex faith, and its consequences differ in differing contexts. What I have said may well apply to the medieval West, where in fact technology made spectacular advances. But the Greek East, a highly civilized realm of equal Christian devotion, seems to have produced no marked technological innovation after the late 7th century, when Greek fire was invented. The key to the contrast may perhaps be found in a difference in the tonality of piety and thought which students of comparative theology find between the Greek and the Latin Churches. The Greeks believed that sin was intellectual blindness, and that salvation was found in illumination, orthodoxy—that is, clear thinking. The Latins, on the other hand, felt that sin

was moral evil, and that salvation was to be found in right conduct. Eastern theology has been intellectualist. Western theology has been voluntarist. The Greek saint contemplates; the Western saint acts. The implications of Christianity for the conquest of nature would emerge more easily in the Western atmosphere.

The Christian dogma of creation, which is found in the first clause of all the Creeds, has another meaning for our comprehension of today's ecologic crisis. By revelation, God had given man the Bible, the Book of Scripture. But since God had made nature, nature also must reveal the divine mentality. The religious study of nature for the better understanding of God was known as natural theology. In the early Church, and always in the Greek East, nature was conceived primarily as a symbolic system through which God speaks to men: the ant is a sermon to sluggards; rising flames are the symbol of the soul's aspiration. This view of nature was essentially artistic rather than scientific. While Byzantium preserved and copied great numbers of ancient Greek scientific texts, science as we conceive it could scarcely flourish in such an ambience.

However, in the Latin West by the early 13th century natural theology was following a very different bent. It was ceasing to be the decoding of the physical symbols of God's communication with man and was becoming the effort to understand God's mind by discovering how his creation operates. The rainbow was no longer simply a symbol of hope first sent to Noah after the Deluge: Robert Grosseteste, Friar Roger Bacon, and Theodoric of Freiberg produced startlingly sophisticated work on the optics of the rainbow, but they did it as a venture in religious understanding. From the 13th century onward, up to and including Leibnitz and Newton, every major scientist, in effect, explained his motivations in religious terms. Indeed, if Galileo had not been so expert an amateur theologian he would have got into far less trouble: the professionals resented his intrusion. And Newton seems to have regarded himself more as a theologian than as a scientist. It was not until the late 18th century that the hypothesis of God became unnecessary to many scientists.

It is often hard for the historian to judge, when men explain why they are doing what they want to do, whether they are offering real reasons or merely culturally acceptable reasons. The consistency with which scientists during the long formative centuries of Western science said that the task and the reward of the scientist was "to think God's thoughts after him" leads one to believe that this was their real motivation. If so, then modern Western science was cast in a matrix of Christian theology. The dynamism of religious devotion, shaped by the Judeo-Christian dogma of creation, gave it impetus.

An Alternative Christian View

We would seem to be headed toward conclusions unpalatable to many Christians. Since both *science* and *technology* are blessed words in our contemporary vocabulary, some may be happy at the notions, first, that, viewed historically, modern science is an extrapolation of natural theology and, second, that modern technology is at least partly to be explained as an Occidental, voluntarist realization of the Christian dogma of man's transcendence of, and rightful mastery over, nature. But, as we now recognize, somewhat over a century ago science and technology—hitherto quite separate activities—

joined to give mankind powers which, to judge by many of the ecologic effects, are out of control. If so, Christianity bears a huge burden of guilt.

I personally doubt that disastrous ecologic backlash can be avoided simply by applying to our problems more science and more technology. Our science and technology have grown out of Christian attitudes toward man's relation to nature which are almost universally held not only by Christians and neo-Christians but also by those who fondly regard themselves as post-Christians. Despite Copernicus, all the cosmos rotates around our little globe. Despite Darwin, we are *not*, in our hearts, part of the natural process. We are superior to nature, contemptuous of it, willing to use it for our slightest whim. The newly elected Governor of California, like myself a churchman but less troubled than I, spoke for the Christian tradition when he said (as is alleged), "when you've seen one redwood tree, you've seen them all." To a Christian a tree can be no more than a physical fact. The whole concept of the sacred grove is alien to Christianity and to the ethos of the West. For nearly 2 millennia Christian missionaries have been chopping down sacred groves, which are idolatrous because they assume spirit in nature.

What we do about ecology depends on our ideas of the man-nature relationship. More science and more technology are not going to get us out of the present ecologic crisis until we find a new religion, or rethink our old one. The beatniks, who are the basic revolutionaries of our time, show a sound instinct in their affinity for Zen Buddhism, which conceives of the man–nature relationship as very nearly the mirror image of the Christian view. Zen, however, is as deeply conditioned by Asian history as Christianity is by the experience of the West, and I am dubious of its viability among us.

Possibly we should ponder the greatest radical in Christian history since Christ: Saint Francis of Assisi. The prime miracle of Saint Francis is the fact that he did not end at the stake, as many of his left-wing followers did. He was so clearly heretical that a General of the Franciscan Order, Saint Bonaventura, a great and perceptive Christian, tried to suppress the early accounts of Franciscanism. The key to an understanding of Francis is his belief in the virtue of humility—not merely for the individual but for man as a species. Francis tried to depose man from his monarchy over creation and set up a democracy of all God's creatures. With him the ant is no longer simply a homily for the lazy, flames a sign of the thrust of the soul toward union with God; now they are Brother Ant and Sister Fire, praising the Creator in their own ways as Brother Man does in his.

Later commentators have said that Francis preached to the birds as a rebuke to men who would not listen. The records do not read so: he urged the little birds to praise God, and in spiritual ecstasy they flapped their wings and chirped rejoicing. Legends of saints, especially the Irish saints, had long told of their dealings with animals but always, I believe, to show their human dominance over creatures. With Francis it is different. The land around Gubbio in the Apennines was being ravaged by a fierce wolf. Saint Francis, says the legend, talked to the wolf and persuaded him of the error of his ways. The wolf repented, died in the odor of sanctity, and was buried in consecrated ground.

What Sir Steven Ruciman calls "the Franciscan doctrine of the animal soul"

was quickly stamped out. Quite possibly it was in part inspired, consciously or unconsciously, by the belief in reincarnation held by the Cathar heretics who at that time teemed in Italy and southern France, and who presumably had got it originally from India. It is significant that at just the same moment, about 1200, traces of metempsychosis are found also in western Judaism, in the Provençal *Cabbala*. But Francis held neither to transmigration of souls nor to pantheism. His view of nature and of man rested on a unique sort of pan-psychism of all things animate and inanimate, designed for the glorification of their transcendent Creator, who, in the ultimate gesture of cosmic humility, assumed flesh, lay helpless in a manger, and hung dying on a scaffold.

I am not suggesting that many contemporary Americans who are concerned about our ecologic crisis will be either able or willing to counsel with wolves or exhort birds. However, the present increasing disruption of the global environment is the product of a dynamic technology and science which were originating in the Western medieval world against which Saint Francis was rebelling in so original a way. Their growth cannot be understood historically apart from distinctive attitudes toward nature which are deeply grounded in Christian dogma. The fact that most people do not think of these attitudes as Christian is irrelevant. No new set of basic values has been accepted in our society to displace those of Christianity. Hence we shall continue to have a worsening ecologic crisis until we reject the Christian axiom that nature has no reason for existence save to serve man.

The greatest spiritual revolutionary in Western history, Saint Francis, proposed what he thought was an alternative Christian view of nature and man's relation to it: he tried to substitute the idea of the equality of all creatures, including man, for the idea of man's limitless rule of creation. He failed. Both our present science and our present technology are so tinctured with orthodox Christian arrogance toward nature that no solution for our ecologic crisis can be expected from them alone. Since the roots of our trouble are so largely religious, the remedy must also be essentially religious, whether we call it that or not. We must rethink and refeel our nature and destiny. The profoundly religious, but heretical, sense of the primitive Franciscans for the spiritual autonomy of all parts of nature may point a direction. I propose Francis as a patron saint for ecologists.

The New Mythology of "Man in Nature"

DANIEL McKINLEY

EMPTY WORDS, like blimps in the wind, tear our feet from the Earth. The Web of Nature is held up approvingly for us to admire, but rarely without a phrase on some uniqueness in man that puts him outside that net. Ecology becomes a magic symbol aimed at the awesome task of picturing the interrelations of nature; but its knowledge is manipulated as freely by professional fox killers, exterminators of crabgrass, and paid promoters of chemical pesticides as by earnest naturalists. The person who finds man uniquely human to that extent negates any attempt to present man as one miracle among many others; there is always the implication that man is more different from nonhuman nature than African elephants are different from non-elephant nature. To put man in nature, while insisting sanctimoniously that we ought to avoid desiring wildernesses where we can escape a little from too many people, is not to allow much. To say that man is "natural" may prevent us from seeing his danger to himself. To claim that the ecology of suburban lawns and city junk-piles is a valid whole in ecology will surely lead to trouble.

One never gets far from intimations of man's exemption from ecological rules and his superiority over beasts. In this there are no claimants more strident than the admirers of corporate human activities who insist that people must not be interfered with, since

Perspectives in Biology and Medicine, 7(1): 93–105, Autumn 1964. Reprinted by permission of the University of Chicago Press. Copyright 1964 by the University of Chicago.

"man is a part of nature" and, therefore, what he does is natural. This
essentially leaves man the role of
Destroying Angel as the only one
worthy of him. Our most fearful destructiveness today is a result of col-
lusion among great numbers, so that
one is denied a clear taste even of his
own powers of devastation. Yet, the
human individual is the vessel which
sifts beauty and morality from events;
to relegate responsibility to a corporation is as deadening as to allow that
corporation to tell you what is beautiful
or to let it mutter such magic words
as "ecology" while thrusting a piece of
crabgrass into your questioning fist.

I do not imply that lawns and city
lots do not have plenty of mysteries
left. The honest student of crabgrass
has a great story to tell. He might, for
example, shame the practices that make
weeds inevitable, as Aldo Leopold
once did in a classic composition of
unpopular truths on how "Cheat Takes
Over." He might pioneer and teach us
that enriching our landscape with native plants is a surer way to a gardener's dream than chemical crabgrass
killers. A true account cannot fail to
honor mankind, but one wants no
shallow anthropocentrisms masquerading as ecology. I have no quarrel with
research into the ecology of city lots;
but I do not wish it to become another
counting of sheep in order that we can
sleep more soundly while carefully
marshaled forces of technology impoverish the world still further.

No doubt our plant and animal weeds
have much to teach us. They have
been at this business of civilization as
long as we have, and the lusty weeds
that clung to muddy lanes of a Stone
Age village in Europe were probably
the ones that you commonly see in the
barnyard and city lot of much of the
Westernized world today. But should

we study house sparrows, we shall
have a report merely upon house sparrows. They are barnyard cockneys,
too similar to the rest of us to teach us
all we want to know. We need the uncivilized aloofness of mudwasps and
Canada geese and whooping cranes
and sea.anemones and rhinoceroses
and white-footed mice to tell us how
man's points are oriented within Creation's compass box. And there are pas-
senger pigeons, dodos, and Carolina
parakeets from which we shall not now
learn. More importantly, the "flower in
the crannied wall"—any one species of
plant or animal—can tell no more than
its own tale; it is the whole story that
we desire: from the hum of the sea in
a spiralled shell to an account of the
arrangement of the conch-shell's molecules of calcium carbonate.

Ecological Sophistries

It is time for men to commit themselves
to a contemplative study of nature,
however hard that may be for us to begin. In a hard-headed sense, man is
much too green to have a "for" for
every fact, and we are far from knowing all the facts. We need more information. It is too easy to say that people
prefer their landscapes humanized and
that we adore wilderness only after it
no longer howls. The presumed fact
that men like to tame wilderness does
not prove that men are well off without
wilderness. We are still ignorant of
what men, in the deepest levels of
their brains, need from the world that
has always, at least previously, had
vivid mysteries that could not be as
easily dismissed as the shallow enthusiasms of the hobbyist and the
learned but dry specialisms of the
microscopist and astronomer, whose
experiences lead onto plains of learning that are austere and of limited
meaningfulness. It is no answer to

shrug and say that wild forms adjust to altered surroundings or that there has always been somewhere room for most wild things to persist. These are dangerous ecological sophistries, because much of the biotic catastrophe that we face is not organic change. This is probably true of all regions opened to the West within historically recent times. England has been changing slowly since the Stone Age, and in many ways that country appears healthier than our America after the massive wave of uprootedness that has hit it in three centuries and less.

It is unrealistic to excuse ourselves by saying that man has always changed nature. With our eyes tempered less by contact with nature, with our activities less intimately guided by the individual capacities of a biotic region than in the past, the degree and rate of change that people are now implementing make the statement so simpleminded that our esthetics, ethics, and economics demand that we look into its emptiness. "Man in Nature" becomes another excuse for the things that men do, while doing less than its share to guide their actions.

In the sense that we are free at any moment to attempt anything we choose with knowledge that we have, the gods are indeed neutral. Centuries of Western culture have been sterilized by empty arguments that man is peculiarly free. We mistake, as we so often do, certain attractive ideas for concrete reality. As a matter of fact, Determinism and Freewill are merely missiles in the artillery of professional philosophers, useful only to them in shooting down each others' trial balloons. The emptiness of our words does not mean, however, that the results of applying our knowledge will be innocuous. It is

to our shame that the commonest excuse when a scheme aborts is that we did not know the gun was loaded.

Any credo or tradition can be revered. Only time can tell us the ecological effects of a society's activities. Since abstract thought is often held up as man's most human characteristic, and since thought is claimed to be free and not controlled by material environment, men's thoughts and activities are to that extent chaotic and must be judged not by the rules of physics and chemistry but by those of ecology, whose wheels grind slowly and whose scales patiently weigh all contingencies. Ecology's causal relations are none the less as precise as a million impinging events will allow. It is ourselves who lack four-dimensional eyesight, not ecology which lacks balance and precision. No such circumscribed philosophies as economics or religion or ethics can be our sole guide. I do not propose scrapping our value judgments. Values tell us where we think we want to go. Ecology *may* help us to get there; my particular hope is that it will show us along the way many riches that a mechanical guide, even if such were possible, could never do. My trust is that close contact with reality may cause us to fear the sterility promised by some of the ecologically wrongheaded doctrines that formerly seemed so precious to us. Values that do not in some way heighten human sensitivity are false gods. Even at the risk of being thought prejudiced and didactic, I submit that men need to experience nonhuman nature deeply.

Nature's Richness Depends on Its Complexity

It is always open season on other peoples' hobby horses. No old nag, even when quite harmless, can avoid

353

the fun that is poked at silliness. The most dedicated offenders are people who have reduced all human beliefs to either conventions or prejudices. Clarity is to be treasured, but it is a little too easy to play games with the eviscerated symbols that others cherish. You may, for example, laugh off Romanticism, with its love of the exotic, the dead, the too-sweet "natural" world, its rather optimistic clutching at platonic postulates of an infinity of worlds peopled by all possible gradations of beings. But if Romanticism was a social fashion, so is a belief in communism or democracy or the idea of inherent equal rights. It is still possible that Romanticism generated some salvageable truths that previous centuries had failed to disclose. Even though one would now prefer to talk about the ecological rule of competitive exclusion or the uniqueness of functional roles of species in the natural community, Romanticism, in its reverence for the integrity of the exotic and its presuppositions of a divine fullness in kinds of things, helped lay the groundwork for modern ecology and natural history. Ecologist Paul Shepard has aptly considered in an essay on "The Artist as Explorer" (*Landscape*, Winter 1962–63) the possibility of a core of sense in what may have seemed just another fad. Shepard reviews the ways in which Western artists broke with tradition to see truly that there were integrated "typical" landscapes in other lands; but one gathers that many volumes could hardly document the failure of other Westerners to act upon that wisdom, for the essay's warning is clear enough: "It is in just such exotic worlds as the European found in the South Pacific that he brought the most catastrophic changes."

You can have genetics, anatomy, physiology, or almost any other conventional "science" you wish on a city lot that is luxuriant in nothing more complex than crabgrass. But you cannot have a very challenging ecology without a considerable temporal and biotic continuity that exceeds that of any laboratory or any city lot. The ecological community is worthy of study in a search for valid principles, as geologist Luna B. Leopold says in a publication of the U.S. Geological Survey, "only if natural biological and physical processes are in operation." "To describe a biota there is no substitute for a sample," he says again, a statement that ought to make those who sneer at natural areas and wilderness feel a little uncertain. Quite legitimate proponents of nature conservation can also take comfort from another of Leopold's observations: "In some instances, visible signs of accomplishment of conservation, signs of having done something, may be less important than visible signs of having done nothing. When you find . . . a little remnant of prairie flowers, you may thank your lucky stars for this visible sign that man has done nothing here."

All of this implies order in nature, perhaps many orders in nature. But I think that very little of that order can be found in a city. No doubt ecological processes operate in a city park or even on a sidewalk. But conceptually, the order of difference is that between a simple melody and a Beethoven symphony. Ecologically, we are fooling ourselves not by the objectivity of our facts but by their triviality and lack of relatedness. Nature's richness, surely, is outside of man and prior to him, and dependent upon its priority, its outsidedness and, to some as yet unknown extent, upon its complexity.

"The presumed fact that men like to tame wilderness does not prove that men are well off without wilderness." (Photo by Grant Heilman.)

Our Danger Consists in Doing

Yi-Fu Tuan, a geographer in the Southwest, argues persuasively for the preeminence of the personal in architecture ("Architecture and Human Nature," *Landscape*, Autumn 1963), and twits our definitions of man's nature by maintaining that it is the planner and the missionary who stand most in need of a clearly defined, sloganized

"Human Nature." I too am worried about what Professor Tuan terms disembodied philosophers and town planners and I agree that Human Nature is suspect. Aside from the fact that most professional fields have limited touch with the human scene (and so have limited solace to offer us), the term "Human Nature" must bridge the gap between the experiential methodology of George Catlin's "Mandan Torture Ceremony" and the reflective patience of Gautama Buddha; between the most perfect love and the degradation imposed by man upon his fellows in his organized cruelties; between the man who commits suicide if his honor is impeached and the existentialist who shrilly affirms that if life is worth living at all it is worth living at all times. I think there must be common denominators of human nature, some of them possibly quite rarefied, others of great importance that we have smothered with ignorance or not yet learned about, but in meaningful terms at both individual and societal levels, it may conceivably be just to speak of a multiplicity of human "natures."

These strictures upon archetypal thinking are, of course, sobering to the ecologist, but I submit that ecology is not a science whose validity is determined by popular vote. Nor is its fate as a point of view solely dependent upon the huckster whose task it is to encapsulate his stimuli and feed them into the carefully cultivated human slot-machine whose responses have been stabilized. If there are as many human natures as there are individuals and as many humanities as there are cultures, an individual man's ecological relatedness to his environment is not lessened and a culture's drive to transform or deform the biotic landscape to fit its own ideas of propriety is not ecologically neutralized. It is difficult to see how such attitudes can fail to adjust sooner or later, intentionally or not, to ecological reality, if a temporal dimension is counted relevant to causal connections among thought and action and a chain of resulting events. As a human ecologist, I should say: Preserve nature and human nature will take care of itself.

The smug and the shallow carry a lot of weight in public opinion today. From their ranks and from those of the counterrevolutionaries, whose sources of inspiration are no greater credit to human thought, come most of the planners and the missionaries of a variety of Promised Lands. The variety is proof of confusion although this does not seem to act as a brake upon the multiplication of new programs of action. Contemplation of nature's "laws," like the estimable dodo, became extinct soon after modern man discovered and named it; when a vast majority of people treasure a technique (how can one say law?) only if it works, the cassandras of our day are mostly those who vainly point out the vanity of looking for final causal relations. The latter people, of course, do nothing to halt the aimless manipulation of disembodiedness, for our danger consists in doing, and not in knowing or not knowing. If I allow my uncertainties to alienate me from action, I abdicate to those more willing to postulate their certainties. I do not want to dictate, but opinion polls have their limitations as guides either in taste or ecology. I am among non-doctrinaire planners who want to keep some of our ecological portholes open, so that not only can everyone see his best, he will also have something to see. If this is the scheme of a planner, if this is the trap laid by a missionary, I do not see how we can easily avoid their pitfalls. Too much is at stake to funk out now. I speak as one who remembers better and hopes for no worse and this makes me a missionary. There seem ways to avoid some of our undesirable activities and so I am a planner. One could become a recording dinosaur, while the world is pulled down by his fellows; one might cease all goal-oriented planning and attempt to function as a perennial rear-guard to prevent disaster; but both these concepts seem somehow to lack organic wholeness. With all my awareness of dangers, I believe a rich nonhuman environment for many reasons is worth keeping.

Any action presumes the possibility of mistake, but the missionary claiming to speak for eternity and the bureaucratic planner whose embalmed pomposities stand a fair chance of lasting a millennium, compound mistakes. "Majority-rule," "justice," "free enterprise," or even "existentialism" are all ways of getting things done, even if the doing is doing nothing whatsoever. Perhaps the answer is not so much doctrinaire drift or doctrinaire action, as unique talents applied to a unique job in a spirit of awe and full search for knowledge, under the guidance of such embodied philosophers and town planners as we can discover. If we find what we ought to stand in awe of —and then leave it alone—we shall be considerably better off than we now are.

I do not deny that I am a materialist asking for moderation in application of our technology. It seems to me that our danger lies in man acting materially as a part of material nature. It is in the realm of the actual and what we do there (not in esoteric art or in high-flown philosophy, whose practitioners have often talked as if man were outside of nature) that the danger exists. Some of these dangers are possibly peculiar to men; perhaps, for example, we can deform the world to the point that men go mad in it. Other dangers man shares with his animal relatives, as when food fails or when he demands such ecologically expensive items as hierarchy, territory, and, maybe, the freedom to think and see beautiful things.

Bird-watching and People-watching
Mankind appears at times to aim at a technocracy where faceless bureaucrats and mindless technicians make the wheels go round. Its especial prophets are those whom I shall call people-watchers. Bird-watching and nature study elicit a yawp of contempt from them, and deliberately treasured wilderness and natural areas are laughed off as "living museums." Forgetting that there are those who sneer at other museums, too, they also ignore the fact that men now have power enough to destroy a great part of the world. Such people have the responsibility of demonstrating how men, who have always worshipped their palpably human illusions and who have so often considered nature something to be feared or exploited, can avoid setting ecological traps for themselves that ignorant cultures in a "state of nature" rarely or never have to face. Perhaps neither in man nor in non-man are there enough guideposts for all the future, but in the non-human landscape lie certain excellences, both economic and esthetic, and I do not intend to surrender them thoughtlessly to empty verbalisms. A study of the true wealth of a piece of land dedicated quite simply to being itself might easily be worth a man's lifetime.

Can it be that men are going to blanket the Earth and that, in suggestions that people-watching supplant study of natural areas, we are being told to make a virtue of necessity? It may become necessity, but I can think of no possible virtue in it.

What if it is not necessity?

It seems to me that a major failing of people-watching, apart from the smug tastelessness of it, is that you have only insipid fragments when you are through. People, cities, and societies prevaricate shamelessly, especially when they know they are being watched. Psychiatrists can go deeper than the ordinary people-watcher and so shape up for scrutiny more of our human reality. Novelists and poets may use their arts to achieve a more satisfying wholeness than simple observation ever gives; and they may also notoriously ignore the nonhuman environment.

But what has all this to do with ecology? Or nature? Or human nature?

The answer is not easy. Certainly, one ought to be curious about his neighbors and sensitive to his community's needs and characteristics. But most of what his neighbors do will not be very exciting, and certainly most of it will not be of immediate ecological import; one will have to look beyond his nose's end and shed some of his meekly good-humored nosiness before he can sharpen the teeth of his ecological saws.

City-watching and people-watching leave you with no norm. You cannot measure the health of the city against itself. There are those happy enough with concrete under their eyes; I still think that their children ought to have a chance to see some of the unpaved parts of Earth. There are others who like to have cozy landscapes that blossom into dahlias and tea-roses; others yearn for trees and parks, sometimes even without tennis court and golf

course. I also hope that great wildernesses, without any trace of people-watcher, will not be denied a place in this graduated series. Perhaps all is indeed relative; if so, we have only the greater to measure the lesser against. Both the greater and the lesser are outside of us and all can be hurt by our fiat.

It seems appropriate that a human community ought to be a pleasant place to live in. Cities surely have slums because of the ideals of those who live there, but I do not think that anyone can prove, as some have hinted, that many of the people there are so straining after their Thoreauvian Waldens that they allow their city to fester because of it. On the contrary, Paul B. Sears was probably nearer truth when he wrote that "an ugly landscape is a diseased one, and . . . an effective landscape is satisfying to the eye." Sears' statement is not the ultimate answer but its appreciation would certainly help in some quarters. Such a proposal would find its most vigorous opponents in the slum itself, where many adult residents (as well as most of those who make slums economically fairly probable) would hardly bother to sniff at one of Thoreau's wilderness idylls; much less would they learn the difference between blackjack oak and yellow poplar; probably a majority of them would feel uncomfortable both morally and in matters of morale in any place wilder than a paved street. On every score, their life is a denial of the fitness of nonhuman nature as a subject for either conversation or conservation. To leave city life to their ideals is to prescribe myopia as a cure for ugliness.

We have before us in his various forms European Man, ready at a flash to fight for some of the most high-flown and empty ideals that the mind of man has devised. Yet so peculiarly is he conditioned that nature preservation for its own sake (or for man's sake) is a foolish doctrine to him. It is not political systems alone that entomb the body, to the mind's detriment. Social complexities, mores, and mere numbers of men will do as well. Thoreau could cut across back yards in his day. Could he today? What if his swamps and forests had lain miles away or existed only in his memory of pre-suburbia?

If We Lose the Vision of Living Things

What of the suggestion, then, that we ought to watch people rather than wilderness organisms? Are naturalists with broad horizons, in effect, being called maladjusted individuals who are intentionally or incidentally fouling their city worlds? If this is the charge, one would like to find the roots of such societal narcissism, to see whether there is not some need in the charger for a host of lives into which to snoop. Edmund Selous characterized the end result of this sort of thing many years ago in his quizzical, philosophic book *Bird Life Glimpses:*

The wonder of man, therefore, is unchecked by the wonder of anything else. . . . So an image is put up in a temple, and joss-sticks lighted before it. Service is held. It is church, in fact, with man and religion inside it. Outside are the animals and science. In such an atmosphere field natural history does not flourish. You may not bring dogs into church. That, however, is what I would do, and it is just what the Society ought to do. With man for their sole theme they will never, it seems likely, get beyond a solemn sort of mystic optimism. If they want to get farther they should let the dogs into church.

Edmund Selous would have made a good people-watcher.

Just what kind of adjusted "maturity" do our people-watchers want? What do they hope to see emerge from the massive numbers that few of them seem worried about? Have they forgotten Jacquetta Hawkes's fear of "the terrible forces our cleverness has put into our unworthy hands"? Are they not equating man the hunter who, as with all species of animals, is a robber of nature, or early man, the plodding creator of domesticated plants and animals and of resilient landscapes where men seem at home, with our modern man rushing, as Miss Hawkes says in *Man on Earth,* blindly into industrialism, where mutilation of the countryside is followed by its dereliction? What kind of blindness is it to preach that the best use of brains is to contemplate benevolently what men do in fact do? How much better to suggest with Miss Hawkes that Britain with its fifty-five million brains is not by any means giving us proportionally as much poetry and song as five millions of the old Elizabethans. How much better to agree that all that men do is not natural, as S P R Charter says in a book that is also called, appropriately if repetitiously, *Man on Earth.* If our people-watcher can show that he is vividly concerned about the great positive evil that huge numbers of people automatically bring with them, then I shall gladly admit that here is people-watching that I can admire!

The quality of people-watching, too, is something to worry about, when we look benignly only at people and have no measuring stick from the rest of nature by which to judge results. It is a little like leaving politics to the politicians. My fear is not so much that certain naturalists are not aware that man is a part of nature as that the mass of men will not see that nature is a part of man. Attitudes will certainly have to change. We need a point around which

359

facts can cluster meaningfully, in the sharpest and most modern terms. The feeling of ecological kinship with the rest of the natural world is such a creative center, whether you have an elaborate science of ecology or not. Relatedness is still the order of both the day and the geological age, and that relatedness is the blood and spirit of ecology.

A pious claim that man is in nature seems so often another way to separate man from nature. It is a token of affection that denies itself. It is a lonely man becoming more insular with every syllable that he utters in assuring himself that men are not islands. Love surely is in the doing rather than in the saying. On another hand, as I have said, "Man in Nature" becomes a veiled warning that one has no business interfering with what men do. However, I do occasionally find a man saying in sufficiently uncompromising terms that "man is not only in the Universe but of it," as psychiatrist Harold F. Searles does in his book on *The Nonhuman Environment*. Searles goes to great trouble to delineate a palpably real nonhuman world.

For my part, I suspect that we have reached a stage, at the crossroads or even beyond, where we fear that we have lost contact with nature. Such a

"What if we lose the vision of living things—. . . Forget the feeling for the patterning of living things in the world we move through?" (Photo by Grant Heilman.)

feeling could not have occurred to a peasant or to anybody else in medieval Europe, for example, where nature was the undoubted, assumed, and proper backdrop for the acting out of men's lives. They could not lose contact with nature; we can! Rather, we can lose functional, meaningful contact, just as we do when we try to comprehend the astronomer's distances, the atomist's smallnesses, the mathematician's varieties of infinitude.

My small daughter tries to learn to spell the word "blue"; she shuts her eyes and squints at the word, trying, as she says, "to get it in her 'funny papers,'" meaning that she has an image of the word filed somewhere in her head. What if we lose the vision of living things—not the word, but the remembrance of blueness or birdness themselves? Forget the feeling for the patterning of living things in the world we move through? Forget that the function of living things is to be seen? We shall be left with empty yearnings that have no instinct to facilitate the recognition of our need, and only ugliness will remain and we shall not be able to escape from it.

One sees scare articles in national magazines, in which psychiatric research and experimentation with vision-inducing drugs (some of it phony, no doubt) are coupled neatly with legitimate fears of glue-sniffing, goofballs, and tranquilizers. Such colorlessly literal and puritanical lifting of skirts misses the point that the world is becoming too drab for some of its occupants. It is just possible that the stock market and the ecology of crabgrass are not enough to delight them; they revert to dream and psychic landscapes when their own landscape is degraded by the preponderating influence of the dull in mind. It begins to look as if our very civilization has left us with no

place, in the elementally physical sense, to run; and, worse still perhaps, we have little knowledge of what to run from.

If one in any way needs the non-human environment in becoming personally and individually mature, as Searles suggests we do, this is but one step from the vaguely felt but perhaps genetically determined needs for some aspects of natural landscapes (built-in "ideals" possibly, that we have only just begun to look for and worry about); above these larger needs are the practical needs of keeping our large semi-natural holdings in agriculture and related fields stable and going. And here we run right into the ecological perspectives of community complexity that English ecologist Charles Elton has brought into thoughtful focus in a book, *The Ecology of Invasions by Animals and Plants*, that unfortunately could be written only now, when for much of the world it is already the dead stuff of history.

While Elton does not dig very deeply into the philosophy and psychology of human ecology, he concentrates with great success on showing solidly practical reasons for preserving variety in nature. He gives evidence from many fields of ecological research for thinking that a natural community's complexity is the basis of its stability. The relation between this stability and human happiness is one of the threads that holds my story together.

"Nature" is More than a Variable Verbal Artifact

"Man in Nature" can become, like the homely maxim that "Man has always changed his environment," a platitude aimed at cutting man off from nature. It can be another shield of ignorance for men tired of thinking. "Nature"

must be made more than a verbal artifact. As an entity of our wishing, it is
no more true than "Human Nature."
Nature is not the godly powers that the
Greeks believed to bow the heads of
stiff-necked men; nor is it the wayward
God of the old Jews. It is the river of
events within which the artificialities
of men have their reality. In it, living
is translated from the definitional into
the real. Men have within them the
power to attempt to live in a world
impoverished with definitions. It may
be that in experiences in nature (perhaps even "against" nature) we have
more in common with our fellow men
than we have in verbal symbols that
so often separate us from one another.
With his eye upon man, how can one
escape artifice and, eventually, a nonhuman world that is totally technological? How can one preserve the
challenge that is not alone that of
balancing the teacup upon one's knee
or of launching oneself vertically upon
spike heels? One can be named a
traitor to mankind if he wants a breath
of fresh air or a burst of flowers that
comes in its time and not from order of
the city council. How can one keep his
eye on security programs, taxes, sput-
niks, and rockets to the moon and not
yearn for something better? I suspect
that one might deal better with the
rockets, and even taxes, if he took to
heart the problems of albatrosses in
their shy search for the little specks
of island solitude that they require,
in a world too full of men and rats. But
what a fate if the nonhuman environment must become nothing more than
a recreational venture to refurbish us
for our dull jobs. In such recreation,
no standards of taste can exist; it is
merely therapy whose proof is the cure.
Creativity demands greater depths, and
if a few souls drown, and if some of
Earth is spent in making our world

richer than our other-worldly materi-
alists think it has to be to hang together, that is a risk worth taking.

The Modern Retreat from Function

PETER van DRESSER

A curious aspect of a cultural movement is that it may generate a countercurrent which, while never seriously threatening the main direction, tends to balance or even mask it. Some demon, it seems, delights in confusing the real course of social change so effectively that observers may misunderstand completely the meaning of events in which they are immersed.

For example, Americans encourage the roughest sports—football, hockey, boxing —but are probably the least physically fit people anywhere. All children are required to "get an education," but the scholar is relatively without honor. The debasement of women is hidden behind a phony, exaggerated momism; destruction of natural resources is made invisible by a host of conservation publications; the psychic impact of environmental deterioration and loss of functional contact with nature strikes us beneath a mass hypochondria whose essence is a misinterpretation of symptoms.

Such a double face to everything gives the wavering individual a choice both of roles and of "objective" opinion with regard to every issue. By choosing "facts" he can argue with some logic that American life is not one thing but is, instead, just the opposite. In this demonic game, he is not necessarily aware of the alternative and his background and experience may obscure the option. Moreover, there is usually some truth to both of the conflicting views.

THE EDITORS

Landscape, *10(3):15–17, Spring 1961. Reprinted by permission.*

AS A PEOPLE, we have not ceased congratulating ourselves on our remarkable escape from the obsessive genteelness, the overriding concern with propriety, facade and pseudo-elegance which we associate with the past century. Victorian manners and customs are perennially good for a condescending chuckle, and the voluminous garments in which the ladies and gentlemen of that epoch swathed themselves still serve as a sort of subconscious, contrasting background to the tanned mobility of bathing-briefed humanity (on billboard, beach and screen) which accompanies our neo-Hellenic savor of the joys and beauties of the flesh. Surely we have by now achieved a collective *joie de vivre* sufficient to flood away the dark world of anxieties, tensions, repressions which festered in that murky climate of self-fear within which our ancestors are said to have been reared.

But there is evidence that our psychic liberation is still only skin-deep, so to speak; that the current relaxation of tabus against exposed epidermis and musculature has been countered by the proliferation of a system of far more pervasive inhibitions and pruderies than our great grandparents could have imagined. Where the Victorian culture seems to have conditioned primarily against the direct recognition of, or exposure to, the raw phenomenon of sexuality, the modern American is being perhaps even more effectively conditioned against an entire complex of physico-physiological processes.

The Triumph of the Container

Probably the most obvious indication of this conditioning and the one most frequently commented on, is the role that the motor-car has assumed in our society. With its polished exterior and padded interior, it has become a sort of sanitary carapace within which the contemporary psyche shelters itself from the rigors of the physical world. Beginning by progressively eliminating the need for walking and for managing draft animals—two effective modes of contact with the organic environment —the automobile has evolved into the "womb with a view," and on wheels; the concrete embodiment of revulsion against a disturbing underworld of dark fears of germs and physical contact, of exertion, effort and dirt.

The preparation of food, in a parallel fashion, has retreated to an esoteric domain of immaculate and hermetically sealed machinery, the culmination of which is the inevitable cellophane package or tinned container. All the old lusty smells and sensations attendant upon the grinding of corn, roasting of coffee, the fermenting of yeast in bread or beer, the pressing of apples or grapes, have been banished in favor of a hushed operating room asepsis. Gourmets have long lamented the resulting blandification of foodstuffs— the average American child now cannot tolerate foods of marked flavor and character; he subsists on an emolient of homogenized peanut-butter, triply ground hamburger and emulsified chocolate milk. Country life, which used to provide an enclave sheltered from such degeneration, has now of course become as much or more invaded by these practices as the city and suburbia.

The submergence of all operations of a physiological or physical nature beneath a cosmeticized camouflage can be seen at work throughout our technology. The Victorian took an honest pleasure in the construction of his machinery. He embellished its members with scrollwork and gilding, but

he did not hide them. To the Modern, even the play of gear trains, connecting rods and levers has become in bad taste and his mechanisms increase in salability to the extent that they can be shrouded in nubile housings. There is of course a measure of technical justification for this kind of evolution, but the drive behind it is certainly as much psychological as functional, and the fabrication, repair and maintenance problems are often vastly complicated.

A perhaps inevitable result of this trend has been, of course, the withdrawal of the repairing of machinery— especially of automobiles—to the pastel-toned laboratory of smocked specialists. The grimy, grease-stained mechanic is still to be found in an occasional backwater garage, but he is on his way out, and the typical modern repair operation tends to consist in the deft installation of a packaged "factory fresh" component, rather than the painful personal reworking of broken or worn mechanisms. And as for the old-time blacksmith-machine shop, with its Piranesilike interior, its maze of shafting and slapping leather belts, its awesome wrestlings with red-hot metal—this traditional point of contact with the elemental Haephestic world has almost completely vanished.

The Do-It-Yourself renaissance which has aroused so much comment may be cited as a counter-movement against this general professionalization and sanitization of daily life. It seems true that the submerged need for personal manipulation of creative forces has indeed stimulated this thriving new segment of our tertiary economy. However, an examination of Do-It Yourself-ism reveals that it too has gone through the same process of degermination which has affected our whole way of life. It is precisely in the rough elemental stage of extracting and forming

364

In southern mountain communities a chairmaker planes wood with a draw knife. He uses no glue or nails but wets the wood, which then shrinks as it dries, making joints tight. (Photo courtesy Asheville Chamber of Commerce.)

A Navajo artisan creating a blanket on a home-made loom. (Photo courtesy Santa Fe Railway.)

raw materials that the How-to-do-it kit bypasses contact with the crude real world. One plays with plywood or ductile aluminum extrusions or ready tanned and cut leather, or pre-compounded clay and glazes—in extreme cases one even fills in color-coded areas in a prefabricated painting. But all these operations are incomplete, emasculated, predigested. They are, in fact, hardly more than extensions of the childhood manipulations of guaranteed non-toxically colored pegboards in the hygienic nursery.

Indeed, in an ideally laid out suburban development, one gets an overwhelming impression of a gay toyland peopled with brightly painted lawnmowers, baby garden tractors, prefabricated pergolas and aluminum clothes dryers. The toyland picture is completed with the gleaming two-toned icecream-sundae-colored automobiles parked beneath the carports. (Their beautiful but obscene engines and members are of course concealed beneath softly-rounded and magically glittering frostings.)

The Blenderized Environment

The psychological shock of rough textures is carefully avoided here; walls and floors are dulcet planes of featureless plastic or enamel; lawns are uninterrupted velvet. Only an occasional token fireplace chimney of ashlar masonry, or a carefully varnished panel of knotty pine is allowed to symbolize a pioneering heritage.

In this careful cosmetic world there are no gnarled people, no mature or older men and women whose faces, bodies and hands have been formed and indented through direct contact with the brines, caustics and tannins of elder nature. When these people, in response to vestigial urges, penetrate the wilderness briefly on summer vacations, they do so sheltered in their hydromatically propelled perambulators, cared for and distracted by the multitude of gay gadgets such as folding stoves, shirt-pocket radios, collapsible plastic furniture; nourished through the umbilical cord of intricate transport and communications. The Grecian exposure to sun and wind is after all achieved only in carefully selected beaches, resort spots or dude ranches, guaranteed free of chiggers, abrasive gravel and blackflies. Painful effort, sweat other than that which can be quickly removed in the locker room showers, gruelling and permanently disfiguring contacts with the elements—such ingredients are discreetly missing.

More even than in play, this general and tacit evasion of the crudities of our root-contacts with the planet, permeates our mode of organization of work. The rough physical tasks are still to be done; foodstuffs and fibers must still be brought forth from the dirt; animals killed and gutted; minerals wrested from rock veins, smelted and forged; massive objects moved, lifted, piled; trees felled and shaped; mountains of refuse disposed of. In the past all these processes, subdivided into a thousand lesser tasks, were undertaken by men —men with muscles, nerves: men who sweated. Uncounted deeds of individual valor, judgment, skill, seasoned with anxiety, effort and pride, formed the network of man's economic relationship to his globe. Men were marked physically, spiritually and mentally by the demands of their occupations— sometimes honorably, sometimes painfully.

In our emerging automated world this intimacy with the physical processes of existence is not in good taste. As on a small scale we conceal the play of vital activities behind euphemic shroudings, so on the larger stage entire regions are segregated to the massive chemurgies of our industry. Broad piedmonts and prairies are devoted to the dreary but efficient monoculture of cotton, corn, wheat or tobacco; mineralized basins and littorals to the monstrous extractions and smeltings of iron, copper, coal; prodigious intrametropolitan complexes to wildernesses of interlocking manufacturers and processings. In sheer physical extent, such areas overwhelm suburbia; psychologically they are nevertheless subservient to it. The powerful and capable men who operate the great machines here are blighted with its fatally genteel pruderies. Wherever physically or economically possible, their housing developments and shopping centers caricature the dream world of chrome store fronts, picture windows and unctuously curving asphalt motorways; wives move in a hypnotic orbit of easy-pay-plan color-styled bathrooms and living room suites, of shopping expeditions to the nearest glittering super market and its attendant beautician, seeking, unconsciously, escape from the overwhelming brutality of the technology about them.

In this environment, no balance of the physical, the intellectual and the esthetic may be expected to evolve. Here, especially, because of the sheer economic pressure towards ever mounting production, labors that demand participation of body and nerve are being reorganized into cerebrally guided, automatically coordinated mechanical processes.

The Need for Roughage
Examples could be multiplied indefinitely and have been discussed exhaustively since the days of Ruskin and William Morris, but the general tendency away from human-to-nature contact with our environment and towards impersonal, cerebral, specialized manipulation continues and no doubt will proceed to a much greater degree of perfection.

Without questioning the basic benefits of applied science—release from drudgery, power over the blind vagaries of nature—one may entertain doubts as to the particular ends towards which the present technological evolution is rushing us. Whether we think we like it or not, it is quite probable that the healthy human psyche requires a proportion of roughage in its figurative diet. We are the heirs of a million years of a generally victorious struggle against cold, hunger, difficult terrain, carnivorous cunning; our nervous and glandular balance has evolved under the stress of exertion, effort, endurance. Individuals reared in the complete absence of such stimuli are not apt to be healthy or sane. A prudish avoidance or concealment of physical challenge in the world about us is much more apt to result in a pseudo-refinement, a pseudo-spirituality with an accompanying drive towards cruelty and violence in some specialized department of civilization, than it is to result in the development of full-blooded humans capable of the exercise of all the nobler human emotions. "Overcivilized" (i.e., culturally imbalanced) societies of the past are notorious for mass exercises in cruelty —gladiatorial combats, animal baiting, gang slave labor, massacres of prisoners and the like. After the experiences of the last world war and in the face of mounting statistics of mechanical violence in our own cities and highways, can we confidently assert that such a compensation mechanism is not at work in our own society?

367

To an indeterminate but certainly very large extent, the shape and structure of our economy is being fixed by a mistaken urge to escape all demands upon, and challenges to, our somas. "Our abundant society," says Paul Goodman, "is at present simply deficient in many of the most elementary objective opportunities and worth-while goods that could make growing up possible. It is lacking in enough man's work. . . . It is lacking in the opportunity to be useful . . . it thwarts aptitudes and creates stupidity . . . it dampers animal ardour. . . ." Is it pure coincidence that at the same time the economy as a whole is being shaped towards releases of destructive energy and collective violence on an utterly unprecedented scale?

It does not follow that the alternative to this mode of evolution lies in a regression towards a Spartan or a primitive social pattern. What is required is the opening up of our productive arrangements to a new intensity and opportunity for personal skill, personal creative mastery or useful processes, personal contact with the basic aliment of life. This implies a re-organization of the technical and economic landscape, a retreat from over-centralization, over-organization and over-mechanization; a re-emphasis of the human scale, a closer symbiosis between the human community, the soil and the total pattern of indigenous—both living and inorganic—resources. It implies a re-direction of the enormous social energy now consumed by the Frankenstein drive towards endlessly increasing complexity, power, size and fake refinement. Such a shift, one can guess, would result in a society boasting far less applied horsepower but far more applied science, skill and artistry; less plate-glass, plastic and chrome and more lovingly-laid masonry

and beautifully worked wood; fewer superhighways but more richly diversified countrysides, towns and cities; less speed and multiplication but greater fruitfulness. Above all, the insensate lust for aggrandizement and technological-mercantile conquest which characterizes our culture would diminish before the lure of self-conquest, of internal, personal and community cultivation. But without a renaissance of pride and delight in grasping and manipulating the stubborn but priceless realities of the soil, of rock, of timber; of growth, muscular effort, discomfort and even danger, the glitteringly sterile domination of unrelieved mechanism will crystallize about us into the nightmare environment fore-shadowed by a Capek, a Huxley or an Orwell.

Land Use and Urban Development

GEORGE MACINKO

SOME YEARS AGO I read a passage from one of Bertrand Russell's writings which had a lasting effect. When asked to summarize the major differences to be noted between 19th and 20th century life Russell said that there was vastly less humbug in the twentieth century world of ideas than was true of the earlier period, and for this he was grateful; but that, on the other hand, almost every place he had visited after a long absence showed a marked deterioration in beauty and for this he was profoundly sorry. (1)

Russell's observations were in accord with my own judgment and with what I believed to be the collective but poorly articulated sentiments of much of the American public. More and more often I had read reports in the popular press of housewives who linked arms around or even perched in trees trying to stem the tide of the developer's bulldozers; of civic groups who protested the building of highways through park and field; and of sportsmen's groups who bemoaned the fouling of water bodies and the loss of open lands. These reactions, based essentially on sentiment, I believed to be symptomatic of a deeper distress and I waited for my betters to provide me with some rational explanation to this complex and baffling situation in which the most affluent society the world has ever known seemed to be growing increasingly dissatisfied with the evolution of its public environment. I read avidly, gained some insights, but nothing sufficed to remove

Adapted from an address delivered April 13, 1967, at the Travelers Research Center, Inc., Hartford, Conn.

the nagging doubt that though there was an abiding assumption that something was being done about this disaffection, in fact, short-term palliatives were the rule, and nothing that would be effective over the long term was even projected. I would have to see for myself.

My investigation began with a study (2) of the Brandywine Valley Association, a local conservation organization which, stimulated to action by the marked decline in the quality of Brandywine Creek, was attempting to arrest and reverse a process of more general environmental deterioration in Northern Delaware and Southwestern Pennsylvania. The major conclusion of this initial study was that conservation measures designed to enhance farm productivity, wildlife resources, stream improvement, and rural esthetics could not withstand the onslaught of residential and industrial development which the free play of economically motivated and technically induced forces could unleash. Land renovation, achieved only after much effort, was being rendered futile and senseless by continuing and accelerating suburban sprawl. The simple process of growth, unforeseen as a problem when the Association laid out its initial program, had become the most serious threat to its hopes of realizing a pleasant habitat.

Faced with the prospect of a continued decline in the effectiveness of its program the Association turned to the land planner for help and my examination entered its second phase in which I would attempt to determine how land planning works in theory and in practice, and especially how it copes with the phenomenon of industrial and residential growth.

This second study (3) provided confirmation that growth presented the land planner with his most important

369

problem. Because there was reluctance or outright refusal to face the implications of this fact, land planning was shown to rest on a series of accommodations to the growth phenomenon. Under the guise of flexibility plans are altered to accommodate more industrial and residential growth than was originally planned. These accommodations and their companion increases in space allocations to parking lots and expressways at the expense of parks, playgrounds, and nature areas commonly resulted in deterioration in environmental quality. This was held to be unfortunate but inevitable. I believed this study demonstrated that contemporary planning practices, such as the advocacy of cluster housing and garden apartments as substitutes for the single-family home on its uniform plot of ground, though ostensibly designed to guarantee the indefinite perpetuation of green and open spaces would at best slow the rate at which open land was disappearing. But it was trends, not rates, which were crucial because use of open land, even at reduced rates, would, if continued, eventually use up all open lands. This was incompatible with the publicly announced goals of land planning, and, consequently, a serious examination of the long-term implications of sustained growth appeared to be a vital necessity to the planning movement. Further, I had naively assumed that publication of a logically unassailable argument to this effect would thereby result in the investigation of the growth phenomena so much needed.

This evidently was not to be and again I was forced to seek my own way, for, if growth led to chaos on the local scene, this might be attributed to purely local conditions, and I wished

to work out the relationship between growth and environmental conditions on the broadest scale possible. To focus on this wider topic I have chosen to examine the most ambitious, most conspicuous, and most widely publicized environmental planning proposal I have yet encountered.

Doxiadis, Ekistics, and Ecumenopolis
A dozen years ago Constantinos A. Doxiadis, an energetic Greek planner with a flair for showmanship, coined the word ekistics which he defined as "the science of human settlements." (4) Shortly thereafter he founded the Athens Center of Ekistics to promote his brand of urban and regional planning. Since then his influence has grown tremendously, many urban planners are numbered among his disciples, and he has captured prime contracts throughout the world. Christopher Rand writing in the *New Yorker* says, "in terms of the number of human beings involved, Doxiadis is the greatest planner . . ." (5) Though Doxiadis' Ekistics viewpoint is not universally shared, even his opponents ruefully admit that it is perhaps the single most important planning influence extant and must be reckoned with.

It is important to point out at the outset that Doxiadis and his associates are to be highly commended for their recognition that there is a future which extends beyond the end of this century and this future is worthy of our serious attention now. Furthermore, Doxiadis has provided planning with a valuable service through his insistence that planning efforts must pay heed to all man's senses, not simply the visual, and must be responsive to a wide variety of human interests. A final point worthy of mention is the difficulty encountered in attempting to separate the man (Doxiadis) from the viewpoint (Ekistics). Because everything emanating from the Ekistics Center bears the strong imprint of the Doxiadis personal philosophy all efforts at criticism may give the appearance of an attack on the man. Such, however, is the peculiar relationship between Doxiadis and the Ekistics doctrine that this may be unavoidable.

I will direct my probe toward Doxiadis' handling of growth for here he has been much lauded:

More than any other planner, he has given importance to the problems of growth. They excite his wild imagination by demanding predictions of the future, and they draw the best from him. In this faculty he has yet to be challenged . . . (6)

While I confirm his wild imagination I would challenge him, for I find his handling of growth far from satisfactory. Notably absent is the thorough analysis one might expect to find behind his widely advertized and much quoted predictions. An impressive technical facade diverts attention from the many, varied, and highly dubious assumptions which comprise the heart of the Ekistics approach. I would especially challenge the contention that over the next century we are limited to shaping and directing population and urban growth but must not attempt to interfere with or blunt that growth. (7)

In their "City of the Future" (COF) project Doxiadis and his associates have carried out a series of projections into the future which would have one believe that the present "explosive" phase in the development of human settlements can be expected to last from 100 to 150 years so that at the earliest by the mid 21st century and at the latest by the beginning of the 22nd century projected population curves will slow down when a point

of physical saturation is expected to be reached. We are told that at this time a "static" phase in human settlements will occur because all physical space on earth that can be economically inhabited will be occupied at the highest practically obtainable densities within these areas. (8)

At this time some 90 to 95% of the world's peoples will live in urban areas and it is suggested that the term "Ecumenopolis," meaning "the city spanning the entire habitable portion of the earth," be given to this development. (9) Achievement of Ecumenopolis is expected to be reached at a total world population ranging from 12 to perhaps 100 billion, with 30 billion considered most probable. (10) One should note that the ultimate Ecumenopolis population is determined by resource availability and not by intellectual decision. It is assumed that population will press on resource availability and will grow to the limit imposed by such availability. (11) Furthermore, not only will the "better" areas be settled to the point of saturation but even the "difficult" areas will be inhabited to maximum capacity. However, these difficult areas, though settled at greater densities than at present, will prove uneconomical to settle at high densities and will represent forcibly low densities of development.

One apparently does not argue the desirability of this Ecumenopolis development for this is held to be a natural and inevitable occurrence and cannot be forestalled.

It would be illogical to discuss the desirability or undesirability of Ecumenopolis and try to escape from what seems to be the natural course of evolution. Even more, to fight natural trends would be a lack of recognition of reality, and the energy spent in such a futile effort would constitute a

"... it is imperative that man do his utmost to avoid situations wherein a powerful sheer necessity compels the adoption of technological measures before their safety has been proven or even reasonably tested." (Photo courtesy Standard Oil Co., N.J.)

real waste of valuable effort. It seems, therefore, that a logical attitude would be to assume Ecumenopolis as a tentative target. (12)

Evaluation of the ecumenopolis concept. Because I am going to suggest that the assertion that logic compels one to assume Ecumenopolis as a target is nonsense, and because I don't want to be accused of illogical procedures, it is necessary to look in more detail at the process by which this conclusion forming the heart of the COF program is arrived at. Such an examination discloses the disconcerting trait of leap-frogging from disputable premises to conclusions then advanced as the logical derivatives of presumably universally accepted premises.

For example, the conclusion noted above is arrived at in this fashion:

If the concept of Ecumenopolis, as developed within the project, is assumed to constitute a probable model for patterns of urban life in the future, it would be wise to conceive the development of urban settlements toward the static stage as a continuous flow without too many fluctuations. Since, therefore, it is considered probable that we are tending towards such a state, it would be illogical to discuss the desirability or undesirability of Ecumenopolis ... (13)

This switch from the probabilistic "if" statement in the premise to the deterministic "is" statement in the conclusion is a convenient but unconvincing transformation.

Now I maintain it is perfectly defensible to argue the desirability or

"... one need not be a misanthrope to hold that a world-wide landscape everywhere peopled to the density of lower Manhattan is an unattractive prospect." (Photo courtesy Tennessee Valley Authority.)

undesirability of any future condition independent of its probability of occurrence. More to the point, however, it is quite obvious that if one does not accept the premise that Ecumenopolis is the probable model of the future then all subsequent derivations fall of their own weight. (14)

Should one accept Ecumenopolis as the probable model of the future? Donald J. Bogue, professor of sociology at the University of Chicago and past-president of the Population Association of America, evidently would not. Bogue argues that new and recent developments make it plausible to expect rapid strides in fertility control.

These developments are so new and so very different from the past that population trends before 1960 are largely irrelevant in predicting what will happen in the future. Demographers who continue to try to foresee the future of world population growth right now by carefully fitting curves to time series or seek the roots of matrices summarizing masses of age-specific historical information in the search for hidden indicators of the future are making extrapolations from invalid premises. (15)

Bogue concludes that population growth rates may well decline to zero or nearly so by the year 2000 when the total world population will be about 5 billion. (16) One can disagree with Bogue's conclusions which he admits to be contingent on a "crash program" of fertility reduction, but he does set forth the data and the reasoning used to arrive at his conclusions. Unfortunately, the material emanating from the Ekistics school and especially that concerning the COF project is of a sort that defies testing for it relies heavily on reference to materials unavailable to any but project insiders; to so-called expert testimony with, in some cases, no documentation on who the expert was, in many cases no indication of the reasoning process by which the expert arrived at his opinion, and in most cases no reference to the raw data furnishing the basis for such opinion.

I have found no way to determine how much information was fed into the COF evaluation effort and how much was sheer brainstorming. Some of the methods used to carry out the COF project appear superficial in the extreme. For example:

A second method consists in imagining that one has been "parachuted" in the year A.D. 2100 or thereabouts. An attempt is then made to determine an order of magnitude for certain basic phenomena under a number of predetermined assumptions . . . For instance, total world population values have first been determined under a number of assumptions and then checked against resource availabilities. As a result, relative probabilities have been assigned to the various assumptions. (17)

But if resource availability is to be used as the criterion for assigning relative probabilities to future levels of population, then it is imperative to get accurate assessments of such future resource availability. I fail to see how the imaginary act of parachuting into the year 2100 A.D. gives one knowledge sufficient to assess resource availability 135 years in the future. (18) And unless one can determine resource availability one cannot determine population levels. For—remember—the COF study assumes population presses hard on the limit of resource availability.

But such speculations on future resource availability and population levels I regard as of distinctly secondary importance. As a member of the human community I am more concerned to note that no consideration has been given to the possibility that societies may choose to settle at densities somewhat less than the maximum allowed by environmental and economic constraints. Moreover I am puzzled by what happens after "D" day—that is after Ecumenopolis has been achieved. If, as asserted, resource availability is the only constraint on population growth, and if Ecumenopolis represents a static phase in human settlements, the logical implication is that technology then comes to a standstill and is incapable of expanding the resource base. If, however, technology and resource availability continue to grow, the population also must continue to grow, and you do not have Ecumenopolis, for only resource availability was to limit population size.

Previous criticism notwithstanding, my main criticism of the Ecumenopolis concept is Doxiadis' assertion that the growth leading to such a state is a *natural* process which *cannot* and *should not* be headed off. Taking these in reverse order I would ask why should not growth be headed off? Only the most recalcitrant can oppose action toward this end. Frederick Seitz, president of the National Academy of Sciences, introduces the academy's report *The Growth of World Population* in words emphasizing our present responsibilities:

The problem of uncontrolled population growth emerges as one of the most critical issues of our time since it influences the welfare and happiness of all the world's citizens. It commands the attention of every nation and society; the problem is no less grave for the technically advanced nations than for the less developed. (19)

Nor can one simply wait around hoping for external events to bring about a solution, for we are reminded that:

Economic progress will be slower and more doubtful if less-developed areas wait for the supposedly inevitable impact of modernization on the birth rate. They run the risk that rapid population growth and adverse age distribution would themselves prevent the modernization they count on to bring the birth rate down. (20)

That we cannot stem the tide of rapidly rising growth is an assumption more dogmatic than axiomatic. While I am not overly optimistic about the chance of reducing growth rates to the extent needed to relieve the stresses and pressures now shaping the future, I maintain that any present efforts in that regard hold promise of enormous future benefits, and are, therefore, worthy of encouragement.

The argument that present growth is the manifestation of a natural process gives me pause, for unless natural is used in an entirely trivial sense— whatever is, is natural (21)—then it apparently is used to signify a normal or average condition. But when I look either into the past or into the future, I find that present growth, referred to as natural, represents a highly unusual condition. Current growth rates have had no precedent in the past, and more importantly, they are incapable of extension into any but the most immediate future.

But, if natural cannot be used in the above context, then perhaps it is to be used to signify that man has some inherent tendency to grow up to the limit imposed by his environment. Now I can find but one argument for man pushing to the limits of his environment—this maximizes the number of

humans. The arguments for stopping short of the limit are many, of which the most important may be that a population living at the limit of resource availability is vulnerable to all perturbations in the resource system. Any downward fluctuation in available resources would cause untold hardship. Further, the recent and the immediately prospective future growth in population is intimately tied to the harnessing and use of fossil fuels and exhaustible high-grade mineral resources. In the absence of specific information to the contrary it is possible that rapid population growth continued through the period of availability of these industrial raw materials may result in a population well above the long-range equilibrium level. Finally, and perhaps most important to a society with any pretentions to civilization, it is necessary to add that man is not the only sentient being on earth and his ever-increasing numbers pose the very real threat that he will become, in the words of Charles Elton, "an all sterilizing force" obliterating all other life forms in his relentless and uncontrolled expansion into their living space.

Some, aware of the fossil record, may argue that many life forms have suffered obliteration in the past, but while it is true that extinction can be regarded as an inevitable consequence of evolution it is equally true and more pertinent to note, as does Marston Bates, that:

the rate of change through human action is much faster than anything in the geological past. And it is a single species that is responsible for the elimination of these hundreds of others, and they are not being replaced in the biological community by newly evolving forms [as was true under "natural" conditions]. Man is acting purely as an agent of destruction, and destructiveness is not a value esteemed in any system of human ethics—however common it may be in human practice. (22)

A growing body of evidence similar to the above and pointing to the undesirable concomitants of growth has not yet altered the tendency to push responsibility off into the future, thus vindicating Kingsley Davis' judgment that contemporary planning continues "to treat population growth as something to be planned for, not something to be itself planned." (23) Still one might well ask why land planning exhibits such a serious weakness in its handling of growth. Here one must consider the very nature of the planning movement, which is of recent origin and is essentially an attempt to synthesize a vast array of information. Because of its recency and its synthetic nature it is critically dependent on other disciplines for its supply of accurate information and working principles. In this respect it has all too often been ill-served by the greater intellectual community.

The attempt to debunk the necessity of honestly and forthrightly facing population-resource problems often takes the form of evasive action of which an outstanding example is to be found in a recent annual report of Resources For the Future. We are told that if the world's population continues to increase at its present rate, the year 2500 A.D. will see the globe peopled like one vast anthill, with an average density over all land areas equal to that now found on Manhattan Island below Central Park during the daytime. We are, however, also told that this "standing room only" crowd could easily fit in the Grand Canyon and thus hardly be noticed if the crowd was packed

into a box the shape of a cube, allowing a space 6 feet by 2 feet by 1 foot for each inhabitant. From these two observations the conclusion is drawn that the way one looks at population and resources is all important, for it is held that such examples are but "fantasies," otherwise of no help to persons seeking to mitigate the many problems growing out of the population-resources relationship. (24) Supposedly, we are to believe that the population explosion is a fiction because it has just been demonstrated that "it's all in the way you look at it."

However, one needn't be able to predict the future with unvarying accuracy to conclude that given a continuation of present growth trends the population of the future is far more likely to be distributed over the landscape in a pattern approximating that of Manhattan than it is to be placed in a box and dumped into the Grand Canyon. And one need not be a misanthrope to hold that a world-wide landscape everywhere peopled to the density of lower Manhattan is an unattractive prospect. Reflection, therefore, suggests this to be a strained attempt to eliminate an obviously undesirable situation without abandoning a priori philosophical ideals—presumably, the bigger the better. Saving the philosophical postulates of a position untenable in the light of reality involves a curious use of facts. Facts are not to be explained, but are rather to be explained away.

Such argumentation serves to obscure a serious problem that will demand more of humanity than recourse to scholastic dialectics. Implicit in the above example is the presumed futility of the long term look into the future. However salutary this skepticism may be in some respects, it is inapplicable in the context used, for the arithmetic of population growth and space is unarguable. Any positive rate of population growth must, if sustained, result in densities exceeding the physical bounds of any given finite space. Since, then, continuous growth is impossible, the important consideration becomes what is gained and what is lost in its continued pursuit.

An excessive reliance on technology as the solution to all problems and the assumption that all problems are most effectively ordered by means of economic evaluation are other factors contributing to the legacy of misinformation which is the land planner's. The net result of this is that attention is directed away from the role growth plays in emerging problems. Boulding provides a trenchant comment on the present scene:

There is need to devote a substantial intellectual resource to this problem [population growth], and this we are not doing . . . We are all guilty of ignorance, frivolity, and blindness, and the accusing fingers of billions of the unborn are pointed angrily toward us. (25)

Some suggestions for reform. My main concern in man's effort to develop and sustain a satisfactory environment will be with ruling or guiding principles rather than with institutional changes or innovations. I am fully aware of the current search for institutional means for bringing research and technological competence to bear more effectively on the problem of land use and urban development. I am not unmindful of the importance of ways and means. I am, however, convinced that institutions are, or should be, created to fulfill some purpose. Thus far our purposes in manipulating and planning environments remain ill-defined. Therefore it is not surprising that we

are dissatisfied with the present institutional mechanisms. This dissatisfaction is likely to continue until we have better defined the purposes that should determine the shape of the institutions needed.

It seems that one of man's most fundamental purposes is to insure the existence of a healthy, pleasant, varied, and interesting environment with maximum possibilities for human choice for as long into the future as is possible. At this stage in the human endeavor one cannot dispute the necessity of an advanced technology. But such a technology which makes possible vastly increased powers of environmental manipulation can be used for ill as well as good. Man would do well to heed the advice of Mumford when he exercises these new found powers: "The question always must be: What essential human need, viewed in historic perspective, is being fulfilled or is being sacrificed?" (26) Man's most serious threat to a satisfactory answer to this question is that his ever-increasing numbers will require that he adopt technological measures which, though necessary to sustain his swelling numbers, may override fundamental human values and purposes.

Given this broad perspective, what are some guiding principles that might usefully be invoked in planning the human environment?

First—one must realize that meaning, value, and purpose are what distinguish man from the rest of the biotic community. Unless man's behavior is merely random activity, it must be goal-directed, at least in part. His goals are many and are not immutable. They must be continually redefined by each generation and by each individual. They are often vague and poorly articulated, but they are a fact of existence nonetheless. Therefore, if man's

377

primary goal is to maximize his numbers, he need do little other than continue what he is now doing and Doxiadis' Ecumenopolis prescription may be fulfilled. If, however, this is not his overriding objective, and I submit there are far worthier aims, then it is a denial of the human heritage to dogmatically assert that he should make no attempt to influence his future. My first suggestion is that man engage in a conscious and continuous dialogue on where he is heading, where he wishes to go, and then attempt to so arrange his institutions as to make possible the latter. Only then can his institutions truly serve his basic needs. Time should figure prominently in this discussion—a long time. For when one attempts even the most cursory glimpse into the future over a period of time equal to man's past, a perspective on growth emerges that is compellingly different from that which now guides action.

For the moment it is likely that only an educated minority will be capable of meaningful participation in such a dialogue. This thoughtful minority is growing fast, but, meanwhile, it is absolutely necessary that those now in a position to exercise a leadership function do so with more candor and less flippancy than that evidenced in the past.

Second—the life of modern man is bound up in economics and technology, but for each a new perspective seems called for if man is to be well served. With respect to economics I suggest that a long term look into the future is absolutely essential to reconstruction of economics. Such a look would disclose that the basic problem facing twentieth-century man is ecological—the survival of the species in a humane environment for the longest period possible.

Boulding has made some preliminary gestures in this direction in his attempt to assess the economics of planet earth conceived of as a space-ship or closed system without unlimited reservoirs for either extraction or pollution, and where man must exist in a cyclical ecological system. (27) Boulding also tells me that his attempt produced little response, and economists continue in their preoccupation with production, consumption, and GNP. It is commonplace knowledge that Galbraith has long inveighed against the preoccupation with traditional economic concerns. One can hope these efforts will be emulated, and perhaps Weiskopf's sensitive and perceptive analysis of the impasse caused by our purely economic approach to the problem of means, ends, and human life presages a trend in that direction. (28)

While it is true that we cannot do without economics, it is equally true that we cannot long afford to indulge ecologically unrealistic economics. Gomer provides some insight here when he suggests that though cybernetic analogies are much overworked, the idea of feedback is useful because it emphasizes that only those changes which produce sufficiently strong inhibitory responses can be self-correcting while others will continue unchanged or be magnified. Though he addresses himself to the technological revolution in general his point that negative feedbacks have been slow to be felt, or are made manifest in subtle ways and thus have been obscured by the more clearly visible positive gains, is particularly applicable to our programs of environmental manipulation. Here strong positive feedbacks, largely economic, have tended to promote unplanned expansion. Gomer expresses it as "pressure for doing things most cheaply regardless

of ultimate cost to the society . . . If it is a little cheaper to build a steel mill on a lake dune, no matter how unique, chances are the mill will be built there." (29)

If, as Gomer suggests, this proclivity is merely a reflection of the values of our Society, then it becomes idle to talk about restructuring environmental planning without a previous alteration in values. Unless and until we change our sentiments, loyalties, and affections, constructive counterpressures will remain weak and relatively ineffective. The cultural readjustment required will depend heavily on the wisdom and statesmanship of the economist, for only by shifting attention from the narrowly economic to the more broadly ecological aspects of man's predicament can we reasonably expect to create and maintain a satisfactory environment.

With respect to technology I believe a much shorter term look is sufficient to provide evidence that we have not yet gotten on top of our technology, and, in most places, we are running rather fast in order to stand still. My study of the Brandywine showed this to be true with respect to stream pollution—increased pollutants effectively kept pace with a program of pollution abatement. The same appears true for automobile induced pollution.

Even more important than the ability of growth to negate technological advances, or to diminish their hoped-for benefits, is the fact that growth acts as a powerful forcing function causing the adoption of measures otherwise deemed unwise. In a recent paper I have suggested that Egypt's fantastic population growth has been such as to cause its leaders to invest heavily in the Aswan High Dam. The dam, justified on the basis that it will greatly increase needed agricultural outputs, will also create ecological conditions favorable to the spread of the fresh water snails acting as intermediate vectors for a debilitating parasitic disease known as schistosomiasis. This disease has so many and such far reaching undesirable concomitants that the wisdom of constructing the dam in advance of adequate control measures is open to serious question. (30) However, given Egypt's enormous population pressure as an accomplished fact, there appeared to be little choice but to construct the dam and hope that medical science will be able to mitigate the health hazard it represents.

Because vast technologically induced manipulations of the environment of the magnitude now contemplated can result in unknown changes that may be destructive as well as beneficent it is imperative that man do his utmost to avoid situations wherein sheer necessity compels the adoption of technological measures before their

safety has been proven or even reasonably tested. For this reason I find myself in full accord with the sentiments expressed recently by two officers of Travelers Research Center. Malone, speaking at a recent meeting of the AAAS, is reported to have warned that the possible consequences of weather modification must be weighed "before we are called upon to deal with them" and "the point is that there is still time for reflective thought, for setting objectives, for weighing alternative courses of action—in short, to act responsibly." (31) And Brooks cautioned that one must do more than "hope" that large scale intervention with natural processes will benefit mankind, but must "assure" that they do so. (32)

I see little hope that we can go from 3 to 30 billion people in less than a century without losing the time for the sober, reflective thought necessarily a prelude to such assurance. Instead I believe it is highly likely that such growth will force the adoption of otherwise indefensible measures. Which statement is simply to assert that there definitely are irreconcilable conflicts between quantity and quality of life.

Third—because quantity and quality of life have points of direct conflict and because the number and severity of such conflicts are likely to increase with a rapidly accelerating growth in population I propose that humanity engage in a great social experiment designed to reduce this conflict by getting to its source. More specifically, I would propose that each generation adopt as its goal the halving of the growth rate experienced by its predecessor. In order that this end might be accomplished a vast educational job will be required.

If man and his environment form a single interacting system, and if the reciprocal fit of man and environment is a focus of concern, then rationally induced change in man's behavior is fully as reasonable as is rationally induced change in his environment. Further elucidation of some simple facts and relationships and their widespread dissemination would disclose that the seemingly bold proposal calling for a reduction in growth rates does not ask humanity to make great personal sacrifices. It should be noted, for example, that if the next generation reduced its growth rate to 1% per annum, this would be equivalent to the fastest rate of growth mankind ever experienced until World War II, and, further, that the new rate would be achieved with far less deaths than was necessary to sustain the previous 1% rate of increase. The second future generation with a growth rate of 0.5% would be increasing at a rate equal to the fastest ever experienced until the twentieth century.

As background it should be reiterated that no society has ever managed to sustain its full reproductive capacity. Checks have always operated—consciously or unconsciously, by choice or by default. Today one notes that in North America, Europe, and Australia we already have a pattern of deliberately controlled births and this pattern is beginning to spread. The question then is not whether to control births—this we are already doing—but, rather, at what levels such controls should operate.

Economists in particular and social scientists in general might be brought into the venture to inform the public that a population approaching an equilibrium condition need not imply stagnation in economic, educational, and related social functions, but could instead provide the setting for qualitative increases in these functions, and would maximize the amount of freedom for individual growth and development. (33) Finally, in the new mood so generated, land planners could depict environmental alternatives to those now presented which are merely variations on Doxiadis' assumption of continued growth.

Fourth—despite the recency of planning as a profession and practice, I have encountered no dearth of plans, but instead note that existing plans rely heavily on expedience (lately ofttimes masquerading as incremental planning); are characteristically of limited scope, and, Ecumenopolis notwithstanding, of limited vision. Superior plans are unlikely to be forthcoming in the absence of a framework more amenable to the nurturing of such plans. Such a framework will require a much different vision of the future than is now commonly contemplated.

Barnett and Morse, presumably speaking for twentieth century man, state that ". . . unlike Mill, we do not look forward to a stationary state, with endless time to contemplate and devise a steady, costless improvement in the quality of life." (34) Because I regard the attainment of population stabilization to be an absolute ecological necessity in the not too distant future, and, for reasons suggested above a marked reduction of population growth rates to be a social desirability in the immediate future, I maintain that rapid evolution toward Mill's stationary state must be the cornerstone of any viable conservation position. Only then, with time as friend, not foe, would there be realistic hopes of devising environmental plans of more than limited scope and vision.

More than thirty years ago Aldo Leopold exclaimed:

We of the industrial age boast of our control over nature. Plant or animal, star or atom, wind or river—there is no force in earth or sky which we will not shortly harness to build "the good life" for ourselves.

But what is the good life? Is all this glut of power to be used for only bread-and-butter ends? Man cannot live by bread, or Fords, alone. Are we too poor in purse or spirit to apply some of it to keep the land pleasant to see, and good to live in? (35)

A serious consideration of Leopold's question is long overdue. But we have been too busy growing, too infatuated with the sheer exercise of power to give it more than passing notice. I believe adoption of the conservation position suggested would release man from his frantic and often frenzied efforts to keep abreast of the times. He might then contemplate the human condition in which the marriage of science and technology little more than a century ago gave man enormous powers, which, coupled with the exaggerated anthropocentrism of his Judeo-Christian heritage, has seen these powers exercised in ways increasingly destructive of the natural order. (36) Perhaps this contemplation might see a controlled and humane use of power replace power used merely for the sake of control. If this comes to pass, then one might even answer affirmatively that not at all frivolous question recently posed by an astronomer, "Is there intelligent life on Earth?" (37)

References

1. Russell, Bertrand, *The Future of Science*, pp. 83–84. New York: Philosophical Library, 1959.
2. Macinko, George, "Resources management and conservation; the approach of the Brandywine Valley Association." *Land Economics* 50(3): 318–324, 1964.
3. ———, "Saturation: a problem evaded in planning land use," *Science* 149: 516–521, 1965.
4. See inside cover of any issue of *Ekistics*.
5. Deane, Philip, *Constantinos Doxiadis*, p. 2. Dobbs Ferry, New York: Oceana Publications, 1965.
6. Ibid, p. 3.
7. This contention is not unique to Doxiadis but, instead, merely makes explicit the attitude toward growth that is implicit throughout contemporary planning thought.
8. *Ekistics* 20(116): 15, July 1965. This entire issue is devoted to a discussion of the City of the Future Project (COF) and the Ecumenopolis concept.
9. Ibid, p. 18.
10. These figures are taken from a lecture delivered by Doxiadis at the University of Michigan on September 28, 1966. Though they differ slightly from those given in the source cited above they are the most recent figures I have come upon.
11. That man may choose to behave differently—choosing deliberately to restrain growth in numbers, stopping short of that size imposed by external constraints—is a possibility seemingly never entertained.
12. *Ekistics*, op. cit., p. 51. This quote smacks of the "self-fulfilling forecast." For a discussion of the idea that such forecasts tend to create the future they predict see Dan. B. Luten, "Parks and People." *Landscape* 12(2): 5, Winter 1962. Luten observes that "the predictions of continued growth for California are themselves generating that growth."
13. *Ekistics*, op. cit., p. 11.
14. In examining the COF study I could find no evidence that serious attention was given to the distinction Mumford makes between the "probable" future and the vastly more numerous "possible" futures. Mumford suggests that if the probable future is not to one's liking, then man can and indeed is obliged to oppose it and by so doing help bring into being one of the more satisfying future possibilities. The COF study maintains not only that Ecumenopolis is the probable model of the future but that it is the only possible future. See Lewis Mumford, "Closing Statement," in *Future Environments of North America*, ed. F. Fraser Darling and John P.

Milton. Garden City, New York: 1966, pp. 718–719.

15. Bogue, Donald J., "The prospects for world population control (multilithed), p. 2, 1967.

16. Ibid, p. 11.

17. *Ekistics*, op. cit., p. 8.

18. A measure of the difficulty inherent in such an attempt might be gained by imagining that one parachuted an equal number of years into the past. How accurately might such an imaginary parachutist in 1833 assess resource availability for the year 1968?

19. Seitz, Frederick, from the Introduction to "The growth of world population: a report prepared by the Committee on Science and Public Policy (NAS-NRC publ. No. 1091, Washington, D.C. 1963).

20. "The growth of world population," p. 19.

21. For a counter to the argument that this or that aspect of behavior cannot be changed because it is a reflection of "human nature" see Clyde Kluckhohn, *Mirror for Man*, pp. 280, 287–288. New York: McGraw-Hill, 1949.

22. Bates, Marston, "Can animals survive in a fast-changing world?" (Part II). *Audubon* 65(6): 372, Nov.–Dec., 1963.

23. Davis, Kingsley, "The urbanization of the human population." *Scientific American* 213(3): 53, September 1965.

24. Fisher, Joseph L., "Perspectives on Population and Resources," Annual Report, Resources for the Future, Inc. 1963, p. 2.

25. Boulding, Kenneth E., *The Meaning of the Twentieth Century*, p. 135. New York: Harper and Row, 1964.

26. Mumford, op. cit., p. 727.

27. Boulding, Kenneth E., "The Economics of the Coming Spaceship Earth," in *Environmental Quality in a Growing Economy*. Baltimore: Johns Hopkins Press for Resources for the Future Inc., pp. 3–14, 1966.

28. Weiskopf, Walter A., "The Psychology of Abundance," in *Looking Forward: The Abundant Society* (pp. 3–12). Santa Barbara, California: Center for the Study of Democratic Institutions, 1966.

29. Gomer, Robert, "The tyranny of progress." *Bulletin of the Atomic Scientists* 24(2): Feb. 1968.

30. Macinko, George, "The Aswan High Dam: A Study in Tropical Resources Development." Presented before 62nd Annual Meeting, Association of American Geographers, Toronto, August 29, 1966 (unpublished).

31. Malone, Thomas F., *Science* 155:271, 1965. From a quote by J. V. Reistrup.

32. Brooks, Douglas L., "Looking Ahead," Annual Report, Travelers Research Center Inc., Hartford, Conn., 1966, p. 3.

33. Weiskopf, op. cit., p. 26. Weiskopf does not elaborate on this point and his setting is different from that suggested above but it provides a preliminary to some much needed studies. Ikle observes that a few decades ago the prevailing view was that demographic "stagnation" was bad, but that many now favor a stable population. He suggests that by the year 2000 more of us may favor John Stuart Mill's "stationary state" not only in the demographic sphere but also in the economic sphere—though not in culture. It is important to note, as does Ikle, that "stagnation" in one area (a stable population) need not imply stagnation elsewhere (in either the economic or cultural spheres).

 Ikle, Fred C., "Can social predictions be evaluated?" *Daedalus* 93(3): 750, Summer 1967.

34. Barnett, Harold J., and Chandler Morse, *Scarcity and Growth: The Economics of Natural Resource Availability*, p. 262. Baltimore: Johns Hopkins Press for Resources for the Future Inc. See Ikle, 1967, op. cit., for a different reaction to Mill's "stationary state."

35. Leopold, Aldo, *Game Management*, p. vii. New York: Charles Scribner's Sons, 1933.

36. White, Lynn, Jr., "The historic roots of our ecologic crisis." *Science* 155: 1203–1207, 1967.

37. Anonymous, Annual Report, Travelers Research Center Inc., Hartford, Conn., 1966, p. 4.

Science and the Study of Mankind

LAURA THOMPSON

The same American public that gets an undiluted diet of hostility toward "beings from outer space" from the communications media has had similar pap spooned to it for many years about primitive, i.e., non-industrial, people. Any show of intelligent compassion for whatever or whomever may be found on Mars or in the interior of New Guinea in fiction, films, or comic strips must be hailed as a sign of some ultimate unwillingness of the human spirit to be duped. At best, the usual portrayal of possible extraterrestrial life is humdrum and repetitive, however hard it tries to evoke images of a universe filled with ferocious antipathy to man. There is almost nothing good that can be said of the treatment of the primitive personality and society in our movies of the past 40 years unless it is that such slander was bound to provoke a reaction sooner or later. Nor have the graceless lies and unprovoked malevolence been limited to cheap media. The view of the world's dark-skinned people as quaint and ignorant has been as much a part of the National Geographic with its Great White Father complex and as much a part of history-as-taught-in-schools as the popular conviction that time began in 1492.

The misrepresentation of wild animals, of the possible nature and temperament of life elsewhere than on earth, and of the mentality of primitive people remained, over most of our history, unaffected by a persistent minority who believed differently, who were "soft," "emotional," or "romantic" in their conviction that tenderness and intelligence and complexity were no prerogatives of white Christian men. The change that is beginning to appear is largely due to cultural anthropology and to ethology, the science of animal behavior.

The truth is that contemporary primitives, like men for the past thousand generations, were "born equal" to us. Similarly, their cultures, which, even as ours, may be regarded as an interface between themselves and the world, are surely in some ways superior to our own.

THE EDITORS

THE REVOLUTION that has been taking place in science in the last century is apparently changing our conception of reality and the function of science regarding it. Indeed it seems to be overthrowing what we regard ordinarily as plain common sense: namely, the view of reality that is deeply embedded in, and perpetuated by, the peculiarities of Western European languages.

As is well known, our bias is related to the subject-predicate bifurcation of our sentence structure, which makes it impossible for us to formulate a sentence without a substantive either stated or implied, and which compels us to separate noun from verb, actor from action, form from function, etc. This linguistic peculiarity helps to condition us to the twofold slicing of experience so characteristic of Western civilization: i.e., our traditional division of "matter" from "mind," and our notion of matter as in itself inert and acted on only *externally* by forces. These and other grammatical forms characteristic of Western European languages are now recognized as having played an important role in structuring our world view, which we generally accept as simple common sense (*4; 13*, p. 53; *15; 16*).

Science, III: 559–563, 1950. Reprinted by permission.

On the other hand, fundamental to the revolution in modern science seem to be the following basic assumptions (*4*, p. 63; *10; 13*, p. 90; *17*):1. The external world is real and exists quite apart from any esthetic intuitions or logical assumptions on the part of man. 2. The external world is ordered and bound by immanent formative process or law according to which all of nature is interrelated and each event is an outgrowth of past events and a forerunner of future events. 3. The primary aim of scientific inquiry is not to understand what, ontologically speaking, these events are—since the nature of ultimate reality is beyond our reach as scientists—but rather to discover their inner dynamic relationships or structure.

All the sciences are gradually undergoing this revolution; but the social sciences, owing partly to their dependence on language as a basic means of expression and communication, are the last to be drawn into the great transformation. Since this lag in the development of the social sciences seems to be a crucial factor holding up the resolution of the current world crisis, it is important that social scientists concern themselves with it.

Actually, when we attempt to extend the new view of science to the study of mankind, it follows logically that man, as an integral part of nature, is a component in the dynamic natural order just postulated, and that the sciences of man are natural sciences. Furthermore, the ultimate aim of the scientist of mankind is recognized as that of attempting to understand man as part of the inherently lawful, dynamic natural order, that is, to understand man in his interrelationship with the world of nature, including other men. The significant units of research in the human sciences become human events

viewed as complex wholes in space and time; they become nature-culture-personality events and occasions in space and time. The meaningful type of problem concerning these units becomes the investigation of their dynamic structures, that is to say, their inner relationships in full environmental context. Logically, the solution of such types of problems requires the cooperative, integral efforts of the major sciences of man with the help of other basic sciences.

We may infer, furthermore, that by increasing our knowledge of the inner dynamic structure of a nature-culture-personality whole, we shall also increase our ability scientifically to predict future events to the extent that they are predictable; namely, to the extent that they are manifest within and determined by the structural whole (*7*, p. 59; *13*, pp. 90–91; *14*, p. 250). Finally, following through this hypothesis, it seems probable that, once we begin to describe nature-culture-personality wholes from the viewpoint of their inner dynamic structures, we shall be able to compare them and to establish scientifically valid similarities and differences in basic structures between them.

From these general considerations let us turn to a specific research project which has attempted to test the hypothesis. The Hopi Indians are one of five tribes[1] studied as part of the Indian Personality and Administration Research, sponsored jointly by the U. S. Office of Indian Affairs, the University of Chicago's Committee on Human Development, and the Society for Applied Anthropology. The Hopi

[1] The Navaho, Papago, Sioux, and Zuni tribes were also investigated as part of the project. For a list of project publications see reference 8. The writer was coordinator of the project from its inception in 1941 to its termination in 1947.

group consists of some four thousand Indians who, for more than fifteen centuries, have inhabited a few square miles of desert and semidesert highland in northern Arizona. A representative sample of two Hopi communities, expressing differing kinds and degrees of Euro-American influences, was investigated in total environmental setting and in historical perspective. Techniques from many sciences, including ecology, cultural anthropology, sociology, psychology, psychiatry, clinical medicine, and linguistics, were used integratively. From this broad-gauged, relatively precise analysis of the complex Hopi event in space and time have emerged facts and generalizations of theoretical and practical moment.[2]

Analysis of the Hopi nature-culture-personality integrate suggests that for at least fifteen centuries the Hopi tribe has played its life drama dependent on a relatively limited and isolated geographic area of such a nature as to allow a narrow range of choice regarding the group's adjustment to it. The arid northern Arizona plateau posed unyielding imperatives which had to be met habitually and unerringly if the tribe were to survive and reproduce itself generation after generation. Specifically, the existence of this group of sedentary agriculturists in Hopiland has always been linked with the regional water supply. The tribe's survival has depended on the presence of a few semipermanent springs used for drinking water and garden irrigation, on the retention of moisture in sand dunes used for dry farming, and on the fanning out of water at a time of flood in such a way as to allow arroyo

flood farming. Agriculture in Hopiland has always been limited and hazardous because of low rainfall and humidity, frequent droughts, floods, and storms, killing frosts, and pests. Although these Indians supplemented their farming by hunting in the vicinity of their mesas, subsistence was an ever present problem. No matter how industriously they stored up food to tide over their frequent crop failures, drought occasionally outlasted the food supply. Theirs was indeed an economy of scarcity. Thus the Hopi had constantly to cope with the problem of actual group survival and, although they solved this problem, it is likely that their precarious existence tended to take a physical toll in undernutrition, illness, and premature death, especially among the children.

Faced with these constant and intense environmental pressures, the Hopi through the centuries developed a social system which was apparently well adjusted to their indigenous needs. In brief, Hopi traditional society expresses a complementary relationship, a mutual dependence between a female-centered kinship system and a male-centered secret society system, integrated through an annual ceremonial cycle. The relationship between the kinship and secret society systems gives a fine balance to Hopi social organization and tends to equilibrate the status of men and women in Hopi society. Each sex has its unique and indispensable place, role, and function. The complementary biological functions of male and female are institutionalized in a complex, correlatively balanced social order. The system has been extended by means of totemic devices to include all classes of phenomena important to the Hopi life-way, so that it functions as a sort of cooperative supersociety

[2] Detailed documentation of the findings and generalizations from the Hopi project are presented in references 10 and 11.

embracing man and the world of nature. All phenomena of value in the Hopi world are traditionally believed to work together in a complex, interdependent relationship, for the common good, and no one class is dominant or subordinate to the others. The concepts of "rugged individualism" and "exploitation" are completely absent, for no individual functions for himself alone, but only as a member of a group that is a responsible part of the complex, reciprocally balanced whole.

In a traditionally organized Hopi pueblo every individual is expected to fulfill his obligations to the group with a minimum of supervision and with a minimum of external controls exercised by centralized authority or by physical force. Characteristically, social controls are diffused and internalized. They tend to extend inward in the form of a group-structured individual conscience which reflects the group's ethical code, and also they tend to extend outward to the farthest reaches of the Hopi natural and supernatural world. Traditional leadership is self-effacing, obligatory, and socially responsible. Indeed, exposed as the Hopi have been through the centuries to all the hazards of the external environment, including out-group attacks, they have developed a social system which apparently allows and encourages the development of their human potential to a high level of efficiency and a high degree of intensity.

We do not know how great a psychological toll in anxiety and frustration was exacted in ancient times by all these pressures. But the personality findings from children of the First Mesa community, where the ancient

Walpi, a Hopi pueblo—". . . of such a nature as to allow a narrow range of choice regarding the group's adjustment to it." (Photo by Milton Snow, Navajo Service, Window Rock, Arizona.)

social structure persists virtually intact, suggest that the balanced social system of the Hopi was reflected in a characteristically balanced and healthy personality structure, distinguished by its subtle complexity within definite boundaries; by its social, emotional, and artistic maturity within allowed areas; by its many-sided and deep-rooted control system; by its high puzzle-solving type of intelligence; and by its abstract, holistic, and at the same time practical, type of mental approach.

While the Hopi's basic-discipline training is definitely permissive and Hopi babies are characteristically happy and smiling, indigenous patterns of inducting the child into the social group, although nicely adjusted to the Hopi developmental curve, are relatively more systematic and concentrated and also more ritualized, than those of the other tribes studied in the Indian Personality and Administration Research, and relatively sterner methods are likely to be used when a child fails to meet social and moral expectations within the prescribed age range. Apparently these training patterns, in the context of Hopi social and cultural environment—which is both complicated and integrated in a balanced manner—tend to stimulate the child to a personality development that is somewhat precocious but at the same time emotionally balanced and socially mature, and of the kind needed to cope with Hopi life problems.

Finally, the findings suggest that the Hopi symbol system, expressed in language, mythology, ritual, and art, reflects a complex, subtly balanced, organic type of world view (2; 6). While the world is believed to be very dangerous, it is not unpredictable or erratic, nor is man at the mercy of

"... attempting to understand man as part of the inherently lawful, dynamic natural order ... to understand man in his interrelationship with the world of nature, including other men." (Photo at left courtesy Union Pacific Railroad. Photo at right by Milton Snow, Navajo Service, Window Rock, Arizona. Photo below courtesy Taos Chamber of Commerce, Taos, New Mexico.)

unpredictable or erratic forces. On the contrary, the universe is seen as a complex correlative system, controlled and regulated by natural law. There is no vagueness or inconsistency about man's role in this system, nor is it a subordinate or dependent one. And not only the character traits, but also the degree of intensity of emotional and mental energy needed to fulfill his role, are explicitly formulated and stressed. Indeed, the intensity of the Hopi's emotional and social atmosphere, as compared to that of the other tribes studied in the Indian Personality and Administration Project, seems directly to reflect the severity of environmental pressures and tensions that the tribe habitually sustains.

Thus, when the Hopi nature-culture-personality whole is analyzed as a multidimensional pattern of events in space and time, it reveals not only a high degree of integration, but also a delicately balanced, self-regulating type of structure.

Now I wish especially to point out that the type of structure described here appears to be similar to that which distinguishes ecologically balanced natural communities. Ecology teaches us that natural plant and animal communities tend in the course of time to move toward a delicately balanced, self-regulatory ecological arrangement in environmental context (5). In an ecologically balanced community the group supports the individual and the individual has to perform his particular function in the group. Characteristically, every individual has a place, a role, and a function in the whole arrangement, and this place, role, and function usually involve a certain unequivocal responsibility to the whole. The individual is an indispensable part of the whole

and is of vital importance to it. Moreover, the values of functions and roles are not weighted. The balance of the parts and the whole is self-adjusting and self-regulating—in other words, it is organic. Furthermore, by a process of symbiosis, accommodation, and competition, isolated plant and animal communities in the course of time tend to move toward an optimum or climax type of organization, in which characteristically every niche tends to be used to full advantage and every individual tends to function with minimum waste of energy or potential energy. The Hopi analysis suggests that, like isolated plant and animal communities, isolated human communities under certain conditions tend to develop in the course of time toward an ecologically balanced optimum or near-climax type within the total environment.

On the other hand, the analysis suggests that whereas optimum or near-climax types of plant and animal communities are characterized by a high degree of organic integration in the context of the total environment, such types of *human* communities are integrated, not only organically and functionally, but also symbolically. In other words, the whole tends to be integrated not only in the manner of natural communities but also in a distinctively *human* manner; that is, esthetically and logically (*1*, pp. 24–25; *6*).

An intensive study of the covert aspects of the Hopi culture, and especially an analysis of the Hopi language from the conceptual point of view and its interrelation with the world view, ritual, art, myth, social organization, and group personality structure, led to the inference that the whole had an inner coherence which was logical as well as esthetic. And this logico-esthetic integrating dynamic seemed to give to the

"In an ecologically balanced community the group supports the individual and the individual has to perform his particular function in the group." (Photo by Milton Snow, Navajo Service, Window Rock, Arizona.)

culture configuration its unique and persistent style [reference 7, p. 61].

Analysis of the Hopi nature-culture-personality integrate also reveals that the tribe is in the grip of a severe crisis of considerable historical depth and scope (10). This disturbance may be traced from its origin in the tribe's first contacts with the Spaniards in the 16th century through the period of Franciscan missions, Spanish wars, and Navaho raids, to more recent influences, especially those expressed in Protestant mission teachings, traditional Indian Service policies, and new federal policies. The analysis indicates that Mennonite mission influences tend to have a distintegrating effect on the Hopi socioreligious system, reflected in a disorganizing trend in male personality structure (12); that the traditional Indian Bureau policy in Hopiland has had a negative effect on Hopi welfare, modified somewhat by the inaccessibility and cultural resistance

of the tribe; that although federal policy and program have been changed officially, many individuals in Hopiland (both Indian and non-Indian) still express, in feeling, thought and behavior patterns, ideologies, and rationalizations similar to those underlying the traditional policy; and finally, that the new, integrative Indian Service policy, based on a positive philosophy regarding the creative nature of man and of society in environmental context, has had a markedly beneficial effect on the personal and social welfare of the tribe. The analysis also indicates, however, that, in Washington, and in the general American population, there is considerable misunderstanding of, and resistance to, the new federal policy and program in Hopiland.

The findings suggest that, although the Hopi crisis has a tribe-wide spread in its ecologic and biologic dimensions, it has reached acute proportions in its sociologic, psychologic, and symbolic dimensions only in communities where the traditional ceremonial and social system has broken down under white pressures. The findings viewed as a whole lead to the conclusion that the core of the crisis is cultural.

These findings and generalizations also suggest that in ancient near-climax types of human communities like those of the traditional Hopi, wherein an ecologically balanced and self-regulatory type of structure and a high degree of organic and logico-esthetic integration with the total indigenous environment have developed, new cultural elements and patterns may be added and many of the accoutrements (or much of the so-called "content") of the culture may change or even disappear, but under favorable circumstances the ancient culture structure will endure. Culture crisis is engendered not so much by changes in culture content as by disturbances in culture structure which generate a condition of imbalance in one or more essential dimensions of the culture and generate thereby a strain through the whole structure.

In an acculturation situation, aside from extermination or forced dispersal of the culture group, the factors most deeply disturbing to the balance of an optimum or near-climax type of culture thus seem to be intrusive influences which dislocate the logico-esthetic integration of the symbol system with the total environment. Next in importance as radically disturbing to such a culture type are attacks or influences which bring about a severing of the bond between the culture group and its geographic environment. Such radical disturbances may operate as determining factors in disintegrating the culture and the conditions which foster its particular type of personality.

Such cultural shocks—the deep disturbance of the symbol system, throwing off balance the distinctively human component of the culture, and the severance of the life line between man and nature whereon the culture developed—engender major crises. If not resolved, such crises may be fatal to the cultural whole and to the personality type it fosters. Somewhat less radical in effect, since they do not necessarily disintegrate the culture quickly—although they may do so in the long run—are alien influences which throw the sociological structure out of balance by attempting to superimpose incompatible political or economic systems.

Thus this research project suggests that in broad perspective, acculturation problems are problems in the dynamics of culture structures. A culture structure may endure, it appears, long after many of its outer accoutrements have disappeared or changed almost beyond recognition. Furthermore, the findings underscore and clarify the close relationship between acculturation problems and practical administrative problems of the community. They indicate that, basically, problematic situations of community administration may be reduced to scientific problems in culture structure analysis. In other words, it is the culture structure of a community in environmental context that sets the form of the administrative problem of that community from the viewpoint of community welfare. It follows, for example, that the integrative type of governmental administration, effectively implemented at the community level by social action research (3, 9), may be expected to be successful and psychologically healthy in human terms, from the long range community welfare viewpoint, because it allows the group to function by means of the structures of its culture in environmental context and to find its own solutions to new problems mainly through those structures. An integrative community administration and social action research allow indigenous solutions, indigenously structured. On the other hand, exotic, arbitrarily imposed types of administration may be expected, in the long run, to be unsuccessful and psychologically unhealthy in human terms because they attempt to superimpose arbitrary, rigid, and foreign culture structures on the community and tend thereby to dislocate indigenous structures and to engender culture crises.

According to the holistic, community-centered approach which emerges from the findings, the applied social scientist's primary role is viewed, not as one of adjustor, mediator, or troubleshooter, but rather as one of diagnostician and integrative leader in co-operation with the administrators and the residents of the community itself. Such an approach, it should be noted, logically implies that community governmental administration shall be designed to *serve* the community, that its personnel shall be selected and professionally trained according to the biosocial personality needs and trends and the resources of the particular local area, tribe, or community wherein they are to serve. It logically implies, furthermore, that administrative organization shall be decentralized to the extent that creative community administration is made possible, encouraged, and rewarded.

The findings, therefore, logically point to an integrative, democratic type of long range administrative policy, implemented by a program of social action research, as appropriate and effective in promoting the welfare of

the Hopi community and helping to resolve the Hopi crisis, and they explicitly define the structural foundations whereon such an administrative policy and program, if it is to be effective, has to be built.

Finally, we are given a clue as to the kind of community planning and self-cultivation that may be required for the development of enduring peace and mutual well-being in the world. The inference is that social planning need no longer be envisaged as "management" in either the gross meaning of the term or any of its subtle refinements. It may be viewed as self-discipline and self-cultivation.

According to this view . . . social planning would become a function of cooperative action research, initiated and implemented by the society (or the community) itself. In a self-perpetuating process of discovery, during which the members of the group come to understand their distinctively *human* potential, through the cooperative leadership of social scientists and with the aid of physical and biological scientists, the society's self-made plans might become actualities. Men would be able to discover for themselves through their own experience that by cooperating with one another and with the world of nature *as human beings*— as systematic symbol-builders and symbol-integrators—they might grow in the course of time to their full stature in a pluralistic world, logically and esthetically articulated for mutual prosperity and peace [reference 7, p. 63].

Hence from the inquiry have emerged significant clues regarding the development of universal, pluralistic, local community norms and methods for their implementation, whereby the findings of science may be applied to community-wide and world-wide practical problems—problems of political, economic, social, religious, and psychological import. Discovery and formulation of such pluralistic cultural norms and research methods in the sciences of man, adequate to the needs of the current world crisis, may be expected to open the way for the development of a more mature science of mankind which will have far-reaching practical significance.

References

1. Cassirer, E., *An Essay on Man.* New Haven: Yale Univ. Press, 1944.

2. Collier, J. and I. Moskowitz, *Patterns and Ceremonials of the Indians of the Southwest,* chap. 6. New York: E. P. Dutton, 1949.

3. Dobbs, H. A. C., *Operational Research and Action Research.* Washington, D. C.: Institute of Ethnic Affairs, 1947.

4. Korzybski, A., *Science and Sanity: An Introduction to Non-Aristotelian Systems and General Semantics.* Lancaster: International Non-Aristotelian Library, 1933.

5. Sears, P. B., *Life and Environment,* p. 100. New York: Teachers' College, Columbia University, 1939.

6. Thompson, L., *Amer. Anthrop.* 47: 540, 1945.

7. _____, *Phil. Sci.* 13: 53, 1946.

8. _____, *América Indígena* 10: 35, 40, 1950.

9. _____, *Sci. Mon.* 70: 34, 1950.

10. _____, *Culture in Crisis: A Study of the Hopi Indians.* New York: Harper and Bros., 1950.

11. Thompson, L., and A. Joseph, *The Hopi Way.* Chicago: Univ. of Chicago Press, 1944.

12. _____, *Amer. J. Sociol.* 53: 17, 1947.

13. Whitehead, A. N., *Science and the Modern world.* New York: Macmillan, 1930.

14. _____, *Adventures of Ideas.* New York: Macmillan, 1933.

15. Whorf, B. L. *Language, Culture and Personality: Essays in Memory of Edward Sapir.* Menasha: Sapir Memorial Publication Fund, 1941.

16. _____, *Tech. Rev.* **43**, No. 6, 1941.

17. Whyte, L. L., *The Next Development in Man.* New York: Henry Holt, 1948.

The Steady State: Physical Law and Moral Choice

PAUL B. SEARS

The crucial question about the relationship between science and ethics in our century has been exemplified in the development of the atomic bomb and personified by Robert Oppenheimer. Whether or not scientists can be held responsible for the uses to which their discoveries are put is not the question, but is perhaps only a device in a society looking for scapegoats. Nor is the question one of choosing deliberate ignorance over knowledge when the consequences of that knowledge could be perilous or the information put to wrong use.

The question is whether there are any ethical implications in or moral inferences to be drawn from the information accumulated by science. To take a concrete example, evolution is substantiated by a large body of data from paleontology, embryology, genetics, demography, behavior, comparative anatomy, physiology, and biogeography. Does all that information arrive in the hands of philosophers and metaphysicians as an amoral mass? Or does its internal logic and momentum carry the human situation with it in such a way as to inform the ethical decisions men must make?

Of course there is no fixed answer. An understanding of the valence of the oxygen atom in another context may not necessarily help in choosing a course of action. But that same valence is related to atmospheric stability and, by extension, to the continuation of life. It therefore implies a moral imperative, assuming a previous ethic recognizing the integrity of life.

The Key Reporter, 24(2): 2-3, 8, Jan. 1959.
Reprinted by permission of the publishers.

There are not many scientists who can interpret scientific data ethically, primarily because there are not many men of any sort capable of creative insight into ethical dilemmas. On the other hand there is nothing inherent in science or its practice which blinds its professors to ethical questions or to the wider relevance sometimes apparent and sometimes hidden in their studies. A few scientists are foolish enough to give their impressions too quickly; most are smart enough to resist that temptation altogether; and a very few are wise enough to translate directly from one sphere of knowledge to the other.

THE EDITORS

THE DREAM OF universal harmony is an ancient one. Often it has taken the nostalgic form of a Golden Age, long past. Again it appears as future promise. The dreamer who looks ahead often sees it all very simply. Let him and all who think alike with him have their way. Never has this been better set forth than by Dr. Rabelais.

"Then, ah then!" continued Homenas, ". . . then plenty of all earthly goods here below. Then uninterrupted and eternal peace through the universe, an end of all wars, plunderings, drudgeries, robbings, assassinates, unless it be to destroy these cursed rebels, the heretics."

In an earlier chapter Rabelais had given us a glimpse of a far nobler harmony—that of the Abbey of Thélème. Peopled by the generous and enlightened who could trust each other and tolerate differences, its motto was *Do What Thou Wilt*. But in the Prophetic Riddle just following he pictures a world disordered, too much like the present for comfort. It is here that one may see, if so minded, a brief, graphic, uncannily prescient forecast of the revolution that was to come less than three centuries later.

There are today four times as many human beings in the world as when those words were written. Old and stable social orders have broken up. New powers, through new knowledge, are at man's disposal. He has, in truth, become a geological force. The dream of ultimate harmony still persists, but the old cleavage remains. There are those who think the blessed state must come by eliminating all who do not think as they do. There are others who hope for a condition of mutual tolerance and restraint, founded upon some measure of common understanding.

These are moral problems, using that term in its broad and classic sense. But morality today involves a responsible relationship toward the laws of the natural world of which we are inescapably a part. Violence toward nature, as the Tao has it, is no less an evil than violence toward fellow-man. There can be no ultimate harmony among our own species in defiance of this principle. But more than that, we can find in certain concepts of natural science an invaluable guide as we struggle to attain a better order in our own affairs.

A disturbing paradox of this scientific age is the fact that its most profound implications have not sunk into our minds and become manifest in our behavior. Commonly—too commonly—we hear such glib phrases as "man's control of nature," "the necessity of an expanding economy," and "the conquest of space." As Ortega y Gasset has said, the effect of the industrial revolution has been to create an illusion of limitless abundance and ease, obscuring the ancient doctrine that effort and struggle are the price of human survival.

Thus in one sweep are brushed away the lessons of history, the wisdom so painfully gained through disciplined thought and intuition in the fields of ethics and aesthetics, as well as those aspects of natural science that could afford us perspective, rather than immediate convenience. A subtle and dangerous symptom of this last is the recurring objection to physical and biological analysis of man's estate.

Whatever else he may be, a human being is a physical object and a living organism. He is by no means an inert particle, nor is he exempt from physiological limitations. Enough of us have been caught, afoot or on wheels, in traffic jams, have been hungry and thirsty, and are sufficiently familar with birth and death to appreciate these facts. To mention them is not to say that human beings are mere particles or mere animals. Yet certainly one must be free to weigh any consequences that may result from a particular quality or property of mankind, without being condemned for applying physical or biological analogy to the demi-god, man.

There is precisely here a most delicate and important job of identification and discrimination. Could we clarify it, it might help lower the costly barriers that hamper free intercourse between scholars in the humanities and those in science—indeed, among scientists themselves.

An initial difficulty comes from confusing analogy with proof. Yet no matter how much the role of analogy may be abused, its importance as an aid to scientific investigation is very great indeed. Wisely selected parallels, or analogies, are the source of models that science can then test. A new situation, structure, or process suggests a familiar one, and we go on from there. The brown discoloration of a peeled apple suggests oxidation, and so it proves to be.

We can also isolate certain qualities in a system and study them profitably on their own merits. A notable instance is afforded with respect to mere increase in human numbers within a finite space. Obviously we cannot apply the laws that govern the dynamics of gas molecules strictly unless we are all playing blindman's buff with motion at random. This we are not doing, for eyesight and judgment enable human beings to pick open pathways, which molecules cannot do. Yet the general principle that freedom tends to diminish (or stress to increase) as numbers multiply not only applies in theory, but in historical fact.

The application may be pressed still further. When energy is introduced into a system, the stress increases. This obviously applies to the molecules in a kettle of heated water. I am unable to see why it does not apply with equal rigor to modern man who, through the internal combustion engine, is drawing upon the fossil energy of oil deposits, now being consumed at an estimated rate one million times faster than they have accumulated. By virtue of this process the average American moves, I should judge, some ten times faster than he did in 1900, and if so, covers one hundred times more territory. The evidence of stress as a function of numbers and energy is manifold. Yet we have reassuring voices telling us not to be disturbed, because the earth can support an indefinitely increased population.

Perhaps, with so much at stake, it is time to make certain we understand what science is, and what is its role in human affairs.

Science is the discovery and formulation of the laws of nature. In our enthusiasm we may forget that a law not only tells you what you can do, but what you cannot do. When we use our knowledge of natural law for specific problems we are practicing technology, not science. And because scientific technology has placed an estimated minimum equivalent of three dozen servants at the disposal of the average American, we are, quite naturally, more inclined to listen to promises than to warnings.

Yet the necessary warning can be stated quite simply. *The applications of science must be guided, managed, controlled, according to ethical and aesthetic principles and in the light of our most profound understanding.* Unfortunately we cannot set up an equation to show that because a thing is possible, it is necessarily wise and proper. If we could, it might simplify matters.

Certainly the application of science has been selective. An astute student of cultural processes, examining the western world, would note that science has been applied in spectacular fashion to the elaboration of consumers' goods, the reduction of mortality rates, and the tapping of fossil energy. He would also note certain consequences of this situation. Among them would be an explosion of human population without known precedent in the biological world, a lessening of the need for muscular effort, increased leisure, a startling multiplication of the rate of individual movement, dissipation of non-renewable resources, and disruption of natural cycles in the landscape. Nor would he be likely to overlook the signs of increasing tension upon the individual and the disintegration of value systems, which, whatever their limitations, have always exerted a stabilizing effect on human societies.

Our observer would find the question of man's relation to environment relegated to the fringes of serious scientific inquiry. He would uncover a wide-spread belief in the possibility of and necessity for a perpetually expanding economy. He would find economists well pleased if they could look ahead twenty-five years while a few scientists try honestly to peer much farther into the future. He would see that a great deal of effort is being given by the latter group to estimating the maximum number of human beings that could possibly be kept alive on earth, such estimates ranging from three to ten more times the present population. Concerning the quality of existence possible under such conditions he would discover a strange silence broken only by such bold prophets as Orwell, Huxley, and Sir Charles Darwin, the physicist.

Persisting, he would recognize other interesting conditions. Although the devising of means of human destruction continues uninhibited, frontal attack on the control of population pressure—difficult enough for technical reasons—is largely taboo. So are suggestions that human happiness might well be possible under a far less wasteful and consumptive economy. And while analysts are beginning to demonstrate that, beyond a certain limit, the expansion of any urban center means economic loss, not gain, their warnings carry little weight.

Modern society seems incalculably rich in means, impoverished in ends. The dazzling success of science in placing facilities at our disposal has left us all, including the scientist, a bit confused. Yet wisely enough the editor of a recent collection of studies on population points out that while the scientist possesses no special magic or superior methods for reaching policy decisions, he can offer sound knowledge, highly relevant to the making of value judgments.

There appears to be some consensus on one point: that an improved level of living for mankind is desirable. Such a blanket statement covers a multitude of possibilities, of course, although it clearly implies adequate nutrition, a better distribution of benefits, and relief from unnecessary hardship and suffering. But on the means of attaining this objective, we find ourselves in a bipolar atmosphere of world politics. One doctrine holds the individual generally competent to take part in decisions and provides elaborate safeguards to ensure him this privilege. The other sets up a monolithic structure in which the individual is submerged, ostensibly for his own good.

It would clarify, if not resolve, matters if we were to admit frankly that our Cold War is the third great religious conflict of the western world. The two previous ones were abated, not simply by military means, but more basically by concession to the idea of survival through dynamic equilibrium. Hope today lies in arriving at some similar agreement in principle, powerful enough to carry conviction, broad enough to tolerate the inevitable diversity that should enrich rather than impoverish human culture.

This brings us inescapably to a well-worn topic—the need for a better entente between the sciences and the humanities. Granting freely that science has frightfully disturbed the orderly world of the humanist, the latter has not, in my judgment, risen to the full opportunities that are his.

One cannot generalize about either humanists or scientists with any assurance, good manners aside. But this restriction does not apply so strictly to the fields they represent. A safe proposition is that neither of these vital activities should be carried on in isolation from the other.

"... I am far less interested in guessing how thickly mankind can be amassed on this planet and still survive than I am in the optimum quality of existence for those who do." Lake Anne Village, Reston, Virginia. (Photo by Blue Ridge Aerial Surveys, Leesburg, Virginia.)

Complicating the situation is the prevailing conviction that science holds the key to man's future. Julian Huxley has described this mood as "the airy assumption that 'science' will surely find a way out," a mood intensified by recent developments in the exploration of outer space. Yet it is clear enough that the fundamental problems of mankind are no longer technological, if they ever were, but rather cultural.

The need, in this neo-technical world, for the best that the humanities can offer is well-nigh desperate. It is the business of science to minimize the areas of uncertainty in human affairs. They remain large enough when this is accomplished. At this point we must begin to draw on the accumulated experience and wisdom of mankind to formulate, refine, and dramatize the ethical and aesthetic values that will guide us.

Values are the business of the humanities, and values clearly determine the direction of human effort. With incalculable powers at the disposal of mankind, the need for responsible control is correspondingly great. People shape their values in accordance with their notions of the kind of universe they believe themselves to be living in. The basic function of science is to illuminate our understanding of that universe—what it may contribute to human ease and convenience is strictly secondary.

399

Personally I am far less interested in guessing how thickly mankind can be amassed on this planet and still survive than I am in the optimum quality of existence for those who do. It is on this issue that the humanist must not desert us. We need his tempered judgment, his knowledge of great human achievement, his sensitive awareness of the creative human spirit to help us understand what, indeed, constitutes the good life. Doubtless this is an issue that can never be completely settled, but with each step that clarifies it, we shall have more guidance in our quest for a worthy goal.

Yet this goal must be sought with a realistic understanding of the natural world of which we are a part. We must know its possibilities and respect its limitations. We must scan it for hints and models, remembering that the organized system of life and environment has been operating more than a thousand times as long as the experience of our own species. Our knowledge of the vicissitudes of geological and climatic change, of organic competition, conflict, even extinction, should not blind us to the essential order behind it all. In our consumptive age we hear much talk of the danger of depleting our environment. A far more profound threat lies in our power to disrupt its orderly transformations of material and energy.

The confidence with which the physical scientist faces his task rests essentially upon a few basic assumptions with respect to the orderly behavior of energy and matter. One of the important concepts corollary to these principles is that of the steady state. Systems tend toward conditions of minimum stress and least unbalance —that is, toward equilibrium. Energy flowing into a system operates to upset this trend, unless the system is so organized as to transform that energy in orderly fashion, using it meanwhile to keep the system in good working condition. Such a system, that is, an open steady state, is approximated in living communities. Green plants utilize solar energy to build carbon compounds that sustain themselves and animals as well, while complementary processes return materials for fresh re-use.

The heat from a stove—energy—will keep the pot boiling so long as there is water in it. But it will not replace the water when it is gone, nor mend the pot when it melts. By contrast, an organized pattern of living communities is self-maintaining if energy is available.

These circumstances have long since caught the imagination of men. Harrison Brown and other analysts point out that if man continues to increase in numbers and per capita requirements his fate will depend on his success in tapping additional energy sources rather than on lack of materials. For example, the mineral content of a ton of granite or a cubic mile of sea water is most reassuring. The hitch comes in the energy cost of reclamation, yet the literature abounds in optimistic assurances that man is clever enough to turn the trick. Now and then, but not always, we see the added proviso that he must first learn how to behave himself better than he does. On a less responsible plane we continue to hear talk of an expanding economy, the conquest of nature, and man's unlimited future.

Poking about such an imposing edifice of technological statesmanship is creepy business, not unlike that of being near neighbor to a high-tension wire or an unguarded atomic pile. Yet certain naive probings seem unavoidable. Why not, for example, divert more of our scientific enterprise to studying the model that is before us, that has operated for more than a billion years, and has made our own existence possible?

Again, why continue, not only to tolerate, but to sponsor reckless and irresponsible multiplication of human numbers? Why accede to the notion that in a world where millions are hungry and malnourished through failure to apply the knowledge we now have, industrial enterprise must concentrate so largely on the mass production of what a philosopher would consider toys for adults?

Why worry so much about the other side of the moon when our cities, bursting at the seams, are erupting into an unplanned chaos? Why dream of escape to other planets when our own would respond generously to kinder treatment? Right and proper it is to push knowledge to the uttermost limits, but why not use what we have to clean the open sewers we call rivers, purify the air we must breathe, slow down the tragic waste of human ability, and get things about us shipshape? We are sweeping too much stuff under the bed, locking up too many closets.

Probably men will always differ as to what constitutes the good life. They need not differ as to what is necessary for the long survival of man on earth. Assuming that this is our wish, the conditions are clear enough. As living beings we must come to terms with the environment about us, learning to get along with the liberal budget at our disposal, promoting rather than disrupting those great cycles of nature —of water movement, energy flow, and material transformation that have made life itself possible. As a physical goal we must seek to attain what I have called a steady state. The achievement of an efficient dynamic equilibrium between man and his environment must always, in itself, have the challenge and the charm of an elusive goal. The infinite variety and beauty of the world about us, the incalculable facets of human experience, the challenge of the unknown that must grow rather than diminish as man advances in stature and becomes at home here— these are sufficient guarantee that a stable world society need never be a stagnant one.

The Land Ethic

ALDO LEOPOLD

WHEN GOD-LIKE Odysseus returned from the wars in Troy, he hanged all on one rope a dozen slave-girls of his household whom he suspected of mis-behavior during his absence.

This hanging involved no question of propriety. The girls were property. The disposal of property was then, as now, a matter of expedience, not of right and wrong.

Concepts of right and wrong were not lacking from Odysseus' Greece: witness the fidelity of his wife through the long years before at last his black-prowed galleys clove the wine-dark seas for home. The ethical structure of that day covered wives, but had not yet been extended to human chattels. During the three thousand years which have since elapsed, ethical criteria have been extended to many fields of conduct, with corresponding shrink-ages in those judged by expediency only.

The Ethical Sequence

This extension of ethics, so far studied only by philosophers, is actually a process in ecological evolution. Its se-quences may be described in ecological as well as in philosophical terms. An ethic, ecologically, is a limitation on freedom of action in the struggle for existence. An ethic, philosophically, is a differentiation of social from anti-social conduct. These are two defini-tions of one thing. The thing has its origin in the tendency of interdepen-dent individuals or groups to evolve modes of co-operation. The ecologist

calls these symbioses. Politics and economics are advanced symbioses in which the original free-for-all compe-tition has been replaced, in part, by co-operative mechanisms with an ethical content.

The complexity of co-operative mechanisms has increased with popu-lation density, and with the efficiency of tools. It was simpler, for example, to define the anti-social uses of sticks and stones in the days of the mastodons than of bullets and billboards in the age of motors.

The first ethics dealt with the rela-tion between individuals; the Mosaic Decalogue is an example. Later accretions dealt with the relation between the individual and society. The Golden Rule tries to integrate the individual to society; democracy to integrate social organization to the individual.

There is as yet no ethic dealing with man's relation to land and to the ani-mals and plants which grow upon it. Land, like Odysseus' slave-girls, is still property. The land-relation is still strictly economic, entailing privileges but not obligations.

The extension of ethics to this third element in human environment is, if I read the evidence correctly, an evolu-tionary possibility and an ecological necessity. It is the third step in a se-quence. The first two have already been taken. Individual thinkers since the days of Ezekiel and Isaiah have asserted that the despoliation of land is not only inexpedient but wrong. Society, however, has not yet affirmed their belief. I regard the present con-servation movement as the embryo of such an affirmation.

An ethic may be regarded as a mode of guidance for meeting ecological situations so new or intricate, or in-volving such deferred reactions, that the path of social expediency is not discernible to the average individual. Animal instincts are modes of guidance for the individual in meeting such situations. Ethics are possibly a kind of community instinct in-the-making.

The Community Concept

All ethics so far evolved rest upon a single premise: that the individual is a member of a community of interdependent parts. His instincts prompt him to compete for his place in that community, but his ethics prompt him also to co-operate (perhaps in order that there may be a place to compete for).

The land ethic simply enlarges the boundaries of the community to include soils, waters, plants, and animals, or collectively: the land.

This sounds simple: do we not already sing our love for and obligation to the land of the free and the home of the brave? Yes, but just what and whom do we love? Certainly not the soil, which we are sending helter-skelter downriver. Certainly not the waters, which we assume have no function except to turn turbines, float barges, and carry off sewage. Certainly not the plants, of which we exterminate whole communities without batting an eye. Certainly not the animals, of which we have already extirpated many of the largest and most beautiful species. A land ethic of course cannot prevent the alteration, management, and use of these "resources," but it does affirm their right to continued existence, and, at least in spots, their continued existence in a natural state.

In short, a land ethic changes the role of *Homo sapiens* from conqueror of the land-community to plain member and citizen of it. It implies respect for his fellow-members, and also respect for the community as such.

In human history, we have learned (I hope) that the conqueror role is eventually self-defeating. Why? Because it is implicit in such a role that the conqueror knows, *ex cathedra*, just what makes the community clock tick, and just what and who is valuable, and what and who is worthless, in community life. It always turns out that he knows neither, and this is why his conquests eventually defeat themselves.

In the biotic community, a parallel situation exists. Abraham knew exactly what the land was for: it was to drip milk and honey into Abraham's mouth. At the present moment, the assurance with which we regard this assumption is inverse to the degree of our education.

The ordinary citizen today assumes that science knows what makes the community clock tick; the scientist is equally sure that he does not. He knows that the biotic mechanism is so complex that its workings may never be fully understood.

That man is, in fact, only a member of a biotic team is shown by an ecological interpretation of history. Many historical events, hitherto explained solely in terms of human enterprise, were actually biotic interactions between people and land. The characteristics of the land determined the facts quite as potently as the characteristics of the men who lived on it. Consider, for example, the settlement of the Mississippi valley. In the years following the Revolution, three groups were contending for its control: the native Indian, the French and English traders, and the American settlers. Historians wonder what would have happened if the English at Detroit had thrown a little more weight into the Indian side of those tipsy scales which decided the outcome of the colonial migration into the cane-lands of Kentucky. It is time now to ponder the fact that the cane-lands, when subjected to the particular mixture of forces represented by the cow, plow, fire, and axe of the pioneer, became bluegrass. What if the plant succession inherent in this dark and bloody ground had, under the impact of these forces, given us some worthless sedge, shrub, or weed? Would Boone and Kenton have held out? Would there have been any overflow into Ohio, Indiana, Illinois, and Missouri? Any Louisiana Purchase? Any transcontinental union of new states? Any Civil War?

Kentucky was one sentence in the drama of history. We are commonly told what the human actors in this drama tried to do, but we are seldom told that their success, or the lack of it, hung in large degree on the reaction of particular soils to the impact of the particular forces exerted by their occupancy. In the case of Kentucky, we do not even know where the bluegrass came from—whether it is a native species, or a stowaway from Europe.

Contrast the cane-lands with what hindsight tells us about the Southwest, where the pioneers were equally brave, resourceful, and persevering. The impact of occupancy here brought no

"The fallacy that economic determinists have tied around our collective neck . . . is the belief that economics determines *all* land-use. This is simply not true." (Photo by Soil Conservation Service, Courtesy U.S. Department of Agriculture.)

bluegrass, or other plant fitted to withstand the bumps and buffetings of hard use. This region, when grazed by livestock, reverted through a series of more and more worthless grasses, shrubs, and weeds to a condition of unstable equilibrium. Each recession of plant types bred erosion; each increment to erosion bred a further recession of plants. The result today is a progressive and mutual deterioration, not only of plants and soils, but of the animal community subsisting thereon. The early settlers did not expect this: on the ciénegas of New Mexico some even cut ditches to hasten it. So subtle has been its progress that few residents of the region are aware of it. It is quite invisible to the tourist who finds this wrecked landscape colorful and charming (as indeed it is, but it bears scant resemblance to what it was in 1848).

This same landscape was "developed" once before, but with quite different results. The Pueblo Indians settled the Southwest in pre-Columbian times, but they happened *not* to be equipped with range livestock. Their civilization expired, but not because their land expired.

In India, regions devoid of any sod-forming grass have been settled, apparently without wrecking the land, by the simple expedient of carrying the grass to the cow, rather than vice versa. (Was this the result of some deep wisdom, or was it just good luck? I do not know.)

In short, the plant succession steered the course of history; the pioneer simply demonstrated, for good or ill, what successions inhered in the land. Is history taught in this spirit? It will be, once the concept of land as a community really penetrates our intellectual life.

The Ecological Conscience

Conservation is a state of harmony between men and land. Despite nearly a century of propaganda, conservation still proceeds at a snail's pace; progress still consists largely of letterhead pieties and convention oratory. On the back forty we still slip two steps backward for each forward stride.

The usual answer to this dilemma is "more conservation education." No one will debate this, but is it certain that only the *volume* of education needs stepping up? Is something lacking in the *content* as well?

It is difficult to give a fair summary of its content in brief form, but, as I understand it, the content is substantially this: obey the law, vote right, join some organizations, and practice what conservation is profitable on your own land; the government will do the rest.

Is not this formula too easy to accomplish anything worth-while? It defines no right or wrong, assigns no obligation, calls for no sacrifice, implies no change in the current philosophy of values. In respect of land-use, it urges only enlightened self-interest. Just how far will such education take us? An example will perhaps yield a partial answer.

By 1930 it had become clear to all except the ecologically blind that southwestern Wisconsin's topsoil was slipping seaward. In 1933 the farmers were told that if they would adopt certain remedial practices for five years, the public would donate CCC labor to install them, plus the necessary machinery and materials. The offer was widely accepted, but the practices were widely forgotten when the five-year contract period was up. The farmers continued only those practices that yielded an immediate and visible economic gain for themselves.

405

This led to the idea that maybe farmers would learn more quickly if they themselves wrote the rules. Accordingly the Wisconsin Legislature in 1937 passed the Soil Conservation District Law. This said to farmers, in effect: *We, the public, will furnish you free technical service and loan you specialized machinery, if you will write your own rules for land-use. Each county may write its own rules, and these will have the force of law.* Nearly all the counties promptly organized to accept the proffered help, but after a decade of operation, *no county has yet written a single rule.* There has been visible progress in such practices as strip-cropping, pasture renovation, and soil liming, but none in fencing woodlots against grazing, and none in excluding plow and cow from steep slopes. The farmers, in short, have selected those remedial practices which were profitable anyhow, and ignored those which were profitable to the community, but not clearly profitable to themselves.

When one asks why no rules have been written, one is told that the community is not yet ready to support them; education must precede rules. But the education actually in progress makes no mention of obligations to land over and above those dictated by self-interest. The net result is that we have more education but less soil, fewer healthy woods, and as many floods as in 1937.

The puzzling aspect of such situations is that the existence of obligations over and above self-interest is taken for granted in such rural community enterprises as the betterment of roads, schools, churches, and baseball teams. Their existence is not taken for granted, nor as yet seriously discussed, in bettering the behavior of the water that falls on the land, or in the preserving of the beauty or diversity of the farm landscape. Land-use ethics are still governed wholly by economic self-interest, just as social ethics were a century ago.

To sum up: we asked the farmer to do what he conveniently could to save his soil, and he has done just that, and only that. The farmer who clears the woods off a 75 per cent slope, turns his cows into the clearing, and dumps its rainfall, rocks, and soil into the community creek, is still (if otherwise decent) a respected member of society. If he puts lime on his fields and plants his crops on contour, he is still entitled to all the privileges and emoluments of his Soil Conservation District. The District is a beautiful piece of social machinery, but it is coughing along on two cylinders because we have been too timid, and too anxious for quick success, to tell the farmer the true magnitude of his obligations. Obligations have no meaning without conscience, and the problem we face is the extension of the social conscience from people to land.

No important change in ethics was ever accomplished without an internal change in our intellectual emphasis, loyalties, affections, and convictions. The proof that conservation has not yet touched these foundations of conduct lies in the fact that philosophy and religion have not yet heard of it. In our attempt to make conservation easy, we have made it trivial.

Substitutes for a Land Ethic

When the logic of history hungers for bread and we hand out a stone, we are at pains to explain how much the stone resembles bread. I now describe some of the stones which serve in lieu of a land ethic.

One basic weakness in a conservation system based wholly on economic motives is that most members of the land community have no economic value. Wildflowers and songbirds are examples. Of the 22,000 higher plants and animals native to Wisconsin, it is doubtful whether more than 5 per cent can be sold, fed, eaten, or otherwise put to economic use. Yet these creatures are members of the biotic community, and if (as I believe) its stability depends on its integrity, they are entitled to continuance.

When one of these non-economic categories is threatened, and if we happen to love it, we invent subterfuges to give it economic importance. At the beginning of the century songbirds were supposed to be disappearing. Ornithologists jumped to the rescue with some distinctly shaky evidence to the effect that insects would eat us up if birds failed to control them. The evidence had to be economic in order to be valid.

It is painful to read these circumlocutions today. We have no land ethic yet, but we have at least drawn nearer the point of admitting that birds should continue as a matter of biotic right, regardless of the presence or absence of economic advantage to us.

A parallel situation exists in respect of predatory mammals, raptorial birds, and fish-eating birds. Time was when biologists somewhat overworked the evidence that these creatures preserve the health of game by killing weaklings, or that they control rodents for the farmer, or that they prey only on "worthless" species. Here again, the evidence had to be economic in order to be valid. It is only in recent years that we hear the more honest argument that predators are members of the community, and that no special interest has the right to exterminate them for the sake of a benefit, real or fancied, to itself. Unfortunately this enlightened view is still in the talk stage. In the field the extermination of predators goes merrily on: witness the impending erasure of the timber wolf by fiat of Congress, the Conservation Bureaus, and many state legislatures.

Some species of trees have been "read out of the party" by economics-minded foresters because they grow too slowly, or have too low a sale value to pay as timber crops: white cedar, tamarack, cypress, beech, and hemlock are examples. In Europe, where forestry is ecologically more advanced, the non-commercial tree species are recognized as members of the native forest community, to be preserved as such, within reason. Moreover some (like beech) have been found to have a valuable function in building up soil fertility. The interdependence of the forest and its constituent tree species, ground flora, and fauna is taken for granted.

Lack of economic value is sometimes a character not only of species or groups, but of entire biotic communities: marshes, bogs, dunes, and "deserts" are examples. Our formula in such cases is to relegate their conservation to government as refuges, monuments, or parks. The difficulty is that these communities are usually interspersed with more valuable private lands; the government cannot possibly own or control such scattered parcels. The net effect is that we have relegated some of them to ultimate extinction over large areas. If the private owner were ecologically minded, he would be proud to be the custodian of a reasonable proportion of such areas, which add diversity and beauty to his farm and to his community.

In some instances, the assumed lack of profit in these "waste" areas has proved to be wrong, but only after most of them had been done away with. The present scramble to reflood muskrat marshes is a case in point.

There is a clear tendency in American conservation to relegate to government all necessary jobs that private landowners fail to perform. Government ownership, operation, subsidy, or regulation is now widely prevalent in forestry, range management, soil and watershed management, park and wilderness conservation, fisheries management, and migratory bird management, with more to come. Most of this growth in governmental conservation is proper and logical, some of it is inevitable. That I imply no disapproval of it is implicit in the fact that I have spent most of my life working for it. Nevertheless the question arises: What is the ultimate magnitude of the enterprise? Will the tax base carry its eventual ramifications? At what point will governmental conservation, like the mastodon, become handicapped by its own dimensions? The answer, if there is any, seems to be in a land ethic, or some other force which assigns more obligation to the private landowner.

Industrial landowners and users, especially lumbermen and stockmen, are inclined to wail long and loudly about the extension of government ownership and regulation to land, but (with notable exceptions) they show little disposition to develop the only visible alternative: the voluntary practice of conservation on their own lands.

When the private landowner is asked to perform some unprofitable act for the good of the community, he today assents only with outstretched palm. If the act costs him cash this is fair and proper, but when it costs only forethought, open-mindedness, or time, the issue is at least debatable. The overwhelming growth of land-use subsidies

in recent years must be ascribed, in large part, to the government's own agencies for conservation education: the land bureaus, the agricultural colleges, and the extension services. As far as I can detect, no ethical obligation toward land is taught in these institutions.

To sum up: a system of conservation based solely on economic self-interest is hopelessly lopsided. It tends to ignore, and thus eventually to eliminate, many elements in the land community that lack commercial value, but that are (as far as we know) essential to its healthy functioning. It assumes, falsely, I think, that the economic parts of the biotic clock will function without the uneconomic parts. It tends to relegate to government many functions eventually too large, too complex, or too widely dispersed to be performed by government.

An ethical obligation on the part of the private owner is the only visible remedy for these situations.

The Land Pyramid

An ethic to supplement and guide the economic relation to land presupposes the existence of some mental image of land as a biotic mechanism. We can be ethical only in relation to something we can see, feel, understand, love, or otherwise have faith in.

The image commonly employed in conservation education is "the balance of nature." For reasons too lengthy to detail here, this figure of speech fails to describe accurately what little we know about the land mechanism. A much truer image is the one employed in ecology: the biotic pyramid. I shall first sketch the pyramid as a symbol of land, and later develop some of its implications in terms of land-use.

408

Plants absorb energy from the sun. This energy flows through a circuit called the biota, which may be represented by a pyramid consisting of layers. The bottom layer is the soil. A plant layer rests on the soil, an insect layer on the plants, a bird and rodent layer on the insects, and so on up through various animal groups to the apex layer, which consists of the larger carnivores.

The species of a layer are alike not in where they came from, or in what they look like, but rather in what they eat. Each successive layer depends on those below it for food and often for other services, and each in turn furnishes food and services to those above. Proceeding upward, each successive layer decreases in numerical abundance. Thus, for every carnivore there are hundreds of his prey, thousands of their prey, millions of insects, uncountable plants. The pyramidal form of the system reflects this numerical progression from apex to base. Man shares an intermediate layer with the bears, raccoons, and squirrels which eat both meat and vegetables.

The lines of dependency for food and other services are called food chains. Thus soil-oak-deer-Indian is a chain that has now been largely converted to soil-corn-cow-farmer. Each species, including ourselves, is a link in many chains. The deer eats a hundred plants other than oak, and the cow a hundred plants other than corn. Both, then, are links in a hundred chains. The pyramid is a tangle of chains so complex as to seem disorderly, yet the stability of the system proves it to be a highly organized structure. Its functioning depends on the co-operation and competition of its diverse parts.

In the beginning, the pyramid of life was low and squat; the food chains short and simple. Evolution has added layer after layer, link after link. Man is one of thousands of accretions to the height and complexity of the pyramid. Science has given us many doubts, but it has given us at least one certainty: the trend of evolution is to elaborate and diversify the biota.

Land, then, is not merely soil; it is a fountain of energy flowing through a circuit of soils, plants, and animals. Food chains are the living channels which conduct energy upward; death and decay return it to the soil. The circuit is not closed; some energy is dissipated in decay, some is added by absorption from the air, some is stored in soils, peats, and long-lived forests; but it is a sustained circuit, like a slowly augmented revolving fund of life. There is always a net loss by downhill wash, but this is normally small and offset by the decay of rocks. It is deposited in the ocean and, in the course of geological time, raised to form new lands and new pyramids.

The velocity and character of the upward flow of energy depend on the complex structure of the plant and animal community, much as the upward flow of sap in a tree depends on its complex cellular organization. Without this complexity, normal circulation would presumably not occur. Structure means the characteristic numbers, as well as the characteristic kinds and functions, of the component species. This interdependence between the complex structure of the land and its smooth functioning as an energy unit is one of its basic attributes.

When a change occurs in one part of the circuit, many other parts must adjust themselves to it. Change does not necessarily obstruct or divert the flow of energy; evolution is a long series of self-induced changes, the net result of which has been to elaborate the flow mechanism and to lengthen the circuit.

410

Evolutionary changes, however, are usually slow and local. Man's invention of tools has enabled him to make changes of unprecedented violence, rapidity, and scope.

One change is in the composition of floras and faunas. The larger predators are lopped off the apex of the pyramid; food chains, for the first time in history, become shorter rather than longer. Domesticated species from other lands are substituted for wild ones, and wild ones are moved to new habitats. In this world-wide pooling of faunas and floras, some species get out of bounds as pests and diseases, others are extinguished. Such effects are seldom intended or foreseen; they represent unpredicted and often untraceable readjustments in the structure. Agricultural science is largely a race between the emergence of new pests and the emergence of new techniques for their control.

Another change touches the flow of energy through plants and animals and its return to the soil. Fertility is the ability of soil to receive, store, and release energy. Agriculture, by overdrafts on the soil, or by too radical a substitution of domestic for native species in the superstructure, may derange the channels of flow or deplete storage. Soils depleted of their storage, or of the organic matter which anchors it, wash away faster than they form. This is erosion.

Waters, like soil, are part of the energy circuit. Industry, by polluting waters or obstructing them with dams, may exclude the plants and animals necessary to keep energy in circulation.

Transportation brings about another basic change: the plants or animals grown in one region are now consumed and returned to the soil in another. Transportation taps the energy stored in rocks, and in the air, and uses it elsewhere; thus we fertilize the garden with nitrogen gleaned by the guano birds from the fishes of seas on the other side of the Equator. Thus the formerly localized and self-contained circuits are pooled on a world-wide scale.

The process of altering the pyramid for human occupation releases stored energy, and this often gives rise, during the pioneering period, to a deceptive exuberance of plant and animal life, both wild and tame. These releases of biotic capital tend to becloud or postpone the penalties of violence.

This thumbnail sketch of land as an energy circuit conveys three basic ideas:

(1) That land is not merely soil.

(2) That the native plants and animals kept the energy circuit open; others may or may not.

(3) That man-made changes are of a different order than evolutionary changes, and have effects more comprehensive than is intended or foreseen.

These ideas, collectively, raise two basic issues: Can the land adjust itself to the new order? Can the desired alterations be accomplished with less violence?

Biotas seem to differ in their capacity to sustain violent conversion. Western Europe, for example, carries a far different pyramid than Caesar found there. Some large animals are lost; swampy forests have become meadows or plowland; many new plants and animals are introduced, some of which escape as pests; the remaining natives are greatly changed in distribution and abundance. Yet the soil is still there and, with the help of imported nutrients, still fertile; the waters flow normally; the new structure seems to function and to persist. There is no visible stoppage or derangement of the circuit.

Western Europe, then, has a resistant biota. Its inner processes are tough, elastic, resistant to strain. No matter how violent the alterations, the pyramid, so far, has developed some new *modus vivendi* which preserves its habitability for man, and for most of the other natives.

Japan seems to present another instance of radical conversion without disorganization.

Most other civilized regions, and some as yet barely touched by civilization, display various stages of disorganization, varying from initial symptoms to advanced wastage. In Asia Minor and North Africa diagnosis is confused by climatic changes, which may have been either the cause or the effect of advanced wastage. In the United States the degree of disorganization varies locally; it is worst in the Southwest, the Ozarks, and parts of the South, and least in New England and the Northwest. Better land-uses may still arrest it in the less advanced regions. In parts of Mexico, South America, South Africa, and Australia a violent and accelerating wastage is in progress, but I cannot assess the prospects.

This almost world-wide display of disorganization in the land seems to be similar to disease in an animal, except that it never culminates in complete disorganization or death. The land recovers, but at some reduced level of complexity, and with a reduced carrying capacity for people, plants, and animals. Many biotas currently regarded as "lands of opportunity" are in fact already subsisting on exploitative agriculture, i.e. they have already exceeded their sustained carrying capacity. Most of South America is over-populated in this sense.

In arid regions we attempt to offset the process of wastage by reclamation, but it is only too evident that the prospective longevity of reclamation projects is often short. In our own West, the best of them may not last a century.

The combined evidence of history and ecology seems to support one general deduction: the less violent the man-made changes, the greater the probability of successful readjustment in the pyramid. Violence, in turn, varies with human population density; a dense population requires a more violent conversion. In this respect, North America has a better chance for permanence than Europe, if she can contrive to limit her density.

This deduction runs counter to our current philosophy, which assumes that because a small increase in density enriched human life, that an indefinite increase will enrich it indefinitely. Ecology knows of no density relationship that holds for indefinitely wide limits. All gains from density are subject to a law of diminishing returns.

Whatever may be the equation for men and land, it is improbable that we as yet know all its terms. Recent discoveries in mineral and vitamin nutrition reveal unsuspected dependencies in the up-circuit: incredibly minute quantities of certain substances determine the value of soils to plants, of plants to animals. What of the down-circuit? What of the vanishing species, the preservation of which we now regard as an esthetic luxury? They helped build the soil; in what unsuspected ways may they be essential to its maintenance? Professor Weaver proposes that we use prairie flowers to refloculate the wasting soils of the dust bowl; who knows for what purpose cranes and condors, otters and grizzlies may some day be used?

Land Health and the A-B Cleavage

A land ethic, then, reflects the existence of an ecological conscience, and this in turn reflects a conviction of individual responsibility for the health of the land. Health is the capacity of the land for self-renewal. Conservation is our effort to understand and preserve this capacity.

Conservationists are notorious for their dissensions. Superficially these seem to add up to mere confusion, but a more careful scrutiny reveals a single plane of cleavage common to many specialized fields. In each field one group (A) regards the land as soil, and its function as commodity-production; another group (B) regards the land as a biota, and its function as something broader. How much broader is admittedly in a state of doubt and confusion.

In my own field, forestry, group A is quite content to grow trees like cabbages, with cellulose as the basic forest commodity. It feels no inhibition against violence; its ideology is agronomic. Group B, on the other hand, sees forestry as fundamentally different from agronomy because it employs natural species, and manages a natural environment rather than creating an artificial one. Group B prefers natural reproduction on principle. It worries on biotic as well as economic grounds about the loss of species like chestnut, and the threatened loss of the white pines. It worries about a whole series of secondary forest functions: wildlife, recreation, watersheds, wilderness areas. To my mind, Group B feels the stirrings of an ecological conscience.

In the wildlife field, a parallel cleavage exists. For Group A the basic commodities are sport and meat; the yardsticks of production are ciphers of take in pheasants and trout. Artificial propagation is acceptable as a permanent as well as a temporary recourse—if its unit costs permit. Group B, on the other hand, worries about a whole series of biotic side-issues. What is the cost in predators of producing a game crop? Should we have further recourse to exotics? How can management restore the shrinking species, like prairie grouse, already hopeless as shootable game? How can management restore the threatened rarities, like trumpeter swan and whooping crane? Can management principles be extended to wildflowers? Here again it is clear to me that we have the same A-B cleavage as in forestry.

In the larger field of agriculture I am less competent to speak, but there seem to be somewhat parallel cleavages. Scientific agriculture was actively developing before ecology was born, hence a slower penetration of ecological concepts might be expected. Moreover the farmer, by the very nature of his techniques, must modify the biota more radically than the forester or the wildlife manager. Nevertheless, there are many discontents in agriculture which seem to add up to a new vision of "biotic farming."

Perhaps the most important of these is the new evidence that poundage or tonnage is no measure of the food-value of farm crops; the products of fertile soil may be qualitatively as well as quantitatively superior. We can bolster poundage from depleted soils by pouring on imported fertility, but we are not necessarily bolstering food-value. The possible ultimate ramifications of this idea are so immense that I must leave their exposition to abler pens.

The discontent that labels itself "organic farming," while bearing some of the earmarks of a cult, is nevertheless biotic in its direction, particularly in its insistence on the importance of soil flora and fauna.

The ecological fundamentals of agriculture are just as poorly known to the public as in other fields of land-use. For example, few educated people realize that the marvelous advances in technique made during recent decades are improvements in the pump, rather than the well. Acre for acre, they have barely sufficed to offset the sinking level of fertility.

In all of these cleavages, we see repeated the same basic paradoxes: man the conqueror *versus* man the biotic citizen; science the sharpener of his sword *versus* science the searchlight on his universe; land the slave and servant *versus* land the collective organism. Robinson's injunction to Tristram may well be applied, at this juncture, to *Homo sapiens* as a species in geological time:

Whether you will or not
You are a King, Tristram, for you are one
Of the time-tested few that leave the world,
When they are gone, not the same place
    it was.
Mark what you leave.

The Outlook

It is inconceivable to me that an ethical relation to land can exist without love, respect, and admiration for land, and a high regard for its value. By value, I of course mean something far broader than mere economic value; I mean value in the philosophical sense.

Perhaps the most serious obstacle impeding the evolution of a land ethic is the fact that our educational and economic system is headed away from, rather than toward, an intense consciousness of land. Your true modern is separated from the land by many middlemen, and by innumerable physical gadgets. He has no vital relation to it; to him it is the space between cities on which crops grow. Turn him loose for a day on the land, and if the spot does not happen to be a golf links or a "scenic" area, he is bored stiff. If crops could be raised by hydroponics instead of farming, it would suit him very well. Synthetic substitutes for wood, leather, wool, and other natural land products suit him better than the originals. In short, land is something he has "outgrown."

Almost equally serious as an obstacle to a land ethic is the attitude of the farmer for whom the land is still an adversary, or a taskmaster that keeps him in slavery. Theoretically, the mechanization of farming ought to cut the farmer's chains, but whether it really does is debatable.

One of the requisites for an ecological comprehension of land is an understanding of ecology, and this is by no means co-extensive with "education"; in fact, much higher education seems deliberately to avoid ecological concepts. An understanding of ecology does not necessarily originate in courses bearing ecological labels; it is quite as likely to be labeled geography, botany, agronomy, history, or economics. This is as it should be, but whatever the label, ecological training is scarce.

The case for a land ethic would appear hopeless but for the minority which is in obvious revolt against these "modern" trends.

The "key-log" which must be moved to release the evolutionary process for an ethic is simply this: quit thinking about decent land-use as solely an economic problem. Examine each question in terms of what is ethically and esthetically right, as well as what is economically expedient. A thing is right when it tends to preserve the integrity, stability, and beauty of the biotic community. It is wrong when it tends otherwise.

It of course goes without saying that economic feasibility limits the tether of what can or cannot be done for land. It always has and it always will. The fallacy the economic determinists have tied around our collective neck, and which we now need to cast off, is the belief that economics determines *all* land-use. This is simply not true. An innumerable host of actions and attitudes, comprising perhaps the bulk of all land relations, is determined by the land-user's tastes and predilections, rather than by his purse. The bulk of all land relations hinges on investments of time, forethought, skill, and faith rather than on investments of cash. As a land-user thinketh, so is he.

I have purposely presented the land ethic as a product of social evolution because nothing so important as an ethic is ever "written." Only the most superficial student of history supposes that Moses "wrote" the Decalogue; it evolved in the minds of a thinking community, and Moses wrote a tentative summary of it for a "seminar." I say tentative because evolution never stops.

The evolution of a land ethic is an intellectual as well as emotional process. Conservation is paved with good intentions which prove to be futile, or even dangerous, because they are devoid of critical understanding either of the land, or of economic land-use. I think it is a truism that as the ethical frontier advances from the individual to the community, its intellectual content increases.

The mechanism of operation is the same for any ethic: social approbation for right actions: social disapproval for wrong actions.

By and large, our present problem is one of attitudes and implements. We are remodeling the Alhambra with a steam-shovel, and we are proud of our yardage. We shall hardly relinquish the shovel, which after all has many good points, but we are in need of gentler and more objective criteria for its successful use.

Fullness of Life Through Leisure

JOHN COLLIER

A new and significant development in the character of the ecology of man lies ahead. While its exact form cannot be foreseen, it will attempt, in terms of a functional relationship, to reconcile mankind with biological reality. No single area of creative endeavor will be outside of this emergent awareness, for its essence will be an awakening of a new sense of community.

The foreshadowing of that event does not permit description of it in precise terminology. Our sense of its coming is not from prophets so much as from men who see that there is no alternative for human survival, who find their world crowded with signs of the new ecology's necessity and who have faith in nature and mankind. The language of such men is likely to sound strange, even mystical. But it would be a serious mistake to confuse their statements with vagueness or demagoguery.

Much is written and yet lost in the cacophony of voices and the avalanche of communication. But when the time comes to look back on these events, historical retrospect will center on a few strangely beautiful essays that were nearly overlooked in the confusion of their time.

THE EDITORS

FULLNESS OF LIFE through leisure: this is a problem and an opportunity of eternal human nature.

No group, and no individual, can permanently solve the problem or realize the opportunity and then rest upon the achievement. Life, to use the symbol often employed by Elie Faure, is a dance over fire and water. Whole societies, which have veritably existed, have danced that dance of life, though they have not called it leisure life or recreation. There are existing groups which continue that dance.

We want fullness of life for average men, not only for occasional Goethes, Huxleys or Leonardo da Vincis. Intensity of enthusiasm, and an effort sustained, diversified and organized, are demanded precisely in the measure that we seek fullness of life not for exceptional geniuses but for average people—for whole populations. Not geniuses, but average men, require profound stimulation, incentive toward creative effort and the nurture of great hopes.

We cannot escape the problem and opportunity of leisure. The life activity never stops. It never stops in anybody. It may stretch on the rack of ennui. It may dissipate into sensation whose fruitlessness is known at the time and whose bitterness at the core, whose mockery even of pleasure, is known before the end. It may revolve hypnotized about psychic fixations, may flood or palsy the soul as a neurotic misery. It may even be buried by habit and sophistication out of reach, until life seems what it never is, a mere polyp-like periphery. But the life activity never stops. And there is an art of life which, in many times and lands, has guided or builded this essential activity into beauty, into power—into habitual experiences and collective achievements which appear superhuman and miraculous. . . .

Fullness of life in leisure depends upon and, in fact, essentially is, an integration of body with emotions, of emotions with thought, and of individual with group. Saying this, have we said anything? "Body," "emotion,"

from **Mind-Body Relationship,** *Vol. 1, pp. 217–256, ed. Jay B. Nash. (South Brunswick, N.J.: A. S. Barnes, Inc., 1931.) Reprinted by permission.*

"thought," "individual," "group"— these are words grown hackneyed in educational parlance. Usage has killed them. Can we resurrect their meanings through examining life in its concrete manifestations?

That examination will require some attention to history and to present-day group life remote from our own, during this hour. There are societies far from our own in time and in development, which have realized an integration of body, mind and group, more intensely than ours. They have faced what we call the challenge of leisure, with a consciousness greater than our own and with more determination and more success. Some of these remote societies have furnished us with high-water marks showing what it is that men in groups can achieve. They have shown how much of fullness of life—what a dazzlingly diversified fullness of life— is possible for great numbers of men, and what vibration and flame of wonder can be diffused through the whole mass of life by creative traditions operating amid fortunate social arrangements. They show us, or have actually created for us, those values which at once sustain us and fill us with despair. And they suggest what guiding principles must be relied on if a great leisure-life, or any fullness of life, is to be attempted. Of course, they do not show us how to apply these principles in our own fundamentally altered society. They help us to space our problem, but imitating them will not solve it.

In this lecture I shall try to suggest how our own problem of leisure and of life differs from that of other societies. I shall touch on the primitive social group; on the use of leisure, and the art of social life, in ancient Greece; and on what minimum goal should be

our own. Throughout, I can only hope to be suggestive. . . .

Our own age, as President Hoover, John Dewey, and Stalin of Russia have pointed out, is witnessing an economic and social integration, more complex than the world has ever known, and ultimately world-wide. And in exact reverse correspondence, our age is witnessing *a human and psychic disintegration* possibly more profound, possibly more world-wide, than any previous age has known.

The leisure problem becomes clear when these various disintegrations are mentioned.

Technology has separated the worker from his product; has confined him within one or another minutia of the process of making his product. It has destroyed home industry, community industry, apprenticeship and the craft guilds. Technology has largely separated work from body activity—from generalized or large-muscle activity.

Secondary effects of our technological processes are the diminishment of family life, the destruction of village life, the establishment of slight contacts at long range in place of massive contacts face to face.

Technology has created the habit and expectancy of depending on machines not only for the production of things but for the production of satisfactions.

Technology through indirect influence has created our system of compulsory free education—free education in a different sense than free of money charge. It is an education freed from sacrifice, from obligation, from the necessity or opportunity of wholesouled cumulative expression, pursuit of interest or pursuit of work by young people.

Finally, within our system of competitive money economy, technology has created a world-view which assumes, sometimes explicitly, sometimes implicitly, that money can buy anything, even life. Machines can make anything, even life; money can buy anything, even life.

Looking abroad over the planet, we see that technology has blown into shreds, or blown utterly away, blighted or altogether killed, the primitive and ancient group life of all continents. We shall note some exceptions.

Technology has created problems of social control, of population control and distribution, of race relations and of concentrated power, so urgent and so enormous that every brain reels when trying to visualize them. These problems must be met by average men— by majorities, or, at least, by groups numbering tens of millions; and no arrangements yet have been forged out, not for the solving of these world problems by the masses, but even for informing the masses that the problems exist.

This extremely concentrated picture, which omits a hundred lights and shades and saving clauses, is all that we have time for. I have tried to sketch it with just one object in view. That object is to suggest the size and kind of burden which has been thrown on leisure through the effects, direct and indirect, of technology.

But we are not yet done with technology. I have already suggested the kind of predisposition which our young and old people bring to leisure, through their experience with technology and with its social by-products. We almost universally take it for granted that machines, and external arrangements and activity outside ourselves, can, and even that they alone can, supply the needs of leisure. Almost as universally, we associate leisure concerns with the spending of

of money; we think that we can buy our leisure life and we do buy it.

But the effects of technology are more direct than this. Technology has furnished the appalling arsenal of labor-saving machines designed to substitute receptive pleasure for active pleasure. The movie and the radio and phonograph are, of course, our top instances.

Technology and the economics of technology have created the newspaper of today, which typically is simply commercialized amusement.

All of these factors together (the indirect and direct consequences of technology) have brought about the reign of commercialized amusement, of which the commercialized theatre and our daily press are types. And commercialized amusement knows how to find and to exploit every one of the predispositions toward sensationalism, passivity, money-mindedness and crowd-mindedness which I have tried to state or to imply in the last five minutes. Devastating reversal has taken place through commercialized amusement. Once upon a time, social organization and organized leisure aimed at the highest common denominator, and in varying degrees and ways they succeeded in bringing average human nature up toward highest human nature. Commercialized amusement seeks out, exploits, socializes, moralizes, and makes dominant, the lowest common denominator, and our humanity, rendered passive through the effects of technology, seems to be momentarily helpless within this operation.

Let us abruptly pause, remarking that the diagnosis which I have tried to give is not original or new in any particular. How is the familiar situation reacted to by minds variously circumstanced?

418

To some it appears as an inescapable, fated by-product of cosmopolitanism, racial mixture and the diffusion of leisure and of technology and the money economy. They say: "This problem of leisure and of life, approached in any direct fashion, is not for our own day at all. It is for a future day, after economic and racial integration have run their cycle, or after some revolution or some evolutionary change greater than a revolution. Our own day is given to the conquest of material power and the organizing of utilitarian human-relationships. That is our own age's particular work in the world and no other work can be greatly done." These, sometimes pessimistic, sometimes remotely optimistic, have closed their eyes to the perspective of leisure and their ears to the challenge of leisure.

Others say: "The day of groups is past—of all groups, that is, existing with the immediate aim of enriching life rather than controlling power. Future experience is individual experience; neither now nor forever can the primitive oneness and fullness of life be realized within or directly through the instrumentality of groups. Most men are and will remain 'hommes moyens sensuels.' Individuals will raise the plane of their lives through an essentially solitary striving and achievement. The soul shall be freed through physical medicine, through surgery, through psychotherapy and psychoanalysis; ultimately it may be enhanced through eugenics. But whenever freed, whenever enhanced, now or hereafter, it will be an individualized, essentially a detached and solitary soul, above the crowd, outside the group, living in the heat of its own flame." This type of mind views collective effort toward fullness of life as a movement reversionary toward outlived primitive forms, a concession to the infantile, or at best a means toward individual or social catharsis.

And third, are the pallid and faint-hearted hopes of professional recreation workers. They do believe that recreation can achieve the highest. Some of them personally have far visions. But they find themselves trying to construct amid a social tornado. Or their enterprise is like a ship caught in the polar ice and moving with the drifts of uncontrollable currents. They do what they can; and what they can do, in the midst of the situation which I have tried to describe and shall later describe in another way, is, as none more clearly know than they, ephemeral and meager, indecisive alike in terms of individual character and psychic formation and of world events. Their practically-sought goals become very near and very few, and mediocrity swallows not necessarily themselves but their enterprise.

If you have followed me to this point, you will think that we have arrived at the bottom of a well, and you would like to know how we can get out.

We have arrived at the bottom of a well. Otherwise stated, it is an enveloping fact that deep disintegration of human institutions has taken place and is going forward; and with it, deep disintegration of human and psychic life.

Let us postpone any attempt at a pedantic verbal solution. Instead, let us move over into concrete experience.

Is there any case showing that in our present world an integrated, passionate, worldly-wise and reposeful life by average men in groups is possible? Does there exist anything showing that childhood can burgeon into an un-diminished adult life? Is there any-thing showing that in our world today, not some ancient world, the vital joy, which is an individual and biological property of childhood, can be main-tained and broadened and deepened through cooperative actions between grown men and women who are not living in cloisters, who are not in-toxicated with drugs, who are not self-surrendered into one or another hypnotic cult, and who are not tasting an instant's collective exaltation as an incident to the mowing-down of nations in war?

There is this proof; there are these concrete instances, and they are in-side the United States. I refer to cer-tain of the American Indian tribes. They bring some of our visions of leisure possibilities out of the far past into a present which we can ex-perience; out of the far future into a present which we can experience. These tribes have been shot through with influences from our white world for centuries. These tribes are now embarked on social adjustments noth-ing less than gigantic. They may succeed; they probably will largely fail; but they are consciously embarked. These tribes not only permit the magical fires of youth and of adoles-cence to burn on; they know how, and practice it, to re-kindle or dis-entomb the fires extinguished or buried through compulsory schooling practices more hostile to life than any that are inflicted on our white children. These tribes contain within themselves, and ap-parently always have contained, dis-ruptive and anti-social factors which, if one's examination were concentrated on them and on their potency, would seem to outlaw any possibility of serene and immense common joys, of com-munal flights into the regions of the

soul, of long and bitter toil performed without reward or applause as part of an industrial-esthetic-religious life jocund or solemn or ecstatic. Yet the disruptive factors do not disrupt the life of common joy, or block the cooperative, creative striving which brings the joyful life. The oldest Americans have their special answer to our newest American problem, the problem of leisure. Can their answer be part of our answer? They have reasons for pessimism, stronger than our own. Can we learn something from their victory over pessimism?

The integrations of life among these Indian tribes are achieved within and through the mechanisms of the primary social group. I use Professor Cooley's term. Groups whose members are associated face to face are primary social groups. All primitive society exists in such groups. Greek society was essentially a primary social group down to and until the end of the great Attic period. The primary social group is hardly less essential for the realiza-tion of human life than language itself, or than some essential organic struc-ture. It can and must be regenerated, and the future of leisure—of realized life—depends on the discovery of how to regenerate the primary social group and enrich it until it is adequate to human nature, and how to charge it with burdens of work grievous and exciting enough to call the deeper energies into action. How this can be done in the new world order; how primary social groups, interacting with each other, and basically intended to free and shape life itself, can be enabled to rise throughout the whole world as the makers of a new life tide; this is the deepest problem of sociology, and its full solution will not come in our lifetime. But it will come with the passing times, if men can recapture the vision of what it is that life is meant to be.

The primary social group looms in our background enormous from the standpoint of historical duration, enormous from the standpoint of the human nature which it has made possible through at least 100,000 years. The primitive primary social group, as actually experienced by its members, may have been more massive and far more versatile and complex than the whole American nation of today as experienced by any one of its members. How enormously complicated a primary social group could be is illustrated by any of the Pueblo Indian tribes of today. They contain two hundred, five hundred, a thousand members; but a descriptive survey of any one of the groups would require a volume, and no two of them are alike. The laws and language, the racial bible and folklore and poetic literature, are carried in memory alone. Their mnemonic vocabularies, in number and range and subtle distinctions of words, dwarf our print-reading man-on-the-street's vocabulary. Yet when recorded, the language, with all the record which it carries, yields but a shadowy sketch, with many blank interludes, of the social life and personal expressiveness of the members of the tribe.

Why is this the case? The answer bears startlingly upon our thought of human and psychic life as an integration, and suggests the disintegration amid which we, "the heirs of all the ages," are more or less contentedly abiding. This is the answer:

The expressed intention of language is, for so-called primitives, not the exclusive and not even the major expression. Esthetic handiwork vies with language in importance. Song is universal and is the crown of language.

But all—handiwork, language, song—is crowned with, is enhanced by, is carried into an illusion of infinitude by, dancing. Dancing is, in primitive life, personal integration, social integration, and a real or illusory transcendence of personal limitations, of place limitations, even of human limitations. Pueblo children, long before they walk or crawl, are inducted into the dance; I have seen a mother dance through an entire night, her young baby on her shoulder, the baby kept awake in order to be made a participant. I have seen many babies danced hours long by many mothers, in the gleam of fires out on the tremendous sacred mountain above Taos Pueblo, to the roaring of night-winds in the forest, blended with the millenial song poured from hundreds of Indian voices.

We are risking too much abstraction, too many truncated dogmatic statements. For relief, let us pause on this subject of the dance. It connects with so much else that has been given by other lecturers in this series; it was for so long, through all or nearly all races, man's perfect uniting of body with soul, of self with community, of self and tribe with God; it was so preeminently the integrating mechanism, and could so abundantly still be ours—ours—no matter what changes of world-view have come, no matter what irreversible perfectings of technology and of organization and degradations of human work have taken place; and its decay is so fearfully the measure of our human disintegration and our psychic or esthetic decadence. Let us pause for a moment on the dance.

"A savage does not preach his religion, he dances it," remarks an anthropologist. Havelock Ellis quotes Livingstone: "When a man belonging to one branch of the great Bantu division of mankind met a member of

"... personal integration, social integration, and a real or illusory transcendance of personal limitations, of place limitations, even of human limitations." A group of nomadic aborigines performing one of their ritual dances, known as corroborees. (Photo courtesy Australian News and Information Bureau.)

another, he asked: 'What do you dance?' What a man danced, that was his tribe, his social customs, his religion." Were the Bantus compelled to dance by deficiency in other vehicles of expression? A competent philologist declares the Bantu language to be one of the master-languages of the world. "The Bantu languages," says Crisp, before the British Association of Science in 1905, "will express any idea, however esoteric, and will do it with extraordinary precision and often with great felicity. A foreigner who has acquired one of them will often leave his own language to use a Bantu word, because it conveys his thought more aptly and tersely. Bantu proverbs and metaphors are often most incisive, emphasizing with much power and delicacy what it is intended to say. The Bantus are masters in the art of

destructive criticism, and their native shrewdness, observation and wit render them dangerous disputants."

Why is Bantu religion, as Dr. R. R. Marett states, "not so much thought out as danced out?" The Professor of Missions in Africa, at the Kennedy School of Missions, W. C. Willoughby, answers in his richly informing volume, "The Soul of the Bantu:"

When tribesmen strive to kiss the hem of the garment of the unseen, unspeakable thoughts clamour within them for the garb of the ritual, and will not be denied; hence it is that every tribe in Africa has a ritual of politeness, as well as of worship, and a ritual of affection, of respect, of authority, of hospitality, of medicine, of war, and of social organization; all of which, like art, try to express what words are too small to utter,—not the trifles of the soul, but its immensities.

The Bantu handicrafts were triumphs of audacious and subtle forms; a hint can be obtained from the African musical instruments at the Natural History Museum.

Rene Fulop-Miller writes: "Among the Russian peasants the dance is not yet degraded to a form of social entertainment. It is a rite of religious activity; in many respects it assumes the dignity of a prayer. Everything for which his speech is inadequate, his emotions, impulses and intuitions, receive in the dance their most powerful and liberating form, and the movements of the dancer express the incomprehensible yearning for the infinite, the immemorial melancholy as well as the exultant primitive joy of the creature in being alive. The saint who preaches, and then when words are no longer adequate continues his sermon dancing, is a comprehensible, understood phenomenon."

What of races not "primitive?" Ritual life in Egypt was one mighty yet structural and delicate, thousand-year-never-ending dance. Sophocles at Athens danced in his own dramas, Plato made of dancing the primordial art; Aristotle derived the Greek tragic drama from the dance, and it is correct to say with G. Ware Cornish: "The Greek drama is a musical symphonic dance-vision, through which the history of Greece and the soul of man are portrayed." In the great age of Christianity, dancing known as such was usual in the cathedrals; and the Catholic mass is a beautiful and aweful dance-drama. In Dante's paradise Christ danced forever amid those who on earth had been warriors of God.

But we are now looking at the dance as an institution of the primary social group. In such a group, aboriginal, primitive, the dance is often hardly if at all less stupendous in execution and in meaning than was the Greek

"What do you dance? What a man danced, that was his tribe, his social customs, his religion." (Photo by Nathan Liskov.)

tragic drama. The Red Deer dance at Taos Pueblo, the Shalako at Zuni Pueblo, the Night Chant of the Navajos, probably represent our nearest contact in space and in time with the sources of Greek drama; and through these dances the Indians pass to where you and I cannot go, deeply shaken and deeply nourished though we may be, for we are but half-understanding witnesses, while they are creators, united with the creative process of the universe itself, borne on a mystic tide of racial life which their own activity engenders. Not the exceptional, not the privileged few of the tribe, but, though of course with varying intensities of consciousness, all the members of the tribe.

Let us note two other aspects of the primary and primitive social group. Less universal than the use of the dance, they are yet worldwide, and knowledge of them helps to make known what mankind has lost.

All work in primitive life is craftsmanship. All work-forms are conventionalized into beauty. All work is social. And all work has magical or mystical implications. No stuff upon which one works is dead stuff. The earth where one ploughs and reaps is a living titanic being; its soil is the body of God. The state of being of the emotions of the worker passes into the fabricated product. Beyond the resistant stone or wood is a resisting or co-operating will. In ways that no material technology can hint of, the worker's quality and intensity of life are controlling in the technological process, and give predestination to his implement of peace or war, to the seed which he plants, to the house which he builds. Hence, invocation, song, magic spells, purifications of body and soul—the concentration of the whole nature, of all the creative powers; the worker must be an athlete and a magician in body and in soul. It is from this high point, occupied during tens of thousands of years, not perhaps amid all, but amid many races, that work—any and all industrial operation—has declined to the unintegrated, repetitive, physically void, indifferently objective manipulations of today. This devolution we can neither reverse nor regret; but we can acknowledge it, we can seek to compensate for it in other regions of life, and we can learn from it one of the gravest truths: Mastery of things, if our attention be fixed solely on such mastery, may be loss of life.

The final aspect of the primary and primitive social group, to which we have time to give note, surely is the strangest of all. The strangest, I mean, in contrast with our own life. I refer to the uses made of the crises of adolescence. It is far too extended a subject to permit of more than a reference; I refer you to Hutton Webster's "Primitive Secret Societies," and to Stanley Hall, for descriptive detail. We have the recent incident of a whole Pueblo tribe, in 1925, defying the United States government and announcing its readiness to go to jail and stay there, over the issue of the suspension of the initiation training of its boys. Our government knew nothing, but assumed that boys are bad boys, and of course Indians are bad Indians. The tribe knew that its hold upon the future, the persistence of its tradition, of its religion, of its emotional orientation, of its ancient soul which involved the world-soul, were dependent on the adolescent disciplines. The tribe prevailed. We who were close to the Indians watched the disappearance of boys from public view. Even their fathers saw them no more. After sometimes a year, some-

424

times eighteen months, the boys returned—from the underground kivas,
from the pathless areas of the Sangre
de Cristo range, from the hidden crag
where perhaps burns the mythical
everlasting fire. Radiant of face, full-
rounded and powerful of body, modest,
detached: they were men now, keep-
ers of the secrets, houses of the Spirit,
reincarnations of the countless generations of their race; with "reconditional
reflexes," with emotions organized
toward their community, with a connection formed until death between
their individual beings and that
mythopoeic universe—that cosmic
illusion—that real world—as the case
may be, which both makes man
through its dreams and is made by
man's dreams.

The supreme moment for coordination, integration and orientation,
destined to be permanent, is adolescence. That is a truism to ourselves,
and to our world of today a sterile
truism, an affirmation with no prag-
matic consequences. Our control of
the adolescent tides is less than our
control of floods of the Mississippi.
We are grateful when, like floods, they
subside. Preachment and negative
control we still do faintly essay, but
adolescence rightly, and uncompromisingly, rejects and reverses us. What
have we to offer to it? And we call
them the "uncivilized," those aborigines—not our Red Indians alone but
the aborigines of all continents—who
do offer to their adolescents life; who
do give to their adolescents tasks the
most romantic, the most solemn, the
most mysterious, the most burdened
with fate, that inherited tribal wisdom
can devise; who do make of adolescence the crisis of second birth, and
the marriage of the individual with
the race, and the marriage of the race
with the universe.

Incredulity, or at least a suspicion of
unreality, may have been aroused in
some of you by what I have told of the
primitive community. It is hard indeed
for us, children of an age of giant
external power, to conceive that the
psychic and human powers and values,
which on their eternal march are
traversing our moment of social time,
or which perhaps are waning from our
society, were not created by ourselves.
Let us try to grasp through one
example what the dawn-man innately,
biologically, was, and then let us understand what necessity drove the Stone
Age community to discover and maintain the arts of fullness of life. There
are caves in France and in other parts
of the world, where men left their
record—men who were actually,
literally the dawn-men—the first men.
I quote from H. J. Massingham's delightful book, "The Golden Age," one
of a series edited by Professor G. Elliot
Smith:

There, 700 feet from the mouth of the cave,
and fenced within the primeval darkness,
is a little steppe horse cantering over the
meadows, with every line, curve, muscle
and tendon of his workmanlike body realized
in some casual strokes with a dash of
shading. A bison rampant with eyes of fire,
a toy mammoth filled with comedy . . . At
Cap Blanc, high up in the scoop of the
cliff looking towards the 12th-Century-
Chateau of Comargnes . . . is a sculptured
horse standing in his rock stable with a
repose and majesty as though he had come
to rest here from his plunging fellows in
the Parthenon frieze.

Line drawings in black and red, shaded
black drawings, frescoes in brown or black
monochromes, slight or full polychromes,
stipples, flat tints, even impressionistic
designs of reindeer herds. They were crafts-
men all through, and worked in their tough
and elementary material as though they
had made the rocks for the glory of scratching them. But, however astonishing their

technical mastery in a medium so intractable, the supreme fact is that their art is flawless, the flower of perfection blossoming in the inchoate beginnings of human life just taking human form.

[Their materials:] Pointed flints, stone saucers of flickering grease, palettes daubed with pounded earths.

Anthropologist and man-in-the-street alike are so obsessed with their Cave-Man fantasy that the art of the Cro-Magnons, though known for 20 years, has had no influence whatever upon modern thought . . . Owing to candle and electric light, and the superb vandalism of visitors who carve their names upon the first and, of their kind, the greatest works of pictorial art achieved by the human race, many of the drawings are going back into the rock.

Now, for that reason in necessity which coerced the primitive community toward fullness of life and many-sidedness.

Such a community faced the two worlds of man and of nature without any of those impersonal instruments which experimental science has created—the myriad instruments of power machinery, of laboratory precision, of accumulated written record and of the organic control furnished by scientific medicine. It engaged in a life-long grapple, naked-handed, with antagonists now banished from our civilized life; more often with antagonists not banished, but with whom we cope at long range through technologies relegated to specialists. The dawn-man's body was engaged in this grapple; his intuitions, his broodings and his emotions were engaged; his family life and group life, his imagination and his mystical perceptions were engaged. That he should feel power, should feel exultation, was a pre-condition of that biological vigor whose insufficiency might mean tribal extinction or enslavement. And his magical world-view led him to assume and to work

over into his institutions the assumption that to feel power, to feel exultation, to feel joy, happiness and beauty, were means to the end of the magical control of nature through co-partnership with the gods. This necessity and illusion, and lifelong group stimulation, and the individual experience of "beauty and anguish, walking hand in hand the downward road of death:" all of these causes cooperated toward building and sustaining the life-art. A short life was the individual dawn-man's, though racially it was ninety-five per cent of human time until now; a fragile and unweaponed life, from our modern collective standpoint; a life clouded in primordial mists, in comparison with what we collectively, with our mere intellect, know. But it was warmed with central fires of communal and of cosmic emotion which are buried far from our present reach; it was energized through stimuli both external and internal which our privileged world does not concede to us, and which our adult habits and resistances would exclude and inhibit if they were conceded to us. Perhaps, being so hazardous and so strenuous an existence, it experienced the repose that follows any unwithholding total rhythm of life, any complete giving of the self—that repose which our privileged and our humanly and psychically disintegrated condition denies to us. At least, the dawn-man whom we can ourselves observe, the tribal Indians, do experience a repose within mighty movements of life.

How true was the intuition of Tennyson, writing long before social anthropology was born:

We are not idle ore,
But iron dug from central gloom
And heated hot with burning fears
And bathed in baths of hissing tears
And tempered with the shocks of doom.

"Rise after rise bow the phantoms behind me," wrote Whitman—the phantoms of the dawn-man. We, biologically, are the dawn-man; nothing has been added, and as yet little or nothing has been lost. All the additions and losses have been social; the innate man, who upbore, if he was not created by, the hundred thousand or quarter-million years of pre-history, sleeps, dreams or awakes in us; his is the stake in the future. On his fulfillment, and not, except infinitesimally, on our fulfillment, the future waits.

Let us pass to our immediate, direct spiritual ancestry. An abrupt passage it must be, and a hopelessly brief pause on the watershed of the modern world. But concerning Greece, many of you know much more than I.

There is a famous dictum of Sir Henry Maine, "Except the blind forces of nature, all that moves in the modern world is Greek in its origin." Much of the old and the far was gathered into the Greek system and was there reintegrated but not originated. Some highest achievements of the modern world were rather anticipated by the Greeks than inaugurated by them. But at least, we can say that for students of leisure and of the social principles influencing fullness of life, Greece is the crown of history, the extremest outpost, the perfect and unattainable type and ideal, the eternal challenge.

Greece rose out of primitive life; even the miracle of Homer was completed within the primitive stage.

The dominant social values of Periclean Athens, and many of the dominant institutions, were direct heritages from the primitive stage, and their contemporaries knew them as such. The Attic festivals, the Attic drama as a form, the Orphic cults, the Dionynsian cults and conceptions, and much of the specific content of the dramas of Aeschylus and Sophocles, were derived immediately from the primitive stage, and their contemporaries knew it. Chronologically, more than a thousand years may have separated the age of Pericles from that age in the Greek islands to which our highest American Indian civilizations are reasonably comparable. But it was a thousand years of institutional continuity, of interaction between folk-institutions and energizing ideals embodied in the most living language that collective genius has yet produced. Self-activity, many-sidedness and integration through the whole range from body to group, where the hygienic and moral imperatives consciously affirmed, with applications always broadening and deepening through the whole period. The pursuit flagged only on one great line—the realization of woman as woman; and fearful and dramatic was the retribution, but it waited long.

The temple at Delphi bore two inscriptions, "Know thyself" and "Nothing in excess." These precepts must have preceded by hundreds of years the rise of Protagoras with his philosophy: "Man is the measure of all things." Hellenic ethnic or communal loyalty was Hebraic or Roman in its sternness; and the integration of Greek life is exemplified when Socrates, the standard-bearer for all time of free conscience and free thought, in his defense before the jury and again in his refusal to flee from the death penalty, expounds the principle of loyalty as a limiting and final principle.

But throbbing, flashing and straining as in a chariot race, within the control of these self-imposed ideals of loyalty, balance, many-sidedness and self-examination, were the dynamic principles of beauty as a way and an end, and of the pursuit of knowledge as a way and an end. Homer gave these two dynamic and transforming principles their expression, destined to rule the popular and the esoteric mind alike clear through the age of Pericles and even of Alexander the Great. One was the Achilles ideal, "ardent, adolescent, passionate," as characterized by John Addington Symonds. One was the Ulysses ideal, "to follow knowledge like a sinking star beyond the utmost verge of human thought. . . . I cannot rest from travel." Again quoting Symonds, Ulysses was "stern in action, ruthless in hatred, subtle, cunning; persuasive in eloquence, wisest in counsel, bravest and coolest in danger."

The Ulysses impulse carried the primary social group out to the world; fertilized the native group with influences from the whole accessible world; established the mercantile dominion of Greece; systematized discovery into knowledge, and based internal and external action on discovery. The Achilles ideal of a beauty not made and then possessed, but lived with passion, brought youth and age into confluence through all of Greek history. It was Achilles more than Ulysses who found expression in "Man is the measure of all things." Socrates' final word: "The unexamined life is not worth living," unites the two ideals.

We are less concerned, for present purposes, with these ideals of Greece and their results in achievement, than with the social mechanisms which they created and which served as their instruments. Mechanisms, institutions, disciplines, customs. These, in Greece, were the master-works of art. More than the Acropolis, or the sculptures of Pheidias, or all the poetry and philosophy, these disciplines, institutions and customs were the crowning art of Greece. Being only human, being only

life, and not made with hands, they have now vanished as utterly as the disciplines and institutions of California's Indians or the pre-mediaeval Germanic institutions described in that perfect book, "The House of the Wolfings" by William Morris.

Greek gymnastic training, which moved hand in hand with rhetorical training, was controlled by the test of beauty. Essentially, it was training for and through the dance, and as a matter of course, the training through group dancing. For five hundred years or more this dual training in gymnastic and rhetoric prepared the way for the Great Age of Athens. Writes Symonds: "The foundation of the highest Greek art was being laid (800 and 1000 years before Christ) in the cultivation of the human body. The sentiment of beauty shows itself in dances and games, in the races of naked runners, in rhythmic processions and the celebration of religious rites. The whole race lived out its sculpture and its painting, rehearsed, as it were, the great works of Pheidias and Polygnotus in physical exercise, before it learned to express itself in marble or in color." Walter Pater gives exquisite details in his "The Age of Athletic Prizemen." "'Now on one, now on another' as the poet tells 'doth the grace that quickeneth (quickeneth, literally, on the race course) look favorably.' The actual prize, as we know, was in itself of little or no worth—a cloak, in the Athenian games, or at the greater games, a mere handful of parsley, a few sprigs of pine or wild olive. . . . It was a gymnastic which, under the happy conditions of that time, was already surely what Plato pleads for, already one half music, a matter, partly, of character and of the soul, of the fair proportion between soul and body, of the soul with itself."

"The whole race lived out its sculpture and its painting, rehearsed, as it were, the great works of Pheidias and Polygnotus in physical exercise." Relief from a statue base, from the Kerameikos, Athens. (Photo by Alison Frantz.)

What was the monument built by Athens at Plateia? It was the monument to Kallikrates because he was the fairest of the Greeks who died on that battlefield. The authentic records of the great festival of Athenae depict an entire society achieving self-activity in beauty. And note that women shared equally with man in the effort and the splendor of this as of the myriad Greek festivals. . . .

Paralleling or, more accurately, containing the gymnastic and rhetorical expressions, was the Greek ceremonial drama. This did not suddenly flower in that century of miracle following the Persian Wars. Rather, as an institution more of the gods than of man, it moved through the common life of all the Ionian Greeks for a thousand years and more before the Persian Wars, much as the Shalako gods at Zuni Pueblo, coming from out of the desert at sundown, move through the streets and fraternise in the homes of the Zuni Indians. These ceremonial dramas were themselves gymnastic in all their developments, to the most elaborate mass dancing; they were song and epic narrative, and they were as heavy with mystic symbolism and

traditional reference as was the mediaeval Catholic mass.

And it was into these ceremonial dramas, after the Persian Wars, that Athens poured its genius until more than four thousand gigantic dramatic poems were written in less than a hundred years by a population smaller than that of East Orange, New Jersey. The folk drama thrust itself with bewildering quickness across into that political and ethical forum which it became in the hands of Euripides and of Aristophanes. . . .

We must cease from the Greeks. Perhaps their clearest meaning to us, or the meaning which we might best appropriate, is the significance of activity. Greek life was an activity life. Greek education was based exclusively on activity. The activity principle was carried into the highest reaches of Greek philosophic thought. The "diagogic" life, which the citizen of Athens had earned when middle life had passed, was nothing but a freed and more versatile activity. Yet where is there any repose like that of men and women and beasts in the Parthenon friezes? The function of the Sophists, as insisted throughout the Socratic Dialogues, was to compel self-activity in the thinking process. The Sophist frequented the market place, and his task was accomplished when he forced men to substitute genuine self-searching and audacious thought for whatever traditional or crowd-judgment might be unconsciously possessing them. That the Greeks did not press forward (as their mathematics had prepared them to do) the invention of machines and of power instruments, was due perhaps to their pre-occupation with, and their horror of jeopardizing, this total human self-activity which they viewed as the beginning and the end. Their neglect of machinery did not lead to their downfall, for their competitors were equally neglectful.

The Great Age came to an end because the Attic synergy or integration was disrupted. We know some of the causes or can speculate about them. Others of the causes may remain forever unknown. But we do know what immediate event plunged Athens into subjugation—into a ruin that was never restored. That act was the decision to embark on the war against Syracuse. The Ulysses impulse tore itself out of the balance of Greek life, and under what impulsion? Under the impulsion of Alcibiades. Pericles had foreseen the menace: Aspasia had foreseen it; Pericles and Aspasia were gone, and Athens plunged to destruction, obeying the incitement of a disintegrated man of genius, narcissistic, perhaps hermaphroditic, certainly exhibitionistic and crowd-minded. Such was Alcibiades. Not Aspasia, but woman, had she been enabled to play her part in Athens, might have changed history, at this, one of the critical moments, about which the ages past and to come must mournfully speculate.

Since ancient Athens, there has been no perfect integration of body, soul and society among civilized occidental peoples. Plato himself had controverted the humanist philosophy and had laid the foundation for intellectualism and for asceticism. Christianity and the neo-Platonists and the Epicureans divorced body and soul. Once the social voluntarism of Athens had plunged to death, social coercion became the necessary resort. In a world become a melting pot, no other device, under the then conditions, could be successful. Social coercion has remained down the ages the substitute for that social voluntarism which would reach beyond conduct and opinion and automatism to the buried fountains of passion and of will. These incidents are not of a mere historic interest. Dewey and James, Schiller, Bergson and Whitehead battle against their workings in our philosophy and world view at this hour, and in our pedagogy, our morals, our esthetics and politics at this hour. Havelock Ellis suggests, in his early volume, "The New Spirit," and again in his recent masterpiece, "The Dance of Life," that the word "disintegration" is not adequate to describe the movement since Plato; he thinks that the word "decadence" is more adequate.

There have been compensations which will seem to have filled the measure to overflowing if, but only if, we can re-achieve the lost integration. Unless we can achieve it, the immense progressions since ancient Greece will have been in vain for the masses of men and for the long future stretching before us. What are some of these compensations? What new reaches of life?

Athens incorporated a whole citizenship in an ambition and attainment of radiant excellence; the excellence reacted on the average human brain and that average brain gave forth a

430

myriad incandescence. Since that bright beauty passed from the world, a solitude has entered the human spirit such as perhaps no Greek ever knew. The highest and deepest communings became communings with the dead—as Dante's were; with the universe and the inner soul, its shadow, or the inner soul and the universe, its shadow—such were the communings of Virgil, of Marcus Aurelius; again, the intensest communings were those held with the God of All: the "journey of the Alone to the Alone" of Plotinus, the Beatific Vision of the Christian mystics. And from Christ through to St. Francis, there came such a universal pity, such a universal love as neither the Greeks nor any ancient Western peoples had understood. And science, diminishing the human equation which it can never wholly elude, began that search, through instruments and experiments, into the cosmos which (science must assume) knows not man. Newton, "forever voyaging through strange seas of thought alone," and Darwin, the perfect seeker, are prototypes. Greece indeed laid the foundations of our natural science. But Aristotle was not an Athenian; his work was done at the court of Macedonia; and night descended upon it for two thousand years.

What Athens might have done had that Athenian miracle persisted and developed, from Pericles until now, we cannot guess. But Greece, as we know it, produced no Christ; no Dostoievsky or Dante, no Abelard and Heloise; no Florence Nightingale or Emily Bronte; no Mona Lisa; perhaps not even any Virgin of the Rocks. We search in vain through any Greek frieze for such nameless hints of new abysses of beauty and insight as Leonardo da Vinci strewed through a hundred notebooks. Vantage-points

far, very far out in the soul and in nature have been conquered, with vistas such as Greece never knew. They remain isolated vantage-points, and we, because our psycho-social mechanisms have long been wrecked, take it for granted that the vantage-points must remain isolated, outside the possibilities of most men forever. In spite of William Blake, and of Dostoievsky, and of Emerson, that is what we tacitly believe. . . .

Reintegration will be accomplished by our age or by some future age. World-wide and instantaneous that reintegration can never be. I am speaking, of course, of human and psychic reintegration—regeneration—not of political and economic integration.

I dare not now pause again in social anthropology or history. But they do teach us that fullness of life and many-sidedness require time for their accomplishment; roots striking very deep into human earth must nourish the social flowering; standardized, hurriedly pursued, world-wide or even, in our population arrangements, community-wide achievement is impossible as a matter of the first instance. If immediately sought, it necessarily censors or constrains the life-enterprise into mediocrity or worse.

That is what history teaches, but history teaches also that the social growth process does not require physical or economic isolation. On the contrary, it depends on social interaction. Renaissance history is crowded with evidences of this truth.

Cosmopolitanism, though it be world-inclusive, and though it be cultural as well as economic, does not in and of itself forbid or foredoom the regeneration of the human spirit—the reintegration of life through group institutions; nay, it favors that redemption which has become the peculiar task, hardly

431

yet even envisaged, of our age. The machine and the competitive money economy, including of course competitive nationalism, are far graver hindrances. Whether the handicaps that they impose are insuperable, will be answered when effort, in the spirit of the primitive community and the spirit of the Greek state, is perseveringly set under way, whether in America or in some other part of the world. It has not yet been carried forward anywhere. That effort will be chiefly, at the beginning, an effort toward creative popular leisure.

Is there any prescription, of principles or of method, which I can state here? The justification for all that I have quoted from primitive life and history, lies in this alone—that the facts are heavily burdened with prescription. I shall not ask you to go over them a second time, but shall conclude with propositions which do rest on these experiences of the old, wide world, but which must now rest on their own brief and, I admit, dogmatic statement.

Leisure should be uncompelled, voluntary, uncalculating, free. Yet leisure is fatally emasculated if it be divorced from work. From world's work, I mean, as distinct from the restricted labor called wage work.

Nothing short of world's work can make the searching, irresistible appeal to our voluntary nature, on which a great leisure must depend.

I do not mean world's work casually performed, at no sacrifice to the young person. Getting what we do not pay for is one of the demoralizing facts of American life. Being forced to take what we do not need, and what we will not pay for, and what, therefore, we are not required to pay for, seems to be a condition of formalized education from the first grammar grades up,

growing worse in the upper grades and worst in college, and no early escape appears probable. By paying, I mean paying with life, not paying with money. We have made education compulsory, have created the school as an artificial institution not within life but self-contained in its own world. Through increasingly blocking the careers of those without college diplomas, we have increased the dictatorship of colleges over all lower education, while expediting, through these same policies, the degradation of college standards. The school casts on leisure a heavy burden which the school, under happier conditions, might be foremost in shouldering. It casts upon leisure a demoralized youth for leisure to moralize.

We have all read William James's essay "The Moral Equivalent of War." With self flattery or pathetic optimism, many have said: "Organized recreation, the kind we now have, is the moral equivalent of war." James would have repudiated the assertion. Organized recreation as at present is neither the moral antagonist of war, nor the substitute for those life values which war in ancient times offered at a price not too great to pay; which war today still offers, but at many prices too great to pay. For war has now become a machine, and furthermore, it has become a duel across a handkerchief by which, with little moral force or skill or romance entering the decision, nations, cultures and races murder one another.

James states the facts uncompromisingly. The moral equivalent of war is public work—strenuous and uncompensated public work. Nay, far more. War had its moral values, which were universal and deep-reaching, *because* it was public work. War, through the intermediate ages since the socially

432

complete and illusion-endowed primary social group perished (Athens being the latest of such groups and the supreme one), has furnished the moral equivalent of the ancient primary group facing the wilds of nature, of the gods and of man: its stimulus deep-probing and constant, its organizing sway laid upon emotion and thought, its comradeship in peril and death, its apotheosis of the individual into the community with the resultant intensification of individuality, its loyalty rooted as a passion and a law, and its emancipation from personal calculation and from personal fear. These values war had because war, through these intermediate centuries, provided for the mass of men their only experience in great public work. Why has war been adored by mankind through this era behind? Because it was the means of individual redemption, of fullness of life infused with iron and with reality through bitter effort and through hazard and sacrifice with comrades.

And now the primary group as a dynamic system has long gone past, until it be recreated; and science and the integrations of races and of economic systems have stripped war of its moral uses to the individual and have made it the master-curse of our time. What moral equivalent remains?

Our answer must be: Fullness of life through leisure. But we must cleave to our understanding of what life is. Fullness of life is integration of life lived at intensity—body life, emotion life, thought life and imaginative life; and of all these with community or race life; and under the control of the principle that life is a striving, exploring and creative activity and not a synchronization of automatic movements or a titillation of sensations inertly or casually apperceived. Fullness of life is a wrestling match. It is a battle. It is

a hunt conducted while famine waits but will not wait long. It is a searching of the unknown and of peril. It is construction. It is the repose that comes in the pauses of absolute effort. It is union with others in effort and in labor. It is the dance over fire and water.

Now let us return to the thesis of James. The moral equivalent of war is public work. Fullness of life is public work. Leisure must be organized and inspired as public work, toward public ends. For the masses there is no other way—there never has been, since the dawn of social life. For all, including the minority with irrepressible temperamental hungers, public work is a necessity for complete manhood. For the masses it is the only way to fullness of life.

A formal recognition is given to this truth by our civic clubs, our Boy Scout and Girl Scout and Camp Fire Girl organizations. The significance of the recognition is not faint but immense. But the development of program or even of hopes, after years and decades of recreational enterprise, simply does not square with the problem. It does not space the problem at all. It presumes an evanescent relation of youth with groups whose advantages, whose challenges and demands, fail even to hint of the mighty world. It presumes a casualness and a softness, and a small-town-mindedness, a passivity, a mediocrity of imagination and of life-standards, a predestined psychical parasitism, which, did they exist as finalities in our young people, would tempt toward despair and suicide. These words will be heard or read as excessive words. But we are dealing with a grave subject, and one should speak his belief if he speaks at all.

I would not under-value these youth organizations. Nothing else in American life—this is said thoughtfully—is worth as much as they, actually and potentially. The extreme limitations are forced on them by the social situation. But must they be forced? Must they be accepted?

One reason for these pigmy programs seeking pigmy results amid giant opportunities is the lust for numbers, for hurried extension and universality. That lust is carried across from public education, surely the worst exemplar that could be forced upon leisure time workers. But though the lust for numbers were cast off, still recreation workers would have legislatures to cope with, taxpayers, philanthropists, and lay boards of directors. The difficulty lies deeper still. If childhood and adolescence are to be united with public work, public authority must be brought to recognize the necessity as an urgent one justifying many changes in governmental policy. And beyond government, the parents stand. I hasten to recite these handicaps, in order to suggest that it is no accident which has dwarfed our leisure provisions for childhood, and no mere dearth of creative, audacious professional leadership. Rather, such leadership finds itself suffocated by the conditions, and is driven to other spheres to do its work; and few and fewer in American education life are the spheres not pre-empted by Philistia.

Suppose that recreational leaders were freed, and were helped, to unite leisure organization with public work. Suppose that the upsetting of the wage levels was not an obstacle and that organized labor consented and bureaucracies cooperated. Suppose that school calendars, routines, crediting systems were accommodated. What could be attempted?

I preface with a recent incident from one of our Pacific seaports. A sailing vessel forty years old had been purchased by Swedish interests. A four-masted, square-rigged, iron ship, battered by service in the Alaska packing trade. No auxiliary engine, no radio and no modern conveniences. Destined to become a training ship for Swedes preparing for nautical careers.

A Swedish naval officer had come to take it home, not through the Panama Canal but around the Horn. For five months or longer, it would not make port or send or receive messages.

The captain offered, in exchange for a nominal sum, to take six 'prentices on board, housing them in his own quarters, serving them officers' fare, and training them in the ways of the sea. In all that city, known as a place of adventurous spirits, he found two families, each with one son prepared to take the risks. Yet this may be the last freight-carrying sailing craft that will ever round the Horn.

Two boys, aged sixteen and eighteen, determined that they would ship, not as apprentices, but as crew. They overwhelmed every parental scruple and the captain signed them on. The whole crew initially signed on had deserted; a new crew was being assembled with difficulty. A cargo of grain—in certain eventualities a dangerous cargo—was being loaded. Few or none of the crew had ever sailed in sailing ships. Was the captain appalled, or were any of these adolescent Ulysses? They were not. The ship went out into a January storm. Possible danger, gruelling work and scant comfort for many months, but the playing of one's whole nature against a mighty opponent, marriage with the sea, and conquest of the sea! It was not public work initially, but the day that ship took the sea a new group life was born, the ship became an imperiled command, and on a "further side of silence" an immitigable public work conscripted every youth of the crew. . . .

Social conflict is an essential of social energy and social health. Our best public work often is pitted against the commonwealth—that is, against those in power or against the *status quo* which they must defend. This is a fact of objective necessity, and more; it is a fact of human nature, and peculiarly of the psychical orientation of adolescence.

Today, in America, education, public recreation and commercialized recreation unite in setting their faces to deny, to suffocate, to crowd off from the stage of conscious life, this multitudinous conflict within our own society which we, as sociologists, know to be indispensable to social progress, to social energy and social health and to the generation of the desired social passion: hardly less essential than is, for example, the functioning in our bodily economy of the supra-renal glands.

It was an unavoidable step but a dangerous one, which made education compulsory and placed both education and leisure organization under the immediate control of the state—the monistic and authoritative state. It was more unavoidable, more beneficent than Herbert Spencer or Tolstoy conceded, but not less dangerous than they insisted. It may have been fatal—one cannot yet tell. Here is no place or time to elaborate this thought which carries us to the heart of the problem of government and of public opinion and of democracy. I mention it at all, only because the facts bear grievously on our problem of awakening and organizing the life forces of our young people through bringing them at the earliest age, and progressively, into important, sternly demanding public work.

Let me point the question. There are subjects which have agitated the public mind, or some minds, in the last two years. To mention examples. The Sacco-Vanzetti case in the East, and the Mooney case in the West. The revelations about prison conditions, Federal and State, dramatized in a glare of hell-light at Auburn and in Colorado. The Samoan, the Nicaraguan and Haitian situations, the power trust question, public ownership, birth control, the recognition of Russia. The long-term imprisonment of Southern California women for conspiracy to hang a red flag above a children's camp. The violations of civil liberty in various strike areas in recent months. The battle waged against Federal authority, to check the slow massacre by starvation and germs of our American Indians—a battle provisionally won on March 4th last. What leaders of Boy Scouts, Girl Scouts, Camp Fire Girls, public playground groups, community center groups, have used any one of these subjects or like subjects as a means to kindle into flame the social consciousness of their groups and to enlist them self-sacrificingly or militantly in public work and public struggle? Nay, have not local and national organization policies definitely outlawed any such use of such subjects? Is this not true equally of our public recreation systems and our privately financed recreation systems?

Tooth and claw are not absent from our common life. Conflict, contest, controversy, shake the whole body of our common life, and they must continue to shake it until changes beyond our power to imagine have taken place, and perhaps thereafter, by the very nature of man and of society, until the end of time. In our schools we would never know it. In our commercialized amusements we would never know it.

435

Fugitive and distorted impressions in our daily press yield hints of these social realities and hardly more. I speak of ninety-eight per cent of the daily press. Our magazines of mass circulation suppress these realities as a matter of policy, save for rare exceptions. And we wonder that a generation of political, economic and social illiteracy and of crowd-mindedness; and of Babbitry is swallowing us up. But here is not the place to generalize, beyond one statement.

If our commonwealth wants our young people to take it seriously, it must take them seriously. If it wants them to take themselves seriously, it must enable them to function seriously in relation to urgent real matters. It must not lie to them, and it must not wall them off from its own real problems and its own real work.

America has such power, and such responsibility, as no nation has ever had. A worldwide power, and a worldwide obligation which cannot be evaded, which must be faced, though it can be betrayed. We will move, with our unparalleled resources and resourcefulness, yet ultimately as nothing but a blind economic power, possibly to some unpredictable happy outcome, but from all historic precedent, including the most recent, not to any such outcome but to our own and the world's diminishment or ruin. Or we will move as an informed and knowing agent, studious of the indirect effects of what we do, increasingly wise, with values increasingly rich and true, with a spirit grown mighty through its tasks, toward the healing and the making of our own world and the whole world. It depends on ourselves; it depends on our youth. It depends on a changed national and local social policy—a policy designed to bring our entire public, but most of all our children, into contact with those world's work opportunities and those challenges and realities and problems, burning and abysmal, which are within our own life and beyond it in Europe, in Asia, in all the continents and islands. . . .

A Woman as Great as the World

JACQUETTA HAWKES

THERE WAS ONCE a woman as great as the world. She was of a placid disposition, and, knowing everything, had no cares. Indeed, she would hardly have been conscious of her beautiful and complete existence had it not been for the visiting Wind who came to disturb her peace. He would blow round her where she lay, fluffing the clouds that lapped her idle limbs; sometimes he would caress her tenderly, his touch like that of a firm hand that feels the bone and quickens the flesh; sometimes he would blow stormily until her hair streamed out among the clouds. Always when he came he filled her mind with images of herself which hung before her and seemed by their mere presence to demand an explanation. She wished he would not come to trouble her, and when he did not come she hungered after him.

Sometimes, though rarely, he would arrive as a whirlwind, gathered together in a single rod, like a twist of molten glass. Then he would order her to open herself to him, and she would obey, to find her swooning consciousness sucked down into the caves and sea-beds of her being. After these visitations she would feel heavy, full of yawns and drowsiness, until at last she would part her thighs once again, allowing a new creation to come forth.

Perhaps her progeny would be fishes, many smooth and simple in their silver scales, others intricate with fins, barbels and spines; some delicate and lovely, their fins and tails like veils of iridescent silks; some ferocious and

ugly with faces that were masks of anger. Or it might be a fantastic creation of reptiles, gigantic monsters plated and armed as though to endure the collision of planets; or birds, each species with its own songs and cries housed within it, its own skills in the shaping of nests, and plumage that was specific to the faintest bar on the smallest feather. All these creatures displayed in their every part the endless inventiveness, the immeasurably powerful imagination of the generating Wind; they became one with the Woman, increasing her beauty like a fine garment.

The Wind stayed away for a very long time; to the Woman it seemed aeons since he had so much as breathed along the channels on the back of her hand or stirred a single hair on her forehead. All her old reluctance to receive him had been forgotten; without him she was listless and lifeless; her beautiful body began to grow cold, to freeze and destroy its own life. Then at last the Wind was upon her—she heard his quick sighs and saw where the clouds were parting before him like a flock of springtime sheep. He butted through them and without caress or tenderness entered into her; all the particles of her vague knowledge of herself were blown together, given force and swept through her as though she were flooded by a pebble-laden wave.

The Woman was left sunk in her usual heaviness; indeed, it was deeper than ever before, while the images that came to her were more than ever clear and disturbing; she felt herself to be close to understanding the secret of her life. When the time came for the parting of her thighs she expected to give birth to a creation of surpassing wonder, to creatures stronger than the reptiles or more exquisite than the birds. When her womb brought forth

from **A Woman as Great as the World and Other Fables** (New York: Random House, 1953). Reprinted by permission of the author, and of A. D. Peters & Co.

"The Sleeping Lady" from the Hal Saflieni Hypogeum, Malta. (Photo courtesy National Museum of Malta.)

ugly little mommets who walked clumsily on two legs and presently began to hang themselves with leaves and skins she was at first downcast; this progeny, surely, could do nothing to glorify and enrich her. But then the Woman was puzzled to feel in herself some new disturbing thing, a persistent self-consciousness as though the Wind were always with her, as though he were present among the tissues of her body. She began to be pleased by what had happened, thinking, with a clarity that before would have been beyond her reach, "Now I am as clever and imaginative as the Wind; I can be his equal and no longer merely his obedient mistress—the instrument upon which he plays."

Soon, however, she discovered that the new relationship did not suit her; she and the Wind were forever quarrelling; beating up terrible storms, floods, earthquakes and volcanoes in their anger. Some of their quarrels were provoked by the Woman's attempts to argue logically, some by her jealousy when she found that the Wind liked to loiter among the new creatures, whispering to them and, she suspected, caressing them. Soon, too, the mommets themselves became troublesome. They tormented her skin and flesh in a hundred ways by their restless activity; they were spoiling her physical beauty even while they were destroying her age-long peace of mind.

Her quarrels with the Wind and her jealousy, her bodily and mental discomfort at length proved too much for the Woman's native idleness and good nature. Her body was her own and hers the completeness of being. She rolled over and over, she scratched and slapped herself, and as she scratched and slapped and rolled she began to laugh; laughed louder, altogether abandoned herself to laughter.

When she grew quiet and the clouds could again fold softly round her, she

Additional Readings

was at peace once more, knowing everything and caring not at all. She did not even care if the Wind never returned, being unable to forgive her for her wanton destruction. As any woman may enjoy the sight of her clean, warm flesh stretched before her in the bath with steam curling lightly from the pale landscape of the body, so she now surveyed herself appreciatively, heedlessly, as she rested among clouds.

To avoid repetition, titles have not been included in lists of "Additional Readings" if they are cited in individual papers in the anthology. Titles have generally been listed only once, although there are a few exceptions to this practice. The full usefulness of the reading lists can be realized only when the reader uses works cited by contributors as well as those listed in one or another of the five separate lists. All bibliographic material, taken together, can hardly be defended as "complete," either historically or currently, since the subject is such a vast one. But the lists are meant to be useful, rewarding, provocative, and even irritating. Most of all, the lists offer evidence that an intellectual ferment that may save us from ourselves has roots in some unexpected facets of our culture. On the other hand, of the pieces that make up the anthology, a preponderance were written by biologists. This is the result of many biases, one of which is that the editors are biologists and wish to show that a viable ecology of man is already foreshadowed in biology. Beyond this, it may be that biologists—particularly the biologists we have in mind—present a view of man that is useful in a social and political context. The lists are not primarily for the purpose of shoring up the establishment but are submitted in the hope that a new age need not be generated by either doctrinaire verbiage or empty activism.

1. Men As Populations

A CHAPTER IS NOT an airtight container and of the title of this one particularly it could be said that the things men do as individuals or have done to them are effected through some sort of population structure of whose gene-pool they are a part. Readings listed here emphasize not only relevant modern ideas on the evolution of man as a biological species but also those ideas that inform a realistic picture of the distribution, production, and mortality of human protoplasm, past, present, and future. Finally, the question of controls, rational or otherwise, enters into what becomes increasingly *the* population problem. We now approach realization of our species' unhampered biotic potential, an aspect of the geometric progression of numbers that our society has not yet fully apprehended.

Anon., "War on hunger." *Intercom* (Foreign Policy Association), 8(6):24–72, November–December 1966.

Baker, Paul T., and J. S. Weiner, eds., *The Biology of Human Adaptability*. New York: Oxford University Press, 1966.

Baumhoff, Martin A., "Ecological determinants of aboriginal California populations." University of California Publications in American Archaeology and Ethnology 49:155–236, 1963.

Berkner, Lloyd V., "Man versus technology." *Population Bulletin* 22:83–94, 1966.

Bonner, James, "The upper limit of crop yield." *Science* 137:11–15, 1962.

Brereton, J. Le Gay, "The evolution and adaptive significance of social behaviour." Proceedings of the Ecological Society of Australia 1:14–30, 1966.

Brown, Harrison, *The Challenge of Man's Future*. New York: Viking, 1954. (Also Viking Compass Book C3.)

———, James Bonner, and John Wier, *The Next Hundred Years*. New York: Viking, 1957. (Also Viking Compass Book C135.)

Brown, Lester R., "The world outlook for conventional agriculture." *Science* 158: 604–611, 1967.

Budowski, Gerardo, "Middle America: the human factor," in *Future Environments of North America* (pp. 145–155), ed. F. F. Darling and J. P. Milton. Garden City, N.Y.: Natural History Press, 1966.

Buettner-Janusch, John, *Origins of Man; Physical Anthropology*. New York: John Wiley, 1966.

Calhoun, John B., "Social welfare as a variable in population dynamics." Cold Spring Harbor Symposia on Quantitative Biology 22:339–356, 1957.

———, "Population density and social pathology." *Scientific American* 206(2): 139–148, February 1962.

———, "Psycho-ecological aspects of population." Bethesda, Maryland: U.S. Public Health Service, Dept. of Health, Education and Welfare; Laboratory of Psychology, National Institute of Mental Health. Mimeographed, 1966.

Campbell, Bernard, *Human Evolution; An Introduction to Man's Adaptations*. Chicago: Aldine Publishing Co., 1966.

Caspari, Ernst, "Selective forces in the evolution of man." *American Naturalist* 97: 5–14, 1963.

Ciriacy-Wantrup, S. V., and James J. Parsons, eds., *Natural Resources—Quality and Quantity*. Berkeley: University of California Press, 1967.

Clark, J. Desmond, "The later Pleistocene cultures of Africa." *Science* 150:833–847, 1965.

Cole, LaMont C., "The ecosphere." *Scientific American* 198(4):83–92, April 1958.

Cook, Robert C., "Population and food supply." United Nations Freedom from Hunger, F.A.O. Basic Study No. 7, 1962.

———, "World Population Projections 1965–2000." *Population Bulletin* 21:73–93, 1965.

———, "California: after 19 million, what?" *Population Bulletin* 22:29–57, 1966.

Coon, Carleton, "Climate and race." Smithsonian Annual Report, 1953:277–298, 1954.

———, "Growth and development of social groups," in *Man and His Future* (pp. 120–131), a Ciba Foundation Volume, ed. Gordon Wolstonholme. London: J. & A. Churchill, 1963.

Corner, E. J. H., "The evolution of tropical forest," in *Evolution as a Process* (pp. 34–46), ed. J. S. Huxley, A. C. Hardy, and E. B. Ford. London: Allen and Unwin, 1954. (Also Collier paperback 09308.)

Cowles, Raymond B., "Missiles, clay pots and mortality rates in primitive man." *American Naturalist* 97:29–37, 1963.

Crook, J. H., and J. S. Gartlan, "Evolution of primate societies." *Nature* 210:1200–1203, 1966.

Crow, James F., "Mechanisms and trends in human evolution." *Daedalus*, Summer 1961:416–431.

Currie, Lauchlin, "Economics and population." *Population Bulletin* 23:25–38, 1967.

Davis, Kingsley, "Population policy: will current programs succeed?" *Science* 158: 730–739, 1967; comments, 159:481–482, 827–829, 1968.

Deevey, Edward S., Jr., "Recent textbooks of human ecology." *Ecology* 32:347–351, 1951.

———, "The human crop." *Scientific American* 194(4):105–112, April 1956.

Desmond, Annabelle, "How many people have ever lived on Earth?" *Population Bulletin* 18:1–18, 1962.

Ehrlich, Paul R., *The Population Bomb.* San Francisco: Sierra Club; Ballantine paperback 73031, 1968.

Emlen, John Merritt, "Natural selection and human behavior." *Journal of Theoretical Biology* 12:410–418, 1966.

Etkin, William, "Social behavioral factors in the emergence of man." *Human Biology* 35:299–310, 1963.

Goodhart, C. B., "Biological fitness in man." *Eugenics Review* 52(2):83–85, 1960.

———, "The evolutionary significance of human hair patterns and skin colouring." *Advancement of Science* 17:53–59, 1960.

Gregg, Alan, "Is man a biological cancer?" *Population Bulletin* 11:74–78, 1955.

Hardin, Garrett, "The myth of space travel as a solution to the population problem." *Journal of Heredity* 50:68–70, 1959.

———, "A second Sermon on the Mount." *Perspectives in Biology and Medicine* 6: 366–371, 1963.

———, *Population, Evolution, & Birth Control; A Collage of Controversial Readings.* San Francisco: Freeman, 1964.

———, "The semantics of 'Space.'" *ETC.: A Review of General Semantics* 23:167–171, 1966.

Hawkes, Jacquetta, *Man on Earth.* New York: Random House, 1955.

Hoagland, Hudson, "Mechanisms of population control." *Daedalus*, Summer 1964: 812–829.

Howell, F. Clark, "Recent advances in human evolutionary studies." *Quarterly Review of Biology* 42:471–513, 1967.

Howells, William White, *Ideas on Human Evolution.* Cambridge, Mass.: Harvard University Press, 1962. (Also Atheneum Paperback 98-h.)

———, *Mankind in the Making: The Story of Human Evolution* (rev. ed.). Garden City, N.Y.: Doubleday, 1967.

Hutchinson, G. Evelyn, "Prolegomenon to the study of the descent of man," in *The Ecological Theater and the Evolutionary Play* (pp. 78–94). New Haven: Yale University Press, 1965.

Huxley, Aldous, "The double crisis," in *Themes and Variations* (pp. 225–260). London: Chatto & Windus, 1950.

———, "The Politics of ecology; the question of survival." Occasional Paper on the Free Society, Center for the Study of Democratic Institutions, Santa Barbara, Calif., 1963.

Huxley, Julian, "World Population." *Scientific American* 194(3):64–76, March 1956.

Kortlandt, A., *Tussen Mens en Dier.* Inaugural Lecture, University of Amsterdam-Groningen, 1959. (English summary, courtesy of author.)

———, (Comment upon) "On the essential morphological basis for human culture." *Current Anthropology* 6:320–326, 1965.

Lyle, David, "The human race has, maybe, thirty-five years left." *Esquire*, September 1967:116–118ff.

Morris, Desmond, *The Naked Ape: A Zoologist's Study of the Human Animal.* New York: McGraw-Hill, 1967.

Mudd, Stuart, ed., *The Population Crisis and the Use of the World Resources.* Bloomington, Ind.: Indiana University Press, 1964.

Napier, John, "Early man and his environment." *Discovery*, March 1963:12–18.

Odum, Howard T., "Limits of remote ecosystems containing man." *American Biology Teacher* 25:429–443, 1963.

441

Osborn, Fairfield, *Our Plundered Planet.* Boston: Little, Brown, 1948. (Also Little, Brown paperback LB9.)

———, ed., *Our Crowded Planet: Essays on the Pressures of Population.* Garden City, N.Y.: Doubleday, 1962.

Paddock, William, and Paul Paddock, *Hungry Nations.* Boston: Little, Brown, 1964. (Also Little, Brown paperback LB61.)

———, *Famine—1975! America's Decision: Who Will Survive?* Boston: Little, Brown, 1967.

Price, Daniel O., ed., *The 99th Hour—the Population Crisis in the United States.* Chapel Hill: University of North Carolina Press, 1967.

Roe, Anne, "Psychological definitions of man," in *Classification and Human Evolution* (pp. 320–331), ed. S. L. Washburn. Chicago: Aldine Publishing Co., 1963.

Schreider, Eugène, "Ecological rules, body-heat regulation, and human evolution." *Evolution* 18:1–9, 1964.

Scientific American, *Human Variation and Origins,* introductions by W. S. Laughlin and R. H. Osborne. San Francisco: Freeman, 1967.

Sears, Paul B., "The ecology of man." Condon Lectures, Oregon State System of Higher Education, Eugene, Oregon, 1957; *also* Smithsonian Annual Report, 1958: 375–398, 1959.

———, "Pressures of population; an ecologist's point of view." *What's New* (Abbott Laboratories, North Chicago, Ill.), 1959; *also, Atlantic Naturalist* 15:80–86, 1960.

Simpson, George Gaylord, "The nonprevalence of humanoids." *Science* 143:769–775, 1964. (Also in *This View of Life,* Harcourt, Brace paperback H-052.)

Steward, Julian H., "Cultural evolution." *Scientific American* 194(5):69–80, May 1956.

Tappen, N. C., "Primate evolution and human behavior," in *Men and Cultures* (pp. 725–731), ed. A. F. C. Wallace. Philadelphia: University of Pennsylvania Press, 1960.

Vogt, William, *Road to Survival.* New York: William Sloane Associates, 1948.

———, "Population patterns and movements," in *Future Environments of North America* (pp. 372–389), ed. F. F. Darling and J. P. Milton. Garden City, N.Y.: Natural History Press, 1966.

von Foerster, Heinz, P. M. Mora, and L. W. Amiot, "Doomsday: Friday, 13 November, A.D. 2026." *Science* 132:1291–1295; comments, 133:936–946 and 1931–1937, 1960.

Washburn, Sherwood L., ed., *Social Life of Early Man.* Chicago: Aldine Publishing Co., 1961.

Weaver, Warren, "Dreams and responsibilities," *Bulletin of the Atomic Scientists* 19(5):10–11, May 1963.

Wittfogel, Karl A., "Developmental aspects of hydraulic societies." Pan American Union, Social Science Monograph 1:43–52, 1955.

Wynne-Edwards, V. C., "Population control in animals." *Scientific American* 211(2): 68–74, August 1964.

2. The Environmental Encounter

IT IS CONVENIENT to isolate the individual from his environment. We have, however, hardly begun to sort out the contributions of environments to individual development. Unfortunately, our emphasis is often more upon some political, economic, or religious relation to environment, rather than upon the quality of the total environmental encounter by the individual. The readings for this chapter are diverse. They elaborate upon the subtle interplay between personality and place that this anthology epitomizes. The readings also expound historical roots, describe alternative exposures, and press, at times, the point that the role of the blood, flesh, and gristle individual as "experiencer" is not fully understood. Our society's accounts of transactions— and our *expectations* of such transactions—seldom get deeper than conventional symbols. While it is customary to laugh at bird-watchers, the bird-watcher characteristically watches the continuity of interchange between man and nature. He is not content to assume that a bird song put on tape is enough.

Audy, J. Ralph, "Measurement and differential diagnosis of health." Paper in press, George William Hooper Foundation, University of California, San Francisco Medical Center, 1967.

Bachelard, Gaston, "The house protects the dreamer." *Landscape* 13(3): 28–33, Spring 1964.

Baker, Paul T., and J. S. Weiner, eds., *The Biology of Human Adaptability*. New York: Oxford University Press, 1966.

Bates, Marston, "Human ecology," in *Anthropology Today* (pp. 700–713), ed. A. L. Kroeber. Chicago: University of Chicago Press, 1953. (Also, pp. 222–235 in Sol Tax's paperback version, 1962.)

———, "Man and nature," in Proceedings of the Lockwood Conference on the Suburban Forest and Ecology (pp. 22–30). Connecticut Agricultural Experiment Station Bulletin 652, 1962.

Calhoun, John B., "The role of space in animal sociology." *Journal of Social Issues* 22(4):46–58, October 1966.

Campbell, Joseph, "The imprints of experience," in *The Masks of God: Primitive Mythology* (pp. 50–118). New York: Viking, 1959.

Charter, S P R, "Why preserve nature?" *Man on Earth* 1(2):1–8, 1965.

Clark, J. Desmond, "The later Pleistocene cultures of Africa." *Science* 150:833–847, 1965.

Cloos, Hans, *Conversation with the Earth*. London: Routledge & Kegan Paul, 1954.

Collier, John, Sr., "The Indian as ancient man; and ancient man as the primal ecologist. With a remark on Indian material poverty and its meaning to the Indian," in *Homenaje à Juan Comas en su 65 Aniversario*, Vol. I, pp. 15–22. Mexico City, 1965.

Coon, Carleton, "Climate and race." Smithsonian Annual Report, 1953: 277–298, 1954.

Crowe, Sylvia, "Civilization and the landscape." Smithsonian Annual Report, 1962:537–544, 1963.

Darling, F. Fraser, "The unity of ecology." Smithsonian Annual Report, 1964:461–476, 1965.

Dasmann, Raymond F., "Man in North America," in *Future Environments of North America* (pp. 326–334), ed. F. F. Darling and J. P. Milton. Garden City, N.Y.: Natural History Press, 1966.

Driver, Harold E., and William C. Massey, "Comparative studies of North American Indians." American Philosophical Society, Transactions, 47:165–456, 1957.

Dubos, René, *Man Adapting*. New Haven: Yale University Press, 1965. (Also Yale paperback Y197.)

Ekirch, Arthur Alphonse, Jr., *Man and Nature in America*. New York: Columbia University Press, 1963.

Eliade, Mircea, *Cosmos and History: The Myth of the Eternal Return*. New York: Harper Torchbooks TB2050, 1959.

Ellis, Havelock, "The love of wild nature." *Contemporary Review* 40:180–199, 1909.

Glacken, Clarence J., *Traces on the Rhodian Shore: Nature and Culture in Western Thought from Ancient Times to the End of the Eighteenth Century*. Berkeley: University of California Press, 1967.

Glikson, Artur, "Man's relationship to his environment," in *Man and His Future* (pp. 132–152), a Ciba Foundation Volume, ed. G. Wolstonholme. London: J. & A. Churchill, 1963.

Goodhart, C. B., "Threat display in monkeys and men." *Animals* 7(6): 142–147, August 24, 1965.

Hall, Edward T., *The Hidden Dimension*. Garden City, N.Y.: Doubleday, 1966.

Hallowell, A. Irving, "The structural and functional dimensions of a human existence." *Quarterly Review of Biology* 31:88–101, 1956.

Halprin, Lawrence, "The gardens of the High Sierra." *Landscape* 11(2):26–28, Winter 1961–62.

Harris, Marvin, and George E. B. Morren, "The limitations of the principle of limited possibilities." *American Anthropologist* 68:122–127, 1966.

Hawkes, Jacquetta, *A Land*. New York: Random House, 1952.

———, *Man on Earth*. New York: Random House, 1955.

Hutchinson, G. Evelyn, "The Gothic attitude to natural history," in *The Itinerant Ivory Tower* (pp. 28–35). New Haven: Yale University Press, 1953.

———, "The electronic Antichrist" and "The uses of beetles," in *The Enchanted Voyage and Other Studies* (pp. 44–49, 90–97). New Haven: Yale University Press, 1962.

———, "Prolegomenon to the study of the descent of man," in *The Ecological Theater and the Evolutionary Play* (pp. 78–94). New Haven: Yale University Press, 1965.

Huth, Hans, *Nature and the American: Three Centuries of Changing Attitudes.* Berkeley: University of California Press, 1957.

Isaac, Erich, "Religion, landscape, and space." *Landscape* 9(2):14–18, Winter 1959–60.

———, "The act and the covenant: the impact of religion on the landscape." *Landscape* 11(2):12–17, Winter 1961–62.

Jackson, John B., "The westward-moving house." *Landscape* 2(3):8–21, Spring 1953.

Kates, Robert, "The pursuit of beauty in the environment." *Landscape* 16(2):21–25, Winter 1966–67.

Kuttner, R., "Cultural selection of human psychological types." *Genus* 16(1–4):3–6, 1960; reprinted in *Culture, Man's Adaptive Dimension* (pp. 286–289), ed. M. F. Ashley Montagu. New York: Oxford University Press, 1968.

Leroi-Gourhan, André, "The evolution of Paleolithic art." *Scientific American* 218(2):59–79, February 1968.

Lowenthal, David, "Is wilderness 'Paradise Enow'? Images of nature in America." *Columbia University Forum* 7(2):34–40, Spring 1964.

McHarg, Ian L., "Ecological determinism," in *Future Environments of North America* (pp. 526–538), ed. F. F. Darling and J. P. Milton. Garden City, N.Y.: Natural History Press, 1966.

McKinley, Daniel, "A clamor of gulls: journal of a Maine island summer." *Contact* No. 11, 3(3):22–31, August 1962.

Martin, A. F., "The necessity for determinism." Transactions and Papers, Publ. No. 17, Institute of British Geographers, 1951.

Meggers, Betty J., "Environmental limitation on the development of culture." *American Anthropologist* 56:801–824, 1954.

———, "Environment and culture in the Amazon Basin: an appraisal of the theory of environmental determinism," in *Studies in Human Ecology,* Pan American Union, Social Science Monograph 3:71–89, 1957.

Napier, John, "Early man and his environment." *Discovery,* March 1963, pp. 12–18.

Nash, Roderick, *Wilderness and the American Mind.* New Haven: Yale University Press, 1967.

Ottersen, Signe Ruh, "Readings on natural beauty: a selected bibliography." U.S. Dept. of Interior Library, Bibliography No. 1, 1967.

Pichler, Walter, "The lesson of Precolumbian architecture." *Landscape* 13(3):24–25, Spring 1964.

Ritter, William E., "Feeling in the interpretation of nature." *Popular Science Monthly* 79:126–136, 1911.

Rockefeller, Laurance S., et al., The White House Conference on Natural Beauty: Report to the President; The President's Response. Washington, D.C., 1965.

Schreider, Eugène, "Ecological rules, body-heat regulation, and human evolution." *Evolution* 18:1–9, 1964.

———, "Possible selective mechanisms of social differentiation in biological traits." *Human Biology* 39:14–20, 1967.

Scully, Vincent, *The Earth, the Temple and the Gods: Greek Sacred Architecture.* New Haven: Yale University Press, 1962.

Searles, Harold F., "The role of the non-human environment." *Landscape* 11(2):31–34, Winter 1961–62.

Sears, Paul B., "Science, life, and landscape." University of Hawaii Occasional Paper 68, 1962.

Sewell, Elizabeth, *The Orphic Voice: Poetry and Natural History.* New Haven: Yale University Press, 1960.

Shepard, Paul, "The cross valley syndrome." *Landscape* 10(3):4–8, Spring 1961.

_____, "The artist as explorer." *Landscape* 12(2):25–27, Winter 1962–63.

_____, The wilderness as nature." *Atlantic Naturalist* 20:9–14, 1965.

_____, *Man in the Landscape: A Historic View of the Esthetics of Nature.* New York: Alfred Knopf, 1967.

Sommer, Robert, "Man's proximate environment." *Journal of Social Issues* 22(4):59–70, October 1966.

Sperry, Robert W., "Mind, brain, and humanist values." *Bulletin of the Atomic Scientists* 22(7):2–6, September 1966.

Stapledon, Sir George, *Human Ecology,* ed. Robert Waller. New York: Hillary House Publishers, 1964.

Thomas, William L., Jr., ed., *Man's Role in Changing the Face of the Earth.* Chicago: University of Chicago Press, 1956.

Tuan, Yi-Fu, "Architecture and human nature." *Landscape* 13(1):16–19, Autumn 1963.

von Foerster, Heinz, "Circuitry of clues to platonic ideation," in *Aspects of the Theory of Artificial Intelligence* (pp. 43–81), ed. C. A. Muses. New York: Plenum Press, 1962.

Watts, Alan W., *Nature, Man, and Woman.* New York: Pantheon Books, 1958. (Also Mentor New American Library MD282.)

_____, *The Book: On the Taboo Against Knowing Who You Are.* New York: Pantheon Books, 1967. (Also Collier paperback 06812.)

Wittfogel, Karl A., "Developmental aspects of hydraulic societies." Pan American Union, Social Science Monograph 1:43–52, 1955.

Wolfe, Roy I., "Leisure: the element of choice." *Journal of Human Ecology* 2(6):1–12, 1952.

3. Man and Other Organisms

THE SEARCH FOR a life-substance, independent from the organisms that are alive, has proved an interesting failure. Albert Szent-Györgyi has said that, after his investigations took him from rabbits to bacteria to molecules to electrons, "on the way I lost life; it had run out between my fingers." While it is not difficult today to get a detailed account of deterioration of the environment, it is hard indeed to find a convincing report on the environment's nonhuman complexity, especially as it was before human activity so disturbed it. This refers not to the complexity of processes merely, but to the elaborate flush of differences in species of organisms and their activities and roles and delicately balanced functions. We now see the impending emergence of a man-centered engineering—designed, we must suppose, to put Humpty Dumpty back upon the wall—a wall whose architectural details we unfortunately never learned beyond determining its elevation, longitude, latitude, and chemical composition. Much of the effort to rebuild nature seems as unreal as the previous world view that it was all either indestructible, inexhaustible, or infinitely malleable; it somehow ignores the fact that, aside from a few physical activities of air and water, only living individuals of the various species of organisms perform most of the ameliorative and restorative functions of nature.

Anderson, Edgar, *Plants, Man and Life.* Berkeley: University of California Press, 1967.

Anon., "Scientific Aspects of Pest Control." U.S. National Academy of Sciences—National Research Council Publ. 1402. Washington, D.C., 1966.

Ardrey, Robert, *The Territorial Imperative.* New York: Atheneum, 1966.

Audy, J. Ralph, "Ecological aspects of introduced pests and diseases." *Medical Journal of Malaya* 11(1):21–32, 1956.

_____, "Medical ecology in relation to geography." *British Journal of Clinical Practice* 12(2):102–110, 1958.

————, "Man and the land," in *Tomorrow's Wilderness* (pp. 101–106), ed. F. Leydet. San Francisco: Sierra Club, 1963.

Bates, Marston, "Man and nature," in *Proceedings of the Lockwood Conference on the Suburban Forest and Ecology* (pp. 22–30). Connecticut Agricultural Experiment Station Bulletin 652, 1962.

Bouillenne, Raymond, "Man, the destroying biotype." *Science* 135:706–712, 1962.

Braidwood, Robert J., and Charles A. Reed, "The achievement and early consequences of food-production: a consideration of the archeological and natural-historical evidence." Cold Spring Harbor Symposia on Quantitative Biology 22:19–29, 1957.

Bullen, F. T., "Locusts and grasshoppers as pests of crops and pasture—a preliminary economic approach." *Journal of Applied Ecology* 3:147–168, 1966.

Burkill, I. H., "Habits of man and the origins of the cultivated plants of the Old World." *Proceedings of the Linnean Society of London* 164(1):12–42, 1953.

Carter, George F., "Ecology—geography—ethnobotany." *Scientific Monthly* 70:73–80, 1950.

Clark, J. G. D., *Prehistoric Europe: The Economic Basis*. Stanford: Stanford University Press, 1966.

Corner, E. J. H., "The evolution of tropical forest," in *Evolution as a Process* (pp. 34–46), ed. J. S. Huxley, A. C. Hardy, and E. B. Ford. London: Allen and Unwin, 1954. (Also Collier paperback 09308.)

————, "The tropical botanist." *Advancement of Science* 20:1–7, 1963.

Cowles, Raymond B., "Missiles, clay pots and mortality rates in primitive man." *American Naturalist* 97:29–37, 1963.

Dasmann, Raymond F., *Environmental Conservation*. New York: Wiley, 1959.

————, "Man in North America," in *Future Environments of North America* (pp. 326–334), ed. F. F. Darling and J. P. Milton. Garden City, N.Y.: Natural History Press, 1966.

Dubos, René, *Man Adapting*. New Haven: Yale University Press, 1965. (Also Yale paperback Y197.)

Dunn, Frederick L., "On the antiquity of malaria in the Western Hemisphere." *Human Biology* 37:385–393, 1965.

Egler, Frank E., "Wildlife habitat management for the citizen." *Atlantic Naturalist* 22:166-169, 1967.

Etter, Alfred G., "Why nothing gets done about pesticides: a case history." *Atlantic Naturalist* 19:28–36, 1964.

Flannery, Kent V., "The ecology of early food production in Mesopotamia." *Science* 147:1247–1256, 1965.

Goodhart, C. B., "Threat display in monkeys and men." *Animals* 7(6):142–147, August 24, 1965.

Harris, Marvin, "The cultural ecology of India's sacred cattle." *Current Anthropology* 7:51–66, 1966.

Hediger, Heini, "Man as a social partner of animals and vice-versa." Symposium, Zoological Society of London, 14:291–300, 1965.

Hinkle, Lawrence E., Jr., "Studies of human ecology in relation to health and behavior." *BioScience* 15:517–520, 1965.

Hoagland, Hudson, "Mechanisms of population control." *Daedalus*, Summer 1964: 812–829.

Hudson, E. H., "Treponematosis and man's social evolution." *American Anthropologist* 67:885–901, 1965.

Hutchinson, G. Evelyn, "The electronic Antichrist" and "The uses of beetles," in *The Enchanted Voyage and Other Studies* (pp. 44–49, 90–97). New Haven: Yale University Press, 1962.

Huth, Hans, *Nature and the American: Three Centuries of Changing Attitudes*. Berkeley: University of California Press, 1957.

Isaac, Erich, "Influence of religion on the spread of citrus." *Science* 129:179–186, 1959.

Kates, Robert, "The pursuit of beauty in the environment." *Landscape* 16(2):21–25, Winter 1966–67.

Koprowski, Hilary, "Future of infectious and malignant diseases," in *Man and His Future* (pp. 196–216), a Ciba Foundation Volume, ed. G. Wolstonholme. London: J. & A. Churchill, 1963.

Kortlandt, A., *Tussen Mens en Dier*. Inaugural Lecture, University of Amsterdam-Groningen, 1959. (English summary, courtesy of author.)

Kuenen, D. J., "Man, food, and insects as an ecological problem." Proceedings, XVI International Congress of Zoology, 7:5–13, 1963.

Laughlin, William S., "Acquisition of anatomical knowledge by ancient man," in Social Life of Early Man (pp. 150–175), ed. S. L. Washburn. Chicago: Aldine Publishing Co., 1961.

Leeds, Anthony, and Andrew P. Vayda, eds., Man, Culture, and Animals: The Role of Animals in Human Ecological Adjustments. American Association for the Advancement of Science, Publ. 78. Washington, D.C., 1965.

Leroi-Gourhan, André, Treasures of Prehistoric Art. New York: Harry N. Abrams, 1967.

Leyhausen, Paul, "The communal organization of solitary mammals." Symposium, Zoological Society of London, 14:249–263, 1965.

Lorenz, Konrad, On Aggression. New York: Harcourt, Brace & World, 1966. (Also Bantam paperback Q3511.)

May, Jacques M., "The ecology of human disease," in Studies in Human Ecology, Pan American Union, Social Science Monograph 3:91–113, 1957.

Morris, Clarence, "The rights and duties of beasts and trees: a law teacher's essay for landscape architects." Journal of Legal Education 17:185–192, 1964.

Morris, Desmond, ed., Primate Ethology. Chicago: Aldine Publishing Co., 1967.

Morris, Ramona, and Desmond Morris, Men and Apes. New York: McGraw-Hill, 1966.

Murray, E. G. D., "The place of nature in man's world." American Scientist 42:130–135, 142, 1954.

Pearson, Oliver P., "Metabolism and bioenergetics." Scientific Monthly 66:131–134, 1948.

Reed, Charles A., "Animal domestication in the prehistoric Near East." Science 130:1629–1639, 1959.

Salaman, Redcliffe N., "Influence of food plants on social structure." Nature 166:382–383, 1950.

Sauer, Carl O., "Theme of plant and animal destruction in economic history." Journal of Farm Economics 20:765–775, 1938. (Reprinted in Land and Life, University of California Press paperback 132.)

Sharp, A. J., "Responsibilities and opportunities of the taxonomist today." Economic Botany 16:49–52, 1962.

Shepard, Paul, "Reverence for life at Lambaréné." Landscape 8(2):26–29, Winter 1958–59.

———, Man in the Landscape: A Historic View of the Esthetics of Nature. New York: Alfred Knopf, 1967.

Thompson, Laura, "The basic conservation problem." Scientific Monthly 68:129–131, 1949.

Washburn, Sherwood L., and David A. Hamburg, "The implications of primate research," in Primate Behavior (pp. 607–622), ed. Irven DeVore. New York: Holt, 1965.

4. Men in Ecosystems

THE INTERPLAY IN NATURE that, aside from man's own efforts, keeps our mankind Humpty Dumpty on the wall may be thought of as defining man's place in nature. Man's functional place in nature can be taken "hot"—as feelings and tastes, as species of animals and plants seen, collected, cultivated, hunted, or eaten, as bones broken and trails hiked. Or, it can be taken "cold," as patterns and amounts of energy expended, as cyclic movements of minerals through nature, as intergeared feed-back mechanisms, as processes and chemistries of communities. In the latter the sharpness of individual borders are smudged, rather as in population dynamics: the statistics of mass-behavior comes into its own and free-will is a dubious term. Perhaps it is a matter of whether we focus upon forests or upon trees; both are defensible realities. A little outside reading in community processes suggests that ecosystem chemistry differs from purely test tube science in its unique temporal and structural complexity.

Åberg, Bertil, and Frank P. Hungate, eds., *Radioecological Concentration Processes*. New York: Pergamon Press, 1967.

Adams, C. C., "The relation of general ecology to human ecology." *Ecology* 16:316–335, 1935.

Albrecht, William A., "Wastebasket of the Earth." *Bulletin of the Atomic Scientists* 17(8):335–340, 1961.

Anon., "Restoring the Quality of our Environment." Report of the Environmental Pollution Panel, President's Science Advisory Committee. The White House, Washington, D.C., 1965.

Anon., "Scientific Aspects of Pest Control." U.S. National Academy of Sciences—National Research Council Publ. 1402. Washington, D.C., 1966.

Audy, J. Ralph, "Types of human influence on natural foci of disease," in *Theoretical Questions of Natural Foci of Diseases* (pp. 245–253), ed. B. Rosický and K. Heyberger. Czechoslovak Academy of Sciences, 1965.

———, "Man-made maladies," in *The Air We Breathe* (pp. 100–112), ed. S. M. Farber and R. H. L. Wilson. Springfield, Ill.: C. C. Thomas, 1961.

Bates, Marston, "Human ecology," in *Anthropology Today* (pp. 700–713), ed. A. L. Kroeber. Chicago: University of Chicago Press, 1953. (Pp. 222–235, in Sol Tax's paperback version, 1962.)

———, "Man and nature," in Proceedings of the Lockwood Conference on the Suburban Forest and Ecology (pp. 22–30). Connecticut Agricultural Experiment Station Bulletin 652, 1962.

Baumhoff, Martin A., "Ecological determinants of aboriginal California populations." University of California Publications in American Archaeology and Ethnology, 49:155–236, 1963.

Braidwood, Robert J., and Charles A. Reed, "The achievement and early consequences of food-production: a consideration of the archeological and natural-historical evidence." *Cold Spring Harbor Symposia on Quantitative Biology* 22:19–29, 1957.

Bresler, Jack B., ed., *Human Ecology: Collected Readings*. Reading, Mass.: Addison-Wesley, 1966.

Budowski, Gerardo, "Middle America: the human factor," in *Future Environments of North America* (pp. 144–155), ed. F. F. Darling and J. P. Milton. Garden City, N.Y.: Natural History Press, 1966.

Cain, Stanley A., "Man and his environment." *Population Bulletin* 22:96–103, 1966.

Caldwell, Lynton K., ed., *Environmental Studies*. Bloomington: Indiana University, Government Department, Institute of Public Administration. Parts I–IV, 1967.

Ciriacy-Wantrup, S. V., and James J. Parsons, eds., *Natural Resources—Quality and Quantity*. Berkeley: University of California Press, 1967.

Clark, J. G. D., *Prehistoric Europe: The Economic Basis*. Stanford: Stanford University Press, 1966.

Clark, J. Desmond, "The later Pleistocene cultures of Africa." *Science* 150:833–847, 1965.

Coe, Michael D., and Kent V. Flannery, "Microenvironments and Mesoamerican prehistory." *Science* 143:650–654, 1964.

Cole, LaMont C., "The ecosphere." *Scientific American* 198(4):83–92, April 1958.

———, "Pesticides: a hazard to nature's equilibrium." *American Journal of Public Health* 54(1, Pt. ii):24–31, 1964.

———, "Man's ecosystem." *BioScience* 16:243–248, 1966.

———, "Can the world be saved?" New York *Times* Magazine, March 31, 1968, pp. 35 ff.

Commoner, Barry, *Science and Survival*. New York: Viking, 1966. (Also Viking Compass Book C212.)

———, "Nature unbalanced; how man interferes with the nitrogen cycle." *Scientist and Citizen* 10(1):9–13, 28, Jan.–Feb. 1968.

———, et al., "The integrity of science: a report by the AAAS Committee on Science in the Promotion of Human Welfare." *American Scientist* 53:174–198, 1965.

Coon, Carleton S., "Race and ecology in man." *Cold Spring Harbor Symposia in Quantitative Biology* 24:153–159, 1959.

Crook, J. H., and J. S. Gartlan, "Evolution of primate societies." *Nature* 210:1200–1203, 1966.

Daniels, Farrington. "Direct use of the sun's energy." *American Scientist* 55:15–47, 1967.

Darling, F. Fraser, *West Highland Survey: An Essay in Human Ecology.* New York: Oxford University Press, 1955.

————, "Simplicity and complexity," in Proceedings of the Lockwood Conference on the Suburban Forest and Ecology (pp. 39–44). Connecticut Agricultural Experiment Station Bulletin 652, 1962.

————, "Conservation and ecological theory." *Journal of Ecology* 52(supplement):39–45, 1964.

————, and John P. Milton, eds., *Future Environments of North America.* Garden City, N.Y.: Natural History Press, 1966.

————, et al., "Implications of rising carbon dioxide content of the atmosphere." New York: The Conservation Foundation, 1963.

Dasmann, Raymond F., *Environmental Conservation.* New York: Wiley, 1959.

Deevey, Edward S., Jr., "Recent textbooks of human ecology." *Ecology* 32:347–351, 1951.

————, "The human crop." *Scientific American* 194(4):105–112, April 1956.

Driver, Harold E., and William C. Massey, "Comparative studies of North American Indians." American Philosophical Society, Transactions, 47:165–456, 1957.

Egler, Frank E., "Pesticides in our ecosystem: communication II." *BioScience* 14(11):29–36, 1964.

Elton, Charles S., *The Ecology of Invasions by Animals and Plants.* London: Methuen, 1958.

Etter, Alfred G., "Why nothing gets done about pesticides: a case history." *Atlantic Naturalist* 19:28–36, 1964.

Eyre, S. R., and G. R. J. Jones, "Introduction" to *Geography as Human Ecology* (pp. 1–29). New York: St. Martin's Press, 1966.

Flannery, Kent V., "The ecology of early food production in Mesopotamia." *Science* 147:1247–1256, 1965.

Fuller, R. B., and John McHale, *Inventory of World Resources, Human Trends and Needs.* Carbondale: Southern Illinois University. World Resources Inventory, World Design Science Decade 1965–1975, Document 1, 1963.

Goodman, Gordon T., et al., *Ecology and the Industrial Society.* New York: Wiley, 1965.

Hainline, Jane, "Culture and biological adaptation." *American Anthropologist* 67:1174–1197, 1965.

Hardin, Garrett, "Pop research and the seismic market." *Per/Se,* Fall 1967, pp. 19–24.

Harris, Marvin, "The cultural ecology of India's sacred cattle." *Current Anthropology* 7:51–66, 1966.

Hines, L. G., "The myth of idle resources: a reconsideration of the concept of non-use in conservation." Transactions of the Eighteenth North American Wildlife Conference, pp. 28–35, 1953.

Hutchinson, G. Evelyn, "On living in the biosphere." *Scientific Monthly* 67:393–398, 1948.

————, "Prolegomenon to the study of the descent of man," in *The Ecological Theater and the Evolutionary Play* (pp. 78–94). New Haven: Yale University Press, 1965.

Jarrett, Henry, ed., *Environmental Quality in a Growing Economy.* Resources for the Future, Inc., 1966 (Baltimore: Johns Hopkins University Press).

Jennings, B. H., *Interactions of Man and his Environment.* New York: Plenum Press, 1966.

Komarek, Edwin V., Sr., "Fire—and the ecology of man." Tall Timbers Fire Ecology Conference, Proceedings, 6:143–170, 1967.

Kroeber, Alfred L., *Cultural and Natural Areas of Native North America.* Berkeley: University of California Press, 1963.

Kuenen, D. J. "Man, food, and insects as an ecological problem." Proceedings, XVI International Congress of Zoology, 7:5–13, 1963.

Leopold, Luna B., "Water and the conservation movement." U.S. Geological Survey, Circular 402, 1958.

————, "Conservation and water management." U.S. Geological Survey, Circular 414, 4 parts, 1960.

Livingstone, Daniel A., et al., "Biological aspects of weather modification." Bulletin, Ecological Society of America, 47(1):39–78, 1966.

McHale, John, *The Ecological Context: Energy and Materials.* Carbondale: Southern Illinois University. World Resources Inventory, World Design Science Decade 1965–1975, Document 6, 1967.

McKinley, Daniel, "Human ecology: some thoughts on brash pioneering in an orderly world." *Atlantic Naturalist* 19:165–174, 1964.

Major, Jack, et al., "An ecological context for the use and conservation of natural resources." Bulletin, Ecological Society of America, 45(1):13–17, March 1964.

Meggers, Betty J., "Environmental limitation on the development of culture." *American Anthropologist* 56:801–824, 1954.

———, "Environment and culture in the Amazon basin: an appraisal of the theory of environmental determinism," in *Studies in Human Ecology,* Pan American Union, Social Science Monograph 3:71–89, 1957.

Miettinen, Jorma K., "Radioactive food chains in arctic regions" (mimeographed). Department of Radiochemistry, University of Helsinki, 1964.

Odum, Eugene P., "The new ecology." *BioScience* 14(7):14–16, 1964.

Ottersen, Signe Ruh, "Readings on natural beauty: a selected bibliography." U.S. Dept. of Interior Library, Bibliography No. 1, 1967.

Pearson, Oliver P., "Metabolism and bioenergetics." *Scientific Monthly* 66:131–134, 1948.

Platt, John R., "The step to man." *Science* 149:607–613, 1965.

Pruitt, William O., Jr., "Lichen, caribou and high radiation in Eskimos." *Audubon Magazine* 65:284–287, 1963.

Rienow, Robert, and Leona Train Rienow, *Moment in the Sun.* New York: Dial Press, 1967.

Rudd, Robert L., *Pesticides and the Living Landscape.* Madison: University of Wisconsin Press, 1964. (Also University of Wisconsin Press paperback W58.)

Sargent, Frederick, II, "Taming the weather." *Scientist and Citizen* 9(5):81–88, 96, May 1967.

Sauer, Carl O., "Theme of plant and animal destruction in economic history." *Journal of Farm Economics* 20:765–775, 1938.

(Reprinted in *Land and Life,* University of California Press paperback 132.)

———, "Foreword to historical geography." Annals, Association of American Geographers, 31:1–24, 1941. (See note, Sauer, 1938, above.)

Sears, Paul B., *Deserts on the March.* Norman: University of Oklahoma Press, 1935.

———, "Integration at the community level." *American Scientist* 37:235–242, 1949.

———, "The ecology of man." Condon Lectures, Oregon State System of Higher Education, Eugene, 1957. (Also, Smithsonian Annual Report, 1958:375–398, 1959.)

———, "Pressures of population: an ecologist's point of view." *What's New* (Abbott Laboratories, North Chicago, Ill.), 1959. (Also, *Atlantic Naturalist* 15:80–86, 1960.)

———, "Ecology—a subversive subject." *BioScience* 14(7):11–13, 1964.

Shepard, Paul, "The place of nature in man's world." *School Science & Mathematics* 58:394–403, 1958.

———, *Man in the Landscape: A Historic View of the Esthetics of Nature.* New York: Alfred Knopf, 1967.

———, "Whatever happened to human ecology?" *BioScience* 17:891–894, 911, 1967.

Snow, Joel A., "Radioactive waste from reactors." *Scientist and Citizen* 9(5):89–96, May 1967.

Spilhaus, Athelstan, ed., "Waste Management and Control." U.S. National Academy of Sciences Publ. No. 1400, Washington, D.C., 1966.

Stapledon, Sir George, *Human Ecology,* ed. Robert Waller. New York: Hillary House Publishers, 1964.

Taylor, Griffith, "Human ecology in Australia," in *Biogeography and Ecology in Australia,* ed. A. Keast, et al. Monographiae Biologicae No. 8:52–68. The Hague: Junk, 1959.

Thomas, William L., Jr., ed., *Man's Role in Changing the Face of the Earth.* Chicago: University of Chicago Press, 1956.

Tindale, N. B., "Ecology of primitive man in Australia," in *Biogeography and*

Ecology in Australia, ed. A. Keast, et al. Monographiae Biologicae No. 8:36–51. The Hague: Junk, 1959.

Treichel, Georg, "Man, nature, and the landscape," in *Three Papers on Human Ecology* (pp. 9–18), ed. Darl Bowers. Oakland: Mills College, 1966.

Vogt, William, "Population patterns and movements," in *Future Environments of North America* (pp. 372–389), ed. F. F. Darling and J. P. Milton. Garden City, N.Y.: Natural History Press, 1966.

Wedel, Waldo R., "Some aspects of human ecology in the central Plains." *American Anthropologist* 55:499–514, 1953.

White, Leslie A., "The energy theory of cultural development," in *Ghurye Felicitation Volume* (pp. 1–10), ed. K. M. Kapadia. Bombay: Popular Book Depot, 1954.

Wittfogel, Karl A., "Developmental aspects of hydraulic societies." Pan American Union, Social Science Monograph 1:43–52, 1955.

Woodwell, George M., ed., "Ecological effects of nuclear war." Upton, N.Y.: Brookhaven National Laboratory, 1963.

———, "Radiation and the patterns of nature." Brookhaven National Laboratory, Lecture Series BNL 924 (T-381), No. 45, 1965.

———, "Toxic substances and ecological cycles." *Scientific American* 216(3):24–31, March 1967.

5. Ethos, Ecos, and Ethics

THE DOCTRINES THAT men live by finally weave a fabric within which societies flower, or fall. The flowering requires roots that reach into the heart of good earth. Our beliefs about the environment, whether thought of as sacramental ties or bonds of frustration and alienation, whether or not we have unconsciously to obey them or can create them at will, are our roots that reach into the responding earth. The ultimate irresponsibility is to assert that there is nothing "out there."

Bertram, Colin, *Adam's Brood: Hopes and Fears of a Biologist.* London: Peter Davies, 1959.

———, "What are people for?" in *The Humanist Frame* (pp. 373–384), ed. J. Huxley. London: Allen and Unwin, 1961.

Birch, L. C., "Concept of Nature." *American Scientist* 39:294–302, 1951.

Bonifazi, Conrad, *A Theology of Things; A Study of Man in his Physical Environment.* Philadelphia: J. B. Lippincott, 1967.

Calhoun, John B., "A glance into the garden," in *Three Papers on Human Ecology* (pp. 19–36), ed. Darl Bowers. Oakland: Mills College, 1966.

Charter, S P R, *Man on Earth: A Preliminary Evaluation of the Ecology of Man.* Sausalito: Contact Editions, 1962.

———, "Why preserve nature?" *Man on Earth* 1(2):1–8, 1965.

———, "Homo ex machina: man-from-a-machine." *Man on Earth* 1(7):1–20, 1966.

Ciriacy-Wantrup, S. V., and James J. Parsons, eds., *Natural Resources—Quality and Quantity.* Berkeley: University of California Press, 1967.

Collier, John, Sr., "The Indian as ancient man; and ancient man as the primal ecologist. With a remark on Indian material poverty and its meaning to the Indian," in *Homenaje à Juan Comas en su 65 Aniversario,* Vol. I, pp. 15–22. Mexico City, 1965.

Commoner, Barry, et al., "The integrity of science: a report by the AAAS Committee on Science in the Promotion of Human Welfare," *American Scientist* 53:174–198.

Darling, F. Fraser, "The unity of ecology." Smithsonian Annual Report, 1964:461–476, 1965.

———, "A wider environment of ecology and conservation." *Daedalus,* Fall 1967:1003–1019.

———, and John P. Milton, eds., *Future Environments of North America.* Garden City, N.Y.: Natural History Press, 1966.

Dubos, René, *Man Adapting.* New Haven: Yale University Press, 1965. (Also Yale paperback Y197.)

Eliade, Mircea, *Cosmos and History: The*

Myth of the Eternal Return. New York: Harper Torchbooks TB2050, 1959.

Elton, Charles S., "The reasons for conservation," in *The Ecology of Invasions by Animals and Plants* (pp. 143–153). London: Methuen, 1958.

Farber, Seymour M., "Quality of living—stress and creativity," in *Future Environments of North America* (pp. 342–354), ed. F. F. Darling and J. P. Milton. Garden City, N.Y.: Natural History Press, 1966.

Galbraith, John Kenneth, *The Affluent Society.* Boston: Houghton Mifflin Co., 1958. (Also Mentor New American Library MT534.)

Glacken, Clarence J., *Traces on the Rhodian Shore.* Berkeley: University of California Press, 1967.

Glikson, Artur, "Man's relationship to his environment," in *Man and his Future* (pp. 132–152), a Ciba Foundation Volume, ed. G. Wolstonholme. London: J. & A. Churchill, 1963.

Hallowell, A. Irving, "The structural and functional dimensions of a human existence." *Quarterly Review of Biology* 31: 88–101, 1956.

Hardin, Garrett, *Nature and Man's Fate.* New York: Holt, 1959. (Also Mentor New American Library MT338.)

———, "A second Sermon on the Mount." *Perspectives in Biology and Medicine* 6: 366–371, 1963.

———, "Pop research and the seismic market." *Per/Se,* Fall 1967, pp. 19–24.

Harris, Marvin, and George E. B. Morren, "The limitations of the principle of limited possibilities." *American Anthropologist* 68:122–127, 1966.

Hawkes, Jacquetta, *Man on Earth.* New York: Randon House, 1955.

Hocking, Brian, *Biology—Or Oblivion; Lessons from the Ultimate Science.* Cambridge, Mass.: Schenkman Publishing Co., 1965.

Hutchinson, G. Evelyn, "On living in the biosphere." *Scientific Monthly* 67:393–398, 1948.

———, "The Gothic attitude to natural history," in *The Itinerant Ivory Tower* (pp. 28–35). New Haven: Yale University Press, 1953.

Huth, Hans, *Nature and the American: Three Centuries of Changing Attitudes.*

Berkeley: University of California Press, 1957.

Huxley, Aldous, "The politics of ecology: the question of survival." Occasional Paper on the Free Society, Center for the Study of Democratic Institutions, Santa Barbara, California, 1963.

Iltis, Hugh H., "To the taxonomist and ecologist—Whose fight is the preservation of nature?" *BioScience* 17:886–890, 1967.

Isaac, Erich, "Religion, landscape and space." *Landscape* 9(2):14–18, Winter 1959–60.

———, "The act and the covenant: the impact of religion on the landscape." *Landscape* 11(2):12–17, Winter 1961–62.

Joranson, Philip N., "Conservation—theological foundations." Faith Learning Studies No. 6. Faculty Christian Fellowship, New York, 1964.

Juenger, Friedrich Georg, *The Failure of Technology.* Hinsdale, Ill.: Henry Regnery, 1949. (Also Gateway Editions paperback 96030.)

Kates, Robert, "The pursuit of beauty in the environment." *Landscape* 16(2):21–25, Winter 1966–67.

Krutch, Joseph Wood, "Conservation is not enough." *American Scholar* 23:295–305, 1954.

McKinley, Daniel, "A clamor of gulls: journal of a Maine island summer." *Contact* No. 11, 3(3):22–31, August 1962.

———, "My eye is on the sparrow." *Contact* No. 15, 4(1):10–20, July 1963.

Murray, E. G. D., "The place of nature in man's world." *American Scientist* 42: 130–135, 142, 1954.

Rickover, Hyman G., "A humanistic technology." *Nature* 208:721–726, 1965.

Rockefeller, Laurance S., et al., The White House Conference on Natural Beauty: Report to the President; the President's Response. Washington, D.C., 1965.

Sears, Paul B., "Integration at the community level." *American Scientist* 37:235–242, 1949.

———, "Ecology—a subversive subject." *BioScience* 14(7):11–13, July 1964.

Shepard, Ward, "Our indigenous Shangri-La." *Scientific Monthly* 62:158–164, 1946.

Simpson, George Gaylord, "The world into which Darwin led us." *Science* 131:966–974, 1960. (Also in *This View of Life*, Harcourt, Brace & World paperback H-052.)

Sperry, Robert W., "Mind, brain, and humanist values." *Bulletin of the Atomic Scientists* 22(7):2–6, September 1966.

Thompson, Laura, "The basic conservation problem." *Scientific Monthly* 68:129–131, 1949.

Watts, Alan W., *Nature, Man, and Woman.* New York: Pantheon Books, 1958. (Also Mentor New American Library MD 282.)

Williams, George H., *Wilderness and Paradise in Christian Thought.* New York: Harpers, 1962.

Wolfe, Roy I., "Leisure: the element of choice." *Journal of Human Ecology* 2(6):1–12, 1952.

BCDEFGHIJ–R –7654321O/69